Supply Chain Management

PROCESS, SYSTEM, AND PRACTICE

N. CHANDRASEKARAN

Director
Centre for Logistics and Supply Chain Management
Loyola Institute of Business Administration, Chennai
and
Vice President – Corporate Affairs
Take Solutions Ltd, Chennai

OXFORD
UNIVERSITY PRESS

OXFORD
UNIVERSITY PRESS

Oxford University Press is a department of the University of Oxford.
It furthers the University's objective of excellence in research, scholarship,
and education by publishing worldwide. Oxford is a registered trademark of
Oxford University Press in the UK and in certain other countries

Published in India by
Oxford University Press
YMCA Library Building, 1 Jai Singh Road, New Delhi 110001, India

© Oxford University Press 2010

The moral rights of the author/s have been asserted.

First published 2010
Fourth impression 2015

ISBN-13: 978-0-19-806302-5
ISBN-10: 0-19-806302-4

Typeset in Baskerville
by Tej Composers, New Delhi
Printed in India by Multivista Global Ltd., Chennai

Third-party website addresses mentioned in this book are provided
by Oxford University Press in good faith and for information only.
Oxford University Press disclaims any responsibility for the material contained therein.

We can see God in the unblemished love of our parents and their commitment to nurturing us with values.
I respectfully dedicate this work to my mother, Annapoorani Nagarajan, my wife, Prabha, and my daughter, Sangeetha.

Foreword

I first came across Dr N. Chandrasekaran while setting up the CII Institute of Logistics where he joined us to provide a roadmap for the institute. During the two years he worked on this task, his knowledge and performance impressed me.

Logistics or supply chain, sometimes used interchangeably, is the key to India's growth and competitiveness. Though we may not reach accurate results every time, it is generally agreed that the cost of logistics in India is around 13–15 per cent of GDP as compared to the world average of 5 per cent of GDP, thus making it uncompetitive.

This book will take readers through experiences and journey to illustrate and define the various issues of supply network. Whether it is the Dabbawalas of Mumbai or Maruti Suziki, the objective remains the same, of enabling the readers to relate to these examples and understand the concepts better. Case studies have been used to explain the importance of logistics in the chapters.

The author has tried to cover all the important aspects of supply chain management in this book, which are vital not only for the development and progress of large companies but also for the smaller ones. Further, logistics is a key factor not only in manufacturing but also in the defence services and cellular companies. This has been elaborated upon in detail. The old adage, 'A penny saved is a penny earned' holds true for companies too. The book also traverses the entire gamut of industries and retail in detail. The book not only covers the current logistics practices for the practitioner but also covers the future trends. The coverage includes inventory management as well as the various elements of transportation, financial costs, and internal supply chain, thus discussing the complete cycle of the network.

Technology is an important ingredient and is critical in managing a supply chain network. The book discusses in detail various aspects of technology and its application for supply chain planning, collaboration, and execution. The author has also succinctly pointed out in a chapter the various players and the scope of their offering. The book also includes discussions on pure technology play in supply chain, such as RFID and bar code and how these help in warehousing and distribution. In today's world the other key issue in the supply network is ethics and corporate governance. The author has talked about this area in the book, showing that in all our actions 'hygiene' is the key—and this extends to supply chain functions such as sourcing, inventory, facilities and transportation—and must be given due importance.

I am extremely happy that the author has written a couple of chapters on 'green supply chain'. Green supply chain would be compelling, especially for those who are export oriented and reach out to developed markets. As is the case with any other good management practice, the rest of the market will catch up sooner or later on green supply chain. The author has rightfully focused readers to take cognizance of the same ahead of the compulsions of trade. I believe that this book as a whole is well researched and covers the subject in a 'complete sense' and has thought of logistics holistically. It has covered all aspects of the cycle with case studies and examples so as to clearly bring out the important issues. I believe the readers, whether practitioners or students, will find this book an important piece of arsenal in their weaponry to take on the competitive world.

I congratulate the author on this brave step to educate the world of 'to be' supply chain professionals.

N. Kumar
Vice Chairman, The Sanmark Group

Preface

Supply chain management relates to how a firm organizes receipts of material and components, adds value, and delivers goods and services to the customer through efficient planning, sourcing, manufacturing, and distribution by engaging multiple stakeholders in the supply network. Increased proliferation of products and services, with demanding customers who expect product differentiation at lower costs, poses several challenges to a supply chain professional. Firms which can establish a unique supply chain network and create it as a strategic asset gain a competitive edge and, in fact, can acquire a leadership position across industries and markets.

Some of the international companies who have created intangible assets through supply chain networks are Wal-Mart and Seven-Eleven Japan Co. Ltd, and Zara in Europe and Toyota in Japan. Some examples of such distinctive supply chain networks of corporates in India include the ones established by Gujarat Cooperative Milk Marketing Federation (GCMMF) (the brand owner of AMUL), Maruti Suzuki India Limited (subsidiary of Suzuki Motor Company Ltd), Tata Motors, ITC Ltd, PepsiCo India, and HUL, to name a few.

Supply chain management cuts across various functional areas, including production and operations, marketing, finance, and information technology. Until recently, there has been a tendency to push supply chain problems more towards finding logistical solutions, which are typically taken at the operational level, across functional areas. However, this is changing and a broader level of involvement of managers is being brought in these days. Technology explosion has also led to a significant change in supply chain processes. Over the last two decades, firms operating in a fiercely competitive environment have been increasingly focusing on an efficient supply chain network managed by dedicated professionals with an inter-disciplinary skill sets.

ABOUT THE BOOK

The aim of this book is to provide a clear, well-structured, and comprehensive treatment of the subject. It brings out the interrelations among the drivers of supply chain across the various functions in an organization. The text provides a logical approach to the key activities of supply chain management and relates principles with practice, predominantly with examples from India, Southeast Asia, and other developed nations such as the US and UK.

The book covers issues across various spectra of business and public life. It attempts to provide a comprehensive approach and a new outlook, with a range and variety of situations and cases of supply chain network for the readers to relate to.

PEDAGOGY

Each chapter starts with a set of learning objectives. The content is explained through suitable illustrations and examples. Supply chain management is a practical subject driven by theoretical concepts. Most of the chapters contain theory, applications, and examples, either real world or hypothetical. The book includes a number of real-life case studies for analyses and discussions in the classroom.

The book is targeted at students of supply chain management in a management course or a specialization course and also at working professionals. Each chapter contains questions, critical thinking questions, project assignments, and references that also serve as further reading.

A CD with digital content accompanies the book, which contains Excel worksheets on the problems discussed in the text. It also contains interactive sessions-interviews with leading industrialists and professionals on issues of supply chain. The presentation of real-life supply chain issues and products are also discussed.

Some key features of the book are as follows:

- Discussions on new business models and applications of technology in detail
- Real-world examples from Indian cases to facilitate better understanding of the concepts
- Chapters exclusively on supply chain structure and supply chain assessment
- An entire chapter comprising case studies on Redington (India) Limited and Cargomen Logistics (India) Private Limited, with exercises

COVERAGE OF THE BOOK

The book covers various processes, systems, and practices of supply chain management. These terms are used interchangeably and the reason to use them independently is discussed below.

Process It includes those decision areas that facilitate decision-making processes. Some of these areas are strategic in nature, while a lot in this domain are policy driven. Strategy, being one of the most important aspects of SCM, is being covered in various chapters. For instance, Chapters 6 and 7 talk about the key strategic decisions for transportation chains and network design, respectively. Policy is the guiding principle that is critical for successful operations and planning in any organization. It plays a major part in forming decisions across the supply chain domain. For example, sourcing has certain strategic orientations like structuring of alliances and partnerships, and setting up JIT and VMI, discussed in Chapter 11. A substantial portion of this is explained in the chapter on planning, where policies guide procurement and operational issues such as SOPs for buying, VMI and JIT, and in-plant movements.

System This refers to putting the policy in a framework that is implemented with technology and SOPs. These aspects of supply chain management are discussed in Chapters 15 to 19.

Practice Various practices have been discussed throughout the book, which are linked to different processes and systems in this field. Chapter 20 includes a number of Indian case studies that will help the readers relate the theory discussed in earlier chapters with practice.

The chapter-wise structure is as follows:

Chapter 1, on supply chain perspectives, discusses the evolution, definition, and nomenclature of logistics and supply chain management and the role of the supply chain manager.

Chapter 2, on supply chain structure, brings out the difference between efficient supply chain and responsive supply chain as well as the push and pull classification of supply chain and the key parameters for enabling the same. The agility of supply chains in certain and uncertain times is also discussed.

Chapter 3, on supply chain drivers, helps understand the role of the drivers—namely, facilities, transportation, inventory, sourcing, pricing, and information—in supply chain performance. The various components of the drivers and their influence on the competition, by linking business with supply chain strategies, are discussed as well. The chapter also focuses on gaining an insight into each driver, each strategy, and the competitive force relevant for a chosen focus and driver.

Chapter 4, on decision environment, focuses on understanding decision-making in supply chain management, which is determined by a host of internal and external factors. External factors include government rules and regulations relating to warehousing, transport movement, carriers and direct controls such as pricing and licensing. It lends an insight into the opportunities and constraints of resource-driven decision environment and the support system for mapping decision environment.

Chapter 5, on strategic decision in supply chain management, focuses on the nature of strategic decisions in business and their linkages with the supply chain domain at the corporate, strategic business unit, and functional levels. It also brings out the importance of third party or integrated logistics services, the key strategic partner that provides support for supply chain activities.

Chapter 6, on the role of transportation in supply chain management, discusses the key role players and factors that influence transport decision, transportation mode selection and speed of delivery and choice of mode, inventory aggregation and transportation cost management, and vehicle scheduling and routing.

Chapter 7, on network decision, helps understand the different choices of network configurations and the impact of any specific configuration on service and cost factors, the tools and models for decision-making with respect to facility location, facility capacity, demand allocation, and also sensitivity analysis and use of simulation as a tool.

Chapter 8, on the role of sourcing in supply chain management, defines purchasing, procurement, and sourcing. It gives an insight into the sourcing grid matrix and guidelines, strategic sourcing comprising outsourcing strategies, and the role of technology for enabling buying decisions.

Chapter 9, on supply chain tactical planning, provides insight into demand planning and forecasting, the importance of aggregate planning processes, and how planning relates to sales and operations planning. It also discusses the evolution of CPFR and ECR.

Chapter 10, on the role of inventory management in supply chain management, helps understand the importance of inventory in system, inventory models, and the role of inventory in supply chain with respect to efficiency and effectiveness.

Chapter 11, on current and emerging operational practices in supply chain, helps understand the key operational aspects that influence supply chain operations, such as just-in-time (JIT), vendor managed inventory (VMI), and ethical supply chain management practices.

Chapter 12, on managing obstacles and enabling coordination in supply chain, helps understand the importance and management of the financial flows and identifies the causes of obstacles in coordination of the supply chain.

Chapter 13, on global supply chain perspectives, gives an insight into the various aspects of the global supply chain, discusses the cost drivers and their impact on the global supply chain configuration, the responsiveness-based global supply chain configuration, the challenges in establishing a global supply chain, the supply chain risks, and the approach for an effective global supply chain as well as the changing perspective of logistics infrastructure.

Chapter 14, on new business models with technology and process integration, explains the scope of creating new supply chain networks and business models, technology applications for recreating business through the reconfiguration of supply chain, the role of supply chain in success of e-business models, and pure technology applications in supply chain.

Chapter 15, on information technology in supply chain management, explains the application of IT in supply chain management and the capital investment requirements, identifies enterprise applications domains and their relevance to business, especially e-SCM, and also appreciates the key challenges of supply chain management systems.

Chapter 16, on the application of technology in supply chain management, discusses supply chain management information systems, technology devices, and risks and benefits of supply chain information systems projects.

Chapter 17, on the approach to supply chain assessment and excellence, details the need for assessment, helps understand the importance of validating current processes and their effectiveness, measuring efficiencies of resources and eliminating redundancies, and barriers to audit and improvements, and provides an insight into supply chain assessment services in India and service providers in India.

Chapter 18, on supply chain organizational issues, focuses on aspects such as corporate size, business complexity, ownership pattern, and the level of decision-making in supply chain. It gives an insight into intra-organization decision-making versus outsourced supply chain.

Chapter 19, on supply chain performance management, highlights the importance of measuring performance both with the traditional as well as the contemporary approaches and the application of frameworks and tools from the perspective of the management accountant.

The Cases Studies section covers various issues in supply chain management, ranging from transportation scheduling and strategic issues to inventory analysis and organizational issues. The cases are drawn from various industries, such as textiles and garments, perishables, engineering, and fertilizers, and also from consumer products group such as the one on retailing of mobile phones.

ABOUT THE CD

The book is accompanied by a CD that contains a power point presentation (PPT) and three folders.

The PPT has

- 7 audio interviews, with leading professionals in the industry discussing various concerns of the supply chain network. Along with the transcripts for these interviews, two additional transcripts have also been provided. Special links are provided to access these interviews and transcripts.
- Excel snapshots, including selected exercises along with their illustrations related to chapters on network decision, supply chain tactical planning, and role of transportation in supply chain. These are formulae based and any change in the entry would show changes in the solution as well as the graph.

The three folders have audio interviews, transcripts, and Excel snapshots for the readers to view them separately.

ACKNOWLEDGEMENTS

I must thank Mr N. Kumar, ex-President, CII, Chairman, CII Institute of Logistics, Chairman, Take Solutions Ltd, and Vice Chairman, Sanmar Group of Companies, for his continued support over the years and for giving me the opportunity to interact with people of various corporates across India and to work in this domain. I immensely thank Mr Srinivasan HR, Vice Chairman, Take Solutions Ltd, for his continued support and encouragement on all my academic endeavours along with business requirements. Without his understanding and open-minded approach, this initiative could not be accomplished. Rev. Fr Christie, Director, LIBA, Chennai, has been constantly a source of strength and was personally involved in making me pursue this effort.

I owe a lot to my teachers who have helped me evolve over the years. I would like to put on record my sincere gratitude to those who have at different stages of this work been very encouraging and supportive: Dr T.V. Subramaniam, Prof. P.S. Anantha Narayanan, and Prof. G. Raghuram. I would like to thank Mr Johnson, St. John's, Tuticorin; Mr Ravichandran, President, TVS Logistics; Mr Thiru Kumar, Vice Chairman, Janson Business School; Mr S. Mohan, Director, Janson Business School; Mr S. Rathinam, Director, BGR Energy Ltd; Mr Sadasivam, DGM, SBI; Mr B. Sridhar, Director, Bengal Tiger Line Services; Mr S. Sriraman, Bee-Hive Ventures; Mr Rajesh Menon, CII; Mr Anathanarayanan, AGM, SBI; Mr B. Saravanan, IFS; Mr Kamal Jain, Cargomen; Mr K. Krishna Kumar, Avon Logistics, Chennai; Mr Jeyakar S, Mr S. Ramanan, Mr Suresh Joseph, and Prof. G. Balasubramaniam, IFMR.

My friends and colleagues from Take have given me immense support. I would like to acknowledge the support of Mr S. Sridharan, Managing Director, Take Solutions Ltd; Mr R. Seshadri, Mr D.V. Ravi, Mr G. Ramesh, Ms Neera Baburaj, Mr R.M. Alagappan, and all my other colleagues from the HR department. I also would like to thank my colleagues at LIBA, Prof. P. Chandiran, Mr Sai Sridhar, Dr M. Ramasubramaniam, Mr V. Krishna Kumar, and Aarthi Nanadakumar, along with Neera, who read, critically evaluated, and contributed to my writing. This team effort, especially of Sai Sridhar and Neera, who were involved throughout this project, is greatly appreciated.

I acknowledge the following persons for their support in preparing the case material in Chapter 20. Some of the businessmen, who are leaders in their own way in running their business, spared time to educate me on these issues. I may not have adequately captured their passion and commitment. The material used here is for academic discussions only.

1. Dr T.V. Subramanaian, Management Consultant, Chennai
2. Mr K. Krishnakumar, Founder, Avon Solutions & Logistics Private Limited, Chennai
3. Mr Devarajan, Chairman and Managing Director, Sambandam Spinning Mills Ltd, Salem
4. Prof. P.S. Anathanarayanan, Director, Sambandam Spinning Mills Ltd, and faculty in Strategy and Operations Management
5. Mr Naveen, Clifton Exports Ltd, Tirupur, and Mr N. Srinivasan, Clifton Exports Ltd
6. Info Media Ltd for permission to reprint an interview
7. Mr R. Arunachalam, General Manager – Supply Chain Business Initiatives, Redington (India) Ltd
8. Mr Nagarajan J., Deloitte Consulting India Pvt. Ltd, Hyderabad, Mr Kamal Jain, Mr Hari Prasad, and Mr Jayakar, Cargomen Logistics India Pvt. Ltd

9. Mr Subramaniam, President of Pollachi Lorry Owners Association, and other office bearers, and Mr Guna Sekar, lorry owner and operator
10. Mr Venkat Ramakrishna, Beroe Inc.
11. Messers Krishna Kumar Velayudham, Padmanabhan, Vinoth Raja, Bharathi Sathya, Manoj Mishra, Yuvaraj, and Achutharam participants in the LIBA Centre for Logistics and Supply Chain programme course in 2007–08, and Murthinathan, Rajesh Seshadri, and Syamsundar participants at the LIBA Centre for Logistics and Supply Chain Management Programme batch III, 2008–09
12. Mr S. Ramanan, HP India, Chennai, and Mr V. Sankaran, Precision Software, New Delhi
13. Mr Vijay Shrinivas, Chennai
14. Mr Sachin Garg, Manager – Investor Relations, Take Solutions, Ltd

I would also like to thank my students at LIBA, BIM, and IFMR and other industry practitioners whom I have trained across many locations. Most of the learning and clarity in my thoughts came through these interactions.

I am also thankful to Oxford University Press for providing me constant support.

I am grateful to my mother, Mrs Annapoorani Nagarajan, and also my siblings and their families who have been constantly motivating me in my academic endeavour. Last but not the least, I must thank my spouse, Prabha, for her patience and tolerance while I was working on this title.

I would appreciate all suggestions towards the improvement of the book. Readers may contact me at enchandru@yahoo.com or nchandrasekaran@takesolutions.com/nc@chandrasekaran.in.

Chandrasekaran Nagarajan

Contents

1

Introduction to Supply Chain Management

Learning Objectives

After studying this chapter, you will be able to:

- Discuss the evolution of supply chain management
- Define supply chain management
- Comprehend the similarity and difference between logistics and supply chain management
- Delineate the role of a supply chain manager
- Understand the concept of value chain and its correlation to supply chain
- Describe the macro processes of supply chain
- Explain the nodes and processes of supply chain
- Comprehend how the interface of technology, process, and people has revolutionized supply chain management
- Understand the hierarchy and span of supply chain decisions
- Discuss the importance of professional excellence in supply chain management

1.1 SUPPLY CHAIN IN DAY-TO-DAY LIFE

On a Sunday morning, when a hawker walks into a neighbourhood with his basket of vegetables and fruits, one may wonder how he knows the demand pattern of the families living in the area. It may be that one of his regular clients—an elderly lady—chats with the hawker about the other households in the locality. Equipped with surprisingly precise knowledge about the demand pattern of each household, his basket would be stocked with the exact amount of perishables. If we observe his selling pattern a little more, we will find the hawker completes his round through the neighbourhood by 11 a.m.—a total work time of six hours—and has made a decent margin of profit with less variability in price, stock-keeping items, and quantity. It's amazing! The customers are happy with the fresh stock and fair prices. The vendor is happy with his service, realization, and stability of earnings. The cash-to-cash cycle is so perfect that his sourcing and distribution plans are also clear and well established. The synchronization with supplier relationship management and customer relationship management—the macro processes of supply chain management—is well in place.

Critics may feel this is no earthshaking achievement as the entities involved are small in quantity and insignificant in economic value. However, big players like

---

Exhibit 1.1 Innovation from a Paint Manufacturing Company

In preparation for the festive season, the head of a household wants his house to be painted. His daughter comes up with the idea of painting streaks of varying colours on the ceiling, walls, and doors. The father is a little sceptical at the idea—he can envision the painter coming in with a few colours of large SKUs and mixing them up to provide different shades. In the process, there will be wastage because of the uneconomic size of the packs, the number of brushes used, and so on. But his little daughter knows better. When the father expresses his reservation to her, she tells him about the website 'my painting room' where one can mix all shades virtually and forward the selected shade to the company. The father does so and gives the company the contract for painting his house. The company engages a local service provider who accomplishes the very colourful job to the delight of everyone!

Toyota and Dell work through the same method with corresponding stress on processes, people skills, and application of technology.

The evolution of trade in civilization is a fascinating study. From the days of barter in self-contained societies to the modern era of technology-led trade growth, society has benefited mainly through organizing demand and supply through planning and execution of production, storage, and movement of goods and services. Prima facie, commerce and trade could not have existed without logistics. The nomenclature itself could be recent and different but not the purpose and spirit. What is striking is the centrality of the art and science of logistics and supply chain management in a successful business, whether large or small, recent or ancient. Not just business but even public life, government, and military operations are extremely focused on logistics and supply chain efficiency, effectiveness, and evolution.

However, there also exist phenomenal supply chain innovations and reconfigurations impacting business models, and thereby, the fortunes of stakeholders. Exhibit 1.1 gives an example to explain the concept of supply chain network.

The explosion in technology and its adoption across networks, people capability, and structuring of business processes have enabled innovations in supply chain networks. Even product/service flows are synchronized with informational and financial flows for efficiency and effectiveness of the supply chain. At the end of the day, it is not only the focal organization that benefits but also every stakeholder, including the customer.

1.2 EVOLUTION AND LANDMARKS

In the brief period of just above ten years before he died in 323 BC, the great Macedonian general Alexander conquered countries including Greece and Persia because he had included logistics in his strategic planning (Van Mieghem 1998). According to Engels (1980), '... (W)hen the climate, human geography, physical geography, available methods of transport, and agricultural calendar of a given region are known, one can often determine what Alexander's next move will be.' Engels elaborates how Alexander used logistical tactics to ensure an open supply chain by maximizing speed and flexibility, forging alliances, and aligning the route along the transportation corridor and supplies tie-up. This could be one of the earliest links to this domain on supply chain management.

Recent history would show that new ideas and technologies have revolutionized supply chains and changed the way enterprises work. With industrialization, capital-intensive mechanized production systems have come to replace labour-intensive production systems. Infrastructure development, such as railroads, national highways, seaports, aerospace, and the new communications media expanded markets and made supply chains effective and efficient. Population growth and the formation of regional and international trade unions accelerated the development of communities and the demand for goods and services, which could not have been met without the maturity of logistics and supply chain domain.

In the early 1900s, a man called Henry Ford successfully established an automotive company in the US, where he integrated car manufacturing process for the first time, enabling mass production. Ford can be said to have created the first moving assembly line, which reduced the time required to build a car from 728 hours to 1.5 hours. This brought down the cost of manufacturing as well, so Ford could sell his first car, Model T, at a relatively low price. In this sense, Ford can be said to have ushered in the mass production era. Over the next sixty years, American manufacturers became adept at mass production and streamlined supply chains with the help of scientific management methods and operations research techniques.

Post World War II, economies were resurrecting and a new world economic order was emerging. European economies, especially Germany, Belgium, and France, were gaining prominence because of the development in manufacturing and trade. Similarly, in the East, Japan was emerging strongly, rising like a phoenix from the ashes of war. The sudden growth in the Japanese economy was due to a leap in the manufacturing industry. Starting in the early 1970s, Japanese manufacturers such as Toyota changed the rules of production from mass to lean. Lean manufacturing focuses on flexibility and quality more than on efficiency and quantity. The significant lean manufacturing ideas include six-sigma quality control, just-in-time inventory, and total quality management, which will be explained later in the book.

It was in the 1970s that the US's superiority in manufacturing was challenged by firms in many global industries which made higher quality products at lower costs. Global competition forced the US manufacturers to concentrate on improving quality by reducing defects in their supply chains. The US also started focusing on quality initiatives while maintaining cost effectiveness. This was the beginning of the information technology (IT) boom when many IT companies set up shop in the US. These companies started revolutionizing trade with new generation business models, which required a responsive supply chain. The customer's preference was now finding place in the chain.

In the 1990s, the manufacturing and service industries started producing mass customized products and services with the help of the Internet and other technological advances. Dell revolutionized global business, being one of the earliest companies to adopt mass customization. Dell didn't have to stock in-house finished goods inventories and the customers were delighted as they got products that suited their needs. Following Dell, many firms started effectively using new information technologies to improve their service and delivery processes. Secure cyber-based communication and web technologies led to the growth of e-commerce and e-business, changing the way supply chain network was structured. Online stores such as amazon.com, departmental store chains such as Walmart, and financial services companies opened a new era. Hence, one can observe how supply chain has evolved dramatically over the last four decades.

1.3 SUPPLY CHAIN MANAGEMENT

A number of authors and institutions have tried to define supply chain management over the years. Many a times it is seen as logistics, operations management, procurement, or a combination of the three (Lambert and Cooper 2000), but today the broader definition given by the Global Supply Forum is generally accepted: 'Supply Chain Management (SCM) is the integration of key business processes from the end user through original suppliers that provides products, services, and information that add value for customers and other stakeholders.' This definition mentions key business processes without limiting itself to processes such as buying, movement or storage, and their integration. It also uses terms such as original suppliers and adding value to customers and stakeholders, which are quite interesting and appreciable.

Another interesting description: 'SCM is the term used to describe the management of the flow of materials, information, and funds across the entire supply chain, from suppliers to component producers to final assemblers to distribution (warehouses and retailers), and ultimately to the consumer.' This description talks about managing three flows—physical, informational, and financial—across the chain and also the importance of the customer. The objective of SCM is to manage a '... network of organizations that are involved, through upstream and downstream linkages, in the different processes and activities that produce value in the form of products and services in the hands of the ultimate customer' (Christopher 1998). This connotes that a supply chain involves two or more organizations for serving the ultimate customer, which happens by articulating flow of material, finance, and information. It may be worth reiterating here that the key to the existence of a supply chain is the presence of an ultimate customer and its value to him.

A network of organizations, generally, links up nodes and flow of multiple entities. Some of the flows could be divergent while others could be convergent. An organization would focus on the flow of goods and services to a set of customers for which a value is being enabled. One of the interesting cases in India is the Amul supply chain—its success story is widely portrayed among business leaders, scholars, and academia. Appendix 1.1 gives an idea of the complexity of the Amul supply chain in terms of customer spread, sales and distribution network, manufacturing and process facilities, number of product ranges, procurement centres, and support services. It may be interesting to note that the initial success of this is what led to Operation Flood being sanctioned by the World Bank, which dramatically over four tranches changed India's fortune from a net importer to a leading dairy products processor in the world.

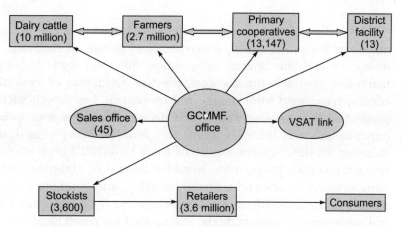

Figure 1.1 The Amul supply chain (all figures are estimates)

Figure 1.1 shows linkages among various inter-organizational entities for achieving value for the focal organization, namely GCMMF (Gujarat Cooperative Milk Marketing Federation), in serving its customers across different geographical locations in India and abroad. The effectiveness and efficiency of the SCM involves deploying various business approaches, concepts, and methods.

1.4 LOGISTICS AND SCM

There has been a tendency to use both nomenclatures interchangeably. It may be useful to understand the focus areas of both of these so we can find both the commonality between the two and the niche of each. The evolution of each process has benefited from the other. As mentioned earlier, logistics functions have existed for a long time and contributed in civic life, military operations, and business. Logistics is all-pervasive. For instance, it is amazing to understand the logistics operations for holding parliamentary and assembly elections in India. Till 2004, the activities involved moving physical ballets across the length and breadth of the vast country. Today, there are electronic voting machines, which have phenomenally improved the process of holding elections and have reduced the cycle time and cost of managing elections. Similarly, the use of voter's identification cards and building an electronic database of citizens have facilitated managing logistics in public life. It may be worth understanding some of the definitions of logistics management.

In 1991, the international Council of Logistics Management (CLM) defined logistics as: 'The process of planning, implementing, and controlling the efficient, effective flow and storage of goods, services, and related information from the point of origin to the point of consumption for the purpose of conforming to customer requirements.' This definition describes logistics as the management of movement and storage of goods and services of an entity from the point of origin to the point of consumption, based on consumer needs. The definition sounds more operational, dealing with a single entity, and is customer focused. Typically, when competition is restricted or focused, in cases such as military operations, such definitions clearly depict the function.

This definition was later modified as: 'Logistics is the process of strategically managing the procurement, movement and storage of materials, parts and finished inventory and the related information flows through the organization and its marketing channels for the cost effective fulfilment of customers' orders.' This encompasses, apart from storage and movement, key aspects such as strategic focus, product and information flows. This definition is more appropriate for commercial organizations and business. Over the decades, many organizations have started focusing on the logistics aspect of their business. Large engineering companies realized that their progression depended upon their ability to efficiently manage the transportation of inbound material, stocking, and handling outbound goods, which many a times involved an over-sized cargo. Such cargo required specialized vehicles and movement on project mode, and so on. One could handle such complexity only with a good knowledge of logistics operations such as managing transport operators, yard management, and contract logistics service providers.

Some of the terms such as logistics, inbound logistics, materials management, physical distribution, and supply chain management are used interchangeably. Inbound logistics covers the movement of material, components, and products received from the suppliers. Materials management is about the handling of material and the movement of goods and components within the factory or firm. Physical distribution refers to the outward movement of the finished goods from the shipping or despatch department. Logistics describes the entire process of material and products moving into, through, and out of a firm. The gamut of logistics management includes:

- Order management
- Outbound transportation and distribution management
- Inventory management
- In-plant logistics such as stores, movement towards line and shops
- Inbound transportation
- Procurement
- Information management

It may be inferred from this that logistics management is oriented towards cost minimization for the focal firm/group. This gives the sense of logistics management being limited to internal supply chain management. But current thinking on supply chain management and experience has evolved from a broader perspective, where one needs to go beyond logistics operations.

1.5 SUGAR INDUSTRY—LOGISTICS AND SCM

In India, plantation white sugar is a regulated industry which is dependent on agro-economic conditions. It's not simply role agents in the environment who decide the fortune of this business. Logistics and supply chain operations too are critical for its success. This is a seasonal industry, operating on an average for about seven months in a year. A teaspoon of sugar takes approximately twenty-two to twenty-nine months cycle time to get into your beverage. Imagine a plant with a daily cane crushing capacity of 5,000 tonnes. In this plant, the tasks of the supply chain manager, who is generally head of the plant, would be:

1. **Planning:** Plan cane plantation, growth, and supplies. Draw up plant management, stocking, and sales management plans.

2. **Operations:** Cane management begins with seed cane and goes on to getting the harvest cane to hopper at plant. This is a highly planning and operations-oriented activity, as about 50,000 units of farms and farmers have to be managed. Typically, in a country like India, where mechanization of cane harvesting is not possible, a group of thirty people can harvest and load about 6–9 tonnes a day. To avoid the risk of stoppages from a particular route, cane harvest plan and supply to a plant is scheduled in a phased manner. One can imagine the logistics coordination required by the cane department, which is a key procurement team. Similarly, sugar process plants run with crushers, mills driven by motors, and a number of vessels handling boiling and condensing of juices, which are again impacted by the corrosive nature of the juice and dependability of pumping motors. Proactive plant maintenance and plant logistics, including management of byproducts like molasses, bagasse and pressmud, are critical to the success of sugar plant economics. One can see that logistics-intensive operations such as movement and storage are sensitive in a traditional low-profit, high-volume business.

3. **Stock and sell:** Sugar plants in India cannot sell sugar in the open market as desired. Since sugar is listed under essential commodities, the sale and distribution of sugar takes place as per the release order of the government. The government decides the quantum and limits the sale of sugar within a period, say a month. So what is produced over seven months is sold over fourteen months. In such a scenario, planning to hold stocks and selling on time are going to be critical decisions. Generally, sugar plants maintain stock within the plant considering the volume, ease of handling, and tariff, especially duties, to be paid. More often, sales contracts happen at the plant and outbound handling is minimal. All the same, it is important that goods are stocked in order and movement is supported so that volume permitted for sale is fully utilized. Again, this is logistics-intensive functionality as warehousing and outbound facilitation are critical for this.

4. **Managing physical, financial, and informational flows:** As mentioned earlier, physical flow management requires careful planning, both in terms of farms and harvests, so that the plants continuously receive a definite capacity, say 5,000 tonnes of cane per day or about 230 tonnes per hour. If one has to manage such physical flow successfully, information flow management must be efficient and effective. Right from the planning stage, wherein field and farmers are registered for procurement, to the stage of monitoring growth at frequent

intervals with the support of input materials such as fertilizers, to harvesting, to engaging harvest labourers and inbound transportation, there is an immense need for information coordination between the planning and operations departments. Good information systems and equipment, including handheld devices, are deployed to manage this. Another equally important flow that needs to be organized is the financial flow as one would deal with farmers who are dependent on timely and fair payment of proceeds. Since farmers operate on an annual crop with bunched pay-out during the early stage of planting and during the final stages, such as harvesting and transportation, financial flow is critical for the success of this industry. Else, farmers have a tendency to switch crops, affecting plant economies. In India, switching has one more aspect: agriculture on wet lands like cane plantations tend to be driven by availability of contiguous lands for plantation (even though there are multiple owners) and volumes can swing due to reasons beyond the control of the plant.

One can see the sugar business fits in the definition of logistics and supply chain mentioned earlier. This adds up to the question: Where is the divide and commonality between logistics and SCM? The definitions by the Council of Supply Chain Management Professionals (CSCMP) are given in Appendix 1.2. Using experience and definitions given by the council, let us throw more light on both the topics.

Logistics primarily focuses on order management, inbound transportation, in-plant management, outbound transportation, storage and procurement, and managerial phases of strategic, planning, and operational decisions. The focus is more on internal organization, especially with regard to cost, service, resource/asset utilization, and quality. Primarily, it is inward-looking. In the sugar business discussed above, the process is more logistics centred, with inward-looking focus of optimizing sugar production from a satellite area of farming, managing farmers, time window, process plant, and so on.

On the other hand, supply chain management is more outward-looking and inter-organizational in approach. It involves collaboration, partnering, and co-ordination across entities serving the nodal organization. Relationship management depends heavily on logistics effectiveness and efficiency. Hence, supply chain is a super set of activities, which is more strategic in nature and performs the specific function of managing demand and supply.

As a profession, both logistics and supply chain have their own areas of orientation and specialization, which must be enriched and worked in unison for achieving excellence. Logistics professionals would like each of the perspectives—warehousing, transportation, inventory, and information—to be optimized, micro-managed, and aligned. Primarily, most of it is a scientific and routine decision system. On the other hand, supply chain professionals would look at the process more from the point of view of relationship management and could be behavioural in approach. Supply chain professionals would also approach management from a logistics perspective. Appreciating this difference is important for long-term sustenance of goals and objectives of a business and its evolution.

To cite an example, in the sugar business, a strategist in logistics must use an engineering-centred approach for the development of produce with ease, design improvements in warehouse operations, and so on. At times, the logistics strategist must engage with civil bodies of government for improving roads, availability of water storages, and so on. All these actions would be informed by the goals of plant optimization and long-term growth. In the same case, a supply chain strategist would look into managing relationships with farmer communities, improving relationships with transport operators, harvesting ties with labourers and financiers, and so on. Thus, both logistics and SCM help an organization achieve high growth and remain competitive. In an organization, specificities of supply chain and logistics initiatives must be clearly defined and pursued.

Logistics infrastructure could largely be government-initiated and driven by public and private partnerships. Many countries in the US and Europe, and of late China, are achieving improvements in supply chain mainly because of investment in building logistics infrastructure such as highways, seaports and airports, cold chains, and so on. India must also invest in this sector at an aggressive pace to meet the increasing demands of the industry and achieve improvements in efficiency. Hence, logistics investment leads to supply chain improvements. As logistics infrastructure is a separate branch of study, this book will focus more on supply chain.

1.6 VALUE CHAIN, VALUE SYSTEM, AND SUPPLY CHAIN

As one observes the relationship between logistics and supply chain management, it may be useful here to discuss another useful concept, namely value chain, developed by Porter (1985), and relate it with supply chain. Figure 1.2 gives a flow chart of value chain. According to Porter, value chain analysis can be used to identify an organization's internal business processes and how they interact. An organization, in the process of creating value for different customers, performs numerous value activities. These could be a part of development, production, sales, or distribution of its services and products. The customer's perspective is given more importance than the cost parameter, as the organization is open to increasing cost for a premium product or service. According to this rule, value is more important than the cost as it is

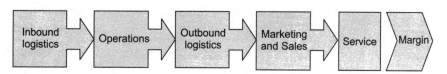

Figure 1.2 Value chain outline

believed that a customer will be willing to pay a higher price for a value-added product.

According to Porter, there are five generic categories of primary activities involved in competing in any industry, as shown in Table 1.1. Each of the main activities in Table 1.1 is divisible into a number of distinct activities that depend on the particular industry and organization strategy. One may observe that two of the five categories, namely inbound logistics and outbound logistics, are the key focus areas of logistics management and play a significant role in value chain activities. The other categories—operations, manufacturing, marketing and sales, and service—also involve supply chain and logistics management. Hence, the primary activities of value chain have a strong connection with logistics and supply chain management. One could argue that the essence of value chain arises from efficient management of supply chain. Value chain for competitive advantage could only be possible if strategies like cost leadership, differentiation, and focus are applied to primary activities. For example, in an industry like auto manufacturing, a player may gain an edge over competition by using effective just-in-time inventory management to reduce cost and provide value to customers. The advantage could be due to strategic initiatives deployed over years. The key point here is that synchronization of logistics is important for managing value chain activities.

Table 1.1   The value chain of a washing machine manufacturer

Category	Activities	Washing machine example
Inbound logistics	Associated with receiving, storing, and disseminating inputs into the product, such as material handling, warehousing, inventory control, vehicle scheduling, and returns to suppliers.	Receiving components such as motors, electrical switches, controls, metal sheets, and paints.
Operations	Associated with transforming inputs into the final product form, such as machining, packaging, assembly, equipment maintenance, testing, printing, and facility operations.	Assembly of components and conversion into the final product.
Outbound logistics	Associated with collecting, storing, and physically distributing the product to buyers, such as finished goods warehousing, material handling, finished goods inventory control, delivery vehicle operation, order processing and scheduling.	Movement of finished goods into mother warehouses, dealers, and own stores.
Marketing and Sales	Associated with promoting a product and providing means by which buyers can purchase the product and inducing them to do so.	Marketing functions such as pricing, promotions, appointment of channel partners and sales force management.
Service	Associated with providing service to enhance or maintain the value of the product, such as installation, repair, training, parts supply, and product adjustment.	Installation of the product at the customer's place on purchase, warranty management, and parts availability.

Support activities, according to Porter, can be divided into four categories: procurement, technology development, human resource management, and the firm's infrastructure, including general management, planning, finance, accounting, legal, government affairs, and quality management. Of these, procurement is more of a logistics-related function. Porter defines procurement as the function of purchasing inputs used in the firm's value chain and not purchasing inputs per se. According to him, the cost of procurement activities is usually a small portion of the total cost but often has a large impact on the firm's overall cost and differentiation. Improved purchasing practices can strongly affect the cost and quality of inputs, as well as of other activities associated with receiving and using the inputs, and interacting with suppliers.

If one looks at the value chain activities, they are mainly inward-looking and organization-centric. Porter's framework on industry analysis discusses the 'five forces model', in which he reckons the bargaining power of buyers and sellers, and the intensity of rivalry among firms in an industry with respect to the five factors that shape competition and drive strategic decision-making of firms. It is natural for Porter to extend in value chain analysis the spectrum of relationships for competitive advantage.

According to Porter, a firm's value chain is embedded in a larger stream of activities termed as value system. A value system links up the value chain of a firm with the value chain of the supplier and the value chain of the channel and buyer (shown in Figure 1.3). In the upstream linkage with the supplier, the firm must synchronize its value chain with that of the supplier.

The value system is not merely the movement of goods from a supplier. It involves much more because it is crucial for an organization to understand the value-creating activities of the supplier, including margin, for competitive advantage. In the same way, value mapping and understanding are critical for downstream linkages with buyers. A firm could gain competitive advantage and sustain it by not merely understanding value chain but the whole system. This holistic appraisal is what the concept of supply chain targets. Today, companies no longer compete for products or services, but mainly on the strength of their supply networks. Hence, it is important for a supply chain manager to understand nuances of value chain and value system and work with strategic management orientation for driving success. Exhibit 1.2 relates this for a capital goods manufacturer.

Exhibit 1.2 Supply Chain of a Capital Goods Equipment Manufacturer

Let's look at the supply chain of an engineering company, which could be a multinational company (MNC), manufacturing food industry capital goods equipment. Typically, this could cater to the domestic food industry like dairy, juices, alcohol, and so on. This company will have to look at value chain internally for all primary activities, namely inbound, operations, outbound, marketing, and post-sale support; and secondary activities such as procurement. There could be number of suppliers, such as component-vendors, including those dealing in sheets and metals, motors, electrical parts, and so on. The same vendors may be supplying components to competition as well. Unless this company synchronizes the value chain of the supplier with its value chain, margins would not improve. Similarly, the company could have channel partners, who could be project implementers or direct customers, whose value chain must also be synchronized with its own.

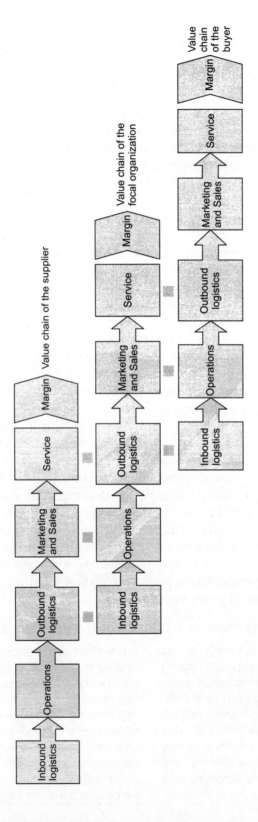

Figure 1.3   Value system

Hence the essence of a value system is to strategically manage suppliers, channel partners, and customers, which are key to supply chain management.

1.7 SUPPLY CHAIN MACRO PROCESSES

To enhance our discussion in Section 1.6, it could be useful to have an understanding of the macro processes of supply chain. One may cite the linkages among supply chain processes as being key to synchronization of activities and delivering value to customers. Process orientation links identifiable flows and value-adding activities. The debate about value addition and value creation is kept outside this discussion and these terms are used here interchangeably. Figure 1.4 shows the supply chain macro processes.

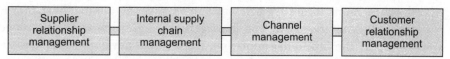

Figure 1.4 Supply chain macro processes

Traditionally, logistics were looked upon as a functional activity. The orientation was towards the accomplishment of tasks by grouping various resources. This was a silo approach (that is, 'acting independent of others') and led to suboptimal decisions. There was a complete lack of systemic thinking. For example, an inventory-control manager would look at reducing inventory holding so that the cost is reduced. The inventory policy could be at times independent of the market situation wherein consolidation could have been initiated. With reduction in ordering cost, frequent orders could be placed, leaving the scope of price negotiation to the procurement department. The conflict would become more pronounced with the procurement department as well as with marketing, which may prefer responsiveness. Apart from poor managerial effectiveness, another major problem would be behavioural concerns and playing the blame game, which would lead to further loss of effectiveness in supply chain. The worst cases were those where the lost sales could not even be mapped and escalated as behavioural issues which superseded managerial demands of growth and customer satisfaction. Thus, the functional approach was effective only where the boundaries of operation were clear with definite deliverables and adequateness of resources.

Given the drawback of the functional orientation, one may look upon process orientation for supply chain efficiency and effectiveness. Process orientation emphasizes on 'how' of an activity rather than 'what'. Each process has a set of certain flows and defined activities. With respect to supply chain at the macro level, informational, physical, and financial flows are paramount. At the macro level, activities would pertain to supplier management, the focal organization's internal supply chain, channel management, and customer relations. Each of the macro activities could be seen as a nodal point for decisions that are inter-linked, and the three flows ensure that the deliverables are achieved. A good process orientation would have defined procedures and policy for such activities so that quality is adhered to.

Supplier management process would include the goal of ensuring supplies at the best cost and terms, depending on whether it is a tactical purchase, a strategic buy, a negotiated purchase, or an engineered item. Each of these would have a different process. By and large, the process would include analysing information on supplier capabilities and pricing. Strategic buying and engineered buying would have more activities in the process of evaluation, especially at the initial stage of collaboration. It must be clearly understood that the entire supplier management process is driven by the nature of purchase and linked to the product manufactured.

In the case of Amul, supplier development formed a key component with process orientation. The development of dairies depended upon the commitment of the supplier, for which collection and payments had to be carried on schedule. More importantly, information flow was also critical, which was also enabled. Apart from these, a number of strategic initiatives such as animal husbandry support, bio-technology intervention, feed management, and so on were committed. If Amul had used only the functional approach, much of its developmental activities would have been limited to transactions and disparate handling of processes, lacking synchronization for growth.

Internal supply chain process includes a number of activities with respect to receiving, conversion, and despatch of finished goods. During this process, goods are internally value added through in-plant logistics operations such as stores management, movement and storage, and so on. All these activities are heavily linked to supplier collaboration like just in time (JIT), kanban (a technique of inventory management discussed later in the book), and design collaboration, and also with channel partners and customers. One may note that automated information flow and physical movement are synchronized for supplier-maintained inventory at the plant. The same would be true if one were to consider the importance of information flow from the customer's end to plant operations, especially with regard to changes in the weekly production as per the change in market conditions. Financial flows are fundamentally essential in these. Hence the functional approach to manufacturing would be limited to excellence in manufacturing but may lack supply chain synchronization unless it is explicitly pursued.

It could be useful here to cite an example noticed in a jewellery manufacturing unit wherein electronic kanban is practised. The internal operations are organized as per the cellular manufacturing concept and the production schedule clearly provides design and studding pattern. The vendor supplying gems and stones for studding at the cellular desk delivers to the daily requirement as per the production schedule. This kind of synchronization is enabled by process orientation, equipped by electronic kanban, leading to zero inventory on speciality items. But such sophistication in operations and supply chain management cannot be achieved in every scenario, specially in the continuous process industries.

The next important macro process is **channel management**. One can look at this as the key distribution functionality. Instead of looking at distribution as a function, one may treat this as a process. It is important to note linkages in distribution with multi-tier arrangements, depending upon the type of products moved. In case of fast-moving consumer goods (FMCG) and the consumer products group, it may have a multi-tier structure. In case of heavy capital goods, it may be a simple channel structure but with complicated movement and handling activities. The goal at this stage is mainly to reduce channel cost and improve availability to customers. Channel conflicts emerge because of priorities and conflicts in objectives between channel partners and the focal organization. Unless flows are synchronized and trust is created among stakeholders, the supply chain would suffer in terms of effectiveness and efficiency.

One may understand the importance of this macro process with the example of a consumer electronics supply chain and the role of a dealer in the channel. A dealer selling X brand of television must be expected to link up with the focal organization, namely the brand owner of X, and his own dealership brand where he would be a large retailer of consumer electronics selling multiple brands. The dealer brand value could be because of location factor, availability of SKUs, quickness to launch new brands, and so on. In the X supply chain, his role is to mainly ensure the sale of X to customers who would like to own the brand. Unless the dealer passes on the discounts and promotions offered by X to its customers, there could be a choking of sale. The dealer may not lose a customer as he can cross-sell another brand by manipulating the promotion structure, but X fails to optimize its supply chain in this case. The failure in process orientation here is due to the lack of right flow of information and inability to involve dealers in promotions and so on. Hence, a synchronized supply chain thrives on process orientation and not just on functional approach.

Another important macro process is **customer relationship management**. As mentioned earlier, the purpose of a supply chain network is to serve the ultimate customer of the focal organization. The focal organization orients itself to synchronize its role agents and processes to serve its customers. Customer delight happens only if the product meets the customer's satisfaction in terms of time, quantity, responsiveness, and cost. Also aspects like warranty, service support, and parts availability are critical. Customer retention and upgradation would be the main objectives of the focal organization, which could happen only if financial, informational, and product flows are managed effectively. The interdependence among processes and role agents must be well-appreciated and synchronized for effective and efficient supply chain network. Customer relationship management from supply chain management perspective must take care of responsiveness, reliability, and flexibility. These could be possible only when the focal organization seamlessly integrates all processes.

If one were to look at the same situation of a consumer electronics distributor from the customer's perspective, customer value is enhanced only when the brand of a customer's choice is delivered on time and installed appropriately. In other words, customer value is about making the product functional. Over and above these, the customer must be provided with operational warranty, post-sale support from installation to maintenance and replacement with spares on failure. When the customer experiences such committed service which has linkages to other processes, he would be delighted. For example, a television chosen by a customer must be installed and after-sale service support must be provided. The replacement of spares requires production and distribution tie-up for spares.

Hence it is important to enable process orientation and linkages among macro processes for running an effective supply chain network. Many successful organizations have identified their macro processes and synchronized them seamlessly.

A process view of supply chain is discussed by Sunil Chopra and others (2007). According to Chopra, 'A supply chain is a sequence of processes and flows that take place within and between different supply chain stages and combine to fill a customer need for a product.' There is the 'cycle' view, according to which the processes in a supply chain are divided into a series of cycles, each performed at the interface between two successive supply chain stages. Alternatively, the 'push/pull' view divides the processes in a supply chain into two categories, depending on whether they are executed in response to a customer order (pull) or in anticipation of a customer order (push).

There are typically five nodes—namely the customer, retailer, distributor, manufacturer, and supplier—and four stages in a supply chain. The cycle view clearly defines processes involved in each stage and the owner of each process. This view specifies the roles and responsibilities of each member and the desired outcome of each process. The four processes in four stages are:

1. Customer order cycle (customer–retailer)
2. Replenishment cycle (retailer–distributor)
3. Manufacturing cycle (distributor–manufacturer)
4. Procurement cycle (manufacturer–supplier)

It can be observed that these are closely linked to the macro processes discussed earlier. One may also note that the number of stages is decided on the basis of the number of intermediaries. For example, traditional businesses, such as the dairy industry, have a number of stages as intermediaries are more. On the other hand, businesses such as capital goods manufacturing may have fewer intermediaries. However, such operations would have severe process intensity within the level of operation. The importance of the cycle view approach is that it is useful in specifying roles and responsibilities of different players in the supply chain network and establishing rules and procedures across the various stages in supply chain operations.

A supply chain is mainly aimed at serving the ultimate customer and processes get triggered in relation to customer demand. The processes could be initiated either in anticipation of a demand or in response to a demand. The concept of 'pull' in supply chain is about the execution of processes in response to a customer order. This concept is reactive but brings value creation to customers by allowing flexible configuration of products. The advantage to the focal organization in this process is that it reduces finished goods inventory by postponement. For example, dial-a-pizza is normally a pull-based supply chain wherein the focal organization provides the customer the flexibility of selecting the toppings of his choice. At the same time, the focal organization manages its inventory better.

The idea of 'push' in supply chain means the execution of processes is initiated in anticipation of customer orders. This mainly depicts the speculative character of a supply chain where production and stocking happens on the basis of demand forecasts. This process would be more driven by economies of scale in operations and for low-value items. For example, popular models of two wheelers are produced in India on the basis of demand estimates. These are stocked and await customer demand. However, it is important to understand the boundary of push and pull in any supply chain network. Even in the above example of dial-a-pizza, the final choice of pizza could be customer driven but the base and common ingredients must be ready for serving on time. Push and pull processes are useful in considering strategic decisions relating to supply chain design as one gets a more global view of how supply chain processes relate to customer orders. Based on such a global view, facility locations, which could be split or consolidated, and other facets of the supply chain can be designed accordingly. One may also note here that the balancing of push and pull processes and their relative importance will have an impact on the supply chain process. Generally, it is believed that a push process would be cost-based and a pull process would be based on responsiveness. Now let's look at the Dell direct model explained in Exhibit 1.3.

Exhibit 1.3   Dell Direct Model

The Dell Corporation business model is based on the supply chain strategy of direct-to-customer, which was a source of competitive advantage, especially in the home PC segment. Dell differentiated from competition by providing a channel for customers to place orders of their configuration from a set of choices, cutting intermediaries. Dell's aim was to achieve fulfilment of orders at the least cost. For customer satisfaction, logistics operations had to be streamlined to ensure the timely delivery of customized products. Dell was required to design its supply chain appropriately across the globe to give similar experience to all customers, wherever they may be. This involved defining strategy with respect to the location of facilities and structuring of relationships among suppliers, assembly centres, and delivery operators.

The Dell Direct Model facilitates immediate market feedback as the company has direct links with customers. With such an advantage, the company can quickly influence demand trends. Another important aspect of this model is that all players are accountable as roles and responsibilities are clear and management is through metrics. The model lays tremendous emphasis on fulfilling customer orders, an approach which requires the customer to be treated with respect.

The key attribute of this model is 'build to order' as the customer order initiates the process of finalizing the product. This gives the firm the advantage of postponing material ownership until the point of sale. The focus of operations is to ensure resource productivity so that cost advantage is created. The operations run 24 X 7 and matrix form of organization is deployed for organizational efficiency. All these are followed up with commitment and dedication for value creation across the chain.

Dell Direct Model has also defined boundaries of push and pull. Components and accessories need to be available commonly across SKUs, whereas the delivery process from the hub would be initiated after an order is received. The customer order cycle would be in response to a demand, and hence pull-based, whereas aggregation of common items at the hub would be on push basis. The engineering of common products and demand estimation is critical in this whole process.

1.8 INTERFACE OF TECHNOLOGY, PROCESS, AND PEOPLE IN SUPPLY CHAIN

The quality measures and technological advances have revolutionized supply chain in the last two decades. The various process opportunities for supply chain configuration could be understood from the models so far discussed. Business processes mapping and documentation have attained sophistication because quality initiatives are being increasingly adopted across the globe. Rather, quality adherence has become mandatory and transparent for global business.

At the same time, global business has been transformed by technological advances. Technology can be divided into information technology and purely business-specific technology. The advancement of each of these independently triggered growth for the other, and customers were the biggest beneficiaries. A classic example would be e-business, especially trading in goods from apples to apartments, books to boutiques, cards to cars, and so on. One could see success achieved in different models such as B-to-B, B-to-C, G-to-C, and so on. Today, in India, one can buy a bouquet of flowers off the web and get it delivered in any corner in the country. This is how technology empowers customers. Selling flowers online is a simple idea but a great effort from the supply chain perspective. One is now able to send flowers to the remote parts of India, which are not easily accessible and where bouquets may not be available. Aggregators deliver this service at an affordable price because technology has opened up new business opportunities that thrive on economies of scope and collaboration rather than on the simple model of economies of scale.

Of course, there are other less dramatic but still remarkable applications of technology in business which have streamlined the supply chain. These will be discussed at length in chapters that follow. But to provide a window to them, it can be said that business applications have moved from the simple use of technology for transactions and management information system to real-time connectivity and integration with partners, reducing time and eliminating the need to stock information and cash.

Today manufacturing firms have supplier networks linked to their servers. Their visibility in production plans and schedule is enabled for efficiency and effectiveness in the supply chain. It is difficult to imagine life and business without the interface of technology, which is now more like a routine and close to being a universal truth.

The performance of people in the supply chain domain has also been improving dramatically. The competencies of people are critical at the operating and planning levels, and the advances in technology have enhanced their output. For instance, while delivering a courier, the delivery personnel usually take the confirmation of receipt on a document. It leaves one wondering when they would confirm delivery to the consigner. Nowadays some delivery personnel carry a small handheld device and take signature on the monitor of the same. This allows one to track from anywhere in the world the delivery status of one's consignment on near real-time basis. Similarly, stores staff, which handles a huge number of documents for reordering and analysis, is able to do so efficiently because of new technology. The personnel have not changed but their performance has improved dramatically. One can go on listing such examples from around us. These could be in public life, in services like banking, insurance and education, or in manufacturing like engineering and pharmaceuticals. The productivity of people has moved up due to new business models and developments in the supply chain. The relationship is illustrated in Figure 1.5.

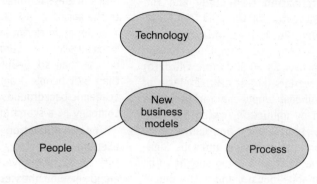

Figure 1.5 Relationship among technology, process, and people

It is important to note that development of new business models is happening not just because of technological advancement or process improvement or quality of people. It is rather due to the ability to interface all of these in a systematic way. In reality, improvements in one leads to the other and new improved models evolve. One would be amazed at the changes that have occurred during this decade in financial services, especially in stock broking. The players are able to assimilate information and act quickly because of the availability of information, improvements in processes, and heightened skills of people who assimilate and make use of such changes. The interface among technology, process, and people has benefited all stakeholders. Similarly, one can look at how many purchasing decisions at the corporate level have improved. It is important to note here that the level of interface would vary according to the business. However, it is certain that interfaces among technology, process, and people are facilitating the configuration of new supply chains, either directly or indirectly, and have dramatically improved supply chain performance. Exhibit 1.4 demonstrates one such story in India.

1.9 SUPPLY CHAIN DECISION HIERARCHY

Supply chain management decisions could belong to one of the three levels—strategic, planning, or operational—based on the time bucket of decision. Figure 1.6 shows the three levels of decisions in a hierarchy. Decisions on the strategic level would set the conditions under which planning and operational level decisions would be made. The strategic level would involve non-routine and critical decisions, planning would engage more of scheduling and structuring a framework for effectiveness, and operational level would concern activities related to execution.

The strategic decisions would have three characteristics: they are long term, capital in nature, and may not be easily reversible. These are related to network design wherein issues such as plant and warehouse location are decided. Other facets such as

---

Exhibit 1.4   The Story of Metal Junction

mjunction services limited operating at the cutting edge of information technology and the Internet, is a 50:50 venture of SAIL and TATA Steel. Founded in February 2001, it is today not only India's largest eCommerce company (having eTransacted worth over Rs 30,800 crore till date) but also runs the world's largest eMarketplace for steel. The steel and coal supply chain in India has been transformed by mjunction, which has ushered in efficiency, transparency, and convenience to the way steel and coal is bought and sold. Similar transformational change is being sought to be made in the automobile industry and in the sale of fixed priced branded products with the launch of autojunction and straightline respectively.

Business volume of the company in terms of transaction value has soared from Rs 94.35 crore in fiscal year 2002 to Rs 14,393 crore in fiscal year 2009, registering a spectacular CAGR of 105 per cent. mjunction's growth has not only been in terms of transactional value, revenue, and profits. In the space of just eight years, it has established a national footprint with offices at twelve locations all over the country. Starting out with a team of less than six people at inception, today more than 375 people from different professional and academic backgrounds are working on growing the company at a scorching pace.

Today, mjunction offers a wide range of eSelling, eSourcing, eFinance and eKnowledge services across diverse industry verticals that empower businesses with greater process efficiencies. mjunction has service offerings spanning the entire eCommerce spectrum and operates through metaljunction.in, buyjunction.in, coaljunction.in, autojunction.in, straightline.in, valuejunction.in, financejunction.in, and mjunctionedge.

Source: http://www.mjunction.in/about_us/, accessed on 30 December 2009.

inventory management, supplier development through alliance network, transportation modelling, and so on are also decided at this level. The decisions made at the strategic level are interrelated. For example, decisions on the mode of transport are influenced by decisions on the geographical location of plants and warehouses, and inventory policies are influenced by the choice of suppliers and production locations. Modelling and simulation are frequently used for analysing these interrelations, and the impact of making strategic level changes in the supply chain.

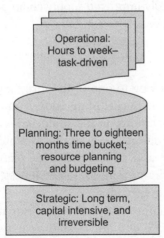

At the planning level, quarterwise demand estimates help in arriving at production plans, decisions about tie-ups with suppliers, aggregate planning for personal care products, quarterwise inventory policy, and so on. The decision hierarchy at this level is mainly based on resource planning and budgeting for achieving efficiency and effectiveness of supply chain. For example, an automotive plant would arrive at an annual budget and indicate the same to the suppliers for their preparedness. Then, it would release a quarterwise production plan, which would give the suppliers an estimate of the quantity of components they should be

Figure 1.6   Hierarchy of supply chain decisions

prepared to supply. This estimate would be fine-tuned and adjusted from month to month.

At the operational level, decisions and activities are meant for accomplishing immediate tasks on set parameters and policies. These are routine and a fixed number of functions which could be happening repetitively. The focus is to accomplish the function without any error or loss of resources. Some operational activities could be production scheduling, executing delivery, movement of a consignment, and so on.

It is important to note the nature of decisions for resource requirement and competence requirement vary widely among the hierarchy of a supply chain. Hence, the preparedness of suppliers and the execution capability of a firm must factor in the same. Many a times, strategic decisions are driven from top management, planning decisions are structured and anchored by supply chain experts, and operational decisions take place at the ground level. However, supervisory management is responsible and accountable for these decisions in reality.

1.10 SPAN OF DECISIONS AND PROFESSIONAL EXCELLENCE IN SCM

It may be pertinent here to highlight the span of supply chain decisions. The rationale is to highlight the importance of supply chain professionals and the nature of decision areas where they may concentrate. Here, it is more indicative to stress the importance of professional approach to SCM and orient a supply chain professional towards opportunities and challenges.

First, strategic decisions involving the supply chain domain and linkages of supply chain strategy with other functional strategies—Strategic Business Unit (SBU) level strategy and corporate strategy—must be clearly understood. This is a decision which would involve top management and a team of functional managers. Hence, a supply chain champion must be able to spearhead decision-making for getting required attention for resources and domain specialization so that value creation for customers could be ensured. A supply chain champion must clearly map information systems required for the chain strategy framework and involve a review mechanism and feedback to other functions and strategic decision-makers.

Second, responsiveness and the efficiency spectrum calls for a trade-off between cost management and service factors. It may be noted that increasing service costs disproportionately is harmful and hence understanding this trade-off is critical. Also this decision needs the support of top management, as service and cost are key competitive features on which the company could be operating in the market. The supply chain manager, who should ideally be a part of the top management, must champion this. If there is no such role, he must be able to draw the attention of the top management.

Third, the span of decision would involve planning functionality like aggregate plans, coordination of production plans, inventory plan, and so on. All these would require functional capability to handle and coordinate. Though technology has been increasingly deployed and decision support systems are available, it is important to appreciate time sensitivity and relational sensitivity of these decisions. Relational sensitivity is how a decision criteria is inter-related within the supply chain domain and across other domains. For example, a manufacturing company may consider a production drop for a product that is to be replaced. If it is planned during a particular planning bucket, the supply chain manager must ensure all stakeholders in the supply chain system are informed and adjust their volume to this requirement.

Four, another area of supply chain decision would be in relation to operational issues, which may involve coordinating inbound and outbound transportation, in-plant logistics, day to day handling with suppliers for daily production schedule, and so on. These decisions, as mentioned, would be taken at a supervisory level. It is critical to understand the occurrences and escalate to the next level. Going back to the sugar plant, in such an enterprise daily reports are critical to understand whether certain production areas are susceptible to failure and need adjustment. This may affect the flow of cane from fields or yield or efficiency parameters. A supply chain analyst must relate such operational data to various parameters and bring it to the attention of appropriate managerial hierarchy.

Five, supply chain managers must coordinate with technology support managers, process owners, and people managers for an interface of the three functions for supply chain improvements. This requires a supply chain manager who can focus on these three aspects with adequate background on contemporary developments and understanding of competition moves on these. The business values of these applications can be mapped by a supply chain manager as he understands the system from the ultimate customer's perspective.

Professional excellence in supply chain is important for any organization to be a high performer. Supply chain focuses on strategically and operationally linking all stakeholders in serving the ultimate customer. Unless the domain is given due share of representation in senior and top management functions and professionally qualified personnel are engaged, the organization would find it difficult to be competitive. Professional excellence is not gained by experience alone. There must be organized effort from the individual and the organization, stakeholders like academia and government, and other professional bodies like Confederation of Indian Industries (CII), Indian Institute of Materials Management (IIMM), and so on. Academia is giving importance to this domain with engineering and management institutions and universities now offering courses in SCM. CII has made an excellent effort by creating a centre of excellence. IIMM has been imparting knowledge on the subject. International programmes and affiliations like Council of Supply Chain Management and others have certification to train professionals in this domain.

SUMMARY

Supply chain management (SCM) is defined as 'the integration of key business processes from the end user through original suppliers that provides products, services, and information that add value for customers and other stakeholders' (the Global Supply Forum). A supply chain involves two or more organizations for serving the ultimate customer, which happens by streamlining the flow of material, finance, and information. Supply chain is more outward looking and inter-organizational in approach.

Collaboration, partnering, and coordinating across entities serving the nodal organization are the key to success.

Logistics is the process of strategically managing the procurement, movement, and storage of materials, parts, and finished inventory. The related information flows through the organization and its marketing channels for the cost-effective fulfilment of customers' orders. Logistics primarily focuses on order management, inbound transportation, in-plant, outbound transportation, storage and procurement, and managerial phases of strategic, planning and operational decisions. The focus is internal organization-centric, primarily on cost, service, resource/asset utilization, and quality parameters.

Value chain, value system, and supply chain management interface, complementing the approach to value creation to customers by defining activities and systems. According to Porter, there are five generic categories of primary activities involved in value creation by any firm competing in an industry: inbound logistics, operations, outbound logistics, marketing and sales, and service. While discussing procurement, Porter defines it as the function of purchasing inputs used in the firm's value chain and not purchasing inputs per se. According to him, the cost of procurement activities themselves usually represents a small if not significant portion of total costs, but often has a large impact on the firm's overall cost and differentiation. Value chain analysis can be used to identify an organization's internal business processes and how they interact. A firm's value chain is embedded in a larger stream of activities termed as value system. Value system links up the value chain of the firm with that of the supplier, channel, and buyer.

While defining macro processes in SCM, it may be noted that process orientation emphasizes on 'how' of an activity rather than 'what'. With respect to supply chain at the macro level, the activities would pertain to supplier management, focal organization's internal supply chain, channel management, and customer relationship management. Supply chain management is entrenched in process orientation and adherence. Many successful organizations have identified their macro processes and synchronized them seamlessly.

There are typically five nodes—the customer, retailer, distributor, manufacturer, and supplier—and four stages in supply chain. According to the cycle view, the four processes in the four stages of supply chain are: customer order cycle, replenishment cycle, manufacturing cycle, and procurement cycle. 'Push' in supply chain means the execution of processes is initiated in anticipation of customer orders. This mainly depicts the speculative character of supply chain where production and stocking happens on the basis of demand forecasts. The concept of 'pull' in supply chain is about the execution of processes in response to a customer order. This concept is reactive but brings value creation to customers by allowing flexible configuration of products.

The trilogy of technology, process, and people plays a key role in improving supply chain effectiveness. The advance in technology and its successful deployment for business, process improvements driven by quality measures, and enhanced people's skills due to technological development contribute to the efficiency of supply chain.

KEY TERMS

Business model: A business model refers to an estimate of revenues and costs incurred in conducting a business. It includes an asset and liability structure, which shows margins and return on investment. The model is fundamental to product/service offering and approach to competition.

Cycle view of supply chain: The cycle view clearly defines processes involved in a supply chain and the owners of each process. This view specifies the roles and responsibilities of each member and the desired outcome of each process. There are normally four stages and five stakeholders, namely the customer, retailer, distributor, manufacturer, and supplier. Each of the two successive nodes are connected to form a cycle.

Hierarchy of supply chain decision-making: This refers to the management level, the level at which decisions are made. Supply chain could be strategic, planning-related, and operational, based on factors such as the time window, the significance of resource deployment, whether the decision is routine or not.

Inbound logistics: Activities associated with receiving and storing material, disseminating inputs from suppliers, inspection, inventory management, transport management, and so on, are categorized as inbound logistics.

Logistics management: Logistics management is about defining a system and managing the same. It ensures that the movement of material, the storage of goods in intermediary stages, and the movement of finished goods to customers are in line with the business strategy of the organization. Logistics management is inward looking and is focused on cost optimization and service level of the focal organization.

Outbound logistics: Activities associated with order processing, order picking and packing, shipping, delivery vehicle operations, and dealer/distributor network are categorized as outbound logistics.

Pull in supply chain: The execution of processes in response to a customer order. This process is reactive but brings value creation to customers by allowing flexible configuration of products.

Push in supply chain: Push in supply chain means the execution of processes is initiated in anticipation of customer orders. This mainly depicts the speculative character of supply chain where production and stocking happen on the basis of demand forecasts.

Strategic business unit (SBU): This level of strategy pertains to a geography or a product group, and so on.

Supply chain management (SCM): SCM is the integration of key business processes of a focal organization with downstream players (customer and customer's customer) on one side and upstream players (supplier and supplier's supplier) on the other side. It also includes managing three flows, namely products/services, information, and finance.

Value chain: A value chain identifies primary activities such as inbound logistics, operations, outbound logistics, marketing and sales, and service; and related support activities such as human resources, procurement, product R&D, technology and systems development, and so on.

Value system: A focal organization's value chain is linked to the value chains of its suppliers and customers. Together these are addressed as a value system.

CONCEPT REVIEW QUESTIONS

1. Analyse supply chain management perspectives in managerial decisions with examples.

2. Define value chain and its linkages in upstream and downstream activities. Identify a focal organization's value chain and elucidate how it works within the industry it operates. Discuss whether value chains of different firms within an industry could be different. If yes, cite an example.

3. Discuss the role of technology application and process adherence in effective supply chain management and cite examples from real life.

4. What do you understand by macro processes in supply chain and how are they related? Explain the concept with an example.

5. 'The role of a supply chain manager is more like a functional manager and has a limited scope.' Comment on the statement with different industry situations.

CRITICAL THINKING QUESTIONS

1. Imagine that you are the supply chain manager of a power equipment engineering company. You have ancillaries who do product-related work. Your customer is erecting a power plant. You have been asked to demonstrate your value system to your management and suggest a fair distribution of supply chain profits among the players involved. Point out the focal points for your discussion with your management.

2. Assume you are in charge of the internal supply chain of a construction site where a residential complex is being built. Discuss the important processes and approaches for effective supply chain management.

3. Assume that you are in charge of the supply chain of a retail chain's large store. How would you approach technology, process, and people integration for in-store supply chain management? It is recommended you visit a store and apply your experience accordingly.

REFERENCES

Chopra, Sunil, Peter Meindl and D.V. Kalka, *Supply Chain Management: Strategy, Planning and Orientation*, Pearson, 2007

Christopher, Martin, *Logistics and Supply Chain Management: Creating Value-adding Networks*, Financial Times Prentice Hall, Third Edition, 1998

Engels, Donald W., *Alexander the Great and the Logistics of the Macedonian Army*, University of California Press, 1980

Lambert, Douglas M. and Martha C. Cooper, 'Issues in Supply Chain Management,' *Industrial Marketing Management*, Vol. 29, No. 1, pp. 65–83, 2000

Porter, Michael E., *Competitive Advantage*, Free Press, 1985, Export edition 2004, pp. 36

Van Mieghem, Timothy, 'Lessons Learned from Alexander the Great,' *Quality Progress*, Vol. 31, No. 1, January 1998, pp. 41–46

http://cscmp.org/Council of Supply chain management Professionals

www.amul.com/organisation.html

www.mjunction.in/about_us/

www.supply-chain.org/

Appendix 1.1 — Gujarat Cooperative Milk Marketing Federation

GCMMF: AN OVERVIEW

Gujarat Cooperative Milk Marketing Federation (GCMMF) is India's largest food products marketing organization. It is a state level apex body of milk cooperatives in Gujarat which aims to provide remunerative returns to the farmers and also serve the interest of consumers by providing quality products which are good value for money.

CRISIL, India's leading Ratings, Research, Risk and Policy Advisory company, has assigned its highest ratings of 'AAA/Stable/P1+' to the various bank facilities of GCMMF.

Details of GCMMF

Members: 13 district cooperative milk producers' unions

No. of producer members: 2.7 million

No. of village societies: 13,141

Total milk handling capacity: 10.21 million litres per day

Milk collection (total 2007–08): 2.69 billion litres

Milk collection (daily average 2007–08): 7.4 million litres

Milk drying capacity: 626 Mts per day

Cattle feed manufacturing capacity: 3090 Mts per day

Sales Turnover	Rs (in millions)	US$ (in millions)
1994–95	11,140	355
1995–96	13,790	400
1996–97	15,540	450
1997–98	18,840	455
1998–99	22,192	493
1999–2000	22,185	493
2000–01	22,588	500
2001–02	23,365	500
2002–03	27,457	575
2003–04	28,941	616
2004–05	29,225	672
2005–06	37,736	850
2006–07	42,778	1,050
2007–08	52,554	1,325

Products Marketed

Bread spreads	3 products
Cheese range	8 products
Mithaee (Ethnic sweets) range	6 products
UHT milk range	7 products
Pure ghee	3 products
Infant milk range	3 products
Milk powders	4 products
Sweetened condensed milk	1 product
Fresh milk	6 products
Curd products	4 products
Amul ice creams	6 products
Chocolate and confectionery	2 products
Brown beverage	1 product
Milk drink	2 products
Health beverage	1 product

Source: http://www.amul.com/organisation.html.

Appendix 1.2   **SCM Definitions by CSCMP**

As supply chain covers a broad range of disciplines, the definition of supply chain management can be variable and confusing. Often, supply chain management is confused with logistics management. The definition given by the CSCMP board of directors, comprising industry experts, is accepted as the official definition of supply chain management.

CSCMP's Definition of Supply Chain Management

Supply chain management encompasses the planning and management of all activities involved in sourcing and procurement, conversion, and all logistics management activities. Importantly, it also includes coordination and collaboration with channel partners, which can be suppliers, intermediaries, third party service providers, and customers. In essence, supply chain management integrates supply and demand management within and across companies.

Supply Chain Management—Boundaries and Relationships

Supply chain management is an integrating function with primary responsibility for linking major business functions and business processes within and across companies into a cohesive and high-performing business model. It includes all of the logistics management activities noted above, as well as manufacturing operations, and it drives coordination of processes and activities with and across marketing, sales, product design, finance, and information technology.

CSCMP's Definition of Logistics Management

Logistics management is that part of supply chain management that plans, implements, and controls the efficient, effective forward and reverses flow and storage of goods, services, and related information between the point of origin and the point of consumption in order to meet customers' requirements.

Logistics Management—Boundaries and Relationships

Logistics management activities typically include inbound and outbound transportation management, fleet management, warehousing, materials handling, order fulfilment, logistics network design, inventory management, supply/demand planning, and management of third party logistics services providers. To varying degrees, the logistics function also includes sourcing and procurement, production planning and scheduling, packaging and assembly, and customer service. It is involved in all levels of planning and execution—strategic, operational, and tactical. Logistics management is an integrating function, which coordinates and optimizes all logistics activities, as well as integrates logistics activities with other functions, including marketing, sales manufacturing, finance, and information technology.

Source: http://cscmp.org/aboutcscmp/ definitions.asp.

2

Supply Chain Structure

After studying this chapter, you will be able to:
- Comprehend the definition of supply chain structure
- Understand the difference between efficient supply chain and responsive supply chain
- Understand the push and pull classification of supply chain and the key parameters for enabling the same
- Understand the key parameters of cost-based supply chain
- Gain an insight into the managerial levers for achieving cost efficiency in supply chain
- Comprehend the agile supply chain in uncertain times and during certainty
- Understand the trade-off between push and pull systems

2.1 STRUCTURE OF A SUPPLY CHAIN

The structure of a supply chain network refers to the pattern or manner in which constituent parts are arranged together. The characteristics of a supply chain network that exercise a strategic influence on competitive forces are referred to as structural factors. These factors include sharing of profit across the supply chain constituents and the level of customer service within the network. In other words, it is these characteristics that play an important role in the conduct and performance of organizations participating in the supply chain network and provide competitive advantage to the focal organization.

Figure 2.1 represents the network of organizations in a supply chain. It illustrates the relationship between the focal organization's supplier, the supplier's supplier, the intermediaries' logistics service providers, the customer, and the customer's customer, and so on. The design of a supply chain must take into account such 'where' and 'how' issues as: where and how products are produced, where and how they enter the market, where they are stored, and how they reach a customer. However, this approach is manufacturing centric and not really supply chain-centric, that is, it is not customer-centric. One key aspect that this book stresses is that is the supply chain should be set from the customer's perspective, as the whole end is to serve a customer.

The key or starting point for designing a supply chain structure is the purpose and command, or hierarchy, which is all about striking a balance between the cost of

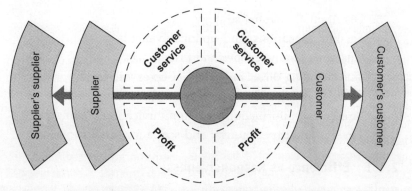

Figure 2.1 A supply chain structure

storing and moving goods and services from the supplier to the customer. Figure 2.2 shows the generic perspective of a supply chain structure.

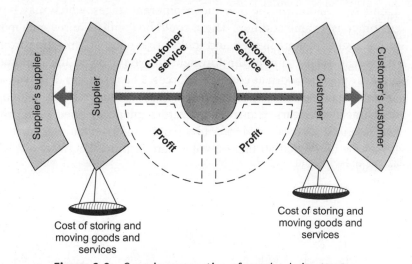

Figure 2.2 Generic perspective of supply chain structure

In the set-up, customer service needs special attention. Hence, the supply chain horizon extends from efficiency on one side to responsiveness on the other side. Often, these are extreme and mutually exclusive options. Managerial challenges have been in bringing both ends close so that a high degree of efficiency and responsiveness is achieved, giving competitive advantage to the focal organization.

As there is no formula or framework that can prescribe the right balance, the optimal supply chain structure would typically differ not only from company to company but also among product and market groups. This is mainly because each product and market group is unique and the company's competitive approach would vary based on the resources it commands and other strategic factors like focus and vision. A number of factors influence the structural features of a supply chain:

1. Character and type of product
2. Nature, type, and size of market

3. Distribution channel strategy
4. Facilities, locations, and options available
5. Customer characteristics and preferences
6. Tax including direct and indirect taxes and levies
7. Strength of logistics services and intermediary options
8. Strength of information and communication channels
9. Level of industry maturity and scope for innovations

2.1.1 Efficiency vs Responsiveness

Efficiency refers to output to input ratio. In a supply chain, output needs to be defined in terms of revenue realized from customers on a product or service. Every player, right from the supplier to the channel partner of the nodal organization, is involved in revenue generation from the customer (see Figure 2.3). The objective of all these agents is to maximize the revenue in different stages, which may be passed on to the customer as a value addition. There could be conflicts in revenue maximization if any of the agents is short-sighted and looks at revenue optimization from the perspective of a single stage, without the foresight to pass it on to the customer. This is where market dynamics work as corrective forces. The resources deployed are the key inputs in any function in such a chain activity. These resources could be people in the form of warehouse operators, transport operators, planning specialists, inventory analysts, and so on. Resources could refer to the time involved and the functional value as well. It may be noted that all these involve certain money equivalents, which are mapped as costs.

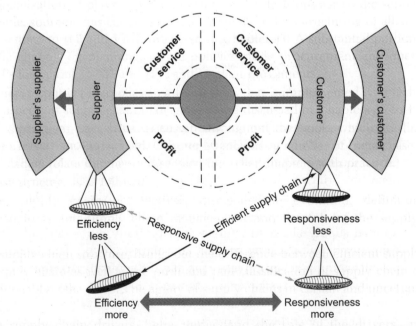

Figure 2.3 Efficiency and responsiveness orientation in supply chain structure

Efficiency could be simply defined as the ratio of revenue to cost or profit generated. As it is easier to measure cost as compared to profit, cost is more often used as a measure of efficiency. According to Fisher (1997), the primary goal of an efficient supply chain is to serve demand at the lowest cost. Hence, one may conclude an efficient supply chain keeps costs low. Typically, this approach is common in cases of necessity items, utility products, and standard goods. In such cases, the product market is mature and normally goods or services are commoditized. Some examples of such product categories include food items, dairy products, popular models of functional consumer products segments, and automobiles. The other key parameter of an efficient supply chain is that product design and facilities management are oriented towards minimizing costs. A higher utilization of facilities and effective product design, with standard usage and functionality for the customer, are likely to be the key focus points for an efficient supply chain. Products should be designed in such a way that they are essentially functional; the customer would not require add-ons at high prices in these cases.

Similarly, the inventory level would be cost focused, which means that the nodal organization would reduce its inventory. It may be asked if facilities minimization and inventory reduction can work together. The answer is: yes, they can, in only the standard and matured product/services market. Another aspect, namely lead time reduction, would also be a part of an efficient supply chain. Lead time reduction leads to inventory reduction and thus to efficient supply chain. However, lead time reduction is challenging to achieve as it could impact responsiveness in terms of customer service level. Thus, an efficient supply chain is one end of the supply chain structure spectrum, which works well for items in demand. These are low- to medium-value items, which are standardized and have a matured market.

Responsiveness is a measure of the speed of reaction to a customer demand. It is measured as a unit of time in normal parlance and some authors include in it rightfully the level of customer service. That is, if demand for a product is 100, the level of service measures the percentage of orders served. There could be different measures like the fulfilment of demand, the fulfilment of promise, and complete fulfilment, which will be discussed in detail in Chapter 19. In simple terms, responsiveness is the speed and level of customer service.

According to Fisher, the primary goal of a responsive supply chain is to respond quickly to a demand. Besides a quick response, the ability to serve demand and the customer service level are also important factors. Hence, one may conclude that a responsive supply chain focuses on the time and level of service to customer demand. Typically, this is common in cases of high-value items, personalized items that require customization, and new products that are at early growth stages of a product lifecycle. In such cases, either the product market would be in early stages or the products would be of high value or specific to a group or individuals. For example, trendy motorcycles with high horsepower targeted at the youth segment are highly priced. Other examples are: hi-tech goods, medical equipment, garments, fashion jewellery, mobiles, electronic goods, home furniture, and selected automobile segment in passenger cars, commercial vehicles and two wheelers, and agriculture equipment including tractors. The other key parameter of a responsive supply chain is that product design and facilities management should be configured towards creating modularity, allowing postponement of product completion. Modularity allows product differentiation and high degree of customization. It may require more common items but allows variety on completion.

A higher flexibility in manufacturing, allowing for uncertainty in demand and accommodating product variation based on demand, would be the key manufacturing strategy for a responsive supply chain. Supplier relationship management would be driven by the ability to respond quickly to demand variation, provide flexibility in manufacturing, and the ability for concurrent engineering. Quality management is one of the key aspects, which is more than the threshold requirement for a responsive supply chain. Similarly, inventory strategy would be focused on creating a buffer to meet service level and enable quick response to demand. This would also help meet demand and supply uncertainty, allowing flexibility in demand. One may question whether facilities flexibility and inventory buffering would result in high investment and commitment of resources. Obviously, such concerns are genuine for any supply chain manager and they have to be addressed through a functional strategy of effective pricing and high margins. When we speak of high margins, aspects of both absolute and relative margins must be considered. Absolute margins refer to gross margin in currency compared to standard items. Relative margins are net margins compared as percentage of cost of production or offering of service. Often, the responsive supply chain exerts pressure on relative margins, especially during a downward trend in the economic cycle when sentiments are weak across the board.

Another aspect, namely lead time reduction, irrespective of cost would also be part of a responsive supply chain. This sounds very theoretical and seems to contradict the appropriate management perspective. How can one recommend lead time reduction irrespective of cost? To understand this, one has to interpret the term with respect to customer service level and the relationship between increasing service level or availability vis-à-vis cost of providing that level of service. After a point, increasing responsiveness would require more than proportionate increase in costs and would affect margins. However, contemporary manufacturing management practices are addressing this issue with new techniques such as just in time (JIT), lean, and so on, which would be discussed in later chapters.

Thus, a responsive supply chain works well for items that have uncertain characteristics, especially high-value items, new products, and products that lend for customization and for which the market is in early stages of growth in product lifecycle. It also works for products where innovation is the basic character of the product group, such as electronics and medical equipment.

2.1.2 Boundary for Efficient and Responsive Supply Chain

Efficiency is a measure of cost. Supply chain efficiency would focus on reducing cost, which would lead to reduction in customer service level, response time, and so on. As mentioned earlier, efficiency would focus on fewer variants and on standardization of products and manufacturing set-up. On the other hand, responsiveness is the speed at which one services customer requirement. Often, such a speed can be achieved with higher inventory, expensive and reliable movement, and so on. Thus a responsive supply chain would be high on cost. Thus there is a direct relationship between responsiveness and efficiency as shown in Figure 2.4. Here, cost depicts efficiency.

Ideally, any supply chain manager would like to reverse this relationship, which is a big challenge in supply chain management. A manager would want to achieve the dual objective of cost minimization and increased customer service. As can be observed from Figure 2.4, an increase in responsiveness entails a proportionate increase in cost, and this prospect becomes less attractive after a point. When a firm focuses on increasing responsiveness, it must question the ability to pass on the increase in cost to the customer. Different firms approach the quandary differently, based on their strategic focus and resource capability. Exhibit 2.1 on Avaya IT Communications shows how responsiveness and cost efficiency can be balanced to compete in the market.

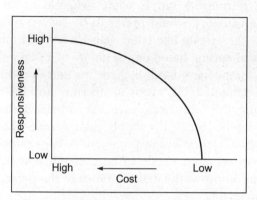

Figure 2.4 Trade-off between cost and responsiveness

Exhibit 2.1   Avaya

Avaya delivers intelligent communications solutions that help companies transform their businesses to achieve marketplace advantage. More than one million businesses worldwide, including more than 90 per cent of the FORTUNE 500 companies, use Avaya solutions for IP telephony, unified communications, contact centres, and communications-enabled business processes.

In June 2008, Avaya selected Singapore as the hub for its Asia Pacific supply chain management. Avaya established a finished goods distribution centre in Singapore as part of its new supply chain management strategy for Asia Pacific, which would see an annual turnover of over 500 tons of IT equipment worth over $100 million out of Singapore. As part of the new strategy, all Avaya products manufactured in Asia Pacific were consolidated and shipped to regional customers and business partners from the island nation. Avaya's manufacturing facilities located in China, Thailand, and Indonesia serve the region, including Australia, China, India, Southeast Asia, Korea, and Japan. The company budgeted a cost savings of up to 80 per cent and a reduction in lead time for delivery of products from fourteen days to as short as two days for most of the region.

The three main drivers for choosing Singapore as the hub were cost savings, shorter delivery times, and close proximity to customers and business partners. Avaya is now able to respond more quickly to orders from business partners and pass on these cost savings as freight. Other locations that Avaya considered include Hong Kong and Malaysia. Singapore's strategic location in Asia and its world-class infrastructure were key factors for the company to establish its regional supply chain management centre here. In addition, the hub's close proximity to Singapore's award-winning Changi Airport means Avaya is now able to fulfil orders to customers and business partners faster than ever before.

Source: Adapted from http://www.avaya.com/gcm/master-usa/en-us/corporate/pressroom/pressreleases/ 2008/pr 080613.htm&Wrapper=Print.

It may also be noted that with low-cost electronics manufacturing shifting to China, Singapore has moved into high value-adding activities like product design and high-end manufacturing. Be it a multinational corporation (MNC) with regional production or a regional small to medium enterprise (SME), responsiveness in supply chain is becoming key for firms in Singapore to be competitive.

Thus, certain markets focus on the responsive supply chain, whereas in other markets, customers falling in the same category would prefer to be served by an efficient supply chain. For example, a conglomerate like Hindustan Unilever Limited (HUL) would have a different focus in structuring, based on the nature of a particular product—whether it is a personal care, home care, food, hygiene, or dairy product. For most of the segments in which it operates, HUL needs to structure an efficient supply chain. However, it has to balance this with responsiveness as market share depends upon the ability to service customers. Hence, the supply chain managers and system have the pressure to balance both efficiency and responsiveness. For example, while the popular body wash and soap segment needs to be cost efficient, it is important to introduce new products and improve the existing range in the personal care products category to attract customers.

Products like sugar will have a cost-efficient configuration. Similarly, paper and pulp manufacture would be cost-efficiency driven. Products like cycles and popular models of two wheelers would be somewhat efficiency-driven with less degree of flexibility as manufacture and marketing would be based on demand estimates. However, product groups such as tractors, commercial vehicles, middle and high-end car segments, and electronic goods for mass consumption would have a somewhat responsive supply chain. This is mainly because the products are more expensive and product demand may change in a short period, based on environmental or external factors. Finally, hi-tech items such as iPods, mobile phones, and medical equipment; fashion goods such as apparel and jewellery; and premium automobiles would require a responsive supply chain. For these segments, demand forecasts are difficult and customers are not primarily concerned with price when compared to the value of possessing the product.

It may be observed from our discussion in this section that responsiveness and efficiency are two ends of the supply chain spectrum. The supply chain strategy would be to understand the positioning and structure of the supply chain network accordingly. Industry structure, competitive conditions, and behaviour of firms decide the evolutionary trend. As one may notice, there are many situations which vary from industry to industry, from firm to firm within an industry, from market to market for a firm, and also within product categories or groups. The challenge is to manage this dichotomy of cost versus responsiveness, which would run through all managerial aspects of a supply chain while satisfying a customer demand. Decisions such as inventory management, transportation, facilities management, sourcing, pricing, and information management are twined around the choice of efficiency and responsiveness as the purpose of the supply chain network.

2.2 PUSH-BASED SUPPLY CHAIN

One of the broad classifications of the supply chain is the push- and pull-based supply chain, which is based on process view. Prima facie, pull-based supply-chain relates to responsiveness whereas push-based supply chain is related to cost efficiency. Both push- and pull-based supply chain are processes and strategies of a supply chain network whereas cost efficiency and responsiveness are more like the purpose and philosophy of a supply chain network.

The push-based supply chain, in simple terms, is work in anticipation of customer orders. For this reason it is seen as a speculative supply chain. One needs to consider a few questions while analysing a push-based supply chain:

1. Why should a manufacturer prefer to set up his production function and incur huge marketing and sales support in order to woo customers?
2. Are there inherent product, market, and industry characteristics that warrant push strategies?
3. Are there certain process or structural features which facilitate only push strategies?
4. What is the relationship between cost efficiency and responsiveness if push strategies are to be pursued?
5. What are the managerial levers available in order to make the strategy both push effective and cost efficient?

It is obvious that there are aspects of business that require push strategies in supply chain and the management must apply all its efforts and resources in ensuring cost minimization when there is a lack of certainty in demand. Over the years, business and industry development has facilitated streamlining approaches towards cost-efficient push-based supply chain strategies. A multidisciplinary orientation is important for the successful implementation of these strategies, so they should be well executed at the planning and operations stages. It is important to understand the drivers for success in terms of cost efficiency. A wrong approach or implementation practice would lead not only to failure of the supply chain network but also affect the nodal organization negatively.

2.2.1 Key Conditions Enabling Push-based Supply Chain

The enablers of a push-based supply chain could be industry factors, the organization of the distribution structure, the nature of the product, and the strength of support services, including logistics service providers. These are the aspects the first three questions raised above refer to. They could be addressed as shown in Table 2.1.

One of the key enablers of a push-based supply chain is the manufacturing strategy of 'made to stock' (MTS). MTS strategy is one where the product is produced so that it can be stocked for meeting an expected or estimated demand. Based on experience, a production plan is drawn so that at any point of time, a deliverable based on a sales order may be made from the existing stock. One may appreciate that MTS strategy would work in situations where lot sizes would require production in large lots and

Table 2.1 Factors influencing push-based supply chain structure

Features	Example	Focus	Remarks
Character and type of product	Steel	Efficiency	Standardized product used as raw material for many goods.
Nature and size of market	Perishable market such as fruits and vegetables	Efficiency	Definite timeframe for market reach and life of product. Must be sensitive to demand.
	Global market	Efficiency	Products in global market may adopt efficient supply chain using multiple plant location and distribution centres.
Distribution channel strategy	FMCG goods such as personal care products, beverages, and so on with a number of intermediaries	Efficiency	More intermediaries, larger inventory across the chain and the need to be cost-centric.
Facilities locations and options available	Centralized facility such as Amazon	Efficiency	Time to service could be longer but cost efficiency would be the focus.
Customer characteristics and preferences	Standard product choice and price sensitive.	Efficiency	Staple food items and necessary goods
Tax including direct and indirect taxes and levies		Efficiency	Tax and levies addded to the cost. A prudent approach is to minimize the same by consolidating stock points and related activities.
Strength of logistics services and intermediary options	Matured LSP (Logistics Service Providers) who can handle DCs, transportation, and so on, especially for manufacturing standard products	Efficiency	As in the case of bulk chemicals, pharmaceuticals, and engineering industry wherein made to stock (MTS) is practised.
Strength of information and communication channels	Structured information and communication channel	Efficiency	Supportive systems for planning and distribution management. Would apply to industries mentioned above as well.
Level of industry maturity and scope for innovations	Matured industry situations—Popular two wheeler segment in India	Efficiency	As industry matures, there would be stable growth and cost competitiveness.

releases have to be made in batches. In such cases, the manufacturing set-up would be based on a standard size of operation. However, sometimes the MTS strategy is adopted for operating efficiency rather than demand requirements. The manufacture of products such as cement and chemicals is driven by product economics. Besides the demand pattern and operating efficiencies, the supply of raw materials also determines the MTS strategy. The classic examples would be the manufacture of sugar and dairy products. The manufacture of plantation white sugar is determined by cane availability and sucrose content in cane which is seasonal. Similarly, dairy products such as cream and butter oil are produced and stocked during the peak season and recombined as milk during the off season. Many ancillary and component manufacturers also follow the MTS strategy to maintain operating balance and viability of business, as such firms have limited resource capability to manage flexibility and huge variations in demand.

2.3 MANAGERIAL LEVERS FOR ACHIEVING COST-EFFICIENT SUPPLY CHAIN

As mentioned earlier, if a firm focuses on cost efficiency, it may have to compromise on responsiveness. Any manager would like to understand how one can balance both the factors, or arrive at a cost that can be borne by the customer with a healthy profit and a reasonable service level. Here we will discuss the managerial levers to achieve cost efficiency in supply chain.

1. Facilities consolidation and achieving economies of scale in production would be a key factor. In India, over the decades, cement plants have been able to establish economies of scale in production and now there are many plants with a capacity of a million and above tonnes per annum, which is about 3,000 tonnes per day. If one looks at the manufacturing strategy, production automation and savings in process costs have driven the rise in economic size. Though demand has been growing phenomenally, scaling of size is one of the key contributors for the growth of the industry. Hence, by nature, the production process and the product may require cost-efficient supply chain traditionally.

   Other aspect of facilities consolidation would include aggregating distribution centres so that inbound transportation and finished inventory are consolidated. This could be difficult in certain types of industries like FMCG because of disbursed demand points. Though commodities like steel and oil would also have disbursed demand characteristics, there is a tendency for consolidation due to difficulty with multiple levels of handling.

2. Inventory management is another lever for the cost-efficient supply chain. In this, inventory must be optimized and cost efficiency can be achieved only if the stock is minimized. Stock minimization can happen only when there is certainty and transparency in the system, especially when demand is unknown and speculative as in the case of MTS strategy. Given that, one can always work more easily on upward linkages of a supply chain. Among the downward linkages, the most critical problem arising due to inventory reduction would be lost sales when there is no stock. Hence this management lever works only for stable, low-to-medium value items in matured markets and product groups.

3. Transportation management towards push would be to consolidate and economize. This may work in tangent to inventory policy and hence one would have to work out savings carefully. Like with consolidation of facilities, transportation to distribution facilities in the downstream supply chain activities can be economized. This may increase outbound cost from distribution centres. Under normal conditions, customers are spread out and outbound transportation tends to be more. Moreover, outbound transportation generally carries finished good of

one stage whereas inbound transportation is for raw material and intermittent process goods. Looking at these, there is adequate scope for transportation-led economies in a cost-efficient push-based supply chain.

4. Sourcing and supplier relationship management is a major supply chain activity in the downstream. For instance, because of the development and growth in the automotive supply chain over the past few decades, there has been a phenomenal progress in sourcing and supplier relationship management. Apart from industry-led initiative, quality movements, especially in the automotive and electronics sectors, have led to further advancement in sourcing and supplier management. These practices again facilitate cost-efficient push strategies in the supply chain. When a nodal organization adopts initiatives such as vendor managed inventory and kanban system, there could be surplus inventory in the supply chain network. But due to transparency and cost of handling being lower at the supplier end, the overall supply chain costs also come down. Similarly, quality initiatives like pre-approved vendors for supplies, supplier partnership, and collaborative initiatives in product development and engineering reduce supply chain costs. Push-based strategies can be effective in such cases.

5. Information management could be another useful managerial lever for an efficient and cost effective push-based supply chain. An information system must focus on visibility, effective utilization of stock and demand, and price information to optimize profits across the system. To cite an example, a nodal organization involved in the manufacture of consumer electronic goods has scheduled a milk run to collect components from vendors on a daily basis from an industrial area. On a particular day, the manufacturing units decide to skip a component vendor as there is a change in production schedule. If there is an information network among the manufacturer, supplier, and transport operators, the vendor and the transport operator would be timely informed about the change in schedule. There would be many such instances as production plan and schedule are based on a uniform demand pattern which have to be modified in reality.

6. Pricing can also be used for a cost-efficient push-based supply chain. As mentioned earlier, push-based supply chain is based on demand estimations, which also determine prices of products. Due to a poor estimate of demand or change in competitive environment or any such factor, demand may fall short of estimate and there could be excess stock requiring action to liquidate. If the nodal organization could work a pricing strategy which would facilitate stock movement, then cost efficiency can be achieved. This is a reactionary approach. However, if the nodal organization works out a plan of using pricing strategy while implementing MTS strategy itself, cost-efficient supply chain can be managed well.

7. There are other generic levers available for managing a cost-efficient push-based supply chain. These include improving forecasting techniques, operational efficiencies in all supply chain activities, and establishing strong feedback

mechanism and information flow for monitoring and evaluating performance. This would also help in taking timely actions. It is important to map industry practices constantly and deploy innovative strategies in order to succeed. Many firms, which have been thriving on push-based supply chain, have successfully implemented the same. One of the classic examples in India is the growth of organized retailers operating in a competitive market with millions of SKUs.

Hence cost-efficient push-based supply chain could be successfully deployed if industry, market, and product characteristics warrant the same. The ability of organizations to be innavative and meet the challenges of such a strategy has been established over the years and across markets. Supply chain managers must be conscious of such developments and deploy initiatives for being a competitive player in the market.

2.4 COMMODITY AND COST-CENTRIC SUPPLY CHAIN

Commodities mean goods which are traded. In this context, one would look at products which are homogenous in character or with less variation, and commonly traded under commodities. These could be agricultural produce such as rice, wheat, pulses, oilseeds, spices, sugar, and fruits and vegetables. Or these could be minerals and mineral-based products such as iron ore, steel, bauxite, and so on. The trade of these commodities is widely regulated in different countries through various agencies and international bodies. Some commodities are covered under the Essential Commodities Act and regulated through market operations, support mechanism, and so on. Hence, understanding the dynamics of commodities supply chain is critical for those who are in this business or are using these products as raw material and intermediaries. For example, those in the business of personal care products such as hair oil are directly dependent on oil and oil extracts as their raw material. Similarly those who are in the business of food products such as wheat flour, ready-to-eat food items, and processed spices, would also be directly influenced by the commodities market. On the other hand, though pharmaceutical companies use sugar syrup in their compounds, syrups constitute a small portion of the total value add and may not be sensitive to raw material commodity price. It is important to note here that there are various customer categories to these segments.

One can similarly look at commodities such as iron ore, steel, and bullions for which there are various kinds of customer groups located in different geographies. In the supply chain for these commodities, especially in the case of bullions, customer preference would vary from utility function and store function to protect value of investment. Hence, the supply chain of such a commodity has to be mapped for the nodal organization with respect to the customer group. For example, many commodity buyers may not even take physical possession but would have rights and stocks through common agents. In such cases, a financial supply chain would be required. Since this subject is exhaustive, it is out of the scope of this book to cover it in detail. One example of the commodities supply chain, that of edible oil in India, is discussed in Table 2.2.

Table 2.2   Oilseeds production in India (in million tonnes)

	1960–61	1970–71	1980–81	1990–91	1999–00	2000–01	2001–02	2002–03	2003–04	2004–05	2005–06	2006–07
Oilseeds*	7	9.6	9.4	18.6	20.7	18.4	20.6	14.8	25.2	24.2	28	23.8
Kharif	NA	7	5	9.8	12.5	11.9	13.2	9	16.7	14.1	16.8	13.9
Rabi	NA	2.6	4.4	8.8	8.2	6.5	7.4	5.8	8.5	10.2	11.2	9.9
Groundnut	4.8	6.1	5	7.5	5.3	6.4	7	4.1	8.1	6.8	8	4.9
Kharif	NA	NA	3.7	5.1	3.8	4.9	5.6	3.1	6.9	5.3	6.3	3.3
Rabi	NA	NA	1.3	2.4	1.5	1.5	1.4	1	1.2	1.5	1.7	1.6
Rapeseed/Mustard	1.4	2	2.3	5.2	5.8	4.2	5.1	3.9	6.3	7.6	8.1	7.1

*Includes groundnut, rapeseed and mustard, sesame, linseed, castorseed, nigerseed, safflower, sunflower, and soya bean
Source: Economic Survey 2008 Statistical Tables, Government of India.

It can be seen from Table 2.2 that groundnut and rapeseed/mustard seeds are the major oilseeds. Oil is marketed in bulk, in large packs and consumer packs, for sale in markets through agents and distribution network. It may be noted that the oilseed crops are dependent on both the southwest monsoon and the northeast monsoon. Also, the cropping pattern varies across geography. Groundnut is primarily grown in Gujarat, Karnataka, Tamil Nadu, and Andhra Pradesh, and rapeseed/mustard is grown in Rajasthan, parts of Uttar Pradesh, and Madhya Pradesh. So there is wide variability at source, and the availability is also seasonal. Moreover, the Essential Commodities Act, 1955 does not permit stocking beyond a certain period. Hence there is a need to transact goods within a fixed time period. These are major supply side limitations. There would be a gap between demand and supply, especially if the supply is hampered due to failure of monsoon during periods of peak demand. The government regulates the market with import of palmolein (palm oil) and other vegetable oils. With commodity exchanges operating systematically, there is better price discovery and operating leverage availability, improving the supply chain efficiency. Thus, industry characteristics like seasonal availability of produce, fragmented process units, established market operations of traders across the country, prevalence of loose edible oil usage, increasing brand awareness, and demand for quality oil improve the efficiency of the supply chain which may be based on estimated demand.

However, regulatory markets, multiple-level handling of produce and processed products, and presence of unorganized intermediaries across the chain complicates the cost efficiency. Any nodal organization across the chain has no choice except to apply managerial levers effectively to improve efficiency to be successful in this business. A typical edible oil supply network is shown in Figure 2.5.

2.5   PULL-BASED SUPPLY CHAIN

Pull-based supply chain is configured to produce customized products as per the customer's demand. If such an execution is warranted, then there is a need to know with certainty the arrival of the customer and preparedness to serve the customer. Pull-

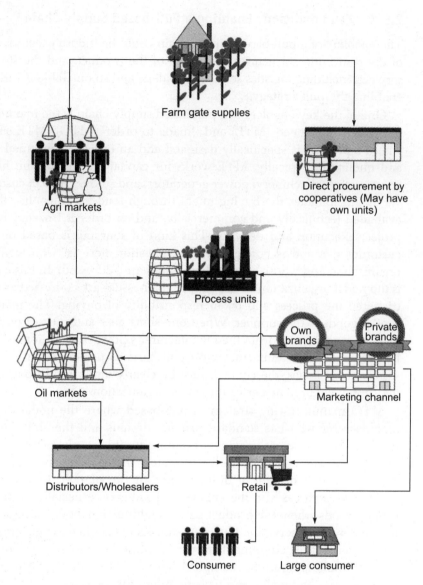

Figure 2.5 Edible oil supply chain

based supply chain is more a reactionary process as it reacts to customer demand. The simplest example is dial-a-pizza where a pizza is prepared and delivered on order. It must be noted that most of the pull-based supply chains are on downward stream wherein an inventory framework and capacity dedication are available. Also, the ability of delivery mechanism is to use quick, responsive, and customized outbound transportation. Over the years, improvements in industry practices have enabled pull-based supply chain for upstream activities as well. Just in time (JIT) in manufacturing is one of the classic applications of pull strategy in downstream activities wherein the supplier is encouraged to deliver components at production line to save time and inventory, and also have flexibility and responsiveness towards servicing customer demand.

2.5.1   Key Conditions Enabling a Pull-based Supply Chain

The enablers of a pull-based supply chain could be industry factors, the organization of the distribution structure, the nature of the product, and the strength of support services, including logistics service providers, and so on. Table 2.3 lists certain factors enabling the pull strategy.

One of the key enablers of a pull-based supply chain is the manufacturing strategy of 'made to engineer' (MTE) and 'made to order' (MTO). MTE strategy is applied where a product is specifically designed and an order is confirmed based on tender and quotation. Typically, MTE works for capital machinery and high-value capital goods such as machinery, power generators, and so on. Often, a customer directly, or via agents, initiates the buying intent through tenders. After this, the responses are evaluated technically and commercially, and an order is frozen. This is common in project execution and delivery. This kind of sourcing is based on pull strategy as customer demand is configured. The question here is: who would be the nodal organization and whose supply chain issues are addressed? In this case, the customer is the nodal organization whose supply chain issues are addressed as the customer has triggered the process and taken responsibility of buying. The manufacturer of the capital goods is the supplier. When one shifts gear and focuses on the supply chain issue of capital goods from the manufacturer's point of view, it may be observed that he organizes his manufacturing on pull basis as per customer orders. In handling supply chain issues, the context must be clearly understood from the perspective of the supply chain manager of the nodal organization.

MTO manufacturing strategy is pull-based where the nodal organization is the manufacturer who has standard product designs and the ability to configure final demand—this strategy provides the opportunity for mass-customization. A classic example of this would be Dell Computers in the personal computers and laptop segment, which became a differentiator in the market. One can come across a number of such cases in the engineering industry, especially in the manufacture of capital, goods where the product design and functionality are standardized, and offer little variation to serve the final demand. Examples include generator sets, auxiliary power generation equipment, electrical fitments, and so on. The food served in luxury hotels is another example where MTO strategy can be deployed as the customer gets high value and pays premium for the same.

2.5.2   Managerial Levers for Achieving Effectiveness in Pull-based Strategy

If a firm were to achieve effectiveness in pull-based supply chain, then it may have to deploy certain managerial capabilities and levers, which are discussed here.

1. Facilities planning for pull-based strategy would require a decentralized set-up. Facilities can include manufacturing unit and distribution centres. In case of products that are assembly based, the manufacturing and consolidation of components could be centralized. Once the products have been manufactured, they are distributed to distribution centres. On receiving orders from their regions, the distribution centres configure the product and deliver the same. This would

Table 2.3 Factors influencing pull-based supply chain structure

Features	Example	Focus	Remarks
Character and type of product	Medical equipment	Responsiveness	High-technology items, likely to have short product lifecycle with new developments surfacing quite often.
Nature and size of market	Food	Responsiveness	Especially fast food such as pizzas, which are made to order.
	Local market	Responsiveness	Local market-oriented products could follow the responsive chain as there could be flexibility.
Distribution channel strategy	Fashion jewellery, fewer intermediaries	Responsiveness	High-value items, sensitive to demand changes.
Facilities, locations, and options available	Decentralized facility	Responsiveness	Quick response and flexibility is enabled.
Customer characteristics and preferences	Fashion items such as apparel and jewellery, and electronic goods such as mobile phones	Responsiveness	Trend matters. Price is not a constraint, rather premium on product is preferred.
Tax, including direct and indirect taxes and levies		Responsiveness	Tax and levies add to the cost and a prudent approach is to minimize the same by postponing configuration to the final point of delivery to the customer.
Strength of logistics services and intermediary options	High maturity of LSP (Logistics Service Providers)	Responsiveness	As in the case of automotive and consumer product segment wherein JIT and VMI are matured, more intermediation may lead to less responsiveness.
Strength of information and communication channels	Strong information and communication channel	Responsiveness	As there is increased visibility and transparency, higher the responsiveness more the certainty for planning.
Level of industry maturity and scope for innovations	High innovations and early stage of growth—hi-tech goods	Responsiveness	The demand is likely to change with new introductions and product functionality.

improve service level for multiple SKUs in the same product category and postponement would also help customers to configure the product to personal choices. Again, a typical example would be that of personal computers. One can see global business firms deploying this strategy in order to achieve responsiveness. The company gets the product in 'completed knocked down' (CKD) form and configures at the local country to serve the demand. This is also common in the automobile industry, especially the luxury imported car segment and hi-tech equipment.

2. The management would deploy inventory in such a way that customer service could be provided on demand. Typically, inventory would be near-completed stage to achieve variety and deliver value to the customer. Pull-based strategy can be effective in downward linkages, especially close to the customer, if there are more common items to different SKUs. Product designing, SKU proliferation, and inventory management policy must facilitate the same. At the upstream level, pull-based strategies are practised using techniques like JIT, vendor managed inventory, kanban systems, and so on. Since the customer service level in terms of time and number of items filled in an order is important, inventory optimization, rather than cost efficiency, would be the approach.

3. Transportation as a management lever in pull-based strategy would use a small package and specialized dedicated service to serve the order on time. The cost of outbound is likely to be higher but the customer would be able to bear the incidence of the same. The classic example in manufacture is of a tier I automotive component (such as car wheel steering) vendor, which supplies every four hours to the production line of a major car plant in Chennai. This gives complete flexibility and there is no need of stocking steering wheels for the production schedule in the car manufacturer plant, as JIT is being practised. This requires frequent movement of steering systems from the tier I supplier to the plant, increasing the transportation cost, but at the same time gives advantages of pull-based strategy, such as effortless micro management of inventory, bill of materials validation, and so on. Many such examples are possible in the downstream supply chain close to the customer point.

4. Sourcing and supplier relationship management is another lever which is critical for effective pull-based strategy. This is a key aspect in upward stream of supply chain for the nodal organization in the supply chain network. Typically, in manufacturing, one would look at this feature as the most important factor for achieving production economies. As mentioned earlier, supplier relationship strategies such as JIT, vendor managed inventory, kanban, and quality management would facilitate effective management of pull-based supply chain. Other factors include capability in concurrent engineering, ability to participate in product development, involvement with customer directly for delivery and erection of certain components at site, which may not have required value addition at plant. Hence, relationship with the supplier is key to success, not only in manufacturing but also in other formats of business such as retailing and channel partnership in forward linkages for coordinating delivery of goods.

5. Information management is another important lever for managing effectiveness of the pull strategy. A leading brand of cycle has few dealers in a city like Hyderabad in India, which has a population of more than six million. Suppose a customer walks into a store to buy a specific SKU. The dealer notes that the SKU mentioned in the catalogue is not available in stock. Instead of turning

down customer demand or trying to convert it into a different order, the dealer cross-checks data with an alternate dealer in Hyderabad and serves the customer. By this, the dealer has ensured that the customer is delighted with his order and the brand-owner has also not lost a sale. This kind of optimization for improving the level of customer service using pull strategy is possible only if all dealers can be linked and the role is changed from dealer to dealer-cum-stockist. The dealer-cum-stockist will serve as a competitive dealer well and share margins, ensuring that the overall supply chain profits are increased. Similarly, one can look at numerous examples where information systems improve transparency and visibility.

6. Pricing is another important lever for managing certain pull-based supply chains. The pull factor does not focus on cost and, after a point, responsiveness more than proportionately increases the cost. The premium for such responsiveness must be factored in pricing decisions. Also, certain cost structures get shifted because of adoption of pull strategies. When vendor managed inventory (VMI) is practised, the vendor manages stock. In the cost statement of a manufacturer, material cost would also include vendor managed inventory cost which should reflect as the manufacturing cost of goods, plus inventory holding cost. The difference between vendor managed inventory and value of goods stocked at manufacturing location would be different if inventory managing costs between the two vary. The advantage it provides is flexibility in production, for which the customer has to pay a premium.

7. Certain generic levers like deploying experienced logistics service providers, demand management, effective customer management, and deploying innovative business practices are critical for the success of pull-based strategies. For example, a number of automotive companies have linked their dealers' showrooms to capture customer responses in order to effectively manage sales and customer delight. This would be part of the pull strategy as the dealer here can quickly interact with the manufacturer and retain the customer for a couple of days to serve an odd demand in the selection of a model of a vehicle. Such flexibility was not available earlier and even now not everyone is able to effectively handle the same.

Hence, the responsive pull-based supply chain could be successfully deployed if the industry, market, and product characteristics warrant the same. It takes a few years for a firm to successfully meet the challenges presented by such a strategy and be innovative. Supply chain managers must be conscious of such developments and deploy initiatives for being competitive players in the market. Pull strategies are increasingly practised both in upstream and downstream supply chain activities. They assume more significance at the down trend of the business cycle as they give the manufacturer the flexibility with regard to supplies—the manufacturer can act after receiving a demand and thus improve profit margin.

2.6 AGILE SUPPLY CHAIN

Agility was initially introduced as a manufacturing paradigm in 1991 by the Iacocca Institute of Lehigh University, USA, in its report '21 Century Manufacturing Enterprise Strategy: An Industry-Led View' (Kidd 1994). The report described how US industrial competitiveness will—or might—evolve during the next fifteen years. It proposed that significant changes were needed in manufacturing companies in order to achieve or improve their ability to cope with continuous and unanticipated changes in the business environment, and proactively capture opportunities from the turbulent business environment. Thus, from the start, agility has been a change-proficiency paradigm.

Agility is based on time-based competition and fast-cycle innovation which led to a highly volatile business environment. If a firm were to survive and grow, it has to be necessarily agile to adapt to the changing environment. Agility in manufacturing has more interface with lean thinking as principles of agility are embedded in lean manufacturing as well.

According to Preiss (2005), 'Agility is a comprehensive response to the business challenges of profiting from rapidly changing, continually fragmenting, global markets for high-quality, high-performance, customer-configured goods and services. It is dynamic, context-specific, aggressively change-embracing, and growth-oriented. Agility is a comprehensive response to new competitive forces that have undermined the dominance of a mass production system.'

According to this definition, agility is more a strategic initiative to face dynamic environmental changes in business with a heavy focus on manufacturing, but also rather customer-centric in its approach. The definition provided by Goldman et al (1995)—'Agility is the ability of an enterprise to quickly respond to changes in an uncertain and changing environment'—fits exactly the concept from a strategic perspective, especially in context of the external environment to a firm.

According to other authors, agility is the ability to respond quickly to changes in the market demand and to meet customer demands sooner—be they changes in volume, variety, or mix, but at an acceptable cost (Christopher 2000, Christopher and Towill 2001, Gunasekaran 1998). This definition is more organization-centric. In reality, if agility is to meet volatile market conditions, then perspective must go beyond the organization and encompass the supply chain network as discussed by researchers (Power and Sohal 2001).

The European Agile Forum (2000) defined agility as: '(T)he ability of an enterprise to change and reconfigure the internal and external parts of the enterprise—strategies, organization, technologies, people, partners, suppliers, distributors, and even customers—in response to unpredictable events and uncertainty in the business environment.' This definition covers the span of supply chain network clearly. Harrison and van Hoek (2005) emphasize the extended enterprise nature of the concept by defining agility as 'a supply-chain-wide capability that aligns organizational structures, information systems, logistics processes and, in particular, mindsets.' So agile characteristics for the supply chain domain could be:

1. Speed of response in serving new products and customers markets
2. Robust ability to withstand the turmoil in market due to changes in market forces
3. Ability to create new relationships and alliances to face changing environment
4. Managerial capability in quickly putting in place strategy, structure, and people
5. Ability to capture knowledge and embed the same in offering to customers

In short, agility in a supply chain is the ability of a supply chain to rapidly respond to changes in the market and customer demands. A supply chain evolves because of a customer demand or anticipated demand, and when one realizes that the industry situation in which one operates is fluid and highly volatile, there is a need to be agile. Thus, agile supply chain is driven by various factors:

1. Change in business environment
   (a) Customer preference and tastes
   (b) Social factors
   (c) Competitive forces
   (d) Industry factors like technology or increase in capital costs and so on
2. Based on the industry and market in which a firm operates, it would decide on the level of agility it should maintain to be competitive. For example, recessionary conditions would affect a developing country like India more adversely, especially in comfort and luxury goods, compared to developed nations. Even the classification of goods as comfort and luxury may vary. Another example could be the prices of petrol and diesel. A rise in prices could affect the usage in the salaried group as compared to the segment of high net worth individuals. A firm must understand its supply chain network by relating to the customer it serves.
3. Agile supply chain capabilities would be responsiveness, flexibility to adjust variations in demand and supply, competence, including market intelligence, learning capability of the organization, and speed at it which it can react.
4. Agile supply chain goals would be time and cost efficiency and robustness to withstand turbulent conditions and convert challenges into opportunities.
5. Agile supply chain can be enabled successfully if the organization has strong collaborative relationship with its network partners, strong information infrastructure with good alert systems, and the ability to capture ahead of competitors a change in system and strong customer relationships.

An example of an agile supply chain can be observed in the two wheeler industry in India. Originally, India was a prime market for scooters. Because a large population had low affordability, companies focused on low engine power (in the range of 50 cc), low cost vehicles. Not only was the capital cost of acquiring the vehicle a concern, but also fuel consumption and mileage. Buyers mostly focused on fuel efficiency. One company launched motorcycles with the fuel efficiency of four stroke engines, and the pattern of demand changed. The market leader in the scooter segment was challenged and had to necessarily move over to this segment as well. Currently, India's two wheeler industry is driven by motorcycles for men and scooters are predominately bought by women. Unless firms understand this and turn agile, especially with respect to the launch of motorcycles models for men in two categories—high end and energy efficient—they may not be competitive in the Indian two wheeler segment.

Agile supply chain works both for predictable and unpredictable markets. Industries such as consumer electronics, mobile phones, computers, fashion clothing, jewellery, and so on, need agility. A supply chain manager must look at this as part of responsiveness and structure the supply chain network accordingly.

2.7 SUPPLY CHAIN FOR FACING CALAMITIES AND EMERGENCIES

A vast geography like India faces different challenges from nature by way of calamities such as floods, earthquakes, tsunami, and famines due to crop failures, and so on. It is quite possible that varying degrees of calamities happen more or less around the same time in different parts of the country. The challenge is to ensure logistics and supply network support in facing such hardships. In India, the government has established a National Institute for Disaster Management. (Exhibit 2.2)

The key issue with agility in such cases is preparedness, the ability to pool resources, both pecuniary and non pecuniary, and leadership and command on ground to execute the operations. The services of logistics and supply chain network are twofold—one, strategizing and planning under normal conditions for an eventual calamity, and two, seamless execution with high speed on incidence of the calamity. There must be initiatives and exercises in risk-prone areas to constantly learn and communicate risk mitigation strategies and reactionary approach on incidence.

Something which is similar to this is emergency management initiatives taken by some organizations in India, especially on private and public partnership mode. With the development of highways, road safety and handling of accidents on emergency has become essential. A number of hospitals, health care companies, and NGOs are involved in this. This would require an agile logistics service and an agile supply chain approach from the services perspective. Exhibit 2.3 shows one such operation in India. Thus, not only in business but also in public life, there is a need to deploy the principles of logistics and supply chain for managing unforeseen situations and normalizing them.

2.8 VIRTUAL ORGANIZATION—PULL-CENTRIC

The virtual organization is composed of people who are linked by computers, faxes, computer-aided design systems, and video teleconferencing, and who may rarely, if

---

Exhibit 2.2 National Institute of Disaster Management

The National Institute of Disaster Management (NIDM) is a premier national organization working for human resource development at national level in the area of disaster mitigation and management. The NIDM came into existence on 16 October 2003 by a Government of India order upgrading the National Centre for Disaster Management (NCDM), which was located at Indian Institute of Public Administration, New Delhi. The NCDM was established by the Ministry of Agriculture, Department of Agriculture and Cooperation, Government of India, in March 1995. The NCDM had been functioning as a nodal centre for the human resource development in the area of disaster management.

NIDM will be gearing up the national, state, and district level administration to tackle natural calamities and will also be coordinating research projects, training programmes, and will build a database on natural disasters with case studies.

The mission of NIDM is to work as a think tank for the government by providing policy advice and facilitating capacity building services including strategic learning, research, training, system development and expertise promotion for effective disaster preparedness and mitigation.

The strategy behind forming NIDM was to build a national hub to share and learn and to create a critical mass of institutions, trainers, and trained professionals.

Objectives of NIDM

• To undertake quality research covering both natural and human induced disasters, with a multi-hazard approach.

• To work as a national resource centre for the central and state governments in the country through effective knowledge management and sharing of best practices.

• To professionalize disaster risk reduction and emergency management in India and other neighbouring countries by developing an independent cadre of professionally trained emergency and mitigation managers.

• To promote formal training and education for disaster management in India and in the region.

• To build working partnerships with the Government, universities, NGOs, corporate bodies, and other national and international institutes of eminence.

• To link learning and action by building a synergy between institutions and professionals in the sector.

Source: Adapted from http://nidm.gov.in/vision1.asp, accessed on 5 January 2009.

---

ever, see one another face to face. People come and go as and when services are needed. It is increasingly becoming a challenge for supply chain managers and organizations to coordinate between people who are linked virtually. By design, such a system is pull-centric as resource and services are engaged only on demand. The deployment of outsourced partners for outbound transportation, third party warehouse management, design consultancy for product configuration and implementation of postponement, engagement of intermediaries for document processing, information consultants, IT service providers for reverse auctioning while sourcing, are all examples of such an organization.

The key aspects that a supply chain manager must evaluate while engaging virtual resources would be:

1. Reliability
2. Robustness
3. Cost efficiency
4. Delivery capability and validation

Exhibit 2.3   Emergency Management and Research Institute (EMRI)

The EMRI was established in April 2005 in a public private partnership mode. The Institute provides comprehensive emergency management services for medical, police, and fire related emergencies in the states of Andhra Pradesh, Gujarat, Uttarakhand, Goa, Chennai, Rajasthan, Karnataka, and Assam, using a single three-digit toll-free number (108) (www.emri.in). The author had the opportunity to visit the Chennai EMRI, which is linked with medical, police and fire services, and the state government and provides phenomenal support. The ambulances are well equipped and information technology provides key support. The transport for reaching the place of incidence and hospital is well routed and coordinated. The integration with various agents is carefully planned and executed for every case, which is key to the success of this agile network.

---

5. Track record
6. Financial diligence
7. Adequate documentation for protecting risk

The years have taught us important lessons, especially in the field of reverse auctioning for the procurement of goods and services. Often bidders collude, which leads to delay and non-performance. Over the years, organizations and supply chain managers have been able to effectively network for validating bidders. There must be more industry-led initiatives and forums by organizations such as CII Institute of Logistics in India to facilitate this.

2.9   TRADE-OFF BETWEEN PUSH AND PULL STRATEGIES

There are wide differences among firms in different industries/markets and even within an industry in adopting push and pull strategies. Certain general guidelines on the trade-off between push and pull strategies are discussed here.

The processes in supply chain can be divided into a series of cycles—customer order cycle, replenishment cycle, manufacturing cycle, and procurement cycle (Figure 2.6). Certain actions or incidence by a player set off the trigger in each cycle. For example, customer order cycle triggers on the arrival of a customer. Hence, for a certain action to trigger, aggregation has to take place. For a manufacturing cycle to trigger, distributors must demand goods from the manufacturer. From this, it is clear that pull strategies are fairly easier to be configured close to the customer demand as they are based on the initiation of order, whereas push strategies would be configured wherever production has to take place based on anticipated demand. So the first trade-off is the point of incidence of the ability to serve on demand and the need to anticipate for demand and for manufacture to stock.

A number of examples of each of these can be discussed. The demand for standard business jackets can be easily anticipated based on a pattern and stocked. However, personalized garments for various occasions are made to order even by big brands as the customer buys them for occasional wear. It would be difficult to break this chain.

A second situation where the trade-off is applicable is the goal of a supply chain network. If the goal is to be cost efficient, then the cost-efficient push strategy would be preferred. Typically, popular segment products are of this nature. As mentioned

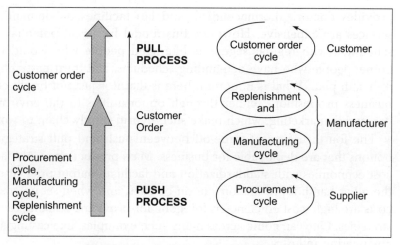

Figure 2.6 Processes view of supply chain

earlier, bicycles used by the common man can be placed in this category. When one looks at fitness cycles in the same industry or the children's cycles segment or the technically more advanced cycles such as geared vehicles, these are based more on responsiveness and pull-based strategy. The most common day-to-day application of push- and pull-based strategies is in the restaurants of luxury hotels where in the same building one restaurant would serve buffet meals which offer a wide choice at low prices, but with choice limited to the spread of the day, whereas speciality restaurants would cater to customer preference at a high price. These restaurants aim at achieving total responsiveness wherein buffet hotel chains offer preferences which are both cost-focused and based on limited responsiveness.

The third situation where there could be a trigger for trade-off is product configuration and the ability to postpone the product completion to customer preference. When products are standardized and the demand is stable and predictable, it is better to deploy push-based strategies. A number of products such as perishable services of air transportation on fixed schedules, hotel rooms, standardized financial products, home furniture for poplar segment, automotives for the same segment, and FMCG can fall in this category. On the other hand, there are products requiring modularity and need to be configured close to the point of consumption. These could be speciality furniture, capital goods, engineering goods, computers for personal, home and office segments, and hi-tech equipment, including medical equipment, and so on.

This trade-off must be handled with innovation. There is abundant material on how Dell Computers were innovative when they introduced made-to-order strategy in that segment. There are a number of earlier cases such as the business model of US food chain Wendy's, where a customer could drive in with an order while entering and pick it up as he or she exits. Business dynamics changed in the fast food segment and competition came up challenging Wendy's model. This is typical of competitive forces. There are other cases where the marketing idea is innovative enough but mass customization may be needed. One such is 'Doc Medical Services' at Chennai that provides doctor, pharmaceutical, and lab facilities on demand. Obviously, such services are expensive. However, this model has great potential if demand can be scheduled with regular segments like aged people who would require support at home, people who have demanding schedules, and third party engagements as part of health plan. What is important here is that it is just not bright concepts but viable business propositions, either through opportunities in the environment or through persuasive marketing, which make such hybrid supply chain to work.

The fourth trigger of trade-off between push and pull strategies are production options that are deployable for business. Mass production would facilitate production cost economies with standardization and facilitate output price at normal profits. On the other hand, if production run on batches, and when set-up cost and change-over costs are high, cost efficiency is foregone for providing responsiveness and pull-based strategies. One can come across many such examples, like casting and forgings, in the engineering industry.

The fifth trigger of trade-off could be linkages from the supply chain perspective, such as inventory policy, sourcing, transportation choices, facilities plan, information systems, and linkages of supply chain strategy to overall business strategy. If resources are limited and industry is mature, a firm would prefer cost-efficient, push-based strategies. On the other hand, if a firm is at the stage of product introduction, especially of a new product, or in the highly volatile product shelf-life business, such as consumer electronics, mobile phones, and apparel, the responsive pull-based supply chain is preferred. One may ponder how pull-based system could work in mass customers demand goods like the ones cited above. Here is where one may apply the cycle view concept and pull work at customer order cycle level where retailers serve through stores and at replenishment stages. The feedback mechanism and agile manufacturing is what would help in such cases.

2.10 IDENTIFYING APPROPRIATE PUSH AND PULL STRATEGY

There is nothing like a prescribed push or pull strategy for a business or a supply chain network. Industry practices mature over a period of time, leading to the evolution of approaches, which commonly benefit the industry, market, and customers. However, our discussion on the trade-off between push and pull strategies does give some guidelines. One may also look at the following aspects in identifying appropriate pull- and push-based strategies:

1. Resource availability with the organization
2. Strategic vision with respect to business and differentiation initiatives
3. Innovativeness
4. Demand and supply characteristics of products and market
5. Technology and its obsolescence
6. Maturity of logistics service providers and support system

The choice of push and pull strategy is a behavioural attribute of a firm which would be strongly influenced by the above industry structural factors, competitive forces, and performance attributes. A supply chain manager must be sensitive to these and involve a multi-disciplinary approach while addressing the choice of push and pull strategies. As mentioned earlier, customer satisfaction and growth should not be seen as mutually exclusive but rather complementary to each other.

SUMMARY

The supply chain structure is about setting up a framework that strikes a balance between the cost of storing and moving goods and services from the supplier to the customer. As there is no formula or framework for the right balance, the structure may vary from company to company and within products of a company.

An efficient supply chain is cost-centric, which works well for standardized items that have more certainty with respect to demand estimate, low to medium value items, standardized goods and services in a market which is matured.

On the other hand, a responsive supply chain is a measure of speed of serving customers and the level of customer service. Typically, high-value items, fashion products, personalized demand goods where customization is required, and the new products segment fall in this category.

A push-based supply chain strategy is configured in anticipation of demand. Hence, there an element of speculation and uncertainty in demand. A push-based supply chain would be more akin to cost-efficient supply chain, and by and large be implemented in those situations.

Made to stock (MTS) manufacturing strategy is complementary to the push strategy, which means that goods are produced to be delivered on stock.

MTS is deployed where production economies arise because of lumpiness of production capacity, set up and change, supply constraints and lumpiness of the supply of raw material, and where demand estimates are reliable.

The managerial levers for effective push-based strategy would be with facilities management, inventory policy, transportation choices, sourcing plan, pricing, and information management. Similarly, pull-based strategy is also managed with same levers. Their application and support tools such as demand forecasting and management are critical for proper implementation.

The commodity supply chain is dependent upon supply and demand economics with typical characteristics of external forces playing a significant role. For example, it was observed that agricultural supply chain is more dependent on monsoon and weather conditions. Some of the commodities demand is derived demand and hence its efficiency depends on the understanding and strength of principal demand items.

A pull-based supply chain is configured to execute a customer order. This strategy is akin to responsiveness in supply chain where the main aspect is the ability to serve with speed and achieve a higher level of service. Cost efficiency is compromised in the favour of responsiveness in pull strategy.

Made to engineer (MTE) and made to order (MTO) are complementary to pull-based supply chain strategy. MTE is deployed in situations where design confirmation and project engineering is required. There may not be ready-to-assemble components which satisfy a demand situation. On the other hand, MTO strategy is adopted mainly to provide variants of SKUs— the fundamental product functionality and engineering is frozen.

Agile supply chain is the ability of supply chain to rapidly respond to changes in market and customer demands. This is similar to responsiveness except that agile is drawn more from agile manufacturing concept, which discusses rapid changing environment and volatility in business and demands manufacturing systems to adopt the same. Agile supply chain can be viewed both for certain and uncertain business condition; however while the first is induced the latter is autonomous of the system.

Virtual organization is a part of strategy increasingly adopted by utilizing non-dedicated available resources on demand for satisfying demand. This would be more common in services supply chain where physical engagement is limited.

The trade-off between push and pull is driven by many factors such as structure of the industry, market, competitive forces, and performance attributes. The demand and supply factors, technological changes, innovativeness, and resources command, along with strategic thinking of the firm, would determine the balancing of push and pull strategies.

KEY TERMS

Agile supply chain: Agile supply chain is development based on agile manufacturing, which focuses on responsiveness of manufacturing systems to changes in business environment, rather to short periods because of turbulence in the market. It is the ability of the supply chain to rapidly respond to changes in market and customer demands.

Just in time (JIT): The goal of JIT is to time activities so that components or goods or services arrive at production line just in time for transformation. There must be absolute synchronization of item, quantity, quality, and time for achieving success in JIT.

Kanban: Kanban refers to a system of signalling, originally using cards or bins or dedicated space area for goods used in the manufacturing process. It mainly streamlines the flow of inventory into the process.

Made to order (MTO): MTO strategies are those where production is specific to customer order. Made to engineering (MTE) is a step ahead of this where engineers custom products to the consumer's specific requirement. In case of MTO, specification, basic product design, and engineering are frozen, variability is provided to customers, and manufacture is triggered on arrival of demand.

Made to stock (MTS): MTS strategies in manufacturing are characteristic of industry where there is reliable forecast, and where production economies are achieved by lumping order size.

Pull strategy: In a pull strategy, supply chain activities are triggered on arrival of customer rather than on forecasted demand. The firm does not hold any inventory and only respond to specific order. This works for hi-tech and high-value items, fashion goods, technology intense products, and so on.

Push strategy: In a push-based strategy, supply chain activities are based on long-term forecasts. The push approach could be for achieving production economies. However, there could be diseconomies in transportation and inventory related costs. The deployment of push strategy depends on overall advantage.

Vendor managed inventory (VMI): VMI is when the supplier assumes responsibility and actually manages the inventory. This was initially adopted in a retail supply chain where the category owner took VMI responsibility. Increasingly, this has been applied in backward linkages of supply chain as well in manufacturing.

Virtual organization: A set-up where resources are used in supply chain activities on demand for specific purposes and there is flexibility on deployment and resource cost.

CONCEPT REVIEW QUESTIONS

1. Describe efficiency and responsiveness in supply chain with examples.
2. Analyse push and pull strategies of supply chain and their advantages and disadvantages.
3. Discuss management levers for the effectiveness of push and pull strategies in supply chain. Use practical experience in explaining the same.
4. What are the critical issues in commodity sup-

ply chain? Describe an agricultural commodity and mineral-based (commodity) supply chain.

5. What are the various industry and market factors which can influence push and pull strategies? Explain by applying to a company in a chosen industry and market with which you are familiar.

6. Discuss the boundary of pull and push strategies and how it is designed with the two complementing each other.

7. Explain made to stock (MTS) and made to order (MTO) with examples.

8. 'Effective agile supply chain depends upon collaborative relations and strength of information systems.' Elucidate.

9. Use a two-by-two grid with cost economies and responsiveness as axes, and high and low as levels. Provide illustration for each of the four quadrants.

CRITICAL THINKING QUESTIONS

1. Consider a company which intends to manufacture bio-fuels in a SEZ in Chennai by importing vegetable oil from Malaysia and wants to export the bio-fuel to Europe. If you are hired as logistics and supply chain consultant, how would you apply push-based strategies? What are the key parameters?

2. Consider a branded fresh coffee retailer like Café Coffee Day in India. What are the key supply chain issues that you would focus on and how would you deploy push and pull boundaries for the business?

3. Consider recessionary economic trends as experienced in the late 2008. You are a supply chain manager with an auto major. How would you make your supply chain agile? Alternatively, what recommendations would you suggest for the management for a near-term handling of the situation?

4. Take the case of hi-tech products such as high-end mobile phones. The product is marketed directly, through cyber sale, agents, and other possible channels. There are diversified channels of sale and the product needs to be be refreshed. How would you go about deploying push and pull strategies and draw the boundary between the two for a supply chain in case of such a product?

REFERENCES

Christopher, M., 'The Agile Supply Chain: Competing in Volatile Markets,' *Industrial Marketing Management* 29, 2000, pp. 37–44

Christopher, M. and D. Towill, 'An Integrated Model for the Design of Agile Supply Chains,' *International Journal of Physical Distribution* & *Logistics* 31 (4), 2001, pp. 234–246

Economic Survey 2008 Statistical Tables, Government of India

Fisher, Marshall L., 'What is the Right Supply Chain for Your product?,' *Harvard Business Review*, March–April 1997, pp. 83–93

Goldman, S.L., R.N. Nagel and K. Preiss, *Agile Competitors and Virtual Organizations*: *Strategies for Enriching the Customer*, van Nostrand, Reinhold, 1995

Gunasekaran, A., 'Agile Manufacturing: Enablers and an Implementation Framework,' *International Journal of Production Economics* 36 (5), 1998, pp. 1223–1247

Harrison, A. and R. van Hoek, *Logistics Management and Strategy*, Prentice Hall, 2005

http://nidm.gov.in/vision1.asp, accessed on 5 January 2009

Kidd, P.T., *Agile Manufacturing: Forging New Frontiers*, Addison-Wiley London, 1994

Power, D.J. and A.S. Sohal, 'Critical Success Factors in Agile Supply Chain Management: An Empirical Study,' *International Journal of Physical Distribution and Logistics* 31 (4), 2001, pp. 247–265

Preiss K., 'Agility—The Origins, the Vision, and the Reality,' In Andersin H.E., E. Niemi, Hirvonen V. (eds), *Proceedings of the International Conference on Agility—ICAM, Otaniemi, Finland*, July 2005, Helsenki University of Technology, pp. 13–21

www.emri.in
www.avaya.com/gcm/masterusa/enus/corporate/pressroom/pressreleases/2008/pr-080613.htm&Wrapper=Print, accessed on 2 January 2009

CASE STUDY: HOME FURNITURE SUPPLY CHAIN

We are looking at the supply chain of home furniture marketed by Delight Home Depot (DHD) and specifically, simple mica topped dining tables and chairs sold at leading private stores. Typically, timber is procured from local wood forests which may be at a distance of 700 km on an average from an urban centre like Chennai. The wood gets processed and shaped in the manufacturing station. DHD stores and dealers would be selling mass customized tables and sets of chairs, which would be based on standard or what is referred to as popular demand. And then the firm would have a catalogue of multiple variants to suit customer choices: these would be customizable to each customer's preferences and tastes and delivered to promise. The variants are critical for DHD to attract customers and grow in the fragmented industry. Also a customer prefers to buy from such private brands instead of getting a dining table set made to order. This could be prohibitively expensive, and demands enormous effort in pooling and organizing resources.

To understand the differences in responsiveness and efficiency more, one may probe the making of home furniture—the product category here being dining table sets. Generally, the popular version with standard mica top would be shipped to distribution centres and then to stores. The focus of the nodal organization, namely DHD, would be to achieve efficiency in cost so that there is price competitiveness. All its activities from purchase of timber, inbound transportation, yard management of timber stock, purchase of all process materials, including chemicals, to finishing mica sheets, processing timber into dining tables and chairs, to outbound, to distribution centres and stores, and delivery are all cost focused. There would be clearly defined policies and procedures for sourcing material, movement engagement, and conversion costs. Often

delivery cost is always borne by the customer wherein delivery services are organized through stores. While analysing economics of manufacturing and selling popular dining table and set of four chairs, the following data were collected.

Component	In Rs
Material cost	4,000
Transportation at various stages	800
Conversion cost	1,600
Marketing cost	800
Overheads	800
Cost of product	8,000
Margin	2,000
Market price	10,000

DHD works for target cost and plays around margins to give price attractiveness in this popular version as the product volume is critical. Any deviation from target costs in any of the heads would lead the economics astray. For example, if a customer who is far away from store or distribution centre wants to buy a popular version, DHD would find it difficult to serve the customer as the outbound transportation cost would go up, which would cut on price advantage. Hence, the market for such a product exists within fairly rigid physical boundaries, as not only transportation but also post-sale service overheads get affected by distance, even if it is for one time. Hence, such a supply chain is driven by cost efficiency rather than responsiveness.

On the other hand, one may look at the responsive supply chain in the DHD market for dining sets. This product category would also include items in a catalogue. Ideally, customers look at these promotion materials and arrive at a demand. The product is either assembled at distribution centres or finished in special batches at conversion units and delivered to customers. Thus, it differs from the cost-efficient supply chain of the popular version. The following data as of August 2008 gives an understanding of the market:

Component	In Rs
Material cost	4,000
Design offering	2,400
Transportation at various stages	1,200
Conversion cost	1,600
Marketing cost	1,600
Overheads	1,200
Cost of product	12,000
Margin	4,000
Market price	16,000

It may be observed that costs are higher except for material and conversion. There is a new head of cost called 'design offering' which includes the creativity of designs and the making of promotions pieces and material. The responsiveness of supply chain of such pieces is limited to defined creativity, hence DHD can create a price band which works out for the customer. Also since this kind of product category can be easily engineered and adopted by competition, even such markets are fragmented. One main advantage in competition here is that DHD gives customers a choice and there are a group of customers who would be willing to exercise such options.

In a standardized market like this where there are national and international brands selling variants, private brands like DHD can be competitive only if they combine efficiency and responsiveness in the supply chain. It may be observed that the popular category where the margins are less compared to the customized product segment will have larger share of volume of business. In such situations, the ability of DHD to be creative in the customized product segment and improve on margin would be key to success. Unless DHD provides reasonable variants for customer choice, and at the same time, price variants are affordable, the strategy would not work. In such a market, it is the production economics of private brands, including the location of conversion, distribution centre and store facilities, and marketing capability in convincing customers of variants that are important. There is scope for DHD to apply cost principles such as activity-based costing in order to improve business efficiencies.

Questions

1. What are the key cost components which differ in both supply chains of DHD?
2. 'DHD success is based on the ability to compete on supply chains.' Elucidate.
3. Identify a private brand food restaurant business with the scope of efficient and responsive supply chain and explain its supply chain configuration.

3

Supply Chain Drivers— Role and Relevance

Learning Objectives

After studying this chapter, you will be able to:

- Understand the role of drivers in supply chain performance, their components, and their influence on competition by linking business and supply chain strategies
- Understand the definition of drivers—namely, facilities, transportation, inventory, sourcing, pricing, and information—and their importance in supply chain management
- Gain an insight into each driver and the strategic focus, and the competitive force relevant for a chosen focus and a driver
- Comprehend the likely decision-making situations with respect to a driver and competitive force
- Understand the trade-offs in designing supply chain networks
- Gain an insight into the elements influencing the selection of a specific configuration
- Understand the opportunities and challenges in reconfiguration and in providing flexibility

3.1 SUPPLY CHAIN DRIVERS AND SUPPLY CHAIN PERFORMANCE

Supply chain drivers are key to the performance of supply chain constituents and role players across the network. In fact, a network is operational only when supply chain drivers are in place. They are the pillars for supply chain operations. In a way, supply chain drivers are the operating tools for implementing supply chain strategies and carrying out operations. They could be logistical in nature, such as warehouse facilities, inventory, and transportation, as well as cross-functional, such as pricing, sourcing, and information. Apart from these drivers, external factors such as tax system and logistical infrastructure may also impact the performance of the supply chain indirectly through the configuration of drivers. Hence, it is important to understand the role of drivers in supply chain performance.

Supply chain strategy cannot be independent of other functional strategies or business unit level or corporate level strategies. The alignment of a specific business strategy to a corresponding supply chain strategy is achieved through the proper deployment of supply chain drivers. For instance, when a firm introduces a new product group and moves on to building the product's share in the market, it requires a responsive supply chain strategy, which is based on product lifecycle and customer response. If there is a need for a responsive supply chain, supply chain drivers like facilities, inventory, supplier relationship, and transportation are to be organized accordingly. At the introduction stage, when there is uncertainty with regard to demand, higher levels of inventory may be utilized to achieve responsiveness by enhancing product availability. Product availability at the introduction stage translates to market share. Similarly, the remaining supply chain drivers of information, facility, and transportation are deployed to achieve alignment between business and supply chain strategies at the introduction stage.

Let's see how ITC, a conglomerate with multinational ownership structure in India, adopts the strategy of localized approach for growth and introduces ready-to-eat food business in India. The company may be in a position to exploit economies of scope in distribution as well as in sourcing. As the company has been a leader in the fast-moving consumer goods (FMCG) business, foods could be added to its distribution network. However, the addition of food products would require additional effort in terms of applying learning and experience, capacity, and managerial effort in coordinating new relationships in the channel for widening reach. Since the firm has a fair understanding of Indian agriculture, extending sourcing practices for increasing variety of food business is also appreciable. But the challenge lies in achieving success in the introduction stage of products, keeping in mind the variations in cultural and culinary preferences of the diversified ethnic populations of India. Exhibit 3.1 gives details of ITC food business in India.

Supply chain drivers enable a balance between responsiveness to the customer and efficiency in supply chain that allows the company to be competitive in its chosen strategic arena. As one may note, there is need for synchronization of supply chain strategy with functional strategies such as product, marketing, and finance, and

---

Exhibit 3.1 ITC Ltd: Ready-to-Eat Food Business

Indian Tobacco company (ITC) made its entry into the branded and packaged foods business in August 2001 with its brand 'Kitchens of India'. In June 2002, it entered the confectionery, staples, and snack food segments. Here the discussion would be on packaged food business.

ITC's competitive headway in areas of hospitality and branded cuisine, and packaging and sourcing of agricultural commodities is its competitive strength in packaged foods business. ITC's restaurants, significantly popular and known for their quality, cater to high income groups in urban India. As this segment already identifies ITC with good quality food products, it would be the obvious target segment for ready-to-eat packaged foods business.

The foods business focuses on providing quality products to the customer, and the range of products is designed after extensive market re-

search. ITC believes in developing and launching new innovative products. The company has a state-of-the-art production facility at Bengaluru. It may be noted here that the introduction of new products, market research, and the support of the product development centre are important for success in this product group.

A deep understanding of the supply chain of agricultural produce is important for achieving leadership in the foods business. The agricultural produce supply chain is complex, with different regional, socio-economic, and environmental factors influencing it. Unless a company has experience and strong inter-personal relationships, it would be difficult to deploy growth strategies in this sector. ITC has nearly a century of close business relationship with the farming community in India—it is currently in the process of enhancing the Indian farmer's ability to link to the global markets through the e-Choupal initiative, and produce the quality demanded by its customers. This long-standing relationship is being leveraged in sourcing the best quality agricultural produce for ITC's foods business.

The foods business of ITC is currently represented in four categories in the market. These are:

- Ready-to-eat foods
- Staples
- Confectionery
- Snack foods

In order to assure consumers of the highest standards of food safety and hygiene, ITC is engaged in assisting outsourced manufacturers in implementing world-class hygiene standards through HACCP certification. The unwavering commitment to internationally benchmarked quality standards enabled ITC to rapidly gain market standing in all its six brands—Kitchens of India, Aashirvaad, Sunfeast, Mint-o, Candyman, and Bingo!

Here one may look at the Kitchens of India ready-to-eat segment. Each one of these legendary delicacies has been created by the Master Chefs of ITC Hotels, following rare, closely guarded recipes over generations. These delicacies are available in imported four-layer retort pouches that keep them fresh for as long as twenty-four months (vegetarian) and twelve months (non-vegetarian and desserts) from the date of packaging.

It is a challenge to market such brands across India, suiting tastes of each region and culture. ITC has been successfully doing this. Apart from product proliferation, the other challenge is setting process technology, packaging, and delivering. That is where supply chain drivers, namely, facilities management, inventory to assure freshness of stock, transportation, and pricing become important.

To comprehend the complexity of manufacturing ready-to-eat segment, it is important to understand the technology involved. The pioneering introduction of retorting technology is what has made the sale of ready-to-eat food products commercially viable. The inspiration of this technology could be from the usage of the same in military operations where soldiers carry light but nutritious food, with an assured long shelf life. Retorting technology was used by the US in its Apollo Space missions. Today it is the mainstay of US military rations. Retorting is also widely used in packaged foods in Japan and Europe.

The efficacy and effectiveness of the retorting process depends on the sterilization process and the retorting pouch. The sterilization process ensures the stability of the ready-to-eat foods in retort pouches, on the shelf and at room temperature. The application of sterilization technology completely destroys all potentially harmful microorganisms, thereby making sure that the food product has a very long shelf life. However, in the current commercial context, the shelf life is limited to one year.

Retort pouches are flexible packages made from multi-layered plastic films, with or without aluminium foil as one of the layers. Their most important feature is that they are made of heat-resistant plastics, unlike the usual flexible pouches. This makes retort pouches uniquely suitable for the processing of their food contents at temperatures around 120 degrees Celsius. That is the kind of ambient temperature prevalent in the thermal sterilization of foods.

The three-ply laminate consisting of PET/Al oil/PP is the most common material used in retort pouches and is the only one used in India. ITC uses four-layered pouches. The use of PET or polyester as the outer layer gives the required strength to the pouch. The aluminium foil serves as a barrier layer, ensuring a shelf life of more than one year. The nylon layer provides strength to the pouch, reassuring additional shelf life. The innermost layer of polypropylene provides the critical seal integrity, flexibility, strength, and taste and odour compatibility with a variety of food products.

These above discussion highlights the complexity of packaging, which is also critical in supply chain network. It may be concluded in this case that it is inventory and facilities, apart from product innovation, which are critical drivers for success in business.

Source: Adapted from http://www.itcportal.com/sets/foods_frameset.htm, accessed on 26 January 2009.

competitive strategy. This can be accomplished through the effective deployment of supply chain drivers. It may be important here to identify these drivers—facilities, inventory, transportation, sourcing, pricing, and information. We would now discuss each of the drivers separately and analyse its components and importance in supply chain.

3.2 FACILITIES AND SCM

Facilities in supply chain are defined as the physical location where a product or service is being fabricated, assembled, produced, processed, or stored. Planning the location of facilities has been widely discussed in the area of industrial economics. Von Thünen (1966) notes that the cost of transporting goods consumes some of Ricardo's economic rent. He notes that because of facilities, transportation costs and economic rents would vary across goods. Also, different land uses and usage intensities will result in economic rent based on distance from the marketplace. Prior to this, a notable contribution was made by Weber (1909). Weber applies freight rates of resources and the finished goods along with the finished good's production function to develop an algorithm that identifies the optimal location for the manufacturing plant. He also introduces distortions induced by labour and both agglomerative and deglomerative forces. Weber then moves on to discuss groupings of production units, anticipating Lösch's market areas.

Theorists later developed a proposition that volume-based goods tend to be located near the raw material source. Mineral-based businesses like steel, cement, aluminum and sugarcane, and agro-based goods are located near the source of raw material supply. Other categories of goods which are value-based and involve assembly units tend to be located near the market. For example, MNCs locate manufacturing facilities near the market, as in the case of automobiles such as cars, as assembly and delivery in the host country could be cheaper and more efficient in the supply network. Similarly, facilities for FMCG goods such as personal care products and staple foods are generally located near the market.

3.2.1 Role of Facilities in Supply Chain

Facilities are of two categories as shown in Figure 3.1. The role of production facilities in supply chain is derived from the supply chain strategy on whether to achieve responsiveness for given level of efficiency or to aim for efficiency at a desired level of responsiveness. Though in our discussion in the previous section, we saw economists define location as being determined by transportation cost and weight of the material processed, a supply chain manager typically decides the location and number of units with the aim of achieving customer satisfaction.

In the supply chain, manufacturing facilities determine where goods are produced. Considering the growth of mobile phones in market and brand acceptance in India, Nokia set up its production facility in Chennai. Exhibit 3.2 details reasons for the selection of this facility. It is to be noted that the choice of facility is interwoven with other drivers for delivering value to customers.

Exhibit 3.2   Nokia Facility at Chennai

Nokia set up a manufacturing facility for mobile devices at Chennai in India. The manufacturing unit in Chennai was Nokia's tenth mobile device production facility globally. Nokia invested around USD 100–150 million in the India production plant.

The reason to select Chennai as the location was the availability of skilled labour, friendly business environment, support from the state government, good logistics connections, and overall cost-efficiency.

This was an important step for Nokia towards the continuous development of their global manufacturing network.

Mobile penetration in Asia Pacific was expected to be a major contributor to the global mobile subscriber base. Therefore, India, which is set at the heart of the region where mobile communications were growing rapidly, was a natural location of choice for the new production facility.

Source: Adapted from http://www.nokia.com/A4136002?newsid=-6134, accessed on 26 January 2009.

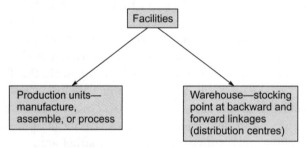

Figure 3.1   Categories of facilities

A manufacturing facility provides product configuration relationship through assembly or manufacturing process. As explained in Supply Chain Operations Reference (SCOR) model of Supply Chain Council, this is one of the key processes in supply chain which is driven by sourcing and supported by distribution management function. When one discusses both pre and post activity of manufacturing facility, the other aspects of facility management, namely warehousing and distribution centre, come into play.

The warehousing set-up varies from industry to industry and across firms. It has also been changing over time. For instance, in the contemporary business world, corporates follow practices, such as just in time and vendor managed inventory, third party logistics service, and so on. The heavy engineering industry would require stocking capacity for work in progress and goods in yards, and stores for value addition in stages. In chemical units which use imported material, the imports have to be in bulk, so the warehousing activity during the pre-manufacturing stage assumes greater importance. On the other hand, FMCG, pharmaceuticals, home furniture, building materials, including paint, and food depend upon forward linkages of distribution. Hence dependence on warehousing is high and assumes greater significance in their supply chain.

3.2.2   Facilities as Drivers and Competitive Forces

The importance of facilities in the supply chain varies, depending upon industry structure, practice, nature of goods, buyer characteristics and strategic intent of the focal organization. These are the typical competitive factors that may influence the role and importance of the supply chain driver. A number of competitive forces may impact the choice of location.

Apart from the factors shown in Table 3.1, the competitive structure too influences facility location. When a market is oligopolistic with a large number of buyers and few sellers, firms would be differentiating products and markets in order to maximize profit. In such cases, a nodal organization decides on location based on its strategic intent and focus on market share. It would not look at efficiency as customers would be able to absorb cost but prefer responsiveness by way of differentiated products.

On the other hand, in a monopolistic market when there are few sellers competing aggressively for market share and profits, efficiency becomes important. The facility location could be driven by cost factors and firms follow the dominant firm in price fixation. In a near perfectly competitive market with numerous buyers and sellers, the decision for location is driven more by the strategic intent of the firm. The efficiency in supply chain would be critical as the product would be near-homogenous with peripheral or no variation.

In case of monopoly where there is a single seller, the competitive approach is to exploit the buyer group as there is no alternate source of supply. Such monopoly arises mainly due to a command over resources. The supply chain strategy is indifferent to efficiency and responsiveness in such a case. Over a period, either through regulatory intervention or customer opinion, responsiveness may improve but efficiency is generally given a slip as buyers in the market can absorb inefficiency.

There are other industry features and time-based factors which may impact location decisions. For example, capital cost, entry and exit barriers, and control over distribution channels could impact the decision on location. Similarly, the intensity of rivalry among competing firms and the strategic intent of the nodal organization, that is, whether take the competition head on or through passive strategy, influence facility location decision.

Given these hosts of factors, a supply chain manager could lose focus on decision-making. A supply chain manager must limit his decision inputs to key demands of efficiency versus responsiveness and how costs relating to drivers would impact decision. When the supply chain manager is part of decision group, he must be able to appreciate trade-off between strategic factors and supply chain driven factors and formulate initiatives for overall organizational success.

3.2.3 Key Facilities Decisions

Key facility decisions, whether it be a manufacturing or warehousing facility, would include location, capacity sizing, and operations methodology. As explained above, location decisions are driven by host of factors like competitive conditions, which include rival firm's behaviour, resource availability, buyer behaviour, and entry and exit conditions. Many of these factors are strategic in nature. The fundamental trade-off in most situations is between cost efficiency and responsiveness to customer.

The capacity sizing decisions would be driven both by strategic and planning level decisions. At the time of capacity creation, the focus would be more strategic, looking

Table 3.1 Competitive forces and approaches

Competitive factor	Supply chain focus	Remarks
Cost leadership	Cost efficiency as it would be in conflict with responsiveness.	Generally, economies in production to reduce cost of manufacture and at the same time optimize distribution cost by minimizing transportation and warehousing costs.
Product differentiation	Responsiveness and customer satisfaction	Multiple SKUs and flexibility in production would be the focus of manufacturing. Supply chain strategies will have to provide proliferation of products in the group and provide wide range of goods and services. This would increase inventory and handling charges and cost of manufacture. Change-over in production would be common.
Focus strategy	Low-cost focus strategy in a narrow segment. Alternatively, focus strategy with differentiation. Balancing between efficiency and responsiveness.	Low-cost focus would be on volume based businesses where customers could be price-sensitive and the product group could be the focus of the nodal organization. Alternatively, product differentiation to build customer loyalty with a broad product group may lead to responsiveness.
State of industry in lifecycle: introduction and growth stage (stable demand and average growth rate; product at nascent stage; accleration could be critical at growth stage)	Responsiveness	Nodal organization's strategic focus with respect to market determines the choice of facility. Flexibility in manufacturing and product variation could be key. Responsiveness in meeting customer orders through volume and product variation would drive distribution centre facility configuration.
State of industry in lifecycle: matured (stable demand and average growth rate; product standardized)	Cost efficiency	Nodal organization's strategic focus with respect to market determines the choice of facility.
Decline stage (decreasing demand and survival of product category demanding repositioning)	Balancing efficiency and responsiveness	Nodal organization, depending upon its future business focus, balances facility by closing unviable locations and refocusing on production capability to beat the industry trend and competition.

at long-term demand and supply conditions, plant cost and economies of scale in production and other managerial functions. But once capacity is created, it is the near-term business cycle that influences capacity utilization depending on demand and supply conditions. There is a need to have flexibility, which is the built-in capacity to adjust to the changing market scenario.

The manufacturing design and production choices are again driven by many competitive and technology-related factors. They are driven by the maturity level of the technology deployed, associated capital which provides flexibility, the ability to handle flexibility and its impact on operating cost efficiency. For example, some companies have moved from batch processes to cell manufacturing, which is an important facility decision as it has a lot to do with the facility design, machinery deployment, and skills of production employees. Such a change-over gives certain advantages in sizing, especially to handle product group demand changes in the short run. It may be observed here that the decision regarding production facility design would either be driven by responsiveness, in terms of increasing product variation and deploying capacity to produce multiple products in a group, or by efficiency—focused only on cost economies through lumping capacity on limited products or even SKUs.

In case of warehouse and distribution centres, facility designs are related to location, number of warehouses, and level of investment in warehouses. The trade-off there is decided by responsiveness, which leads to decentralization and increased number of warehouses, and cost efficiency that involves centralization of facilities.

Overall, the facility decision depends upon a number of competitive factors. From a supply chain perspective, it is important to achieve a balance of efficiency and level of service to customer and cost of providing the same.

3.3 INVENTORY AND SCM

Inventory plays a key role in supply chain as demand and supply often tend to mismatch. There are many reasons for this mismatch. It could be because of lumpiness of production demanding a certain size, which would be over and above immediate demand, or could be due to seasonality, or due to randomness of estimates, and so on. By the sheer character of production and value creation, inventory in supply chain is required.

For example, a nodal organization may have to carry stocks of raw materials or intermediate goods which go in the chain for value creation. For instance, a company which is producing tyres in India will have to have necessarily different kinds of inventory to successfully manufacture and market tyres. This is especially true when companies also face competition from international players. Apart from being capital intensive, the tyre industry is highly raw material intensive. Any change in the prices of raw materials affects the profitability of tyre companies. The raw materials used in the manufacture of tyres are rubber and petroleum derivatives like nylon tyre cord, carbon black, styrene butadiene rubber, and poly butadiene rubber. The most important raw material is rubber—natural and synthetic. Natural rubber (NR), with 29 per cent weightage in the cost of raw materials used by tyre industry, is the most expensive item. Also, this can be imported as a raw material though the options of rubber import are restricted and manufacturers have to rely on the domestic market for procuring rubber. Unless inventory is well managed, supply chain would be inefficient in this cost-efficiency driven supply chain, especially for the standardized product category.

One may look at how different forms of utility of product impact inventory decisions in the supply chain. The five forms of utility which go in a product to build value are: time utility, place utility, form utility, information utility, and possession utility. Form utility involves changing raw material or assembling parts or processing of materials to create or add value to the customer. Manufacturing process takes care of the same. Most goods are carried in split forms as raw material or intermediary and the final shape to customer is given close to demand in terms of time and place. Inventory management becomes significant in assessing demand and value in different forms and providing support to optimize the same across stages through different stakeholders. Place utility comes in when the product's usefulness is increased because of location. Time utility makes a product available at the right time.

Though these are all mundane functions in value creation, they are highly critical to the success or failure of the supply chain process. For example, a national pizza food brand has an inbound logistics service provider for dry and wet consumables from Chennai, who aggregates buying and movement to restaurants in different locations. A pizza form utility is added on when add-ons like mushrooms, nuts, and sauces are available. On a weekend, when sale peaks, all these must be in-stock for the restaurant to ensure that there are no lost sales. Approximately on a weekend, sale could be worth Rs 2,00,000, assuming Rs 200 per table cover and an order of four covers per family. If, for example, the order system misses garlic sauce, the potential sale could be less than 10 per cent of value ordered on the day. However, likely loss is just not the garlic flavour, but total order loss as the customer shifts dining to other restaurants or choice of food, which is termed as 'lost sales'.

This highlights the importance of inventory providing time, place, and form utility. In the same case, information utility and possession utility become important. Possession utility refers to the ability to aid customers in owning goods. Information utility is about usefulness added to product through communication across supply network for ensuring product availability at the right form, place, time, and price to the right person. In the case of the pizza chain, all forms of utility are fulfilled through inventory function across the supply chain. This is true of any product or service, which one may consider in any supply chain network from pin to perishables, amplifiers to aeroplanes, and consumer electronics to combat equipment.

3.3.1 Inventory as Driver and Competitive Forces

Inventory plays a significant role not only in supply chain but also in competitive strategy. A company's competitive leadership could be impacted in certain industries because of effective inventory management practices. If the supply chain strategy is responsiveness, the competitive situation must be the one where the customer is keen on product variability and quick response rather than cost. Leadership here would depend upon the ability to accomplish this with the highest degree of responsiveness and being perfect or near perfect in the fulfilment of orders.

For example, if one is in the home electronics appliances segment, post sales service and parts availability are going to be critical for brand success and upgrades. For post-sale servicing, inventory management of parts and spares and providing service on demand is going to be a critical competitive factor which has to be responsive. Similarly, if one looks at certain products where cost efficiency is fundamental to supply chain, competitive situation would also be one where cost leadership could be a critical factor for success rather than serving the customer with multiple variants. If one looks at the footwear industry in India, especially in semi urban and rural markets, cost and functionality, rather than fashion, are driving factors. The company would focus more on aggregation of order with centralized distribution warehouse system to reduce cost and be competitive.

Inventory as a force in competition is also influenced by business cycles and the need of a firm to adjust inventory, facility management, and production in response to movement in business cycles as shown in Exhibit 3.3.

Inventory management policies are interwoven with stages of the product lifecycle. During the introduction stage, product availability is the key factor in capturing the market share. In this stage, the firm would focus on responsiveness and not on cost. The high level of demand uncertainty at the introduction stage does not lend itself to effective demand planning. At this stage, the firm is far from finalizing supply chain strategy as customer acceptance and growth plans are yet to be frozen. In such conditions, holding high levels of inventory in the emerging product supply chain network assures product availability, failing which a firm not only incurs lost sales but

---

Exhibit 3.3 China's Handset Markers Face Growing Competition

The fourth quarter of 2007 was tough for mobile phone sales in China. International brands such as Nokia and Samsung continued to hold their market share, while domestic Chinese manufacturers and brands saw a steep decline in sales. Some are merging with rivals and many have been forced out of the market altogether due to inventory oversupply. Many of them were taking advantage of a flexible and low-cost baseband chip integration platform offered by local vendor Spreadtrum Communications Co Ltd and Taiwan-based Mediatek Inc (MTK), in order to survive in the highly competitive market.

Inventec, China's biggest PHS (Personal Handy-phone System) handset maker with the OKWAP brand, focused on the dual-mode PHS/GSM market, as well as on increasing its GSM product mix. The company saw little demand from the Chinese market in the short term and shifted focus to the developing market.

In China, MTK dominated second-tier handset markets. As much as 100 million cell phones with MTK chips were shipped in 2007, accounting for at least a 30 per cent share of the total Chinese handset market. The company worked closely with upstream players such as Longcheer Holdings Ltd and Sim Technology Group to integrate the MTK platform onto printed circuit board assemblies (PCB-A), which were sold to hundreds of handset assemblers in China. These assemblers, mostly based in Shenzhen in southern China, sourced their own casings, keypads, and LCD screens, and integrated them into MTK's PCB-A platform for a complete phone. Thus, Mediatek did a lot to change the game in China by making it cheaper for small companies to assemble phones. They offered ready-made software and hardware packages that allow reduced development time.

Another Chinese competitor, Spreadtrum Communications Inc., had begun to threaten MTK's market share in China. Spreadtrum started as a GSM baseband provider, but had moved to the TD-SCDMA chipset business and is now one of the largest TD-SCDMA baseband providers for China's homegrown 3G handset market.

Source: http://techon.nikkeibp.co.jp/article/HONSHI/20080304/148428/, accessed on 31 January 2009.

also the intangible loss of image in the market. Therefore, overstocking is a preferred tactic.

During the growth stage, inventory becomes a less important factor to ensure responsiveness as compared to the introduction stage. As demand uncertainty decreases, the accuracy of demand forecasting improves, which in turn helps assure product. Another approach could still be responsive as one may not like to lose sales opportunity during the growth phase and this would be critical for building the brand image. The competitive strategy would be to augment market share and cost may not be the focus. Since it is the growth phase, the ability to pass on cost would also be there.

At the product's maturity stage, efficiency is the dominant supply chain strategy. At this stage, the product becomes standardized and the growth rate is stable and predictable. A firm would focus on economies of scale to lower unit cost. In such a competitive situation, inventory becomes a cost factor in profit and loss account and a liability in the balance sheet. The focus would be to reduce inventory to an optimal level given demand predictability. The production focus would also move on to increasing commonality among products in a group and configuration close to demand point so that the value of inventory held is low.

The falling sales volume and product prices are the key features in the decline stage. A firm would focus on liquidating stocks in order to reduce losses due to inventory obsolescence. Cost would be the main driver in such conditions. This need not necessarily be in a situation when a SBU or a firm is in the declining phase. It could be a product in a product category or group. For example, a design in a fashion may die out at the end of the season. Liquidation is the only way the inventory can be managed and cost could be recovered.

Thus, inventory management becomes crucial and is related to strategic intent and competitive situation in which a firm operates. Apart from product lifecycle, many industry factors like stage of industry and competitive responses from stakeholders may also influence inventory policies which need to be understood by the supply chain manager.

3.3.2 Components of Inventory

Inventory could be raw material, intermediary or in-process, and finished goods inventory. The need for each of these is based on how it contributes to role players and value creation towards the ultimate customer. Also, categories of inventory form the basis for inventory decisions relating to the order phase, uncertainty handling, and seasonality factors.

The raw material goods are those which go as input in a process. The raw material forms a part of the total value in goods produced in the supply chain at every stage in the network. For a sugar manufacturer, the raw material is cane or beet and the output is sugar. Cane is the raw material for white sugar in India whereas in Brazil it could be beet based raw sugar or refined sugar. In the refinery process, raw sugar becomes the input. In the manufacture of chocolates or in syrups, sugar or refined sugar could be the input for different product category output. It is important to understand the different classifications of inventory in any production process and its criticality to design an inventory-holding policy. Though it is rudimentary in concept, it is basic in process mapping and plays a vital role in policy making.

To decide on the balance of efficiency and responsiveness, one may have to understand cycle inventory, seasonal inventory, and safety inventory. Cycle inventory is the average amount of inventory used to satisfy the demand between receipts of shipments. The choice is between large inventory with longer cycle time and less inventory with frequent offering, thereby reducing average lot size. Seasonal inventory refers to beefing up or slashing inventory for peak and slack seasons respectively, based on experience and predictability. Seasonality could be due to demand or supply or both factors. It would be a managerial challenge to decide on the quantum of seasonal inventory based on the efficiency level for a desired level of responsiveness.

For example, an export-oriented sweater manufacturer deals in sweaters that are used in a particular season in cold regions. The firm works out a plan with dealers and distributors in advance. By understanding the customer's preference towards design and material in the sampling stage, the firm would consolidate its order for each season. The company factors in seasonal influence and inventory build is based on demand projection. It produces garments based on orders placed by leading brands to different locations; the number of sweaters runs into millions of pieces. Though the firm has a certain amount of flexibility to increase labourers and their time window with spare production capacity to increase production for despatches, it would be difficult to keep spare capacity idle for most of the year. The firm would thus follow the two-pronged strategy of running popular standard sweater production during the normal period and fashion designed sweaters would be produced close to season, based on the confirmation of orders after the acceptance of patterns by customers.

Safety inventory is a build-up to counter uncertainty in demand. If demand is certain, one may handle managerial decisions with inventory, firmly based on experience and customer research. However, sudden factors unexpectedly increase demand. Firms may not like the opportunity to sell and corner market share during such spurts in uneven demands. Any firm will have to carefully balance between likely lost sales for want of stocks and excess stocks due to over-estimation and attempting to be responsive.

It may be noted that inventory plays a key role in the supply chain and the competitive position of the firm in the industry, irrespective of form of inventory. Value creation takes place due to the utility it brings to all players across the supply chain network. The overall objective of balancing responsiveness and cost in terms of efficiency needs to be achieved.

3.4 TRANSPORTATION AND SCM

Transportation plays a key role in supply chain management of a nodal organization as the movement of goods across the supply network to the ultimate customer is an important value creating activity. From the available array of transportation options, the nodal organization opts for a specific mode at every stage, with supply chain focus on cost efficiency and responsiveness. If a firm operates on a supply chain focus of efficiency, it chooses low-cost transportation, which may not necessarily be responsive. On the other hand, if a firm operates on a supply chain focus of responsiveness, then speed of delivery is the most important criteria and cost is given lesser importance, because the customer is able to absorb the incremental cost for the desired service level. The choice of transportation is driven not only by efficiency and responsiveness but also by a host of other factors within the framework of decision making. For example, high-value products like medical equipments, electronic products, or critical parts like spares of high-value items, are all moved through air cargo, which is expensive. Thus, choosing high-speed transportation could be due to the criticality, value, or perishable character of the product.

For a supply chain manager, it is important to be able to balance transportation cost with responsiveness. Also, the spread of the customer group to be served and the efficiency of operations could be the influencing factors for a transportation decision. It may also be noted that in a supply chain, the transportation decision is influenced by the location of facilities, inventory, and information efficiency. Let us consider the case of a capital machinery manufacturer located in south India. Since India experienced fast-paced business growth till September 2008, the firm received an increasing number of orders and saw a compounded annual growth of 40 per cent for the last seven or eight years. Most of its customers are in the north, south, and west of India. South India, where it is located, contributes to approximately 18 per cent of the firm's business. Transportation is key to the business of this firm because it receives large volumes of steel from the regional yards of Steel Corporation located in east and central India and also imports steel from Chennai, which is not far away from the plant. The plant also receives a lot of material and parts from nearby ancillaries and subcontracting units. Inbound transportation is intense and needs to be efficiently done on schedules supporting the production plan. Similarly, outbound transportation of capital machinery is also critical as about 30 per cent of the material moves by rail and road. Of this, a sizeable volume of goods goes on specialized trucks for over-sized cargo. Planning and executing the movement of such cargo is done on a project mode. Given the criticality and intensity of the cargo to be moved, vehicle availability and management of trips are big challenges to overcome in order to maintain an on-time, efficient, and effective supply network.

3.4.1 Transportation as Driver and Competitive Forces

Table 3.2 shows transportation as driver and supply chain focus with respective competitive factors.

Apart from individual strategies employed by firms or product groups, supply chain efficiency and effectiveness can also be achieved by borrowing the industry's best practices. For example, the transport operators in India have strong associations that constantly endeavour to improve their services. They also have a strong network to exchange information and optimize resource utilization, thus positively affecting the overall economy of business that contributes to cost efficiency in transportation.

Table 3.2 Competitive forces and approaches

Competitive factor	Benefits and trade-offs	Solutions/Outcomes
Cost leadership	Cost efficiency as it would conflict with responsiveness	Generally, economies in production aim to reduce the cost of manufacture and also at the same time attempt to optimize the distribution cost by minimizing the cost of transportation. Inexpensive, bulk transportation in full truckloads could be choices.
Product differentiation	Responsiveness and customer satisfaction	Multiple SKUs and varied customer groups would be the normal trend. Transportation could be in small parcels and in disaggregated outbound movements, which would be expensive. Customers could be in a position to absorb the cost.
Focus strategy	Low-cost focus strategy in a narrow segment. Alternatively, focus strategy with differentiation. Balancing between efficiency and responsiveness.	Low-cost focus would be on volume-based businesses where customers could be cost conscious and the product group could be the focus of the nodal organization. Transportation in such a case should focus on efficiency and low cost. It is possible to provide customized transportation for a narrow segment of customers, where responsiveness or quick delivery is more important than the cost.
State of industry in lifecycle: introduction and growth stage (stable demand and average growth rate; product at a nascent stage of customer acceptance; acceleration could be critical at growth stage)	Responsiveness	Introduction stage is characterized by low sales volume and high demand uncertainty. Quick response transportation modes such as direct shipping from the production site or from the distribution centres are normally implemented at this stage. At the growth stage, with increased demand visibility, the number of distribution centres is increased and the network is decentralized. Outbound transportation is based on 'Direct Shipping with Milk Runs' and 'All Shipments via Central Distribution Centre'.
State of industry in lifecycle: mature (stable demand and average growth rate; product standardized)	Cost efficiency	In the mature stage, products are stocked into and/or moved from increased number of distribution centres. As products are placed in closer proximity to customers, less responsive transportation methods are needed. The supply chain strategy of efficiency is achieved by employing the least unit cost transportation

Contd.

Contd.

Competitive factor	Benefits and trade-offs	Solutions/Outcomes
		networks of shipping via central DC (distribution centre) with crossdock, shipping via DC using milk runs, and tailored network.
State of industry in lifecycle: decline stage (decreasing demand and survival of product category demanding repositioning)	Balancing efficiency and responsiveness	At this stage, because demand is less and infrequent, the cost of excessive stocking is more harmful than having no stock at all. To achieve the strategic imperative of high efficiency, a low-cost transportation mode must be utilized. The supply chain network may deploy less complicated transportation network such as shipping via DC using milk runs or arranging for all shipments via central DC.

Similarly, there are operators' associations at the regional and district levels that procure orders for movement from major industries and distribute demand and supply for streamlining operations. Such initiatives over the years are bound to strengthen industry practices and a number of competitive advantages are likely to come up. In the same way, manufacturers, especially those who move their products in specialized trucks like car haulers and containerized trucks, are promoting good practices through cooperation among themselves for better utilization of assets and resources. All players in a supply chain network stand to benefit from such an activity.

For example, a plant located in the west of India that manufactures and distributes consumer durables like refrigerators may have to deploy containerized trucks to transport its products to east or south of India. The trip turnaround time could be approximately eighteen days. If the return loads are empty, the cost of transport in containerized cargo goes up, thus adding to the overhead costs. In such cases, the supply chain manager may tie up with counterparts who have to send their products in the reverse direction to ensure that the transport cost is shared. Thus, transportation as driver in supply chain could be challenging but provides a lot of scope for improvements in supply chain management and creating strategic advantages to a focal organization.

It may be noted that key transportation decisions that a supply chain manager looks into include selection of transportation mode and designing a transportation network. As mentioned earlier, there are a number of alternative modes of transport for movement of cargo available. However, the choice is determined by the cost of transportation and the ability of the network to deliver the designated goods to the customer on time. For example, a Canon digital SLR EOS 1DS Mark III camera, bought by an end customer, has a warranty covering lens servicing. The lens happens to be the costliest component of the camera and also has the least failure rate. If the end customer is in a remote location like Patna in eastern India, servicing this lens would require repossession of the camera and replacing the lens. The customer would expect responsiveness and the company would also prefer a mode of transportation that is the fastest and the safest, independent of the cost involved.

On the other hand, a regular raw material used in the manufacturing industry has a standard flow and its transportation mode is fixed based on the cost and flow-time factors. For example, in automobile manufacturing, components that go into production are defined by the production plan, and the schedule and arrival pattern are defined according to a stocking plan. Transportation is defined according to the bulk of the material, distance to be covered, and also according to the options available to the nodal organization. In this case, network selection is also involved as material may come from multiple points or vendors and aggregation through routes is possible.

Thus, transportation as driver plays a critical role in deciding a supply chain network. It is also an important competitive factor that could influence the business of both nodal organizations and other participating players.

3.5 INFORMATION AND SCM

Information plays a key role in supply chain management, as information is a bi-directional flow that helps a nodal organization communicate on the physical and financial parameters of the product and service a requirement on time. Information flow is critical throughout the supply chain whether it is backward linkage from the nodal organization to the manufacturer or forward linkages from the manufacturer to dealers (both primary and secondary distribution).

Recent trends are that FMCG companies are focusing on linking secondary distribution through real-time and near-real-time linkages. Understanding the customer needs and organizing to service them at an efficient cost or with a high degree of responsiveness is possible only with information linkages across the network. Visibility, which is one of the key features of supply chain, is possible only with right information tracking, dissemination, and collaboration based on the same. Collaboration fails if information is not transparent.

Apart from strategic decisions, information is a key driver at the operational level of supply chain. Production scheduling, linkages with suppliers for receiving bill of materials at plant from suppliers or through logistics service providers, distribution management at forward linkages, coordination with transport operators, and so on, warrant strong information linkages across players and processes. Any lapse in information at these stages leads to a drop in production or even exigencies at the shop floor, in supplier relationship, or at the distribution centres.

A typical example of such situations could be in a manufacturing plant where there is a breakdown of machinery that requires a resetting time of eighteen hours. This may require the adjustment of supplies of inbound material accordingly. Depending upon the nature of the industry and the level of storage available, the impact would vary. For example, if it is an assembly plant for passenger cars where supplies are every four hours from ancillaries and suppliers around the plant, it may be important to stop inbound movement. Similarly, if it is a sugarcane crushing plant for manufacturing sugar, such stoppages would require a readjustment of receipt of raw material. Alternatively, if it is a pharmaceuticals plant where storage is driven by the capacity of tankers and large vessels and godowns, then the adjustment process is easier. It may be noted that in all situations, it is important to share information appropriately to adjust supplies.

Thus, information as a driver plays a key role in supply chain management and interacts with other drivers for achieving a balance between resources, cost, and customer service.

3.5.1 Information as Driver and Competitive Forces

Information technology is fundamental in today's business, and must make the best use of the information that businesses create and use the same for value creation to all stakeholders. A wide spectrum of increasingly convergent and linked technologies help to process information to collaborate, partner, and co-perform along with entities and players across the supply chain to create value for customers, suppliers, intermediaries and to the nodal organization. Such linkages throughout are being managed by the nodal organization. Earlier companies used to compete through IT as a differentiator. However, current evolution of technology and reduced costs have made information technology a threshold competence for an organization.

Information technology changes the industry structure and fundamentals of competition with the application of new generation technology and process speed. This is true for the supply chain domain as well. One of the examples in business is the application of a technology platform for business processes like sourcing, buying, and selling through cyberspace. Post-sales customer-service engagements are now applied across industries and have become the order of the day. This is clear from Exhibit 3.4 given on the next page.

This clearly shows the competitive advantage that technology can bring into a company and its supply network. Information technology can also create a competitive advantage by giving companies new ways to outperform rivals, as Dell Corporation did in its growth strategy in the home-computer segment, and it can create a new business model for existing business operations. IT can set new trends as in the case of amazon.com, which started selling books through cyberspace, or in case of mjunction, which was discussed in Chapter 1.

One could relate the role of information technology as driver during the product lifecycle. At the introduction stage, product-specific activities and transactions are limited to the focal firm, its closely located divisions, and a few trading partners. The underlying business processes of the introduction stage tend to be less complex with respect to the number of entities. The focus here would be to ensure that the product meets customer acceptance and the model is scalable. Hence, the range of IT capability requirements is limited to this ambit, which is a simple structure. Thus, during the introduction stage, the focus would be on a reliable, cost-efficient information system for an efficient supply chain, although the supply chain focus would predominantly be responsiveness.

Exhibit 3.4 TATA Motors

In 2001, Tata Motors in India experienced a decrease in its operating margin and product development expenses gradually got out of control. To make matters worse, new competition continually arose. In 2000, there were only eight other domestic competitors, but by 2010, there are expected to be more than fifteen. The company realized that something needed to be done to regain its lead and truly become a world-class organization.

According to Ravi Kant, Managing Director of Tata Motors: 'In 2001, Tata lost five billion rupees. That was the first time something on that scale had happened in the company and our reaction was to try to understand what had gone wrong and to create a path for the future to ensure that we never got into that situation again.' To combat the issues it faced, Tata Motors established a three-tiered plan focused on turnaround, growth, and leadership. It also made the decision to partner with Ariba to achieve those goals. The procurement team wanted to reduce costs as much as possible and soon discovered the potential cost cutting that would become available by using Ariba Sourcing. A key objective was to drive major reductions in costs. Utilizing Ariba's team of category specialists and spend management professionals, Tata conducted a benchmark of its competitors and evaluation of its own products to see where savings could be achieved. The company then implemented Ariba Sourcing to drive these savings to its bottom line. In the short-term, the team needed to improve growth by strengthening their sales and services networks and creating products that would meet market needs. Its long-term goals included becoming a global leader that created world-class products, as well as to become a dominant, international business that used globally benchmarked processes.

Source: Adapted from http://www.allbusiness.com/company-activities-management/operations 10590151 -1.html.

As sales and market share increase quickly during the growth stage, the focal firm establishes more trading partners and suppliers with increased interaction across the network. Therefore, information becomes a critical driver as it helps coordinate activities across the supply chain. At this stage, information systems such as ERP and domain-based SCM systems are deployed to improve supply chain execution. The mature product's supply network extends over wide geographic locations. In such a case, efficiency is the dominant supply chain strategy. Stable market share and mature relationships with trading partners facilitate the establishment of complex transaction systems across the supply network. The supply chain becomes more complex and highly networked with multiple tiers and partners. The reach requirements include the ability to interact over the entire supply chain network including customers irrespective of technologies at specific network locations. The range requirements can be as extensive since the capabilities to execute complex transactions are demanding. Information technology investment could have reached a maturity level but needs to be responsive to market requirements based on technology obsolescence and the needs of the supply chain network.

For example, let us take the case of a fashion jewellery manufacturer who receives orders from direct or franchise stores through its customer relations management system. In fact, a customer can directly book an order through a store with advance payment. If this category is not in a batch process, it may need a separate production plan and schedule. This requires coordination with the vendor on the specific design and preferred material for studding to fulfil the order. The information driver helps to achieve responsiveness by enabling coordination across the entire supply network and functional integration across various transactions. Types of IT technologies for the mature stage include enterprise portals, enterprise integration tools, and supply chain transaction systems. An organization can grow only when it responds efficiently to each of these demands.

During the decline stage, as the focal firm loses trading partners, the supply chain shrinks. The focus would be to be cost efficient. Technology should be very effective too, even if it cannot be updated and made contemporary. This is mainly because of decline stage of business.

Apart from these, technology can be a key input in many strategic situations involving supply network. The fundamental trade-off is to prioritize between efficiency and responsiveness, which could be related to the 'push and pull' strategy of supply chain. Investment in technology is largely driven by budget and ease of implementation without constantly changing the business process. Though process improvements and changes are welcome, frequent intervention irks the partners and learning time needs adjustment along the supply chain network. Hence, while deploying technologies, a supply chain manager would consider such soft issues as acceptability and ease of implementation.

3.6 SOURCING AND SCM

Sourcing has a key role in supply chain and would be considered as one of the drivers in many businesses like automobiles, heavy engineering, electronics, machinery manufacture, agro food processing, and pharmaceuticals and chemicals. Sourcing refers to a number of strategic activities that go into supplier relationship management, right from selecting a vendor, engineering and configuring the product along with vendors, to strategic investment for committing the vendor as a competitive differentiator and single vendor, and proprietary commitment on resource and technology.

Sourcing, a set of business processes required to purchase goods and services for the ultimate customer, is important in the supply network. However, supplier development and synchronizing supply for production, product development, and cost management are big challenges. If one looks at a capital machinery manufacturer, say textile machinery, there is demand for machinery for new capacity creation, expansion, and replacement, which is known as derived demand. The new capacity creation and expansion depend upon the growth of the textile industry. The replacement would be based on the age profile of the machinery deployed, technology advancement, and industry cycle. However, textile machinery manufacturers will have to keep their suppliers engaged as per the requirement of business. During a recessionary trend, derived demand may not be high. But critical component suppliers have to be taken into confidence and engaged. Suppliers at this stage would expect transparency and commitment for being involved in future growth plans when the textile business turns around. Hence, it may be noted that suppliers need to be categorized based on their position with respect to bargaining power, criticality, and value of items procured. It is important to invest time, effort, and at times even finances for effective supply chain management, as these would decide long-term cost efficiency and responsiveness.

3.6.1 Sourcing as Driver and Competitive Forces

Table 3.3 shows sourcing as a driver and supply chain focus.

Thus, sourcing plays a key role in managing responsiveness and cost efficiency in any supply chain network as per the chosen focus of the nodal firm. Specific business

Table 3.3 Competitive forces and sourcing as driver

Competitive factor	Sourcing as driver and supply chain focus	Remarks
Cost leadership	Cost efficiency as it would conflict with responsiveness	Generally, economies in production try to reduce the cost of manufacture and also optimize sourcing efficiency by minimizing inefficiencies in buying like wastages due to quality, adjustment costs in input, or number of defects, and so on. Long-term contracts on volume and commitment on purchase give price efficiency.
Product differentiation	Responsiveness and customer satisfaction	Multiple SKUs and varied customer groups would be the normal trend. Flexibility in supply as per the demand of the nodal firm's production plan is the key. It may involve incremental cost due to low volume and change over. Customers could be in a position to absorb cost.
Focus strategy	Low-cost focus strategy in a narrow segment. Alternatively, focus strategy with differentiation. Balancing between efficiency and responsiveness.	Low-cost focus would be on volume-based businesses where customers could be price sensitive and the nodal organization's focus could be on the product group. Sourcing options in such cases are to focus on efficiency and low-cost mode. Alternatively, it is possible to create differentiation by building customer loyalty with a broad product group. This may serve responsiveness to customers and require sourcing for product variability. The speed of service would require customized approach which could be at an increased cost.
State of industry in lifecycle: introduction	Responsiveness	Introduction stage is characterized by low sales volume and high demand uncertainty.

Contd.

Contd.

Competitive factor	Sourcing as driver and supply chain focus	Remarks
and growth stage (stable demand and average growth rate; product at a nascent stage of customer acceptance; acceleration could be critical at growth stage)		Quick response sourcing such as material or parts reconfiguration and improvements are normally implemented at this stage. At the growth stage, with increased demand visibility, product categories and levels stabilize. Focus is more on cost efficiency with flexibility to increase volume at short notices.
State of industry in lifecycle: mature (stable demand and average growth rate; product standardized)	Cost efficiency	In the mature stage, products are market driven with a stable growth rate. The supply chain strategy of efficiency is achieved by employing the least unit cost sourcing with self-certified vendors and automatic replenishments, and so on. Interface with inventory policies are key at this stage.
Decline stage (decreasing demand and survival of product category demanding repositioning)	Balancing efficiency and responsiveness	At this stage, the growth rate of the firm declines. Sharing production plans and reworking on shorter intervals supplies are important. Supplier relationship, especially on critical parts and with strategic vendors, is important for reviving and repositioning products.

sourcing could play a larger role as product development, ownership of the resource, and engineering may decide industry competition. The supplier may have a strong bargaining power, thus compelling the nodal firm's supply chain manager to work on a partnering mode.

There are certain country-based factors that give a firm a competitive advantage over firms that are its sourcing partners. These advantages bring value to the firm and also drive the industry to a higher level of maturity. There are Indian companies that are involved in product/component development. Bharat Forge and Sundaram Clayton are acclaimed to be involved in product planning (including designing and supply of components) for automobile manufacturers in the USA and across the globe. India is highly competitive in value-added, precision-machined forgings and castings, which the global companies 'prefer' to source from India. There are players like Hinduja Foundries Ltd, Kirloskar Ferrous Industries Ltd, and Nelcast Ltd, who are in the forgings and casting business and manufacture for the automotive sector.

Foreign players have also chosen India as a preferred destination for setting up their sourcing plants. Delphi has relocated a part of its supplies from Johnson Controls, China, to the Igarashi Motors plant in India for manufacturing armatures of DC motors. Honeywell has shifted its requirement for detailed engineering work from China to Chemtex, India (for chemical plants). The other advantage a country like

India has is leadership in quality initiatives, which helps to improve supplier development and relationship. Like India, every region and country has its own natural factors and endowments and policies, which improve sourcing decisions in supply network. China has emerged as a manufacturing hub with developments in infrastructure. SEZs have contributed to the same. It is important to note the advantages that a supply network can exploit by aligning with such sourcing partners and how sourcing could be a competitive tool for a firm.

The decisions on sourcing processes would involve aspects like supplier scoring and assessment, supplier selection and contract negotiation, design collaboration, procurement, sourcing planning and analysis including scope of outsourcing vis-à-vis manufacturing internally. Some of these decisions are strategic decisions, while others could be either planning related or operational decisions, which are discussed in the later chapters of the book.

3.7 PRICING AND SCM

An efficient supply chain means to move the right product, at the right time, right place, right quantity, and right quality to the right customer at the right price for everyone in the supply chain network. Hence, it is clear that price is one of the drivers of supply chain. With one's understanding of supply chain focus, in the trade-off in supply chain structure between efficiency and responsiveness, price has a connotation in both. An efficient supply chain is one where customers would prefer the best price at close-to-market efficient levels. Price is one of the key factors that decides demand. Though simple economics states that price is determined by demand and supply factors, in real life, businesses decide on supply under normal conditions keeping in view the demand and realizable price. Therefore, price is necessarily a factor while defining and configuring a supply network.

On the other hand, when the supply chain manager focuses on responsiveness where customer service is of paramount importance, it is believed that the customer would be able to pay a premium price and price setting would take this into consideration. Supply chain network players reckon this while defining and executing their activities so that the incremental cost and margin could be borne by customers. In this case, price is based on the level of customer service, and monopolistic practices like price fixation, product differentiation, and so on, are based on realizable price. Therefore, price is one of the drivers of supply chain network irrespective of whether the focus is on efficiency or responsiveness. The other drivers influence and are influenced by the price factor.

One may look at the biscuits business in India, which is more than Rs 5,000 crore, a large share of which is unbranded and in the rural market. Till 2003, Britannia and Parle were the two companies that dominated the branded biscuits market. For any company to be successful in this arena, apart from selling high-margin cream biscuits in the urban segment, the company must have deep impact on the 'bread-and-butter, low-margin, high-volume, popular, low-priced, small-pack, glucose biscuit segment'. A typical customer is from a low-income group or is a daily-wage earner in society who looks for energy supplements during breaks from work. The selling points there are price and availability. Brand loyalty and recall matter least when price and availability are ignored. In this market, since the product is standardized for a branded player, price is the key differentiator. Price, coupled with supply chain efficiency, especially in distribution management, is the competitive force that determines success.

Another interesting area is the sale of perishables in Indian supermarkets. The perishables segment, especially in the case of fruits and vegetables, is one of the items in the basket that determines the success of a store. Perishables are sensitive to price and freshness. Price is a function of freshness as well. A challenge of the supply chain manager here is to ensure that fresh stocks are available at a competitive price. When a customer walks into a store and is unable to find perishables of the right quality and price, the customer moves on to the next store, and the store manager loses a large basket of buy. So, to overcome this problem, stores work on daily low-price, time windows by which they liquidate a stock of perishables at low price points. This increases the number of visits to the store at non-peak hours and also increases the volume of sales. The stores later replenish fresh stocks for peak-hour buys, thereby improving price realization. Thus, price plays a key role to be competitive. One may note that this strategy of price discounting and liquidation is not limited to perishables alone but also to many other commodities where models decay fast and functionality changes, including electronics and automobiles.

The role of pricing as a supply chain driver is crucial in supply chain effectiveness as every intermediary completes a transaction at a price that forms cost for the next stage. The ultimate customer, for whose value the focal organization works, pays up for it. Competition and industry structure have a role in pricing. Traditionally, economists have given various theories on how price fixation happens in markets and how non-price factors can influence business. One must realize that all non-price factors can be expressed in terms of cost and price. These are customer service driven factors where the customer is willing to pay a premium for a desired level of service. Hence, price is an aspect that a supply chain manager has to reckon with in order to achieve the overall business objective of synchronizing the value chain of all the players linked to the nodal organization.

3.8 BALANCING THE CONFIGURATION OF DRIVERS AND STRATEGIC FOCUS

One often comes across interesting observations on fiercely competing players in industries like automobiles, consumer electronics, FMCG, and capital goods, having different approaches in configuring supply chain drivers. One may note differences in the location of their facilities, including warehouses, inventory policy, delivery network, transportation, and so on. One may note numerous endogenous factors that would impact a firm. These could be product portfolio, budget allocation, market focus, brand strategy, and the strength of channel partners. For a supply chain manager, it is important to understand the endogenous factors like the ones mentioned above and many other exogenous factors that influence the choice of a configuration. Individually, each driver has a role and selection criteria and together they form a framework. While deciding the framework, a few conflicting situations could arise and the managerial decision would be to arrive at a trade-off in such situations. One broad principle, as explained in the earlier chapters, is that these are driven by the strategic focus of a firm on the supply chain horizon with respect to responsiveness and cost efficiency.

3.9 TRADE-OFFS IN DESIGNING SUPPLY CHAIN DRIVERS

Trade-off situations arise when there is competing demand for configuration. Any managerial decision, which involves resource commitment and is strategic in nature, with a potential to impact earnings and balance sheet, has some peculiarities. Supply chain driver configuration, by way of creating facilities or using third-party facilities, inventory policy, and distribution network involving transportation and distribution centres, is influenced by many factors. Though it is natural that evolution of an industry would standardize the supply chain drivers' configuration, it seldom can be taken as a static framework. One may understand that while arriving at a strategic decision on a location or while structuring an inventory policy based on the development of suppliers, a supply chain decision maker has to consider many factors. It is important to see how the manager constantly reviews these decisions, because the factors are dynamic and influenced by competitive situations. The manager should also be able to assess at what frequency such conflicts are to be reckoned and resolved.

3.9.1 Demand-and-Supply Conditions

Changes in the character of demand-and-supply conditions considerably influence the configuration of a supply chain driver. One may see such macro factors influencing all players but the responses could be different. Though recession is a macro event, it affects each firm differently.

For example, take the case of tier-1 auto component suppliers in India. There are clusters of auto majors in north, west, and south India. One may consider two players in the same component area: one servicing with a single location and the other with two locations. Under normal business conditions, having multiple plants with transport operations and increased inventory holding are feasible, whereas under recessionary conditions there can be a cut in production and the cost of operating two plants can be too high. In this case, a different competitive response needs to be triggered. Although the auto major is likely to lend support in such a situation, it hampers the supply chain configuration. What looked good at the designing phase is now in transition trouble till the economic cycle revives! This is common to many businesses. While configuring supply chain drivers itself, firms must understand such risks and define configuration accordingly. Here, the trade-off is between demand risk and positioning with respect to logistical drivers.

Similarly, one can look at supply-driven conflicts in the configuration of drivers. There are certain products for which facility location decision is driven by the availability of raw material, volume-based output constraining transportation or sizing issues, globalization, and so on.

For example, in India, cement manufacture is driven by limestone deposits available in certain regions. The decision on where to locate the manufacturing facility is driven by the availability of raw material. With a spurt in construction across the country, there is a need to transport and move the product on a larger radius. This requires establishment of distribution centres, effective usage of rail network along with roads, necessity to beat seasonality in construction, which is tapering, and so on. The seasonality in construction is driven by many factors—budget allocation for public works by the government, agricultural fortunes influencing rural construction, and monsoon-related factors. Recently, governments in some states allowed foreign trade, which influenced supply conditions phenomenally. A configuration of supply network for any firm is driven by demand across regions and competing manufacturers' supply factors, potential of foreign trade, monsoon, especially in India where there is prevalence of two monsoons, multiple agricultural seasons linked to monsoon, and so on. A supply chain manager needs to be sensitive to these factors and quick to respond. Though least connected by the character of product, many FMCG, consumer electronics, and two wheeler manufacturers are also affected by similar conditions.

3.9.2 Negotiating Power of Suppliers

While configuring logistical drivers, namely facilities like manufacturing and distribution centres (DCs), inventory, and transportation, one may have to consider the extent of power and its changing character when it comes to supplier relationship. If a supplier is a dominant player or single manufacturer who possesses superior technology and the component is critical to the product, then the manufacturer is driven by the supplier's decisions. Exhibit 3.5 cites one such product, of computer chips and dominance of Intel.

Logistical drivers could be configured in collaboration with supplier involvement. This also affects cross-functional drivers like pricing and sourcing, as the component price is not a competitive price but rather a profit-making price as determined by the supplier. The focal organization has to pass on the price inefficiency to the customer. The sourcing decision is less complicated in these situations because there are fewer choices. However, the sourcing department has to ensure a strong and influential relationship to manage price and quantities commitment in such cases. (See Exhibit 3.5.)

Similarly, a configuration issue would arise if the group bargaining power of suppliers increases due to the natural clustering of business. As a strategy, firms support the formation of clusters because there could be economies of scope for the players in the cluster. Further, it facilitates product development and provides easy-to-market conditions. However, the downside of this is that the bargaining power of the supplier increases and failure at the supplier's end makes it difficult to reconfigure the supply chain, especially in the case of critical components. Such strategic focus is necessary while structuring such a relationship. A relationship like this should also be

---

Exhibit 3.5   EU Charges Intel with Monopoly Abuse

The EU regulators had charged Intel Corp. with monopoly abuse for blocking rival computer chipmaker Advanced Micro Devices (AMO) Inc.'s access to customers. Intel immediately said its conduct had been lawful and said it welcomed the chance to finally respond to allegations made by its main competitor.

The European Commission claimed that Intel gave 'substantial rebates' to computer makers for buying most of their x86 computer processing units, or CPUs, from Intel; that it made payments to manufacturers to get them to delay or cancel product lines using AMD chips; and that it sold its own chips below cost on average to strategic server customers on bids against AMD products to try to muscle into that business.

It said each of these alone broke EU law by shutting out AMD from the market. Together they amounted to a strategy that damaged the rules of fair play in an effort to keep AMD from eroding Intel's market leadership, it said.

Intel, the world's biggest chipmaker, was confident that the microprocessor market was functioning normally and that Intel's behaviour had been lawful, pro-competitive, and beneficial to customers.

Intel stated that the case is based on complaints from a direct competitor rather than customers or consumers. The evidence that this industry was fiercely competitive and working was compelling. When competitors perform and execute, the market rewards them. When they falter and underperform, the market responds accordingly.

Intel had 10 weeks to reply to the preliminary charges and could seek an oral hearing to defend its case.

The EU's executive arm had been investigating Intel's business behaviour since 2001, looking into complaints from AMD and computer manufacturers that it used its power as a market leader to shut out rivals for chips that run on Microsoft software.

The case had run hot and cold for several years. EU regulators had to shut down one line of inquiry when Taiwan's Via Technologies withdrew its complaint about computer circuits—or chipsets—in 2002. At the time, they also said they did not have enough evidence to pursue an AMD complaint on microprocessors. AMD filed another complaint in 2004 and EU officials said they had no choice but to investigate, or risk AMD taking them to court for negligence.

In 2005, EU regulators raided Intel offices in Britain, Germany, Spain, and Italy two weeks after AMD filed another set of lawsuits in Japan and the United States. The EU investigation widened later to include AMD's allegations that Intel had pressured Europe's largest consumer electronics retailer Media Markt not to offer computers that carried AMD chips.

Microprocessors from Intel continue to dominate the global market in desktop computers that run Microsoft's Windows operating system.

Source: Adapted from http://www.washingtonpost.com/wpdyn/content/article/2007/07/27/AR2007072700421_pf.html.

---

closely monitored to avoid challenges of such a configuration. The disruption in configuration calls for a quick reaction which is the biggest challenge. The best way to approach such challenges is to be sensitive to disruptions and to allocate a higher budget during the disruptive period.

It is important for a supply chain strategist to reckon the bargaining power of suppliers in different scenarios and understand the configuration of the drivers accordingly. Adjustments and reworking of strategies are important to establish an effective supply network.

3.9.3 Negotiating Power of Buyers

Porter's five forces model on competitive analysis explains the importance of the bargaining power of buyers. One may look at how it is relevant for the configuration of supply chain drivers. In most of the cases, where differentiated products are available in the market, customers are conscious of the brand, expect high level of post-sales service, and thus, the bargaining power of the customer is high. In such scenarios, the supply chain structure would be responsive. The configuration has challenges because there is a need to establish more facilities and stock inventory, and outbound transportation must be customer specific. If the customer pays for it, it becomes easier. Once volume increases, challenges go up because the character of the product changes and it becomes difficult for the constituents to provide service. Under such circumstances, the configuration of supply chain drivers also needs to be reassessed. For example, a change in inventory is a smooth function compared to demand for warehouse space, which could be a step function. When buyers are powerful, the firm gets affected because the buyer would tend to go for competitive products. To avoid loss of market share, the firm will have to increase its cost of service, thereby resulting in a conflict in supply chain configuration: an increase in cost when responsiveness is also tough.

The condition of strong buyer behaviour arises when the buyer is a captive or single customer. This imperfect competition is a situation of monopsony. Though the nodal organization may have structured its supply chain drivers to suit such a condition, any circumstantial situation like a spurt in demand would lead to a situation where re-configuration of supply chain drivers would be warranted. Under this circumstance, the buyer would expect the firm to strengthen the facility and catch up with demand parameters. Unless the firm responds on time irrespective of cost, it runs the risk of jeopardizing the relationship with the buyer.

There are situations where a group of buyers have strong bargaining power, which may be due to psychological factors or due to some extraneous factors like political power, and so on. For example, in India, mass consumers of staple food articles and agro-based commodities like sugar and vegetable oil would have a high collective bargaining power as the media and the government are sensitive to price rise and availability. Hence, supply chain managers of such commodity groups must be able to quickly reconfigure supply chain drivers whenever such a commodity market is distorted.

These disruptions and sensitivities in supply chain configuration are not just limited to agricultural products. Even manufacturing goods face such situations during movement in business cycle. For example, in the case of some manufactured goods, like capital goods, buyers have strong bargaining power just because of the size of the operation. The suppliers could be ancillaries or components vendors who are expected to support a large-scale buyer. Small players absorb more pressure on adjustments in the supply network. Hence, the bargaining power of buyers leads to conflicts in configuration and adjustment of supply chain drivers, which a supply chain manager has to strategize and respond during times of demand.

3.9.4 Innovations and Competitive Behaviour

There are certain businesses in which innovation is a regular feature impacting competitive behaviour of firms. In such businesses, the supply chain strategy configured is to be responsive and not to be cost efficient. However, innovation as a strategy would work only when customers are able to absorb the extra cost or the firms are able to bring out cost-saving and efficient products so that the customers realize incremental value at a decreased cost. In the latter situation, product delay is treated as a strategy and a firm must be able to provide spares and service supports for certain SKUs. This is possible only when there is a combination of responsiveness and cost efficiency, which is a conflict under normal circumstances. Any firm in such a business must be prepared with a strategy to combat disruptions due to frequent innovations. Few good examples of such industries are consumer electronics and communication. One would often come across new-generation mobile phones, entertainment devices, and home appliances with increased functionality and features introduced in the market at regular intervals. A supply chain manager is expected to service the customers who have older versions of the models and also satisfy another set of customers who demand new-generation products. This is a challenging responsibility, because one part of the supply network needs efficiency and the other responsiveness. Hence, innovation as a strategy brings pressure on the supply chain configuration.

3.9.5 Resource-based Strategy Decisions

Resource-based factors strongly influence the configuration of supply chain drivers. As it is commonly understood, supply chain configuration like facility, transportation, and inventory consume a lot of resources, both physical and financial. A nodal firm's command over resources determines the choice of supply chain drivers. However, the availability and quality of the resources change dynamically according to the firm's earnings and market conditions. Once when there is an increase or decrease in resource command, the configuration needs to be reworked. Any supply chain strategist would aspire to improve responsiveness and cost efficiency when there is ease of resource availability. However, this needs to be justified by fundamentals of capital budgeting decisions.

Apart from resource availability and command, market factors would also immensely influence supply chain driver configurations. For example, when competition builds a large facility or increases the number of distribution centres across the channel, a firm is compelled to re-assess the configuration of its supply chain drivers. At the outset, this may look like more a problem of competition and less of a supply chain issue. However, an innovative supply chain manager must resort to practices that address the competition given his/her own drawback on resource command. For example, in India, when new generation car manufacturers came with new models and improved features, the market leader Maruti faced the challenge of competition reach and customer value chain. To address this issue, Maruti improved its value chain by aggressive marketing and an increase in the number of dealers so that the overall value to the customer was comparable to what

---

Exhibit 3.6   Maruti Udyog Ltd: Performance in the Year 2006–07

The year 2006–07 was significant for the success of all of Maruti Suzuki's new product launches, its entry into cars powered by diesel and LPG, development of new markets for exports, and the continued rapid expansion of its sales and service network. Net sales increased by 21.6 per cent during 2006–07. Profit after tax grew by 31.4 per cent over the previous year. The company was able to increase its net profit to net sales ratio from 9.9 per cent in 2005–06 to 10.7 per cent in 2006–07.

Maruti's new car assembly plant and diesel-engine plant at Manesar became operational. In a short span, both the plants had attained full capacity. The company launched the new WagonR, WagonR Duo, Zen Estilo, and Swift Diesel in 2006–07, and SX4 and Grand Vitara in the early part of 2007–08. All of these models received a very good response from customers. The company developed new export markets, and its sales to countries outside of India increased by 65 per cent.

The success of Maruti Suzuki in India was based on a sharp understanding of the needs of a typical Indian car buyer, and its ability to meet their changing needs in a satisfactory manner.

The customers continued to expect their cars to be reliable, fuel efficient, with low cost of ownership, requiring spare parts that are affordable, and a service network that was extensive and of high quality. But they were no longer satisfied with this. Without sacrificing any of the above attributes, they also wanted their cars to look stylish, sport a contemporary design, and come loaded with features.

More and more customers seemed to be scaling up. Among entry-level cars, the share of air-conditioned variants was growing at the cost of standard variants. Variants with power steering were increasingly preferred to those without. Even in the compact to premium segments, customers seemed willing to stretch a little extra for better looks and superior features, reflected in the growing share of higher variants within models.

Related trends, like more than one car per family and shorter ownership cycles, also seemed to be gathering pace. The large number of entry-level customers continued to offer tremendous opportunity. Considering these trends, Maruti Suzuki's strategy had been to widen the choice for the Indian customer. This was evident not only in the large number of models the company had launched, but also in diverse segments and with multiple fuel options.

Increasingly, the approach for India cannot be price *versus* features. It has to be price *and* features. It cannot be value *versus* style. It has to be both. Nor can it be looked at as petrol *or* diesel. Multiple fuel options will have to be offered. The way forward, clearly, is to be able to expand the range of offerings, across segments and fuel types.

This evolution of the Indian customer coincided with a major transformation at Suzuki. This process started a few years ago, when Suzuki consciously decided to expand its brand image from being the leader in mini cars and compact SUVs, to becoming a 'complete car maker'.

In line with this, it decided to design its new products with a distinctly stylish and European flavour. The first outcome of this transformation was the Swift. The Swift reflected the new design philosophy, focusing on bold and aggressive designs and European styling. It was based on the design of Mini Cooper and Skoda Fabia. It received overwhelming acclaim, not only in India but in all the four countries where it was launched almost concurrently.

Since then, Suzuki has designed and launched three new globally strategic models, including the SX4 that reflects the new approach. All the new models launched in India have been well received.

Source: Adapted from http://www.maruti.co.in/sb/chairman.asp?ch=4&ct=3&sc=0.

was offered by the competition. Though Maruti might have faced the heat of the competition, its resource availability and command helped to meet its competitive challenge. Exhibit 3.6 summarizes this case.

In the exhibit below, one could observe how a command over resources helped Maruti overcome competitive pressures. Availability of resources, though not explicitly mentioned, as observed in strategic focus on new model introduction depicts the ability to handle competition. There are umpteen firms that have resource constraints and are unable to reconfigure quickly, which leads to their businesses dying untimely deaths. It is not just logistical drivers alone but also cross-functional drivers like pricing, information, and sourcing that play a significant role in managing such firms that face collapse. The tools available to face such distress situations are mainly supply chain strategic adjustments like managing facility, inventory, information, and pricing.

When a firm is on a cash crunch due to competitive pressure and facilities need to be slowed down, it requires resource adjustment. This adjustment comes through reducing the flow rate and increasing the cost per unit, as economies of scale would go disarray. Such a situation would lead to cash losses that are to be funded temporarily. If the supply chain manager fails to understand and synchronize with the finance manager, there is a lack of coordination. Here is a situation where costs increase and responsiveness lowers, and resource adjustment is what can provide a lifeline. A firm needs to judicially manage such situations keeping in mind the strategic perspective of supply chain drivers in order to reposition and face such challenges successfully. Thus, resource-based factors support conflicts in managing supply chain drivers in critical situations of business.

3.9.6 Technology

Technology as a competitive force would impact the configuration of supply chain drivers. Technology could be related to both products/services as well as processing of data and information. Here, both are discussed.

Product technology is that which is embedded in product features and value is created because of technology applications, through manufacture or processes that are deployed in creating products.

For example, the supply of mobile phones is basically driven by demand and regulatory conditions in the country of operation and the level of maturity the industry has reached. Within such operating parameters, any manufacturer has a wide variety of customers from a simple telephone instrument for communication to a business organizer, communicator, and entertainment set, which again widely varies in range. The ability of the company to bring in new models in every customer segment group and service them is going to be critical. Model proliferation and availability are the challenges faced by facilities and distribution management. Supply chain drivers are to be configured to provide such responsiveness. Also, there could be times of change in the orientation of business linked to the economic cycle. During recessionary times, the firm's activities could be less volatile, demanding stable drivers, whereas during market boom, the same firm will have to have a more aggressive configuration.

A supply chain manager must understand that product technology gets obsolete and that new products need to be introduced at a regular interval. He/She should accordingly strategize supply chain driver configurations. This is common in the consumer electronics and home appliances segment.

Another interesting segment in India where product technology has an impact on supply chain configuration is the industrial product segment, especially in companies that provide battery backups and power support systems. A wide range of UPS systems and power conditioning solutions are marketed by players to companies that use them according to their requirements, such as for manufacturing units, offices, hospitals, data centres, BPO and IT companies, and so on. The latest generation of products embed Clean Power technology products in order to provide environment-friendly and reliable applications. The market is inundated with players applying international technology and quality standards. The competition is severe and these products are marketed and distributed both directly and through channel partners. A supply chain configuration needs to be responsive and efficient as price and speed of sale and support services are critical success factors. Supply chain strategy is key to the success of this business and more importantly, configuration by way of facilities, inventory, movement, and pricing must be internationally competitive and customer focused. Players like Numeric Power Systems Ltd, Crompton Greaves, Bharat Bijlee, Honda SIEL, Techno Electric, and few others fiercely compete in this market.

One may also note how developments in information technology have impacted supply chain configuration. Information is one of the critical drivers and advancement in information technology is impacting other supply chain drivers because the decreasing cost and ease of application of information technology are bringing in transparency and visibility in the supply network. This is reflected in the way facilities in manufacturing and warehousing are reconfigured. Safety inventory is getting reviewed closely and companies are reducing demand risks with better information availability. Again, the application of technology has facilitated track and trace in movement, which improves transportation efficiency. Thus, supply chain drivers are extremely sensitive to technology advancements because the competition quickly adopts new applications for improving value across the system.

3.9.7 Government Policies

Government policies impact the configuration of supply chain drivers. Facilities, like manufacturing and warehousing locations, are influenced by government policies. At the global level, since the late 1980s, governments have been focusing on reducing trade barriers and encouraging the setting up of plants. Some of the classic examples are China and India in manufacturing, and Thailand and Taiwan in electronics. Malaysia and Singapore have also been actively leading such a change by being open to the location of facilities. The configuration of network would change strategically with a change in government policy. For example, India liberalized the automotive sector in 1992 and attracted leading players into the market. At one point, Hyundai was considering setting up a world car project in India in association with other players like DaimlerChrysler and Mitsubishi. However, the other players backed out of the project.

The bulk of India's annual passenger car market of around 1.2 million cars is made up of small cars with an engine capacity of 1 litre or even lower. The car market has been growing at a fast pace since 1993, when the government removed restrictions on local car production, prompting global car majors like GM, Ford Motor Co., Mercedes Benz, Honda Motor Co., Daewoo Motor Corp., and Toyota Motor Corp. to set up facilities. The geographical location of India is what makes it very attractive. A production base in India could cater to the entire South Asian region, which does not provide infrastructure facility like India. One may note that another major market like the Middle East is close by. It may be noted from Exhibit 3.7 that Toyota is looking at the small cars market in India in a big way.

Exhibit 3.7 clearly indicates that government policies influence global players on supply chain configuration. Similar situations arise domestically as well when there is a change in state-level duties and taxes or incentives provided by the central/federal government to encourage a region to grow. For example, in India, when the Uttaranchal State was formed, the central government announced a number of incentives that encouraged some firms to set up manufacturing base in Uttaranchal. This encouraged reconfiguration of supply chain drivers that provide economies in production and distribution.

Exhibit 3.7 Toyota Eyes Small Car Market in India, to Invest $350 Million in New Plant

Toyota Kirloskar Motor (TKM), the automotive joint venture between Japan's Toyota Motor Corp. and India's Kirloskar Group invested Rs 1,400 crore ($350 million) on a new plant in Bangalore from where it will roll out its small car in a bid to tap the largest segment of car market in India.

Toyota Motor Corp. is developing the small car from scratch in Japan, and by 2010, the car will be ready to roll out from the Indian plant.

The facility, TKM's second in India, will come up at Bidadi in the vicinity of the existing plant and will be able to produce 100,000 cars when it starts production. The company's current plant has an annual production capacity of 63,000 units.

From this plant, TKM will roll out a strategic new small car which is now being developed at their research and development facility in Japan. The new car will meet the market demand of Indian consumer. The dealership network would also be expanded.

TKM is a joint venture set up between Toyota Motor Corp. and Kirloskar Group in 1997 with a shareholding ratio of 89:11. The company, which has a market share of about 2.6 per cent in India, has enjoyed immense success with its sedans such as the Corolla and the Camry, the multi-utility vehicle Innova, and the sport-utility vehicle Land Cruiser Prado. In 2007, it managed to sell 54,000 vehicles, achieving a turnover of Rs 4,000 crore ($1 billion). The company now hopes to expand its market share by increasing its production capacity to 600,000 units by 2015 and the launch of its small car, which market analysts feel, will be from the stables of Daihatsu, a company in which Toyota owns 51 per cent. Daihatsu is known for its compact cars globally.

TKM is one of the many automobile companies keen on tapping India's four-wheeler market as the country's booming economy has led to increased consumer spending. In 2007–08, the passenger car market saw a total sale of 12,03,531 units as against 10,76,582 units in the previous fiscal, registering a growth rate of 11.79 per cent. Annual passenger vehicle sales are expected to rise to 2 million units by 2010 in India and analysts say Indian car sales would more than quadruple to $145 billion by 2016.

Source: Adapted from http://in.ibtimes.com/articles/20080416/toyota-motor-kirloskar-small-car-tata-nano-plant.htm.

CavinKare is a good example of this initiative. Their plant is situated in Sidcul Industrial Estate, Haridwar, where it manufactures its entire portfolio of products. It also outsourced its manufacturing to third-party manufacturing units located across India in places like Pondicherry, Noida, Assam, and Faridabad. The plant is environment friendly with effective waste management systems in place and has vertically integrated manufacturing (manufacturing to packaging) with very minimal human intervention during the process.

Exhibit 3.8 describes the Industrial Policy 2003, and throws light on the role of government policies in supply chain configuration.

The sales tax system has greatly influenced warehouse and distribution centres as mentioned earlier. The rationalization of central and state government sales tax (CST and SST) and value added tax (VAT) has greatly influenced setting up of distribution centres. Due to a dual tax structure (CST and VAT), most of the companies maintain CFA and warehouse in every state, leading to fragmented, small, and inefficient warehouses apart from higher inventories. Implementation of GST (general sales tax) would lead to consolidation and change in supply chain drivers.

Government policies not only influence the location of facilities and thereby other drivers but also other drivers directly. As seen above, tax policies influence inventory configuration. Similarly, improvements in policies like just in time and VMI have

---

Exhibit 3.8   Industrial Policy 2003

The aim of the policy is to provide a comprehensive framework to enable a facilitating, investor-friendly environment for ensuring rapid and sustainable industrial development in Uttarakhand and, through this, generate additional employment opportunities, and to bring about a significant increase in the State Domestic Product and eventual widening of the resource base of the state. The policy shall remain in force for a period of five years.

Selective investment incentives are listed below. A detailed list is available on the website.

- 100 per cent central excise exemption for 10 years on items other than those mentioned in the negative list in the concessional industrial package announced by the central government.
- 100 per cent income-tax exemption for the first five years and 30 per cent for the next five years for the companies and 25 per cent for others.
- CST @ 1 per cent for five years.
- Capital investment subsidy @ 15 per cent up to a maximum of Rs 30 lakh (Rs 3 million).

- Central transport subsidy extended till 2007.
- Exemption from entry tax on plant and machinery for setting up industry or undertaking substantial expansion and modernization.
- Land use conversion and development charges and regime will be rationalized.
- Stamp duty concession will be provided in respect of land in specialized commodity parks, including IT parks.
- Interest incentive @ 3 per cent up to a maximum of Rs 2 lakh per annum, per unit. For the purpose of the interest incentive, modernization of new existing industrial units means additional investment to the extent of 25 per cent of the underpreciated book value of plant and machinery, made in acquisition of plant and machinery and technical know-how for such modernization.
- In the case of sick non-SSI units, government will sympathetically consider measures required under revival/rehabilitation package drawn by Operating Agency/Financial Institutions/Banks.

Source: Adapted from http://www.uttaranchalonline.info/Business-and-Industries/Policy_Framework.html, accessed on 18 February 2009.

helped change the configuration and deployment of third-party and fourth-party logistics service providers.

Similarly, investments in infrastructure like roads, seaports, and airports have led to a considerable change in the transportation network. In India, new roads have increased the speed of transfer of goods, which has knocked off some capacity creation either by way of facility or storage. The ability to deploy high-powered vehicles enables the movement of large-size cargo and thereby initiates reconfiguration of supply chain drivers.

Apart from these, government policies with respect to investment in Special Economic Zones (SEZs) have led to the reconfiguration of supply networks in manufacturing and trade in India. SEZs get tax incentives which changes economic profits and hence supply network, especially those involved in export reassess the network configuration.

Thus, government policies influence supply chain configuration and changes in policies constantly drive the need for reassessment and reconfiguration of supply network.

3.9.8 Changing Structure of Logistics Service Providers

Logistics service providers, especially in India, are more of splinter groups and small firms run on ownership and partnership structure rather than being professionally run through corporate structures. This feature is increasingly changing during the last decade because of following reasons:

- Globalization and foreign players are bringing in professional organizations and international players to the forefront.
- There's a consolidation of logistics service providers across the globe and in India as well. At least companies are getting into strategic alliances if not changing ownership, and also improving the quality of service.
- The intensity of competition is forcing small and marginal players to employ professionals and improve their overall systems in order to thrive.

Thus, for focal organizations to exploit such a healthy change and remain competitive during this changing industry profile, they have to consider reconfiguring their supply chain network. A typical case is given in Exhibit 3.9.

Exhibit 3.9   Hyundai Motor India Limited

This is a case of a leading auto major from southeast Asia setting up a manufacturing unit in India at Chennai and continuously increasing its capacity over 15 years. After introducing new models and focusing on multiple segments, the company is also focusing on the export market. This company has applied supply chain drivers configuration like facilities, transportation, sourcing, information, and pricing to its best advantage for growth and has also reasonably reconfigured to accommodate the exogenous and endogenous factor influences.

Hyundai Motor India Ltd (HMIL) has grown significantly from its initial set-up in 1993 in India. It has set up its second manufacturing unit within its existing plant in Sriperumbudur, near Chennai in March 2008. The production capacity at the new plant takes Hyundai's total capacity to build 5,30,000 units annually, up from the earlier 3,00,000 units. Once the plant goes on full steam

HMIL would be capable of manufacturing 6,30,000 units per annum, second only to the market leader Maruti Suzuki, who is ramping up production capacity to one million units per year by 2010–11. Hyundai Motor India will play its role of a global manufacturing hub for all of Hyundai's small car models. At this stage, HMIL's facility in Sriperumbudur is Hyundai's largest in the world, but would be overtaken by its China facility in 2009, which would be able to produce one million cars a year. The larger plan is to export as much as 50 per cent of the production from India. The company would be exporting its car from the Chennai port. It is understood that the company is working on a plan to get a rail connectivity to transport its cars from the factory to the Chennai port, to make the process more efficient and safe.

Source: http://www.automonitor.co.in/article/Second-Hyundai-plant-up-on-stream/page1.html, accessed on 17 February 2009.

Exhibit 3.10 will further help you understand the importance of the reconfiguration of supply network in this changing scenario.

Exhibit 3.10 International Flavours and Fragrances

International Flavours and Fragrances India Ltd is a part of International Flavours and Fragrances (IFF), a global leader with a $1.9 billion business in flavours and fragrances.

The company has been growing in double-digits in recent years. The growth in developed markets like the U.S.A. could be as marginal as 2 per cent. However, that market is more than ten times that of the Indian market. The demand for the products is derived demand based on segments like beverages, bakery, sweets, and confectioneries. The competition is tough. There is a tremendous pressure on the margins because there are small and marginal players who indulge in slashing prices and undercutting the market. IFF drives business through volumes. The competition for IFF is stiff, with consolidation happening in India where it is reported that the top six players enjoy a market share of 70 per cent. IFF has a market share of 30–35 per cent in flavours and caters to the bakery, confectionery, savoury, beverages, and pharmaceutical businesses. India is one of the few markets where fragrance is bigger than flavours because the food processing industry is underdeveloped.

This is linked to high GDP growth, continuing reforms, and business in rural India picking up. Then the markets would develop faster. The change in food habits is already noticed with strong roots of FMCG brands in the rural segment. They have aspirations; they are willing to experiment with new foods, use lifestyle products. There is tremendous scope for the industry to grow and there's no reason why IFF should not grow in an emerging market as this.

The production centre of IFF is based in Chennai, India, and it serves institutional customers, dealers, and channel partners through its warehouses located in Chennai, Chittoor, Bangalore, Ernakulam, Mumbai, Hyderabad, Ghaziabad, Kolkata, and Delhi. As mentioned earlier, the increased number of warehouses may be due to the dual sales tax structure of central sales tax and value added tax at the state level. With a reduction of tax rates and rationalization of the tax regime, this is likely to change. But there are still operational constraints in tax administration and companies like IFF could be comfortable in handling distribution with multiple warehouses.

It is understood that the company has recently set up a plant in Jammu. Obviously, such a location of facilities would demand a reconfiguration of supply chain drivers. Again, while it looks like a niche and narrow focus business with an established brand, companies like IFF face challenges in setting up and managing the configuration of supply chain drivers due to the pressure of competition, government polices, and strategic initiatives driven by the top management.

Source: Adapted from www.iff.com.

SUMMARY

The alignment of a specific business strategy to a corresponding supply chain strategy is achieved through proper deployment of supply chain drivers. The supply chain structure defines such a strategic focus for the supply chain, which needs to be accomplished through effective deployment of supply chain drivers, namely, facilities, inventory, transportation, sourcing, pricing, and information.

Facilities by definition in supply chain refer to the physical location of the nodal organization or its partners, for example, where a product or service is being fabricated, assembled, produced, processed or stored. The role of production facilities in the supply chain is derived from the supply chain strategy. To achieve responsiveness for a given level of efficiency, one would go for decentralized facilities, and for efficiency at a desired level of responsiveness, the facilities would be centralized. The importance of facilities in a supply chain varies depending upon industry structure, practice, nature of goods, buyer characteristics, and the strategic intent of the focal organization. The decision of setting up a facility depends upon a number of competitive factors. From a supply chain perspective, it's the choice between frequency and level of service to the customer and the cost of providing the service, which matter most.

Inventory plays a key role in supply chain as demand and supply would tend to mismatch. Mismatch could happen because of lumpiness of production demanding a certain size that would be over and above the immediate demand, due to the factor of seasonality, or due to randomness of estimates, and so on. By sheer character of production and value creation, inventory in supply chain is required. The overall objective of balancing responsiveness and cost in terms of efficiency needs to be achieved.

Transportation plays a vital role in supply chain management of a nodal organization as the movement of goods across the supply network to the ultimate customer is an important value creating activity. A nodal organization opts for a specific choice at every stage based on whether cost efficiency responsiveness is the supply chain focus. It may be noted that key transportation decisions that a supply chain manager may look into would include selection of transportation mode and designing a transportation network.

Information plays a key role in supply chain management because information is a bi-directional flow that helps a nodal organization communicate on physical and financial parameters of the product and servicing a need on time. Information flow is critical throughout the supply chain whether it is backward linkage from the nodal organization to the manufacturer or onward linkages from the manufacturer to dealers (primary distribution) and later on to secondary distribution.

Sourcing refers to a number of strategic activities that go into supplier-relationship management, right from selecting a vendor, engineering and configuring the product along with the vendors, to strategic investment. Sourcing plays a key role in managing responsiveness and cost efficiency in any supply chain network depending upon the chosen focus of the nodal firm. There are certain country-based factors that give a firm a competitive advantage over other firms to be sourcing partners. These advantages bring value to the firm and also drive the industry to a higher level of maturity.

An efficient supply chain is one where customers would prefer the best price that is close to market efficiency levels. When the supply chain manager focuses on responsiveness where customer service is of paramount importance, it is believed that the customer would be able to pay a premium price and price setting would take this into consideration.

Numerous endogenous factors like product portfolio, budget allocation, market focus, brand strategy, and strength of channel partners would impact a firm. For a supply chain manager, it is important to understand the endogenous factors and manage the configuration of supply chain drivers.

Similarly, exogenous factors like government policies, market factors, globalization of business, cluster development, and environmental factors influence the choice of a configuration.

Individually, each driver has a role and selection criteria and they together form a framework. While deciding the framework, a few conflicting situations could arise in which the managerial decision would be to arrive at a trade-off. The firm's actions are driven by the strategic focus the firm has on the supply chain horizon with respect to responsiveness and cost efficiency.

Demand and supply conditions, negotiating power of suppliers, negotiating power of buyers, innovations and competitive behaviour, resources, technology, government policies, and the changing structure of logistics service providers are some of the factors that influence a supply chain network and are responsible for the reconfiguration of supply chain drivers.

KEY TERMS

Cost leadership: A low-cost leader in any market gains competitive advantage from being able to produce goods at the lowest cost. Factories are built and maintained, and labour is recruited and trained to deliver the lowest possible costs of production. 'Cost advantage' is the focus.

Cycle inventory: Cycle inventory is the average inventory in a supply chain due to either production or purchases in lot sizes that are larger than demanded by the customer.

Design collaboration: Involvement of suppliers in product engineering, designing, and planning to reduce cost, improve quality, and decrease time to market.

Facility: Facility by definition in supply chain refers to the physical location chosen by a nodal organization where a product or service is fabricated, assembled, produced, processed, or stored.

Focus strategy: Where an organization cannot afford a wide scope cost, leadership, or a wide scope differentiation strategy, a focus is deployed by which an organization focuses its effort and resources on a narrow, defined segment of a market.

Inbound transportation: Inbound movement of goods in the supply chain network, especially from the supplier to the manufacturer and from the manufacturer to mother warehouses.

Just in time (JIT): The goal of JIT is to time activities so that components or goods or services arrive in the production line just in time for transformation. There must be absolute synchronization of item, quantity, quality, and time for achieving success in JIT.

Lost sales: Sometimes a customer cannot be serviced because the supply with the nodal organization falls short. This results in the customer moving his demand to a competitor, and termed as a lost sale.

Outbound transportation: Outbound movement of goods from the manufacturer to dealers, and further down the network.

Procurement: It is the purchase of material both directly and indirectly by consolidating orders with the objective of reducing cost

Product differentiation: Products that are differentiated satisfy the needs of customers and provide a sustainable competitive advantage. This allows companies to desensitize prices and focus on value that generates a comparatively higher price and a better margin.

Product lifecycle: A product goes through a sequence of stages from introduction, wherein a product is in an early stage of acceptance by market, to growth, where market acceptance gallops to a stage of maturity where the product and the market stabilize with normal demand. Finally, the demand starts slackening, leading to the decline stage.

Safety inventory: Safety inventory is inventory held in case demand exceeds expectation; it is held to counter uncertainty.

Seasonal inventory: Seasonal inventory is built up to counter a predictable variability in demand.

Sourcing: Sourcing refers to a number of strategic activities that go into supplier relationship management, which include selecting a vendor, and engineering and configuring a product along with vendors. It also includes strategic investment for committing the vendor as a competitive differentiator with single vendor and proprietary commitment on resource and technology.

Special Economic Zones (SEZ): SEZs are specially demarcated geographical regions that have more liberal economic laws as compared to the centralized laws of the country. The very purpose of a SEZ is to develop the area covered under the special economic zone by supporting with special economic policies. For example, the basic motive behind developing SEZ in India or in China, primarily in the developing countries, is to attract mass foreign investments in the country.

Stock keeping units (SKUs): The variants of a product in a category to serve varying units of demand are generally referred to as stock keeping units or SKUs.

Third-party logistics service providers: These firms are either asset- or non-asset based, who own and operate transportation equipment and warehousing buildings and provide service to nodal organizations.

Vendor managed Inventory (VMI): VMI is when the supplier assumes responsibility and actually manages inventory. This was initially adopted in the retail supply chain where a category owner took VMI responsibility. Increasingly this has been applied in backward linkages of supply chain as well as in manufacturing.

CONCEPT REVIEW QUESTIONS

1. Define a supply chain driver and its relation to supply chain focus with a couple of examples.
2. Explain the role of manufacturing facilities and their importance in supply chain. Highlight the importance of facilities with respect to product lifecycle relating to a product of your choice.
3. What are the different forms of utilities that create value to products? How are they related to supply chain effectiveness?
4. Analyse the role of transportation in creating value in a supply chain network. Discuss its relevance in backward linkages and forward linkages with examples.
5. How could the choice of transportation mode

be impacted by competitive force? Explain any situation where competition was intensified by the choice of transportation mode.
6. Explain the role of cross-functional drivers, namely information, pricing, and sourcing in a supply chain, with examples. Discuss how competitive forces can influence the deployment of those drivers.
7. Explain the various factors that lead to the reassessment of configuration of supply chain drivers. Give some examples.
8. Analyse the impact of government policies on supply chain drivers. Use a typical situation in which reconfiguration could be triggered.

CRITICAL THINKING QUESTIONS

1. You are responsible for supply chain management of an engineering firm, which is into textile machinery manufacture. Your company was growing at 40 per cent during the last three years and you had projected a similar growth rate for the next three years. Earlier you had an inventory of 90 days. During the growth phase, you have reduced inventory to 60 days. You have contracted additional warehouse space, production facilities, and movement contract on a long term. With global recession hitting you, how would you approach reorganizing your drivers?

2. You are appointed as chairman of a local fruits and vegetable market, which acts as a hub in your city. How would you assess the driver and improve effectiveness? You must focus more on cross-functional drivers in improving effectiveness. A few observations include: arrivals are in early morning between 3 a.m. and 4.45 a.m. Institutional buyers and resellers buy between 5 a.m. and 7 a.m. Retail and small resellers buy till 1 p.m. At 1 p.m., it is assessed that balance stocks available during the weekend are low at 15 per cent, whereas during midweek it goes up to 36 per cent. If you were to advise participat-

ing traders about selling in the market, how would you approach?

3. After web-based research, look at an industry where there has been a change in the bargaining power of any constituents in the supply chain network that demand reconfiguration of supply drivers. Elucidate with examples.

4. Why are trade-offs critical in the configuration of supply chain drivers? Use a typical case wherein reconfiguration was initiated and major trade-off was engineered for the overall gain in supply network.

PROJECT ASSIGNMENTS

1. Visit a manufacturing facility in your town and map its relevance to the supply chain. Also inquire what are the competitive forces that influence this facility. You may also look at competitive advantages the facility may provide in the supply network.

2. Visit a nearby retail store that sells grocery and perishables. Analyse how price as a driver is used to improve supply chain efficiency.

3. Research on the web and analyse the manufacturing growth in China. Choose a major industry that has repositioned its location to China and analyse the competitive factors that caused the same.

4. Do a structural analysis of the Indian paint industry and find out whether supply chain drivers are reconfigured for effective demand management.

REFERENCES

http://en.wikipedia.org/wiki/Location _theory# cite_ref-0). (Thünen, Johann Heinrich von, *Der Isolierte Staat...*, *Vol I and II* Partial translation into English, by Carla M. Wartenberg, *Isolated State*, New York, Pergamon Press, 1996

http://in.ibtimes.com/articles/20080416/toyota-motor-kirloskar-small-car-tata-nano-plant.htm

http://kirloskarapps.kirloskar.com/kirloskar/aboutkirloskar/kfil.html

http://techon.nikkeibp.co.jp/article/HONSHI/20080304/148428/

Ron De Marines, http://findarticles.com/p/articles/mi_m0UDO/is_2000_June_2/ai_63676742

Ron De Marines http://findarticles.com/p/articles/mi_m0UDO/is_2000_June_2/ai_63676742

Weber, Alfred, *Theory of the Location of Industries*, 1909, Chicago, Translated by Carl J. Friedrich, 1929

www.allbusiness.com/company-activities- management/operations/10590151-1.html

www.automonitor.co.in/article/Second-Hyundai-plant-up-on-stream/page1.html

www.cavinkare.com/corp_manufact.html

www.hindujafoundries.com

www.itcportal.com/sets/foods_frameset.htm

www.maruti.co.in/sb/chairman.asp?ch= 4&ct=3&sc =0

www.nelcast.com

www.nokia.com/A4136002?newsid=-6134

www.uttaranchalonline.info/Business-and-Industries/Policy_Framework.html

www.washingtonpost.com/wp-dyn/content/article/2007/07/27/AR2007072700421_pf.html

4

Decision Environment

Learning Objectives

After studying this chapter, you will be able to:

- Understand the external factors that impact decision making in supply chain management
- Understand the impact of macro environment in decision making
- Understand the industry and competitive factors influencing supply chain decisions
- Gain an insight into the opportunities and constraints of a resource-driven decision environment
- Understand the technology environment for mapping decision environment
- Understand the support system for mapping decision environment

4.1 FACTORS IN DECISION MAKING

As in any business, decision making in supply chain management is determined by a host of internal and external factors. External factors could be government rules and regulations relating to warehousing, transport movement, carriers, and direct controls like pricing, licensing, and so on. Similarly, a number of economic factors like group collusion, price setting by dominant players, and trade practices can influence decisions. This section presents a brief overview of various external factors that may influence the decisions of a supply chain manager.. This is intended to be more indicative than comprehensive because, in real life, such factors change very often and a manager has to take cognizance of the latest regulation in vogue.

4.2 EXTERNAL FACTORS RELEVANT FOR SUPPLY CHAIN DECISIONS

As mentioned in the earlier chapter, supply chain management (SCM) is the network of organizations that are involved, through upstream and downstream linkages, in different processes and activities that produce value in the form of products and services in the hands of the ultimate consumer. Logistics is the process of strategically managing the procurement, movement, and storage of materials, parts, and finished inventory, and the related information flows through the organization and its marketing channels for cost effective fulfilment of customers' orders. Logistical drivers are important value creators in the supply chain. One may come across a number of external actors that influence supply chain decisions.

A supply chain manager arrives at a number of strategic, planning, and operational decisions in supply chain domain area. Broadly, the decision could be related to the location of the facility, capacity planning, network design, and so on. Each of these decisions is based on many internal factors and a command on resources. At the same time, external factors also influence decisions. For example, though internally location X may be best suited for supply chain optimization, the decision may depend on external factors like government approval to set up a production unit at the chosen site, which may be based on various sociological, economic, and environmental issues. It may not be a direct responsibility of the supply chain manager to decide on the location and many a time an inter-disciplinary team facilitates such decisions. All the same, it is important that a supply chain manager is aware of the broad aspects of external factors that might impact decision making in the domain (Figure 4.1). These would include:

1. Macro environment covering: economic, societal, political, legal, demographic, and environmental—health, safety, and ecological—factors.
2. Industry and competitive factors
3. Technology environment

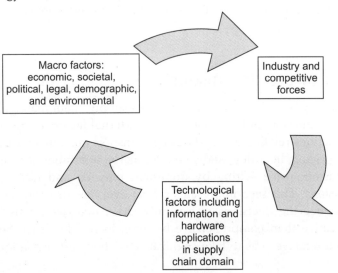

Figure 4.1 External forces impacting supply chain decisions

4.2.1 Macro Environment

A macro environment is one that directly and/or indirectly impacts strategic decisions, and planning and operations of a company. All organizations operate in a macro environment consisting broadly of the following:

- Economic and demographic factors
- Societal value and lifestyles
- Government legislation, both at the federal and state levels
- Technology factors

- Immediate industry standards
- Competitive environment

The macro environment includes all relevant forces outside the company's boundaries but would have a bearing on the operations and strategy of the company. Although the macro environment is outside the control of the company, it is important to monitor macro variables on a continuous basis because it impacts company decisions. Some of these factors are evolutionary and allow some adjustment time during transitions. There are some factors that are dynamic and at times the changes are drastic in nature. Hence, there is a need to monitor these factors regularly. For example, the global economic crisis from late 2008 has had a drastic impact on many supply chain-related decisions like operations of facilities in certain geographies where demand became weaker and the currency exchange rate turned unfavourable for the nodal organization, and so on. A supply chain manager must take cognizance of those factors while making decisions. This section provides a brief coverage of the macro factors that might impact decision making. It is suggested that a supply chain manager must constantly keep an environment monitor to validate the decision horizon.

Facilities could be setting up a manufacturing unit or a warehouse or distribution centre. Generally, choosing the location for a facility requires regulatory clearances like licence for manufacture. Otherwise, there must be a clear policy that such manufacturing activity is not controlled under licensing or under a reserved category for SSI or any such regulatory mechanism (Exhibit 4.1). For example, if an entrepreneur wants to set up a sugar plant, one may have to get a licence from the central government. This licence from the central government would depend on a certificate issued by the state government (where the facility will be located) for possible demarcation of lands from where cane can be procured, and so on. Once it is

---

Exhibit 4.1   Policy Measures in India

Policy measures

(i) Liberalization of Industrial Licensing Policy

The list of items requiring compulsory licensing is reviewed on an ongoing basis. At present, only six industries are under compulsory licensing, mainly on account of environmental, safety, and strategic considerations. Similarly, there are only three industries reserved for the public sector. The lists of industries reserved for the public sector and of items under compulsory licensing are at Appendix III and IV respectively of Industrial Policy.

(ii) Introduction of Industrial Entrepreneurs' Memorandum (IEM)

Industries not requiring compulsory licensing are to file an Industrial Entrepreneurs' Memorandum (IEM) to the Secretariat for Industrial Assistance (SIA). No industrial approval is required for such exempted industries. Amendments are also allowed to IEM proposals filed after 1.7.1998.

(iii) Liberalization of the Locational Policy

No industrial approval is required from the Government for locations that do not fall within a 25-km radius of cities with a population of more than one million except for those industries where industrial licensing is compulsory. Non-polluting industries, such as electronics, computer software, and printing can be located within a 25-km radius of cities with a population of more than one million. Permission to other industries is granted in such locations only if they are located in an industrial area so designated prior to 25.7.91. Zoning and land use regulations as well as environmental legislations have to be followed.

(iv) Policy for Small-Scale Industries

Reservation of items of manufacture exclusively for the small-scale sector forms an important focus of the industrial policy as a measure of protecting this sector. Since 24 December 1999, industrial undertakings with an investment up to Rs 1 crore are within the small-scale and ancillary sector. A differential investment limit has been adopted since 9 October 2001 for forty-one reserved items where the investment limit of Rs 5 crore is prescribed for qualifying as a small-scale unit. The investment limit for tiny units is Rs 25 lakh.

A total of 749 items are reserved for manufacture in the small-scale sector. All undertakings other than the small-scale industrial undertakings engaged in the manufacture of items reserved for manufacture in the small-scale sector are required to obtain an industrial licence and undertake an export obligation of 50 per cent of the annual production. This condition of licensing is, however, not applicable to those undertakings operating under 100 per cent Export Oriented Undertakings Scheme, the Export Processing Zone (EPZ) or the Special Economic Zone Schemes (SEZs).

(V) Non-Resident Indians Scheme

The general policy and facilities for Foreign Direct Investment as available to foreign investors/companies are fully applicable to NRIs as well. In addition, the government has extended some concessions especially for NRIs and overseas corporate bodies that have more than 60 per cent stake held by NRIs. These inter-alia include: (i) NRI/OCB investment in the real estate and housing sectors upto 100 per cent and (ii) NRI/OCB investment in domestic airlines sector upto 100 per cent.

NRI/OCBs are also allowed to invest up to 100 per cent equity on non-repatriation basis in all activities except for a small negative list. Apart from this, NRI/OCBs are also allowed to invest on repatriation/non-repatriation under the portfolio investment scheme.

(vi) Electronic Hardware Technology Park (EHTP)/Software Technology Park (STP) scheme

For building up a strong electronics industry and with a view to enhancing exports, two schemes, viz. Electronic Hardware Technology Park (EHTP) and Software Technology Park (STP), are in op-

eration. Under the EHTP/STP scheme, the inputs are allowed to be procured free of duties.

Directors of STPs have powers to approve fresh STP/EHTP proposals and also to grant post-approval amendments for the EHTP/STP projects, as have been given to the Development Commissioners of Export Processing Zones in the case of Export Oriented Units. All other applications for setting up projects under these schemes are considered by the Inter-Ministerial Standing Committee (IMSC) chaired by the Secretary (Information Technology). The IMSC is serviced by the SIA.

(vii) Policy for Foreign Direct Investment (FDI)

Promotion of foreign direct investment forms an integral part of India's economic policies. The role of foreign direct investment in accelerating economic growth is by way of infusion of capital, technology, and modern management practices. The department has put in place a liberal and transparent foreign investment regime where most activities are automatically opened to foreign investment without any limit on the extent of foreign ownership. Some of the recent initiatives taken to further liberalize the FDI regime, inter alia, include opening up of sectors, such as:

- Insurance (up to 26 per cent)
- Development of integrated townships (up to 100 per cent)
- Defence industry (up to 26 per cent)
- Tea plantation (up to 100 per cent subject to divestment of 26 per cent within five years to FDI)
- Enhancement of FDI limits in private-sector banking
- Allowing FDI up to 100 per cent under the automatic route for most manufacturing activities in SEZs
- Opening up B2B e-commerce
- Internet Service Providers (ISPs) without gateways
- Electronic mail and voice mail to 100 per cent foreign investment subject to 26 per cent divestment condition

The department has also strengthened investment facilitation measures through Foreign Investment Implementation Authority (FIIA).

Source: Adapted from http://dipp.nic.in/evol1.htm, accessed an 13 March 2009.

done, there could be a number of other legislations that one has to go through because the manufacture and distribution of sugar comes under the Essential Commodities Act. If a supply chain manager wants to plan for the optimization of multi-plant locations into aggregation of capacity by the rationalization of plant size, he/she must be familiar with the feasibility of such options.

Similarly, a global player desirous of locating in a country like India must familiarize with innumerable regulatory measures. Apart from licensing, capital investment directives and technology transfer are some of the areas that need attention. Understanding the economic environment also includes understanding international trade treaties, preferred country status, regional cooperation agreement, and so on. A number of such regional cooperation and pacts among a group of countries are effective across the globe. These include EU, NAFTA, SAARC, ASEAN, GCC, and a host of other multilateral trade regimes. A list of such trade regimes is given in Appendix 1. A supply chain manager may not have to worry necessarily about the nitty-gritty of these factors. But certainly one has to take cognizance of the same and get an expert opinion while decision making to ensure that there are no adverse impacts. Exhibit 4.1 on policy measures gives some idea on the subject.

The economic policy shows how the promotion of SEZs across the globe has impacted location decisions. A Special Economic Zone (SEZ) is a geographical region that has economic laws that are more liberal than in a country of location. SEZs may have different categories like Free Trade Zones (FTZ), Export Processing Zones (EPZ), Free Zones (FZ), Industrial Estates (IE), Free Ports, Urban Enterprise Zones, and others. The goal is to promote foreign investment and economic activity. India was one of the first in Asia to recognize the effectiveness of the Export Processing Zone (EPZ) model in promoting exports, with Asia's first EPZ set up in Kandla in 1965. With a view to overcome the shortcomings experienced on account of multiplicity of controls and clearances, absence of world-class infrastructure, an unstable fiscal regime, and with a view to attract larger foreign investments in India, the Special Economic Zones (SEZs) Policy was announced in April 2000. This policy intended to make SEZs an engine for economic growth supported by quality infrastructure complemented by an attractive fiscal package, both at the centre and the state level, with minimum possible regulations. The government has been consistently taking initiatives to promote SEZs for growth of trade in India.

In the twentieth century, export-led industrialization supported by foreign investment and technology (ELIFIT) has become an economic and social development strategy for many third world countries. In the 1950s and 1960s, a group of Latin American and East Asian countries adopted such a strategy and allowed companies in the U.S.A. and Europe to use their cheap labour with the hope that this would lead to economic development. For East Asian countries, originally Hong Kong, Singapore, Taiwan, and South Korea, this strategy worked well and made a substantial contribution for their economic development. Similarly, Special Economic Zones were founded by the government of the People's Republic of China under Deng Xiaoping in the early 1980s. The most successful Special Economic Zone in China, Shenzhen, has developed from a small village into a city with a population of over 10 million within 20 years. Following the Chinese examples, Special Economic Zones have been established in several countries, including Brazil, India, Iran, Jordan, Kazakhstan, Pakistan, the Philippines, Poland, Russia, and Ukraine.

There are a few economic zones focused on logistical activities like warehousing and distribution. Jebel Ali Free Zone (JAFZ) is a free economic zone located in the Jebel Ali area of Dubai, United Arab Emirates. The JAFZ also caters to the Dubai Port, which ranks ninth in the world in terms of container traffic. The Jebel Ali Free Zone also provides warehousing and distribution facilities to international and local corporations (www.jafza.ae/en/). A host of other countries and ports offer such incentives and locational advantage for logistical activities. Places like Singapore, Hong Kong, Antwerp, Bussan, Middle Eastern countries, and China have such strategies for growth. A supply chain manager must constantly monitor and evaluate such locational advantages while devising a supply chain network.

In India, Free Trade & Warehousing Zones (FTWZ) were announced as part of the Indian Foreign Trade Policy 2004–09. The objective was to create trade-related infrastructure to facilitate the import and export of goods and services with the freedom to carry out trade transactions using free currency. The scheme envisages the creation of world-class infrastructure for warehousing of various products, state-of-the-art equipment, transportation and handling facilities, commercial office-space, water, power, communications and connectivity, with one-stop clearance of import and export formality, to support the integrated zones as 'international trading hubs'. These zones would established in areas proximate to seaports, airports, or dry ports so as to offer easy access by rail and road. The FTWZ shall be a special category of Special Economic Zones with a focus on trading and warehousing.

Thus, one may understand that there are a host of external environmental factors that could impact location decisions. Apart from economic factors, societal factors like pressure groups impact location decisions both favourably and adversely. Some of the classic examples in India are the experience of Cargill Seeds and Kentucky Fried Chicken, which went through social pressures. Similarly, when a few large groups wanted to set up branded retail, especially in the groceries and perishables segments in India, there were a few pressure groups that were initially opposed to the idea. But later this was overcome when the advantages were realized. Another classic influence of pressure groups is location-driven economic activities especially related to the engagement of labour. This is common in some cities where local labour unions decide on wages and remuneration. Similar experiences are also common in the transport movement where the local transport association handles allotment of loads to vehicles and manages rates. In one way, it is a pattern of group governance and has its advantages as long as it does not lead to cartelization. One may look at innumerable instances of societal factors impacting location decisions.

There are a number of legal factors that influence supply chain and logistical decisions. Some of the straight legal factors are related to laws governing direct controls, which are more economic and corporate laws. Some are related to licence and price and distribution controls, Foreign Currency Management Act, and so on. There are legal implications with respect to:

1. Entry/exit into a business
2. Export–Import controls
3. Foreign investment and ownership
4. Indian Company Laws and regulations including that of capital markets
5. Permits, exemptions, and provisions of various Acts for trade
6. Environment, safety, and health
7. Labour laws
8. Commercial laws like sales tax, excise, and customs duties
9. Motor Vehicles Act and regulations on transport
10. Airports & Seaports Clearances Act
11. International commercial pacts and legal implications on trade in a country
12. Tariff Authority for Major Ports in India, which fixes tariffs and regulates and controls commercial operations of ports
13. Airports Authority of India (AAI), formed by the merger of IAAI and NAA through Airports Authority Act (No. 55 of 1994), came into existence on 1 April 1995. AAI manages five international airports, 87 domestic airports, and 28 civil enclaves.
14. Indian Railways, Government of India, is largely responsible for development of the rail cargo movement in India. Railways presents its budget annually, and government initiates a number of regulatory measures to promote cargo and passenger movements every year.

It is a near monopoly that owns railroad across India and regulates and controls the movement of cargo. Recently, some privatization initiatives have been launched with the flagship project, the dedicated freight corridors (DFCs). DFCs will have approximately 3,300 km of mostly double, electrified, high-axle-load tracks. These will have a liberal space envelope, will be fit for high-capacity wagons and heavy haul freight trains at cruising speeds of 75 km/hr and top speeds of 100km/hr, and will be constructed between Jawaharlal Nehru Port Trust (JNPT), Tughlakabad, Mumbai to Rewari (western route), and Kolkata to Ludhiana (eastern route). The Government of India is also planning a number of industrial nodes as a part of a related initiative. The Delhi–Mumbai Industrial Corridor (DMIC) alongside the western route of the DFC is one such initiative. A few Mega Multimodal Logistics Parks (MMLPs)—hubs providing state-of-the-art integrated logistical facilities with mechanized handling and intelligent inventory management—are planned at select locations along the DFCs to reduce the overall cost of logistics in the supply chain for the customers, duly leveraging the modern, efficient, high-capacity rail connectivity of the DFCs capable of meeting time-sensitive freight transportation requirement.

Ecological, safety, health, and environmental factors also govern supply chain decisions. Facilities and transport are major drivers impacted by these factors. Transportation naturally adds to air, noise, and water pollution. Similarly, facilities, such as manufacturing and warehouses, must have well-defined, socially responsible policies that take into account ecological factors. Environment boards like Pollution

Control Board, Airports Authority of India (for height clearances), health departments in the central and state governments, and a host of other regulatory bodies streamline this function.

A supply chain manager should not look at the scenario only from the perspective of the organization, but also from the perspective of suppliers and other partners in the supply chain network, including service and product vendors. Organizations must have clearly defined policies about protecting the environment. This could be like avoiding overloading, fixing emission standards for vehicles, and so on. Unless the nodal organization insists, the service providers and vendors would not implement the same. Hence, it is the responsibility of the supply chain manager to understand the ecological, health, and safety factors, and relentlessly strive for the implementation of these factors. A failure in implementing these factors would affect an organization and its network adversely. There is increased awareness about environmental issues across the globe today, and one has to adhere to the same in any situation to avoid penalty and legal action.

There are also positive measures initiated by a number of organizations that instill best practice across the industry. For example, one of the largest pulp factories in Indonesia has implemented the ISO 14001 Environmental Management System that provides the framework for managing the environmental aspects of the forestry operations, thereby minimizing the impact on the environment. For a pulp manufacturing plant, forestry operations and maintaining plantation are key to the business and also for maintaining ecological balance. Unless the top management involves the procurement and logistics teams, it would be difficult to run the organization successfully. Different forums and international bodies including World Bank provide guidelines and support for such activities. By implementing such stringent quality certification, the organization is equipped with the tools necessary to prevent pollution and to comply with the laws and regulations relevant to the business.

It may be thus observed that environmental factors—economic, political, societal, legal, and ecological—have a bearing on supply chain decisions. Though a supply chain manager would involve experts for decision support, it is important for a supply chain manager to be familiar with such factors and constantly monitor the same.

4.2.2 Industry and Competitive Factors

The markets are competitive and the pace of competition critically impacts value creation. Supply chain drivers have emerged as a competitive tool and a differentiator in business. A few classic examples would be Dell, Amazon, and Walmart. These companies have achieved success by deploying a new approach in supply chain, which changed the industry environment. Dell Computers made all home computer manufacturers relook at their distribution models. Similarly, Amazon came up with a model where they could reach customers with a centralized location and process orders for books through their website. An effective delivery management changed the way books are sold in the market.

Walmart, the largest and highest profit retailer in the world, achieved this position by employing innovative and relentless practice of customer needs management. Walmart's goal was simply to provide customers the access to goods and to develop cost structures that enable competitive pricing. To achieve this goal, Walmart replenished its inventory by balancing cost and responsiveness, and implemented effective procurement, transportation, and distribution-centre management. The company deployed a logistics technique known as cross-docking. In this strategy, goods are continuously delivered to Walmart's warehouses, from where they are despatched to stores without adding to the stock of distribution centres. This strategy reduced Walmart's cost of sales significantly and made it possible to offer everyday low prices to their customers. It is important to note that Walmart changed the structure of the retail industry where cost management became the key competitive tool in major retail segments.

Such instances have been discussed in detail in Chapter 3. It may be noted here that though a number of industry structural features and competitive conditions may be relevant for a supply chain, it is imperative that a supply chain manager follows the right model. If an organized retailer in India wants to look at cost as a differentiator, a procurement model adopted by ITC e-choupal could be a good approach. You may note that e-Choupal is a significant two-way multidimensional delivery channel, efficiently carrying goods and services out of and into rural India. By progressively linking the digital infrastructure to a physical network of rural business hubs and agro-extension services, ITC is transforming the way farmers do business, and the way rural markets work. This is a good model for better sourcing and value enhancement as intermediaries are knocked off.

In the FMCG business, Indian companies have successfully deployed various pack sizes and proliferated low-budget stock-keeping units (SKUs) for capturing a vast uncovered market. The approach is more that of product reach and convenience rather than cost per unit. The explosion of volumes gives an advantage in cost management and a supply chain manager faces the challenge of ensuring maximum reach and service rather than cost per unit. The recent competitive trend in most of consumer product groups is of availability, price/budget affordability, and market expansion. Even in recessionary conditions, the competitive focus remains the same because this is peculiar to the country of operation, and its demographic and social factors. There is a need for a supply chain manager to quickly link with the strategist in the company on such ground realities.

It is critical to adopt a methodology to formally scan the industry and the competitive environment, and infuse supply chain-driven practices in the same. It may be important to understand how an industry in which one is operating is influenced by such competitive behaviour. Though no industry would be spared of a structure-conduct-performance relationship, it is important to understand the level at which such a mapping has to be done as well as the role of the supply chain manager in the same.

For example, oil and gas distribution, which is highly controlled in India, is far stable as compared to telecom services, which may be also regulated but is fiercely competitive. A supply chain service manager must constantly provide inputs to the management on emerging trends. Similarly, a number of such industries as fashion goods, jewellery, paints, automotive, consumer electronics, retail, and so on, which are sensitive to behavioural factors and intense rivalry among firms, require the involvement of supply chain managers. This section covers only a broader view of the significance of competitive forces in the industry. However, later chapters present a comprehensive coverage of the various competitive tools and techniques in the domain. A supply chain manager must get away from the operational perspective and see beyond the domain and one's company to ensure the right competitive mapping initiative for decision inputs. Otherwise, a corporate may suffer. There are some classic examples in India and other countries where such failures led to the erosion of the market share of the lead players.

4.2.3 Technological Environment

Technology in a production process refers to the technique of production involved in combining inputs, processes, and skills to produce a certain level of output. It usually causes an exponential growth of output at the same level of input because of capital efficiency. It involves:

- An improvement or change in production techniques and processes
- Knowledge or soft skills—techniques which improve processes and lead to value creation

A supply chain manager has an important role in understanding and mapping the role of technology in the domain area. As mentioned in Chapters 1 and 3, technology explosion has redefined the supply chain network through the deployment of information technology, which has improved value creation to customers. A classic example is mapping of secondary distribution efficiency in the FMCG industry by which a supply chain manager is able to reduce unevenness in distribution. Also in upward linkages of supply chain network, supply chain efficiency is achieved by deploying technology for sharing production planning and scheduling, concurrent engineering for product development, reducing time to market, and inbound transportation.

With an advance in technology, new business models are being created with supply chain as the focal area of thrust. These models involve web technologies, amalgamating new business processes and deploying new-generation service providers. Also, customer expectations have now gone up on information and updates, especially when third-party service providers are involved. Companies are able to meet these expectations by deploying appropriate technology. The proliferation of technology has led to greater supply chain efficiency and business growth.

Apart from these, domain-centric technology, especially in inventory management and storage handling, is increasingly becoming important. Bar coding is widely applied in many industries involving mass volume of goods, retail sale, and spares and parts management. Efforts are constantly made to improve the efficiency of the bar code reader to capture information for inventory management. Similarly, Radio-

Frequency Identification (RFID) is being applied, which is considered as an improvement over bar coding, for managing stocks and order management. We will discuss these topics in detail in Chapter 15. Here, it is important to understand that a supply chain manager must have competitive information on two aspects—one, advancement in domain technology and how it is being applied, and two, the competitive edge enjoyed by players in the industry by adapting such technology and initiating domain-driven strategies for achieving a competitive advantage.

Although it is common that the technology team and/or the strategy team would be mapping such technology advancements, it is important for a supply chain manager to understand the applications of technology. He/She should understand the innovations in not only hard and soft technologies but also material and product specific technology intelligence.

For example, vendors may give information about a new raw material for a product. Unless a supply chain manager is sharp in appreciating the same and transfers the knowledge to the strategy team, the company may lose its competitive advantage in the market. Technology has brought about a number of advancements in sourcing efficiencies. Also, research teams constantly use web search engines to achieve price and information efficiencies and economies in buying. Even small and medium companies are able to use this option to their advantage. A supply chain manager who doesn't keep himself updated on the latest development in technology is out of the competitive arena today. Hence, it is critical for supply chain managers to appreciate and map the technology environment and constantly strive for a competitive advantage in the supply chain.

4.3 RESOURCE-DRIVEN DECISION ENVIRONMENT—OPPORTUNITIES AND CONSTRAINTS

One may observe that there are significant differences in how two companies command their resources in an industry. Resources refers to capital, assets, income generating avenues and wherewithal, and so on. According to Penrose (1959), the growth of a firm is focused on an internal process of development, leading to the cumulative movement of the firm in a particular direction. It is the management whose knowledge and skills will influence the capability of other resources on productive services. It is not resources per se but the services of the resources that determine output and growth. The two together create a subjective opportunity set that is unique for each firm. Thus, managerial capability is the binding constraint that limits the rate of the growth of the firm—the so-called Penrose Effect.

On the contrary, a number of management professionals and theorists believe that a company's success belongs not only to the management but also the resources, which include skill sets, assets (physical, intangible, organizational, and human), competitive capabilities, brand value and command over key resources, location, and so on. A company would be better off if its resources can lead to a distinct, unique, or strategic value. According to Collis and Montgomery (1995), there are four tests of competitive value in which a company must qualify:

- Is the resource hard to copy?
- How long would the resource last?
- Is the resource really competitively superior?
- Can the resource be trumped by the different resources/capabilities of rivals?

A supply chain manager must understand the importance of resource-led strategic opportunities and constraints, especially when one has to do industry and competitor analysis. For example, a strategic asset for supply chain could be a dedicated and exclusive distribution channel, which is common for success in the FMCG business. Similarly, knowledge and information pool gained through a global organizational network could be an advantage for a number of supply chain initiatives. For example, a global company could have a well-established knowledge initiative which facilitates better negotiation with suppliers, the transfer of product features for manufacture, and quick to market.

Apart from these, if the resource is located in close proximity to the service providers, thus enabling pricing and cost benefits, a company can enjoy some competitive advantage. At times, a supply chain manager may also enjoy some advantages because of being located in a cluster, which leads to buying efficiency or any such advantage in the engagement of a supply chain driver. For example, companies located in Ludhiana and Tiruppur are leading the hosiery and garments business because they have a natural advantage in terms of transport availability, buying, facilities management, and so on. More common examples can be drawn from the engineering and automotive clusters where a group of manufacturers are able to share some common facilities. Across the globe, one comes across logistical advantages arising in clusters. Resource capabilities are also among intangible assets like trade knowledge and expertise, embedded in activities and gained over years of experience. Though some of these are replaced by learning and research, they still command a premium.

For large-scale operations, it is difficult to find a skilled transport manager or facilities/warehouse manager who understands the nuances of the trade, especially with respect to managing costs, disruptions, or any contingency that may arise. This is more common in developing countries where such occurrences are often unprecedented, and unless someone has the skill to react promptly, a company may be hit significantly. Hence, a supply chain manager must appreciate the advantages of resource-led opportunities and constraints and map constantly for the same to increase value in the supply network.

4.4 SUPPORT SYSTEMS FOR MAPPING DECISION ENVIRONMENT

It is clear from the earlier section that a supply chain manager has to constantly map the external environment for which he/she has to have a dedicated approach. Figure 4.2 depicts the same.

A supply chain manager must set a competitive intelligence network to map external factors. One must have a system to capture developments in a macro environment, industry and competition, and also technological changes from different media, industry bodies, conferences, seminars, and peer network. A supply chain manager must also subscribe to information exchanges, which provide scanned reports relevant for one's business. Peer network, supplier information, intermediary and customer feedback are vital and there must be a process to capture and validate such information.

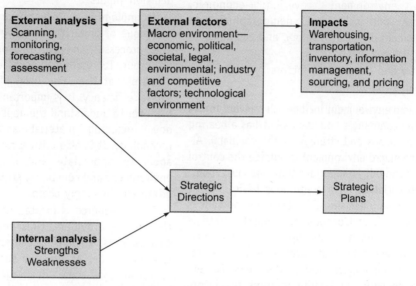

Figure 4.2 Role of external analysis in supply chain

A company must involve the supply chain manager as part of the strategy team and provide cross-functional support in data and information capture. In some of the companies where the supply chain function is critical like large FMCG, CPG, and auto companies, there are systematic methods of having vendor meets and customer-interaction sessions, and the top management gets involved in such forums. In some industries and geographical and industry clusters, cross-organization knowledge and intelligence sharing for logistical improvements are being practised.

In India, government departments and public bodies offer a lot of information about government intents for improvements in logistics drivers, which would impact supply chain efficiency. The Railway Budget, the Economic Survey of India, the pre-budget document, and various other policy documents are transparent and readily available. There are numerous non-profit organizations and academic and research institutions, which publish information on policies. A supply chain manager should be aware of the frequency and source of information related to the same. Thus, support systems required for environmental analysis should be built through concerted efforts of data gathering, tracking of policy, peer interaction, and through inter-disciplinary teams.

SUMMARY

Decision making in supply chain management is determined by a host of internal and external factors. The broad aspects of external factors that would impact decision making in the domain include:

1. Macro environment covering: economic, societal, political, legal, demographic, and environmental—health, safety, and ecological—factors
2. Industry and competitive factors
3. Technology environment

The macro environment includes all relevant forces outside the company's boundaries but has a bearing on the operations and strategy of the company. Although the macro environment is outside the control of the company, it is important that one must monitor macro variables on a continuous basis since it impacts company decisions. A macro environment is one that directly and/or indirectly impacts strategic decisions, and planning and operations of a company. There are a host of external environmental factors that can impact location decisions. For example: a decision on facility requires regulatory clearances like licence for manufacture. A global player desirous of locating in a country like India must familiarize itself with numerous regulatory measures on licensing, capital investment directives, technology transfer, and so on.

Though a number of structural features and competitive conditions in the industry may be relevant for a supply chain, it is imperative that a supply chain manager looks at the relevant model. He/She must get away from the operational perspective and see beyond the domain and one's company to ensure the right competitive mapping initiative for decision inputs.

Technology in a production process refers to the technique of production involved in combining inputs, processes, and skills to produce a certain level of output. It usually causes an exponential growth of output at the same level of input because of capital efficiency. It is important for a supply chain manager to understand the applications of technology, including material and product-specific technology. It is also critical for supply chain managers to appreciate and map the technology environment and constantly strive for a competitive advantage in supply chain.

If the resource is located in close proximity to the service providers, thus enabling pricing and cost benefits, a company can enjoy some competitive advantage. At times, a supply chain manager may also enjoy some advantages because of being located in a cluster, which leads to buying efficiency or any such advantage in the engagement of a supply chain driver. One must have a system to capture—from different media, industry bodies, conferences, and peer network—developments in a macro environment, industry, competition, and also in technology.

KEY TERMS

Cluster: A cluster is a geographic concentration of interconnected businesses, suppliers, and associated institutions in a particular industry, market, or region. Clusters increase the productivity of companies so that they can compete nationally and globally.

Collusive price setting: Collusion takes place within an industry when rival companies cooperate for their mutual benefit. Collusion most often takes place within the market structure of oligopoly, where the decision of a few firms to collude can significantly impact the market as a whole. Collusion would be tacit and non-explicit. Cartels are also referred to as collusion and not normally permitted as legal and economic behaviour.

Dedicated Freight Corridor: A dedicated freight corridor is exclusively for running freight trains at the maximum permissible speed (of 100 kmph in India). It is a double-line corridor (except where a single line is justified due to traffic considerations) running parallel to the existing corridors, so as to maximize the usage of available railway land; and transfer trains from the existing corridor to the DFC and vice versa through predetermined junction arrangement, equipped with grade separators to facilitate smooth transfer of trains between the two networks.

Free Trade & Warehouse Zones (FTXZ): These are a category of SEZs with a focus on trading and warehousing.

Free Trade Zone/Export Processing Zone: A free trade zone or export processing zone is one or more special areas of a country where some normal trade barriers such as tariffs and quotas are eliminated and bureaucratic requirements are lowered in the hope of attracting new business and foreign investments. It is a region where a group of countries has agreed to reduce or eliminate trade barriers.

ISO 14001: It is a series of international standards on environmental management. It provides a framework for the development of an environmental management system and the supporting audit programme. ISO 14001 specifies a framework of control for an environmental management system against which an organization can be certified by a third party.

Mega Multimodal Logistics Parks (MMLPs): These are hubs providing state-of-the-art integrated logistic facilities with mechanized handling and intelligent inventory management at selected locations along the DFCs to reduce the overall logistics cost in the supply chain for the customers. This is achieved by duly leveraging the modern, high-capacity rail connectivity of the DFCs, which are capable of meeting time-sensitive freight transportation requirements.

Social cost: It refer to all the harmful effects that the community on the whole sustains as a result of industrial development. The term includes even certain 'social opportunity costs', avoidable wastes, and social inefficiencies of various kinds.

Special Economic Zone (SEZ): SEZs are locations meant as an engine for economic growth, supported by quality infrastructure, with attractive fiscal packages and the minimum possible regulations, both at the centre and the state level.

Strategic asset: It is an advantage that a company enjoys over its competitors. A strategic asset is long-lasting and cannot be beaten easily by a different resource or capability of rivals.

CONCEPT REVIEW QUESTIONS

1. Describe the importance of the external factors that are relevant for supply chain decisions. Also describe a framework for a supply chain manager to map the same.

2. What are the key economic factors that influence the decision of setting up a facility for a global supply chain manager? Elucidate with an example.

3. Analyse the societal and environmental factors that influence supply chain decisions. How can a supply chain manager handle these factors?

4. Describe the typical inputs that one would consider if one were to look at political factors in an international setting of a supply chain decision. Elucidate with examples.

5. What do you understand by resource-based opportunities and constraints in a supply chain context? Analyse a few examples in different settings for decisions related to supply chain drivers.

6. Explain how one can set up monitoring and assessment of a decision environment for a supply chain domain. Envisage the role of a supply chain manager in the strategy group of a large commercial organization.

CRITICAL THINKING QUESTIONS

1. Analyse the recent announcements by the Indian Railways on the Mega Multimodal Logistics Parks project. How can it help in improving supply chain efficiency?

2. Study infrastructure developments in airports and roads in India. Identify a region and map how it has helped improve operational efficiency.

3. Research on the web to understand cluster development and advantages to organizations in specific regions like the Middle East or Singapore.

4. Map cluster developments in India (such as auto clusters like Pune, Jamshedpur, and Chennai) and discuss their contribution in supply chain efficiency.

PROJECT ASSIGNMENTS

1. Visit a nearby road transportation operators' association and capture the external environmental factors influencing its effective functioning and its overall impact on user firms.

2. Visit a unit located in an SEZ and compare its supply chain effectiveness with a peer in a regular geographic zone. Focus your analysis on the benefits of each in supply chain drivers.

3. Study the implications of environmental acts and quality standards on supply chain decisions made in a large engineering firm. Using your judgement, prepare a report on improving supply chain efficiency.

REFERENCES

Collis, David J. and Cynthia A. Montgomery, 'Competing on Resources: Strategy in the 1990s,' *Harvard Business Review,* 73 (49), July–August 1995, pp. 120–23

http://civilaviation.nic.in/aai/airport.htm

http://dipp.nic.in/evol1.htm

Penrose, Edith *Theory of Growth of Firms*, John Wiley and Sons, New York, 1959

www.airportsindia.org.in/public_notices/noc_document_21_airports.pdf

www.airportsindia.org.in/public_notices/noc_document_21_airports.pdf

www.eximpolicy.net/chapters/free-trade-and-warehousing-zones.htm

www.eximpolicy.net/chapters/free-trade-and-warehousing-zones.htm

www.indianrailways.gov.in

www.jafza.ae/en/

www.sezindia.nic.in/HTMLS/about.htm

www.tariffauthority.gov.in/

www.tariffauthority.gov.in/

Appendix 4.1	**Some of the Major Regional Multilateral Trade Agreements**

1. ASEAN Free trade area
2. GCC
3. SAARC
4. European Union (EU)
5. North American Free Trade Agreement (NAFTA)
6. Free Trade Agreement among CIS countries
7. AFTA (ASEAN Free Trade Area) CER (Closer Economic Relations) Free Trade Agreement (Australia and New Zealand)
8. ASEAN–China Free Trade Agreement
9. Free Trade Area of Americas
10. Central European Free Trade Agreement
11. European Free Trade Association (UFTA)
12. Mexico–EU Free Trade Agreement
13. US–Singapore Free Trade Agreement
14. Japan–Singapore Free trade Agreement
15. WTO

5

Strategic Decisions in Supply Chain

Learning Objectives

After studying this chapter, you will be able to:

♦ Understand the nature of strategic decisions in business and linkages with supply chain domain at corporate, strategic business unit, and functional levels

♦ Understand the nature of strategic decisions involving supply chain drivers

♦ Understand third-party and integrated logistics services, with the key strategic partner providing support on supply chain activities

---

This chapter covers strategic decision-making and its link with functional, business, and corporate strategies. Also, a number of strategic decisions that are taken in the domain of supply chain are introduced and each of these drivers is discussed separately in detail. This chapter also covers third and integrated logistics service providers who have a strategic role as service providers to the focal organization in the delivery of its supply chain functions.

5.1 LINKING STRATEGIC SUPPLY CHAIN DECISION WITH CORPORATE STRATEGIES

Strategic decisions are those that impact an organization for a long term, involve deployment of considerable capital budget, and are not usually reversed. The cost of reversal of a strategic decision is high. A firm's strategy is to achieve a market position, conduct its operations smoothly, attract and retain customers, and achieve organizational goals through effective utilization of its resources. Typically, a strategy is a set of managerial choices among alternatives, and signals organizational commitment to specific markets, competitive positioning, and ways of achieving value for different stakeholders.

Corporate-level strategies relate to those strategic initiatives that impact corporate performance across strategic business units and functions. The top management makes these decisions. For example, a focal organization that is in the consumer home electronics segment decides to venture into eSelling along with traditional channel partners. This is a corporate-level strategic decision wherein a major shift happens in the distribution plan, and the firm has to establish distribution strategies by way of planning for distribution centres, linkages with ordering, and physical distribution and pricing strategy. All this is done without conflicting with the traditional channels employed for business promotion.

Corporate strategic initiatives are triggered by fundamental questions about the business: 'What is our business and where should we be in the next three, five, or seven years?' This can be addressed by the four categories of strategic options given below. Though a few of the options are at the strategic business unit level, the extent and level of the decision hierarchy is at the corporate level, and impact corporate resource and business portfolio composition:

1. Stability—continuing in the same business
2. Expansion—expanding into new business areas by adding new functions, products, and/or markets
3. Retrenchment—dropping of product, market, and/or resources for lack of adequate return on investment or prospect of decline in future
4. Combination—pursuing Options 2 and 3 through vertical/horizontal integration, diversification or mergers, acquisition and divestment, and so on

If one were to analyse the above options, supply chain management decisions interface intensively with corporate strategic decision alternatives. This interface is highlighted below:

1. **Stability decision set:** In this option, the corporate by and large sticks to the same strategic posture without any major change in resources, products, market, or functional mix. The corporate focus is to effectively coordinate resource efficiency through planning and operational efficiency. Supply chain managers must ensure that functional aspects such as utilization of facilities for product mix, inventory planning, transportation, and sourcing are effectively planned and operating efficiencies are achieved for ensuring fulfilment of corporate-level targets. This situation normally arises in a stable and mature business, and especially when the external environment is stable. When the external environment is volatile, either due to a recession or buoyancy in the market, this changes, and appropriate strategic interventions are initiated.

2. **Expansion strategies:** A firm deploys expansion strategies when its current returns are more than the market returns for assumed risk levels. In such a situation, a firm looks for investable options either by adding new functions, products, and/or markets.

   (a) The scope of expansion related to products is in adding a new line of products based on economies of scope. A firm has to initiate a supply chain strategy of reassessing the supply chain configuration and looking at all the processes, namely, supplier, internal supply chain including production, and customer processes. This means the addition of new categories, for example, the introduction of powerful motorcycle by an existing two-wheeler business would require improving the reach in the distribution channel, especially in the urban market where demand is likely to be high.

(b) Another option would be to find new users and/or markets that relate to strategic marketing initiatives. For example, Barnes & Noble, a book store, expanded its customer reach by introducing e-commerce through its website www.bn.com (see Exhibit 5.1).

One can look at a number of such examples in India where companies have gone for new users and new markets. Indian companies, even traditional businesses, have tried e-commerce and various other methods to proliferate into markets. Some were unsuccessful and some others tasted success. Haldiram is a leading manufacturer of snacks in India. They were exporting goods worth $1.7 million in 2001, which grew to $6 million in five years. That was a growth of 40 per cent (http://www.haldiram.com/). They have also been growing in the domestic market by competitively introducing many region-specific products. This required meeting challenges in distribution, tying up production facilities at their plant, and so on. With an increased market reach across geographies and proliferation of products and SKUs, their supply chain strategy is in sync with their business strategy, and the firm has been successfully competing in this market.

Let's now look at the case of a leading dairy brand, which introduced pizzas for the common man. The idea was to extend the customer base by broadening its product range. The brand's ice-cream dealers were expected to store and serve pizzas. This required the supply chain strategy of interfacing two product lines and a skill set at dealer level of warming a pizza in a microwave oven for delivery. As this could not be achieved, customers did not patronize the pizza brand.

3. **Retrenchment strategies:** A firm deploys a retrenchment strategy when its current returns are less than the market returns for assumed risk levels. In such a situation, a firm would look for de-risking by considering exit and sell-offs. A firm may restructure its strategies by exiting in some product category or market, and using its resources by focusing on current strengths. Such strategic initiatives on retrenchment would impact the supply chain configuration of the

---

Exhibit 5.1   Barnes & Noble Expands Its Customer Base

Barnes & Noble is one of the largest booksellers in terms of sales revenue in the United States. At the end of FY 2008, Barnes & Noble operated 778 stores and an online retailer (www.bn.com). Of the 778 stores, 726 were Barnes & Noble book and music superstores and the remaining 52 were mall-based. Its core business model relies on building local bookstores with a comprehensive selection, attractive discounts, and membership discount programmes, and a community-gathering-place environment (apparent in the inclusion of a Starbucks cafe in each Barnes & Noble store).

To counter competition from Amazon.com, Barnes & Noble had to establish a supply chain strategy to cater to a new breed of buyers who used e-commerce. For this, it had to set up a new order management process, take a fresh look at facilities management and stocks at it facilities, and customize outbound transportation to the customer through parcels. It also had to enable a steady financial flow for facilitating all these changes.

focal organization. For example, an organization may sell off a division to a vendor as part of its retrenchment strategy. However, it may outsource the supply of the component manufactured by the division to the same vendor. This is because the focal organization believed that it would not be its core way ahead and hence it may do well by hiving off. Such a move would demand a reconfiguration of the supply chain strategy. Similarly, an organization may sell off a market or a product category to restructure business. One can think of many such examples in business. A fertilizer company went into the manufacture of sugar as they felt there were many interfaces of core competence in both the businesses. After running the sugar business for a few years, the group restructured both the businesses and even opted for a change in the ownership structure. This also impacted the supply chain strategy as asset allocation and the managerial hierarchy of command changed. Thus, there is a strong association between the retrenchment strategy and supply chain strategy adopted by any firm.

4. **Combination strategy:** This refers to pursuing expansion, growth, and retrenchment through vertical/horizontal integration, diversification or mergers, acquisition and divestment, and so on. Strategic intervention of expansion and growth can be achieved through both forward and backward integration. If a focal organization acquires a distribution channel and sets up its own distribution network, it is called forward integration. For example, if an FMCG company selling a competitive product like an aerated drink acquires stakes in regional bottling plants and channel partners in the region, it would be forward integration. On the other hand, when the focal organization acquires the supplier's business for strategic reasons, then it is a backward integration initiative. In the same example of the aerated drinks brand, if the firm buys strategic stakes in the flavours and concentrate manufacturing plant, then it would be a case of backward integration. Such strategic initiatives obviously change the supply chain strategy and configuration. It needs considerable reassessment of both structure and pricing.

5. **Mergers and acquisitions:** Another strategic intervention that would be relevant here is mergers and acquisitions. One may look at a case where a merger is horizontal, similar to horizontal integration. In this case, a cement plant located in Gujarat in western India takes over a plant in Madhya Pradesh, which is in central India. This facilitates the company to grow twofold in size. Since most of the operations of cement plant economies in production come from operations of limestone quarry and power consumption, the supply-side initiative in the supply chain could be limited. On the other hand, demand-side advantages as well as logistical drivers such as distribution management and transportation can be negotiated for achieving economies. With multiple large-size locations, the ability to handle large institutional customers could be high. As responsiveness and market reach would be improved, the return would be

higher. So it requires supply chain strategic initiatives at the corporate level in order to improve returns on investment.

6. **Diversification:** The diversification on related and unrelated businesses can also impact the supply chain configuration. Related diversification is development beyond the present product and market, but still within the broad confines of the 'industry' (that is, value chain) in which a company operates. Unrelated diversification is where the organization moves beyond the confines of its current industry. Synergy is the most common reason for both related and unrelated diversification to happen. Synergy arises when two or more products or services combine to complement each other to the extent that the two products/ services can exploit economies of scope. Related diversification includes backward integration where the nodal organization controls backward linkages of the chain including suppliers. Similarly, one can acquire forward linkages like distribution channel, as explained earlier. Related diversification may also include much broader cases like a sugar plant going in for a bagasse-based, multifuel power plant or an alcohol plant based on the available raw material. Related diversification can also be in the form of achieving process efficiency by co-generation. If one looks at these examples, one can see that diversification impacts resources, costs, and responsiveness apart from a reorientation of the supply chain strategy.

A firm chooses a grand strategy of unrelated diversification mainly when returns from the current business portfolio are less attractive, and the firm chooses the unrelated diversification strategy mainly to improve corporate financial returns. Risk diversification, especially of business risks, is an advantage of diversifying into unrelated areas. For example, when a manufacturer of pharmaceuticals, which manufactures bulk drugs, establishes a fast-food chain in the country on a franchise model with a global brand, then it is a case of unrelated diversification. Logistical and cross-functional drivers are unique and different for each business. Thus, the supply chain manager at the corporate level must understand the nuances of each business and configure the supply chain network accordingly. Thus, the corporate level strategy must be interfaced with supply chain strategy.

5.2 LINKING STRATEGIC SUPPLY CHAIN DECISION WITH SBU-LEVEL STRATEGIES

Supply chain managers need to understand how supply chain management is linked with the strategies of a Strategic Business Unit (SBU). An SBU is a business unit within the overall corporate identity that is distinguishable from other businesses because of the different markets, products, and functions it serves. In an SBU, strategic control is within a defined ambit for effectiveness. When a company becomes really large, it could manage effectively through a number of businesses (or SBUs). These organizational entities are large and homogeneous enough to exercise control over most strategic factors affecting their performance.

SBUs have their own strategic management process. An SBU can encompass an entire company, or can simply be a smaller part of a company to perform a specific task. It has its own business strategy, objectives, and competitors, and these will often be different from those of the parent company. For example, E.I.D. Parry Ltd is one of the largest manufacturers of sugar in India. It has divisions of business such as sugar, bio-products, co-generation of power, distillery and alcohol, property and investments (www.eidparry.com). Even without an insight into its internal management, one can assume that each of these would function as an SBU, and even within the sugar business, one can think of SBUs at the plant level as key strategic decisions are required at the plant. To take it further, procurement plan and facilities creation could be different for each plant and the supply chain strategy has to be specific to that SBU. However, corporate-level issues would interface with the SBU-level supply chain management function. Hence, supply chain managers must understand SBU-level strategies and size up supply chain perspectives for effectiveness of business at the divisional level.

5.3 LINKING STRATEGIC SUPPLY CHAIN DECISION WITH FUNCTIONAL-LEVEL STRATEGIES

Finally, supply chain managers will have to ensure interface of supply chain strategy with functional-level strategies. As shown in Figure 5.1, functional strategies such as production, finance, information technology, marketing, and human resources interface with supply chain drivers for organizational effectiveness. Production strategies such as flexible manufacturing and postponement support a responsive supply chain. Similarly, mass production and concurrent engineering support cost efficiency in a supply chain. Concurrent engineering crashes time to market and hence is responsive as well as cost efficient. The physical flow of a supply chain is mainly driven by production and operations as physical utilities are created during the manufacturing process.

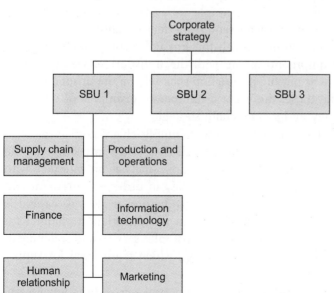

The finance function has a significant interface with the supply chain strategy, as managing financial flow is critical in the completion of a supply chain process. The interface is highlighted here mainly on structuring of financial flows and monitoring the same for synchronization of physical and information flow. This also emphasizes that the ultimate customer receives value for what he pays and there is sharing of profits among all partners in supply chain. Determining the roles, activities, and cost of operations of all partners, and fixing up a profit margin for each component of players are the challenges of the financial interface in a supply chain.

Figure 5.1 Hierarchy of interface of strategic supply decision

The interface of finance with supply chain strategy often affects capital investment decisions. While most of the operating managers are keen to have the best of capital equipment and facility, finance managers rightfully question the financial viability of a project. Though marketing managers would also prefer customers to experience the best of capital outlay, it is important to ensure that the customers pay for it. Thus, understanding such interfaces and soliciting supply chain strategic investments is the key for organizational success. To highlight with an example, in a sugar plant, the manufacturing and processing head seeks a larger cushion in capacity to handle variations in the crushing capacity to an extent of nearly 40 per cent. This means, if the plant's rated capacity of cane crushing is 5,000 TCD (tonnes crushed per day), it can vary between 3,000 TCD and 7,000 TCD. This might require flexibility at the milling section, during the sulphitation process, vacuum pans, centrifuge, and so on. This would also require additional water, varying from 180 per cent to 360 per cent of the original requirement, which would result in a considerable increase in the energy requirement. Though such a facility gives tremendous advantage in managing cane supplies and optimizing output, it impacts profitability. From the marketing aspect, a sugar sales person prefers low ICUMSA (International Commission for Uniform Methods of Sugar Analysis) levels, that is, close to 45 in order to improve the brightness of sugar to realize a higher price. Apart from good processing, he/she expects high standards of warehouse stocking. In this product where moisture levels could affect the product badly, margins are not adequate for the level of sophistication required in process and operation. This case highlights cross-functional demands in strategic decisions, which would impact the supply chain domain as well.

When supply chain interfaces with information technology, it may be noted that information is the fulcrum on which a supply chain moves on. The interface between information technology and supply chain strategies is what has led to the evolution of new business models and service levels. For example, e-business models where goods and services are marketed through the web require perfect synchronization on the back-end to serve the order. At another level, the linkage through technology of supplier and OE (Original Equipment), along with the transport service provider, ensures proper flow of material as per the production schedule on the production line as well as the shop floor. Like these, there are a number of examples of interfaces between information technology and supply chain strategies.

Likewise, people processes have an interface with supply chain strategy as well. The deployment of people and ensuring their productivity are important to the success of supply chain strategy. Another functional area that has an interface with supply chain strategy is marketing. Marketing is the key in order procurement and price setting. Once the order is received and the production triggered, capital is deployed for finishing goods, which again go through the distribution channel for satisfying customer demand. Demand forecasting to post-sales service and soliciting of customer feedback are under the ambit of marketing, which is essential for supply chain strategic initiatives.

Hence, a supply chain manager must be an integral part of a cross-functional team. Every supply chain manager must realize the hierarchy of supply chain decisions and its interface with corporate, SBU-level, and functional-level strategies, and also the relationship between them. The ability to think beyond the supply chain domain and relate the supply chain strategies to the overall strategic vision of the firm, and drive success through inter-functional and inter-organizational strategic initiatives are challenges for a supply chain manager. In the contemporary business environment, a firm may gain competitive advantage in the industry by employing supply chain strategies that have linkages with the corporate, SBU, and functional level strategies. To achieve excellence in business, one needs a thorough understanding of all these.

5.4 NATURE OF STRATEGIC DECISIONS INVOLVING SUPPLY CHAIN DRIVERS

Supply chain drivers include logistical drivers, namely facilities, which include manufacturing and warehouses of all types, inventory, and transportation, and cross-functional drivers such as sourcing, pricing, and information management. As explained elsewhere, these drivers are strategic, planning, and operational decisions that impact supply chain objectives of cost efficiency and responsiveness. Each of these drivers is addressed in detail in different chapters of this book. Here, the scope of strategic decisions is discussed.

Facilities could include a manufacturing plant, a distribution centre, a yard for stocking goods or containers, and so on. Strategic decisions involving facilities would be regarding the location, sizing, and level of capital to be deployed, which is called capital-output ratio. For example, a tier 1 auto component manufacturer supplying steering systems to Suzuki Motors in India (brand owners of Maruti) may have its plant at Gurgaon near Delhi, close to the Maruti manufacturing facility. Once auto manufacturers start growing in Chennai, this component supplier would like to increase its market share, manage costs, and improve responsiveness by setting up a facility at Chennai. It requires an evaluation of facility size and future opportunities to arrive at a strategic decision.

Similarly, a large heavy engineering factory located near Chennai at Gummidipoondy was growing at 50 per cent CAGR, and grew to almost five times its initial revenue in four years. This required huge demand for facilities, including yard management, ancillary development, and so on. Growth became strategically a challenge as space and ancillary units are not easily available and scalable. Finally, this firm managed with increased outsourcing and more acquisition of facilities and partners.

Another logistical driver considered here is transportation. The choice of transportation mode for long-term regular service is one of the critical aspects as this would affect cost efficiency as well as responsiveness. Similarly, some of the options of transportation would involve providing dedicated vehicles and facilities for coordination. For example, a consumer products company finds that moving goods in regular trucks leads to damages, and decides to opt for containerized trucks. Such a decision would involve getting into an agreement with the service provider on guaranteed usage in terms of distance to be covered and taking on a dedicated service. When economics are not favourable, the firm will have to necessarily look at alternative options of soliciting tie-ups with others to improve return traffic and at reasonable rates.

Similarly, an engineering plant may require special trucks for moving oversized and heavyweight cargo for which they need strategic tie-ups with transport operators. Such movements may not again support economics by way of rates and also may require support for capital outlay. Such strategic orientations in transport decisions are common. A cement plant that depends on limestone from quarries may move by ropeways and lay permanent ropeway and support systems for movement. There are liquid processors who import oil and pump it through a pipeline from storage tanks at the port to the site for processing, which could be about 20 km away. Thus, strategic perspectives play a critical role in transportation decisions.

Inventory management is another supply chain driver that is more of a planning and operations decision than a strategic one. Though this is largely true, here are a few aspects of inventory that directly or indirectly lead to strategic decisions. For example, decisions on just-in-time delivery as an inventory policy would require aligning suppliers accordingly, and this goes with the sourcing and vendor development policy. Strategic initiatives like sharing of production plan and schedules, tie-ups with operators, product design, structure, and so on need to be synchronized. The set decision is not easily reversible and the cost of reversal is high. Thus, it qualifies to be a strategic decision.

To cite an example, a firm selling food intermediaries such as flavours and food colouring agents all over India stocks at various points across the country to meet demand from distributors and wholesalers. Each location has a demand pattern and stock is supplied to all the locations to meet the demand for more than a month. Though this improves responsiveness, it may not be an efficient way of handling as freshness of the stock could be lost. Also, production runs are affected by disaggregated forecasts, thus affecting cost efficiency. If the firm has to reassess its inventory turnover, which is less than 12, and improve to a target level of, say, 24, it may have to revisit its stocking policy and set up other support logistical drivers so that there is an overall reduction in cost without compromising on the service level. There are numerous such real-life situations where the inventory policy has led to strategic orientation in managerial decisions for achieving supply chain excellence. The Toyota production system is a classic example of this.

Cross-functional drivers, namely, sourcing, pricing, and information technology, would also have a strategic orientation in decision-making and impact supply chain effectiveness. Sourcing and supplier development as cross-functional drivers involve the production and operations functions along with the supply chain function. A strategic relationship with vendors is important from the point of view of reducing product development cycle, sharing research, and sharing technology and resources. This is especially important for suppliers of high-value and highly critical components for any original equipment manufacturer. Apart from this, post-sales service and maintenance of genuine spares are important and need to be supplied by qualified vendors.

To cite an example, a design jewellery manufacturer in Tamil Nadu was doing batch processes and sourcing precious stones from Mumbai, which has the leading metals market in India. The jewellery-manufacturing firm had strategic tie-ups with vendors during the batch process and carried stock. As part of the reengineering process, the jewellery firm decided to move on to cell manufacturing and brought in contemporary practices in manufacturing. By this, it wanted to move into e-kanban, using which the production schedule and stock levels are shared over the web with vendors who could replenish stocks on a need basis. This initiative involved changes across drivers and the vendor had to respond through technology upgrade and better delivery tie-up for improving responsiveness. Thus, a strategic orientation with sourcing and vendors is absolutely essential for achieving supply chain synchronization.

Pricing strategy plays an important role in supply chain effectiveness. There are certain goods and services that cannot be managed unless there is a clear strategic perspective on approach to pricing and sharing of profit across a supply chain network. Revenue is a function of price and volume of sale, and revenue along with cost is a major determinant of profitability. A focal organization, while arriving at a pricing strategy, will need to understand the dynamics of the competitive situation and strategies it may have to pursue to gain a competitive advantage For example, a fashion garment manufacturer estimates a demand of six pieces of a fashion garment and starts manufacturing accordingly before the beginning of a season. While pricing the garments he knows from experience that only one piece will go on full price, two pieces on a 10 per cent discount, and the remaining three pieces at a 30 per cent discount. He has to price his garments accordingly to realize a normal return on such realization. Within this, he has to provide for channel member profits and be prepared to allow for a squeeze in his profits if estimates go wrong. Another example of pricing strategy could be that of the focal organization being a captive buyer and there being a need to arrive at a transfer price, normalizing profits of both parties and enabling normal profits across the supply chain network. Thus, pricing could be an important strategic tool for supply chain effectiveness.

Finally, information management is one of the key strategic differentiators in a supply chain. This is discussed in detail in Chapters 15 and 16. As mentioned earlier, synchronization of physical, financial, and information flow is essential for effectiveness in supply chain management. For this, a focal organization will have to necessarily invest on IT hardware and systems, and link up partners. To cite an example, it is important for FMCG and electronic consumer products groups to capture secondary distribution data for coordinating production plan and avoiding lost sales opportunity for want of right SKUs. Also, visibility and transparency across players in the network provides adequate confidence and builds the confidence of all the players in the network. Thus, information management system is a critical requirement from a strategic orientation perspective of better planning and coordination, and also to establish relationships across players in the system.

Apart from drivers, even some of the role players have strategic orientation. Here, the roles of the third-party and integrated-logistics service providers are discussed, as they are crucial in delivering services. Their deployment is strategic as a focal organization outsources the activity as a non-core activity to the core delivery organization, whose performance is critical for the completion of value chain activities.

5.5 ROLE OF THIRD-PARTY AND INTEGRATED-LOGISTICS SERVICE PROVIDERS

Companies are increasingly focusing on their core competence and outsourcing non-core activities to those whose core competence is handling of those activities. Earlier, this was quite common in the services industry. Over the last few decades, manufacturing companies too have started outsourcing functions. Such outsourcing could range from the simple activity of a billing process or sales process to an involved function such as manufacturing, where the focal organization is the brand owner and marketer of goods. This has increased over the decades because Asian countries such as China, India, Taiwan, Thailand, and others have emerged as low-cost manufacturers. Technology explosion and bringing trade and commerce closer across the globe has further led to a wider acceptance of outsourcing processes.

One may note that traditionally logistics components such as freight forwarding, warehouse management, document handling, transportation, and so on were outsourced. Over the years, firms have started deploying third-party and integrated-logistics service providers for a number of activities such as distribution management, sourcing, milk runs, just in time (JIT) delivery, vendor managed inventory, and so on, apart from traditional activities. For example, it would make sense for an auto component manufacturer to produce the component with the best possible production process and leave the supply management to OE by a logistics service provider. This trend has caught up with all industries where cost and responsiveness are critical parameters in acquiring, retaining, and upscaling customers.

5.5.1 Deployment of Outsourced Partner for Supply Chain Activities

Supply chain drivers include logistical activities such as facilities management, inventory management, transportation, and cross-functional drivers such as sourcing, pricing, and information technology. In all these components, there is a scope for outsourcing the function. Companies either outsource a process or parts of activities depending upon the availability of the required expertise.

Outsourcing of supply chain activities refers to the function by which the owner of goods outsources various elements of the supply chain to a third party or integrated-logistics service provider that can perform the management function of the client's inbound freight, customs, warehousing, order fulfilment, distribution, and outbound freight to the client's customers. In short, both upward and forward movements, including reverse logistics requirements, if any.

A logistics service provider brings a different perspective, knowledge, experience, and technology to the existing function and can and will work with the firm to re-engineer it into an improved or new process. It is an outcome-based result, not just a pure cost-reduction issue. The new process will interact or be integrated into the company in a way that can bring value, even bottom line and shareholder benefits, to the client.

Outsourcing is a viable option for companies. An organization outsources functions for varied reasons—to increase shareholder value through reducing costs, transforming business, improving operations, and overcoming lack of internal capabilities. It can keep up with competitors, and gain competitive advantage through improvement of capabilities. Outsourcing helps to increase sales and improve service, facilitate reduction in inventory, and thereby increase inventory velocity and turns. It also mitigates capital investment, improves cash flow, turns fixed costs into variable costs and other benefits, both tangible and intangible. By and large, business process outsourcing can be used to create a viable virtual corporation.

5.5.2 Value Propositions of Logistics Service Outsourcing

The value propositions that an outsourced third party or an integrated logistics service provider (LSP) can bring in are as follows:

- Outsourcing logistics operations to an LSP gives the focal organization an opportunity to focus on its core business. Since the LSP is a specialist in logistics operations, it brings value enhancement to focal organization. For example, a company like TVS Logistics Ltd., which specializes in third-party and integrated-logistics services, can operate vendor-managed inventory, JIT, and milk runs quite efficiently for auto and auto component businesses as they have the required expertise. The smooth operation of these functions is core to the growth of the company and thus provides higher value to its clients.

- LSP could leverage on assets and thereby improve the quality and efficiency of assets deployed for supply chain functions. For example, Safexpress Ltd. (www.safexpress.com), a leading parcel company in India, covers over 550 destinations, spread across 28 states and 7 union territories, and manages warehousing space exceeding 3 million square feet. It also manages over 3,000 all-weather-proof ISO 9002 vehicles and covers more than 1,000 routes, linked through 41 super hubs and hubs. These assets, both tangible and intangible, can be used across clients, providing cost advantage and responsiveness as compared to a focal organization trying to build its own assets for supply chain activities.

- Productivity improvements and operational efficiency could be achieved by deploying third party and integrated logistics service providers. For example, Transport Corporation of India (TCI) (www.tciscs.com), a listed company, offers supply chain solutions. It focuses on a single-window enabler of logistics and supply chain solutions, encompassing all domain activities from conceptualization to implementation. An in-house team of supply chain analysts blends the clients' objectives with a supply chain design. These thoughts are put into practice by customizing logistics, warehousing, planning, and information management skills to deliver a sustainable solution as a Lead Logistics Provider (LLP). The uniqueness of the TCI-SCS is achieved by domain knowledge and assets (vehicles, modern warehouses), coupled with a footprint of group companies in freight, express cargo, shipping, freight forwarding, and customs clearance. They work across industries such as auto, retail consumer products, electronic goods, telecom, life sciences and healthcare, and cold chain. A player with such experience can provide productivity improvements and operational efficiency to its clients. Hence focal organizations outsource supply chain functions to such experienced service providers who can help them achieve a competitive advantage.

- Cost reduction across the supply chain function is possible through dedicated third party and integrated logistics service providers. To cite an example, Expeditors (www.expeditors.com), a US-based logistics company operating in India, is able to deliver this globally. The logistics solutions of Expeditors touch on all aspects of the supply chain. For more than three decades, Expeditors have worked with customers to increase order visibility, reduce surplus inventory, control inflated delivery cycle times, monitor and assign accountability, and reduce overall supply chain costs.

5.5.3   Impediments in Third Party/Integrated Logistics Service

The experience and growth of third party or integrated logistics service deployments are laudable and commended by many corporates. But there are certain woes in deploying third party and integrated logistics service providers like in any other service business. Especially, if the engagement moves up from brick and mortar service providers to 'concept owner and contract delivery', as provided by integrated party logistics service providers (LSP), focal organizations will have to critically evaluate their service providers. The key issues with LSPs are low network, competency level, IT enablement, and unviable cost (Exhibit 5.2).

Low network here refers to the lack of adequate number of nodes that may offer solutions support to customers. Most of the players are regional or scattered on selective basis. Hence, focal organizations looking for wide-ranging services are unable to rely on a single LSP. LSPs then network with other service providers to offer solutions that may not be standardized, thus making coordination difficult. The industry may require consolidation or grouping through strategic alliances to be able to deliver value to clients.

The competency level of service providers is also a limitation in engaging LSPs, especially if it is a switch-over group of companies which has upgraded itself from a single service provider to a supply chain solutions provider over a short duration. A good number of LSPs in India have upgraded themselves from single low-end services such as transportation, freight forwarding, and warehousing to become a consolidated service provider. In this process, skills acquisition and broad basing of people resources have been ignored. There is a mismatch between demand and supply of resources, and the scope for skill upgrade is also limited by lack of time and the nature of engagement in business. Many companies do not have resources bandwidth to invest on skills development. These companies are not willing to spend because the return to gestation period is considerable and retaining talent is also a challenge in this industry.

Another issue is the level of information technology enablement. Though this has not been an issue with leading LSPs, especially multinationals, it is not effective across

---

Exhibit 5.2 Keeping the Supply Chain Healthy

Transglobal pharmaceutical organizations offer great challenges in managing their supply chain because of locations, statutory approvals for medicine, expiry, cost of production, pricing, and sensitivity of markets. Challenges usually faced by a service provider are transition, managing and implementing new global business practices while improving visibility, maintaining strict compliance issues, and reducing overall supply chain costs. Such interventions are to be initiated at frequent time horizons because of the competitive nature of business. Expeditors have shared one such challenge, which is given below:

A global pharmaceutical-healthcare company based in North America is in the business of discovery and development of human and animal health products. They have eight major research centres in the United States, Europe, and Japan with manufacturing, chemical processing, drug formulation, and packaging operations that are carried out in thirty-one facilities in the United States, Europe, Central and South America, the Far East, and the Pacific Rim.

Their challenge was to implement contemporary supply chain practices through an integrated service provider so that cost efficiency and responsiveness could be achieved.

Expeditors approached this challenge by creating standardized operating procedures across all business units, utilizing internal systems technology that promotes global communication, regulatory compliance, and cold chain protocols. They followed a seven-step approach which included: site visits, flow-chart processes, development of standard operating procedures (SOPs), process validation, test transactions, and the creation and modification of a quality management review scorecard.

The combined challenge was to reduce overall supply chain costs, eliminating business process duplicity, while maintaining rigorous demands in the areas of export-import compliance, free trade zone protocols, and managing cold chain mandates.

This involvement required operating knowledge in the following areas:

- Understanding temperature control—cold chain management
- Maintaining velocity—on-time delivery
- Delivering door-to-door services
- Managing product integrity—clean, secure environment
- Providing event-driven visibility
- Monitoring FDA compliance
- Supporting free trade zone management protocols

Overall, success in transitioning, implementing, and delivering a sound and measurable product was proven a success by achieving a score of 90 per cent or better at the quarterly quality measurement review (QMR) meeting.

Thus, an expert service provider can bring immense value through experience, systems, procedure, knowledge, and implementation strengths to a customer.

Note: Reader is encouraged to visit the link and interact with Expeditors for more details.

Source: Adapted from http://www.expeditors.com/Services/CaseStudies/Pharm.asp.

---

the industry. With reduction in the cost of technology and communication, this is likely to improve over the years. It is important that focal organization systems can be hooked for quick and near-real-time data transfer for efficiently managing the business processes in supply chain. As one may observe, players like TVS Logistics, Infreight, Expeditors, Safexpress, TCI, GATI, and so on have invested on information technology and are able to provide value to customers. The problem is more with lesser-known and smaller service providers who are not geared up to meet the challenge.

The cost economics and affordability of engaging integrated logistics service providers is an issue. Often, because integrated service providers engage domain experts, salary levels are high. Secondly, in order to get advantage of a multi-user facility, they block more capacity. Till the capacity utilization reaches full level, the per-unit cost is higher. Thirdly, many traditional user organizations have enjoyed low-cost resources in logistics because of vintage deployment of service. Though contemporary services come up with increased service capability, the customer mindset is on vintage models.

Many integrated LSPs have failed at transforming their own businesses. Some LSPs have not moved past their core commodity service to become true multi-service providers. The professional MNC LSPs have problems in coping with domestic traditions and domestic ones have not succeeded at venturing into international logistics services through partnership mode, barring a few.

Another major issue faced by LSPs is that the decision-making is still with the customer and that hampers performance. Customers dominate solutions and delivery, leaving little independence for LSPs to fully convert their expertise into value. Because this is an unorganized sector, the functioning is impacted and customers indulge in unfair comparison of cost and responsiveness.

Though the issues mentioned here are observed and discussed in reality, customers in their anxiety to reduce costs, want to explore integrated LSPs. The potential market opportunity for outsourced logistics service providers, whether domestic, international, and/or global, is huge.

Opportunities and scope for improvement

Customers are looking at consolidating the number of service providers they have to deal with. They also want to monitor service deliverables of LSPs. In turn, LSPs have started improving the quality of service provided, albeit customers are not adequately compensating for the same.

Globalization, increasing focus on core competencies, increasing readiness to outsource, growing solution orientation, growing customer requirements, new technological opportunities, e-commerce challenges, and changes in business environment are the drivers of opportunities for LSPs.

Peters (2005) mentions that in Europe there are significant opportunities for third-party logistics (3PL) companies because of continued globalization, 3PL industry growth, leading to propelling of demand, further integration of supply chain activities, increased operational efficiency, further information systems development, new markets (Eastern Europe; Asia), continued Europeanization, and value-added services. These factors hold good for many developed and developing countries, including India and China, where one can observe a huge growth in demand for services of integrated logistics service providers.

A focal organization would look forward to LSPs differentiating against competition with adoption of technology and capabilities. They must be customer focused and increase efforts for marketing and sales so that the value propositions are clearly defined and made explicit to users, who can monitor the same.

5.6 FOURTH-PARTY LOGISTICS SERVICE PROVIDER

A fourth-party logistics (4PL) is a supply chain management service for managing resources, building capabilities and technology with those of complementary service providers. They act as the first point for delivering unique and comprehensive supply chain solutions. Intellectual solutions design capabilities and technology are the key differentiators of 4PL.

The 4PL fills the service vacuum created by 3PLs. Using a 4PL is different than using the traditional 3PL. The focus is on technology orientation and expertise. However, over-emphasis on technology at times undermines supply chain effectiveness as the user pays for what he does not use or require. The 4PL must note that success is in the interface of processes, people, and technology, and must ensure the right level of interface to achieve success.

This lead logistics provider brings value and a reengineered approach to the customer's need. A 4PL is neutral and will manage the logistics process, regardless of what carriers, forwarders, or warehouses are used. The 4PL can and will even manage the 3PLs that a customer uses. A good 4PL will have a better understanding of the complexity of the customer's requirements, present viable solutions, and ensure customer satisfaction and retention. It positions itself as an extension and part of its customer. The focal organization appreciates the relationship that 4PL can strike with customers.

A successful 4PL should have both strategic and tactical capabilities. It should have a real-world supply chain and logistics experience. One must avoid the temptations of a theoretical model and refrain from attempting solutions that defy real-life situations. Only experience can allow one to see the real issues and hidden agendas. Solution providers must also avoid the 'been there, done that' syndrome. That complacence can affect their efficiency. A solution provider should always be open to changes in the market and be ready to adapt itself to new market conditions to ensure an effective supply chain for its customer.

A 4PL, with real-world supply chain experience, can present a way for customers to take control of their supply chains. They can structure the relationship and the process in a way that best meets the requirements of the customer, rather than the customer having to accept what the outsourcing provider has to offer.

A 4PL concerns itself primarily with the planning, control, and optimization of business processes involving different companies. In contrast to 3PL and LSPs, which have a largely isolated outlook and focus chiefly on optimizing distribution logistics, the objective and the effect of 4PLs cover the interplant logistics systems across the network. This has a positive effect on the client's manufacturing operations by eliminating interfaces, shortening lead times, and minimizing logistics costs in procurement, production, and distribution.

5.6.1 4PL and Value Enhancement

4PLs facilitate reduction of complexity, eliminate redundancy, develop economies of scale, customize solutions, improve customer service at a reduced cost, and provide access to new technology.

To achieve the above, 4PL is required to:

- Link analytical competency with strong implementation and operation capabilities
- Plan logistics and consulting
- Build high customer confidence in outsourcing solutions
- Offer transparent and flexible win-win contracts
- Improve performance and competency across the network along with IT-support, operative and administrative logistics functions, and effective CRM

Thus, the essential characteristics of 4PL include: solutions orientation, logistics know-how, IT capability, management and organizational skills, innovativeness, the ability to develop and train organizations in the supply chain network independent of the focal organization, and best of breed approach.

With these, 4PL can offer value proposition of overall supply chain optimization through reduced/optimized inventory, improved delivery performance, reduced fulfilment cycle time, improved overall productivity, lower supply chain cost, improved order completeness, and improved capacity utilization.

5.6.2 Comparison of LSPs: Including 3PL and 4PL

1. 3PLs target the function. For example, they want to handle containers/shipments/freight, and not the transport management process, whereas the 4PLs target the process.
2. 3PLs manage particular work/tasks. Much outsourcing is work-related, such as warehousing, handling shipments, and delivery of inventory like VMI. 3PL will have to evolve to reach the stage of planning and managing processes; the 4PL is already positioned to manage complete outsourcing.
3. The outsource service provider, to truly meet the needs of his customer, should be neutral. 4PLs should be neutral if they are to manage the process. 3PLs, especially those that are asset-based, struggle to be neutral. 3PLs that seek to push shipments through their transport contracts or through their warehouses are not neutral.

To sum up, a focal organization would evaluate whether 3PLs have fully stepped up to meet the exact needs of customers or look at working with 4PL service providers. 3PL and 4PL do not compete but help each other; hence both have bright opportunities in the Asian region as well as in the global segment. 4PLs have got the greater responsibility of enabling firms to manage a critical part of their supply chain by providing visibility and integration across multiple enterprises. The need for integrated supply chain from a focal organization perspective is to deploy a service provider who would provide innovative solutions encompassing a customer's SCM requirements, enable effective supply chain integration, and operate on cost-effective, technology-enabled service.

SUMMARY

A strategy is a set of managerial choices among alternatives and signals organizational commitment to specific markets, competitive positioning, and ways of achieving value to different stakeholders. Corporate-level strategies relate to those strategic initiatives that would impact corporate performance across strategic business units and functions, and such decisions are made at the top-level hierarchy of management.

Supply chain management decisions interface intensively with corporate strategic decision alternatives relating to stability, growth, retrenchment, and a combination of these. These could trigger through any of the supply chain drivers.

Supply chain managers need to understand linkages between strategic business unit (SBU) level strategies and supply chain management. An SBU is a business unit within the overall corporate identity, which is distinguishable from other businesses because of different markets, products, and functions it serves. Again, SBU-level strategic orientation with respect to supply chain drivers could be a critical strategic focus determining SBU-level success.

Supply chain managers will have to ensure an interface of supply chain strategy with functional level strategies. Functional strategies like production, finance, information technology, marketing, and human resources interface with supply chain drivers for organizational effectiveness.

In the contemporary business environment, a firm may gain competitive advantage in the industry by employing supply chain strategies that have linkages with the corporate, SBU, and functional level strategies. To achieve excellence in business, one needs a thorough understanding of all these. Top-level management must get involved at appropriate levels in such decisions.

Supply chain drivers include logistical drivers, namely facilities, which include manufacturing and warehouses of all types, inventory, and transportation, and cross-functional drivers such as sourcing, pricing, and information management. These drivers, through strategic, planning, and operational decisions impact supply chain objectives of cost efficiency and responsiveness.

Apart from drivers, even some of the role players have strategic orientation. The deployment of third party and integrated logistics service providers is strategic to a focal organization when it outsources non-core activity to a core delivery organization whose performance is critical for the completion of value chain activities.

Third-party Logistics (3PL) is the function by which the nodal organization in the supply chain network outsources various elements of the supply chain to one 3PL company that can perform the management functions of the clients, including inbound freight, customs, warehousing, order fulfilment, distribution, and outbound freight to the client's customers.

The value propositions that an outsourced third party or an integrated logistics service provider (LSP) can bring include: scope to focus on core business, leverage on assets of service providers, improvement of productivity, operational efficiency, and reduction of costs across functions.

The key issues that need attention while deploying logistics service providers are low network, competency level, IT enablement, and unviable cost. Globalization, increasing focus on core competencies, increasing readiness to outsource, growing solutions orientation, growing customer requirements, new technological opportunities, e-commerce challenges, and changes in business environment are the drivers of opportunities for LSPs.

A 4PL is a supply chain management service for managing resources, building capabilities and technology with those of complementary service providers. They act as the first point for delivering unique and comprehensive supply chain solutions. 4PL concerns itself primarily with the planning, control, and optimization of business processes involving different companies.

A focal organization would evaluate whether 3PLs have fully stepped up to meet the exact needs of customers or whether they should look at working with 4PL service providers. 3PL and 4PL do not compete but help each other.

KEY TERMS

Capital–output ratio: It is the ratio of the capital used in a process, firm, or industry to output over some period, usually a year. This ratio for any process depends on the relative cost of different inputs. Where technology makes alternative techniques feasible, firms normally choose the cheapest, so the capital-output ratios tend to be high when the capital is cheap relative to other inputs. For a firm or industry, the capital-output ratio will depend on the mix of different outputs.

Corporate-level strategies: Corporate-level strategies relate to those strategic initiatives that would impact corporate decisions across strategic business units and functions. The top-level management takes these decisions.

Fourth–party Logistics (4PL): A supply chain integrator that assembles and manages the resources, capabilities, and technology of multiple logistic services providers (for example, transport and delivery of goods), including their own, for a focal organization's supply chain activities.

Functional-level strategies: These strategies focus on improving the effectiveness of functions like production, finance, information technology, marketing, and human resources in the long term.

Just in time (JIT): The goal of JIT is to time activities so that components or goods or services arrive on the production line just in time for transformation. There must be absolute synchronization of item, quantity, quality, and time for achieving success in JIT.

Kanban: Kanban refers to the system of signalling, originally using cards, bins, or dedicated space area for goods used in a manufacturing process. It mainly streamlines the flow of inventory into the process. E-kanban relates to kanban implemented through the Internet.

Milk run: In upstream, it refers to a vehicle moving on a predetermined route to collect supplies for a focal organization. In downstream linkages, the delivery to a series of points on a predetermined schedule by a vehicle is referred to as milk run.

SBU-level strategies: A Strategic Business Unit (SBU) is a business unit within the overall corporate identity, which is distinguishable from other businesses because of the different market, products, and functions it serves. SBUs have their own business strategies, and these are often different from those of the parent company.

Strategic decisions: These are policies and plans designed to achieve an organization's mission, vision, and objectives, and involve allocation of resources to implement the policies and plans. By nature, such decisions would have a large capital outlay, could not be easily reversed and could impact an organization in the long term.

Third-party Logistics (3PL): 3PL describes businesses that provide one or many of a variety of logistics-related services. Types of services would include public warehousing, contract warehousing, transportation management, distribution management, and freight consolidation.

Vendor-managed Inventory (VMI): VMI is when the supplier assumes responsibility and actually manages inventory. This was initially adopted in the retail supply chain where the category owner took the VMI responsibility. Increasingly, this has been applied in backward linkages of supply chain as well as in manufacturing.

CONCEPT REVIEW QUESTIONS

1. Explain strategic decisions in supply domain at corporate level, SBU-level, and functional level with examples.

2. 'Strategic supply chain decision could be a key differentiator of a business.' Elucidate with an example.

3. Describe the scope of an SBU-level supply chain decision with an example.
4. Analyse linkages of different functional areas with the supply chain domain. Highlight these linkages with examples.
5. 'Role players like third party and integrated logistics service providers could have strategic orientation.' Elucidate with example.
6. Describe the opportunities and key control factors for deploying third-party logistics service providers by a focal organization.
7. Explain fourth-party logistics providers and compare with third-party service providers.
8. 'Resources could be strategic assets important for supply chain effectiveness.' Elucidate.
9. Discuss the role of information technology from the strategic perspective of enhancing supply chain network effectiveness.

CRITICAL THINKING QUESTIONS

1. Discuss the scope of evaluating the services of third-party and fourth-party logistics service providers for enabling operations of an engineering firm. Use web research for the same.
2. Explain how as a strategic analyst you would look at supply chain as a strategic competitive differentiator in the consumer products business.
3. Analyse investment in a containerized truck by an electronic consumer goods company for dedicated movements. Assume a facility location and various distribution points in India. Use web research to support your analysis.

PROJECT ASSIGNMENTS

1. Visit a manufacturing firm in your locality and map corporate-level, SBU-level, and functional strategic decisions interfacing with supply chain domain.
2. Discuss the strategic importance of outsourced logistics service providers with an auto major's supply chain manager.
3. Analyse an IT firm's strategic IT investments for supply chain efficiency.

REFERENCES

Householder, Brad, *Strategic Supply Chain Management: The Five Disciplines for Top Performance*, PRTM

Melnyk, Steven A., Rhonda Lummus, Robert J. Vokurka and Joseph Sandor, *Supply Chain Management 2010 And Beyond: Mapping the future of the Strategic Supply Chain*, 2 November 2006, www.supplychaincanada.org/user_files/SCM_2010_Final_Report.pdf

Peters, Melvyn, *Europe's 3PL Industry Consolidates on the Road to Pan-European Services*, White paper, 2005 http://peters.ASCET.com

www.bn.com

www.haldiram.com
www.eidparry.com
www.safexpress.com
www.expeditors.com
www.nesupplychainconference.org/present/2005Presentations/Professional%20Development/Householder_NE_Supply_Chain_Conf_Pres_final.pdf
www.tciscs.com
www.expeditors.com/Services/CaseStudies/Pharm.asp
www.tvslogisticsservices.com
www.gati.com

CASE STUDY: DECISION MAKING ON DEPLOYMENT OF A 4PL SERVICE IN FOOD SEGMENT IN INDIA

(This is based on observations and competitive intelligence and strictly meant for academic purpose)

Tasty Pizzas (name changed) is a fast food brand in the food service business, specializing in sale of pizzas all over India. They operate both by setting up own restaurants as well as by allotting franchise rights to partners for particular locations/outlets. The fast food business is based on four business tenets:

1. Offering the same experience to the customer wherever the customer-brand handshake happens, presuming that the carefully thought out engagement is of value to the customer and enhances brand value. Only if the brand value is high enough will they be able to tweak the prices for a larger margin.

2. Growing as fast as you can, so that you can utilize the inherent advantages in volumes.

3. Rolling out promos or other customer engagement changes so as to maintain customer retention in a phased manner and manage associated variations.

4. Optimization on non-core activities by reducing the need for intervention/involvement and by limiting costs.

Same Experience

It's a problem to offer the same experience given the geographic distances, varying skills at the local level, and dependence on franchisees for volumes. Tasty Pizzas invest a lot in training and auditing to enforce rigid discipline on operating process, both on the restaurant floor as well in the kitchen.

Standardizing the customer experience is enabled by a 4PL, which ensures that products that go into the food production are (a) from approved vendors, (b) have been handled properly to retain product quality, and (c) are available on demand at all times.

Furthermore, in the case of franchisees, making it an incumbent on the franchisee to buy from the food-service distributor enforces product quality norms. The brand also is able to control the performance of the outlet by considering the off take of materials from the 4PL.

Growth

Bigger volumes mean higher visibility for the brand as well as the ability to negotiate better rates from the service/product providers. The brand is at an advantage both because they can demand higher royalty from the outlets as well as because it lowers the cost of operation. Investment in centralized services such as merchandizing, marketing, and food production research becomes feasible.

Managing growth in the same geography has its own risks. Scaling up may sometimes mean a higher cost until the investment gets amortized over higher utilization. Sometimes these are issues that create problems in growth execution plans.

Typically, small fast food chains are looking to expand into new geographical areas once the metro areas are saturated. But they are constrained because they cannot set up the logistical infrastructure required to service the distant areas, which is otherwise prohibitively costly for them, cancelling out the advantage that they are seeking to gain. Storage and movement of smaller lot sizes will mean a higher per-unit cost of operation.

Change Strategy

Menu/theme changes are complicated since they involve coordination over a large number of people who have to execute the change at defined time period, especially so when it involves franchisees. The cost of failure is high since it involves food products as well as made-to-order non-food products that may not be of use after the change. Also not being ready with the new items means that a lot of investment on promotion will go waste.

Optimization of Non-core Activities

Sourcing, purchase, stocking, inventory management, and delivery involve a lot of planning, interaction, and activity. Handing them over to a 4PL will enable the fast food chain to concentrate on more core activities such as merchandizing and food production.

Risks are involved in the management of these activities. Typically they are the risks of obsolescence, expiry, damage, and non-availability. Fast food chains would like to avoid the same.

Costs associated with these activities can vary due to local conditions and/or uncertainties or market conditions. Fast food chains would like to be buffered from these tendencies.

HOW DOES A 4PL HELP

Same Experience

4PL standardizes the product quality across locations by buying from approved vendors and centralizing buying decisions. The 4-PL enables through its buying process the same customer experience across outlets and manages stock level to ensure availability across outlets on demand.

Growth

4PLs are willing to invest and wait to amortize the investment as a business strategy. Their amortization happens across brands and hence will be easier to manage. The same goes for new geographies. 4PLs have better geographical reach since they are servicing various clients and hence will be able to share the associated overheads.

Change Strategy

4PLs are trained to look for obsolescence risks, and new product requirements. Products becoming obsolete will be diverted to other areas, used alternatively, and so on.

Optimization of Non-core Activities

KRAs ensure that a fast food chain need not spend time and resources on supply chain management. The cost of risks is capped by the margin that chains need to pay to the 4PL. Any other risk is to the 4PL account. A contractual engagement over a longer time period with a 4PL ensures that chains are insulated from market changes or local conditions.

Questions

1. Is the decision of Tasty Pizzas to engage a 4PL strategic in your opinion? If so, highlight the strategic orientation in this engagement.
2. What are the advantages enjoyed by Tasty Pizzas with the deployment of 4PL?
3. Explain the role and responsibilities of the 4PL in this engagement and map the capabilities which they require to be successful.

6

Role of Transportation in Supply Chain

Learning Objectives

After studying this chapter, you will be able to:
- Understand the role of transportation in the supply chain
- Learn about the key role players and factors that influence a transport decision
- Know about transportation modes, performance characteristics, and selection
- Understand transportation performance, costs, and value measures
- Gain an insight into transportation mode selection, speed of delivery, and choice of mode
- Understand inventory aggregation and transportation cost management
- Understand vehicle scheduling and routing

6.1 ROLE OF TRANSPORTATION IN THE SUPPLY CHAIN

Transportation is one of the logistical drivers of a supply chain and interacts closely with two other logistical drivers: warehousing and inventory. In supply chain, processes such as sourcing, manufacture, distribution, and post sales management are concerned with the movement of goods from a source to a destination either directly or indirectly. The transportation cost forms a substantial portion of supply chain costs and is impacted by the selection of mode, weight/volume of goods, and distance covered. Transportation is significant in an economy because of the number of direct and indirect employment it creates. The growth of the commercial automotive sector is an indicator of the growth in the transport sector. According to Raghuram and Shah (2004), transportation in India accounts for 45 per cent of logistics cost, and logistics cost is estimated at around 12–13 per cent of the GDP.

Transportation is the key to success, especially in businesses where responsiveness and product availability are key competitive factors. For example, Amul, a leading dairy brand in India, which has its plant in Anand in Kaira District of Gujarat, collects milk from villagers twice a day. This cooperative union has established itself as one of the top brands in India because of transportation efficiency in procuring as well as distributing milk. Milk is collected from small village-level primary societies, sent for pasteurizing, and the pasteurized milk is distributed from western India to east India using rail transportation. Another interesting example is that of Walmart, the biggest retailer in the US, which uses transportation as a strategic and tactical tool to lower costs. There is frequent replenishment to the stores from the central hub or from the suppliers to keep the inventory costs low. To lower the cost of transportation, Walmart consolidates inventory at its central hub and thus ensures higher truck utilization for every trip. To ensure faster turnaround for the trucks, Walmart has pioneered the usage of cross-docking where incoming material from various sources is segregated, sorted, and moved on to another truck for outbound deliveries to the same customer. This eliminates the need for storing and multiple handling, thus saving cost and time. This example illustrates both the innovative usage of transportation and also the inter-relationship between transportation and inventory management.

One may note that transportation decisions would have a strategic impact and need to be considered with the long-term horizon in mind. In this chapter, we would limit our discussion to only those transportation decisions that have a strategic impact on the supply chain.

6.2 TRANSPORTATION—KEY ROLE PLAYERS

Transportation decisions are taken by all the members in the supply chain, and role players in the decision making can be classified as shipper, transporter, asset owner, consignee, agents and brokers, the government, Internet, and the public at large. Some of these players have an overwhelming influence on the transportation network, and all the players are significantly influenced by the decisions taken by the government and the local authorities. Figure 6.1 illustrates the relationship between each of the players. It is also useful to look at the individual player's role in the supply chain.

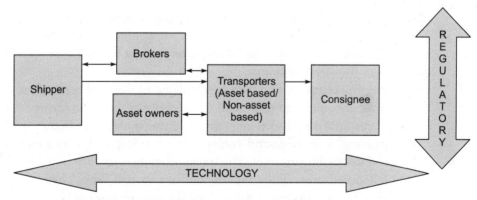

Figure 6.1   Role players in transportation decision making

Shipper and Consignee: The transaction between the shipper and consignee covers movement of goods from a source to the destination, pick-up and delivery schedules, guarantees of safe delivery, and related documentation.

Agents/Brokers: Agents/Brokers are intermediaries who book movement space and vehicles. Alternatively, they may be facilitators who take up the physical movement responsibility on commission basis.

Asset owners: Those who own transport vehicles and accessories, and lease out or deploy the vehicles commercially through carriers and movers.

Transporters: The transporter actually performs the task of loading, transporting, and unloading at the premises. He is guided by the principles of economies of scale and transportation distance. He seeks to optimize his delivery by coordinating the pick-up from multiple shippers so that his costs of transportation are covered and his returns are maximized. The agents/brokers perform the task of matching the shipper to the transporter.

Government: The government has an interest in the smooth and efficient performance of the transportation industry since it has a direct impact on the economic and social well-being. In some cases like the railways, the government enjoys a near monopoly. The government also looks at regulating this sector through multiple laws on the carriage of different types of goods and also through entry and exit timings into the residential zones of the cities or towns.

Technology: The Internet is emerging as the backbone of the industry, primarily through the exchange of information. The earliest usage has been in matching freight to the available shipment in the market. This has changed the role of the various intermediaries in the market. The other role is as a B2B (business to business) marketplace for procurement of fuel, insurance, spares, consumables, and so on. The other major use of technology is to enable the tracking and tracing of shipments from the source to the destination.

6.3 FACTORS THAT INFLUENCE TRANSPORT DECISIONS

Now let's look at factors that affect the transportation decisions in a supply chain. These factors can be looked at from the viewpoint of a transporter or a shipper (company using/contracting the transporter). For a shipper, the factors influencing decisions of transportation are:

Transportation cost: This is calculated as the total cost paid to the transporters for inbound and outbound transportation. Inbound transportation refers to the cost incurred for the movement of raw material and other inputs for manufacturing, and outbound transportation refers to the movement of finished products to the customer. The transportation costs vary based on the product to be handled/moved, the region, and turnaround time. These costs can be considered to be purely variable costs if the shipper does not own the transportation resources.

Inventory cost: These costs are towards holding inventory in various stages of the supply chain. For transportation decisions, these are considered as fixed for short-term transportation and variable when considering the design of the total distribution network.

Facility cost: These are the costs for maintaining the various facilities—factories, warehouses, and so on—and considered as fixed for making transportation decisions.

Processing cost: These are the costs associated with loading, unloading, and handling of goods. These are considered as variable costs for transportation decisions. If the goods have to be transported in containers, these can be quite significant.

A shipper should consider all the above costs while making transportation decisions, since these costs impact the overall cost of the supply chain, the product, and the service level offered to the customer. Within these, there is a scope for making trade-offs where necessary based on the overall supply chain strategy—cost-based or responsiveness oriented.

A transporter would consider the following factors while making transportation decisions:

Vehicle-related costs: These are the costs towards the purchase or lease of a vehicle. These costs are considered fixed for the short term. In the medium or long term, these costs are considered variable, depending on whether or not the vehicle is operating. For strategic and long-term purposes, the vehicle-related costs depend on the number of vehicles owned.

Fixed operating expenses: These are the costs associated with maintaining transportation assets such as insurance, taxes, labour, and so on. If the vehicle operators are paid irrespective of the trips made, they would also fall within this category.

Operations-related expenses: These costs include labour and fuel, which depend on the duration of the trip and are independent of the quantity transported.

Quantity-related costs: The costs of loading, unloading, and handling come under this category. A small portion of the fuel cost also depends on the quantity carried.

Overhead costs: These costs are incurred for planning, coordination, scheduling, and any investment in IT tools and applications.

Transporters should consider all the above costs while making a choice of the markets they wish to serve. If they operate in a market where responsiveness is crucial, then there will be cost implications in terms of the size of the fleet and the operating expenses. But if they focus on serving price-sensitive markets, then the ability to exploit economies of scale in terms of backhaul and so on would be crucial.

6.4 TRANSPORTATION PRINCIPLES

The fundamental economic principles for transportation decisions are economy of scale and economy of distance.

The principle of economy of scale states that as the size of the shipment increases, the cost of weight transported per unit decreases. For example, shipments that use the entire carrying capacity of a truck have a lower cost per unit of weight than those shipments that use a smaller portion of the total truck capacity. The transportation economies of scale operate in such a way that the fixed cost of moving a shipment is spread over a larger weight. Such costs are considered fixed because they do not vary based on the shipment volume. The principle of economy of distance states that the transportation cost per unit weight decreases as the transportation distance increases. This is also referred to as the tapering principle. The working is similar to that of an economy of scale, in that the fixed costs are spread over longer distance, resulting in lower cost per kilometre.

These principles need to be considered while making transportation decisions. The goal should be to maximize the shipment size and the shipped volume for longer distances while offering the desired service level to the customer.

6.5   TRANSPORTATION MODES, PERFORMANCE CHARACTERISTICS, AND SELECTION

The following are commonly used modes of transportation in a supply chain network (Figure 6.2):

- Airlines
- Road transport
- Railways
- Water transport
- Pipelines
- Ropeways
- Multimodal/Intermodal

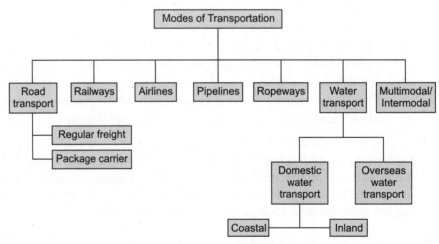

Figure 6.2   Modes of transportation

6.5.1   Airlines

Airlines are the most expensive way of shipment and are primarily used for movement of high-value and low volume/weight goods. Airlines have a high fixed cost compared to the other modes of transport because of the infrastructure and equipment involved. The fuel costs and manpower costs are variable and depend on the number of trips made, but the costs are nonetheless high. The goal of any airline, as is the case with other modes of transport, is to maximize the flying time of a plane (asset utilization factor) and the revenue generated per trip.

For example, Dell uses airlines exclusively for deliveries from plants located in Asia. Even the pharmaceutical industry in India uses this mode of transportation for exports. The general rule for selecting this mode of transportation is the time sensitivity of the product. For instance, for high-fashion clothing or fresh cut flowers, air might be the only feasible mode of transportation. Some of the major air transportation companies are UPS, FedEx, and DHL.

6.5.2 Road Transport

Road transportation is a predominant mode of transportation of goods in a country like India. The trucking industry can be classified based on the size of the vehicle in operation and the capacity as LTL (less than truck load) or FTL (full truck load). The FTL operators charge on the basis of the full carrying capacity of the truck irrespective of the load actually carried. The LTL operators charge on the basis of the weight carried and the distance travelled. The major advantage of road transportation, also known as trucking, is the ability to offer door-to-door pickup and delivery. Though this is a more expensive operation than railways, it is popular because of the ease of delivery. The fixed costs are relatively lower for FTL operations. The idle time and the travel distance between successive shipments impact the costs of operation. The major objective is to minimize the idle time and get return loads from the contracted destination. Some companies producing in large batches and shipping frequently find this option very feasible as they get assured service from the transport operators.

LTL operations are relatively cheaper and used for smaller shipments. LTL operators cannot be contracted for FTL. LTL operators cannot assure the same level of service as an FTL operator because of the need to pick up multiple shipments, consolidate, and then transport.

The effectiveness and efficiency of a road transportation network depends upon the depth and intensity of the highway network in a country. Apart from the network, regulations would impact the ease of transport as well as the cost of movement. The cost of movement would go up with complications in regulatory affairs of road transport, which is an external environmental factor.

6.5.3 Railways

Railroad is one of the cost-efficient means for movement of goods. In India, till recently, movement of goods by rail was a near monopoly. In other countries like North America, there are many private players such as Canadian National, CSX Transportation, Consolidated Rail Corporation, and so on. This mode is used for the transportation of high-density or high-weight cargo over long distances, in cases where the cargo is not time sensitive. For example, transportation of coal from mines to thermal power plants and transportation of food grains from and to the FCI (Food Corporation of India) warehouses are predominantly done through rail. The rail transport has a high fixed cost because of the locomotives, wagons (cars), and the yards. The trip-related expenses such as fuel and labour are independent of the number of wagons but vary according to the distance travelled or time taken. The focus of rail transportation operators is to reduce the idle time or wait time for the train. The costing of rail transportation is economical only when large shipments are transported over very long distances.

The major issues of railways are capital investment on railroad and infrastructure, vehicle and staff scheduling, track maintenance and repair, and availability of empty wagons. In India, demand for rail transportation is growing exponentially but the growth has been less than the road transport because of inadequate investment and expansion of the network. The present capacity is mostly devoted to carrying essential commodities such as coal and food grains, and industrial goods such as iron ore, cement, steel, and petroleum. There is limited capacity available for carrying industrial produce.

6.5.4 Water Transport

Historically, water transport is the earliest form of transportation. It can be classified as:

1. **Domestic water transport:** This involves the transportation of goods within the geographical boundaries of the country. This can be further classified as:
    (a) *Coastal domestic water transport* This involves transport of products through inland waterways as well as within domestic ports.
    (b) *Inland domestic water transport* This uses the rivers, canals, and lakes of the country for transportation of goods.
2. **Overseas water transport:** This is the movement of goods over water across the domestic waterways onto international waterways and boundaries.

Water transport constitutes the majority of the total volumes handled for exports and imports across the globe and accounts for approximately 60 per cent of the total value of foreign trade. This mode of transportation is ideally suited for the transport of very large shipments at low cost. It is, however, the slowest mode of transport because of the slower transit time, dwell time at ports due to loading and unloading, and any other waiting time that may be required. This is not a feasible option for short distances though the domestic water transport is able to operate efficiently through this mode. Domestic water transport depends upon available water network, coastal connectivity, and turnaround time efficiency. Products commonly moved by water transport in India include: cars, food grains, fertilizers, cement, agricultural produce, and so on. Considering the distances and the volume involved, this is the most cost-effective mode of transportation.

In the Indian context, the major issues faced for the growth of this mode of transportation are:

1. Infrastructure, in terms of port facilities, berthing, equipment for handling, congested primary hinterlands, and linkages with intermodal transportation.

2. Poor depth, inadequate dredging facilities, thus preventing large-capacity vessels calling on ports.
3. Lack of sufficient container-handling facilities around ports and high real estate prices, making it less attractive for investment.
4. Presence of unorganized service providers, inadequate technology deployment, and poor coordination among various players.

6.5.5 Pipelines

Pipeline is primarily used for transportation of crude petroleum, refined petroleum products, and natural gas. This mode of transport has a high fixed cost for setting up and operationalizing the pipeline. It is an effective way of transporting liquids and gases when relatively large flows are required. This mode is used along with other modes to cover for any fluctuating demand. For instance, crude is transported through both ships and pipelines.

6.5.6 Ropeways

Though ropeways are not a widely used for transportation, they have specific applications in the industrial sector. Ropeways are used in mining industries to ship raw material from mine heads to processing plants and shipments. They also have some applications for short distances within the premises of manufacturing plants. Also, they are used to connect remote points for transportation of essential commodities.

6.5.7 Multimodal/Intermodel Transportation

The previous discussion focused on the various modes and their performance characteristics and advantages. The shipper could choose to operate on an exclusive basis with some mode or use an appropriate mix of various modes to lower costs and increase responsiveness. This is known as multimodal/intermodel transportation network. This essentially combines two or more modes to take advantage of the inherent economies of each to provide a cost-efficient option for a desired service level.

This mode of transportation has become common with the adoption of containerization for shipping. These are the boxes used for intermodal storage and movement between motor freight, railroads, and water transportation. These are typically 8 ft wide, 8 ft high, and 20 or 40 ft long. Container transport often uses truck/water/rail combination, particularly for global freight.

In India, rail and truck combination is popular and is termed as piggybacking or TOFC (trailer on flatcar). It is a combination of convenience and flexibility of trucking with the long haul economy of rail. Fishyback is a system of transportation requiring the transfer of containers from trucks to ships. Birdyback refers to a system of transportation requiring the transfer of containers from trucks to airplanes.

Table 6.1 Fixed and variable costs for different modes of transportation

Rail	High fixed cost (equipment, terminals, tracks, wagons, and so on) and low variable cost
Road	Low fixed cost and medium variable cost (fuel, maintenance, and so on)
Water	Medium fixed cost (ships and equipment) and low variable cost
Pipeline	Highest fixed cost (construction, pumping equipment) and lowest variable cost
Air	Low fixed cost (aircraft, cargo handling) and high variable cost (fuel labour, maintenance)

The key issue in the use of intermodal transportation is the exchange of information to facilitate shipment transfers between different modes. These transfers often lack coordination and involve considerable delays. Table 6.1 summarizes the fixed and variable costs for different modes of transportation.

6.6 TRANSPORTATION PERFORMANCE, COSTS, AND VALUE MEASURES

It is necessary to understand the underlying economics of transportation in terms of factors and characteristics that drive costs and hence the performance. This deals with four issues, namely 1) the factors that drive costs, 2) the cost structures, 3) carrier pricing strategy, and 4) transportation rates.

6.6.1 Factors Driving Costs

The six critical factors that drive transportation costs are-distance, volume, density, stowability, handling, and liability. Though all these impact the costs, some of these might be specific to product characteristics.

1. **Distance:** Distance is a major influence on transportation cost since it directly contributes to variable expenses such as fuel, labour, and maintenance. Figure 6.3 demonstrates the relationship between distance and transportation cost.

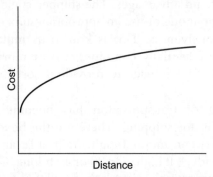

Figure 6.3 Distance–Cost relationship

From the graph it can be seen that the cost curve does not start at the origin but at a higher point, due to the fixed expenses that must be incurred for operating the transportation, irrespective of the distance. Also it can be seen that the cost curve is increasing at a decreasing rate, which is called the tapering effect.

2. **Volume:** The second factor is the load volume. This relationship is shown in Figure 6.4. As the weight of the shipment increases, the cost per unit weight

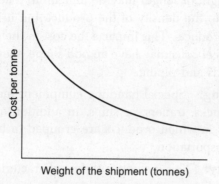

Figure 6.4 Relationship between weight and cost

decreases. This relationship exists because the fixed costs of vehicle operation like loading, unloading, documentation, and manpower get allocated over larger volumes, thus bringing down the per-unit cost. The implication for shippers is that the response time would be highest when a weight equal to the carrying capacity of the vehicle is transported. Hence, small loads should be consolidated into larger loads to maximize economies of scale.

3. **Density:** Density is a combination of weight and volume. Weight and volume are important since transportation cost for any movement is usually quoted in rupees per unit weight. In terms of weight and volume, vehicles are constrained more by cubic capacity than by weight. Since actual vehicle, labour, and fuel expenses are not influenced by weight, higher-density products allow relatively fixed transportation expenses to be spread across more weight. As a result, higher-density products are typically assessed at lower transportation costs per unit weight. The graph in Figure 6.5 illustrates the relationship of declining cost as the product density increases.

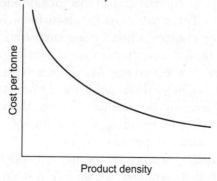

Figure 6.5 Relationship between density and cost

4. **Stowability:** Stowability refers to how the product dimensions can be positioned. Odd-size packaging of different sizes and shapes as well as having excessive weight or length may be difficult to load or position in the vehicle. This is similar to the density of the product, but it is possible to have odd shape and dense products. This impacts the cost in the same way as density. For example, while steel coils may have an odd shape, they are dense and easier to stow than steel rods and piping.

5. **Handling:** Special handling equipment may be required to load and unload from trucks, trailers, or ships. In addition to special handling equipment, the manner in which products are grouped in boxes, pallets, or containers affects the transportation.

6. **Liability:** This includes product characteristics that can result in damage and claims. Transporters must either have insurance to protect against possible claims or accept responsibility for the damages. This can be addressed by improving the packaging and using sufficient material handling equipment for handling.

6.6.2 Cost Structures

Transportation costs are classified into four categories: fixed, variable, joint, and common costs.

Fixed costs: These are expenses that do not change in the short run and must be serviced even when the vehicles are not operating. These include costs that are not directly influenced by shipment volumes or distance travelled. These include information systems, permits, licences, parking fee, and so on. The transporter has to look at spreading these fixed costs over shipment volumes to ensure profits.

Variable costs: These represent the minimum costs that a transporter must charge to pay the running expenses of the vehicle. Hence transportation costs must at least cover the variable costs incurred. The variable costs are incurred for movement of shipments from point to point and are measured as cost per kilometre or per unit of weight. The typical components in this include fuel, labour, and maintenance.

Joint costs: These are costs incurred to provide a particular service and are unavoidable. For instance, when a transporter transports goods from point A to point X, there is an implicit assumption that he would get shipment volumes to start from point X to point A or elsewhere. These costs are usually charged to the shipper who contracted the vehicle from point A. Otherwise, a broker or agent must be approached to assist in the backhaul load for the vehicle. These costs are implied in the freight rates charged by transporters to the shippers and can be reduced by jointly planning for backhaul shipments.

Common costs: These costs are also not apparent but are sometimes charged by the transporter to the shipper. These might include the toll and other movement-related expenses. These are allocated to shippers depending on the level of activity, like the number of shipments.

6.6.3 Carrier Pricing Strategies

Transporters normally use various strategies for pricing the movement of goods. Therefore, no single strategy is right. But based on the observations in the market, the following are the broad strategies that are relevant.

Cost-of-service

This is a cost-plus approach where the transporter adds a margin on his/her base costs. For example, if the cost of transportation is Rs 5,000 and the profit margin desired is 10 per cent, the transporter would charge Rs 5,500. This is the commonly used approach in transporting low-value goods and commodities or in highly competitive markets.

Value-of-service

In this strategy, the transportation calculated is based on the value as perceived by the shipper. For instance, if the shipper thinks that transporting 500 kg of high-fashion goods is more critical than transporting 500 kg of soap because fashion products are worth more, then he/she would be willing to pay more for the transportation service. Hence, transporters use the value-of-service strategy for transporting high-value goods. This strategy is used by the express courier and cargo industry for packages and documents.

Combination pricing

This strategy establishes the cost at an intermediate level between the cost-of-service and the value-of-service. The shippers must understand this for negotiation.

Rate contracts

This strategy is used by shippers for negotiating low transportation rates. Under this, the shipper assures of specific volumes in a period of time in return for committed rates for that period. However, there would be a clause for escalation in this period in case of increase in the prices of inputs such as fuel. This strategy is used by companies to standardize the costing for transportation.

6.6.4 Transportation Rates

In transportation terminology, the price paid to move a unit weight of a product between locations is termed as rate. The rate per unit weight (for the discussion let us consider this as tonne) is usually based on the origin of the shipment and destination points, although the actual rate charged might differ based on the other marginal factors subject to a minimum. The rates are published by the players in the market.

An alternative to the unit weight rate is the per-kilometre charge, which is common to FTL shipments. As discussed earlier, FTL shipments are designed to reduce multiple handling and transfer costs. Since the entire vehicle is used in a FTL movement and there is no requirement to transfer the shipment at different points, a per-kilometre charge offers a more appropriate pricing strategy.

In addition to the variable shipment charge applied on either per-unit weight or per-kilometre, the other charges that are common are: minimum charge and surcharge. The minimum charge represents the rate the shipper must pay to make the shipment irrespective of the weight. For example, if the rate is Rs 500 per tonne and the shipper wishes to transport 1 tonne, then the rate applicable is only Rs 500, which might not cover the fixed cost of the transporter. Therefore, a minimum charge of Rs 1,500 might be specified. The surcharge represents an additional charge designed to cover specific carrier costs to protect the transporter from changes not anticipated when publishing the rates.

Some transporters also perform ancillary or value-added services. The value-added services provided by a transporter are:

- COD—collect payment on delivery
- Inside delivery—deliver product inside a building
- Marking or tagging—mark or tag a product as it is transported
- Notify before delivery—make appointments before delivery
- Reconsignment of delivery—redirect shipments to a new destination while in transit
- Redelivery—attempt a second delivery
- Residential delivery—deliver at a residence without a truck dock
- Sorting and segregation—sort commodity prior to delivery
- Storage—store commodity prior to delivery

6.7 TRANSPORTATION MODE SELECTION

The transportation mode selection process tries to achieve two goals—minimize costs and maximize the service level. The general principles for selecting the mode of transportation are:

1. Match the shipment characteristic with the appropriate mode of transportation. There should be documented proof of performance for a transportation mode.
2. Evaluate on the basis of cost.
3. Developing selection criteria is the final step and the modes should be evaluated on the basis of these criteria.

Table 6.2 ranks the different modes with respect to speed, availability, dependability, capability, and frequency. Note that each has been ranked on a scale of 1 to 5 with 1 being the best option and 5 being the least desirable option. Speed refers to the elapsed movement time. Availability refers to the ability of a mode to service any given pair of locations. Dependability refers to potential variance from expected delivery schedules. Capability refers to the ability of a mode to handle any transportation requirement. Frequency refers to the quantity of scheduled movements. This essentially summarizes the above discussion on the rating of various modes and also enables comparison.

Table 6.2 Rating of various modes of transportation

Operating characteristics	Rail	Truck	Water	Pipeline	Air
Availability	2	1	4	5	3
Capability	2	3	1	5	4
Dependability	3	2	4	1	5
Frequency	4	2	5	1	3
Speed	3	2	4	5	1

6.8 SPEED OF DELIVERY AND CHOICE OF MODE

While establishing price and service strategies for a product, speed of delivery and its impact on inventory and cost would be considered because this is a strategic-level decision at the product and SBU level. Though the decision taken is more at the planning and operational level, the choice of the mode of transportation influences service levels, product price, and thereby supply chain profitability. Hence, a selected mode for continued support for business would be under a strategic decision framework. The decision would be based on:

- Total inventory holding cost, which is a function of cycle inventory, safety inventory, in-transit inventory, and annual cost of holding inventory that results from using each of the alternative modes of transportation.
- Cost of transportation using each mode.

The emerging decision would be that high-value, low-volume goods would be shipped through high-speed mode like air, and low-value, high-volume goods would be shipped through the cheapest mode like water or road transport. The following example explains the same.

A Delhi-based electronics medical equipment company, Farewell Medical Equipments Ltd (FMEL), buys one of its components from a Chennai-based supplier, Chennai Electronics Company Ltd (CECL). FMEL, which is negotiating for supplies, wants to choose the right mode of shipment for the next three years based on current rates with a buffer built in for changes in rates that might occur in the fixed time period. A static decision situation is considered here.

The annual demand for the product is 36,500, with an average daily demand of 100 units. The price at which CECL sells to FMEL is Rs 25,000 per unit. The holding cost per unit internally considered for managerial decision making is 20 per cent of value. Cycle inventory is considered for purposes of evaluation at the fixed rate of $Q/2$. Safety inventory would be equal to 50 per cent of average demand during lead time to meet the variation in demand. Over and above, in-transit inventory is considered as additional inventory. Some professionals assume that safety inventory would take care of the in-transit inventory. Based on the principle of conservatism, here we recommend considering in-transit inventory as well as safety inventory. This is specifically meant for aberrations and is independent of transit.

Table 6.3 Evaluation of various modes of choice for shipment from Chennai to Delhi

Mode	Quantity shipped (unit)	Lead time (days)	Order process time (days)	Replenish-ment lead time (days)	Avg demand per day	Cycle invent-ory= (2) (unit)	Safety inventory (unit)	In-transit inventory (unit)	Total inventory (unit)	Inventory value*	Inventory holding cost*	Transpor-ting cost*	Total cost*
Road	1,000	7	1	8	100	500	400	8001	700	42,500	8,500	2,190	10,690
Air	500	1	1	2	100	250	100	200	550	13,750	2,750	29,200	31,950
Train	2,500	4	1	5	100	12	50,250	500	2,000	50,000	10,000	9,344	19,344

*Rs in 000s

The transportation rate from Chennai to Delhi by road is Rs 60 per unit for a lot of 1,000 units, by air Rs 800 per unit for a lot of 500 units, and by train Rs 256 per unit for a lot of 2,500.

It may be observed from Table 6.3 that road transport is the cheapest mode that can be employed by CECL for shipping from Chennai to Delhi, considering the inventory and transportation cost. It may be observed that both inventory holding cost and transportation cost affect the decision. One may do a sensitivity analysis of the decision set with changes in lot size, for products of different value and different rates of transportation.

Though this decision situation demonstrates a strategic tie-up for movement, this application can be considered for planning. Operations decision would be based mainly on transportation costs if it is a one-off movement.

6.9 INVENTORY AGGREGATION AND TRANSPORTATION COST MANAGEMENT

As discussed, inventory cost plays a significant role in arriving at transportation-related decisions. With increasing e-business enabling virtual ordering processes, firms are selling and distributing products across geographies. This has led to a consolidation of storage and movement of goods after a trigger through small parcel services. Thus, consolidation reduces the safety inventory as the inventory is physically aggregated in a single or a less number of facilities. Standardized products such as pen drives, music CDs, standard size and colour garments, and so on are now popularly sold through e-commerce, leading to aggregation of inventory.

A supply chain analyst must consider a trade-off among inventory management cost, transportation cost, and facility costs while looking at this decision. Though aggregation would result in reduction in facility costs and inventory management cost, it would increase transportation cost mainly because outbound transportation to each customer would be through small and expensive modes like an express cargo carrier. In a large country where there could be the flexibility to handle outbound transportation in a disaggregated scenario with a low-cost regional carrier, such an advantage would be lost as national carriers need to be deployed to have a wider range of service, which could increase the overall cost of transportation.

To cite an example, Pleasant Home Electronics Ltd (PHEL), a home entertainment company based out of Gurgaon near Delhi in India, has distribution points for trade segments at Chennai, Bangalore, Hyderabad, Cochin, and Vizag in south India, and Delhi, Mumbai, Nagpur, Kolkata, Ahmedabad, and Allahabad in north India. PHEL sells both high-value and low-value televisions through trade segments and owns outlets across India. Predominantly the sale happens through dealers. The stores owned by PHEL are more for direct contacts and reassurance of market feedback. PHEL's supply chain manager proposes aggregation of distribution centre facilities and recommends consolidation of one centre in south India based out of Chennai and one in north India based out of Delhi. This proposal would reduce inventory of televisions at distribution centres and also reduce closure of all distributions centres except in Chennai and Delhi. According to this proposal, the inventory would be aggregated at two centres, which would reduce inventory holding costs as safety inventory would be reduced. The outbound cost would go up as PHEL will have to use a dedicated third-party logistics provider (3PL) for delivery to dealers and they would provide the same value-added services earlier provided by the distribution centres.

Generally, inventory aggregation is a good idea when inventory and facility form a large part of supply chain costs. Inventory aggregation is useful for products with a high value-to-weight ratio and for products with high demand uncertainty.

In Table 6.4 on PHEL's inventory aggregation plan, three options are considered. Each option has certain costs and assumptions involved, which are explained in the table. There are two sets of products, namely high-end TVs and low-end TVs. In the first option, there are distribution centres and order is replenished once in four weeks. In the second option, order replenishment is reduced to one week and hence inventory costs come down drastically, but there isn't any change in the transportation cost. In the third option, dealers are served directly at an incremental transportation cost per unit through the carrier service of the same service provider. This option does not reduce inventory-holding cost because in this hypothetical case, inventory reduction due to aggregation is not assumed. If one considers that, aggregation would give advantage. Another point that one has to note here is that the proportion of high-end and low-end TV share is more in favour of the low-end product. The aggregation decision is favourable only when the high-end product has more share in the total inventory cost. Another factor that needs to be noted in this hypothetical case is that there is same-level variability and hence no change in certainty. We have not considered weight as a factor. Rather we have differentiated by unit, which is a surrogate for weight. Since this a product based on volume, weight is not considered as a factor.

Readers may work out such problems in MS Excel and simulate for changes in product cost, variability, shipment cost, and so on. Such simulation exercises would lead to useful inferences.

To sum up, inventory aggregation would affect inventory holding costs and transportation costs. Inventory aggregation decreases supply chain costs if the product has a high value-to-weight ratio, high demand uncertainty, and enjoys large customer orders.

Table 6.4   PHEL stocking options and impact of transportation cost

	Option A	Option B	Option C
Number of stocking locations	12	12	1
Each location mean demand			
High-end television mean demand per week μh	200	200	2,400
Low-end television mean demand per week μl	1,500	1,500	18,000
Std.deviation (σh)—High-end TV	40	40	480
Std.deviation (σl)—Low-end TV	225	225	2,700
Shipping cost per unit of high-end TV (Rs)	900	900	1,200
Shipping cost per unit of low-end TV	400	400	500
Cost per unit of high-end TV (Rs)	30,000	30,000	30,000
Cost per unit of low-end TV (Rs)	12,000	12,000	12,000
Holding cost %	20	20	20
Reorder interval T weeks	4	1	1
Replenishment lead time L week	1	1	1
High-end TV cycle inventory (1)	400	100	1,200
High-end TV safety inventory (2)	246	155	1,865
High-end TV inventory	646	255	3,065
Low-end TV cycle inventory	6,000	1,500	18,000
Low-end TV safety inventory	1,382	874	10,492
Low-end TV inventory	7,382	2,374	28,492
Annual inventory cost (Rs million)	259	87	87
Shipment type: Replenishment or no. of dealers	Replenishment	Replenishment	12
Shipment size—High-end TV	800	200	2,400
Shipment size—Low-end TV	6,000	1500	18,000
Per shipment transportation cost (Rs)	3,120,000	780,000	11,880,000
Number of shipments	13	52	52
Annual transportation cost (Rs million)	486.72	486.72	617.76
Total annual cost (Rs million)	746	573	705
Reduction in cost		77%	94%
Notes:			
1. Cycle inventory = Expected demand during T weeks			
2. Safety inventory = $F^{1(CSL)}$ X Sqrt(T+L) X Std deviation = (NORMSINV(0.997)*std.deviation*SQRT(T+L))			

6.9.1   Trade-off Between Transportation Cost and Responsiveness

Responsiveness refers to speed at which orders can be despatched. Temporal aggregation refers to aggregating of stock despatches over time buckets in order to arrive at a balance between transportation cost and responsiveness. *Ceteris paribus,* temporal aggregation reduces the cost of transportation to the extent of reducing the fixed cost of multiple shipments. By aggregating the goods to be shipped, one can negotiate for better rates and impact variability depending upon the nature of distribution of despatches.

Here, an example of Smart Motor Parts Ltd (SMPL) is considered for analysis (shown in Table 6.5) SMPL, located at Chennai, despatches motors to a Pune-based engineering company every week. SMPL uses a road carrier, which charges Rs 5,000 + 25 per unit of motor sent for any time window to this customer. SMPL, on receiving an order, takes a week to process and the lead time is one week. Every order takes two weeks to be served. SMPL considers the option of aggregating despatches from one-week response to two weeks so that the orders can be aggregated accordingly. With one more week of lead time, the service extends to three weeks. Consequently, three weeks for order response with one week of lead time becomes four weeks response to the customer.

Table 6.5 illustrates that a responsiveness of three weeks gives 12 per cent reduction in transportation costs and four weeks provides lesser reduction. One may note that this is without considering the impact on inventory, which may have to be held for a change in the transportation time bucket. Using MS Excel, you can simulate the impact on cost of transportation with changes in the character of fixed versus variable transportation costs, demand distribution, and so on.

To sum up, temporal aggregation helps to reduce transportation costs for a given nature of fixed and variable costs of transportation and distribution of demand

Table 6.5 Transportation cost with changes in response time

Weeks	Demand shipped	2-week response		3-week response		4-week response	
		Quantity	Cost (Rs) shipped	Quantity	Cost (Rs) shipped	Quantity	Cost Rs
2	600	600	20,000				
3	575	575	19,375	1,175	34,375		
4	550	550	18,750			1,725	48,125
5	720	720	23,000	1,270	36,750		
6	750	750	23,750				
7	500	500	17,500	1,250	36,250	1,970	54,250
8	700	700	22,500				
9	750	750	23,750	1,450	41,250		
10	450	450	16,250			1,900	52,500
11	600	600	20,000	1,050	31,250		
12	700	700	22,500				
13	750	750	23,750	1,450	41,250	2,050	56,250
14	720	720	23,000				
15	650	650	21,250	1,370	39,250	1,370	39,250
			295,375		260,375		250,375
Effect of change in response time					12%		4%
Transportation cost							
Fixed cost (Rs)					5,000		
Variable cost per unit per load (Rs)					25		

pattern. The time bucket for aggregation influences this decision and beyond a point there is less than proportionate increase in savings.

6.10 VEHICLE SCHEDULING AND ROUTING

Vehicle routing and scheduling customers for delivery in a forward linkage or pick up from the supplier in backward linkages are the key aspects of a transportation decision. This is a common decision situation for a service provider or a focal organization in the FMCG sector, consumer products group, or food chains in forward linkages. It is also common among suppliers for OEs, food processing, and dairy products in backward linkages, where vehicle routing and scheduling decisions are important while collecting supplies and engineering ancillaries. A vehicle scheduling and routing decision situation would be related to:

- Number of nodes to be serviced
- Vehicle capacity
- Time window of service

The approach to this problem would be heuristic rather than theoretical. One such commonly used technique, savings matrix, is discussed here. The following is the methodology adopted for deciding which customers are to be serviced in a particular route and which vehicles are to be used for all nodes that are being serviced:

1. Map distance from facility/distribution centre (DC) to each node and use a distance matrix for mapping distance from the row and column of customers. This would be a diagonal matrix.

2. Identify the savings matrix if routes are to be merged. From the distribution centre, one may call each node separately and there could be two trips. Alternatively, if the vehicle capacity permits, the vehicle can pick from node 1, call node 2, and return to the DC by which it saves one run. This is illustrated below (Figure 6.6):

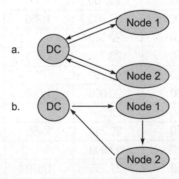

Figure 6.6 Reconfiguration of a transport schedule

3. Choose maximum savings and seed the route. Then, the nodes are added whereby customers are assigned to vehicles or routes based on the availability of capacity.

Table 6.6 Customer location and demand for Saferun Carriers

	x-coordinate	y-coordinate	Order size in tonnes
Warehouse	0	0	
Customer 1	0	5	3
Customer 2	6	5	2
Customer 3	4	9	4
Customer 4	6	12	6
Customer 5	12	4	3
Customer 6	9	0	4
Customer 7	11	–2	5
Customer 8	4	–4	6
Customer 9	2	–6	4
Customer 10	8	–3	5
Max truck load = 12 tonnes			
Number of trucks = 4			

4. Put the customers assigned within routes or vehicles in a sequence to maximize savings.

The tool is illustrated in Table 6.6. It is a hypothetical case of a milk run by Saferun Carriers, which has ten customers from whom an OE is served. Table 6.6 gives x and y coordinates of the customer location on a spatial distribution and load in tonnes for each location. A vehicle capacity is 12 tonnes and there are four vehicles to be deployed.

6.10.1 Distance Matrix

Distance between two nodes (i,j) is calculated using the formula:

$$\sqrt{(X_i - X_j)^2 + (Y_i - Y_j)^2}$$

Table 6.7 on distance matrix gives the distance calculated from each of the nodes and the DC and also the distance between the nodes. For example, the distance between customers 2 and 4 is 7 units. Similarly, each of the cells corresponds to respective columns and rows. Figure 6.7 shows the spatial distribution of nodes on the x and y axes.

Identify the distance matrix:

$$\text{Dist}(A,B) = \text{sqrt}(X_a - X_b)^2 + (Y_a - Y_b)^2$$

6.10.2 Savings Matrix

Based on the principle of savings in cost measured by way of distance, or in cost of running a trip, or both, one must arrive at a savings matrix. As explained earlier, while a vehicle picks up from two nodes independently, it makes four runs. That is,

Table 6.7 Distance matrix for Saferun deliveries

	DC	Cust 1	Cust 2	Cust 3	Cust 4	Cust 5	Cust 6	Cust 7	Cust 8	Cust 9	Cust 10
DC	0										
Cust 1	5	0									
Cust 2	8	6	0								
Cust 3	10	6	4	0							
Cust 4	13	9	7	4	0						
Cust 5	13	12	6	9	10	0					
Cust 6	9	10	6	10	12	5	0				
Cust 7	11	13	9	13	15	6	3	0			
Cust 8	6	10	9	13	16	11	6	7	0		
Cust 9	6	11	12	15	18	14	9	10	3	0	
Cust 10	9	11	8	13	15	8	3	3	4	7	0

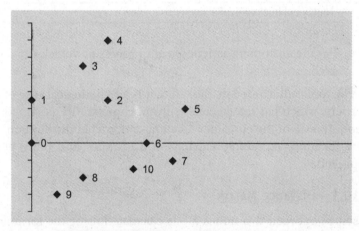

Figure 6.7 Spatial map of nodes to be served

two runs for each trip. If the vehicle has spare capacity, it may alternatively run to node 1, then to node 2, and then return from node 2 to the DC. By this, it saves a run between node 1 to DC and DC to node 2, but involves a run from node 1 to node 2. The savings in total distance is a net of the trips avoided plus the additional trip covered. The savings matrix for Saferun Carriers based on available data is shown in Table 6.8:

Identify the savings matrix:

$$S(x,y) = Dist(DC,x) + Dist(DC,y) - Dist(x,y)$$

6.10.3 Assigning of Customers in a Route or Vehicle

The largest savings value is identified from the table and that node is considered for inclusion. Here, in the example of Saferun Carriers, the largest savings is 21 between

Table 6.8 Savings matrix for Saferun cargo deliveries

	Cust 1	Cust 2	Cust 3	Cust 4	Cust 5	Cust 6	Cust 7	Cust 8	Cust 9	Cust 10
Cust 1	0									
Cust 2	7	0								
Cust 3	9	9	0							
Cust 4	9	10	13	0						
Cust 5	6	14	6	13	0					
Cust 6	4	12	5	11	20	0				
Cust 7	3	12	5	12	21	12	0			
Cust 8	1	8	6	10	17	14	10	0		
Cust 9	0	7	6	10	17	14	11	13	0	
Cust 10	2	11	5	11	20	14	11	5	4	0

customers 5 and 7. Hence, it is proposed to run between DC to customer 5, customer 5 to customer 7, and then from customer 7 to DC. If we evaluate the vehicle capacity for this route, it comes to $3 + 5 = 8$, which is an acceptable value. Then, an additional capacity of 4 tonnes is available and the scheduler can evaluate further additions to the route.

Once these two nodes are accommodated, the scheduler would evaluate for the next highest savings along with customer 5 or 7 and see if it could be accommodated. In this example, customer 5 to 6 gives 20 and similarly, customer 5 to 10 provides 20. Then the constraints are evaluated as below:

Option 1: DC--→5--→ 7--→ 6 = $3 + 5 + 4 = 12$, which is equal to the vehicle capacity and is a feasible option

Option 2: DC--→ 5--→ 7--→ 10 = $3 + 5 + 5 = 13$, which exceeds the vehicle capacity and is hence not a feasible option.

Option 1 is selected, and because it equals the vehicle capacity, an iterative process goes on to select the next route. The iterative process is continued till all the nodes are covered and served. Good routing and scheduling are arrived at by using the following principles:

1. Vehicles must consider a cluster near to each other. This minimizes the inter-stop travel time and the total travel time in a route.

2. Start with the farthest point. Generally, a route must be planned with a call on the farthest point first and then working backward to the DC. Once the farthest point is included, assign nodes that are closer to that point and are tight on cluster. A scheduler may proceed like this till the vehicle capacity is filled. Once the vehicle capacity is filled, the next vehicle is allocated and it starts from the farthest point from the remaining nodes. The iterative process goes on till all the points are served.

3. The sequence of stops while accommodating in a vehicle must follow a teardrop method. This means that the vehicle should not cross points, but move smoothly and appear like a teardrop as shown in Figure 6.9.

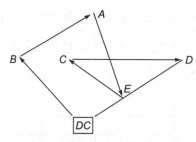

Figure 6.8 Poor scheduling

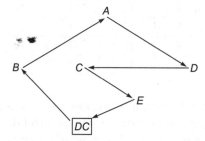

Figure 6.9 Good routing, like a teardrop, where no paths cross each other

4. If there is an option of varying the vehicle capacity for a given per-unit cost, the largest vehicles should be used first. Ideally, using a vehicle with a large enough capacity to accommodate all nodes would reduce cost, time, and distance travelled, and help optimize cost reduction. Many a time, vehicles with a uniform capacity may have to be used because vehicle capacity is subject to statutory regulations.

5. In our example, we have considered only pick-up. In real life, there could be situations of pick-up and drop from a vehicle or in a route. Ideally, the scheduler must apply the principle of teardrop and avoid crossing routes for either pick-up or drop, and schedule both in a trip.

6. In a milk run, if vehicle stops are on different dates, the scheduler may attempt to consolidate pick-ups or drops on a route by tightening days of the week. The daily segments for which routes and schedules are to be developed should avoid overlapping of nodes in a route. This will minimize the number of trucks, and reduce the distance travelled and the time taken. A scheduler must constantly face challenges like storage capacity at facility and the scope of holding stocks to optimize schedule, vehicle capacity, and so on.

7. The Sweep method is a simple tool. Map all the nodes on a graph and draw an arbitrary line. Rotate the line either clockwise or anticlockwise. Evaluate the nodes that appear as the line moves. Check whether the vehicle capacity can accommodate the node. If yes, add the node and continue. If no, continue to accommodate the next node. Proceed till the vehicle capacity is full. Then, start the next vehicle and continue the sweep. Within each route, sequence the stops in such a way that it minimizes distances. The sequencing can be done by fol-

lowing a teardrop method or by using an algorithm on the Travelling Salesman Problem (TSP). (See Figure 6.10).

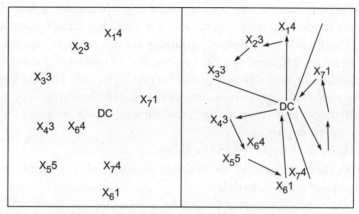

Figure 6.10 Scheduling using the sweep method

Finally, it is the job of the scheduler to sequence nodes in an allocated route while using the savings matrix method. As explained earlier, sequencing can be done heuristically using principles of good scheduling. Once a sequence is identified through an iterative process, further improvements can be studied.

Thus, various tools can be used for scheduling. A number of IT tools are available through SCM software solutions and products to enable scheduling. You can have a hands-on feel of such solutions by going through demos and by trying out Ronald H. Ballou's Logware software.

6.11 MILK RUN

Milk run is a transportation model for the collection and transportation of goods from suppliers with a defined delivery route, in which various stops are planned and executed in terms of quantities and timing. The same concept is applied in forward linkages for the distribution of goods, especially in FMCG, consumer goods, and food and dairy products. A milk dairy plant collects milk from a number of collection centres that are typically located in villages. The challenge is to establish and manage routes so that the milk produced in villages is collected efficiently at a low cost and processed with minimal spoilage, so as to ensure that the farmers benefit. Amul dairy is one of the pioneers in establishing and successfully managing milk runs for collection of milk from suppliers (Chandra and Tirupati 2002). Similarly, for delivery within a town or city, milk unions or marketers establish routes and milk run for various points to drop liquid milk for distribution to ultimate customers and pick empty pallets on return, which is a reverse logistics function.

Though milk run is quite a useful technique for transportation within a defined boundary for less than truck load volume for pick/drop in each node, it also presents complexities at different levels. The key challenge is establishing consolidation hubs for clusters of suppliers and different geographic levels (local, regional, national, and international suppliers). The Hub-and-Spoke model, which is used widely in postal and courier services, where there are consolidation points (hubs) and disbursed pick-up/delivery points (spokes), is more appropriate for a larger area. The Hub-and-Spoke model and milk run are not the same but complement each other.

Vehicle pick-up or delivery routings are not random movements and often need to be planned. Milk run is a proven method of optimizing a service provider's trucking (collection or despatch activities). Increasingly, auto clusters deploy milk run now for the vendor-managed inventory and/or just-in-time inventory management. Even the electronics and engineering industries, which depend upon components or ancillaries, deploy milk run.

Milk run is deployed in the following situations:

- There is demand for multiple pick-up/delivery points in a time window for a production schedule.
- Route optimization by a service provider, especially when the load is less than the capacity of the vehicle and there is scope for multiple pick-up or drop in a route.
- Effective deployment of JIT, VMI, or any integrated service.
- Of late, combining the inbound and outbound logistics chain in a single vehicle is also encouraged for optimizing vehicle use and economizing cost.

Variables that influence a milk run are:

- Distance to be covered, which includes the total distance as well as the distance between two nodes.
- Cost of running a route and adding any particular point in a route.
- The delivery/pick-up schedule may be regular or irregular, depending upon demand/supply from each node, which may be fixed or variable. This is the most commonly used tool for a fixed quantity model, which can be tweaked if needed.
- Cycle-time or longevity of a product.

The success of a milk run operation depends upon the discipline of all the participants in the network of the focal organization, the ability to commit to time and cost, communicate variances, and learning from failures. A milk run operation can succeed if there is a healthy contractual relationship and efficient communication among the focal organization, the service providers, and suppliers. The roles and responsibilities should be clearly demarcated, and there should be rewards and penalties related to performance.

6.12 CROSS-DOCKING

Cross-docking is a practice in transportation of unloading materials from an inbound vehicle and loading these materials directly into outbound trucks, trailers, or rail cars, with little or no storage in between. The purpose of cross-docking is to combine small loads from different points and redistribute, and also save on dwell time, storage, and costs. At times, putaway zones at a distribution centre are used for cross-docking.

Cross-docking is an old concept, which has been used in the parcels, postal, and courier business for ages. It is believed that in ancient times, when jewellery traders of Gujarat used to ship precious metals and stones through camels from northern Gujarat to Mumbai, they used to deploy a technique similar to cross-docking for value addition, trading, and transaction. This was done because of regional variations in preference of design and demand.

In today's business, especially with the boom in the organized retail sector in India and elsewhere, cross-docking is useful for serving multiple locations with varying demand sizes and providing variations in SKUs. Now businesses commonly use LTL (less than truck load) operations. The US has popularized cross-docking, thanks to Walmart, which is credited for deploying this transport strategy effectively.

In the LTL trucking industry, cross-docking is done by moving cargo from one transport vehicle directly into another, with minimal or no warehousing. In retail practice, cross-docking operations may utilize staging areas (putaway zones) where inbound materials are sorted, consolidated, and stored until the outbound shipment is complete and ready to ship.

Advantages of Cross-docking

- Enables effective utilization of vehicle space
- Provides responsiveness as quick turnaround and multiple SKUs are possible
- Reduces costs of storage and inventory, and optimizes transportation cost for a given service level, thus reducing supply chain costs
- Enables better handling of backroom storage space (in the retail industry) in which safety inventory is stocked

Cross-docking is effective in the Hub-and-Spoke model where goods are brought to one location and redistributed. This is all the more useful if receipts and despatches are to the same nodes. Cross-docking can be useful when there is a consolidation of goods. This could be for a batch of similar goods or for complementary goods where two different goods have different manufacturers but are received by the dealer point as one. The same is also true for the backward chain when value additions happen at multiple locations and need to be consolidated. Similarly, deconsolidation could also be possible while cross-docking.

The successful deployment of cross-docking depends upon a number of factors. The most important factor is effective communication among the focal organization, vendors, and service providers. Unless communication is established and the resources are trained to plan and execute cross-docking, it may lead to utter mismanagement. Setting up of standard operating procedures, thereby establishing roles and responsibilities and deliverables, is important. Also, one must clearly spell out contracts, rewards, and penalties while involved in cross-docking. Companies that are in a hurry go with rate contracts find it difficult in reality to manage such situations of variance.

Secondly, while using cross-docking, one must establish a clear boundary of operations. The operations must be confined to a region or location of market where it is easy to manage turnaround times and cost. A huge number of vendors and a larger geography may lead to impediments in the operation of cross-docking.

Thirdly, cost economies as discussed above must be identified and should be deployed only where there is clear advantage.

In many countries including India, cross-docking is playing a critical role in the success of retail, consumer goods, food products, and engineering. Service providers are specializing in this, especially third- and fourth-party logistics service providers (4PL) are playing a critical role in implementing cross-docking. It is more convenient for a third-party player, who is into warehousing and transporting, to implement cross-docking. In India, Expeditor is understood to be one of the leading players in providing this service.

SUMMARY

Transportation contributes to the overall economic activity and provides opportunity for growth. Transportation is a significant cost influencer and has more than 25 per cent share in the total logistics costs. This can influence the price of the end products. It supports greater reach and availability for the products in the marketplace.

The more efficient the transportation, the lower the supply chain costs for a given inventory and facilities configuration. The wider the product distribution and reach, the greater is the role of transportation and more the number of opportunities for companies to exploit the economies of scale.

The transportation activity should not be considered in isolation, but in conjunction with the other supply chain activities and it is more than just a physical delivery. There is a need to deploy and support the transportation planning process with IT tools and techniques.

A shipper should consider inventory costs, facility management costs, and information costs along with transportation costs, while making transportation decisions. These impact the overall cost of the supply chain, the product, and the service level offered to the customer. Within these there is scope for making trade-offs where necessary, based on the overall supply chain strategy—cost-based or responsiveness oriented.

A transporter should consider vehicle-related costs, fixed operating expenses, operations-related expenses, quantity-related costs, and overhead costs while making a choice of the markets it wishes to serve. If he operates in a market where responsiveness is crucial then there will be cost implications in terms of the size of the fleet and the operating expenses. But if he focuses on serving price-sensitive markets, then the ability to exploit economies of scale in terms of backhaul and so on would be crucial.

The economic principles for transportation decisions are: economy of scale and economy of distance. The principle of economy of scale states that as the size of the shipment increases, the cost of weight transported per unit decreases. The principle of economy of distance states that the transportation cost per unit weight decreases as the transportation distance increases. This is also referred to as the tapering principle.

The commonly used modes of transportation in a supply chain network are: road transport, railways, water transport, airlines, pipelines, and ropeways. The choice of mode is determined by many factors, including cost and responsiveness, product characteristics, support infrastructure, and so on. The shipper could choose to operate on an exclusive basis with some mode or use an appropriate mix of various modes to lower costs and increase responsiveness. The latter option is known as multimodal or intermodal transportation network. This essentially combines two or more modes to take advantage of the inherent economies of each to provide a cost-efficient option for decision making.

While establishing price and service strategies for a product, speed of delivery and its impact on inventory and cost would be considered. A selected mode of transportation for a particular business is part of its strategic decision framework. The decision on choice of mode would be based on: total inventory holding cost, which is a function of cycle inventory, safety inventory, in-transit inventory, and annual cost of holding inventory that results from using each of the alternative modes of transportation, and the cost of transportation for a desired service level.

Consolidation reduces safety inventory because inventory is physically aggregated in either a single facility or in just a few centres. Though aggregation would result in reduction in facility costs and inventory management costs, it would increase transportation costs mainly because outbound transportation to each customer would be small and will be through an expensive mode like express cargo carrier.

Temporal aggregation refers to aggregating of stock despatches over time buckets in order to arrive at a balance between transportation cost and responsiveness. Other things being the same, temporal aggregation reduces cost of transportation to the extent of reducing the fixed cost of multiple shipments.

Vehicle routing and scheduling customers for delivery in a forward linkage or pick-up from supplier in backward linkages are one of the key aspects of a transportation LTL decision. A decision situation would be wherein a number of nodes are to be serviced, and the vehicle capacity and time window of service are important to determine the route of customer call or the vehicle to be scheduled. The methodology of arriving at allocation of customers in a route and vehicles for all nodes to be serviced is the savings matrix technique. A number of other support techniques based on heuristic models are available for a supply chain analyst to schedule a vehicle route plan.

KEY TERMS

Asset owners: These are owners of transport equipment and assets like trailers, trucks, railroad, and transport-related infrastructure to facilitate cargo transportation.

Birdyback: It refers to a system of transportation, requiring the transfer of containers from trucks to airplanes.

Brokers: These are intermediaries who facilitate buying and selling of space or services for transportation of goods.

Consignee: The party to whom goods are shipped and delivered, or the receiver of a freight shipment.

Cross-docking: Cross-docking is a practice in transportation of unloading materials from an inbound vehicle and loading these materials directly into outbound trucks, trailers, or rail cars, with little or no storage in between.

Economy of distance in shipment: The principle of economy of distance states that the transportation cost per unit weight decreases as the transportation distance increases. This is also referred to as the tapering principle.

Economy of scale in shipment: The principle of economy of scale states that as the size of the shipment increases, the cost of weight transported per unit decreases.

Fishyback: This is a system of physical distribution of goods, requiring the transfer of containers from trucks to ships.

Full truck load (FTL): FTL operators charge on the basis of the full carrying capacity of the truck, irrespective of the load actually carried. These trucks normally move non-stop from the origin to the final destination.

Inbound transportation: This constitutes the management of materials from suppliers and vendors into production processes or storage facilities by the focal organization in a supply chain network.

Intermodal or multimodal transportation: This involves transporting freight by using two or more transportation modes, such as by truck and rail, or truck and ship.

Less truck load (LTL): LTL operators charge on the basis of the weight carried and the distance travelled. These trucks have multiple points of pick-up and drop.

Milk run: In a milk run, vehicle stops are on different nodes/dates wherein a scheduler may attempt to consolidate pick-ups or drops on a route by tightening days of week.

Outbound transportation: This is the process related to the movement and storage of products from the end of the production line to the end user in a supply chain network with reference to a focal organization.

Package carrier: These are carriers that move small packages. For example, UPS, FedEx, DHL, BlueDart, SpeedPost, Safexpress, and so on.

Piggybacking or TOFC (trailer on flat car): It is a combination of the convenience and flexibility of trucking with the long haul economy of rail.

Shipper: This is the party that tenders goods for transportation. More commonly this would be a focal organization whose supply chain network is considered or any other partner in the network.

Third-party logistics provider (3PL): 3PL is a firm that provides multiple logistics services for use by customers. Preferably, these services are integrated or bundled together by the provider. These firms facilitate the movement of parts and materials from suppliers to manufacturers, and finished products from manufacturers to distributors and retailers. Among the services they provide are transportation, warehousing, cross-docking, inventory management, packaging, and freight forwarding.

Transport operator: Transport operator is the one who undertakes transportation of goods either through self-owned or leased assets.

Transport rates: In transportation, the price paid to move a unit weight of a product between locations is termed as rate.

CONCEPT REVIEW QUESTIONS

1. What are the alternate modes of transportation available to a shipper? Explain the advantages and disadvantages of each mode and rate them on different parameters like cost, speed of delivery, flexibility, and so on.

2. Who are the major role players in a transportation decision? Explain these role players' responsibilities and performance criteria in a decision situation. Give examples.

3. Explain the factors that influence the choice of a mode. What is the reole of inventory in a transportation decision? Elucidate with examples.

4. What do you understand by inventory aggregation? How does it impact a transportation decision? Explain for a high-value, low-weight product situation the concept of inventory aggregation.

5. Explain temporal aggregation. Where can this be useful in making a transportation decision? Elucidate with examples.

6. What are the issues in vehicle scheduling and routing? Explain with examples the various challenges in the same.

7. Explain briefly the following:
   (a) Teardrop method
   (b) Sweep method
   (c) Principles of good scheduling

8. What are the steps in the savings matrix method while scheduling and routing vehicles? Explain the fundamental principles of this technique.

9. Explain the given terms briefly with examples wherever applicable:
   (a) FTL and LTL
   (b) Cross-docking
   (c) Milk runs
   (d) Containerized trucking with an example
   (e) Spot versus contracted rates for trucking

CRITICAL THINKING QUESTIONS

1. Peter, Transportation Sales Manager of Hi-Speed Trucking Company, has considered serving a new customer, Classic Traders (P) Ltd, an importer of cotton, by hauling 12 truck loads of the product each month from the receiving port in Tuticorin, Tamil Nadu, to a converter in Karur, for Rs 24,000 per truck load. Each serving truck must depart from the Hi-Speed terminal, which is 12 km from the seaport. The distance from Tuticorin to Karur is 600 km. Generally, there is no return load from Karur.

   (a) If it costs Hi-Speed an average of Rs 22 per km to operate a truck, should Peter accept the business at the negotiated rate? Why or why not?

   (b) Peter has coordinated backhaul moves for Karur with a new customer in Tirupur. The new customer, Super Spinning, ships garments from its plant in Tirupur to the port of Tuticorin for exporting. Each truck to Karur will be accompanied by a return shipment from Super Spinning (12 truck load per month). Hi-Speed will charge Super Spinning Rs 22 per km of carrying the load. Tuticorin is 700 km from Tirupur. The distance from Karur to Tirupur is 80 km. Trucks must return to the terminal in Tuticorin upon delivering the product from backhaul (before picking up again). The terms of the agreement outlined in part (a) remain intact. How much can Peter expect Hi-Speed to profit (or lose) per month from the new arrangement should the company accept the business?

   (c) Is it worthwhile for Peter to arrange for the backhaul for a committed consignee or pick from the market? Why or why not?

2. An infrastructure company, Goodwill Constructions (GC), based in Delhi in India buys cement from a Madhya Pradesh plant, which is 800 km away, for a daily consumption of about 1,000 tonnes. The cost of cement per tonne is Rs 4,000 and the transportation cost by rail would be Rs 800 per tonne. Rail transportation would buy a rake of 58 wagons of 40 tonnes each. The lead time for train shipment is five days and order would be processed in a day. The holding cost is 20 per cent and the safety inventory would be twice the lead-time demand. Compute the total cost of transportation given the option of moving the stuff by rail. A supply consultant came up with the proposal of reducing lead time to three days and sharing the shipment of the rake along with another infrastructure company exactly by half. How can such an option improve the cost of movement?

3. Ahmedabad Medical equipment Company (AMEC), based out of Ahmedabad in India, has two product categories: one high end and the other low end. The product-related details are given below. A supply chain analyst has given Option B over the current Option A and you are expected to present the case to management. The supply chain analyst also came up with another proposal to deliver direct to dealers. Each territory has ten dealers and they have a uniform demand pattern. Shipping costs would go up to Rs 2,000 per unit of high-end value product and Rs 900 for the low-end value product. All other factors remaining same, you may evaluate the direct delivery model as well.

	Option A	Option B
Number of stocking locations	8	8
Each location mean demand		
High-end product mean demand per week μh	400	400
Low-end product mean demand per week μl	3,000	3,000
Std. deviation (σh)—High-end product	40	40
Std. deviation (σl)—Low-end product	450	450
Shipping cost per unit of high-end product (Rs)	1,500	1,500

	Option A	Option B
Shipping cost per unit of low-end product	600	600
Cost per unit of high-end product (Rs)	50,000	50,000
Cost per unit of low-end product (Rs)	9,000	9,000
Holding cost %	20	20
Reorder interval T weeks	4	1
Replenishment lead time L week	1	1
Shipment type: Replenishment or no. of dealers	Replenishment	Replenishment

Notes:

A. Cycle inventory = Expected demand during T weeks
B. Safety inventory = $F^{-1(CSL)}$ X Sqrt(T+L) X Std deviation

4. Consider the case of a Bangalore-based garments manufacturer, which ships men's shirts (weighing on an average of 500 gm) in containerized dedicated LTL truck. The carrier charges for shipping 500 km at the rate of Rs 6 per km, per tonne on load and Rs 4 per km, per tonne for coming back empty. Trucks return empty to the factory as it is a dedicated service. The response time including lead time is one week. A supply chain analyst comes with the proposal of evaluating alternate response times of two weeks and three weeks. Prepare your analysis accordingly.

Week	1	2	3	4	5	6	7
No. of shirts	8,000	7,500	7,800	7,200	8,200	6,800	8,000
Week	8	9	10	11	12	13	14
No. of shirts	7,500	7,200	6,800	7,800	8,000	6,000	6,800

5. Hi-Speed Logistics Services Company (HLSC) offers milk run service for a cluster of suppliers in Pune. The following data gives details of coordinates of supplier location and order size in tonnes. A truck can carry up to 12 tonnes. Though there are no constraints with respect to availability of trucks, each truck deployed would cost Rs 6,000 per day and a truck would run only one trip in a day. You may use savings matrix and schedule vehicle route for this situation.

Customer location and demand for HLSC

	x-coordinate	y-coordinate	Order size in tons
Warehouse	0	0	
Customer 1	2	4	3
Customer 2	4	0	2
Customer 3	8	10	4
Customer 4	1	10	6
Customer 5	10	6	3
Customer 6	7	2	4
Customer 7	6	−4	5
Customer 8	2	−8	6
Customer 9	3	−9	4
Customer 10	7	−2	5

Maximum truck load = 12
Number of trucks is not a constraint but recommended is 4.

PROJECT ASSIGNMENTS

1. Do a web research on http://neo.lcc.uma.es/radi-aeb/WebVRP/, which is a web-based academic learning site for vehicle route planning. Prepare a report on using algorithms for a hypothetical case: *Lat-Long* Converter, Angle and Distance Calculator.
   Vehicle-Routing Algorithm
   - Cluster *First-Route* Second Algorithm
   - Clustering Algorithm:
     - Sweep Algorithm
   - Routing Algorithm:
     - TSP (Travelling Salesman Problem)
       - Nearest Neighbour Algorithm
   - Load Optimization Algorithm
     - Data Compression Algorithm
   - LZW Data Compression Algorithm
   This would help to firm up discussions of this chapter.
2. Visit a leading retail store chain in your city. Analyse their transportation issues and practices adopted. Do they deploy milk run and cross-docking? If so, what are your observations?
3. Visit your nearest 3PL logistics company. Understand the scope of transportation issues with respect to local supplies and cross-country services and describe how they are scientifically managing to achieve a competitive advantage.
4. Discuss with an export-oriented company about how they are handling issues with respect to container movement and return load management. Are rates negotiated keeping the return load in mind? What are the service factors? How effective is contract negotiation and execution?
5. Meet the supply chain manager of a bulk material company that uses rail transport and map their issues against how they are handled.

REFERENCES

Ballou, H. Ronald, *Business Logistics/Supply Chain Management*, Pearson Education, 5th Edition

Chandra, Pankaj and Devanath Tirupati, 'Managing Complex Networks in Emerging Markets: The Story of Amul,' Working Paper No. 2002-05-06, Indian Institute of Management, Ahmedabad, 2002

Chopra, Sunil and Peter Meindl, *Supply Chain Management: Strategy, Planning and Operation*, Pearson Education, second edition

Indian Supply Chain Analytic Network (ISCAN), Volume I, 2005, Published by CII Institute of Logistics, 2005, www.ciilogistics.com

LOG.india Year book 2008, A DVV Media Group Publication, Vol. I, Issue: 1, www.log-india.com

Raghuram, G. and J. Shah, 'Roadmap for Logistics Excellence: Need to Break the Unholy Equilibrium,' IIMA working paper No. 2004-08-02, 2004

www.inboundlogistics.com

www.indianrailways.gov.in/deptts/commercial/frt-rates0607/frt-tbl-cls220.htm

www.infreight.com/Downloads/INFREIGHT.pdf

www.walmartstores.com/download/2314.pdf

CASE STUDY: INFREIGHT LOGISTICS SOLUTIONS LTD

Transportation Led Logistics Player in India

(This content is based on web research and the author has no intention to comment on the performance and claims of business discussed here and will not be responsible for any pecuniary damage either to the company or readers for arriving at any decision based on this. This is meant for academic purposes only.)

Infreight Logistics Solutions Limited (Infreight) is engaged in the business of logistics operations, consulting, contracting, and technology services such as developing transport management system, vehicle tracking units, warehouse management system, and so on.

Origin and Evolution

Infreight started as a neutral portal for the transport industry after venturing into logistics operations, for transportation in particular, to do price discovery for transportation services in the year 2000. Over a period of time, due to the expertise it had gained in the field of logistics and the transport industry, it has diversified its services to logistics operations, consultancy, and technology services for its corporate clients, identifying right transporters for the right clients through transporter short-listing and contracting. Apart from contracting, Infreight also appraises the service levels of contracted transport service providers in the light of expectations of the clients and as per the industry standards.

Infreight has benchmarked the freight rates for various sectors, segments, and types of vehicle and through this, fixes the ideal freight rates for specific movements all over India. Infreight is a subsidiary of Sundaram Finance Limited. The Infreight Management Team is one of the leading truck financing companies in India. One may appreciate the synergy in Sundaram Finance promoting Infreight for the success of its clients and organizing the sector more effectively because in India, transportation is largely an unorganized sector.

Infreight offerings include:
- 3PL for corporate shippers, both inbound and outbound, with optional transit insurance
- Facilitate JIT and Batch production/despatch
- Expertise in milk run and long-haul operations
- Logistics consultancy to its corporate clients as part of 4PL service
- Technology services like developing transport management system and vehicle tracking units

One may note that the services currently are based on expertise in the transportation sector.

Customers

Infreight customers are from logistics service business, engineering, auto and auto components, food, the consumer products segment, and engineering, apart from others. Some of the major clients as mentioned by them on their website are as follows:
- Amul Dairy Products
- Parle Products Ltd
- Kellogg's
- Mohan Breweries and Distilleries Limited
- L'Oreal
- Pantaloon Retail India Limited—Big Bazaar
- ABRL (Aditya Birla Retail Limited)
- LG Electronics India
- Whirlpool
- Caterpillar India Private Limited (automobile MNC)
- Carborundum Universal Ltd
- BILT
- TVS Tyres
- TVS Logistics Services Limited (largest automobile 3PL in India)
- Binny CFS

Infreight, along with TVS Logistics India Ltd, is understood to have successfully implemented milk run operations for Tata Motors Limited, Pune and entire Maharashtra; line-haul operations for General Motors, Gujarat, and such similar operations across India.

Being the operational service partner to a major automobile 3PL company that has a global presence, Infreight has imbibed global standards by virtue of its thrust for continuous improvement in the area of supply chain. It has also reinforced the experience to serve all sorts of industries such as pharma, FMCG, consumer electronics, automobiles, agriculture, and ODC (over dimension cargo).

Questions

1. Based on web research, evaluate the strengths, weaknesses, opportunities, and threats for Infreight. Evaluate their strategy and provide future direction.

2. Using web-based research and competitive intelligence, map Infreight among 3PL, 4PL, and transport companies on various parameters like business focus, growth, and strategic initiatives.

7

Network Decisions—Key Balancing Issue

Learning Objectives

After studying this chapter, you will be able to:
- Understand the different choices of network configurations and the impact of any specific configuration on service and cost factors
- Understand the challenges in configuring a network option for any business
- Comprehend the tools and models for decision making with respect to facility location, facility capacity, and demand allocation
- Understand sensitivity analysis and use of simulation as a tool
- Gain an insight into analysis and selection of a specific network

7.1 CHOICES OF NETWORK CONFIGURATIONS

In this chapter, you will understand issues relating to designing and managing a network in a supply chain. A distribution network in a supply chain comes into play in backward linkages—the linkages of the nodal organization or the manufacturer with its suppliers—and in forward linkages—the linkages of the nodal organization or the manufacturer to make the product reach the ultimate customer. The latter is more commonly referred to as channels of distribution and management. It has two components: primary distribution and secondary distribution. Primary distribution is from the manufacturer to the mother warehouses, dealers, and CFAs, till the point when the goods reflect on the stock of the nodal organization and move out from the manufacturer's account to that of the channel players'. Secondary distribution is when the product moves from the dealers to the retailers and the ultimate customers. Earlier, companies were focused mostly on primary distribution. There used to be a tendency for lumping the movement of goods in a month or a quarter end to show sales. Many a time, the nodal organization did not get a realistic picture of the final demand pattern, because data capture was difficult. This practice was common in FMCG, pharmaceuticals, consumer products in the electronics and home segment, and so on. Today, companies are deploying technology to capture information as it plays a critical role in the configuration of the distribution network. Information brings immense value to the distribution network as it provides more understanding about the system to the ultimate customer. For example, there may be a demand for a product, which may not be available with the dealer but may be in any part in the system and there could be a demand and supply mismatch within the system. Information makes it possible to track the product and hence facilitate the flow of goods for serving the ultimate customer. For example, a customer asks for a blue motorcycle while finalizing purchase at a showroom. The distributor concerned may not have stock of that particular SKU. If he/she could get into the stock information network and track the availability of a blue motorcycle across systems, including that of nearby dealers, he/she may still not lose the customer. Such is the importance of information visibility in a distribution network.

Distribution network is structuring of nodes and flow through links. Nodes are facilities, which could be manufacturing units, distribution centres, or warehouses, and flows are movements of goods between two points or nodes in order to reach the customer ultimately. Distribution network maps both physical and information flows. The objectives of a distribution network are:

1. The customer needs should be met.
2. Cost should match a given service level.

A distribution network decision could be influenced by:

1. Location of facilities, like manufacturing units and/or distribution centres
2. Movement configuration, speed, and cost of service
3. Level of responsiveness required

Design options would be as follows:

1. Direct shipping
   (a) Supplier to customer site
   (b) Manufacturer to customer
2. Through intermediary
   (a) Manufacturer to customer with in-transit merge
   (b) Delivery responsibility with intermediary
   (c) Delivery responsibility with carrier
3. Customer pick-up
   (a) From distribution centre
   (b) From retail

Each of the above options must be evaluated keeping in mind the cost and service factors. Cost factors are more linked to supply chain drivers, namely, the location of facilities, inventory, transportation, and information, whereas service factors would be response time, visibility, availability, and post-sale service including returns management.

7.1.1 Direct Shipping

Direct shipping in network distribution is an important option, especially in case of capital goods, industrial products, and items that are generally made-to-engineering wherein the nodal organization has to be necessarily in touch with the customer to make custom-designed products. There are two options in direct shipping: direct from supplier and direct from manufacturer.

From Supplier to Customer

The direct shipping design option would be suitable for capital goods in a project site. In such cases, the manufacturer identifies the supplier of certain components that are to be shipped directly to the customer site where value addition would happen. In such cases, there is no intermediary involved except for the transporter, who is a contract operator responsible for the movement of goods. The advantage in such a configuration is that the intermediary is completely eliminated, which reduces dwell time—the customer can directly coordinate with the manufacturer and supplier—and improves the profit margin—no margin has to be set aside for the intermediary.

Few variants of this model are possible, like an order may be booked through an intermediary who could be a selling agent while the manufacturer takes charge of delivery. Direct shipping from supplier to customer is organized in case of spare parts as well as where the manufacturer must only be informed of parts failure and the physical flow need not be through the manufacturer.

From Manufacturer to Customer

In the case of direct shipping from manufacturer to customer, the physical movement of goods would go from the manufacturer's facility to the customer location. In such cases, orders could be direct or through an intermediary, but the delivery is direct. Typically, these are the cases where, like capital goods, the intermediary has a limited role of facilitating order procurement. The requirement finalization and delivery are to be decided directly by the buyer and the seller, and generally the information exchange on technology could be higher.

However, this option is now commonly used for certain kinds of consumer electronic goods and related products where orders can be placed online and the product is shipped directly from the manufacturer's production site. E-business is assuming great significance not only in the case of consumer electronics but also for perishables and low-value items. For example, you can send flowers to any part of India by placing the order online. But business in this case is quite challenging. In this case, the buyer who pays for flowers to be gifted is the customer and the recipient is the customer's nominee. The nodal organization in this transaction is floraindia.com, which is a transaction website. The financial flow is organized through a payment gateway, which accepts payment through credit cards, debit cards, or through online bank transfer. The information flow is ensured through emails after the order is placed on the web. The physical flow happens through the vendors of floraindia.com located at various cities who serve through direct shipping on instructions from floraindia.com. It is a combination of directing shipping from the supplier and the nodal organization, and the responsibility lies with the nodal organization, namely floraindia.com. Exhibit 7.1 provides an insight into such an operation.

It may be observed that direct shipping would work in specific situations and product categories and would impact drivers and service parameters. These factors are summarized in Table 7.1.

Exhibit 7.1   FloraIndia.com: Direct to Customers

FloraIndia.com was formed by a handful of individuals who brought their collective experiences to start this unique business of sending flowers to any corners of India. They set up a nationwide network of florists, flower growers, and export markets to ensure that all the flowers collected are of the best quality and price. They have a well-defined vendor management policy with integrated flash points to identify any variations. Their website showcases all the different flowers/bouquets/packages available and you can place your order online. The fresh flowers are hand-delivered to the receiver by local florists in the respective cities.

Source: Adapted from http://www.floraindia.com/, accessed on 1 March 2009.

It is clear that direct shipping options work in cases where there is an order that requires planning and customization, which could be for capital goods or an order on the web. One of the classic cases is of Dell Computers, which customizes personal computers to the buyers' demand. Once the order is placed, Dell delivers directly to the customer through its partners, making the customer feel special.

7.1.2   Distribution through Intermediary

Channel partners, popularly known as intermediaries, play an important role in the distribution network of a large number of product groups, spanning from FMCG to

Table 7.1   Direct shipping: supplier to customer

Driver/Factor	Comments
Facilities and handling	Aggregation of facilities would reduce cost.
Inventory	Aggregation is possible as facilities are centralized. However, in cases like floraindia.com, where vendors are contracted inventory aggregation is difficult. However, demand management on a large variety of orders reduces inventory.
Transportation	Higher transportation cost as outbound would be disaggregated and could be in small parcels and LTLs.
Information	Significantly high network of information flow is required as order tracking, visibility, and exchange of technical details are critical to ensure smooth transaction. Information flow is key for the financial flow, which happens on the confirmation of the physical flow.
Response time	Response time could be longer because of the nature of transaction and centralization of servicing. However, typically customers who are transacting in this model would be keener on delivery as per their requirement rather than delivery in the shortest possible time. There is a scope for the nodal organization to agree on the delivery time and deliver accordingly.
Order visibility	An important factor from the customer's perspective. The manufacturers are now more transparent. This requires investment on IT and policy.
Availability	High product availability is easy to provide because there is aggregation and also most of these are made-to-order products, which brings in some flexibility.
	Major issue could be in the case of web-based order procurement and contract supplies where availability of product variants could be difficult to manage.
Post-sale service and returns management	Difficult, complicated, and expensive.

capital goods. The role and importance of channel partners vary with the requirements of a network.

Manufacturer to Customer with Intermediary Value Addition

In this case, products undergo value addition during the process of movement. The responsibility of such value addition can be in physical form, in carriage, or by way of packaging, and so on. This value addition happens at the stage of transit as the intermediary can impart value to a product by way of specialized skills, or knowledge, or the capability to meet a customer requirement. For example, a car dealer can add value at the time of delivery to a customer by providing accessories such as upholstery, body-colour bumpers, music system, and so on. A manufacturer would also prefer this part of delivery to the customer to be handled by the dealer, as the customer contact is closest at that level.

Similarly, one can look at the case of goods that are imported in bulk and distributed in a country like India. In this case, the intermediary adds a lot of value by repacking in market lot packs. This happens in case of imported FMCG goods and other consumer items. For example, biscuits, chocolates, fruits and vegetables, dry fruits and host food items, personal care products, and so on, go through this process. Apart from FMCG goods, a number of engineering and capital goods are also subjected to in-transit value addition. These goods are imported through an intermediary and value added either through installation and delivery of engineered items or combined with MRO (Maintenance, Repairs, and Overhaul) operations as it is economically unviable for the OE (Original Equipment) to set up such facilities. The other feature of intermediary value addition are discussed in Table 7.2.

Such intermediary-driven relationships may face problems because of poor relationship management, inadequate economic viability, or change in socio, economic, and political situations. Exhibit 7.2 gives one such example wherein the company was required to take up direct delivery and re-establish networks in order to regain its position in the market.

One can also come across examples of an intermediary providing value addition in backward linkages as well. Classic examples would be a milk run wherein the transporter coordinates with suppliers and schedules pick-up, with the third-party logistics provider taking care of kitting, assembling, MRO, and so on. All such activities have an impact on cost efficiency and responsiveness with respect to supply chain drivers such as inventory, transportation, facility, and information.

Direct-delivery Responsibility of the Distributor

A distributor handles direct delivery only in cases where there are last-mile delivery issues and the manufacturer prefers the distributor to deliver directly at customer locations. A classic example is the bottled drinking water segment in India, which has seen fierce competition among Kinley, Aquafina, Bisleri, and a host of local brands. The bottled water is delivered directly by the distributors so that they can efficiently handle last-mile delivery problems relating to quality and customer contact, and resolve dealer complaints, if any. Exhibit 7.3 mentions one such by Kinley in Chennai, south India.

Exhibit 7.2 UB International and Its Distribution Management in Nigeria

UB International (UBI) drives the marketing and sales of UB's biscuits and snacks around the world. UBI develops markets and ensures availability in many countries. This is achieved either through direct representation in these countries or through an authorized distributor. The role of the authorized distributor is to represent UBI in the country and distribute imported biscuits in the agreed market with SKUs suitable for the market. Canada, USA, Sweden, Greece, Italy, Portugal, Middle East, Australia, India, and Nigeria are identified as key markets.

Their experience in Nigeria is a good example of UB International's marketing and distribution. McVitie's has been a recognized and established brand within Nigeria since the 1980s when it was the number one imported biscuit brand.

A government embargo on imported biscuits resulted in UB's biscuits being banned and subsequently sales were lost in the Nigerian market. In order to maintain a presence in this market, UB set up a local co-manufacturing agreement to make biscuits in Nigeria.

UB International is now re-building distribution and expanding production capabilities to develop a range of Nigerian products produced locally to meet consumer demand.

Although there are around 500,000 stores in Nigeria, only 20 of these are supermarkets. The vast majority of stores are small kiosks or simply tabletops. A successful piece of POS designed to adapt to such stores has been the introduction of a hanger, which is used to hang ten packs of McVitie's Digestives. This is used extensively and has the added advantage of acting as a hanging billboard for the brand.

Source: Adapted from http://www.mcvities.com/, accessed on 3 March 2009.

There are many other products where last-mile delivery by distributor is practised. Consumer electronics for the home segment is another example. Customers buy products from dealers and the dealers deliver and install the products as per the terms set by manufacturers. The manufacturer's call centre calls the customer to ensure that the product was delivered intact and as promised and lists for warranty. The role of the distributor is critical in attracting and serving the customer.

The previous option, of value addition and delivery by an intermediary, and the current option of delivery by the dealers can be considered as variants of the same distribution option except that the latter is more of delivery management. Because it is delivery management, inventory could be less compared to the previous option. The other factors and impacts are almost the same.

Delivery Responsibility with Carrier

In this distribution option, manufacturers engage distributors and/or carriers who would deliver goods to customers. In India, when state sales tax was imposed on goods, air conditioner manufacturers would book sale for delivery from the factory through a dealer, and the delivery would be by a carrier. For example, let's assume

---

Exhibit 7.3 Kinley Water for Home Segment

Kinley Water—a product of the Coca-Cola Company—is the established market leader in the bottled drinking water segment. In Chennai, Kinley Water is produced, bottled, and distributed by S. R. Water Company (P) Limited. The company's state-of-the-art production and bottling plant is the largest bulk water manufacturing plant in South Asia. Kinley Water reaches 10,000 customers through a 40-strong distributor network, backed by a 24-hour customer call centre.

Source: Adapted from http://www.srwater.com/, accessed on 4 March 2009.

Table 7.2 Manufacturer to customer, with intermediary value addition

Driver/Factor	Comments
Facilities and handling	Aggregation of manufacturing facilities would reduce cost but distribution centres are to be disaggregated. The intermediary must be capable of value addition and be able to satisfy customers as it would directly affect the manufacturer's brand value.
Inventory	Inventory would increase as there is disaggregation, and dwell time would depend upon time for value addition. If value addition is like MRO, it is mainly in case of push strategies where goods need to be in order till there's demand. In such cases, the inventory decision is independent of this as it depends on the quality of the demand estimate. In cases of pull and where there is dwell time, efficiency in managing the processes matters.
Transportation	Higher transportation cost as outbound would be disaggregated and could be in small parcels and LTLs.
Information	Significantly high network of information flow is required as order tracking, visibility, and exchange of technical details are critical to ensure smooth transaction. The intermediary should have the required information infrastructure investment.
Response time	Response time could be less than direct shipping as the product is available in stock most of the time. Value addition is possible while in transit.
Order visibility	Important from the customer's and the manufacturer's perspectives as most of the time the manufacturer could be directly in touch or indirectly sensitive to the brand value based on the quality of value addition.
Availability	The product can be made easily available because it is mass produced and is nearing completion. Mostly, the goods are in CKD/SKD forms and need assembling time. SKUs and product variants can also be more as the intermediary handles postponement and customizes the product close to market.
Post-sale service and returns management	Intermediary handles the same.

that an air conditioner is booked for sale by a dealer in a city, say Chennai, for delivery from a state union territory where tax rates are lower. The customer agrees to wait for five days for delivery. The sale is aggregated at the end of the day and sent to the factory. The factory books with the service provider, who is typically a contracted small parcel company like Gati, to handle delivery and coordinate with the customer. This model is not practised anymore because of restructuring of sales tax and introduction of VAT. However, there are many other situations where this model still works. For example, all goods that are sold online are delivered through a carrier who aggregates and brings economies in delivery. These carriers have a network of delivery depots/offices, and managing delivery is their core competence. One can observe this practice in the delivery of credit cards and financial instruments wherein the nodal agency informs the customer that their delivery agent would handle the physical component. This model would also work for medium to fast-moving goods and where delivery expertise is required to give a satisfactory experience to the customers.

As seen in Table 7.3, the distributor plays a key role in the supply chain, especially for FMCG, consumer electronics, and certain other product categories, and wherever

Table 7.3 Delivery by distributor

Driver/Factor	Comments
Facilities and handling	Distributors may reduce display and showroom cost and manage sales through catalogues and samples. Facilities like DCs will have to be effectively used to reduce overall marketing costs.
Inventory	Inventory would increase as there is disaggregation.
Transportation	Transportation may reduce as the goods can be shipped in bulk up to the warehouse, from where small packs are sent to the customer. Customers generally pick up this cost.
Information	Significantly high network of information flow is required as order tracking and visibility are important. The customer must be comfortable with the time window of delivery for every specific transaction.
Response time	Response time could be faster but customers must understand dwell time and movement time between stages.
Order visibility	Important for all stakeholders in a supply chain.
Availability	Standard products and specification, which could be as per catalogue, would be easily available on demand.
Post-sale service and returns management	Intermediary handles the same.

the market is dispersed like in the case of reaching the rural market in India. Strategists focus on building and nurturing a dealer network and the value of such a network is very high in these businesses.

7.1.3 Customer Pick-up

The distribution network can be configured in such a way that customers pick up goods in a supply chain network. It is important to understand situations in which such a configuration would work. Depending upon the distribution network, customers would pick up goods from a distribution centre or from a retail store.

Customer Pick-up from Distribution Centre

In this configuration, dealers and retailers sell goods that are to be picked up by the customer from the distribution centre. Typically, a number of goods in India are sold in this manner, in a slightly disguised manner. For example, in case of home furniture, consumer electronics, and automobiles, the sale process is completed when a customer inspects the product in a showroom and books a sale. As the display pieces in a showroom are not sold, the delivery of brand new pieces is undertaken from the distribution centre. Even the customer wants a brand new piece. As far as delivery is concerned, the retailer/dealer gives the customer an option of taking the delivery himself/herself, or arranges the delivery through a third-party, for which the customer pays. Once the sale gets over, the risk of transportation is with the customer. This is quite common for home goods, consumer electronics, automobiles, and so on.

The rationale for this distribution network is that there may be multiple distributors for a product in an area but only one distribution centre (See Table 7.4). For example,

Table 7.4   Customer pick-up from distribution centres

Driver/Factor	Comments
Facilities and handling	Standard products, where the sale is through the Internet, or through a distributor using catalogues, or in showrooms with product displays. Space management is critical in a DC. The dealer's ability to manage the cost and efficiency of DC operations is vital for success.
Inventory	Inventory would increase as there is disaggregation. Though it is treated as inventory in books of distributors, it certainly affects the overall inventory.
Transportation	Though the transportation cost is borne by the customer, the DC is located at a place where the demand is most concentrated in order to reduce the cost.
Information	Though there are multiple DCs and communication is important, the information network in practice is not developed to that extent.
Response time	Response time is fast as the customer is served instantaneously.
Order visibility	Limited visibility at secondary distribution level.
Availability	Standard products, with specifications as per the catalogue, would be available.
Post-sale service and returns management	Intermediary handles the same.

in case of the cement industry, especially in a rural market, this may be the case. Many times, retail customers also pick up from the distributor's warehouse. This happens in consumer products, home products, building materials, and so on, wherein the territory would be earmarked for distribution rights. There is a tendency in customers to look for landed price arbitrage and choose a distributor based on the convenience of distribution centre operation.

Customer Pick-up from Retail Storage

In this distribution management option, goods are sold by retail in the supply chain network. Customers walk into a retail store and pick up a product on completion of sale. Numerous examples are seen in everyday life. This includes the sale of FMCG goods such as grocery, pharmaceuticals, perishables, consumer electronics, and fashion items such as jewellery, clothing, food, and so on. The rationale behind this structure is that these are all mass demand products that must be distributed through convenience and speciality retail stores that bring in economies in buying for customers and also ensure availability of many goods under one roof. The focal organization is cognizant of the fact that its competition would also be wooing the customer, especially in the convenience and general category of retail, and brand loyalty is going to be critical for the success of business.

It can be seen from Table 7.5 that different configurations of distribution are possible and each has its own impact on supply chain drivers.

7.2   CHALLENGES IN CONFIGURING A NETWORK

There are numerous challenges in setting up distribution management. At the outset, let's analyse the process of distribution and understand its role in the supply chain.

Table 7.5 Customer pick-up from retail

Driver/Factor	Comments
Facilities and handling	Retail business is integrated into a supply chain network with the choice of multiple brands and multiple organizations sold in an outlet for each category. There are some cases where the focal organization maintains its own speciality retail outlet like in the case of Bata, Nike, Tanishq (of the TATA group), and so on. In such cases, it becomes expensive.
Inventory	Inventory would increase as there is disaggregation. Though normally treated as inventory in books of retailers, it has an impact on overall inventory. Speciality stores are improving inventory management through customer relationship management (CRM) and application of technology. Inventory is a key challenge as many a time the absence of an SKU leads to the loss of a basket of sale as a customer walks into the next store. Flooding of inventory increases the cost of inventory management and pricing strategy as it has to be liquidated at a certain point.
Transportation	As customers pick up goods from retail stores, they are not treated as key decision variable. However, the location of the retailer is important. An increase in the number of retail outlets increases the distribution cost of the focal organization. In concepts like Cash & Carry wholesalers, members, mainly small retail stores, pick up goods and are responsible for transportation.
Information	Being a part of secondary distribution, many times a focal organization finds it difficult to get information on stock and movement patterns. Now Point of Sale software and device are being increasingly deployed and linked to various points in the supply chain to analyse data on sales and movement. However, these are still limited to store level tracking except in the case of a speciality store. For example, in a jewellery showroom of a leading brand, the customer did not find a piece of jewellery shown in the catalogue. Immediately, the store manager linked to other stores to find out in which other store the stock is available, and found that he/she could not promise delivery from the stocks of any store. Then the manager linked up to the production-planning department and found that the SKU is in production and promised delivery in twenty-one days. On the evening of the twentieth day, a confirmatory mail was sent and a telephone call was made to the customer to take delivery on the next day. Such CRM with information tie-up, boosting SCM, is being practiced in a few cases.
Response time	The customer is served instantaneously at the retail outlet. Since this is a push-based supply chain for focal organization, they look at this factor from the planning time bucket and for new product categories.
Order visibility	Limited visibility at the secondary distribution level.
Availability	Since this is a push-based supply chain, the product availability is limited to demand patterns. There could be certain non-moving SKUs and categories where there could be the problem of availability. Customer-service level is a predetermined factor in this option.
Post-sale service and returns management	Intermediary handles the same.

According to one definition, a network is more of nodes and movement and can be either in backward or forward linkages. In a supply chain, where a product of a focal organization gains value at different stages—right from the source of the material to reaching the final customer—a distribution network comes into play wherever there is a facility to store, or a scope to add value, or where some movement is involved.

Alternatively, SCOR defines distribution following manufacture. A supply chain analyst should have knowledge about the span of a distribution network. Generally, the definition of distribution management as part of forward linkages is widely accepted. However, a network includes both backward and forward linkages.

A distribution network is evaluated on:

1. Responsiveness, which is the ability to serve the customer
2. Cost of serving the customer

These happen to be the two objectives of a supply chain that work in conflict because any organization would like to maximize the level of service at the least affordable cost. An organization must balance cost and service level; however, if the service level needs to be maximum, cost must not be a constraint.

From the previous section it is evident that configurations are determined by product characteristics, industry practice, customer expectations, and macro policies such as tax structures and so on. These determine the configuration of supply chain drivers for a network decision, and the chosen network gives standard service parameters such as response time, availability, information visibility, and customer satisfaction.

A challenge in configuring a distribution network is how to balance the given constraints to achieve the desired objective of distribution cost management or maximization of profit. One has to necessarily take certain macro factors as given and work on endogenous variables to arrive at an optimal solution.

7.3   TOOLS AND MODELS AVAILABLE

It is evident from the above discussion that trade-offs between supply chain efficiency and responsiveness in a supply chain are unavoidable and co-exist in all firms. A firm needs to consider a lot of competitive factors and have a competitive structure as mentioned earlier. The decision-making process should help the firm to locate the facilities by trading-off responsiveness with cost efficiency, optimally. This section elaborates on the models and tools available for this process.

In order to make this decision-making process more amenable to modelling, it is required to have some level of aggregation and to limit the analysis to crucial factors. Typically, the production costs, inventory-carrying costs, and transportation costs are the crucial factors for the facilities decision, and the discussion is limited to these factors and assumes that the other competitive factors have already been accounted for. So, responsiveness in case of designing new production facilities is basically locating facilities as near to the distribution centre as possible, while achieving supply chain efficiency by minimizing the total production costs, inventory carrying costs, and transportation costs.

However, responsiveness in case of designing new warehouses or distribution centres is locating facilities as near to the distribution centre or retailers as possible, while achieving supply chain efficiency by minimizing the total inventory-carrying costs and transportation costs. The more the responsiveness, the more the number of facilities and the more decentralized the network is, whereas the more the supply chain cost efficiency, the more are the economies of scale.

The facilities decision process involves a number of constraints on the supply chain network. The constraints actually depend on whether the process addresses a strategic-level decision or an operational-level decision. Usually, strategic decisions are limited to factors already discussed earlier and do not consider operational factors such as the seasonality of demand, the amount of inventory in each period, and so on, whereas a tactical decision would involve accounting for these factors. The discussion is limited to the strategic level.

All through the discussion, the choice variables or decision variables that are associated with each supply chain network configuration are not mentioned. The choice variables for the facilities decision-making process include the amount of products to be shipped from each facility to each market and the number of facilities to be opened based on the demand from the markets and total costs.

The course of this decision-making process is too complicated to be solved manually. However, models and computational tools are available to help firms in implementing this process. Problems faced while deciding how to model facilities are covered in the next section. The subsequent discussion covers the various tools available for use in this decision-making process.

The computational tools can be broadly classified into two categories—exact methods (provides optimal solution for the problem) and approximate methods (provides sub-optimal solutions for the problem). Table 7.6 provides the pros and cons of each method.

The selection of a tool depends on the extent of trade-off between the scale of the problem and the computational time available for the decision-making process. The ensuing discussion is limited to exact methods.

7.3.1 A Strategic Facility Location Model with Single Capacity Choice

As mentioned by Daskin, Snyder, and Berger (2003), supply chain management entails not only the movement of goods but also decisions about:

1. where to produce, what to produce, and how much to produce at each site
2. what quantity of goods to hold in inventory at each stage of the process
3. how to share information among parties in the process
4. where to locate plants and distribution centres

In this section, one would look at facility-location decisions. This strategic model is useful in setting up facilities at the right locations given the number of potential facility locations and their associated capacities, fixed costs, and variable costs. The objective of such a model would be to minimize the total cost. The constraints of the model include satisfying the demand from various regions and also not exceeding the capacity of each plant. The decision variables would be: (a) number of units to be transported between facilities and markets/warehouses, and (b) which facilities should serve the market. This decision problem can be formulated as an Integer Programming (IP) problem, the answer to which provides an optimal solution for the

Table 7.6 Pros and cons of various methods

Exact methods	Approximate methods
Uses mathematically sound techniques such as linear programming, integer programming, non-linear integer programming.	Uses rough-cut methods and heuristics (common-sense rules) for the solution.
Provides optimal solution.	Provides sub-optimal solution. The deviation varies from instance to instance.
Computational time varies from instance to instance and is unpredictable. Could go from minutes to hours or even days before giving optimal solution. Useful for small-scale instances.	Computational time varies little from instance to instance and is predictable. Could be used for large-scale instances.
Requires good knowledge of mathematical concepts such as simplex method and so on.	Requires little or no knowledge of mathematics.
Small-scale problems can be solved using software such as MS-Excel. Solving large-scale problems with sophisticated techniques require commercial software tools such as Lindo, Cplex, Xpress-MP, and so on. The downside is, commercial licences are required for business applications.	Requires only commonly used software tools that are available widely. Anybody who has knowledge of a programming language (Excel, C, C++, Java, and so on) can implement. So, virtually a no-cost alternative.

problem. The details of inputs, decision variables, and the model are given in the subsequent paragraphs.

This problem can then be formulated as an IP problem:

$$\min \sum_{i=1}^{n} f_i z_i + \sum_{j=1}^{m} \sum_{i=1}^{n} c_{ij} x_{ij}$$

subject to

$$\sum_{i=1}^{n} x_{ij} = D_j \ \text{ for all } j = 1, 2, 3, ..., m \tag{7.1}$$

$$\sum_{j=1}^{m} x_{ij} \leq S_i z_i \ \text{ for all } i = 1, 2, 3, ..., m \tag{7.2}$$

$$x_{ij} \in \text{ integers for all } i, j \tag{7.3}$$

$$z_i \in \{0, 1\} \text{ for all } i \tag{7.4}$$

where the inputs for the strategic facility location model with single capacity are as follows:

n = Number of possible facilities/locations

m = Number of potential markets

D_j = Annual demand from market j

S_i = Possible capacity of facility i

f_i = Fixed cost (annualized) if facility i is open

c_{ij} = Cost of production, inventory, and transportation from facility i to market j

and the decision variables of the model are as follows:

Table 7.7 Inputs for the mathematical model

Demand centres	Haryana	UP	Orissa	Maharashtra	Fixed cost	Low capacity
Demand regions, Variable costs (Rs/tonne), Fixed Costs (Rs/year), Capacities (tonnes/year), and Demands (tonnes/year)						
Haryana	400	1,500	3,200	3,350	65,000	50
UP	1,500	550	2,100	2,500	75,000	50
Orissa	3,200	2,100	600	2,700	68,000	50
Maharashtra	3,350	2,500	2,700	800	66,000	50
Demand	35	32	25	28		

x_{ij} = Number of units to be transported from facility i to market j

z_i = 1, if facility i is open, 0 otherwise

The objective function minimizes the total fixed cost and variable costs. Constraint 7.1 ensures that the total units produced and shipped across regions from each facility satisfy the demand from each market. The constraint on capacity such that total units shipped from a facility i to market j should not violate the facility's capacity is taken care of by equation 7.2. Then the nature of decision variables: (a) Quantity shipped from a facility to market is continuous and non-negative is taken care of by equation 7.3. (b) The question of whether to open or close a facility is answered by equation 7.4.

As an example of such a problem, consider a hypothetical example of WheatCorp, a roller flour mill unit that caters to different wheat flour distribution centres across India. The management team of WheatCorp is planning to expand the unit. The management has shortlisted the following regions with different demands, capacities, fixed costs, and variable costs after analysing the demand for wheat across various regions, competitive factors, market structure, and product characteristics.

The management of WheatCorp wants to know where the facilities are to be located and how much each facility should contribute to the overall demand. The IP model given above will help in answering the questions faced by WheatCorp.

In order to implement the above example, MS Excel is used. First, the inputs required for solving the model are fed from Table 7.7. The data entered is shown in Figure 7.1:

	A	B	C	D	E	F	G	H	I
1		Inputs for the model: Variable costs (in Rs./Tonne), Fixed Costs (Rs./Year), Capacities(Tonnes./Year) and Demands(Tonnes./Year)							
2									
3			Haryana	UP	Orissa	Maharashtra	Fixed Cost	Capacity	
4		Haryana	400	1500	3200	3350	65000	50	
5		UP	1500	550	2100	2500	75000	50	
6		Orissa	3200	2100	600	2700	68000	50	
7		Maharashtra	3350	2500	2700	800	66000	50	
8		Demand	35	32	25	28			

Note: In order to make it easy for handling numbers, demand and capacity are assumed at two digit levels. In real life, this could be in millions. This applies to all example problems in this chapter.

Figure 7.1 Inputs for the model

Next, the values for the decision variables required for the model are entered in the same sheet (as shown in Figure 7.2) and are set to zero initially:

	A	B	C	D	E	F	G	H	I
1		Inputs for the model: Variable costs (in Rs./Tonne), Fixed Costs (Rs./Year), Capacities(Tonnes./Year) and Demands(Tonnes./Year)							
2									
3			Haryana	UP	Orissa	Maharashtra	Fixed Cost	Capacity	
4		Haryana	400	1500	3200	3350	65000	50	
5		UP	1500	550	2100	2500	75000	50	
6		Orissa	3200	2100	600	2700	68000	50	
7		Maharashtra	3350	2500	2700	800	66000	50	
8		*Demand*	35	32	25	28			
9									
10		Decision variables: Demand Allocation between regions							
11			Haryana	UP	Orissa	Maharashtra	Plants (Open =1)		
12		Haryana	0	0	0	0	0		
13		UP	0	0	0	0	0		
14		Orissa	0	0	0	0	0		
15		Maharashtra	0	0	0	0	0		

Figure 7.2   Demand allocation

Then the excess capacity, unsatisfied demand, and objective function values are entered as in Figure 7.3.

	A	B	C	D	E	F	G	H
9								
10		Decision variables: Demand Allocation between regions						
11			Haryana	UP	Orissa	Maharashtra	Plants (Open =1)	
12		Haryana	0	0	0	0	0	
13		UP	0	0	0	0	0	
14		Orissa	0	0	0	0	0	
15		Maharashtra	0	0	0	0	0	
16								
17								
18		Unutilized Capacity						
19		0						
20		0						
21		0						
22		0						
23								
24		Unsatisfied Demand	35	32	25	28		
25								
26								
27		Objective Function	0					

Figure 7.3   Unsatisfied demand

The cell formulae to be entered in each of the data cells are given in Table 7.8.

The steps given above illustrate only the LHS of a constraint. In order to specify the inequality of constraints, the solver add-in feature of Excel is used. This could be found in the Tools section (MS-Office versions before 2007) or Data section (MS-Office versions from 2007). After invoking this solver add-in, set the target cell to be C27. Then specify the RHS and inequality nature of the model according to Table 7.9, using the Add button in the solver:

After entering the steps, click the Solve button. The results of the solve procedure are given in the screenshot shown in Figure 7.4. From the results table, you can observe the following:

	A	B	C	D	E	F	G	H
10			Decision variables: Demand Allocation between regions					
11			Haryana	UP	Orissa	Maharashtra	Plants (Open =1)	
12		Haryana	35	0	0	0	1	
13		UP	0	0	0	0	0	
14		Orissa	0	25	25	0	1	
15		Maharashtra	0	7	0	28	1	
16								
17								
18		Unutilized Capacity						
19		15						
20		0						
21		0						
22		15						
23								
24		Unsatisfied Demand	1.1268E-09	0	0	0		
25								
26								
27		Objective Function	320400					

Figure 7.4 Objective function

Table 7.8 Cell formulae for the Excel spreadsheet

Cell	Cell formula	Copied to	Remarks
B19	=G12*H4-SUM(C12:F12)	B20:B22	Eqn 4.2
C24	=C8-SUM(C12:C15)	D24:F24	Eqn 4.1
C27	=SUMPRODUCT(C4:F7,C12:F15) +SUMPRODUCT(G4:G7,G12:G15)	–	Objective Fn

Table 7.9 Entering the nature of constraints and RHS in Excel

Cell reference	Inequality/Type	RHS
B19:B22	>=	0
C12:F15	Integer	–
C12:F15	>=	0
C24:F24	=	0
G12:G15	Binary	–

1. Open the facilities only in Haryana, Orissa, and Maharashtra.
2. Serve the demand of Haryana from the Haryana facility.
3. Serve the demand of UP from the facilities located in Orissa and Maharashtra.
4. Serve the demand of Orissa from the Orissa facility.
5. Serve the demand of Maharashtra from the Maharashtra facility.

The total cost of the optimal solution is Rs 320,400 and this can be observed from the cell C27. The IP model for the facility location model considers only a single capacity choice. This model does not take advantage of the economies of scale offered when opening the facility. Investment in a high capacity may be only marginally higher than investing in a low capacity. So, the above model has to be extended to capture this additional feature. This is covered in the next section.

7.3.2 A Strategic Facility Location Model with the Choice of Two Capacities

The strategic facility location model with the choice of two capacities has the objective of minimizing the total costs (both fixed and variable) of opening and operating the facilities, which is the same as the previous model. The constraints of the model given in section 7.3.1 are appropriately extended to ensure that there can be only a low-capacity or high-capacity facility in a demand region. This also requires us to use an additional binary decision variable to identify whether to open a facility or not. The inputs, decision variables, and the IP model are discussed below.

This problem can then be formulated as an IP problem:

$$\min \sum_{i=1}^{n} f_i (z_i + y_i) + \sum_{j=1}^{m} \sum_{i=1}^{n} c_{ij} x_{ij}$$

subject to

$$\sum_{i=1}^{n} x_{ij} = D_j \text{ for all } j = 1, 2, 3, ..., m \tag{7.5}$$

$$\sum_{j=1}^{m} x_{ij} \leq SL_i z_i + SH_i y_i \text{ for all } i = 1, 2, 3, ..., n \tag{7.6}$$

$$z_i + y_i \leq 1 \; for \; all \; i = 1, 2, 3, ..., n \qquad (7.7)$$
$$x_{ij} \in integer \; for \; all \; i, j \qquad (7.8)$$
$$y_i, z_i \in \{0, 1\} \; for \; all \; i \qquad (7.9)$$

where the inputs for the strategic single facility location model are:

$n =$ Number of possible facilities/locations

$m =$ Number of potential markets

$D_j =$ Annual demand from market j

$SL_i =$ Possible low capacity for facility i

$SH_i =$ Possible high capacity for facility i

$F_i =$ Fixed cost (annualized) if facility i is open

$c_j^i =$ Cost of production and transportation from facility i to market j

And the decision variables for the model are given below:

$x_{ij} =$ Number of units to be transported from facility i to market j

$z_i = 1$, if facility i with low capacity is open, 0 otherwise

$y_i = 1$, if facility i with high capacity is open, 0 otherwise

Demand satisfaction of each market is taken care of by equation 7.5. Constraint 7.6 ensures that the total units shipped do not exceed the total capacity. Either a low-capacity or a high-capacity plant alone should be open. Equation 7.7 ensures this. Equations 7.8 and 7.9 are integer and binary restrictions for the decision variables.

In order to implement this model, the hypothetical example of WheatCorp is used. WheatCorp has the option of opening either a low-capacity facility of 40 tonnes or a high-capacity facility of 50 tonnes. The fixed costs of setting up high-capacity facilities and the other input data for the model are provided in Table 7.10:

The Excel solver is used for implementing the model. The screenshot for the data, decision variables, and the constraints are shown below in Figure 7.5:

Table 7.10 Input data for the mathematical model

Inputs for the model: Variable costs (in Rs/tonne), Fixed Costs (Rs/year), Capacities (tonnes/year), and Demands (tonnes/year)								
	Haryana	UP	Orissa	Maharashtra	Fixed Cost	Low capacity	Fixed cost	High capacity
Haryana	400	1,500	3,200	3,350	65,000	40	70,000	50
UP	1,500	550	2,100	2,500	75,000	40	82,000	50
Orissa	3,200	2,100	600	2,700	68,000	40	740,00	50
Maharashtra	3,350	2,500	2,700	800	66,000	40	72,000	50
Demand	35	32	25	28				

	Haryana	UP	Orissa	Maharashtra	Fixed Cost	Low Capacity	Fixed Cost	High Capacity
				Inputs for the model: Variable costs (in Rs./Tonne), Fixed Costs (Rs./Year), Capacities(Tonnes./Year) and Demands(Tonnes./Year)				
Haryana	400	1500	3200	3350	65000	40	70000	50
UP	1500	550	2100	2500	75000	40	82000	50
Orissa	3200	2100	600	2700	68000	40	74000	50
Maharashtra	3350	2500	2700	800	66000	40	72000	50
Demand	35	32	25	28				

	Haryana	UP	Orissa	Maharashtra	Plants (Open =1)	Plants (Open =1)	Total Plants Constraint
				Decision Variables: Demand Allocation between regions			
Haryana	0	0	0	0	0	0	0
UP	0	0	0	0	0	0	0
Orissa	0	0	0	0	0	0	0
Maharashtra	0	0	0	0	0	0	0

Unutilized Capacity
0
0
0
0

Unsatisfied Demand	35	32	25	28	0

Objective Function	0

Figure 7.5   Decision variables and constraints

The appropriate cell formulae for entering the constraints are provided in Table 7.11. After entering the cell formulae, use the solver add-in to specify the constraint cell references and their inequalities as shown in Table 7.12.

The screenshot before solving the model is shown in Figure 7.6.

	B	C	D	E	F	G	H	I	J	K
4	Haryana	400	1500	3200	3350	65000	40	70000	50	
5	UP	1500	550	2100	2500	75000	40	82000	50	
6	Orissa	3200	2100	600	2700	68000	40	74000	50	
7	Maharashtra	3350	2500	2700	800	66000	40	72000	50	
8	*Demand*	35	32	25						

Solver Parameters

Set Target Cell: $C$26

Equal To: ○ Max ⦿ Min ○ Value of: 0

By Changing Cells: $C$13:$H$16

Subject to the Constraints:
$B$19:$B$22 >= 0
$C$13:$F$16 = integer
$C$13:$H$16 >= 0
$C$24:$F$24 = 0
$G$13:$H$16 = binary
$I$13:$I$16 <= 0

[Solve] [Close] [Guess] [Options] [Add] [Change] [Delete] [Reset All] [Help]

Figure 7.6   Decision variables

The screenshot in Figure 7.7 shows the result of solving the above model. From the results, the following interpretations can be made:

Table 7.11 Cell formulae for the Excel spreadsheet

Cell	Cell formula	Copied to	Remarks
B19	=G13*H4+H13*J4-SUM(C13:F13)	B20:B22	Eqn 4.6
C24	=C8-SUM(C13:C16)	D24:F24	Eqn 4.5
I13	=SUM(G13:H13)-1	I14:I16	Eqn 4.7
C26	=SUMPRODUCT(C4:F7,C13:F16)+SUM PRODUCT (G4:G7,G13:G16)+SUMPRODUCT (I4:I7,H13:H16)	–	Objective Fn.

Table 7.12 Entering the nature of constrains and RHS in Excel

Cell reference	Inequality/Type	RHS
B19:B22	>=	0
C13:F16	Integer	–
C13:H16	>=	0
C24:F24	=	0
G13:H16	Binary	–
I13:I16	<=	0

1. Open low-capacity facilities in Haryana and Maharashtra.
2. Open a high-capacity facility in Orissa.
3. Serve the demand of Haryana from the Haryana facility.
4. Serve the demand of UP from the Haryana and Orissa facilities.
5. Serve the demand of Orissa and Maharashtra using corresponding facilities.

	A	B	C	D	E	F	G	H	I	J
10										
11			Decision Variables: Demand Allocation between regions							
12			Haryana	UP	Orissa	Maharashtra	Plants (Open =1)	Plants (Open =1)	Total Plants Constraint	
13		Haryana	35	4	0	0	1	0	0	
14		UP	0	0	0	0	0	0	-1	
15		Orissa	0	25	25	0	0	1	0	
16		Maharashtra	0	3	0	28	1	0	0	
17										
18		Unutilized Capacity								
19		1								
20		0								
21		0								
22		9								
23										
24		Unsatisfied Demand	0	0	0	0				
25										
26		Objective Function	322400							

Figure 7.7 Decision variables—solved model

The strategic models discussed here could be extended to include multiple capacities (more than two options). But the downside of that is the requirement of more binary variables, which increase the computational time for solving the model. So, the decision maker has to use judgement in selecting appropriate number of capacities before solving the model.

Apart from the strategic decisions, mathematical models could also be used for addressing operational decisions. In the next section, a demand allocation model across different facilities with fixed capacities is considered. This could be considered as the operational decision as the model could be reused for different time periods.

7.3.3   Demand Allocation Across Different Facilities with Fixed Capacities

Unlike the mathematical models for strategic facility location mentioned earlier, the model for demand allocation is fairly simple. The objective function is minimization of transportation costs. The operational constraints satisfy the demand exactly without exceeding the capacity of each facility. The decision variables are simply the amount of items to be shipped from different sources to destinations such that the total demand is satisfied. The detailed description of the mathematical model is given here:

This problem can then be formulated as a Linear Programming (LP) problem:

$$\min \sum_{j=1}^{m} \sum_{i=1}^{n} c_{ij} x_{ij}$$

subject to

$$\sum_{i=1}^{n} x_{ij} = D_j \text{ for all } j = 1, 2, 3, ..., m \tag{7.10}$$

$$\sum_{j=1}^{m} x_{ij} \le S_i \text{ for all } i = 1, 2, 3, ..., n \tag{7.11}$$

$$x_{ij} \ge 0 \text{ for all } i, j \tag{7.12}$$

where the inputs for the strategic demand allocation model are given below:

n = Number of facilities
m = Number of markets
D_j = Annual demand from market j
S_i = Capacity of facility i
c_{ij} = Cost of production and transportation from facility i to market j

The decision variables for the model can be defined as:

x_{ij} = Number of units to be transported from facility i to market j

As an example, consider WheatCorp, which has different capacities in four different supply regions. Each of the supply-source combinations involves different transportation costs. WheatCorp is faced with a demand allocation problem of how these demands are to be allocated among the supply regions. The demand allocation model is illustrated using the WheatCorp data in Excel. Table 7.13 shows the inputs to the model. The data for the model, decision variables, and LHS of constraints are shown in Figure 7.8.

Table 7.13 Inputs for the demand allocation model

Inputs for the model: Variable costs (in Rs/tonne), Capacities (tonnes/year), and Demands (Tonnes/year)					
	Haryana	UP	Orissa	Maharashtra	Capacity
Karnataka	4,000	3,600	1,700	1,000	50
Andhra Pradesh	3,100	2,300	1,200	1,300	40
Rajasthan	1,200	1,900	3,500	2,000	40
Gujarat	2,500	2,700	3,600	1,100	45
Demand	30	40	30	50	

Figure 7.8 Inputs for model

The details of cell formulae and constraint details are presented in Table 7.14. Table 7.15 consists of cell references and inequalities for the model.

Table 7.14 Cell formulae for the demand allocation model

Cell	Cell formula	Copied to	Remarks
B18	=G3-SUM(C11:F11)	B19:B21	Eqn 4.11
C23	=C7-SUM(C11:C14)	D23:F23	Eqn 4.10
C25	=SUMPRODUCT(C3:F6,C11:F14)	–	Objective Fn

The results of solving the model are shown as a screenshot in Figure 7.9.

Table 7.15 Nature of constraints, cell references, and RHS for the demand model

Cell Reference	Inequality/Type	RHS
B18:B21	>=	0
C11:F14	>=	0
C11:F14	>=	0
C23:F23	=	0

The results show that the demand in Haryana is to be met using the Rajasthan facility; the demand in UP to be served using the Andhra Pradesh, Rajasthan, and Gujarat facilities; the demand in Orissa using the Andhra Pradesh facility; and the demand in Maharashtra using the Karnataka facility.

		Haryana	UP	Orissa	Maharashtra
9	**Decision Variables: Demand Allocation between regions**				
10		**Haryana**	**UP**	**Orissa**	**Maharashtra**
11	**Karnataka**	0	0	0	50
12	**AndhraPradesh**	0	10	30	0
13	**Rajasthan**	30	10	0	0
14	**Gujarat**	0	20	0	0
15					
16					
17	**Unutilized Capacity**				
18	0				
19	0				
20	0				
21	25				
22					
23	**Unsatisfied Demand**	0	0	0	0
24					
25	**Objective Function**	218000			

Figure 7.9 Demand allocation—solved model

7.3.4 Strategic Gravity Location for a Facility/Warehouse

An alternative and popular method of approach when a single facility is to be located is the gravity location model. The model is simple and allows locating the facility by considering the distance between cities and their corresponding costs and quantity demanded. This model inherently assumes that all the demands of the markets are met.

Then the cost-minimization model is given by the following equation: where,

$$C = \sum_{n=1}^{k} d_n D_n C_n \tag{7.13}$$

The inputs for the gravity location model are:

(x_n, y_n) = Coordinates (in terms of latitude and longitude) of either a source/destination n

C_n = Cost of transporting one unit of product over one km between the facility and either the source or the destination n

D_n = Total number of products to be shipped between the facility and either the source or the destination n

d_n = Geometric distance between the facility at location (x, y) and the source or destination n, with initial location of (x, y) set to zero

The decision variables for the model are:

(x, y) = Coordinates (in terms of latitude and longitude) for the facility, initially set to zero

In order to illustrate the gravity location model, consider the following input data in Table 7.16.

The implementation using Excel includes entering these data and creating a cell each for the x coordinate, the y coordinate, and the total cost of the transportation. The screenshot for the above input data is shown in Figure 7.10.

Table 7.16 Inputs for the gravity location model

Sources	Coordinates (latitude, longitude)		D_n	Cost (F_n in Rs/tonne/km)	Quantity (D_n in tonnes)
	Xn	Yn			
Ambala	30.35	76.86	82.63524	4	45
Yamuna Nagar	32.816	76.833	83.54759	3.5	60
Karnal	29.7	77.03	82.55732	3.5	55
Gurgaon	28.616	77.066	82.20732	2.75	65

	D	E	F	G	H	I	J	K
1								
2								
3		Sources	Coordinates (Latitude, Longitude)		dn	Cost (Fn in Rs./Tonne/Km)	Quantity (Dn in Tonnes.)	
4			Xn	Yn				
5		Ambala	30.35	76.86	82.63524	4	45	
6		Yamuna Nagar	32.816	76.833	83.54759	3.5	60	
7		Karnal	29.7	77.03	82.55732	3.5	55	
8		Gurgaon	28.616	77.066	82.20732	2.75	65	
9								
10								
11		Facility Location				Objective (Cost in Rs.)		
12		X=	0			63006.17889		
13		Y=	0					
14								

Figure 7.10 Inputs for gravity location model

Table 7.17 shows the cell formulae to be used for the gravity location model.

Table 7.17   Cell formulae for the gravity location model

Cell	Cell formula	Copied to	Remarks
H5	=SQRT(($F$12-F5)^2+($F$13-G5)^2)	H6:H8	Distance calculation
I12	=SUMPRODUCT(I5:I8,H5:H8,J5:J8)	–	Objective Fn

The model data using Excel is shown in Figure 7.11.

	D	E	F	G	H	I	J	K
1								
2								
3		Sources	Coordinates (Latitude, Longitude)		dn	Cost (*Fn* in Rs./Tonne/Km)	Quantity (*Dn* in Tonnes.)	
4			*Xn*	*Yn*				
5		Ambala	30.35	76.86	82.63524	4	45	
6		Yamuna Nagar	32.816	76.833	83.54759	3.5	60	
7		Karnal	29.7	77.03	82.55732	3.5	55	
8		Gurgaon	28.616	77.066	82.20732	2.75	65	
9								
10								
11		Facility Location				Objective (Cost in Rs.)		
12		X=	0			63006.17889		
13		Y=	0					
14								

Figure 7.11   Model data

The result of solving the model using Excel is illustrated in Figure 7.12.

	D	E	F	G	H	I	J	K
1								
2								
3		Sources	Coordinates (Latitude, Longitude)		dn	Cost (*Fn* in Rs./Tonne/Km)	Quantity (*Dn* in Tonnes.)	
4			*Xn*	*Yn*				
5		Ambala	30.35	76.86	0.001071	4	45	
6		Yamuna Nagar	32.816	76.833	2.466957	3.5	60	
7		Karnal	29.7	77.03	0.670908	3.5	55	
8		Gurgaon	28.616	77.066	1.745314	2.75	65	
9								
10								
11		Facility Location				Objective (Cost in Rs.)		
12		X=	30.3492			959.3784582		
13		Y=	76.86071					
14								

Figure 7.12   Solved model

From the results it is observed that the facility has to be located in Ambala. The next section covers the decision-making process when uncertainties are involved in the supply chain.

7.3.5 Uncertainty and Application of Probability

The strategic decision models described in the previous sections assume that all the data are deterministic and known a priori. Over a period of time, factors such as demand, prices, exchange rates, and market structure may change, which may affect the responsiveness and supply chain efficiency.

The mathematical models proposed could be appropriately modified to include uncertainty. The uncertainty can be represented as scenarios. Each scenario would involve an associated discrete probability of happening. For example, discrete probabilities for demands can be generated based on the forecasted values and judgement of the decision-maker. The only requirement is that the basic properties of the discrete probability distributions need to be satisfied. That is, each scenario's probability should be greater than zero and the sum of all the probabilities need to be one. Also, demand values for each scenario can be based on forecasted values.

As an example, consider WheatCorp, which is faced with the problem of deciding which facilities to be opened, given the future demand is uncertain, such that the current demand allocation is also in some sense optimal for future. The management is considering the possibility of two future scenarios to occur, with a probability of 0.4 for the first scenario and a probability of 0.6 for the second scenario. The management aims to satisfy the current and future demand for all the markets, without exceeding the capacity of each facility. Assuming the variable costs remains the same, the inputs for the model (fixed and variable costs, current demand, future demand) under each scenario are given in Tables 7.18 and 7.19.

Table 7.18 Inputs for the scenario model (costs, capacities)

Inputs for the model: Variable costs (in Rs/tonne), Fixed Costs (Rs/year), Capacities (tonnes/year)						
	Haryana	UP	Orissa	Maharashtra	Fixed Cost	Capacity
Haryana	600	1,500	3,200	3,350	65,000	50
UP	1,500	550	2,100	2,500	75,000	50
Orissa	3,200	2,100	600	2,700	68,000	50
Maharashtra	3,350	2,400	2,700	800	66,000	50

Table 7.19 Inputs for the scenario model (demand)

Inputs: Demand in tonnes/year				Period	Probability
35	32	25	28	1	1
36	33	20	32	2	0.4
37	40	26	30	2	0.6

This facility location problem could be modelled as an IP problem by including suitable constraints. Since there are three demand scenarios (including the current one), the quantity to be shipped will differ in each scenario. This is captured using separate decision variables for each scenario.

$$\min \sum_{i=1}^{n} f_i z_i + \sum_{j=1}^{m} \sum_{i=1}^{n} c_{ij} x_{ij} + p1 \left(\sum_{j=1}^{m} \sum_{i=1}^{n} c_{ij}\ y1_{ij} \right) + p2 \left(\sum \sum c_{ij} y2_{ij} \right)$$

subject to

$$\sum_{i=1}^{n} x_{ij} \geq D1_j \text{ for all } j = 1, 2, 3, ..., m \tag{7.14}$$

$$\sum_{j=1}^{m} x_{ij} \leq S_i z_i \text{ for all } i = 1, 2, 3, ..., n \tag{7.15}$$

$$\sum_{i=1}^{n} x_{ij} + \sum_{i=1}^{n} y1_{ij} \geq D21_j \text{ for all } j = 1, 2, 3, ..., m \tag{7.16}$$

$$\sum_{i=1}^{n} x_{ij} + \sum_{i=1}^{n} y2_{ij} \geq D22_j \text{ for all } j = 1, 2, 3, ..., m \tag{7.17}$$

$$\sum_{j=1}^{m} y1_{ij} \leq S_i z_i \text{ for all } i = 1, 2, 3, ..., n \tag{7.18}$$

$$\sum_{j=1}^{m} y2_{ij} \leq S_i z_i \text{ for all } i = 1, 2, 3, ..., n \tag{7.19}$$

$$x_{ij}, y1_{ij}, y2_{ij} \ \varepsilon \text{ integer } \textit{for all } i, j \tag{7.20}$$

$$z_i \ \varepsilon \ \{0, 1\} \ \textit{for all } i \tag{7.21}$$

where the parameters are as follows:

n = Number of possible facilities/locations

m = Number of potential markets

$D1_j$ = Annual demand from market j for the current scenario

$D21_j$ = Annual demand from market j for future scenario 1

$D22_j$ = Annual demand from market j for future scenario 2

S_i = Possible capacity of facility i

f_i = Fixed cost (annualized) if facility i is open

c_{ij} = Cost of production, inventory, and transportation from facility i to market j

$p1$ = The probability of scenario 1 happening (= 0.4)

$p2$ = The probability of scenario 2 happening (= 0.6)

And the decision variables for the model are:

x_{ij} = Number of units to be transported from facility i to market j in the current scenario

$y1_{ij}$ = Number of units to be transported from facility i to market j in the future scenario (Period 2), an integer

$y2_{ij}$ = Number of units to be transported from facility i to market j in the future scenario (Period 2), an integer

z_i = 1, if facility i is open, 0 otherwise

Since the first period demand is certain, the demand is to be satisfied completely by the periods units (Constraint 7.14). Equation 7.15 is the capacity constraint. For Scenario 1 in Period 2, the demand is to be met by the units from Period 1 and Period 2 for Scenario 1 (Constraint 7.16). A similar constraint for Scenario 2 in Period 2 is required (Constraint 7.17). Constraints 7.18 and 7.19 ensure that the capacity of the facilities is not exceeded by the corresponding units from both the scenarios.

The above IP problem can be solved by using the Excel solver. Using a procedure similar to those mentioned in the previous examples (the details of Excel implementation are provided in Appendix 7.1), the following result is obtained as shown in Tables 7.20, 7.21, and 7.22.

Table 7.20 Current demand allocation for the scenario model

Decision variables: Current demand allocation between regions					
	Haryana	UP	Orissa	Maharashtra	Plants (Open = 1)
Haryana	35	15	0	0	1
UP	0	0	0	0	0
Orissa	0	17	25	0	1
Maharashtra	0	0	0	29	1

Table 7.21 Future scenario (Period 1) demand allocation

Decision variables: Scenario 1 future demand allocation between regions				
	Haryana	UP	Orissa	Maharashtra
Haryana	1	1	0	0
UP	0	0	0	0
Orissa	0	0	0	0
Maharashtra	0	0	0	3

Table 7.22 Future scenario (Period 2) demand allocation

Decision variables: Scenario 2 future demand allocation between regions				
	Haryana	UP	Orissa	Maharashtra
Haryana	2	8	0	0
UP	0	0	0	0
Orissa	0	0	1	0
Maharashtra	0	0	0	1

These results show that facilities need to be opened at Haryana, UP, Maharashtra, and cater to demands under both scenarios, the optimal objective cost being Rs 326,960. Note that the answer would be different if the future scenarios are not considered and the model provided in section 7.3.1 is used.

The example addresses only two scenarios for modelling. But the model could be extended to include multiple scenarios at the cost of computational time. The following section discusses another representation of uncertainty.

7.3.6   Other Representations of Uncertainty

In the practice model, the input is usually uncertain. Data are based on forecasts and, hence, are likely to be uncertain. As a consequence, we have either deterministic models if the input is (assumed to be) known with certainty, or probabilistic models if the input is subject to uncertainty (Klose and Drexl 2003).

One other important discrete representation of uncertainty is the binomial representation, which is based on the assumption that when moving from one period to another, the value of the factors, such as demand or price, can have only two possible outcomes—up or down. When the variable changes are continuous, such as the asset price in options, stochastic differential equations are used to describe the evolution of the process. Also, one can use the simulation technique for modelling uncertainty, which is discussed in Appendix 7.2. A sensitivity analysis is shown in Appendix 7.3, which would help a manager to know the leeway available in case of deviations to certainty situations.

7.4   ANALYSIS AND SELECTION OF NETWORK

A network has three levels: suppliers, distribution centres, and markets. The questions to be addressed are: which suppliers should replenish the distribution centre? How should each market be served? Which distribution centre is to be opened, and finally, what is trade-off between customer service and cost? These questions are linked as well (Shapiro 2001). However, one may observe that a network selection has different criteria with the broad objectives of efficiency and service level. The criteria would be as follows:

1. Product characteristics such as volume, weight, value, variants, perishable nature, delegate nature such as emotive value, and so on.
2. Demand characteristics such as dispersed demand, spatial characteristics, volume of demand such as high, medium, and low, and price sensitivity, and so on.

Basically it would be supply and demand factors and industry structural features such as technology, level of maturity, ownership of distribution network, entry barriers, cost of setting up a distribution network and competitive pressure, which would impact distribution network configuration. Some generic distribution network options that are practised but are not rules, are as follows:

1. In case of FMCG, it would be through secondary distribution, and last-mile delivery is through retail formats, where customers pick up goods. There are a

number of retail formats such as generic stores, speciality stores, convenience stores of different categories available to customers. A classic case of statutory requirement is petrol and other fuels from gas stations that are mandatory to be sold only to vehicles at dealer points.

2. Consumer electronics, home appliances, and furniture have distributor sale and customer pick up at DCs. In reality, the dealer arranges delivery at the customer's cost and risk.

3. Hi-tech equipments and capital goods are normally under direct shipping and are installed at the customer's place.

4. Capital machinery, say, an alternator in a power generation plant, could be shipped directly from the supplier to the site with the responsibility of delivery clearly earmarked at the project initiation time. We can find many such cases in construction, infrastructure, capital outlays in the project mode, and so on.

5. Medium- to fast-moving spatially distributed goods that are ordered online or over phone are distributed through carriers or intermediaries such as a small parcels company. This includes delivery of credit cards, gifting of flowers, buying of laptops online, and so on.

6. Another popularly used technique in a similar segment is where the dealer or the distributor assumes the responsibility of delivering to a customer. This could be a product where there is sensitivity and emotive values could be higher. Branded drinking water in India is a classic example. There are also other product segments such as home furniture and consumer electronics in India, in which such options work. Paints have also moved into this model wherein a dealer or manufacturer through a dealer arranges the services of painters for the home segment. LPG for cooking gas is another classic example where a dealer delivers refills direct to the customer's residence.

7. Apart from these, one may look at some other options being practised. Though all the cases mentioned are of forward linkages in a supply chain, similar issues come in from backward linkages as well. For example, the location or relocation of a manufacturing/distribution facility entails the consideration of the whole supply chain network, including suppliers, customers, and transportation infrastructure, in addition to traditional considerations, such as costs or profits (Melachrinoudis et al. 2000).

8. The selection of a network based on competitive factors is also important. In certain industries such as soft drinks, brands invest on the exclusivity of dealer network. The proliferation of Internet technologies has restructured the distribution network. There are more options available and delivery from the supplier to the customer is possible through intermediaries.

Other competitive factors such as rivalry among dealers, economies of scale, and economies of scope, all impact distribution networks. The conflict between dealers can be observed in case of electronics goods, especially those sold directly or through dealers. Economies of scope help to utilize the underutilized capacity in dealer networks to increase width. At times it leads to conflicts among channels and suboptimal supply chain profits as there could be undercutting of prices for dealer volumes. One may have to understand such gaps and streamline the structure periodically.

9. New-generation hybrid models do surface the way Dell Computers did in the home PC segment. Players must be conscious of such revolutionary trends and react with their strategic initiatives to combat against erosion of market share.

It may be observed that the selection of network is not tailor-made but needs to be carefully evolved. Apart from factors mentioned here, many other factors such as the structure of tax and duties, urban real estate costs, the culture of customers, and change in the socio-economic factors influence distribution management.

The bottom line for any company is to ensure that cost efficiency and service levels are balanced and total supply chain profits are maximized given the constraints including that of capital budget. It is important to focus both on backward and forward linkages and also on primary and secondary distribution if the best approach has to be adopted.

SUMMARY

Distribution network is structuring of nodes and flow through links. Nodes are facilities, which could be manufacturing units, distribution centres, or warehouses, and flows are movements of goods between two points or nodes in order to reach the customer ultimately. A distribution network maps both physical flow and information flow.

The objectives of a distribution network would be that the customer's needs should be met and the cost should match a given service level.

The design options would be as follows:

1. Direct shipping
   (a) Supplier to customer site
   (b) Manufacturer to customer
2. Through intermediary
   (a) Manufacturer to customer with in-transit merge
   (b) Delivery responsibility with intermediary
   (c) Delivery responsibility with carrier
3. Customer pick-up
   (a) From distribution centre
   (b) From retail

Each of the above options must be evaluated from cost and service factors. Cost factors are more linked to supply chain drivers, namely, the location of facilities, inventory, transportation, and infor-

mation, whereas service factors would be response time, visibility, availability, and post-sale service including returns management.

Network configurations are determined by product characteristics, industry practice, customer expectations, and macro policies such as tax structures and so on. These determine the configuration of supply chain drivers for a network decision, and the chosen network gives standard service parameters such as response time, availability, information visibility, and customer satisfaction. The challenge in configuring a distribution network is how to balance the given constraints to achieve the desired objective of distribution cost management or maximization of profit.

There are certain tools and models for deciding a network. The single capacity model is useful in locating facilities given the number of potential facility locations and their associated capacities, fixed costs, and variable costs. The objective of such a model would be to minimize the total costs. The strategic facility location model with the choice of two capacities has the objective of minimizing the total cost of fixed and variable costs of opening and operating the facilities, which is the same as the single capacity model.

In the model for demand allocation across different facilities with fixed capacities, the decision variables are simply the amount of items to be shipped from different sources to destinations such that the total demand is satisfied. The gravity model is simple and allows locating the facility by considering the distance between cities and their corresponding costs, and the quantity demanded. This model inherently assumes that all the demands of the markets are met.

The selection of a specific network model depends on product characteristics such as volume, weight, value, variants, perishable nature, delegate nature such as emotive value, and so on. It also depends on demand characteristics such as dispersed demand, spatial characteristics, volume of demand such as high, medium, and low, and price sensitivity, and so on.

KEY TERMS

Clearing & forwarding (C&F) agents: Also known as shipping agents, these are the companies that have been authorized and issued a licence by the Customs and Airports Authority of India to get the goods inspected at the customs warehouse. These shipping and clearing agents only prepare the export documents for the nodal firm's shipments. In trade, C&F agents are involved in domestic trade as well, where they serve as intermediaries by linking the primary and secondary member in a distribution channel.

Direct shipping: The direct shipping design option would suit capital goods in a project site where the manufacturer has identified the supplier of certain components that are to be shipped directly to the site. There will be further value addition at the customer site.

Distribution network: Distribution network is the structuring of nodes and flows through links.

Nodes are facilities, which could be a manufacturing unit, a distribution centre, or a warehouse, and flows are movements of goods between two points or nodes and ultimately to the customer.

Primary distribution: Primary distribution from the manufacturer to mother warehouses, dealers, and CFAs till the goods reflect on the stock of the nodal organization and move out from its book finally to that of the channel players.

Secondary distribution: Secondary distribution is from dealers to retailers and ultimate customers.

Stock Keeping Unit (SKU): An SKU is a unique identifier for each distinct product and service that can be ordered from a supplier. An SKU helps in enabling merchants to systematically track their inventory, such as in warehouses and retail outlets.

CONCEPT REVIEW QUESTIONS

1. Explain various criteria preferred for the direct shipping option. Describe the advantages of direct shipping with examples.

2. 'Intermediaries are absolutely essential while managing the distribution of consumer electronics goods in India.' Elucidate. Detail the challenges and managerial levers available to handle the same.

3. Analyse the role of retailers for FMCG in India. What are the challenges for distribution management from the perspective of retailers, focal organization, and the brand owner?

4. What are the advantages and constraints in the customer direct pick-up distribution model? Explain with examples.

5. Describe various criteria to be considered while selecting a network option. Explain network distribution options deployed for products such as steel, cement, sugar, edible oil, and wheat

wherein there's a demand for both large scale (institutional) and retail market.

6. What is the role of facility location in a distribution network? Explain the same for manufacturing and distribution centre locations.

7. What are the two different categories of models used? Explain their pros and cons.

8. Describe how a distribution network can be managed for a global business with manufacturing components and only with the trade component.

9. How do government taxes and duties impact distribution configuration? Elucidate with examples especially for consumer goods.

10. Is uncertainty a factor to be considered while designing a network for distribution management? How could one handle uncertainty?

11. Describe sensitivity analysis. How it is useful in evaluating distribution network options?

12. Explain the demand allocation and facility capacity planning models. Describe their application.

13. What are the factors that influence a distribution network in e-business? Do conflicts arise among channels of distribution? How are such conflicts resolved?

14. Analyse network distribution options deployed in an Internet-based distribution with which you are familiar. Describe three flows, namely, physical, information, and financial. What are the pros and cons of such a structure?

CRITICAL THINKING QUESTIONS

1. A large electronics retail chain company is planning to expand in anticipation of a nation-wide growth in demand for electronics products. After a thorough market research the company has forecasted that the demand would be in the range of 100,000 units in northern India, 75,000 units in east India, 110,000 units in western India, and 140,000 units in south India for the coming year. The management has selected four potential sites for expansion: Hosur, Ahmedabad, Chandigarh, and Kolkata. The stores can operate with a capacity of either 120,000 units or 145,000 units for achieving economies of scale. The annual fixed costs (in '000 Rs) at the four locations along with the production and transportation costs are shown in the table below. How many facilities should the company open? Where should they open and how large should the stores be?

2. A large forging and casting manufacturer is currently operating four foundry units at Coimbatore, Chennai, Bangalore, and Pune. The plants have a capacity of 300 tonnes, 150 tonnes, 200 tonnes, and 150 tonnes, respectively. The company is badly affected by

Fixed and variable costs (in '000 Rs/unit)

	North	West	East	South
Fixed cost for the low capacity plant	250	225	275	260
Fixed cost for the high capacity plant	300	260	310	285
Hosur	13	10	11	9
Ahmedabad	11	8	12	14
Chandigarh	7	11	10	15
Kolkata	13	11	7	10

the ongoing economic recession and forecasts the demand (in tonnes) to come down by 50 per cent in each region it operates. It is no longer viable to operate all the plants. So, the management is considering shutting down at least one plant as early as possible while still catering to the demand from the potential customers. Considering the variable costs of operation, the company wants to minimize the total cost of operation. The data for fixed costs and variable costs are provided in the table.

Variable costs (in '000 Rs/tonne)

	North	East	West	South
Coimbatore	23	16	14	18
Chennai	22	20	22	19
Bangalore	17	14	24	23
Pune	15	22	25	17
Demand	95	100	95	105

Help the company to choose which plants are to be shut down. What it the total cost of operating the network after shutting down?

3. The following questions are based on the above question after shutting down the plant(s).
   (a) At what variable cost does operating from Coimbatore to the north become attractive?
   (b) At what variable cost does operating from Chennai to West become attractive?
   (c) The customers of the foundry have procured new orders and so the demand for castings from the northern region has increased from 95 to 125. What is the new allocation of demand between regions? What is the total cost of the operation?

4. CoolInc, an airconditioner manufacturer, is currently operating at New Delhi and Mumbai. The company is serving demand at Jaipur, Chandigarh, New Delhi, and Mumbai. The demand for airconditioners in the southern region has picked up. So, CoolInc wants to open a new facility that will serve the new markets: Chennai, Bangalore, and Pune. The supply sources for the new facility would be New Delhi and Mumbai. The coordinate location of the existing plants, quantity to be shipped from supply sources and to markets, and their associated transportation costs are given in the table below. Identify where the new facility has to be located.

Demands, costs, and coordinate locations

Sources and markets	Transportation cost (Rs/unit/km)	Quantity (units)	Coordinate location	
			x_n	y_n
New Delhi	25	200	500	700
Mumbai	23	180	240	400
Chennai	33	125	700	200
Bangalore	32	70	300	300
Pune	30	95	250	300
Jaipur	27	80	450	275
Chandigarh	26	85	475	800

PROJECT ASSIGNMENTS

1. The jewellery and gems industry in India is an old industry. This industry of precious and semiprecious stones significantly contributes to India's foreign exchange. There are two sectors, namely organized and unorganized, in the jewellery industry. You are planning to start a jewellery shop in the organized sector. Undertake an analysis to identify what are the key drivers in jewellery supply chain and characterize the sector. What are the economic factors that influence the sector? How do you foresee the demand in the next two to three years? What is the consumption pattern across various regions in the country? Based on the analysis, decide which is the best place to locate your jewellery shop.

2. The Indian cement industry comprises more than 300 manufacturing plants and is dominated by players like Birla, Ultratech, Ambuja, India Cements, and Lafarge. The total installed capacity of the cement industry exceeds 150 million tonnes. However, the per-capita consumption is very low. You have planned to enter into the cement industry by starting a manufacturing plant. What are the key drivers in the cement supply chain network? Identify the entry barriers for both domestic and international players in the cement sector. How do you foresee the demand and consumption pattern for cement in the next year? What is your take on the excise duty front for the cement sector in the next year? Account for this driver in your analysis. Based on the analysis, identify a potential location for your manufacturing plant.

REFERENCES

Daskin, Mark S., Lawrence V. Snyder and Rosemary T. Berger, 'Facility Location in Supply Chain,' Working paper no. 03-010, Department of Industrial Engineering and Management Science, North Western University, Illinois, USA, December 2003

Klose, A. and A. Drexl, *'European Journal of Operational Research'* 2003, www.sciencedirect.com,

Melachrinoudis, E., H. Min and A. Messac, 'The Relocation of a Manufacturing/Distribution Facility from Supply Chain Perspectives: A Physical Programming Approach,' *Advances in Management Science, Multicriteria Applications*, Kenneth Laurence, Editor, JAI Press, Vol. 10, 2000, pp. 15–39

Shapiro, Jeremy F., *Modeling the Supply Chain*, Thomson, Duxbury, 2001

www.floraindia.com, accessed on 1 March 2009

www.mcvities.com, accessed on 3 March 2009

www.srwater.com, accessed on 4 March 2009

Solving the Scenario Model Using Excel

The data for the current and future scenarios are first entered in the spreadsheet. The screenshots are shown in Figure A7.1 and Figure A7.2.

	Haryana	UP	Orissa	Maharashtra	Fixed Cost	Low Capacity
	Inputs for the model: Variable costs (in Rs./Tonne), Fixed Costs (Rs./Year), Capacities(Tonnes./Year) and Demands(Tonnes./Year)					
Haryana	600	1500	3200	3350	65000	50
UP	1500	550	2100	2500	75000	50
Orissa	3200	2100	600	2700	68000	50
Maharashtra	3350	2400	2700	800	66000	50
Current Demand	35	32	25	28		

Decision variables: Current Demand Allocation between regions

	Haryana	UP	Orissa	Maharashtra	Plants (Open =1)
Haryana	0	0	0	0	0
UP	0	0	0	0	0
Orissa	0	0	0	0	0
Maharashtra	0	0	0	0	0

Decision variables: Scenario 1 Future Demand Allocation between regions

	Haryana	UP	Orissa	Maharashtra	Future Excess Capacity (Scenario 1)
Haryana	0	0	0	0	0
UP	0	0	0	0	0
Orissa	0	0	0	0	0
Maharashtra	0	0	0	0	0
Scenario 1 Demand1	36	33	20	32	

Figure A7.1   Current scenarios

Decision variables: Scenario 2 Future Demand Allocation between regions

	Haryana	UP	Orissa	Maharashtra	Future Excess Capacity (Scenario 2)
Haryana	0	0	0	0	0
UP	0	0	0	0	0
Orissa	0	0	0	0	0
Maharashtra	0	0	0	0	0
Scenario 2 Demand2	37	40	26	30	

Excess Capacity (Current Period)				
0				
0				
0				
0				
Unmet Current Demand	35	32	25	28

Unmet Demand scenario1	36	33	20	32
Unmet Demand scenario2	37	40	26	30

Objective Function	0

Figure A7.2   Future scenario

The details of cell formulae and cell references are given in Table A7.1 and Table A7.2.

Table A7.1 Cell formulae for the scenario model

Cell	Cell formula	Copied to	Remarks
B20	=G12*H4-SUM(C12:F12)	B21:B23	Eqn 4.15
C25	=C8-SUM(C12:C15)	D25:F25	Eqn 4.14
O12	=G12*H4-SUM(J12:M12)	O13:O15	Eqn 4.18
J26	=J16-SUM(J12:J15) -SUM(C12:C15)	K26:M26	Eqn 4.16
O20	=G12*H4-SUM(J20:M20)	O21:O23	Eqn 4.19
J28	=J24-SUM(J20:J23) -SUM(C12:C15)	K28:M28	Eqn 4.17
C28	=SUMPRODUCT(C4-:F7, C12:F15)+SUMPRODUCT (G4:G7,G12:G15)+0.4 *SUMPRODUCT(C4:F7, J12:M15)+0.6 *SUMPRODUCT (C4:F7,J20:M23)	–	Objective Fn

Table A7.2 Cell references and constraint types for the scenario model

Cell reference	Inequality/Type	RHS
B20:B23	>=	0
C12:F15	>=	0
C12:F15	Integer	-
C25:F25	<=	0
G12:G15	Binary	-
J12:M15	Integer	-
J12:M15	>=	0
J20:M23	Integer	-
J20:M23	>=	0
J26:M26	<=	0
J28:M28	<=	0
O12:O15	>=	0
O20:O23	>=	0

The screenshot before solving the model is shown in Figure A7.3.

Figure A7.3 Demand and capacity

The results of solving the model are shown as screenshots in Figure A7.4 and Figure A7.5:

	Haryana	UP	Orissa	Maharashtra	Plants (Open =1)		Haryana	UP	Orissa	Maharashtra	Future Excess Capacity (Scenario 1)
Decision variables: Current Demand Allocation between regions						**Decision variables: Scenario 1 Future Demand Allocation between regions**					
Haryana	35	15	0	0	1	Haryana	1	1	0	0	48
UP	0	0	0	0	0	UP	0	0	0	0	0
Orissa	0	17	25	0	1	Orissa	0	0	0	0	50
Maharashtra	0	0	0	29	1	Maharashtra	0	0	0	3	47
						Scenario 1 Demand1	36	33	20	32	

Excess Capacity (Current Period)		Haryana	UP	Orissa	Maharashtra	Future Excess Capacity (Scenario 2)
	Decision variables: Scenario 2 Future Demand Allocation between regions					
0	Haryana	2	8	0	0	40
0	UP	0	0	0	0	0
8	Orissa	0	0	1	0	49
21	Maharashtra	0	0	0	1	49

Figure A7.4   Solved model

					Scenario 2 Demand2	37	40	26	30
Unmet Current Demand	0	0	0	-1					
					Unmet Demand scenario1	0	0	-5	0
Objective Function	326960				Unmet Demand scenario2	0	0	0	0

Figure A7.5   Solved model

Note that there might be some precision issues after solving the model. If this is the case, these cell values could be rounded up or down based on the cell values. From the results it could be observed that the optimal objective value is 3,26,960.

Appendix 7.2   Using Simulation for Network Decision

An important scientific technique, namely simulation, can also be used to study the evolution of the decision-making process when the number and scale of scenarios are too huge to be captured by the mathematical models given in the earlier sections. Another advantage of simulation is its ability to model any kind of business process like manufacturing, service, or financial. Simulation is based on fitting statistical distributions to each activity in the model. These distributions could be identified based on historical data. Once the distributions are identified, random numbers are generated for each of the activities and these are used to study the evolution of the process. Typically, there is commercial software available for simulation such as ProModel, Quest, and Arena, which provide visual representation of process entities and process evolution.

As a hypothetical example, let us consider WheatCorp, which is trying to assess the current performance levels of two existing facilities at Haryana and Uttar Pradesh, both of which supply to a warehouse, 200 km and 300 km away from the factories, respectively. Based on the performance analysis, the management has to decide whether or not to open a new facility. This decision-making process was modelled in ProModel 6. The simulation model is built using general elements: Locations, Entities, Path networks, Interfaces, Resources, Processing, and Arrivals. In most cases, these are the only necessary elements to run a simulation. The software comes with tutorials to get the user started and also detailed documentation on how to feed in relevant data. The hypothetical data for this example is presented below from Table A7.3 to Table A7.9 and screenshots given in Figure A7.6 to Figure A7.11. Most of the data is self-explanatory.

Table A7.3   Location details

Name	Capacity (Units)	Units	Stats	Rule	Cost ($)
Haryana_Factory	5,000	1	Time Series	Oldest, FIFO	2000/hr
Warehouse	2,000	1	Time Series	Oldest	50/hr
UP_Factory	5,000	1	Time Series	Oldest, FIFO	1700/hr

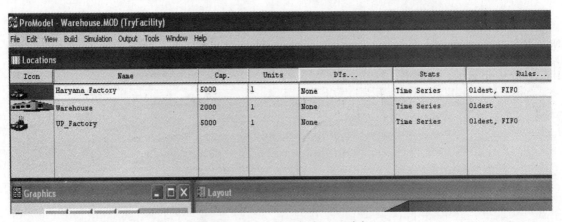

Figure A7.6   Simulation model

Table A7.4 Entities details

Name	Self-speed (metres per minute)	Stats	Cost ($)
Product	0	Time Series	5,000

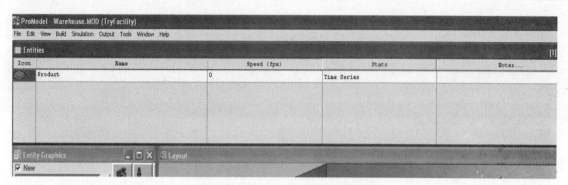

Figure A7.7 Simulation model

Table A7.5 Path network details

Name	Type	Time/Speed	From	To	Bi-directional travel	Dist (m)	Speed Factor
Net1	Passing	Speed & Distance	N1	N2	Bi	200,000	1
Net2	Passing	Speed & Distance	N1	N2	Bi	300,000	1

Figure A7.8 Simulation model

Table A7.6 Interfaces details

Net	Node	Location
Ne	N1	Haryana_Factory
N2	Warehouse	
Net2	N1	UP_Factory
N2	Warehouse	

Table A7.7 Resources details

Name	Units	Stats	Resource search	Entity search	Path	Motion	Cost
Truck	2	By Unit	Closest	Oldest	Net1 Home: N1	Empty: 150 mpm Full: 150 mpm	Rate: 100/Hr 25/Use
Truck2	2	By Unit	Closest	Oldest	Net2 Home: N1	Empty: 150 mpm Full: 150 mpm	Rate: 150/Hr 30/Use

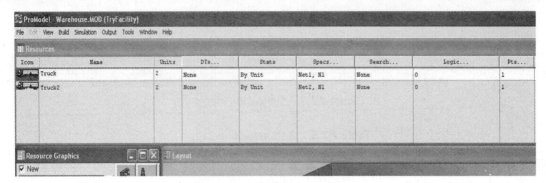

Figure A7.9 Simulation model

Table A7.8 Processing details

Entity	Location	Operation	Output	Destination	Rule	Move logic
Product	UP_Factory	WAIT 1 HR Truck2 FOR U(2,1)	Product	Warehouse	FIRST 1	MOVE WITH Use TRUCK2 THEN FREE
Product	Haryana_Factory	WAIT 1 HR Use Truck2 FOR N(2,1)	Product	Warehouse	FIRST 1	MOVE WITH TRUCK2 THEN FREE
Product	Warehouse	WAIT 10 HR	Product	EXIT	FIRST 1	MOVE

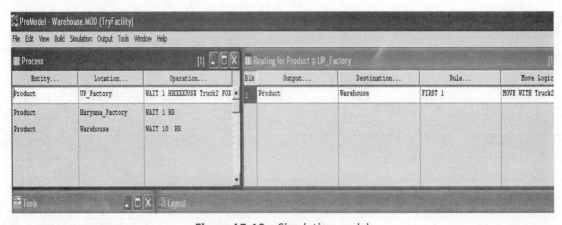

Figure A7.10 Simulation model

Table A7.9 Arrival details

Entity	Location	Qty each	First time qty	No. of occurrences	Frequency of arrival
Product	Haryana_Factory	10	0	INF	0.85 Hr
Product	UP_Factory	8	0	INF	0.75 Hr

ProModel - Warehouse.MOD (TryFacility)

File   Edit   View   Build   Simulation   Output   Tools   Window   Help

Arrivals

Entity...	Location...	Qty Each...	First Time...	Occurrences	Frequency
Product	Haryana_Factory	10	0	INF	1 HR
Product	UP_Factory	8	0	INF	1 HR

Tools   Layout

Figure A7.11   Simulation model

The simulation model assumes that the processing time of the product at the UP and Haryana factories follows uniform distribution (mean, half range as inputs) and normal distribution (mean, standard deviation as inputs). This could be modelled using other distributions also depending on the historical data. The screenshot of the simulation model is shown in Figure A7.12.

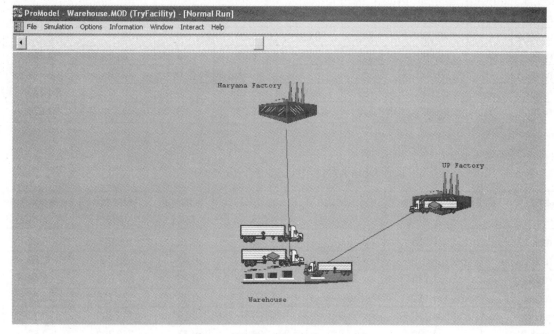

ProModel - Warehouse.MOD (TryFacility) - [Normal Run]

File   Simulation   Options   Information   Window   Interact   Help

Haryana Factory

UP Factory

Warehouse

Figure A7.12   Simulation model

After entering the data for all the elements, the time for simulation is set as 500 hours. With these data, now the simulation model is ready to run. The results of running the simulation model are provided in the form of reports. Note that the results might differ when the same model is run in a different machine because of the random number seed. In order to account for this, in practice, the simulation is run for different replications and average of the results is taken. Three sample reports for the current model are given in Table A7.10, Table A7.11, and Table A7.12.

Table A7.10 Locations report

Name	Scheduled Time (MIN)	Capacity	Total entries (MIN)	Avg time per entry	Avg contents	Maximum contents	Current contents	% utilization
Haryana_Factory	30,000	5,000	5018	22441.5	3753.71	5,000	5,000	75.07
Warehouse	30,000	2,000	32	600	0.64	3	0	0.03
UP_Factory	30,000	5,000	5013	21224.17	3546.559	5,000	5,000	70.93

Table A7.11 Resources report

Name	Units	Scheduled time (min)	Number times used	Avg time per usage (min)	Avg time travel to use (min)	Avg time travel to park (min)	% blocked in travel	% utilization
Truck.1.1	1	30,000	2,353	7.13	5.17	0	0	96.57
Truck.1.2	1	30,000	1,948	8.69	6.70	0	0	100
Truck 1	**2**	**60,000**	**4,301**	**7.84**	**5.86**	**0**	**0**	**98.285**
Truck 2.1	1	30,000	1,957	8.17	7.15	0	0	100
Truck 2.2	1	30,000	2,353	6.90	5.10	0	0	94.142
Truck 2	**2**	**60,000**	**4,310**	**7.48**	**6.03**	**0**	**0**	**97.071**

Table A7.12 Resources cost report

Name	Units	Nonuse cost	% Nonuse cost	Usage cost dollars	% usage cost	Total cost dollars	% total cost
Truck 1.1	1	1,715	28.07	10,7110	0.23	108,825	0.22
Truck 1.2	1	0	0	98,700	0.21	98,700	0.20
Truck 1	**2**	**1,715**	**28.07**	**205,810**	**0.43**	**207,525**	**0.43**
Truck 2.1	1	0	0	133,710	0.28	133,710	0.27
Truck 2.2	1	4,393.5	71.92	141,196.5	0.29	145,590	0.304
Truck 2	**2**	**4,393.5**	**71.92**	**274,906.5**	**0.57**	**279,300**	**0.57**

From the locations report, the first observation one could make is that the number of arrivals in both the factories are higher than the capacity of factories because of which failed arrivals have happened. This cannot be confirmed from the results. This may be because of the higher arrival frequency of the products, which also indicates addition of capacity. The utilization of both the plants is more than 70 per cent. This shows that there is scope for improvement from the utilization perspective.

From the resources report, it is seen that all the trucks operate at more than 94 per cent utilization. Also one truck from each factory is utilized at 100 per cent. Although the utilization is high, any breakdowns (this has not been captured in this model) would cause under-utilization of the resources and this may lead to delayed deliveries. So, it is better to add one more truck at each factory provided the cost is affordable. In order to make this decision, one could look at the resources cost report shown in Table 7.12. From the table one can find that the cost of operating Truck 2, which is under-utilized, is higher compared to the others. So it is worthwhile to consider cancelling Truck 2 and bring in two trucks, which might be cost effective.

Now, coming to the question of whether to open a new facility, first, it is seen from the reports that the existing facilities are operating at around 70 per cent utilization. So, instead of opening a new facility, it would be better to add more capacity at both the plants and look for improving the utilization by better mobilization of resources.

The example shows how simulation models could be used for the facility decision process. The success of the simulation model as a tool depends on the following factors:

1. Understanding the existing system
2. Chalking out the objectives clearly
3. Identifying the appropriate level of aggregation of activities
4. Planning and executing the modelling process effectively

If these factors are taken into account, simulation will be a valuable tool for the decision maker.

Appendix 7.3 — Sensitivity Analysis

Sensitivity analysis is helpful when modelling any decision process as LP problem. The sensitivity analysis is automatically carried out by solvers when solving the linear programme. As the name suggests, they provide us the allowable ranges of objective function coefficients and right-hand side values within which the current set of decision variables remain optimal. This would be really useful for the firms because it allows observing the impact of change in influential factors on an optimal solution without having to resolve the model. It should be noted that sensitivity analysis makes sense only when modelling the problem as an LP. (It has no meaning in a pure IP problem such as those given in sections 7.3.1 to 7.3.2.)

As an example for this analysis, consider the demand allocation example provided in section 7.3.3. The demand allocation example was formulated and solved as an LP. Once the LP is solved, the Excel solver prompts for the type of report required by the user. Here the user can select the sensitivity report. The report snapshot from the solver for the demand allocation model is provided in Figure A7.13:

The solver provides a variety of useful information for the user. In the first set of analysis, the first column denotes the cell that is involved in interpretation. The second column provides the decision variable names. For example, for the decision variable: quantity to be shipped from Karnataka to Haryana (cell C11), the name is Karnataka Haryana. The third column gives the final value of the optimal solution, which is zero for cell C11. The objective coefficient is the cost coefficient of Rs 4,000/tonne for shipping between Karnataka and Haryana. In the fourth column, the solver provides information called 'Reduced Cost'. If this value is non-zero for any variable, this means that the corresponding objective function coefficient has to be increased/decreased by that amount for the corresponding variable to have non-zero value.

Report Created: 3/2/2009 12:22:50 PM

Adjustable Cells

Cell	Name	Final Value	Reduced Cost	Objective Coefficient	Allowable Increase	Allowable Decrease
$C$11	Karnataka Haryana	0	2000	4000	1E+30	2000
$D$11	Karnataka UP	0	900	3600	1E+30	900
$E$11	Karnataka Orissa	0	100	1700	1E+30	100
$F$11	Karnataka Maharashtra	50	0	1000	100	1E+30
$C$12	AndhraPradesh Haryana	0	1500	3100	1E+30	1500
$D$12	AndhraPradesh UP	10	0	2300	400	100
$E$12	AndhraPradesh Orissa	30	0	1200	100	1E+30
$F$12	AndhraPradesh Maharashtra	0	700	1300	1E+30	700
$C$13	Rajasthan Haryana	30	0	1200	500	1E+30
$D$13	Rajasthan UP	10	0	1900	800	500
$E$13	Rajasthan Orissa	0	2700	3500	1E+30	2700
$F$13	Rajasthan Maharashtra	0	1800	2000	1E+30	1800
$C$14	Gujarat Haryana	0	500	2500	1E+30	500
$D$14	Gujarat UP	20	0	2700	100	400
$E$14	Gujarat Orissa	0	2000	3600	1E+30	2000
$F$14	Gujarat Maharashtra	0	100	1100	1E+30	100

Constraints

Cell	Name	Final Value	Shadow Price	Constraint R.H. Side	Allowable Increase	Allowable Decrease
$C$23	Unsatisfied Demand Haryana	0	-2000	0	20	10
$D$23	Unsatisfied Demand UP	0	-2700	0	20	25
$E$23	Unsatisfied Demand Orissa	0	-1600	0	20	10
$F$23	Unsatisfied Demand Maharashtra	0	-1000	0	50	0
$B$18	Unutilized Capacity	0	0	0	0	1E+30
$B$19	Unutilized Capacity	0	400	0	10	20
$B$20	Unutilized Capacity	0	800	0	10	20
$B$21	Unutilized Capacity	25	0	0	25	1E+30

Figure A7.13 Demand allocation model solver

For example, if the current total cost of shipping from Karnataka to Haryana is decreased from Rs 4,000 to Rs 2,000, this decision variable will figure in the optimal solution with a non-zero value. The 'Allowable Increase' column gives the maximum increase in the cost coefficient below, which the current optimal solution will not change. For example, the allowable increase for the cell C3 is 'Infinity'. That is, a change in the objective coefficient for this decision variable in the positive direction does not have any effect on the values of the current decision variables and optimal objective function. 'Allowable Decrease' gives the maximum decrease in the cost coefficient above which the current solution will not change. If one considers the cell E11, the allowable decrease is 100. That is, the current cost coefficient of 1,700 can be decreased till 1,600 but the optimal solution will not change.

The second set of analysis relates to constraints. As before, the first column is the cell involved in interpretation. The second column gives the constraint set name. For example, 'Unsatisfied Demand Haryana' means the constraint in question is 'Unsatisfied Demand' for the location 'Haryana'. The final value is nothing but the value of the constraint after substituting the optimal decision variable values. 'Shadow Price' is the marginal cost that one pays for utilizing one extra unit of resource for each constraint. This can be negative or positive depending on the constraint inequalities. For the demand constraint, increase of every additional unit in demand increases the objective function cost of shipping the extra unit. So, if the current demand of Haryana is increased from 30 to 31, the objective function cost increases by Rs 2,000.

Similarly, for the capacity constraint every additional unit of capacity should decrease cost. So, if one increases the capacity of Andhra Pradesh from 40 to 41, the objective function would decrease by Rs 400. The 'Constraint R.H. Side' shows the current right-hand side value of the constraint. The adjacent column, 'Allowable Increase', shows the value by which one can increase the Right Hand Side (RHS) and still have the same set of decision variables to be non-zero in the optimal solution. For example, it can be seen that the allowable increase for the Haryana demand constraint is 20. This means that the RHS of the Haryana demand constraint can be increased by 20 units, but the optimal solution would not change. Any increase beyond 20 will require the model to be solved again. For the 'Allowable Decrease' column, the constraint RHS can be decreased within the allowable range and still have the same set of non-zero decision variables in the optimal solution. From the discussion, it can be understood how sensitivity analysis helps in observing the impact of change in influential factors on supply chain responsiveness and efficiency.

8

Role of Sourcing in Supply Chain

Learning Objectives

After studying this chapter, you will be able to:
+ Understand the importance of sourcing in a supply chain
+ Comprehend the definition of purchasing, procurement, and sourcing
+ Gain an insight into the sourcing grid matrix and guidelines
+ Understand the purchasing procedures and commonly deployed practices
+ Understand the procurement process
+ Gain an insight into strategic sourcing comprising outsourcing strategies, supplier development, and design collaboration
+ Appreciate the role of technology for enabling buying decisions

Supply chain management is focused on satisfying a customer request at the best-managed cost by adding value from raw material to work-in-progress up to final goods. Such value addition can be through processing at the manufacturing stage or during storage, movement, and distribution across the supply chain network. As mentioned in Chapter 1, supply chain management integrates three macro processes, namely, supplier relationship management, internal supply chain management, that is, activities within a focal organization, and customer relationship management, which includes post-sale functions.

8.1 THE IMPORTANCE OF SOURCING IN A SUPPLY CHAIN

Sourcing is one of the six drivers and it is a cross-functional driver in supply chain management. Sourcing plays a major role in effective supply chain decisions as a focal organization depends upon outsider vendors for material procurement. Once the material is procured, the firm adds value in its business model. Hence strategies and functions with respect to management of sourcing activities would be vital for the success of any supply chain network. The cost-efficiency focus triggers from the point of purchasing the material. Firms similarly work with sourcing partners on product variability and synchronize material or components at the point of purchase. Thus, both for cost efficiency and responsiveness, sourcing policies play an important role.

Exhibit 8.1 Maruti Suzuki's Sourcing Initiatives

Maruti Suzuki is one of India's leading automobile manufacturers and a market leader in the car segment, both in terms of volume of vehicles sold and revenue earned. Though it was started as a joint venture between the Government of India and Suzuki Corporation of Japan, the Indian government exited from this JV in 2007. It sold its stocks to Indian financial institutions. The company was renamed as Maruti Suzuki Motors India Ltd and was listed in major stock exchanges. For understanding the sourcing strategies for the success of this organization, one has to travel back to understand its history and relate to its success.

Maruti Udyog Limited (MUL) was established in February 1981, although the actual production commenced in 1983 with the Maruti 800, based on the Suzuki Alto Kei car. Maruti 800 was launched as a small car meant as a people's car that could be purchased by a large Indian community. Till then, a car was a luxury for the Indian buyer, with only two auto majors, Hindustan Motors and Premier Automobiles Ltd, selling the Ambassador and the Premier models respectively.

Maruti came into the market with a promise of providing an unmatched low-price car that was based on low cost of production. When a company has imported technology and a large portion is typically sourced from outside vendors, the challenge is to maintain the price point. The challenge then for Maruti Udyog Ltd was to indigenize the production of its components and source the OE components domestically. The agreement with Suzuki Motors revolved around developing suitable R&D and transfer of technology to develop vendors in and around the Maruti Udyog plant at Gurgaon near Delhi. The company was able to achieve the indigenization agreement successfully as planned. The sourcing efficiency improved because of proximity of vendors, and improved communication. Costs could be managed because purchases were made in local currency. Thus, the success of sourcing strategies led to the success of Maruti Udyog Ltd.

Now, the company annually exports more than 50,000 cars and has an extremely large domestic market in India selling over 750,000 cars annually. Maruti 800, till 2004, was the India's largest selling compact car ever since it was launched in 1983. More than a million units of this car have been sold worldwide so far. Maruti Suzuki India Limited, a subsidiary of Suzuki Motor Corporation of Japan, has been the leader of the Indian car market for over two decades.

Its manufacturing facilities are located at two facilities—Gurgaon and Manesar, south of New Delhi. Maruti's Gurgaon facility has an installed capacity of producing 350,000 units per annum. The Manesar facility, launched in February 2007, comprises a vehicle assembly plant with a capacity of 100,000 units per year and a Diesel Engine plant with an annual capacity of producing 100,000 engines and transmissions. The Manesar and Gurgaon facilities have a combined capability to produce over 700,000 units annually. More than half the cars sold in India are Maruti cars.

Procurement: About three-fourth of the car, by value, is outsourced. Any improvement in the car in terms of technology and design, quality, or cost has to essentially include the company's vendors and their support. In the year 2007–08, the company signed two joint-venture agreements with global component manufacturers for cost reduction through localization of components for Maruti Suzuki cars. The first was with Magneti Marelli, aimed at the production of electronic control units (ECU) for diesel engines and the second with Futaba Industrial Company, Japan, for the production of exhaust system parts. The company is setting up a Suppliers' Park in Manesar, close to its car plant on an area of 100 acres for just-in-time supplies. Both the joint ventures are located in this Suppliers' Park.

The company's vendors have set up an informal Suppliers' Club and it gives a good forum for building personal relationships, understanding key issues, and exchanging best practices at the CEO level. The company organized a trip for the members to Japan for some plant visits and the Tokyo Motor Show. In the early eighties, the company made significant efforts in trying to develop a component industry from ground zero. Over the next two decades, about 110 foreign technology collaborations were facilitated and Maruti Suzuki engineers worked closely with the vendors' engineers to enable to deliver cars that are both of high quality and competitive in costs. Now, the relationship has matured and most direct vendors or tier 1 vendors are competent enough to work on their improvement, but there is major scope for modernization of some sections of the tier 2 vendors. The company has identified this as an opportunity for further quality upgradation and cost reduction. The second focus area for component cost reduction is improving the yield of raw material across all manufacturing processes, like sheet metal, castings, forgings, and machining. Every component is studied in detail and innovative ideas are tried, to reduce the input material weight for the same component output. The total cost of raw material as a percentage of net sales ranges from 15 to 20 per cent.

The company plans to export 200,000 units from 2010. In view of these developments, the plant's capacity was enhanced from an initial 100,000 units per annum to 170,000 units per annum during the year 2007–08.

Source: http://www.marutisuzuki.com/cars-images/image/pdf/MANAGEMENT%20DISCUSSION%20AND%20ANALYSIS.pdf.

Sourcing strategies also play a role in tandem with other supply chain drivers. The management, while deciding where to set up a manufacturing facility, has the choice of settling for either a committed or a flexible production plan depending upon its integration with the sourcing and manufacturing strategy. Similarly, warehousing or stocking of inbound material is also defined by responsiveness from the sourcing partners. This actually links up to inventory and transportation drivers where there is scope for deploying just-in-time or Vendor Managed Inventory models, where the capability and maturity level of vendors are critical for success. Thus, sourcing strategies are interwoven with supply chain strategies and are responsible for achieving the supply chain objectives of a firm.

Here we would discuss sourcing initiatives that are responsible for the success of these firms. Exhibit 8.1 talks about Maruti Suzuki's sourcing initiatives.

Pepsico in India has achieved major success in the snacks markets with its brand Frito-Lays potato chips. Starting with challenges from the unorganized market and with a scope for selling branded, standardized chips to the Indian community with varied tastes and preferences, Frito-Lays has been a classic marketing and supply chain success story. One of the key reasons for its success is the ability to tie up the sourcing of potatoes for the manufacture of chips. The company had gone in a big way in north India with satellite farming, tying up with farmers for a committed supply of produce and working on supplier development strategies like adoption of best farming practices encouraged by PepsiCo. Exhibit 8.2 gives more information on this.

One can think of many such examples globally and also in the domestic Indian market. It is important to note here that many industries such as automotives, food,

Exhibit 8.2 Pepsi Expands Contract Farming

In December 2008, food and beverage major Pepsico India planned to increase its sourcing of raw materials from contract farming. This is part of the company's $500-million investment plan in India over the next three years. The company's foods business unit, Frito-Lay, procures 50 per cent of potatoes, required for making chips and strips, from contract farming in eight states across the country.

Source: http://www.businessworld.in/index.php/Fianchetto/Fianchetto-29-Dec-08.html.

pharmaceuticals, engineering, consumer products group, retail, and so on depend upon sourcing tie-ups and efficiently managing supplier relationship. These are industries that are in design-based manufacture, components-based, and/or dependent on key material from a single or a few suppliers where relationship management becomes critical. It is also pertinent to mention here that synchronization of sourcing with other drivers is important for effective supply network management.

8.2 DEFINITION OF PURCHASING, PROCUREMENT, AND SOURCING

Purchasing, procurement, and sourcing are used interchangeably by management professionals as well as by organizations. Though all these are intended for acquiring material for a focal organization to add value, there is a subtle difference between these three. It may be important for a supply chain professional to appreciate the same in order to improve functional effectiveness.

Purchasing would be more on the operational aspect of buying, which means acquiring goods or services to accomplish business goals as per policy. There are a number of administrative procedures to be followed while buying, and the core of the purchase process is to maintain such administrative guidelines in acquisition of material. Purchase of consumables to capital equipment may have to follow certain set procedures. A set of such guidelines followed by a manufacturing company in engineering is given in Appendix 8.1 to indicate the approach of Indian companies in the purchase function.

Procurement is the process of acquiring goods or services from preparation of a requisition through receipt, and approval of invoice for payment. It involves activities like purchase planning, standards determination, specifications development, supplier research and selection, value analysis, price negotiation, actual acquisition and possession of material, supply contract administration, and other related functions. Procurement is more of planning orientation and includes technical, commercial, and administrative processes of purchasing. In agriculture-based products such as the manufacture of plantation white sugar in India, a deep analytical procurement plan has to be in place. The functional manager responsible for cane procurement for a season starting from October and ending in next September must plan ahead of a year and execute the plantation plan and register farmers and suppliers for procurement.

In satellite farming conditions in India, where a factory has to develop farming through contracts valid for a limited time period for developing supplies, meticulous planning and execution of procurement strategies are important. In Chapter 3, we had mentioned about the success of ITC in the food business, which is again based on smart procurement initiatives. Engineering companies and many other businesses also rely on an efficient procurement process for establishing success in business. Purchase managers must bring planning orientation when they work on procurement initiatives in supply management.

Sourcing initiatives in supply management have to have a strategic orientation. With a view to development, and to setting up a reliable and effective supply base, a firm must have structured sourcing strategies executed through a procurement plan and efficient purchase processes. For example, an automotive company buys braking systems for its model variants from a tier I company. Though technology and the production plan are standardized, the firm must work closely with the supplier for developing cost-reduction strategies, improving product effectiveness, and work towards developing new models so that the time to market could be faster. Also, the firm must work on such cases with one or two vendor situations where the demand is divided between two as a risk mitigation strategy. However, having multiple vendors can work against product standardization and create unnecessary proliferation in buying.

Thus, purchasing is an operational aspect of buying with an administrative orientation, procurement has a planning orientation and is important for sustained purchases of material, and sourcing is strategic orientation in developing purchases.

8.3 BUYING DECISION—GRID MATRIX AND GUIDELINES

Buying decision can be analysed in a two-by-two matrix with criticality of material on one axis and value/cost in another axis. Both are judged to be on a scale of high and low as shown in Figure 8.1.

1. **Generalized items:** These are low cost/value items and low in criticality, typically consumables such as lubricants, in a production process. These items typically can be purchased off-the-shelf and are highly standardized. Also, these items could not be a competitive differentiator among peers in business. Firms generally go through administrative buying or off-the-shelf or through the web. Let us take the case of computer laser printers, which are used at home or in small offices. Generalized items would be value-added components of buy which may include information kit like user manual, warranty cards, and so on, which are all standardized items.

2. **Volume-based items:** These are items that are standardized through engineering and may be common among competitive products. Product design and engineering may not be a differentiator for such an item. Still it cannot be considered as an off-the-shelf item because the value could be important for negotiation and for achieving a cost advantage. These products may not be critical for performance but are important for product functionality and value. Product groups such as tyres in OE cars can be considered as an important component but not a differentiator in the technology of the focal organization in the network, namely the automotive company. For example, Toyota manufacturers would leave development of tyres to OE component manufacturer. The supply chain manager would be interested in the value he/she can achieve while procuring the same from vendors. Typically, these are products where there are multiple vendors and the firm deals with buying these components by creating competition among the vendors for achieving a cost advantage. In the case of computer printers, which were discussed earlier, these could be electrical and communication cables, paper handling, outer cases, and so on.

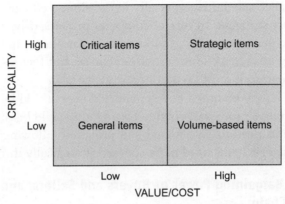

Figure 8.1 Product criticality and value/cost relationship in sourcing

3. **Critical items:** These are the products that may not be very high in terms of cost/value compared to the overall product cost but would be critical in establishing product functionality. It would be like a brake lining in a car's brake system, which is critical for the safety of the car. The quality of manufacture and consistent endeavour to improve by the vendor are important criteria in selecting a vendor. In the case of computer printers, the decision could be based on the quality of the cartridges. Though it is more of a consumable and related to volume usage, it is critical in OE that the right cartridges are selected for a model. Apart from cartridges, it could also be control panels and membrane switches in a printer that could be critical items. The selection of such a vendor would depend upon who provides the best quality and is willing to work closely with the OE and bring about continuous product improvements. Generally, firms have few such suppliers and work closely with them. (Refer to Figure 8.1)

4. **Strategic items:** These are all high value/cost items and are also critical for the performance of the product. The decisions pertaining to the suppliers of these components are strategic in nature. As such suppliers and components are expensive and important in the long term; the manufacturer cannot disown the relationship easily. They become an integral part of the business and are familiar with critical processes, or components, or both. These are suppliers along with whom the focal organization works on design collaboration, concurrent engineering, prototypes, and so on. There is constant dialogue on technology advancements and about bringing in additional features to customers. For any such product, the focal organization would go for either a single-source dedicated vendor or at best adopt a two-vendor policy. At times, the focal organization also enters into a strategic relationship through alliances, joint ventures, or other forms of investments.

For example, parts of a car engine, which are responsible for engine performance, would come under this category. One can think of body metal, which again needs to be of high quality. Although it is classified under commodities, the sheet metal for the body of an automobile needs to meet specific performance standards, especially in developed countries where safety standards are very stringent. In case of computer printers, drivers and memory are critical for the performance of printers and are considered to be of high value. Thus, sourcing of strategic items requires analysis and focuses at a higher level of management, so it must be part of a strategic plan.

It may be noted that generalized items could be purchased following administrative processes; volume-based items could be purchased or procured; critical items need to be planned and procured following a procurement process; and strategic items need to be sourced strategically through long-term relationships.

8.3.1 Bargaining Power of Buyers and Sellers, and Its Relevance in Sourcing Chain

Porter (1975) mentioned five forces that impact industry competitiveness and set the base of strategic initiatives of a firm: threat of entry, substitutes, bargaining power of buyers, bargaining power of sellers, and inter-firm rivalry. In a supply chain, this framework would be useful for the focal organization to understand the bargaining power of sellers and the organization's power while buying from its sellers.

It is important that the focal organization nurture a good relationship with its suppliers. The relationship matures based on experience and trust created by both the transacting parties. Trust is fundamental in building a relationship between the supplier and the focal organization. If both the parties believe that mutual interest would be taken care of as actions are initiated for overall supply chain profit improvements, the trust must be firm.

Trust between the supplier and the focal organization would facilitate:

- Understanding each other's objectives and synchronizing actions towards achieving a seamless supply network.
- Better sharing of information and smooth communication, leading to transparency in actions. This would again avoid speculative initiatives and response by way of back-up plans for supply, over-stocking, and so on. This would also improve productivity as unnecessary efforts are being avoided through timely communication and synchronization of activities for meeting demand and supply.

It is said that organizations do not easily lend themselves for scaling up on a trust-based relationship. A trust-based relationship works mainly when there is mutual dependence and competitive dependence of power is equally relevant for both parties. Trust would also be influenced by the power enjoyed by the buyer and the focal organization.

It may be observed from Figure 8.2 that:

1. When supplier dependence is low on the firm and the firm's dependence on the supplier is also low, there would be a situation of low level of interdependence between the two. This can be a possible situation when there are a large number of buyers and sellers for a product. The situation is common for highly standard-

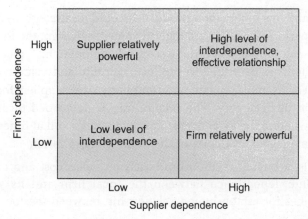

Figure 8.2 Interdependence between a firm and its suppliers

ized and homogeneous products/services with minimal or no differentiation. Typically, these could be generalized items as described in product criticality and value/cost relationship in sourcing.

2. When supplier dependence is high on the firm but the firm's dependence on the supplier is low, there would be a situation where the firm is a dominant partner. This happens when there are a large number of sellers and few buyers. Typically, these could be volume-based items as described in product criticality and value/cost relationship in sourcing. These are standardized products and cost could be a differentiator. Apart from product volume, even purchase value of huge numbers could lead to low supplier power in a buyer relationship of a supply chain network.

3. When supplier dependence is low on the firm and the firm's dependence on the supplier is high, there would be a situation where the supplier gets to play a dominant role. This happens when there are a large number of buyers and few sellers for a product. It could be a niche component, design, or material, with quality and possession being differentiators. For example, Bosch supplies a common rail fuel injection pump for Fiat's 1.3 multijet diesel engine. The same engine is used by Fiat (Palio and Linea), Maruti (Swift, D-zire, and Ritz), Tata (Indica, Manza). Bosch being the only supplier for that engine enjoys a monopoly. By design, the focal firm could have created such suppliers in order to control competition. Typically, these could be critical items as described in product criticality and value/cost relationship in sourcing. For example, the supplier of steering, brake systems, and clutches for car manufacturers could fall in this category. The buyer-supplier relationship is developed through an alliance mode, wherein the focal firm shares technology and leads the R&D efforts of the vendor organization.

4. When both the supplier and the focal organization have a high dependence on each other, there would be a situation of high level of interdependence and effective relationship between them. This can occur when there are few buyers

and few sellers for a product. It could be strategic items that could be critical for performance and are high in value. By design, the focal firm could have created such suppliers in order to control competition. Typically, these could be strategic items as described in product criticality and value/cost relationship in sourcing. For example, engine parts and body steel suppliers for car manufacturers can fall in this category. The relationship is developed through an alliance spectrum, wherein the focal firm shares technology and at times participates in capital and management efforts of the vendor organization.

Thus, a buying relationship based on value/cost and criticality, and matrix mapping interdependence between the focal firm and its suppliers provide suitable guidelines for establishing a relationship between the focal organization and its suppliers.

A focal organization must note that a simple power-based relationship would not be desirable because it would lead to one-stage gains, often at the expense of other stages. It can also hurt a company when the balance of power changes and the less powerful at any stage is not involved or is less cooperative when it comes to improvements. These advantages can be realized if the focal firm initiates trust building exercises and support with deterrence approach, where formal contracts and agreements facilitate to clear certain doubts and suspicions among less powerful players in the system.

Mutual cooperation and building of trust work because they align incentives and goals among partners. When there is trust between the supplier and the focal organization, it is easier to communicate a change in production plan, share the launch programme of a new product, and so on. Costing and effort deployment can be shared and worked on a mutually acceptable basis so that time-to-market can be reduced.

For example, a car manufacturer wants to improve the steering functionality in new versions of a car. Such a firm has to necessarily work with a steering supplier who would be a tier I vendor to the firm and also get involved in the product development process through the vendor. Unless there is trust and cooperation between the two players, such car model improvements cannot be done. Obviously, the focal firm must align not only the goal of improvement but also incentives or profitability improvements on such initiatives with the vendor. One may note that once there is trust, the actions of the players are to coordinate and implement as in this case. The resultant effect is that the supply chain performance measured by profitability and productivity improves by reducing duplication or allocation of efforts to the appropriate stage. This would also encourage greater sharing of information as there is adequate trust and cooperation created even on strategic issues, and hence planning and operations information flow could be enhanced.

Firms may use a deterrence-based approach through the use of formal contracts to start off a trust-based relationship. Normally, contracts should not be seen as mutually exclusive for a trust-based relationship. It may be worth having an appropriate contract in place even if there is perfect trust between the supplier and the firm. One of the problems noticed in practice is that while the going is good, firms do not have a formal contract in place. But once there is a trigger of the slightest issue, the relationship and trust get spoiled. This is seen among firms during times of market fluctuations, deviations in goals, and suspicion about fair and reasonable sharing of incentives. When there is a contract in place, at least it would mirror an agreement entered into consciously and resolve the souring points of any relationship.

It is also pertinent to note that the key aspect in sourcing is that parties would behave in a way that trusting each other would be on self-interest. With increasing competition, firms are highly self-interested in building trust and relationship with engaging partners. As part of corporate governance, firms have well laid-out purchase policy and procedures. They are vocal and open about the same, as corporate governance code has increasingly been deployed. Exhibit 8.3 is an interview with S. Rathinam, Director, Finance, BGR Energy Systems Ltd on the purchase policy of the company.

There is another school of thought that discusses about process-based view. According to this view, trust and cooperation are built over time as a result of a series of interactions. When two firms enter into a dialogue of business as supplier and focal firm in a supply network, there is a detailed evaluation process in which the scope for understanding each other is high. Also, the focal firm may go through evaluation processes and referral checks, and initiate a business that could be a trial or a test order. Such transactions are built over time and mutual trust is established as the business relationship strengthens between two. This is quite common if incentives and goals are transparent and a good information flow is established. Positive interactions strengthen the belief in cooperation from the other party. One would expect the relationship to go through a learning curve and bond faster for the mutual benefit in the supply network.

As mentioned earlier, the focal firm may rely more on a deterrence-based view initially. But then it evolves to a process-based view between the supplier and the focal firm. It is important that firms evolve in building trust but contractual practice may be maintained to capture roles and responsibilities, rewards and penalties, and more importantly, as a risk mitigation aspect. A contractual agreement is the best recommended practice in good corporate governance.

8.4 PURCHASING

Purchasing refers to the activity of acquisition of raw materials, equipments, services, and supplies including consumables. The user department would raise an indent based on which the purchase department would process administratively the transaction of buying. An indicative purchase policy and procedures for an engineering firm are given in Appendix 8.1, which gives an idea of how the various functions are intensely involved in the process of buying. As a supply chain manager, one must be familiar with various facets of buying.

Purchase could be of routine and non-routine items, and capital and current budget items. There are certain purchases that are off-the-shelf, while there are certain

---

Exhibit 8.3   An Interview with S. Rathinam on the Purchase Policy of BGR Energy Systems

Questions & Answers	Questions & Answers
1. Describe your business and key concerns in supply chain management	4. Such instances may impose penalty on the supplier or on you as the case may be. How are those being handled?
We are in the business of design, manufacture, and supply of equipments for power stations, refineries, and petrochemical projects in India and abroad. We construct large power stations (gas-based and coal-based) producing up to 600 MW power at present.	There were many incidents where we had to call off an MTO but there is a system in place to track our orders by continuous review.
Our key concerns are:	5. How do you evaluate the financial stability of a supplier?
• Non-availability of large cranes for loading and unloading	We review the financial statements and check the banking limits before placing orders.
• Lack of heavy duty trucks for transportation	6. What are the key commercial issues covered in your contract, especially with respect to supply risk and shipment risk?
• Increasing freight cost due to increase of oil price	Supply risk—Late deliveries (LD) and risk purchase
• Non-availability of organized transport companies	Shipment risk—Material Despatch Clearance Certificate and pre-despatch instruction
• Lack of regulation to phase out old trucks (resulting in accidents)	7. Are there instances where you have faced such risks? How were the risks handled?
• High corruption in ports and customs, resulting in harassment	Yes, there were many incidents of levy of LD on vendors and most of our contracts insist on pre-inspection.
• On the positive side, good roads will improve supply chain in the future	
2 When you place an order to a supplier, how do you evaluate the supplier's track record especially on Made-to-order (MTO) capital equipments?	8. In your opinion, how are you benefited by technology deployment in buying?
We evaluate the vendor's track record by:	We have implemented SAP, which addresses all concerns in supply chain seamlessly. E-procurement/reverse auction are also practised.
• Past performance of orders placed by us	9. What are the strategic sourcing initiatives that you have undertaken? For example, supplier development, sharing of technical inputs, facilitating financial flows, and support of key management staff, and so on. If any, please give an example.
• Reference list of vendors and reference checks	
• Completion reports	
• Approval by leading agencies like Engineers India, BHEL, and so on	
3. Are there instances when MTO has been called off either by a supplier or your company? If so, under what circumstances?	
We generally call off an MTO when our customer calls off an MTO on us. When we estimate that the vendor will not perform and the project will be delayed and we will be subjected to LD, we call off the MTO and resort to risk purchase.	We have developed tube suppliers from China. We have developed pipe suppliers from east Europe. We have identified steel supplier in Thailand. We have also developed some vendors for tools and spares in the same area as our factory. On many occasions we have provided drawings, and supported them with funds. We have even deputed our personnel to take trials on our vendor's machines.

Questions & Answers	Questions & Answers
10. Are there ethical policies explicitly stated in buying, and if so, how are those monitored?	14. Is supply chain audit part of internal audit? If so, in what time window is a supply network evaluated?
Yes. Our Standard Operating System and Policy (SOSP) required guidelines for the same. Based on that, suppliers are adequately exposed to such guidelines through RFP and bid documents.	Yes, supply chain audit is part of internal audit. Monthly audit is conducted. There is a pre-audit before payment.
11. What are the key aspects of financial flows in both receivables and payables management? How does the company manage the operating cycle in a growth phase like the one you are currently experiencing?	15. Is there a business excellence framework deployed in your company? Is the supply chain process part of the same?
Negotiation of proper payment terms is the key for cash flow management. We tie up adequate working capital funding for our growth phase.	There is no defined business excellence framework. However, all our systems and procedures result in business excellence.
12. Is top management involved in supply chain decisions like facilities management, product mix, transportation choices, sourcing, and so on? If so, please highlight the structure of decision making in the management hierarchy.	16. Any other experience that you would like to highlight?
Yes, top management is involved in supply chain decisions, especially on commercial aspects. As per delegation of powers mentioned in our SOSP, different levels of hierarchy from purchasing executive to purchasing committee, right up to the level of Director (Finance), Chairman, and Managing Director are involved in decision making.	Experience in an import transaction in one of my previous engagements. We placed an order to an American company for the import of scrap for steel manufacture. The terms are FOB terms. However, the American vendor picked up material from more than one port and when the vessel was sailing from one port to another port, it sunk. The vendor claimed payment from us since the insurance was taken by us. However, we initially rejected the claim stating that the ship was not fully loaded when it sunk and it was not in the FOB position. Rather, it was a partial shipment, which was not permitted in the terms of the Purchase Order. However, keeping the vendor relation in mind, we finally made an insurance claim and on receipt of the insurance money, we paid the vendor.
13. How do you build competency in your organization for supply chain management?	
We train manpower in supply chain management and also take experienced manpower from peer companies.	

materials/components/services that are used in regular production for which standing orders are placed. Such orders are called 'Blanket' or 'Master' agreements, which would reduce the cost of order placement. These types of agreements typically have a longer duration and increased scope of managing the price with band of volumes and price related to such bands of buy-ins.

Earlier, the industry practice was intense purchase activity on a day-to-day basis wherein the purchase managers would get involved in getting quotes, analysis, negotiation, placement of orders, and so on till goods were received and the payment was made. There have been significant changes in this with the application of technology, which enables automation of purchase processes. Figure 8.3 gives a generic illustration of purchase processes.

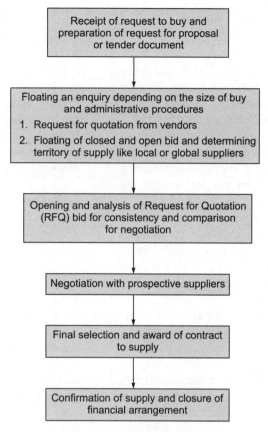

Figure 8.3 Purchase process

8.4.1 Purchase Process

1. Receipt of request to buy and preparation of request for proposal or tender document:

The purchase department receives a request to buy from the user department a material or component that may be required. Depending upon the value of the item to be procured and the nature of the buy, the purchase department may or may not approve the request. For example, in an IT solutions company, the testing department needs to buy an automatic testing tool with a particular number of licenses. Once the purchase department approves the buy, the purchase officer prepares a request for proposal document for the suppliers to understand the technical and commercial terms of the buy. In the case of capital equipments and large purchase, a tendering process is initiated, which requires preparation of detailed technical specifications and commercial terms, and the release of a tender with a deadline. It may be noted that whichever may be the route, the purchase officer must clearly indicate the requirement and terms for the acquisition of material/component/services.

2. Floating an enquiry depending on the size of the buy and administrative procedures:

(a) Request for quotation from vendors   Generally, Request for Proposals and Request for Quotation are commonly used. Here, we would like to mention how both are used. A Request for Quotation (RFQ) is a well-defined request, at times with a pinpointed monetary value for a given set of features and benefits. If one exactly knows what is needed and there are no modifications in the specifications, then RFQ could be the right way to proceed. The RFQ assumes that one has already defined the scope of work, has the necessary textual and graphics materials, and simply needs someone to perform the job. The parameters are finite, and any additional work is addressed as a separate project. An example of this is the purchase of laptops for senior executives of management.

On the other hand, a Request for Proposal (RFP) is a flexible request that provides a base price for the scope of work to be performed. However, it allows for additional billing on an hourly or task-oriented basis or for additional material or features as the case may be. The additional costs should be clearly defined during negotiation or delivery, for which necessary scope must be built in. For example, a project-based company wants to buy a timesheet and resource management tool. The company is not clear whether the scope of the current product would be adequate and prefers to retain the scope for defining and adding features based on experience when the timesheet and resource management software is being built. In such cases, modifications and work effort are billed over and above a base commitment, and RFP is preferred.

An RFQ is more project-oriented with clear definition of tasks, requirement, and resources for a delivery schedule. Normally, budget for RFQ would be fixed with some provision for standard escalation. On the other hand, RFP is process oriented with a flexible budget on approved ranges. Thus, both RFQ and RFP can be used depending upon the requirement of the purchase department.

(b) Floating of closed and open bids and determining the territory of supply (local or global suppliers)   Bid processes can be closed or open. This is decided on the basis of the procedure adopted and on the geography governed by the lender's terms. For example, projects funded by Asian Development Bank (ADB) that are beyond a certain value call for a tendering process that is notified to all the member countries. In some cases, both ADB and World Bank, and many other institutions follow a global tendering process.

Normally, processes vary significantly from stringent to very informal. Large corporations and governmental entities are most likely to have stringent and formal processes. These processes can utilize specialized bid forms that require specific procedures and details. Very stringent procedures require the bids to be opened by several staff from various departments to ensure fairness and impartiality. This is normally a condition applied in closed-bid tendering. Responses are usually very detailed. Bidders who do not respond exactly as specified or do not follow the published procedures can be disqualified. Closed bids are sealed and changes are not allowed during the bidding process. Competitors who participate in the bidding process make their quotes without any knowledge of the price quoted by others.

In open bids, the bidders quote a price for the materials or work that they are going to deliver. However, they have the right to reduce the price to compete with other bidders. In a governmental contract bid, a bidder using an open bid may agree to lower the quoted price if competitors outbid him/her. Smaller private businesses are more likely to have less formal procedures. Bids can be in the form of an email to all of the bidders specifying products or services. Responses by bidders can be detailed or just contain the proposed monetary value.

Thus, the decision of floating an open or a closed bid for a local, global, or selective territory is determined by corporate policy and as per the norms of the lending institutions wherever relevant.

3. Opening and analysis of RFQ/bid for consistency and comparison for negotiation:

Most bid processes are multi-tiered. Acquisitions under a specified value can be as per 'user discretion', permitting the requester to choose a supplier. These are commonly low-value items as shown in Appendix 8.1. The acquisition of low-value items is decided by the purchase department, whereas the acquisition of capital items and high-value items is decided by the top-level management. Closed bids are opened in the presence of bidder representatives to demonstrate fairness. In the case of a multi-tier bid, the technical bids are evaluated first. Only those who clear the technical requirements qualify for the evaluation of commercial bids. Once the bidding process is over, though typically L1 (lowest bid) is chosen, there is a need for detailed analysis, because there could be some commercial implications in the bids submitted.

Depending on the commodity being purchased and the organization, the bid may specify a weighted evaluation criterion. Some bids could be evaluated by a cross-functional committee. Other bids may be evaluated by the end user or the buyer in purchasing. Especially in small, private firms, the bidders could lack necessary skills to evaluate a bid and may end up selecting a less qualified vendor or could be driven more by the quoted price rather than the 'total cost of ownership'. A list of criteria used for the evaluation of a vendor is given in Appendix 8.2. The purchase team prepares the comparative statement and facilitates the key negotiator to make the right commercial decision.

4. Negotiation with prospective suppliers:

Once the comparative statement is ready, the purchase team of the focal firm negotiates on the commercial issues with respect to the delivery mechanism, and the range of acceptance on standards with respect to pricing, warranty, insurance cover, and so on. Negotiation is clearly the key skill that a purchase manager needs to have so that the right value is paid for the acquisition of material. Negotiation is successful only when the negotiator has well-researched information, backed by competitive power and the commitment to deal making. Systematic efforts must be taken in all these three for one to progress as a buyer over the years. The ultimate objective of any negotiation must be to accomplish a deal rather than to show off one's knowledge or power. It would be wiser to pitch for win-win deals so that the relationship can be sustainable. Any short-focused negotiation would lead to disaster in the long run because the inability of the supplier to comply to any of the features will lead to a revision of the 'total cost of ownership'. Hence, in a purchase process, negotiating skills and tact are absolutely essential to achieve effectiveness in a supply network.

5. Final selection and award of contract to supply:

Once the negotiation is complete, an order would be placed with necessary amendments to the specifications and commercial aspects mentioned in the tender. It is important to note that the contract is the final document on which supply would be effected and it is important that both parties are clear and have agreed to all the amendments to the bid document in writing and that the order is placed accordingly. The contract would be signed by the appropriate authority as defined in the delegation of administrative and financial powers, and the milestones for delivery and payment are to be captured in the document. The order must also clearly state rewards and penalties, the escalation process and the scope of amendments within a broader framework.

6. Post-award administration, confirmation of supply, and closure of financial arrangement:

Post-award administration typically consists of making minor changes, additions, or subtractions that in some way change the terms of the agreement or the 'Seller's Scope of Supply'. Such changes are often minor, but for auditing purposes must be documented into the existing agreement. Examples include increasing the quantity of a line item or changing the delivery schedule and sequence of an item, and so on. Post-award management also includes following up the delivery schedule on a project-based purchase. Often in a purchase process, physical, information, and financial flow fail to integrate. It is important that the purchase team coordinates a transaction from beginning to end, and moves from acquisition stage to support post-sale service and user department with the progression of a transaction. For example, the purchase department procures a conveyor for movement of material for the production department. When the conveyor fails, the responsibility of servicing and maintaining the same is with the production department (which is the user). For any service requirement the purchase department would facilitate the same.

Thus, a purchase process is a detailed technical, commercial, and administrative function and involves a thorough understanding and involvement of a supply chain manager to ensure gains across a supply chain network.

Table 8.1 Classification of procurement of goods

Features	Direct procurement	Indirect procurement	
	Raw material and production goods	Maintenance, repair and operating (MRO) supplies	Capital goods and services
Quantity	Large	Low	Low
Frequency	High	Relatively high	Low
Value	Industry specific	Low	High
Nature	Operational	Tactical	Strategic
Example from sugar industry	Cane from farmers	Lubricants, spare parts	Machinery like crushing mills, vacuum pans, boilers, turbines, and IT systems

8.5 PROCUREMENT PROCESS

Purchasing and procurement are used interchangeably in a supply chain. The purchasing process discussed above would cover the procurement function as well. In line with the discussion earlier on differentiating purchasing, procurement, and strategic buying, one may note that the procurement function takes care of the planning function. The process for direct and indirect procurement of materials would be the same except for some of the aspects highlighted here. Table 8.1 shows the nature of procurement decisions.

Procurement activities are often split into two distinct categories: direct or production-related procurement and indirect or non-production related procurement. Direct procurement occurs in a manufacturing set-up where the material goes in for product value creation. It encompasses all items that are part of finished products, such as raw material and components. Direct procurement, which is the focus in supply chain management, directly affects the production process of manufacturing firms. In contrast, indirect procurement activities concern 'operating resources' that a company purchases to enable its operations. It comprises a wide variety of goods and services, from standardized low-value items such as office supplies and MRO items to products and services such as capital goods and services.

During an acquisition process in the procurement phase, apart from other things, the following may have to be considered:

1. Detailed value, financial and economic analysis of the item to be acquired—viability needs to be established.
2. Raw material and such direct items may be contracted through proper planning and must be through committed resources and processes.
3. While regular supply is to be established in a procurement process, having a standard operating procedure, establishing pre-approved vendors, and setting up of quality standards for the same are important.
4. Rest of the purchase processes explained above apply here as well.

8.6 STRATEGIC SOURCING

Strategic sourcing involves activities of the purchase department towards long-term development of vendors wherein the effort and resources are invested for achieving competitive advantages in procurement. Such competitive factors could be with respect to cost, responsiveness, focus, and breadth of product and markets. Traditional purchase functions meet the needs of manufacturing or any other internal requirement, which would predominantly be a purchasing activity. Such an approach sets a narrow focus on the transaction, fails to develop a long-term relationship for competitive intelligence, and is not ideal for the long-term growth of the company.

The following are some aspects of strategic sourcing that would be discussed here:

- Decision to make or buy; criteria for outsourcing
- Supplier development
- Relationship with other functions

8.6.1 Outsourcing

Many manufacturing firms outsource the manufacture of parts and services so that they can focus on their core competencies. They expect their suppliers to deliver innovative and quality products on time at a competitive cost. When a supplier is not capable of meeting these needs, a buyer can bring the outsourced item in-house and produce it internally or switch over to a more capable supplier or help improve the existing supplier's capabilities. All of these options can work. The choice depends on price, volume, or the strategic nature of the procured item.

For low-value, non-strategic commodities, the cost of changing to a new supplier is low and is, therefore, the best option. At the other extreme, if an underperforming supplier provides an innovative product or process technology, the buyer may protect the potential advantage and bring the work in-house by acquiring the supplier. The cases that lie between these two extremes or include these extremes provide adequate scope for 'supplier development'.

Outsourcing is the act of transferring some of the organization's recurring internal activities and the manufacture and supply of components, parts, or services to outside vendors or service providers. The strategic use of outside parties to perform non-core activities is the purpose of outsourcing. Unlike the traditional practice of contracting, outsourcing is a strategic management tool that involves organization restructuring. The rationale for outsourcing is for the organization to focus on its core competencies, adopt 'best-in-class' practices, be more competitive, and thereby reduce cost and advance technologies.

The challenges of outsourcing could be the loss of expertise and dependence on vendors for components or contractual jobs. This may lead to loss of control, thereby increasing the organization's vulnerability as it becomes partially or totally dependent on a service provider. There could also be an increase in risk and uncertainty as the dependence on the vendor increases. But these concerns could be addressed through relationship management between the supplier and the focal firm.

There are three phases of outsourcing:

1. **Internal analysis and evaluation:**   It is important that the top management is involved in the process of outsourcing the manufacture of components or value addition through sub-contracting. Internal analysis would focus on identifying organizational goals and understanding the components or jobs to be outsourced. This has to be preceded by the efforts of the focal firm's team to identify and understand its core competencies. This exercise will allow organizations to identify non-core activities and functions for outsourcing.

   Evaluation must include a comparison of the costs involved in conducting the activities in-house versus the costs involved in outsourcing. Thereafter, a number of non-financial questions are to be addressed. These include: How critical are these functions/activities? What are the dependencies on these activities? Does this activity tend to become a 'mission critical' activity? After having addressed these questions, an analyst must look into long-term cost and investment implications. The total cost of ownership through outsourcing must be calculated. One also could evaluate how outsourcing non-core manufacture would impact work morale and support.

2. **Needs assessment and vendor selection:**   A focal firm may use information within the organization to identify vendors who could supply the components or services being outsourced. Based on this, a Request for Proposal or a bid is floated. This would define the requirements and terms for outsourcing. Vendor assessment and selection are done by a cross-functional team with expertise in legal, finance, human resources, and the specific function being outsourced. The team would evaluate the vendor's financial stability, cultural orientation, and proven track record. If possible, the team would contact existing clients of the vendor to understand and verify the capabilities. Once the evaluation is done and a selection is made, a contract needs to be awarded. The contract would involve negotiation of value, performance criteria, and how they will be measured. Success depends on both the parties' ability to communicate regularly and openly and express the mutual desire to succeed.

3. **Implementation and management:**   Outsourcing depends on defining areas or components to be outsourced, establishing a mechanism of measurement, training and facilitating change management in supplier and focal firm departments, and finally the ability to resolve conflicts to the satisfaction of both the parties.

Thus, outsourcing is one of the key strategic sourcing decisions that needs focus for supply network effectiveness.

8.6.2 Supplier Development

Supplier development is an activity that a buyer undertakes to improve a supplier's performance and/or capabilities to meet the buyer's short-term supply needs. These activities include assessing a supplier's operations, providing support and incentives to improve performance, fostering competition among suppliers, and working directly with suppliers, either through training or other activities. Supplier development requires both the supplier and focal firm to commit financial, capital and personnel resources to the work, to share timely and sensitive information, and to create an effective means of measuring performance.

Continuous long-term improvement of supplier performance is achieved by identifying value creation in the supplier and focal firm interface and also tweaking the model wherein supplier relations management could be a key differentiator. Implementing an integrated supply management strategy to maximize internal and external capabilities throughout the supply chain would be vital for translating strategy into action and value for all players in the network. For example, an auto major that is in the commercial vehicle segment depends upon improvements on castings and forgings for performance improvements.

Also, supply of castings and forgings would depend upon model variants that are produced, and synchronizing with the production plan and schedule. This product requires casting efficiency and continuous improvement of the material used. The auto major works closely with the supplier for new material development, model developments, improving production facilities for cost reduction and productivity improvement, and so on. Unless there is a strategic sourcing initiative, such development cannot happen. In this relationship, the supplier had engineering, design, and volume commitment, and also support of joint R&D. In fact, the top management of the supplier comprised retired members of the top management team of the focal firm (the auto major) working for them.

Although most firms are able to identify suppliers requiring development, few are completely successful in their supplier development efforts. The most commonly used framework for successful supplier initiatives are as follows:

1. Identification of right components/sub contract function for supplier development. As seen in the relationship between value/cost and criticality, supplier development focus is important in areas relating to low-value, high-criticality items and high-value, high-criticality items. Managers must assess the performance of suppliers who supply commodities in the 'strategic supplies' category. These commodities are considered strategically important, as they might be difficult to substitute or purchase from alternative suppliers.

2. Establishing an effective cross-functional team in a supplier development initiative, comprising cross-functional experts on supply chain, purchase, commercial, production, finance, and marketing, depending upon the size, volume, and nature of procurement.

3. Interaction with the top management of the supplier would be another important criterion. It may be noted that establishing processes and information technology could be important. Over and above, one must adopt three-pronged approach to supplier improvement: strategic alignment, supplier engagement through measurement and feedback, and being transparent and professional in approach. These become important as many times suppliers are selected only

on the basis of negotiating power, which could mean that commitment is missing.

4. Constant endeavour to identify improvement areas and put in efforts jointly. After identifying promising opportunities of supplier development, managers must evaluate them in terms of feasibility, resource and time requirements, and potential return on investments. The aim is to decide what the goals should be and whether they are achievable. Once it is done, specific metrics and targets must be agreed upon and it may be good to enter into a formal contract.

Thus, the success factors in supplier development are guided by relative positions of strengths, intention, and efforts to work together for common goals.

Supplier Development—Concern Areas

Though as an initiative supplier development is laudable for improving supply network effectiveness, there are certain concern areas that need management attention for making a supply network effective. These concerns could be specific to the supplier, the focal firm, and/or common to both parties.

Supplier-specific issues could be related to inadequate commitment and resources like people and technical capability. Commitment depends upon understanding and participation in development initiatives and how it would improve the future growth of the supplier. For example, in the case of Maruti Udyog or BHEL, suppliers who participated with commitment grew bigger and some of them have even become large players in the components and sub-contracting business. It is important that the supplier is committed to continuous improvement, both the parties agree on cost reduction targets, and both identify specific opportunities for an improvement within the supplier's manufacturing process. Similarly, most of the suppliers lack the resources such as engineering capabilities, equipment, and people skills especially of managerial talents that are required to implement the improvement ideas identified in a supplier-development initiative. To overcome this concern, the focal firm must at initial stages highlight the need for resources commitment and also support initially by supplementing with their resources. Many a time, organizations train suppliers directly or through third-party vendors in order to cover the gaps. Some of these trainings are specific skill improvements for identified supplier development initiative and generic training skills to improve supplier.

Concerns relating to the focal firm, who is a buyer in this situation, could be reluctance to fully commit to supplier development, primarily when they see no potential benefits. The reluctance could be due to the bargaining power enjoyed, the competitive condition in the supplier's market where there are many players, and lack of strategic focus. A focal firm would narrow down supplier development initiatives to a selective set of suppliers who could be relevant strategically either in terms of criticality, or value, or both. Many buyers optimize their supply bases and use single suppliers to achieve economies of scale. When embarking on such an initiative, developing a chosen supplier becomes important. Apart from the price of the goods it purchases, an organization examines the impact of its important suppliers on the quality and technology of its parts. Going back to the same example of Maruti Udyog, development of lamps suppliers could be important as the quality of lamps would impact customer satisfaction in a big way and customers cannot tolerate failure. Thus, a focal firm would use total cost and long-term strategies as criteria for justifying investments in its suppliers.

It may be important for focal firms to initially set small goals for buyers. When vendors experience the focal firm's initiative with minimum demand on resources, time, and effort, they develop confidence. As there is no fear of failure, the vendors are receptive to improvement initiatives. This also provides a window to experience the transformation of the focal firm from being a buyer to eventually a partner in development. Engineering companies and the auto components industry go through such processes regularly in vendor development initiatives.

Focal firms would use 'total cost of ownership' (TCO) as a measure to decide on investing on supplier development initiatives. TCO includes all lifecycle costs with respect to product or service acquired. This may include direct, indirect, explicit, and implicit costs associated with buying. TCO involves estimating risk component with respect to acquisition and deployment of product or service, and is included as part of costing. TCO is based on the concept that the purchase price is a part of TCO. There is a tendency for purchase managers to look at the landed price of a material while acquiring it; TCO insists on looking beyond the landed price.

Typically, TCO begins with requirements specification. The costs of all possible elements are listed. Explicit costs that need to be considered by the prospective supplier are shared. Implicit and hidden costs are mapped and considered while evaluating bids. However, all elements are identified in the pre-RFP stage itself. Once the tenders are floated, prospective suppliers and the focal firm gather more intelligence on purchase transactions by way of questions, clarifications, and support information, which improve TCO computation. It may be noted that TCO elements are prioritized, and only items of material substance are considered for analysis. The purchase department would choose the bid that is most economical on a TCO basis for awarding the contract.

In fact, an analyst in a supply chain may note that TCO is one option that builds a long-term view of buy and is applied especially for strategic buying. Both the vendor and focal firm would benefit when they apply this concept, especially when they are looking at an enduring relationship. The implementation of a TCO basis of selection would help to get out of a mental make-up for selecting the lowest bid. This will ensure that the buyer understands that it is not the acquisition but the cost of ownership that matters.

As it could be observed while computing TCO in Exhibit 8.4, quality is an important factor in supplier development. Quality standards are a part of requirement and buyers generally pre-approve a vendor after quality processes are adhered to. Once a vendor is in a pre-approved list, random quality checks are made and the rest goes by certification. This can happen only when there is an evolved relationship between the vendor and the focal firm. Quality adherence is important as it reduces various facets of risk like that of product, production schedule, and so on. It may be

---

Exhibit 8.4   Total Cost of Ownership

TCO elements:

- Define/Buy product or service
- Maintain—post-buy activity
- Relocate—post-buy activity
- Fallbacks—failure or any such condition, may cover warranty as well
- Implement or install products or services and costs associated with infrastructure
- Secure and insure
- Upgrade—as and when required due to buyer need or technology change
- Replace—normal circumstances or otherwise
- Handoff and dispose—retire the product or sell off
- Defects—failure to conform to requirements; compute costs of defects
- TCO analysis drives requirements
- Total cost of the procurement process
  - Direct process costs
  - Methods and tasks
  - Reviews/Approvals
  - Inspection and acceptance
  - Risk trade-offs
  - Hard and soft costs
  - Staff satisfaction
  - Internal customer satisfaction
  - Vendor relationship quality

One must also include the following while considering procurement:

- Time
- Infrastructure
- Experts support required and value of same in terms of time and effort cost
- Overhead
- Opportunity cost
- Relationship impact including the disputes that could arise, frequency, and process of settling the same
- Credibility impact

---

important on the part of the vendor and buyer to clearly arrive at a contractual relationship with respect to quality requirement so that the supply network is not jeopardized. Apart from defining expectations on quality standards, procedures for measurements of performance must be clear.

Thus, a TCO-based, quality-driven initiative from the focal organization would help to overcome fears of vendors with buyers.

There are certain concerns with respect to supplier-focal firm interfaces that need to be addressed while embarking upon supplier development initiatives. Concerns may originate in the interface between buyers and suppliers, in areas such as inter-organizational trust, alignment of organizational cultures, and ineffective communication of potential benefits.

One of the biggest challenges in supplier development is to cultivate mutual trust. Suppliers may be reluctant to share information on costs and processes, which may be sensitive and confidential. The concern arises from an assumption that the focal firm would use such data against the supplier and would not share improvement advantages to them. To overcome this, the focal firm may have to use its strategic position and win over supplier confidence and demonstrate fairness in action by being transparent and open to supplier interaction either individually, or in group, or both. The focal firm may also inform third parties like industry forums and even supplier forum to handle the same.

For example, some leading public sectors in India, such as BHEL, are believed to be encouraging suppliers and ancillary association to have openness in resolving issues. The supplier's confidential information must be kept exclusive. Sharing confidential information is unethical when dealing with new suppliers in high-technology areas. Thus, many companies safeguard their interests with nondisclosure agreements and even exclusivity agreements. This means that the supplier provides a specific product only to one buyer. Such agreements are necessary when dealing with high-technology products, to ensure a competitive edge for the buyer. However, legal involvement can be minimized. The buyer should consider the supplier as its extension. Formal contracts should be sparingly used. Alliance agreements between the buyer and the supplier must be established using a single advisor to minimize legal involvement.

Another factor that may affect supplier-focal firm interface is poor alignment of organizational cultures and changes that may occur. When conditions change, the existing supplier development approach, though successful, may no longer be valid. If some change in the supply chain, or plant locations, or any other external or internal factor induced change triggers, then it may affect the supplier development. Supplier development programmes must be designed keeping in mind the local and changing conditions.

There could be insufficient inducement to the supplier because of inadequate understanding of the benefits of supplier improvement programme, which could be either failure of the focal firm to explain the benefits or the buyer's inability to understand the same. Generally, a focal firm needs to communicate potential benefits of investing in the supplier development efforts to suppliers. If not, the supplier's total commitment may be lost. Buyers should offer financial incentives and offer repeat business to suppliers. This effort will gain the supplier's confidence and eventually commitment.

Focal firms, while embarking in their supplier development efforts, may encounter some problems. These problems often arise during meetings between buyer and supplier management teams—while defining development projects or initiatives, while defining agreement terms and determining metrics for success, and while monitoring project status and subsequently modifying strategies.

To avoid these problems, both the supplier and the focal firm must establish transparent and reliable communication. They should openly discuss impediments and resolve issues as soon as possible. The initial projects between the supplier and focal firm should be relatively easy to achieve. This will encourage both to work together in more complex and difficult development initiatives. If the initial targets set for a project are too complex, they usually result in poor follow-up. This is either due to lack of resources or lack of commitment from the supplier's side. The focal firm must sort out problems with the supplier in the initial stages itself. On the other hand, if a focal firm does not commit adequate resources for its proposed development effort, it is difficult to convince the supplier's top management. Therefore, firms should determine the cost they must bear, and the cost and resources to be shared with the supplier, well in advance. Finally, establishing metrics and a timeframe for the follow-up as well as sharing the responsibility of problem solving is critical to a project's completion.

Perhaps these suppliers do not recognize the value of improving the quality or delivery performance. Sometimes suppliers do not even realize that they have a problem. Sometimes front-end managers of the buyers and sellers do not support supplier development to avoid differences of opinion or ego clashes that may ensue. This issue, therefore, needs to be handled carefully by close monitoring and prompt action.

Strategic emphasis on the purchasing and supply chain management is essential for a strong supplier development effort. A strong purchasing mission statement reflects and drives strategic emphasis and alignment. A focal firm (buyer) may pursue its mission through:

1. Developing a world-class supplier base capable of meeting current and future needs.
2. Obtaining the highest quality, most cost-effective goods and services in a timely manner.
3. Establishing long-term relationships with supply partners that meet the company's standards and being committed to the manufacturer.

Relationship management is critical to the success of the supplier development programme. The supplier-focal firm relationship can progress as on an alliance spectrum (shown in Figure 8.4).

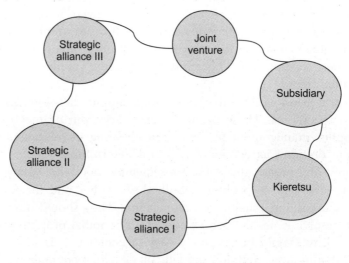

Figure 8.4 Supplier-focal firm relationship spectrum

Strategic alliance I is an option wherein the focal firm is willing to consider a vendor along with other vendors for development initiative without any commitment. Subject to fulfilment of quality and other standards, the focal firm is willing to support the vendor.

Strategic alliance II is an option wherein the focal firm would be willing to support on a volume commitment, subject to quality and other standards. It would be a longer term contract with scope for timely monitoring, evaluation, and scaling up standards.

Strategic alliance III is an option wherein the focal firm would be willing to support a supplier with technology and financial resource commitment along with level II commitments. This comes only after increased understanding and is based on criticality and value factors, and mostly likely the vendor could be supplying critical components for product performance.

Joint ventures are opportunities for enhancing supplier-focal firm relationship by securing business between them and ensuring supply for a focal firm's requirement. The focal firm and the supplier create an entity to monetize the relationship to fulfil its own requirement and supply to competitors and a larger industry base. The basic premise for a JV is that the components business is different from the products business but components per se have a huge potential. Through a JV, the focal firm can achieve certain competitive advantages. For example, an engineering company can invest in a JV with castings and forgings business, which would ensure supply for its own requirement as well as supply to the market. In a JV, the focal firm would not have a controlling interest.

There are cases where a focal firm can have a supplier who is a subsidiary. This is like a JV except for the fact that the focal firm scales up investment to a level of majority holding and the balance sheet can be consolidated. The advantage of having a subsidiary is that the focal firm is the majority stakeholder and would be able to drive strategic initiatives. Kieretsu is another form of relationship common in Japan. Kieretsu could be horizontal or vertical. In case of supplier-based kieretsu, it is vertical, where a focal firm develops a supplier through investment and also management (by deploying its own senior management as top management of the supplier kierestu company). Thus, investment and pecuniary relationship could impact supplier development. As mentioned earlier, apart from this, a power-based relationship would also impact the structure of partnering relationship in business.

Supplier development is an effective method to reduce costs and generate advantages across a supply network. One may note that initiating supplier-performance improvement is a challenging task. Continuous improvement can be achieved by investing time and effort on relationship managers who are determined enough to pay follow-up visits to suppliers, and continually enforce a strong programme of supplier evaluation and performance feedback.

8.6.3 Design Collaboration

One of the strategic aspects that a focal firm needs to focus on is collaborating with suppliers at the design stage itself for critical and strategic supplies. In case of volume-based products, collaboration would be on designing of logistics and support functions for reducing cost. Sustained revenue growth in any industry requires a steady stream of innovative products. Rather, competition has forced manufacturers to shrink product lifecycles and reduce costs, while meeting increased customer demands and supply chain profits. With intensity of globalization of business, teams of engineers, suppliers, and partners being dispersed around the globe, manufacturers are facing a challenge to reduce product time to market, improve quality, and increase corporate profitability (Exhibit 8.5).

Exhibit 8.5   Visteon Supplier Development Initiatives

Pressure on the automotive business across the globe pushes the industry to improve the output of its supply base while reducing costs and maintaining consistent output. Visteon Corporation is in the process of working with its supply base to eliminate waste, and improve design and manufacturing quality. Such initiatives would increase the operating margins of Visteon and its suppliers by employing a combination of short-term quick fixes and long-term collaborative improvements.

The global team of Visteon has set the goals as follows:

- Immediate waste reduction in engineering and manufacturing
- Improvements in design and manufacturing
- Business consolidation with a select number of top performing preferred suppliers

Suppliers that meet their clearly defined requirements enjoy significant financial rewards and enjoy favoured status on future quoting opportunities. The factors that lead to success are meaningful incentives, effective idea generation for supplier involvement, and follow-through and accountability.

Source: http://www.visteon.com/company/features/101602.html.

Making the right decisions at early stages of product development is critical. The need to involve suppliers in design becomes important as creative supply chains are driven by suppliers who enable manufacturers to come up with innovative and higher quality products. According to a research finding on concurrent design, 80 per cent of a product's lifecycle costs are committed in the earliest stages of product design. Furthermore, there is a tenfold cost every time a design flaw moves into the next development cycle. Hence, the focus would be to synchronize with supply chain partners on design collaboration so that one can reduce errors, design changes, and costs.

This is particularly true for short-life products like apparel or computers, where product lifecycles have shrunk dramatically, driving the need for even newer products. However, developing and bringing new products to market is becoming increasingly complex. With the driving forces of outsourcing and globalization, apparel supply chains have been rapidly disintegrating. Product designers, marketers, and manufacturers are no longer in the same building or organization. Hence, getting new products requires squeezing of the design phase and collaborating with all partners from an early stage so that time to market is short. Such an initiative reduces cost, improves the success of the product, and thereby revenue. It also allows high responsiveness as agility helps to rework faster.

One of the reasons for the success of Zara fashions is short lead times. In a traditional retail industry, a fashion store takes anywhere between six to fourteen months to introduce new fashions whereas Zara takes about thirty days to hit the market. This is possible because of constant interaction with customers through market research, especially using innovative practices. It has its own production facility to meet nearly 60 per cent of the total requirement. Design collaboration in this case is quickly identifying fashion trend, confirming, and coordinating with the supplier's unit either in internal supply network or external network, and then, quickly reaching the market to attract customers. Design collaboration from conceptualizing the product, trial version of the model, synchronizing market feedback, to commercial production with suppliers results in reduced cost, improved quality, and decreased time to market.

Let us take the case of automobile manufacture. The car segment in the automotive industry is highly competitive and the ability to launch new models is one of the differentiators. The success of Toyota over the years across the globe and new markets in Asia has led to awareness of cost competitiveness and growth of the industry. If a manufacturer has to succeed, it must reduce time to market and at the same time ensure cost competitiveness. A car manufacturer, being an assembly unit, depends on suppliers. Though a majority of supplies could be common parts across models, variants are required and suppliers need to be involved at early stages of model development so that there is flexibility in production and costs are under control. In the Indian automotive sector, major component manufacturers are believed to be actively involved in collaborative efforts from the design stage.

Not only does fashion, engineering, and the auto industry work on design collaboration but even traditional businesses like agro-based products involve supplier collaboration. Design may not be in product but in material content, thereby improving productivity. For example, the sugar industry in India is in constant collaboration with the farming community through research institutions. There is relentless endeavour to improve productivity and yield quality by improving the quality of sucrose in sugarcane. As mentioned earlier, Frito Lays works closely with farmers on farming practice and improves productivity and quality to give consistency on tastes to customers. Many players of the agricultural input product industry, such as fertilizers and chemicals, work closely with farming community too.

Thus, design collaboration focuses on reduced cost, improved quality, and decreased time to market. It is important to employ design for logistics and manufacturability, and to collaborate with all the partners in the design stage across the supply chain network. Focal firms must become effective design coordinators throughout the supply chain.

8.7 TECHNOLOGY FOR SOURCING FUNCTIONS

Technology would be one of the important enablers of effective sourcing functions. E-commerce, enabled by using electronic data transmission via the Internet, and the use of interactive virtual marketplaces by players are definitely impacting the ways B2B purchasing is taking place across the globe. Technology provides the following advantages for supply chain management:

1. Helps to share information about production plan and schedules.
2. Helps to enable collaboration among supply chain members and functional areas on the design of new products and services.
3. Helps to solicit new suppliers and supplier intelligence.
4. Helps to increase speed and accuracy of exchanging information, thereby reducing cost, time to market, and so on.
5. Helps to reduce cost of administering purchase function.

There are likely to be disadvantages such as difficulty in measuring cost and benefits in the use of technology, less flexibility, and need for professional training for sourcing managers. However, disadvantages are not overwhelming and the success of e-sourcing has proven that it is there to stay in future. Exhibit 8.6 shows e-sourcing success in India.

A detailed discussion on technology application in sourcing is done in Chapter 14.

Exhibit 8.6   E-sourcing Success in India

Tata Motors, which was struggling in the late 90's of the last century, regained its glory and is one of the top ten vehicle makers in the Asia-Pacific region in 2000. This was possible with a bold move to reduce costs, which included e-sourcing. It is believed that Tata Motors has saved more than Rs 100 crore, thanks to e-sourcing, and has conducted close to 300 auctions with the help of e-sourcing major FreeMarkets.

Dabur's first e-sourcing project was held in January 2002, by which it procured saffron, which was traditionally purchased from cultivators in Kashmir who were not the ideal candidates for a technology-driven process. FreeMarkets, the intermediary, facilitated buying trained farmers in the process. With the help of FreeMarkets, Dabur has already conducted a number of initiatives to source products like herbs, honey, spices, and even packaging. It is reported that Dabur has extended e-sourcing to reach international vendors. Today Dabur has not only managed to save costs by close to 8 per cent but has also managed to bring in transparency in the complex, fragmented market for herbs. The aggressive bidding by many vendors has cut costs massively and is reported to have saved substantial costs.

It is important to note that the success of the e-sourcing initiative depends on the quality of the database of suppliers the e-sourcing vendor has.

For instance, before entering the Indian market FreeMarkets spent more than a year in creating a database of suppliers to cater to different business segments.

Another important reason why e-sourcing has succeeded in India has been the timing. For instance, when there's a downturn in a business cycle, most Indian corporates look at cutting costs to survive and go for e-sourcing.

E-sourcing grows up

As more and more Indian companies are getting familiar with the concept of e-sourcing, they spread into other categories. Tata Motors in its first year started out with simple items like oils, lubricants, and fasteners. As confidence in the medium grew, the company added complex materials like castings, injection mouldings, and sheet metals. It is believed that it does close to 20 per cent of its purchases through e-sourcing.

E-sourcing is also happening through the reverse route and helping Indian suppliers access global companies. In the auto components industry many small and medium enterprises have been able to tap global giants to source their requirements. Today, many small Indian auto component players are being invited to participate in auctions. Previously, the same vendors could not even dream of getting an audience with global clients.

SUMMARY

Sourcing plays a major role in effective supply chain decisions as a focal organization depends upon outsider vendors for material procurement.

Once the material is procured, the firm adds value in its business model. Sourcing strategies are interwoven with supply chain strategies and are responsible for achieving the supply chain objectives of a firm.

Purchasing, procurement, and sourcing are used interchangeably by professionals. Though all these are intended for acquiring material for a focal organization to add value, there is a subtle difference among these three. Purchasing would be more on the operational aspect of buying, which means acquiring goods or services to accomplish business goals as per policy. It involves a number of administrative procedures and the core of the purchase process is to maintain such administrative guidelines in the acquisition of the material.

Procurement is the process of acquiring goods or services from preparation of a requisition through receipt and approval of invoice for payment. It involves activities such as purchase planning, standards determination, specifications development, supplier research and selection, value analysis, price negotiation, actual acquisition and possession of material, supply contract administration, and other related functions.

Sourcing initiatives in supply management have strategic orientation. With a view to development and forming a reliable and effective supply base, a firm must have well-thought and structured sourcing strategies, executed through a procurement plan and efficient purchase processes.

It may be noted that generalized items could be purchased following administrative processes; volume-based items could be between purchases and procurement; critical items need to be planned and procured following the procurement process; and strategic items need to be sourced strategically through long-term relationships.

Trust between the supplier and the focal organization would facilitate understanding the objectives of each other and synchronizing towards an efficient supply network, and better sharing of information and smooth communication leading to transparency in actions.

A buying relationship based on value/cost and criticality, and matrix mapping interdependence between the focal firm and its suppliers provides guidelines for establishing the relationship with suppliers for achieving supply chain objective through integration of supplier relationship management with other components. Advantages can be met if the focal firm initiates trust-building exercises and support with deterrence approach, where formal contracts and agreements facilitate to clear certain doubts and suspicions among less powerful players in the system.

Firms may use a deterrence-based approach through the use of formal contracts to start off a trust-based relationship. In a process-based approach, two firms enter into a dialogue of business as the supplier and focal firm in a supply network, and there is a detailed evaluation process in which the scope for understanding each other is high. It is important that firms evolve in building trust but contractual practice may be maintained to capture roles and responsibilities, rewards and penalties, and more importantly, as a risk mitigation aspect and recommended practice in good corporate governance.

A purchase process is a detailed technical, commercial, and administrative function and involves a thorough understanding and involvement of a supply chain manager to ensure gains across the supply chain network.

Strategic sourcing involves those activities of the purchase department wherein effort and resources are invested for long-term development of vendors for achieving competitive advantages in procurement. Such competitive factors could be with respect to cost, responsiveness, focus, and breadth of product and markets.

Outsourcing is the act of transferring some of an organization's recurring internal activities and manufacture and supply of components, parts, or services to outside vendors or service providers. The strategic use of outside parties to perform non-core activities is the purpose of outsourcing.

Supplier development is an activity that a buyer undertakes to improve a supplier's performance and/or capabilities to meet the buyer's short-term supply needs. These activities include assessing a supplier's operations, providing support and incentives to improve performance, fostering competition among suppliers, and working directly with suppliers, either through training or other activities. Success factors in supplier development are guided by relative positions of strengths, intention, and efforts to work together for common goals.

Total cost of ownership' is one model which builds a long-term view of the buy and is applied especially for strategic buying. It includes all lifecycle costs with respect to the product or service acquired.

Technology would be one of the important enablers of effective sourcing functions. E-commerce, enabled by using electronic data transmission via the Internet, and use of interactive virtual marketplaces by players are definitely impacting the ways B2B purchasing is taking place across the globe.

KEY TERMS

Blanket or master agreements: These are certain materials/components/services that are used in regular production, and standing orders would be placed in bulk and delivery staggered so that the cost of order placement is reduced.

Design collaboration: Design collaboration embraces activities from product concept development, trial version of the model, synchronizing market feedback to commercial production between the focal firm and the suppliers to result in reduced cost, improved quality, and decreased time to market.

Deterrence-based approach: Use of formal contracts to start off a trust-based relationship is more common in the deterrence-based approach.

Direct procurement: Direct procurement occurs in a manufacturing set up where the material goes in for product value creation. It encompasses all items that are part of finished products, such as raw material, components, and parts.

Indirect procurement: Indirect procurement activities concern 'operating resources' that a company purchases to enable its operations. It comprises a wide variety of goods and services, from standardized low-value items, such as office supplies and MRO items, to products and services such as capital goods and services.

Multi-tier bid: A multi-tier bid is one where first technical bids are evaluated and only those who clear technical requirements qualify for evaluation of commercial bids.

Outsourcing: Outsourcing is the act of transferring some of an organization's recurring internal activities and manufacture and supply of components, parts, or services to outside vendors or service providers. The strategic use of outside parties to perform non-core activities is the purpose of outsourcing.

Process-based approach: When two firms enter into a dialogue of business as a supplier and focal firm in a supply network, there are detailed evaluation processes in which the scope for understanding each other is high.

Procurement: Procurement is the process of acquiring goods or services, and involves from preparation of a requisition to receipt and approval of invoice for payment. It includes activities such as purchase planning, standards determination, specifications development, supplier research and selection, value analysis, price negotiation, actual acquisition and possession of material, supply contract administration, and other related functions.

Purchasing: Purchasing would be more on the operational aspect of buying, which means acquiring goods or services to accomplish business goals as per policy. It has a lot of administrative procedures to be followed up in buying, and the core of the purchase process is to maintain such administrative guidelines in the acquisition of material.

Request for proposal: A Request for Proposal is a flexible request that provides a base price for the scope of work to be performed, but allows for additional billing on an hourly or task-oriented basis as a job or for additional material or features as the case may be. It becomes clearer when defined during negotiation or delivery, for which necessary scope must be built in.

Request for quotation: A Request for Quotatian is a well-defined request, at times, with a pinpointed monetary value for a given set of features and benefits.

Strategic sourcing: Sourcing initiatives in supply management have a strategic orientation. With a view to development, and setting up a reliable and effective supply base, a firm must have well-thought and structured sourcing strategies, executed through the procurement plan and efficient purchase processes.

Supplier development: It is an activity that a buyer undertakes to improve a supplier's performance and/or capabilities to meet the buyer's supply needs.

Tier I vendors: A firm that supplies parts or services to a focal firm whose supply network is mapped is a tier I vendor as it supplies directly to the firm. A brake system supplier in case of a car manufacturer is a tier I supplier.

Tier II vendors: A firm that supplies to the tier I vendor and thereby is an indirect vendor or derived vendor. OE car manufacturer could ask brake system supplier to procure brake linings from a specific vendor, who is tier II in this case.

Time to market: Time to market is the length of time it takes for a product to move from the conceptual stage to being available for sale.

Total cost of ownership (TCO): TCO includes all lifecycle costs with respect to the product or service acquired.

CONCEPT REVIEW QUESTIONS

1. Discuss the role of sourcing and its importance in achieving supply chain objectives. Give some examples.

2. Explain the benefits of effective sourcing decisions with some illustration.

3. 'Nomenclature of purchasing, procurement, and sourcing with respect to decision hierarchy are different.' Elucidate with examples.

4. Define the various processes in purchasing. What factors should be considered when making purchasing decisions?

5. Analyse the relationship between cost/value and criticality of items in sourcing with examples. Also, describe the role of power dependence between buyers and suppliers influencing sourcing decisions.

6. What do you understand by strategic sourcing? Explain the key facets of strategic sourcing.

7. Explain the importance of outsourcing of components and services including the sub-contracting process. What are the factors that influence outsourcing? Describe ways of managing outsourcing effectively.

8. Explain supplier development, its advantages, and concerns.

9. Why should supply quality be considered in supplier selection decisions?

10. Why should design collaboration capability be considered in supplier selection decisions? How can the focal firm drive collaboration? What are the advantages and challenges of aligning design collaboration with suppliers?

11. What are the technology applications in a sourcing decision and how do these improve sourcing effectiveness?

12. 'Firms focus on external organizations for improving effectiveness and internal sourcing process improvements could be complementary factors.' Discuss.

CRITICAL THINKING QUESTIONS

1. You are a supply chain analyst with a fast growing engineering company, which has components that can be value-added at the site after they are received from vendors. Based out of south India, you are currently growing at 40 per cent. Since your customers are in western and northern India, the Supply Chain Head wants you to evaluate vendor development in a new engineering cluster. Explain after going through the competitiveness of the Indian engineering industry suppliers and prepare a report supporting your analysis.

2. You are a Purchase Head of a leading two-wheeler automotive company located out of western India. You are expected to engage outbound transportation of motorcycles and scooters produced by the company. The top management expects you to evaluate the option of directly coordinating movement through engagement of vehicles from market vis-à-vis a dedicated third-party logistics service provider being given the responsibility of the movement. Prepare your report supporting your decision.

3. You are the Head of Procurement of oilseeds for your vegetable oil brand of a leading food business division of an MNC. Your board is excited at the success of ITC in deploying e-choupal. You are expected to deploy similar technology for procuring groundnut and rapeseed. Explain how you would do the same with clear identification of challenges and resolution in change management.

4. Analyse the following case. Quality is an important issue to consider for the analysis.

Make or Buy Decision Evaluation

High Volt Electricals (HVE) is a leading electrical manufacturer of circuit breakers based in Chennai. It manufactures a die-based moulded case, circuit and switch knob internally. Having purchased consumables and packing material, HVE packs internally, using contract labour. The management has determined that there is a possibility of converting this activity as outsourced function, moving it to a 3PL service provider who would pack, stock, and move. They wanted to compare the cost of packing internally and the cost of service by the 3PL service provider to do the same function.

You are working as a supply chain analyst with HVE. You have negotiated a tentative purchase price under a three-year contract with a long-term supplier, Chennai Logistics Service Providers (CLSP)—a service charge of Rs 20 per piece for moving from unit and packing. The current production volume is 1,000,000 and the growth rate is 10 per cent. The contract will have to be for three years.

The current cost of packing internally for a unit of circuit breaker is as follows:

Purchased material	Rs 12
Labour	Rs 1.50
Depreciation and other charges	Rs 1.50

In addition, variable overheads are 100 per cent of direct labour per unit and fixed overheads are 150 per cent of direct labour. Also, approximately Rs 1,000,000 in discontinuation or switching costs would be incurred if a make-or-buy decision occurs.

Answer the following questions based on the information above:

(a) Develop a make-or-buy analysis for the HVE and report your recommendations in the form of a professional report to the top management.

(b) What type of qualitative issues must the management consider for such type of decisions? List why make-or-buy decisions can have an important impact on a firm's business.

(c) What type of uncertainties may come into picture while taking these decisions and how do you counter them?

PROJECT ASSIGNMENTS

1. Using web research on online exchanges like FreeMarket, 01market (Wipro), and Matex, which are procurement enablers, discuss about procurement exchanges and facilitators. What were the problems faced initially and efforts taken to overcome the same?

2. Visit a nearby engineering plant, auto component supplier, and a retail chain outlet and analyse the various supplier development initiatives that each one is part of. Make a note of your findings.

3. Visit a large organization and study its outsourced components or services business and evaluate the advantages and disadvantages of the same.

REFERENCES

Handfield, R.B., 'Avoid the Pitfalls in Supplier Development,' *Sloan Management Review*, IV Q 2000

Porter, Michael E., *Competitive Strategy*, Free Press, New York, 1980

www.businessworld.in
www.expresscomputeronline.com
www.marutisuzuki.com
www.visteon.com

Appendix 8.1 A Model Purchase Document for an Engineering Manufacturing Firm

PURCHASE

Purchase Policy

1. Company will buy raw materials and components in conformity with the specifications and technical delivery conditions stipulated in the material indents.
2. Purchase department shall be responsible to procure raw materials, bought-outs, consumables, stores, packing materials, tools, tackles, spares, and capital goods.
3. Purchase of raw materials and standard products will be done on a consolidated basis. That is, the annual requirement of all the divisions and group companies will be estimated and procurement action will be taken accordingly. Items other than raw materials and standard products will be procured by the divisions for each project separately.
4. There shall be a minimum of, say, five approved vendors for each material. The purchase department will broad base the vendor list on a continual basis.
5. Purchases will be made on limited tender basis from approved vendors.
6. Orders will be placed on technically acceptable L1 vendors.
7. Other things being equal, purchase preference will be given to Group companies.
8. Company will avail Advance Licence/Project Import Certificate, etc. wherever concessional duties and taxes are available for the project.
9. In respect of single purchase valuing more than, say, Rs 2 lakh, a two-bid system, that is, technical and commercial, will be followed.
10. Company will not open LC or accept bill of exchange for indigenous procurement. As far as possible, direct payment should be insisted for imports also.

Responsibility of Purchase Head

1. Maintenance of database.
2. To attend Contract Acceptance Meeting and seek clarification if any.
3. To attend Contract Schedule Meeting and commit a procurement schedule.
4. Vendor development and approval.
5. Receipt and review of material indents.
6. Floating of enquiry.
7. Evaluation of offers.
8. Placement of purchase orders.
9. Expediting of orders placed, and receiving and monitoring the manufacture and supply schedule of vendors.
10. Supply of materials to the factory, sub-contractors, and site.
11. Processing of vendor payments.
12. Maintenance of purchase records.
13. To submit progress reports.
14. To gather and update intelligence and industry perspective on national and global manufacturers of all raw materials and bought-outs.
15. Submission of request to Finance for opening of LC/order amendments, etc. and follow-up.
16. Follow-up of suppliers' Bank Guarantees.
17. Extension of Invocation of suppliers' Bank Guarantees.
18. Arrangement of material inspection and issuance of despatch clearance.
19. Follow-up for replacement of rejected items or for recovery of payment.
20. To protect intellectual property rights relating to design and engineering.

Systems and Procedures: Procurement Scheduling

1.1 Based on input received in the Contract Acceptance meeting, the purchase department will prepare and commit a procurement schedule consisting of the following during the management meeting:

(a) Schedule for floating of enquiry

(b) Schedule for placement of orders

(c) Schedule for supply of materials to the factory, sub-contractors/site

1.2 The following shall be the broad timeframe for the above activities:

(a) Floating of enquiry	One week from the date of receipt of material indent
(b) Time to be given	One week/Two weeks to vendors to respond to enquiry
(c) Evaluation of offers and negotiation	Two weeks
(d) Placement of Purchase Order and receipt of order acknowledgement	One week
(e) Delivery Period	Depends upon the overall project scheduling

The above schedule is only a general indication. Procurement schedule will in any case meet the project requirements.

1.3 Vendors' request for extension of time to respond to enquiries will be favourably considered subject to a maximum of seven days.

1.4 Purchase department will insist and get validity of offers at least for sixty days from the date of receipt of offer, within which the orders have to be placed; otherwise extension of validity will be secured.

1.5 The Purchase department will get order acknowledgement without loss of time so that all technical and commercial issues are resolved and the delivery period commences without any ambiguity.

1.6 Delivery extension will be granted only with the prior consent of the Projects and Production department and only if the extension does not affect the overall project schedule.

Purchase Procedures: Floating of Enquiry

1.1 The Projects department will ensure that the indent released to the Purchase department includes the following (but is not limited to):

- Technical specification
- Delivery schedule
- Quality Assurance Plan
- Schedule for submission of drawings (civil foundation date, electrical load list, GA drawing, P&I, heat load, Single Line Diagram, and so on)
- Performance guarantees
- Painting and packing requirements
- Special commercial conditions

1.2 The Purchase department will scrutinize the material indent and technical delivery conditions immediately after receipt from engineering department/factory and seek necessary clarification, if any required, immediately without loss of time.

1.3 In parallel, the Purchase department will ascertain the availability of surplus materials in the factory's stock and modify the quantity to be procured accordingly.

1.4 The Purchase department will initiate procurement activity strictly as per approved project execution schedule.

1.5 Vendor approval will be done in an approved format and the head of division's approval is necessary for the addition of any new vendor.

1.6 The enquiries will be floated to all approved vendors within seven days of receipt of clear indent. If the client's list includes any additional vendors, such vendors will also be included for floating of enquiry and in parallel those vendors will also be empanelled. Proof of despatch of enquiry will be maintained in the file. For the purpose of comparison, enquiry can also be issued to non-approved vendors.

1.7 The enquires shall clearly bring out the technical delivery condition, delivery schedule, commercial terms and conditions, inspection plan, packing requirement, and so on, and the enquiry will be floated in an approved, standardized format for each material. A minimum of seven days' time will be given to the vendors to respond to the company's enquiry.

1.8 If any import is to be done against Duty Concession schemes, the Purchase department will co-ordinate with the Projects and Commercial department for securing the appropriate licence from the issuing authorities.

Processing of Bids

1. Offers will be received in sealed covers and the covers will be opened in the presence of the Members of the Committee stated as per Delegation of Powers. Where a two-bid system is adopted, the technical bid and commercial conditions will be opened initially. Until the technical evaluation is completed, the price bid will be in the safe custody of President or any top management as agreed. After completion of the technical evaluation, the President will indicate the target price for procurement and fresh price bids will be called for and opened in the presence of the committee.

   Representative of suppliers shall not be allowed to be present at the time of opening of tenders. A minimum of three offers are required. In case the number of offers received is less than three, prior approval of Head of Division and CC will be taken for opening of the bids.

2. Technical Comparative Statement (TCS) will be prepared wherever necessary and feasible. Head of Engineering will approve such TCS.

3. Technical deviations, if any, will be vetted and approved by Head of Engineering.

4. Commercial Comparative Statement will be prepared within seven days of receipt of offers and submitted to the Head of Purchase.

5. Negotiations will be done by the following tender committee:

S. No.	Limit (Rs)	Committee
(a)	Upto 5L	Purchase Engineer, Project Engineer and Finance Manager
(b)	> 5 L < 50 L	Heads of Purchase, Projects and Finance Manager
(c)	> 50 L < 500L	Head of Division assisted by (b) above
(d)	> 500 L	Head of Division and Director—Finance

Record of negotiations with suppliers must be made available in respective proposal files. Where found necessary, the supplier should be asked to sign the record of negotiation or give a letter confirming the negotiations and conclusions thereof.

6. Import offers will be negotiated through e-mail/fax correspondence.

7. The above purchase procedure is not applicable for cash purchase of items up to Rs 2,500.

8. All the divisions will introduce and install suitable hardware and software for e-Procurement within a period as agreed separately.

Approval of Purchase Proposals

1. The Purchase Proposal along with MI, enquiry, offers received, technical comparative statement, commercial comparative statement, minutes of meeting with suppliers and recommendations of the committee, will be submitted for approval to the competent authority as per the delegation of powers mentioned in Delegation of Powers.

2. All purchases will be by consensus of all members of the tender committee. If any of the tender committee members do not agree to the proposal for reasons to be recorded in writing, the proposal will be approved by the next level of authority. It will be ensured that all the observations of Commercial Controller are suitably addressed.

3. On approval of the purchase proposal, the purchase order shall be released to the successful bidder in the prescribed format within two working days.

4. All import transactions will be governed by the latest version of INCOTERMS unless the terms negotiated by the company are more beneficial.

5. The Purchase Orders will invariably stipulate the packing and handling specifications for each purchase order.

6. The mode of transportation will be stipulated based on the economy of cost of transportation. In case of urgency, other modes of transportation can be resorted to if the cost is within the budget provision.

Commercial Terms and Conditions

1. Liquidated damages (LD)—1% per week; maximum 10%.
2. Warranty—10% value of bank guarantee payable for bought-out items. Warranty period will be as applicable for respective projects or sale orders.
3. Unconditional order acceptance and manufacture and delivery schedule of the vendors will be received immediately after release of order and copies of orders will be circulated to all concerned departments.
4. For regular product business, Company will not pay advance. If the HOD/Committee fails to convince the supplier, then the President can authorize advance against Bank Guarantee valid up to the last delivery date plus four weeks.
5. Deviations, if any, from the commercial terms will require prior approval of the President.

Credit and Payment Policy

1. Company will establish letter of credit 60 days sight for imports above Rs 2 lakh. Interest to be borne by the supplier. LC to be opened 10 days before the readiness of material.
2. For imports less than Rs 2 lakh, company will accept either wire transfer or import on COD basis.
3. Domestic Purchases:

Type	Value	Credit Period
'A' Category	More than Rs 5 lakh	Min. 60 days
'B' Category	Rs 1 lakh to Rs 5 lakh	Min. 45 days
'C' Category	Less than Rs 1 lakh	Min. 30 days

   All efforts should be made by all concerned to pay the supplier bills within due date.
4. No LC will be opened or Bill of Exchange (Hundi) will be accepted for domestic purchases.
5. Payment against proforma invoices shall not be allowed.

6. In unavoidable circumstances, company can accept payment on 'Cash on Delivery' (COD) basis for 'B' category items for amounts up to Rs 5 lakh.
7. No interest will be paid for delayed payment.
8. In respect of high-value, project-specific items, it will be preferable to negotiate back-to-back terms.
9. Some of the 'C' category items of value less than Rs 2,500 can be purchased on cash payment basis. HOD—Purchase to review such purchase prices on weekly basis.
10. All local payments will be made by cheques.
11. All outstation payments will be made by DD. The DD charges will be borne by the vendor.
12. The bank charges will be to the account of respective party.
13. Payments will be handed over to the authorized representatives or will be sent by speed post/courier.
14. All cheque/DD payments will be crossed 'A/c Payee'.
15. The LC amendment will be responsible for amendment/extension.

Procurement Follow-up

1. If a letter of intent is issued to any vendor, the same shall be regularized through a Purchase Order within a maximum period of seven days, but in any case, before the actual despatch of goods.
2. Order amendments will be approved by the respective component authority who approves the Purchase Order.
3. If it is beneficial to the company, a repeat order can be placed on the same vendor on the same terms and conditions, within a period of three months from the date of the original order. This shall be done with the approval of the competent authority.
4. The Purchase department will evaluate the performance of the vendors as per ISO procedures.
5. The Purchase department will generate project-wise pending order status for review in weekly meetings.

6. The Purchase department will arrange appropriate insurance covers.
7. The Purchase and Project departments will co ordinate testing, inspection, and transportation of materials ordered on vendors as the case may be.
8. If there is any rejection of goods at the factory or during inspection at vendor works, the Purchase department will immediately take necessary follow-up action for replacement or re-procurement.
9. If there is any hold up or damage/problem during transit, the Purchase department will take immediate action to inform the Project Manager and Insurance Manager regarding the damage. The Project Manager will co-ordinate for rectification of the damage. The Purchase department will co-ordinate any order amendment/claims on the supplier.
10. The Purchase department will co-ordinate with the Commercial department for appointment of shipping agencies, clearing agencies, and customs clearance.
11. The Purchase department will constantly monitor all the Purchase Orders released by them and in case there is a likelihood of delay in delivery by vendors, the Purchase department will take necessary action for expediting/cancellation and re-ordering/risk purchase as the case may be.
12. It will be necessary to call the vendors of high-value Purchase Orders to our office for mid-term/periodical review of the status of Purchase Orders. The Purchase Orders will stipulate periodical progress reports to be submitted by the vendors.

Criteria for Acceptance of Materials

1. Full compliance with specification, size, quantity, and time of delivery
2. Compliance with the quality plan
3. Compliance with technical delivery conditions
4. Manufacturer's Original Certificates or copy of Manufacturer's certificate endorsed by reputed third-party inspection agency. Wherever Manufacturers' certificates are not available, check tests will be carried out by a reputed inspection agency/company's QC, as the case may be, and the original check test certificates will be reviewed and accepted.
5. Material traceability with heat marks; manufacturer's logo, batch number, serial number, etc. are important requirements for acceptance of materials.
6. Pre-despatch testing shall be carried out and witnessed by the appropriate agency as per the quality plan before the material is accepted.
7. Stage inspection and material identification if stipulated shall be witnessed by the appropriate agency.
8. Visual inspection will invariably be carried out before despatch. However, any stage inspection or pre-despatch inspection or visual inspection will not absolve the supplier of his responsibility under the Purchase Order. The Purchase department shall not agree to any such request or condition of the supplier.

Cancellation of Purchase Order and Risk Purchase

1. The Purchase Orders will invariably contain a clause for premature cancellation of orders as an option for the company with a risk purchase clause. This option will be exercised only when there is a clear indication that the vendor will fail in his/her contractual condition of delivery, quality, etc.
2. Where the supplier is likely to default in supplying the contracted goods and services, the Purchase department should make a personal visit to the vendor and ascertain the factual position. Based on the visit, the Purchase department in consultation with Projects and other user departments shall cancel the order. Care must be taken to ensure that the company is invoking the risk purchase clause contained in the Purchase Order and the entire cost and consequences of such risk purchase shall be passed on to the defaulted vendor. All money payable to that vendor by the group as a whole will stand forfeited including the EMD, Perfor-

mance BG, Advance BG, if any furnished by the vendor.

3. The cancellation will be done by giving sufficient notice in writing to the vendor, preferably with the written consent of the vendor.

4. Before cancellation of orders, alternative firm arrangement should have been made.

5. The Purchase Orders cancelled will have negative marks of appropriate weight in vendor performance evaluation.

6. The Purchase Order shall be in the form given in the Purchase Policy.

7. The work order or sub-contract order shall be in the form given in Responsibility.

8. The general conditions of the contract applicable to the Purchase Order, work order, and sub-contract order are given in System and Procedures.

9. It is the personal responsibility of the Purchase Executive to ensure that a copy of the general terms and conditions is attached with every Purchase Order, work order, or sub-contract order with a link reference to the respective order.

10. It is also the personal responsibility of the Purchase Executive to obtain unconditional acceptance of the vendor of the general terms and conditions of a contract.

11. Where the vendor claims interest for delayed payment on the basis of clause in the invoice or otherwise, the Purchase department must reply immediately to the vendor informing the company's refusal to accept such an interest claim. The said letter of the Purchase department must draw reference of the vendor to the general terms and conditions of contract.

Processing of Vendor Payment

1. The Purchase department will send a copy of the Purchase Order, terms and conditions, amendments, and all important correspondences to the Finance department.

2. The Bills Section will receive the duly accepted Goods Receipt Note (GRN) from the factory or from the site.

3. The Bills Section will receive the vendor's bill

and other related documents from the Purchase department.

4. The Bills Section will compare and correlate all the documents and approve the payment.

5. The Bills Section will make an endorsement on the finance copy of the Purchase Order as a token of having processed the payment.

6. In case of advance/pro forma payment, etc., the Bills Section will prepare adjustment vouchers with necessary supporting documents immediately upon receipt of materials.

7. The Bills Section will also be responsible for processing of freight invoices and deduction of TDS.

8. The Accounts department will issue C Forms, E1 Forms, etc.

9. Wherever feasible, theoretical section weights will be calculated and compared with weight as per bill and actual weighment in a company-approved weighbridge.

Closing of Files

1. After the purchase activity is completed in all respects, all the documents will be properly arranged and the file will be closed after the scrutiny of the Head of Purchase.

2. The Purchase files will be properly stacked for easy access.

Rate Contracting

1. The Purchase department shall sign annual rate contracts for the following items:
   (a) Electrodes, Filler wire, and Flux
   (b) Paints and Zinc wire
   (c) Bearings
   (d) Coolant oil
   (e) Electrical maintenance
   (f) Crane spares
   (g) Lubricants
   (h) NDT items
   (i) Tube expanders
   (j) Packing material including wood
   (k) Grinding wheels
   (l) Flanges
   (m) Nozzles

(n) Fasteners

(o) Gaskets

(p) Gratings

(q) Argon gas

(r) Oxygen

(s) Transportation

(t) C&F Services

(u) Fabrication rates inside the factory

(v) Fabrication rate outside the factory

(w) Job orders like machining, drilling, heat treatment, painting, material testing, X-Ray

2. The rate contract will be finalized by Purchase department and it will be approved by the EC.

3. The rate contract will be circulated to all the potential user departments.

4. Lifting of materials against the rate contract will be done for specific projects and as and when required.

5. The terms of actual purchase can only be better

than the terms finalized under the rate contract.

6. The rate contract will be finalized at least one month prior to the commencement of a financial year and will be valid for the entire financial year.

7. Before finalization of the rates, the rates being paid by other divisions will be compared.

8. No request for change of rates or other terms by the rate contract party shall be entertained during the currency of the rate contract.

9. Rate contracts will be signed with a minimum of two parties for each item.

10. Once rate contracts are signed with vendors, the Purchase department on receipt of MI from the Engineering department will straightaway place the Purchase Order to one of the rate contracted vendors.

11. The Purchase department will ensure that the distributions of orders to the vendors of a particular material are fair and equitable.

Delegation of Powers

S. No.	Description	Committee consisting			
		Head of division on recommendation of lower committee	Head of projects, purchase & CC	Executives of project, purchase, and finance	Internal control
1	Opening of offers, bids, tenders and so on		Any Value	Up to Rs 5 lakh	• Offers must be sealed • Sealed offers must be opened in the presence of the members of the Committee • The committee members must put their initials and the date on all the offers opened in their presence • Overwriting or changes, if any, in the offers opened, must be suitably authenticated by the Finance Executive

Contd.

Contd.

S. No.	Description	Committee consisting			
		Head of division on recommendation of lower committee	**Head of projects, purchase & CC**	**Executives of project, purchase, and finance**	**Internal control**
2	Technical evaluation of offers		Any Value (only by Head of Engg.)	Up to Rs 1 crore	• Compliance with technical specification and technical delivery conditions are to be met • All offers must be technically evaluated on par
3	Approval of revenue	Above Rs 10 lakh	Up to Rs 10 lakh	Up to Rs. 50,000	• On L 1 • Within budget
4	Approval of revenue purchase proposal in excess of budget and contingency	Excess up to 1 %	Nil	Nil	• Reasons to be recorded by the committee • If the committee does not reach a consensus, proposals shall be referred to the CMD for the final decision
5a	Capital Purchase Proposals	Up to Rs 5 lakh	Nil	Nil	• Capex budget/capex indent previously approved by the CMD • The committee to include DF • Firm finance tie-up necessary
5b	Capital Purchase Proposals	Above Rs 5 lakh	Nil	Nil	• The lower committee + CMD • Firm finance tie-up necessary
6	Approval of sub-contract proposals (Other than Factory)	Any Value	Up to Rs 2 lakh		• To L 1 Party • Within budget
7	Award of transport	Any Value	Up to Rs 2 lakh		• To L 1 party • Within budget
8	Vendor registration recommendation of vendor development committee	Based on	--	--	• By EC

Appendix 8.2 — Criteria Used for Evaluation of a Vendor

The following list is only indicative:

1. Supplier viability: technical and financial
2. Supply flexibility
3. On-time performance
4. Replenishment lead time
5. Delivery frequency/minimum lot size
6. Quality process and ability to adhere to quality standards
7. Inbound transportation cost
8. Ability to supply on JIT or VMI
9. Price terms and other commercial terms
10. Design collaboration capability
11. Supply chain coordination capability
12. Impact of taxes, duties, and foreign exchange on commercial terms
13. Track record and referrals
14. Quality of management

9

Supply Chain Tactical Planning

Learning Objectives

After studying this chapter, you will be able to:
- ♦ Understand the planning horizons and the interconnections between the planning decisions
- ♦ Understand the definition of demand planning and forecasting
- ♦ Comprehend the need for demand planning and forecasting in supply chain
- ♦ Understand the importance of aggregate planning processes and how these relate to sales and operations planning
- ♦ Understand the evolution of CPFR and ECR
- ♦ Gain an insight into the collaborative planning forecasting and replenishment process
- ♦ Comprehend the scope of various planning initiatives across the supply chain

9.1 SUPPLY CHAIN PLANNING

All supply chain planning falls into one of the hierarchical planning horizons—short-term, medium-term, and long-term planning.

The long-term or strategic planning covers the planning for more than two years and is reviewed on a yearly or ad hoc basis. Strategic planning represents the highest level of the hierarchy of decision-making activities that occur within a firm or an organization. Ultimately, strategic planning decisions are concerned with defining the long-term objectives of a firm, charting the long-term course that will allow a firm to meet its defined objectives and assuring that a firm has the proper resources and assets necessary to support its long-term objectives. The strategic plan addresses planning decisions such as infrastructure and overall capacity levels.

Medium-term or tactical planning represents the second or intermediate level of decision-making activities that occur in a firm. Quite often, annual planning is viewed as a subset of tactical planning. Tactical planning activities must obtain and use resources effectively to assure the accomplishment of the firm's objectives for a period between six to twelve months. Tactical plans are typically reviewed monthly or quarterly. Tactical planning deals with planning decisions that focus on how to utilize the infrastructure and capacity most effectively.

Short-term or operational planning represents the third or lowest level of the hierarchical planning process. At this level, the decision involves scheduling, rescheduling, and execution for planning periods, ranging from daily, weekly, to less

Table 9.1 Supply chain planning horizons

Horizon	Processes to be Considered
Long-term or strategic planning (More than twenty-four months)	Corporate objectives, products/market mix, manufacturing plans, capacities, facilities, locations, resources
Medium-term or tactical planning (Twelve to twenty-four months)	Aggregate production/distribution planning (Demand planning and forecasting)
Short-term or operational planning (One to eighteen months)	Operations scheduling, including distribution resource planning, master production scheduling, distribution centre work load scheduling, transport scheduling, shop floor scheduling

than six months. Short-term planning has limited flexibility to reschedule resources and is also termed as low-level planning.

A cycle manufacturer based in Punjab in India, which has nearly 58 per cent of the total market share of bicycles in India, wants to continue being the market leader in the bicycles segment. The company would look at increasing their capacity for production of bicycles in the kids and sports segments because these two segments experience high growth, fetch higher margins, and are sensitive to demand changes. Strategic planning decisions would be relating to those of facilities expansion and investment commitment. Typically, supply chain planning would include arriving at an annual demand plan and then from there arriving at a monthly production plan wherein the company would decide capacity allocation for different market segments and fill distribution centres in order to supply to the market. This is an important aspect of the planning function wherein the manufacturer considers the time window of planning resource utilization for a committed investment. Table 9.1 illustrates supply chain planning horizons.

Topics related to strategic planning or long-term planning have been discussed in chapters on decision environment, strategic decision situation, and network decisions (Chapters 4 to 8). This chapter highlights three key tactical planning or medium-term planning practices:

1. Demand planning
2. Collaborative planning, replenishment, and forecasting
3. Aggregate planning

9.2 DEMAND PLANNING AND FORECASTING

Demand planning is the process of arriving at a demand plan that the focal organization will execute to cater to a committed demand obtained from statistical forecasting and other customer intelligence.

The role of demand planning has evolved over time and emerged as a distinct function, separate from the more traditional planning or supply planning functions, with specific responsibilities. These include driving the forecasting process, validating the forecasts, developing norms for stock keeping at multiple echelons of the distribution chain, placing distribution requirements on factories, and managing stock availability. The most important role is driving the sales and operation process. Typically the demand planning horizon ranges from eighteen to twenty-four months.

A demand plan serves the following purposes in demand management:

1. Assists in validating that the sales plan and other operational plans are in alignment with the financial plan and objectives of the company.
2. Facilitates recalibration of capacity and supply plans to meet the demand, in some cases not to meet the demand when it makes business sense.
3. Helps in developing financial reports such as revenue projections, cash flow, and profit margins.

The significance of demand forecasting is shown in Exhibit 9.1.

Exhibit 9.1   Case Study on the Significance of Demand Forecasting

While high volume of sales due to promotions is a good thing, it is imperative to know whether the increased sales of one SKU at a given location is impacting sales at another location (known as cannibalization) and whether there are any other problems due to increased sales. Getting the right product mix out without causing confusion to the end customer is an everyday challenge faced by a retail supply chain.

One such company is a wholesale merchandise company that has branches in more than 70 locations across the United States. They had challenges around providing high customer satisfaction levels due to their enormous growth. As a result of increasing promotional activity, especially in the grocery business, the company had such a large number of SKU location combinations that it could not predict the impact of new product introductions, substitutions, or predict the uplift correctly. They were either facing unwanted stocks on the shelf or were out-of-stock for the more popular brands.

The company decided to focus on demand planning to straighten things out, by automating the forecasting process and by making the forecasts available at an SKU level, in an effort to increase the product availability.

Some of the best practices were followed by the merchandise company. They implemented a sophisticated system that can handle a huge number of SKUs, a predictive demand model that enables predictive analysis by incorporating macroeconomic factors as *causal factors*. The models had the ability to recalibrate to compensate for changes in consumer behaviour. They had refrained from making manual adjustments to handle shift in demand during holidays and promotional periods. They achieved this by introducing festive months and holiday periods as *causal factors* which explained the demand.

The system was able to separate the effect of promotions and the focus was on the total forecasted demand, which included baseline and lift. They utilized the chase strategy (described in section 9.6) to adjust the capacity based on an unconstrained demand forecasting. They centralized the scattered pool of demand analysts into one central demand forecasting-centric organization to focus on customer service levels by concentrating on customer collaboration. This also enhanced their capability of sharing best practices.

By focusing on demand management and forecasting the merchandise, the company improved customer service levels and cash flow. They witnessed a significant improvement in the fill-rate with the existing stock on hand; they observed a noticeable change in inventory levels, which improved their cash flow. Order fill-rates rose from 93 per cent to 98 per cent. They smoothened the impact of promotions and were able to achieve the right product mix at the required levels during peak promotional and holiday seasons. This eliminated overstocking and also drastically reduced out-of-stock scenarios. They were also able to see significant visibility on sudden increases in sales of unrelated SKUs but were able to pin down the causals, enabling them to be prepared well in advance for such spikes (establish dependency).

Forecasting is the process of trying to predict the future demand for a product or service in units or in revenue. Forecasting is subjected to huge amount of uncertainties and hence the accuracy of a forecast continues to be a topic of debate. There are multiple techniques to develop a forecast. All forecasts are characterized by the following:

1. Forecasts are always incorrect.
2. Forecasts are more accurate at an aggregate level than at the SKU level.
3. Forecasts are more accurate for a short planning horizon compared to a long planning horizon.

As mentioned above, forecasting is key to achieving supply chain objectives of efficiency and responsiveness. A wrong forecast may lead to stock piling or stock out. In any case, it would be better to work with a forecast rather than not having it by stating chances of penalty. Based on experience, the human mind learns to adjust and such adjustments are better if a supply chain manager can use proven models that build such parameters. In tactical planning, broad category forecasting would be good, and for operations planning, SKU-level changes can be accommodated.

Forecasts are determined using qualitative and quantitative techniques, a few of which are discussed here.

9.2.1 Qualitative Techniques

1. **Personal insight:** Forecast may be sometimes based upon the insight of the most experienced, most knowledgeable, or senior managers. For example, senior management would have distilled knowledge based on experience and high-level interactions, leading to wisdom on market trends.
2. **Sales force consensus estimate:** Due to close contact with the customer, the sales and marketing executives accumulate a lot of knowledge about customer demand. Hence, the qualitative review of a statistical forecast could be arrived at by using a consensus approach to validate any quantitative forecast.
3. **Management estimate:** In this approach, a panel of senior executives would be involved in a process similar to the sales forecast consensus approach, where they rely on techniques such as pyramid forecasting or historical analogy to arrive at the forecasts.

   The procedure used in implementing the pyramid forecasting approach begins with individual item forecasts at the lowest level, which are rolled up into forecasts for groupings of individual products at the next higher level. The forecasts for product groupings are then aggregated into a total forecast. This is used by the top management to arrive at the final forecast, which then becomes the constraint for the lower-level (disaggregated) forecasts and is used to constrain the product grouping and individual item forecasts, consistent with the final plan (Figure 9.1).

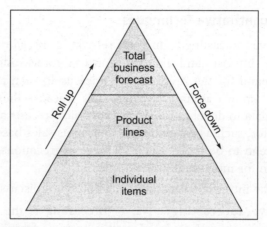

Figure 9.1 Hierarchical approach to forecasting

Historical analogy is used when there is no data on a new product or a service, forecasting is done by studying past patterns of demand for a similar product or service.

4. **Market research:** Market research is the systematic gathering, recording, and analysing of data about problems relating to the marketing of goods and services. Such research is conducted by independent/impartial agencies or their agents.

   Marketing research includes the following approaches:

   (a) Market analysis, including product potential studies, which seeks to determine the size, location, nature, and characteristics of a market

   (b) Sales analysis, or sales research, which undertakes the systematic study and comparison of sales data

   (c) Consumer research, such as motivational research, focus groups, questionnaires, and other methods used to discover and analyse consumer trends, reactions, and preferences.

5. **Delphi method:** Delphi technique uses the exchange of information between anonymous panellists over a number of iterations, taking the average of the estimates on the final round as the group judgement. The carefully selected experts answer questions in two or three rounds. After each round a facilitator provides an anonymous summary of an expert's forecasts and the reasons the expert provided for his/her judgements. This is aimed at the convergence of opinions by hearing the reasoning of the other experts without a bias of who has responded. The Delphi method is used when data is thin or non-existent.

6. **Lifecycle analysis:** Experienced managers who have introduced several products are often able to estimate how long a product will remain in each stage of its lifecycle. This forecast, coupled with other market information, can produce reasonably accurate estimates of demand in the medium to long range.

9.2.2 Quantitative Techniques

Quantitative forecasting techniques rely on historical data. They can be divided into two types—intrinsic and extrinsic. Intrinsic forecasting techniques focus upon data about demand for the product or service itself, such as past sales data. These techniques are known as time series models, because they incorporate chronologically arranged data to develop forecasts. Extrinsic forecasts are based on a correlated leading indicator, such as estimating cement units sales based on housing starts. Extrinsic forecasts tend to be more useful for large aggregations, such as total company sales, rather than for individual product sales.

Some of the intrinsic forecasting techniques are discussed below:

1. **Naive forecasting:** Naive forecasting is the technique in which the last period's actuals are used as this period's forecast, without adjusting them or attempting to establish causal factors. Therefore, all other influences that may impact the outcome are excluded from the forecast. Naive forecasting provides a convenient way to generate a quick and easy forecast for the short-time horizon. It is used only for comparison with the forecasts generated using other sophisticated techniques.

2. **Moving averages:** A moving average forecast model is based on an artificially constructed time series in which the value for a given time period is replaced by the mean of that value and the values for some number of preceding and succeeding time periods. As you may have guessed from the description, this model is best suited for time-series data; that is, data that changes over time. For example, many charts of individual stocks on the stock market show 20, 50, 100, or 200 day moving averages as a way to show trends.

   Since the forecast value for any given period is an average of the previous periods, the forecast will always appear to be less than the observed (dependent) values. For example, if a data series has a noticeable upward trend, a moving average forecast will generally provide an underestimate of the values of the dependent variable.

   The moving average method has an advantage over other forecasting models in that it does smooth out peaks and troughs (or valleys) in a set of observations. However, it also has several disadvantages. In particular, this model does not produce an actual equation. Therefore, it is not all that useful as a medium–long range forecasting tool. It can be reliably used to forecast only one or two periods into the future.

$$MA = \frac{\Sigma \text{ Demand in Previous } n}{n}$$

For example, where, *MA* is moving average and *n* is time period, the Table 9.2 illustrates the actual demand of product A. Table 9.3 and Figure 9.2 show moving average of the product.

Table 9.2 Example data set

Time	Actual demand
2002	180
2003	168
2004	159
2005	175
2006	190
2007	NA

Table 9.3 Estimate using moving average

Time	Demand	Moving total	Moving average
	Y_i	(n = 3)	(n = 3)
2002	180	NA	NA
2003	168	NA	NA
2004	159	NA	NA
2005	175	180 +168 + 159 = 507	507/ 3 = 169
2006	190	168 + 159 + 175 = 502	502/3 = 167.3
2007	NA	159 + 175 + 190 = 524	524/3 = 174.6

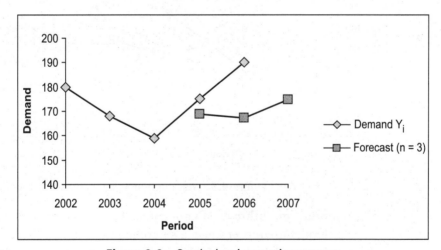

Figure 9.2 Graph showing moving average

3. **Weighted moving averages:** Weighted moving average is similar to moving average, except that it places more emphasis on recent periods. It uses multiplying factors to give different weights to different data points in a time series. The challenging part of weighted average is assigning weights. It also tracks upward trend somewhat better than the unweighted moving averages.

$$WMA = \frac{\Sigma \text{ Demand in Previous } n \times \text{Weight}}{n + (n-1) + (n-2)}$$

In an *n*-day WMA the latest day has weight *n*, the second latest *n* − 1, and so on down to zero. In this example, weights of 3, 2, and 1 have been assigned to demand where weights decrease arithmetically. One may note an illustration on weighted moving average for a data series in Table 9.4 and Figure 9.3.

Table 9.4 Estimate using weighted moving average

Time	Demand	Weighted moving total	Weighted moving average
	Y_i	(n = 3)	(n = 3)
2002	180	NA	NA
2003	168	NA	NA
2004	159	NA	NA
2005	175	$180 \times 3 + 168 \times 2 + 159 \times 1 = 1035$	1035/ 6 = 172.5
2006	190	$168 \times 3 + 159 \times 2 + 175 \times 1 = 997$	997/6 = 166.16
2007	NA	$159 \times 3 + 175 \times 2 + 190 \times 1 = 1017$	1017/6 = 169.5

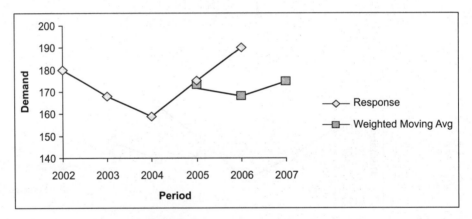

Figure 9.3 Weighted moving average

4. **Exponential smoothing:** Exponential smoothing forecast model is a very popular model used to produce a smoothed time series. While in simple moving average models the past observations are weighted equally, exponential smoothing assigns exponentially decreasing weights as the observations get older. In other words, recent observations are given relatively more weight in forecasting than the older observations.

   In the case of moving averages, the weights assigned to the observations are the same and are equal to 1/N. In simple exponential smoothing, however, a 'smoothing parameter' or 'smoothing constant' is used to determine the weights assigned to the observations.

Exponential smoothing model begins by setting the forecast for the second period equal to the observation of the first period.

$$F_t = \alpha A_{t-1} + \alpha(1 - \alpha)A_{t-2} + \alpha(1 - \alpha)^2 A_{t-3}$$
$$+ \alpha(1 - a)^3 A_{t-4} + ... + \alpha(1 - \alpha)^{t-1} A_0$$

F_t = Forecast value

A_t = Actual value

α = Smoothing constant

$$F_t = F_{t-1} + \alpha(A_{t-1} - F_{t-1})$$

One may observe an illustration of using exponential smoothing for data series shown in Table 9.5 and Figure 9.4.

Table 9.5 Estimate of exponential smoothing

Time	Actual	Forecast ($\alpha = 10$)
2002	180	175
2003	168	175.5
2004	159	174.75
2005	175	173.18
2006	190	173.36
2007		175.02

Sample Calculation
175.00 + 10(180 − 175.00) = 175.50

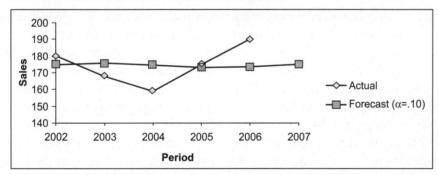

Figure 9.4 Exponential smoothing

Double exponential smoothing—also known as Holt exponential smoothing—is a refinement of the popular simple exponential smoothing model but adds another component that takes into account any trend in the data. Simple exponential smoothing models work best with data where there are no trends or seasonality components to the data. When the data exhibits either an increasing or decreasing trend over time, simple exponential smoothing forecasts tend to lag behind observations. Double exponential smoothing is designed to address this type of data series by taking into account any trend in the data.

Note that double exponential smoothing still does not address seasonality. For better exponentially smoothed forecasts using data where seasonal variation in the data is expected, use triple exponential smoothing.

Extrinsic forecasting techniques base their predictions on factors related to demand for the product, in cases where a demand of one product or service is dependent on another. These are known as associative models, because they analyse data on conditions thought to be associated with changes in demand for a particular item or group of items. This is also known as causal or econometric method.

5. **Regression analysis using linear regression and non-linear regression:** Linear regression is a form of regression analysis in which the relationship between one or more independent variables and another variable, called the dependent variable, is modelled by the least function, called a linear regression equation. This function is a linear combination of one or more model parameters, called regression coefficients. A linear regression equation with one independent variable represents a straight line when the predicted value (that is, the dependent variable from the regression equation) is plotted against the independent variable. This is called a simple linear regression. However, note that 'linear' does not refer to this straight line, but rather to the way in which the regression coefficients occur in the regression equation $Y_t = m X_t + \text{Constant}$, where Y_t is estimated demand at time 't' and X_t is required time period for forecast.

Non-linear regression is a form of regression analysis in which observational data are modelled by a function that is a non-linear combination of the model parameters and depends on one or more independent variables. The data are fitted by a method of successive approximations.

For example, the regression line for the data set in which sales in million INR is defined as dependent variable. Sales is a function of promotional expenses in million INR as shown in Table 9.6 and Figure 9.5.

The resultant regression equation is $Y_t = 381.80 + 0.794X_t$ where Y_t is estimated sales at time 't' and for X_t, which is proposed promotional expenses in million INR is required time period for forecast. Using the equation, the estimates of sales for the thirteenth and fourteenth months are given in the table for given promotional expenses. The difference between estimate and actual is discussed in the 'forecasting error' section of this chapter.

It has been proven that quantitative methods show the greatest accuracy when large changes are involved or much historical POS data is available. However, this is not the case when there is not much data available. This does not mean that you must avoid judgement. Indeed we often need judgement as part of the process, for example, providing inputs or deciding which quantitative procedures to use.

Table 9.6 Estimate of linear regression

Time T	Promotional expenses (in million) X_t	Sales (INR million) Y_t	Regression forecast
1	20	375	398
2	21	410	398
3	22	398	399
4	23	388	400
5	24	420	401
6	26	412	402
7	27	399	403
8	28	425	404
9	30	403	406
10	31	400	406
11	33	390	408
12	34	415	409
	40		414
	50		422

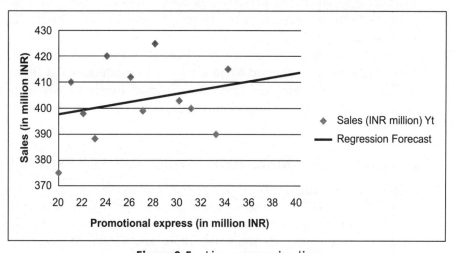

Figure 9.5 Linear regression line

9.3 FORECASTING ERROR

Forecasting involves making projections about future performance based on history and present data. When the result of an action is of consequence, but cannot be known in advance with precision, forecasting may reduce the decision risk by supplying additional information about the possible outcome. Although the models explained above provide a convenient way to analyse the historical data that is captured, this does not guarantee an estimate to be precise. It is equally important that its performance characteristics are verified or validated by comparing its forecasts with historical data for the process it was designed to forecast. Forecast error measures, such as MAPE (Mean Average Percentage Error), RAE (Relative Absolute Error), or MSE (Mean Square Error) may be used for validating the model. The selection of the error measure has an important effect on the conclusions about which set of forecasting methods is most accurate. Most software-based forecasting tools use more than one set of forecasting techniques to provide better forecast accuracy.

A detailed analysis of forecasting accuracy and the way the errors are distributed reveals a great deal about the well-being of the forecasting system. Forecasts should not be biased, that is, persistently too high or too low. Control charts can be set up to ensure that the forecasting system is under control.

The forecast accuracy that can be achieved is different for every business and varies with the level of detail at which it is measured. Regular monitoring against appropriate KPIs is vital to ensure a direction of continual improvement.

The forecast accuracy health check can vary in content depending on the type of business and the data that is available. A review of methods and procedures can be carried out together with an analysis of the levels of forecasting accuracy that are being achieved in the current forecasting system. Forecasts can be checked for overall bias or seasonal bias.

While forecasting provides a way to predict future results, it is important to bear the following limitations in mind while using any forecasting tool. A forecast can never be 100 per cent accurate, and generating a good forecast costs money. Changes in fundamental conditions, and blind assumptions can cause the forecast to vary from the actual results.

9.4   COLLABORATIVE PLANNING, FORECASTING, AND REPLENISHMENT

Collaborative Planning, Forecasting, and Replenishment (CPFR) is the latest in an array of collaborative schemes and is aimed at better coordinating the supply chain, thereby decoupling the inventory from the system. The roots of CPFR can be traced to the Efficient Consumer Response (ECR) and Vendor Managed Inventory (VMI)/ Co-Managed Inventory (CMI) initiatives. Unlike these initiatives, however, CPFR was designed as a balanced collaborative approach where all forecasts and exceptions are communicated to both retailers and manufacturers and the collaborative process of solving these exceptions is carefully laid out. CPFR is a mini Sales & Operations Plan (S&OP) at the customer level. It provides key inputs to the company S&OP with up-to-date data through a weekly planning horizon. It serves as a cross-functional process that translates market opportunity into an optimal, actionable operating plan.

9.4.1   CPFR Components

Collaborative: Collaboration is a structured, repeatable process where two or more people work together towards a common goal by sharing knowledge, learning, and building consensus.

Planning: Planning is the process of thinking about the activities required to create a desired future.

Forecasting: Forecasting is the process of estimation in unknown situations. In more recent years, forecasting has evolved into the practice of demand planning in everyday business forecasting for manufacturing companies. The discipline of demand planning embraces both statistical forecasting and a consensus process.

Replenishment: Replenishment is the act of filling again by supplying what has been used up.

CPFR is the sharing of forecasts and related business information among business partners to optimize product replenishment. It is also designed to quickly identify any discrepancies in the forecasts, inventory, and ordering data so that the problems can be corrected before they negatively impact sales or profits.

It attempts to link sales and marketing best practices to the supply chain planning and execution process, the objective being to increase availability to the customer while reducing inventory, transportation, and logistics costs.

For most companies, a major challenge to implementing CPFR is making the transition to a collaborative culture built on trust. The companies that can vault the 'four walls' that sustain isolated practices, and enter truly collaborative operating arrangements with key trading partners, soon find that trust builds quickly.

The guiding principles behind CPFR are building a trading partner network and developing a single shared forecast of consumer demand. Success for manufacturers will be determined by:

- The commitment within the organization to make the transition to collaboration.
- Implementation of a flexible, robust technology solution that can deliver rapid results at every step of the CPFR journey, and within the enterprise as well.

The CPFR model shown in Figure 9.6 of Voluntary Inter-Industry Commerce Solutions (VICS) is divided into four process areas and three layers of the supply chain, starting from the manufacturer on one side to the retailer on the middle and finally to the consumer for whom the supply chain function exists. The consumer is the central purpose for which supply chain activities are aligned. The trigger for activities happens when the consumer arrives with a demand or is identified for generating a sale. The activities of the retailers and manufacturers are guided by the existence of a consumer with a demand. The four process areas of demand fulfilment are: analysis, strategy and planning, demand and supply management, and finally execution.

Analysis covers processes such as monitoring of the execution phase, managing by exception, evaluating the performance using performance assessment techniques such as score cards and metrices, and suggesting process improvement and changes that will be used to formulate new strategy.

Strategy and planning demarcates processes such as financial, sales, and marketing plans. This stage is crucial to get the buy-in of all stakeholders to arrive at a consensus plan, which will be used by the downstream processes to execute against the agreed-upon plan. This drives the initiation of collaboration and firming up a joint business plan. As the name suggests, the strategic decisions taken during this phase have a long-term impact on the supply chain. Some such decisions are inventory policies, new product introduction decisions, opening of a store in a new location or closing of a store in an existing location, and running promotions and marketing events to promote sales.

Demand and supply management covers processes such as the point-of-sale forecasting based on historical data, analysis of the external data about the market, replenishment planning at the retail level based on the demand forecast, and order planning.

Execution covers the functions of order processing and order fulfilment. It takes care of the supply planning and logistics pieces of the supply chain, thus completing the order fulfilment cycle. Execution involves activities such as order generation, movement of goods, and storing of finished goods ready to be consumed by the consumer in the planned retail and storage houses.

Interface shows the flow of processes where the three layers, namely consumer, retailer, and manufacturer collaborate and work together to achieve an optimum supply chain based on four processes. As Figure 9.6 indicates, it begins with the collaborative arrangement where the level of collaboration and the roles and responsibilities in the collaborative cycle are decided. A sales forecast is generated based on the joint business plan; the order planning, order generation, and order fulfilment take care of the consumer needs; and exception management and performance measurement drive continuous process improvement.

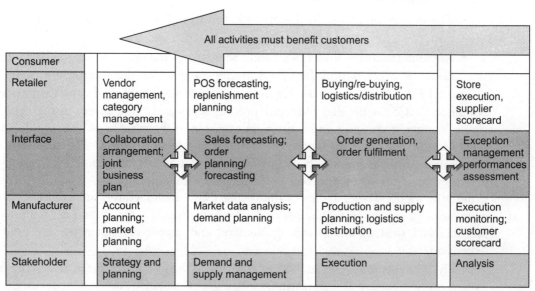

Figure 9.6 CPFR model

There have been multiple reports on the value of CPFR. The benefits are documented by the VICS committee as results of several projects. Some of this is summarized in Table 9.7.

VICS has provided a CPFR road map that will help the focal organization and its trading partners align to common objectives, and provide guidance on forecast exchange, exception management, and the review of performance results. It helps in the rolling out of CPFR practices throughout their organizations.

The VICS-CPFR road map is divided into five steps:

1. **Evaluate your current state:** CPFR begins long before piloting, with an assessment of your company's needs, values, culture, strategies, trading partner relationships, and track record in implementing best practices. This step looks for areas where change is needed to implement CPFR successfully. Only after this step is done will your company be prepared to articulate a meaningful vision for CPFR. In addition, the senior leadership of your company must not only understand the concept of CPFR, but also openly offer their support.

2. **Define scope and objectives:** After you create a CPFR vision, you are ready to begin piloting. Step 2 requires:
   (a) Gaining commitment from your trading partner
   (b) Assigning team members and establishing their roles
   (c) Selecting products and locations that will be included in the process
   (d) Deciding which part(s) of the nine-step CPFR process to test
   (e) Establishing key performance metrics to measure the initiative's success

Before beginning Step 3, the team captain verifies the status and reports it to the project sponsors. The checklist is as follows:

Table 9.7 Typical CPFR benefits

Retailer benefits	Typical improvement
Better store shelf stock rates	5% to 8 %
Lower inventory levels	10% to 40%
Higher sales	5% to 20%
Reduced cost of goods	3% to 4%
Reduced lead time/cycle time	25% to 30%
Lower logistics costs	3% to 4%
Manufacturer benefits	**Typical improvement**
Lower inventory levels	10 % to 40%
Faster replenishment cycles	12% to 30%
Higher sales	8% to 10%
Reduced operating expense	1% to 2%
Decreased account receivables	8% to 10%
Reduced forecast error	+/– 20% (6 wks out) +/– 30%
	(12 wks out)
Better customer service	5% to 10%

- All team members have been assigned, and time has been allocated for team member participation throughout the project.
- Products and locations for collaboration have been identified, and associated personnel have been notified.
- Metrics such as forecast accuracy, inventory reduction, and out-of-stock targets have been established.
- Sources of forecast data have been identified.
- CPFR training session and future project team meetings have been scheduled.

3. **Prepare for collaboration:** In Step 3, the project team studies the details of the CPFR business process, and identifies the technology and additional resources required to support it. Sales and replenishment team members develop ground rules for managing exceptions and changes. Collaboration technology team members install and configure the information systems (purchased, developed, or simple spreadsheets and e-mails) used to support collaboration between partner pilot teams. At the end of this step, the collaboration is ready to begin.

Before beginning Step 4, the team leader verifies the status and reports it to the project sponsors. The following is the checklist:

- All team members have been trained.
- Initial sales and order forecasts for all product/location combinations have been agreed upon.
- Collaboration technology is ready to begin.

4. **Execute:** In Step 4, the sales and replenishment collaboration teams begin to exchange forecasts with each other, modifying them to respond to changing conditions. The collaboration technology team gains experience managing the environment, and prepares for roll out to a large number of locations and projects after the pilot is complete.

Before proceeding to Step 5, the following checklist is verified and reported by the team captain:

- The project team has participated in at least six weeks of online sales and order forecast collaboration.
- The initial results and participant comments have been summarized and reviewed by both trading partners.
- The project team has identified future technology and software modifications that will enhance the process.
- The project team has held a collaboration review meeting, applying ideas from the first four weeks to improving the process in the final two weeks.
- Results have been reviewed by the project sponsor.

5. **Assess results and identify improvements:** In Step 5, the team and its

management review its progress, report results to their respective organizations, and make preparations for broader CPFR roll out. Every six to twelve weeks of collaboration, the business team reviews actual results against the target metrics. The team also considers the business process impact of their partnership.

9.5 EFFICIENT CONSUMER RESPONSE

Efficient Consumer Response (ECR) is a comprehensive management concept based on vertical collaboration in manufacturing and retailing with the objective of an efficient satisfaction of consumer needs. The main components of ECR are supply chain management and category management. (Refer Table 9.8).

The roots of ECR can be traced back to the just-in-time, quick response, total quality, and partnership approaches that transformed the automotive, electronics, and textile industries. In ECR, these ideas were allied with two unique aspects of the supply chain: category management and rich source of consumer data available from electronic point of sale (EPOS). Category management moved the focus away from brands and products to a holistic view of the total category, or consumer or promotional offer. Range rationalization and reduced complexity could be achieved by focusing on customer values and needs. The EPOS data was used to drive the replenishment process and shared with trading partners to help them manage their supply chain.

9.5.1 Core Elements of ECR

Efficient assortment: Product offerings should be rationalized to better meet customer needs and improve supply chain performance. (For example, why is there a need for 100 different SKUs that confuse consumers when 30 SKUs would meet their needs?)

Efficient product introductions: New products should be introduced in response to real customer needs, and only after the impact on supply chain performance has been considered.

Efficient promotions: Prices should be kept as stable as possible. The supply chain impact on promotions and market specials should be carefully considered.

Efficient replenishment: All physical and information flows that link producers to the consumer should be streamlined to cut costs and increase value.

Table 9.8 Efficient consumer response—core elements

Supply chain management	Category management
Efficient Replenishment (ER)	Efficient Store Assortment (ESA)
Efficient Administration(EA)	Efficient Promotion (EP)
Efficient Operating Standards (EOS)	Efficient Product Introduction (EPI)

Table 9.9 summarizes the advantages of using ECR.

Table 9.9   Typical ECR benefits

Manufacturer	Retailer	Consumer
• Efficient manufacturing system	• Reduced capital and inventory investment	• Fresher products
• Minimal inventory	• Lower depreciation	• Greater and more consistent value for money
• Optimal capacity utilization	• Reduced effort on promotion planning	• Improved product availability, resulting in good customer satisfaction
• Assortment of products based on customer preference	• Low out-of-stocks	• Enhanced shopping experience
• Increased sales and market share	• Greater customer loyalty	• Value for money
	• Good understanding of consumer needs	

ECR and other techniques could not address the comprehensive issue of the supply chain though it is trying to achieve inventory reductions by way of linking channel trading partners to achieve the level of continuous, systematic collaboration necessary to link total channel demand and supply. Exhibit 9.2 explains the benefits of ECR in the healthcare industry in India.

9.5.2   HOW CPFR Differs from ECR

ECR's core elements still apply under CPFR. But CPFR extends the business processes to include (shown in the CPFR road map):

- Information systems for capturing and transferring POS, inventory, and other demand and supply information between trading partners
- Formalized sales forecasting and order forecasting processes
- Formalized exception handling processes
- Feedback systems to monitor and improve supply chain performance

While ECR focuses on simplifying the environment, CPFR puts processes in place to handle the added complexity.

9.6   AGGREGATE PLANNING

Aggregate planning is the process by which a company determines levels of capacity, production, subcontracting, inventory, stock outs, and pricing over a specified time horizon. The goal is to maximize profit and reduce cost; the decisions made are at a product family (not SKU) level. The typical planning horizon for aggregate planning is from three to eighteen months. Aggregate planning addresses how a firm can best use the facilities that it has.

Exhibit 9.2   ECR in Healthcare Industry

The Efficient Consumer Response (ECR) movement began in the United States in 1993, to facilitate the retail industry to improve flow of goods and information between retailers and suppliers. The two fundamental principles that guide all ECR are: focus on consumers and working together to overcome barriers that erode efficiency and effectiveness.

ECR encourages companies to pursue continuous improvements under three focus areas:

1. Supply side to achieve reliable operation, continuous replenishment, integrated suppliers, and synchronized production.
2. Demand side by way of understanding and managing the demand for products and services.
3. Enabling technologies focused predominantly on development of the data management and processing capabilities that are needed to permit the rapid communication of accurate and timely information between trading partners. Electronic Data Interchange (EDI) systems and accounting methodologies are the two main requisites to create an enabling technology to operationalize ECR programmes. An EDI system is needed to easily communicate and manage orders, delivery, invoices and payments, both within a company and with its trading partners. EDI allows business partners to exchange a vast amount of information with great speed and accuracy.

Healthcare

The need to reduce costs and operate more efficiently has become important in the healthcare industry. To achieve improved quality at affordable costs requires efficiencies in all the processes that go towards the treatment of patients. Global initiatives such as Efficient Healthcare Consumer Response (ECHR), Global Healthcare Initiative (GHI), Bringing Improvements in Healthcare Practices (BIHP), and the United Nations Drug Control Programme (UNDCP) are the best examples to demonstrate the enormous efforts that have already gone into getting the ECR revolution off the ground.

There are evidences that the effective implementation of bar codes and EDI, based on international standards, can significantly improve the efficiency of healthcare institutions. Improved materials management can be achieved in terms of efficient dispensing of drugs and medical supplies, correct documentation, reduced inventories and lead items. The advantages are:

- Eliminates repetitive administrative duties by the use of advanced technology and help enhance the morale of the staff.
- Increases operations efficiency through improved management of assets through fast and accurate product and asset traceability.
- Reduces operating capital due to cost containment and productivity enhancements.
- Improves quality of care by scanning at the point of use.
- Handles logistic units with consistent accuracy.
- Shared information on product movement leading to accurate planning of activities throughout the value chain, accurate recording of identification, batch number, and expiration date data on products.
- Savings achieved in hospitals can be channelled towards the purchase of needed supplies.
- Use of single identification and codification standards translates into cost savings for suppliers in terms of labelling.

With the growth of e-commerce, the supplier is able to provide structured information on all its products to potential buyers, while the purchaser, using structured product data (such as product group codes) can unlock all relevant information and retrieve the data using EDI. EDI can be conceptualized as paperless trading. A common and useful definition for EDI is 'the transfer of structured data, by agreed message standards, from one computer application to another by electronic means and with a minimum of human intervention.' Organizational change, on the other hand, requires significant effort and time to make e-commerce in healthcare a reality. Without the active involvement of top management this can rarely succeed. The concept here is to form an ad hoc structure, involving all partners with a role in Healthcare EDI, that is, hospitals and clinics, their suppliers of all kinds of products (pharmaceuticals, chemicals, laboratory devices, surgery equipment, food and grocery, disposals, and so on), value-added networks, and software houses.

Source: Rajendra Gupta, 'Effecting efficient consumer response in healthcare in India,' http://www.expresshealthcaremgmt.com/20021231/edit2.shtml.

It gives an idea to the management as to what quantity of materials and other resources are to be procured and when, so that the total cost of operations of the organization is kept to the minimum over that period. The quantity of outsourcing, subcontracting of items, overtime of labour, numbers to be hired and fired in each period, and the amount of inventory to be held in stock and to be backlogged for each period are decided.

The term aggregate implies that the planning is done for a single overall measure of output or, at the most, a few aggregated product categories. The aim of aggregate planning is to set overall output levels in the near to medium future in the face of fluctuating or uncertain demands. Aggregate planning might seek to influence demand as well as supply.

Aggregate planning has certain prerequisites that are inevitable. They include:

- Information about the resources and the facilities available.
- Demand forecast for the period for which the planning has to be done.
- Cost of various alternatives and resources. This includes cost of holding inventory, ordering cost, cost of production through various production alternatives like subcontracting, backordering, and overtime.
- Organizational policies regarding the usage of above alternatives.

The aggregate planning strategies are:

- **Chase strategy:** In this strategy, the capacity is adjusted to match the demand pattern. The firm hires and lays off workers to match production to demand. The workforce fluctuates but the inventory of finished goods remains constant. This strategy works well for make-to-order firms.
- **Level strategy:** This relies on a constant output rate and capacity while varying inventory and backlog levels according to the fluctuating demand pattern. The workforce levels stay constant and the firm relies on fluctuating finished goods inventories and backlogs to meet demand. It works well for make-to-stock manufacturing firms.
- **Mixed production strategy:** This strategy is employed to maintain a stable workforce as the core while using other short-term means, such as overtime and additional subcontracting or part-time helpers, to manage short-term demand.

Options for situations in which demand needs to be increased in order to match capacity include:

- **Pricing:** Varying pricing to increase demand in periods when demand is less than peak. For example, matinee prices for movie theatres, off-season rates for hotels, weekend rates for telephone service, and pricing for items that experience seasonal demand.
- **Promotion:** Advertising, direct marketing, and other forms of promotion are used to shift demand.
- **Back ordering:** By postponing delivery on current orders, demand is shifted to a period when capacity is not fully utilized. This is really just a form of smoothing demand. Service industries are able to smooth demand by taking reservations or by making appointments in an attempt to avoid walk-in customers. Some refer to this as 'partitioning' demand.
- **New demand creation:** A new but complementary demand is created for a product or service. When restaurant customers have to wait, they are frequently diverted into a complementary (but not complimentary) service, the bar. Other examples include the addition of video arcades within movie theatres, and the expansion of services at convenience stores.

Options that can be used to increase or decrease capacity to match current demand include:

- **Hire/lay off:** By hiring additional workers as needed or by laying off workers not currently required to meet demand, firms can maintain a balance between capacity and demand.
- **Overtime:** By asking or requiring workers to work extra hours a day or an extra day per week, firms can create a temporary increase in capacity without the added expense of hiring additional workers.
- **Part-time or casual labour:** By utilizing temporary workers or casual labour (workers who are considered permanent but only work when needed on an on-call basis and typically without the benefits given to full-time workers).
- **Inventory:** An inventory of finished goods can be built up in periods of slack demand and then used to fill demand during periods of high demand. In this way no new workers have to be hired, no temporary or casual labour is needed, and no overtime is incurred.
- **Subcontracting:** Frequently firms choose to allow another manufacturer or service provider to provide the product or service to the subcontracting firm's customers. By subcontracting work to an alternative source, additional capacity is temporarily obtained.
- **Cross-training:** Cross-trained employees may be able to perform tasks in several operations, creating some flexibility when scheduling capacity.
- **Other methods:** While varying workforce size and utilization, inventory build-up/backlogging, and subcontracting are well-known alternatives. There are other, more novel ways that are used in the industry. Among these options

are sharing employees with counter-cyclical companies and attempting to find interesting and meaningful projects for employees to do during slack times.

Aggregate plans are required for medium range resource deployment decisions such as labour force size; financing inventory, and so on. Aggregate forecasts are much more accurate than detailed forecasts.

For a structured approach to aggregate planning, the following guidelines have to be followed in the order given.

1. Set policies on controllable variables
2. Establish forecast interval and horizon
3. Develop demand forecasting system
4. Select unit of aggregate capacity
5. Determine relevant cost structures
6. Apply aggregate planning techniques

9.6.1 Mathematical Techniques

The following are some of the better-known mathematical techniques that can be used in more complex aggregate planning applications.

Linear Programming

Linear programming is an optimization technique that allows the user to find a maximum profit or revenue or a minimum cost based on the availability of limited resources and certain limitations known as constraints. A special type of linear programming known as the Transportation Model can be used to obtain aggregate plans that would allow balanced capacity and demand, and minimization of costs. However, few real-world aggregate planning decisions are compatible with the linear assumptions of linear programming. Chopra and Meindl (2004) provide an application of the use of linear programming in aggregate planning.

Mixed-integer Programming

For aggregate plans that are prepared on a product family basis, where the plan is essentially the summation of the plans for individual product lines, mixed-integer programming may prove to be useful. Mixed-integer programming can provide a method for determining the number of units to be produced in each product family.

Linear Decision Rule

Linear decision rule is another optimizing technique. It seeks to minimize total production costs (labour, overtime, hiring/lay off, inventory carrying cost) using a set of cost-approximating functions (three of which are quadratic) to obtain a single quadratic equation. Then, by using calculus, two linear equations can be derived from the quadratic equation, one to be used to plan the output for each period and the other for planning the workforce for each period.

Management Coefficients Model

The management coefficients model, formulated by E.H. Bowman, is based on the suggestion that the production rate for any period would be set by this general decision rule:

$$P_t = aW_{t-1} - bI_{t-1} + cF_{t+1} + K, \text{ where}$$

P_t = the production rate set for period t

W_{t-1} = the workforce in the previous period

I_{t-1} = the ending inventory for the previous period

F_{t+1} = the forecast of demand for the next period

a, b, c, and K are constants

It then uses regression analysis to estimate the values of a, b, c, and K. The end result is a decision rule based on past managerial behaviour without any explicit cost functions, the assumption being that managers know what is important, even if they cannot readily state explicit costs. Essentially, this method supplements the application of experienced judgement.

Search Decision Rule

The search decision rule methodology overcomes some of the limitations of the linear cost assumptions of linear programming. The search decision rule allows the user to state cost data inputs in very general terms. It requires that a computer program be constructed that will unambiguously evaluate any production plan's cost. It then searches among alternative plans for the one with the minimum cost. However, unlike linear programming, there is no assurance of optimality.

Simulation

A number of simulation models can be used for aggregate planning. By developing an aggregate plan within the environment of a simulation model, it can be tested under a variety of conditions to find acceptable plans for consideration. These models can also be incorporated into a decision support system, which can aid in planning and evaluating alternative control policies. These models can integrate the multiple conflicting objectives inherent in manufacturing strategy by using different quantitative measures of productivity, customer service, and flexibility.

Functional Objective Search Approach

The functional objective search (FOS) system is a computerized aggregate planning system that incorporates a broad range of actual planning conditions. It is capable of realistic, low-cost operating schedules that provide options for attaining different planning goals. The system works by comparing the planning load with available capacity. After the management has chosen its desired actions and associated planning objectives for specific load conditions, the system weighs each planning goal to reflect the functional emphasis behind its achievement at a certain load condition. The computer then uses a computer search to output a plan that minimizes costs and meets delivery deadlines.

HMMS (Holt, Modigliani, Muth and Simon) Model

The HMMS Model uses quadratic functions for the different costs such as overtime, inventory, hiring and layoff, backlog, and so on. For this model, the costs relating to production level with optimal workforce, hiring, layoff, overtime, inventory holding, and back-order are to be considered.

9.6.2 Aggregate Planning in Services

For manufacturing firms, the luxury of building up inventories during periods of slack demand allows coverage of an anticipated time when demand will exceed capacity. Services cannot be stockpiled or inventoried so they do not have this option. Also, since services are considered 'perishable', any capacity that goes unused is essentially wasted. An empty hotel room or an empty seat on a flight cannot be held and sold later, as can a manufactured item held in inventory.

Service capacity can also be very difficult to measure. When capacity is dictated somewhat by machine capability, reasonably accurate measures of capacity are not extremely difficult to develop. However, services generally have variable processing requirements that make it difficult to establish a suitable measure of capacity.

Historically, services are much more labour intensive than manufacturing, where labour averages 10 per cent (or less) of the total cost. This labour intensity can actually be an advantage because of the variety of service requirements an individual can handle. This can provide quite a degree of flexibility that can make aggregate planning easier for services than manufacturing.

9.6.3 What's New in Aggregate Planning?

Hung presents a new, useful idea for aggregate planning called Annualized Hours (AH). Under AH, employees are contracted to work for a certain number of hours (say 1,800 hours) per year, for a certain sum of money. Employees can be asked to put in more hours during busy periods and fewer hours in slow periods. Typically, employees receive equal monthly or weekly payments so that hourly workers in effect have gained salaried status. Overtime is paid only when employees have worked beyond their annual hours.

AH is also known as flexi year, and it can be seen as an extension of flexitime, in which employees can vary their work hours within limits. This concept is used almost exclusively in Europe, particularly in the United Kingdom. The Scandinavian pulp and paper industries pioneered AH in the mid-1970s. Around that time, some West German firms, particularly those in the retail industry, also used AH.

AH gives employers much flexibility. AH serves to cut labour costs by offering employees an annual sum less than their previous annual earnings with overtime. Even though their total earnings may fall, their average earnings per hour would remain the same or even rise. Effective earnings could rise if the employer is unable to consume all contracted hours. Employees have greater income security with no worries about layoffs. There is also increased morale because blue-collar workers are now salaried.

Another development affecting aggregate planning is postponement. This refers to delaying the 'finish' of a product until the moment of sale. Firms that rely on the postponement strategy, such as PC-maker Dell Computers or clothing franchise Benetton Group, depend upon the availability of aggregate inventories of components that can be assembled immediately after an order is taken.

9.7 SALES AND OPERATIONS PLANNING

Sales and Operations Planning (S&OP) is an integrated business management process through which the executive/leadership team continually achieves focus, alignment, and synchronization among all the functions of the organization. S&OP is mostly done monthly, and is an iterative process. Results from one planning cycle are compared with the next to establish trends for the senior management. They evaluate time-phased projections for supply and demand, and ensure that the tactical plans in all business functions and geographies are aligned and in support of the company's strategy.

The monthly S&OP plan includes an updated sales plan, production plan, inventory plan, customer lead-time (backlog) plan, new product development plan, strategic initiative plan, and resulting financial plan (See Figure 9.7). Done well, the S&OP process also enables effective supply chain management.

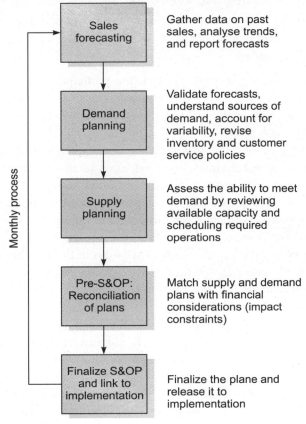

Figure 9.7 The monthly sales and operations planning process

S&OP is drawing attention in the press these days, but analyst firms, consultants, and software providers continue to confuse the market by describing it as difficult, using terms like 'continuous S&OP' and 'real-time S&OP'. These terms only complicate what should be a straightforward monthly planning process. In fact, sales and operations planning is a set of planning and decision-making processes that not only balance product supply and demand but also link business goals with operational and financial plans. The objective of S&OP is to enable executive decision makers to reach a consensus on a single operating plan that allocates critical resources to reach corporate performance targets.

At its heart, S&OP is an aggregated planning process. It is observed that companies reporting the largest gains in revenue, margins, inventory turns, and customer satisfaction, all plan the same way. In general, they practise S&OP at the strategic level—that is to say, not as a tactical, day-to-day or week-to-week planning activity. Rather, it is an aggregated planning activity that includes all lines of business or brands and all factories or regional operational facilities, across product lines.

The S&OP process is the usage of effective management techniques to arrive at one common plan that the company will execute towards agreed-upon goals. The process varies significantly from company to company. However there are a few generalized steps that each organization follows for a successful S&OP, which are:

1. Generate demand, supply, and financial plans based on the existing ones.
2. Perform reconciliation of the plans generated to arrive at one common plan.
3. Conduct review of the 'One Plan', with the help of senior executives and key stakeholders.

Based on the planning horizon, the participants and the frequency of the review meeting vary. This process attempts to integrate the demand and supply side of an enterprise. The review of the demand, supply, and financial plans constitutes the following activities.

The review of demand entails the consolidation of all the forecasts obtained from the different stakeholders involved, such as the marketing and sales forecast, POS forecast/statistical forecast, and the customer forecast. This review helps in identifying the needs for new product development, ascertaining that the sales, marketing, and finance work towards the same demand as opposed to one demand for sales and one demand for production, which would cause an imbalance between the demand and supply side of the supply chain. Any issues in the channel or in meeting the demands of the end customer are discussed. Updates to various plans to work towards one common demand number are done during this review. This also results in the revision of the inventory and customer service policies.

The review of supply plan entails the checking of the ability of the organization to meet the forecasted demand; this is done by reviewing the capacity and scheduling the required operations. This review takes into consideration the capacity constraints, current production performance, status of the current inventory and inventory positions, lead times, and so on. This results in changes in production, inventory, and capacity plans based on whether the review committee chooses to chase the demand or agrees to work within the existing limitations and decides not to meet some of the demand.

While making this decision, existing supplier relationship and issues are considered. It can also result in the introduction of new processes and equipments to meet the demand.

The reconciliation of the financial plan with the rest of the plans discussed above entails the comparison of the existing plans benchmarked against the financial goals and revenue targets of the company. The review committee here will be a team of cross-functional senior executives with the objective of verifying if the current plans and past performance will result in achieving the target set forth, to recommend changes to the joint business plan, and set new strategic directions to meet the objectives.

The final stage of the S&OP process is the executive review that helps in crystallizing the plan and releases it to implementation. This meeting serves as the opportunity for all the key stakeholders to meet and review the business plan. They will suggest changes to the business plan, recommend areas of improvements, and discuss the issues and concerns that hinder progress. This is sometimes conducted to take strategic decisions that have a long-term impact. Therefore, the participants of the meeting could be based on the frequency in which this meeting is conducted. Sometimes these meetings are conducted at a monthly interval where operational stakeholders are involved while the senior executives participate in quarterly meetings.

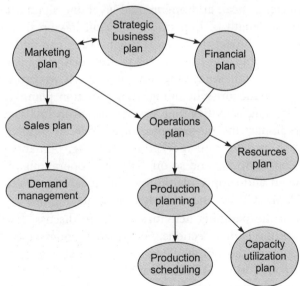

Figure 9.8 Sales and operations process

Figure 9.8 depicts linkages of various plans and forms the basis of sales and operations. A firm's business plan must trickle down to the production schedule for effective sales and operations plan. This would be possible through marketing, finance, and people deployment (resources) planning.

9.7.1 Benefits of S&OP

Some of the benefits of an effective sales and operations planning process include:
- Increased customer service levels
- Improved profitability
- More products to increase revenue
- Lower inventories and obsolescence
- Reduced lead times
- Quicker responsiveness
- Top-down management control
- Predictable operating performance for shareholders

In addition, a sales and operations planning process should also help to answer the following basic questions:
- How does projected demand compare to projected supply?
- What are the projected resource requirements to meet both service and cost targets?
- What actions are required to ensure that the appropriate levels of resources are available when needed?

9.8 SCOPE OF PLANNING INITIATIVES ACROSS SUPPLY CHAIN

At a macro level, the scope of planning in supply chain helps in decision making at the strategic, tactical, and operational level, the significance of which varies with the risk and the length of impact the decision has on the supply chain. The planning activities with respect to the focal organization can be looked at as activities that are performed within the boundaries of the focal organization and impact the intra-organizational efficiency and outcome, such as production planning, inventory planning, production scheduling, transportation planning, warehouse planning, and so on. Planning activities that are performed in interaction with the customers and suppliers impact the performance of the overall supply chain and extended supply chain such as sales and marketing planning, demand planning, supply planning, distribution planning, and so on. Sales and operations planning attempts to integrate the demand and supply planning of the focal organization, and relevant techniques such as VMI, CPFR, and ECR help in achieving this.

Each of the planning activities has been discussed with respect to the planning horizon in the earlier sections. For a better understanding of the scope of planning activities across the supply chain, let us take an example of a two-wheeler manufacturer in south India. We shall analyse the impact of the need for an integrated approach to planning and how aggregate planning is a necessity to simplify planning decisions. The company in question has one manufacturing unit in Chennai and four warehouses in Varanasi, Chandigarh, Nasik, and Chennai. The one in Chennai also acts as the master finished goods warehouse. The manufacturing department prepares a production plan based on the fill requirements, the production planning commences on the 14th of every month, and a finalized production plan and a production schedule is arrived at on the 24th of the month. Sales and marketing provides a marketing plan based on historical customer demand analysis and market intelligence. The procurement department prepares a supply plan, and based on the overall company strategies, the higher management along with finance prepares the revenue plan on a quarterly basis. Though they used an ERP to generate the production plan and a software-based demand plan, there were many issues in the communication of the plans between the internal faculties. This led to many issues in the performance of the supply chain:

1. Increased inventory as a result of mismatch between the supply plan and the production plan
2. Delays in production schedule due to non-availability of resources at the right time and frequent changes in production schedule as long as it was considered to be within the overall broad plan. There was no process to corroborate the scope and impact of the changes in the production schedule.
3. Improper stocking of finished goods at warehouses due to improper alignment of demand with distribution and warehouse planning.
4. Incorrect revenue expectations as sales and marketing plan did not take capacity constraints into consideration.
5. Lack of co-ordination has resulted in a disintegrated approach to planning and each of the departments would act as silos working to execute their own plan, thus resulting in internal competition.

The management recognized the issues early-on and started focusing on streamlining the process; they had embarked on a business process re-engineering project to alleviate the issues once for all. Some of the changes to the overall planning and operations that came out as recommendations, which the company implemented were:

1. Using a statistical demand forecasting tool to arrive at an unbiased demand number.
2. Integration with the external partners to aggregate the sales data on time, and scheduled data feed into the forecasting system.
3. Usage of CPFR techniques to arrive at a consensus forecast—they started using collaboration tools to update the numbers on an agreed-upon frequency to arrive at one demand number for all the supporting departments. This number was used by sales, marketing, procurement, and production departments to create a plan.
4. The S&OP process was used to co-ordinate the individual plans into a unified S&OP plan so that the company will operate on a single plan.

This has resulted in the following improvements (as depicted in Figure 9.9):

1. Proper communication between the supply and demand sides has resulted in the supply side buying inventory based on the constrained production schedule and keeping in mind the desired levels of sales. The focus was on increasing the

inventory turns and reducing the weeks on hand and as a result the overall inventory were reduced by more than 5 per cent in less than six months.

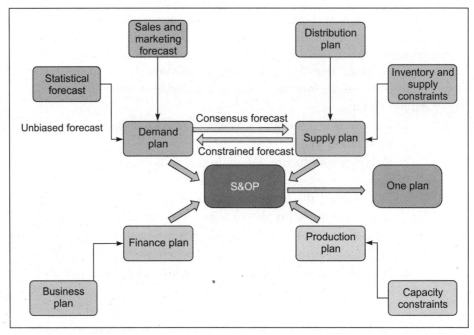

Figure 9.9   Sales and operating plan and its linkages

2. Strict measures have been implemented to restrict the change of production schedule and this was taken up as a special item for review in the S&OP review meetings, which were conducted on a monthly basis. The more strategic decisions were reviewed on a quarterly review meeting by the executive management. This improved the efficiency and responsiveness of the operations to the change in demand signals while optimizing the utilization of resources.

3. Improvements in transaction processing and order management cycles have resulted in shorter customer order backlogs, shorter lead times, and improved customer satisfaction.

4. Organizations achieved more stable production rates due to better integration of the demand and production plan, and shorter supplier lead times due to proper demand supply integration.

5. There is reduced obsolescence as the company works on one single plan that takes into account the inventory positions from all the channels.

6. There is reduced distribution and warehouse management cost as the allocations are streamlined and the movement across the warehouses is minimized.

SUMMARY

Supply Chain planning decisions and activities fall into one of the hierarchical based planning horizons—short-term, medium-term, and long-term planning. Here the focus would be on medium-term or tactical plans which could be for a period of twelve months but reviewed every month or quarter for arriving at an operations decisions.

Demand planning is the process of arriving at a demand plan that the focal organization will execute to cater to a committed demand obtained from statistical forecasting and other customer intelligence. Forecasting is subjected to huge amount of uncertainties and hence the accuracy of a forecast continues to be a topic of debate. Critics may state that forecasts would be inaccurate, more for aggregates than for SKUs, and for short duration rather than long duration. There are multiple techniques to develop a forecast to handle these criticisms.

Collaborative Planning, Forecasting, and Replenishment (CPFR) is a nine-step approach to improving supply chain management, and ties demand planning and supply planning into one process. For any change in the demand cycle— whether a truck breaks down or a seasonal holiday commences—inventory is redistributed and adjusted throughout the entire supply network. Participants can continuously verify the accuracy of each other's demand forecasts and handle exceptions in real time using the same data sets. CPFR also uses performance feedback loops to continually improve the system's efficiency. A major challenge to implementing CPFR is making the transition to a collaborative culture built on trust. Success for manufacturers will be determined by the commitment within the organization to make the transition to collaboration and implementation of a flexible, robust technology solution that can deliver rapid results at every step of the CPFR journey, and within the enterprise as well.

Aggregate planning is the process by which a company determines levels of capacity, production, subcontracting, inventory, stock outs, and pricing over a specified time horizon, the goal being to maximize profit and reduce cost; the decisions made are at a product family (not SKU) level. Aggregate planning addresses how a firm can best use the facilities that it has. Management can also decide as to what quantity of materials and other resources are to be procured and when, so that the total cost of operations of the organization is kept to the minimum over that period, say six to eighteen months. Aggregate plans are required for medium range resource deployment decisions such as labour force size, financing inventory, and so on.

Sales and Operations Planning (S&OP) is an integrated business management process through which the executive/leadership team continually achieves focus, alignment, and synchronization among all the functions of the organization. S&OP is mostly done monthly, and is an iterative process. They evaluate time-phased projections for supply and demand, and ensure that the tactical plans in all business functions and geographies are aligned and in support of the company's strategy. This is the key trigger for efficient supply chain management.

The planning activities with respect to the focal organization can be looked at as activities that are performed within the boundaries of the focal organization and impact the intra-organizational efficiency and outcome, such as production planning, inventory planning, production scheduling, transportation planning, warehouse planning, and so on, and with external partners like suppliers, channel partners, service providers, and customers. Planning activities that are performed in interaction with the customers and suppliers, and impact the performance of the overall supply chain and extended supply chain, need to be managed well.

KEY TERMS

Aggregate planning: Aggregate planning is the process by which a company determines levels of capacity, production, subcontracting, inventory, stock outs, and pricing over a specified time horizon, the goal being to maximize profit and reduce cost; the decisions made are at a product family (and not SKU) level.

Back ordering: By postponing delivery on current orders, demand is shifted to a period when capacity is not fully utilized. This is really just a form of smoothing demand.

Category management: It is a retailing concept in which the total range of products sold by a retailer is broken down into discrete groups of similar or related products; the product groups are known as product categories. Examples of grocery categories may be: personal care products, toothpastes, beverages, ready-to-eat foods, and so on.

Collaborative planning, forecasting, and replenishment (CPFR): A framework in which both the buyer and the supplier share internal information to integrate their plans, forecasts, and delivery schedules to ensure a smooth flow of goods and services. The framework is designed scientifically for synchronization of all partner activities.

Co-managed inventory (CMI): CMI is an inventory replenishment arrangement similar to Vendor Managed Inventory but where replacement orders for the vendor-owned stock are agreed upon by the user prior to delivery.

Delphi method: Delphi technique uses the exchange of information between anonymous panellists over a number of iterations, taking the average of the estimates on the final round as the group judgement.

Demand planning: The process of arriving at a demand plan that the focal organization will execute to cater to a committed demand obtained from statistical forecasting and other customer intelligence is referred to as demand planning. This includes driving the forecasting process, validating the forecasts, developing norms for stock keeping at multiple echelons of the distribution chain, placing distribution requirements on factories, and managing stock availability.

Efficient customer response (ECR): ECR is a comprehensive management concept based on vertical collaboration in manufacturing and retailing with the objective of an efficient satisfaction of consumer needs. The main components of ECR are supply chain management and category management.

Electronic point of sale (EPOS): EPOS is a self-contained, computerized equipment that performs all tasks of a store facilitating a transaction.

Forecasting: Forecasting is the process of trying to predict the future demand for a product or service in units or in revenue.

Mean absolute percentage error (MAPE): MAPE is commonly used in quantitative forecasting methods because it produces a measure of relative overall fit. The absolute values of all the percentage errors are summed up and the average is computed.

Moving average: A moving average is a single estimate, which is an average of the corresponding subset of a larger set of data points. A moving average is commonly used with time series data to smooth out short-term fluctuations and highlight longer-term trends or cycles.

Operations planning: Decisions like scheduling, rescheduling, and execution for planning periods ranging from daily, weekly, to less than six months are part of operations planning. Operations planning has limited flexibility to reschedule resources.

Postponement: This refers to delaying the 'finish' of a product until the moment of sale, providing final product configuration using assembly components close to customer point.

Sales and operations planning (S&OP): It is an integrated business management process through which the executive/leadership team continually achieves focus, alignment, and synchronization among all the functions of the organization on a monthly basis. It is an iterative process.

Strategic planning: Strategic planning decisions are concerned with defining the long-term objectives of a firm, charting the long-term course that will allow a firm to meet its defined objectives and assuring that a firm has the proper resources and assets necessary to support its long-term objectives.

Tactical planning: Tactical planning activities focus on using resources effectively to assure the accomplishment of the firm's objectives for a period between six to twelve months. This deals with how to utilize the infrastructure, labour, and capacity most effectively.

Vendor-managed inventory (VMI): VMI is an inventory replenishment arrangement whereby the supplier either monitors the customer's inventory with own employees or receives stock information from the customer. The vendor then refills the stock automatically, without the customer initiating purchase orders.

Voluntary inter-industry commerce solutions (VICS): Started in 1986, VICS Association facilitates to improve efficiency and effectiveness of supply by pioneering implementation of cross-industry standards, quick response for flow of product, and information between retailers and suppliers.

Weighted moving average: Weighted moving average is a technique that usually places more emphasis on recent periods. It uses multiplying factors to give different weights to different data points in a time series.

CONCEPT REVIEW QUESTIONS

1. Explain different planning horizons and draw examples from real life on each type of planning horizon in a supply chain domain.

2. Differentiate between forecasting and demand planning. What are the different methods of qualitative tools used in forecasting? Explain their merits and demerits.

3. Explain the importance of causal factors in demand planning.

4. Discuss a case to analyse the importance of consensus planning.

5. What is the need for monitoring forecast?

6. What KPIs can be used to measure forecast accuracy?

7. Explain CPFR, facets of collaboration, and challenges in implementing the same.

8. Describe the steps in implementing CPFR. What are the benefits of CPFR?

9. Explain aggregate planning. What are its benefits? In which process of the supply chain is aggregate planning widely used?

10. Explain two econometric techniques with examples using Excel of how to arrive at forecast values.

11. Why is Sales and Operations Planning important for a supply chain manager? Explain with examples the importance of sales plan for a synchronized supply chain network operation.

12. What are the different modules of S&OP? Relate S&OP to other planning models and explain its significance.

CRITICAL THINKING QUESTIONS

1. 'Predicting demand is speculative like being in commodities or stocks price in their respective markets. A supply chain manager would better rely on hunches and trend rather than on application of scientific tools.' Argue for and/or against by choosing a particular product, and use the industry and other economic factors in support of your argument.

2. You are the manager of a watches showroom that sells watches in a territory. You are familiar that there has been a pattern of sales and data from the sales of the last three quarters can be a fair indicator for future sales. You may forecast sales using a 3-period moving average with the following data.

Quarter	1	2	3	4	5	6
Sales Rs	4,500	4,200	4,600	4,800	4,400	4,700

When you submit this to the brand owner and manufacturer of watches, the supply chain analyst wants you to use weighted average. The weight to be arrived based quarter number to sum of quarters so that recent quarters get more weight. Compare both the results and demonstrate sensitivity to recent period sales data.

3. You are Head of East India Marketing of the cement division of a large group. Based on the following data, you have asked the marketing analyst to use different techniques like trend method, linear regression to project demand. What would be the numbers that you could expect from him/her?

Month	Demand for cement in million INR	Spending on construction in million INR
1	INR 375	3,700
2	INR 410	3,888
3	INR 398	4,123
4	INR 388	3,978
5	INR 420	4,123
6	INR 412	3,985

Month	Demand for cement in million INR	Spending on construction in million INR
7	INR 399	4,123
8	INR 425	4,356
9	INR 403	4,120
10	INR 400	3,980
11	INR 390	3,895
12	INR 415	4,300
13		4,100
14		4,000

4. Discuss a case to analyse the importance of consensus planning.

5. What are the core elements of CPFR? Based on web research, discuss cases where CPFR has failed and examine the reasons for its failure.

6. Map the scope of supply chain planning function to a manufacturing activity of a product with which you are familiar.

PROJECT ASSIGNMENTS

1. Use web research on growth of containerization in India and trends in container traffic. You are asked by your management to prepare a policy paper for a local business association demanding the capacity for container terminal in the Chennai port. Develop an approach note with projections and your arguments in support of the same.

2. Approach a nearest consumer products store, tractor dealer, and agricultural produce trader and find out different methods of forecasting used by them. Detail the merits and demerits that they face in using these tools.

3. Visit an automotive plant, a consumer durable, or food manufacturing company. Discuss with the production planning and operations departments the application of aggregate planning. Present a detailed report of the same.

REFERENCES

Armstrong, Jon Scott, *Principles of Forecasting*, Kluwer Academic Publishers, 2001

Chary, S. N., *Production and Operations Management*, Tata McGraw-Hill, 2004

Chopra, Sunil and Peter Meindl, *Supply Chain Management: Stratgey, Planning and Operation*, Pearson, 2004

Crum, Colleen and George E. Palmatier, *Demand Management Best Practices: Process, Principles and Collaboration*, J. Ross Publishing, 2003

Hung, Rerdy 'Annalized Hours and Aggbegate Planning,' Production and Inventory Management Journal, 38(4), 1997

Monks, Joseph G., *Schaum's Outline of Theory and Problems of Operations Management*, McGraw-Hill, 1996

Russell, Roberta and Bernard W. Taylor, *Operations Management: Quality and Competitiveness in Global Environment*, 5th edition, Wiley India Edition, 2005

Shapiro, Jeremy, *Modeling the Supply Chain*, Thompson, 2007

www.ecrnet.org; www.ecraustralasia.org.au;

www.expresshealthcaremgmt.com/20021231/edit 2.shtml

www.vics.org

Autoregressive Moving Average

Autoregressive Moving Average (ARMA) modelling is typically applied for modelling univariate time series data. It is also called the Box-Jenkins model after the iterative Box-Jenkins methodology usually used to estimate them. Given a time series of data Xt, the ARMA model is a tool for understanding and, perhaps, predicting future values in this series. The model consists of two parts, an autoregressive (AR) part and a moving average (MA) part. The model is usually then referred to as the ARMA (p,q) model where p is the order of the autoregressive part and q is the order of the moving average part.

Autoregressive models are defined by:

$$X_{(t)} = \text{XMEAN} + \text{phi}_1 * X_{(t-1)} + \text{phi}_2 * X_{(t-2)} + \dots + \text{phi}_p * X_{(t-p)} + A_{(t)}$$

where $X_{(t)}$ is the series and XMEAN is the mean of the series. $A_{(t)}$ represents normally distributed random errors, and the $\text{phi}_1, \dots, \text{phi}_p$ are the parameters of the model. Autoregressive models are simply a linear regression of the current value of the series against one or more prior values of the series. The value of p is called the order of the model.

Moving average models are defined by:

$$X_{(t)} = \text{XMEAN} + A_{(t)} - \text{theta}_1 * A_{(t-1)} - \text{theta}_2 * A_{(t-2)} - \dots - \text{theta}_q * A_{(t-q)}$$

where $X_{(t)}$ is the series and XMEAN is the mean of the series. $A_{(t-1)}$ represents random shocks of one or more prior points of the series, and the $\text{theta}_1, \dots, \text{theta}_q$ are the parameters of the model. The random shocks are assumed to come from a common (typically normal) distribution with common location and scale. The primary idea behind the moving average model is that the random shocks are propagated to future values of the series. Fitting moving average models require iterative, non-linear fitting techniques.

ARMA models assume that the data are stationary, that is, the data have constant location and scale. Trend can often be removed from a non-stationary series to achieve stationary value.

Differencing is a common approach for removing trend. The first difference is defined as $X_{(t)} - X_{(t-1)}$. In most cases, a single differencing is sufficient. However, more than one differencing can be applied if necessary. You can also fit a linear or non-linear model to remove trend.

ARMA models can also incorporate seasonal terms (and seasonal differencing). ARMA models typically require fairly long series (at least 50 points is recommended by some authors). Also, if the series is dominated by trend and seasonal components, a trend/seasonality/residual decomposition method may be preferred.

Autoregressive Integrated Moving Average (ARIMA)

This model is a generalization of an autoregressive moving average (ARMA) model. These models are fitted to time series data either to better understand the data or to predict future points in the series. They are applied in some cases where data show evidence of non-stationary value, where an initial differencing step (corresponding to the 'integrated' part of the model) can be applied to remove the non-stationary value. Building good ARIMA models generally requires more experience than commonly used statistical methods such as regression.

The ARIMA approach to forecasting is based on the following ideas:

1. The forecasts are based on linear functions of the sample observations
2. The aim is to find the simplest models that provide an adequate description of the observed data. This is sometimes known as the principle of parsimony.

Each ARIMA process has three parts: the autoregressive (or AR) part; the integrated (or I) part; and the moving average (or MA) part. The models are often written in shorthand as ARIMA (p,d,q) where p describes the AR part, d describes the integrated part, and q describes the MA part.

AR: This part of the model describes how each observation is a function of the previous p observations. For example, if p = 1, then each observation is a function of only one previous observation. That is, $Y_t = c + \_1Y_{t-1} + e_t$

where Yt represents the observed value at time t, Y_{t-1} represents the previous observed value at time t–1, et represents some random error and c and $\_1$ are both constants. Other observed values of the series can be included in the right-hand side of the equation if p > 1:

$Y_t = c + \_1Y_{t-1} + \_2Y_{t-2} + \cdots + \_pY_{t-p} + et$

I: This part of the model determines whether the observed values are modelled directly, or whether the differences between consecutive observations are modelled instead. If d = 0, the observations are modelled directly. If d = 1, the differences between consecutive observations are modelled. If d = 2, the differences of the differences are modelled. In practice, d is rarely more than 2.

MA: This part of the model describes how each observation is a function of the previous q errors. For example, if q = 1, then each observation is a function of only one previous error. That is, $Y_t = c + \_1e_{t-1} + et$

Here e_t represents the random error at time t and e_{t-1} represents the previous random error at time t–1. Other errors can be included in the right-hand side of the equation if q > 1. Combining these three parts gives the diverse range of ARIMA models. There are also ARIMA processes designed to handle seasonal time series, and vector ARIMA processes designed to model multivariate time series. Other variations allow the inclusion of explanatory variables.

ARIMA processes have been a popular method of forecasting because they have a well-developed mathematical structure from which it is possible to calculate various model features such as prediction intervals. These are very important features of forecasting as they enable forecast uncertainty to be quantified.

10

Role of Inventory Management in SCM

10.1 NEED FOR INVENTORY MANAGEMENT

Inventory in supply chain plays a crucial role in balancing divergent supply chain objectives, namely cost and responsiveness. Inventory management should facilitate to offer variants of models and SKUs for customers to buy. The top line sale directly depends upon the inventory available. If one's business is not Made to Engineer or Made to Order and is more of Made to Stock, then pressure on inventory is going to be high. For example, in the fashion business, whether it is garments, watches, or jewellery, each requires that the customer have a wider choice at affordable prices. The top line sale is directly linked to finished goods inventory or inventory that is simple to configure or assemble. The latter case, comprising work-in-progress components or items that are close to finishing, is based on the principle of postponement in production.

Though the customer ideally wants a wide choice, the focal firm faces the challenge of managing costs for providing a vast range of goods. If goods are stored in anticipation of sale, then there is an opportunity cost and cost of holding the stock. Once when the products or SKUs lose freshness, then the product needs to be sold at a discounted rate. This obsolescence cost is associated with inventory. A supply chain manager is thus confronted with the challenges of managing cost and responsiveness in customer service with better management of inventory practices. This is true not only in forward linkages but also in backward linkages. Exhibit 10.1 shows the importance of inventory to Titan Industries Ltd in India.

Exhibit 10.1   Titan Industries—Focus on Inventory Management

In an interview, the Managing Director of Titan Industries Ltd pointed out that IT is critical in two areas of operation: managing the supply chain and developing a strong understanding of what the customer wants—something that is vital for lifestyle brands.

This happens at two levels. For one, our retail outlets are highly IT-enabled, and are feeding information on the transactions that the customer has with the company. In addition, the company could capture the customer information and have a loyalty programme. All the information comes through an IT network. Since the transaction information is generated and goes back to the ERP system, data mining gives us useful information.

Reports from various geographies give an idea on trends and customer preferences to take better decisions. This is especially useful while launching new products. IT has also helped us to significantly reduce costs in terms of inventory. This company focuses on not carrying dead inventory.

Source: www.cio.in/view-top/how-titan%E2%80%99s-it-helped-growth.

10.2   DEFINITION AND TYPES OF INVENTORY

Inventory refers to any owned or financially controlled raw material, works in process, and/or finished good or service held in anticipation of a sale but not yet sold. Inventory would also include all those items and goods that indirectly contribute to production processes such as stores and consumables items, which will have a financial impact on the income statement and the balance sheet of the company. Inventory refers to the stock of materials of any kind, such as raw materials, work-in-process goods, finished goods, and any others that are stored for future use. Inventory has a store value but these are practically idle resources. Thus, inventories are materials/resources of any kind having some economic value, either awaiting conversion or for use in future.

10.2.1   Inventory within the Supply Chain Network

The supply chain network of a focal firm extends from suppliers to customers, with intermediaries involved to facilitate moving and adding value for goods and services across the network as shown in Figure 10.1. Whenever inventory piles up in any node or movement, financial commitment begins. One may argue that financial commitment is expressed by contract and physical possession of inventory would matter more. This would mean that the planning function and commitment at the planning stage would not add to the inventory. In such a situation, inventory would not reflect at the same cost head but would be added in the material cost head. To sum up, actual and proposed commitment to add stock for monetizing would be considered as inventory in the system. Figure 10.1 illustrates the inventory process across a supply chain network.

Inventory on a primary network is from the direct supplier to the focal firm, and then to its forward linkage up to the CFA. This inventory is financially critical and would reflect in the focal organization's books. However, in reality, inventory at indirect linkages in a network would impact the supply chain decision. For example, inventory with retail may not be book stock of the focal firm. All the same, movement of goods must be as per plan, because otherwise, the system would clog, affecting all supply chain drivers. Thus, it is critical to have a perception of where inventory is in the system.

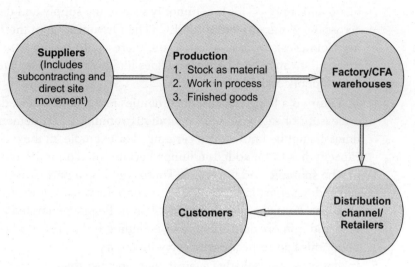

Figure 10.1 Inventory across supply chain network

10.2.2 Importance of Inventory in a System

1. Inventory improves customer service by providing product availability. For example, in the food flavours business, a manufacturer may be producing hundreds of flavours and SKUs, especially in the trade segment, that are supplied through retailers to small bakeries and food manufacturers. Unless the company keeps adequate inventory, it would not be able to ensure product availability and retain its brand value.

2. Inventory encourages production, purchase, and transportation economies. An inventory plan is important for long production runs, especially in case of seasonal products. For example, edible oil seeds in India are available only during certain seasons whereas demand is evenly distributed with small distortions. Unless manufacturers understand this, the seasonal optimization of production runs may not be possible. Similarly, inventory management policy can help to take advantage of quantity based price discounts. Volume buys can facilitate price discounts, and there could be some flexibility in purchase as a manufacturer may trade-off between price discount and inventory-holding costs. Another advantage could be to earn transport economies from larger shipment sizes. An inventory management plan would help to arrive at a trade-off between transportation cost and inventory cost.

3. Inventory would act as a hedge against price changes. The inventory manager must take advantage of purchasing under the most favourable price terms. Though this is important for any kind of purchase, this would be more obvious

in case of seasonal products. The price of edible oilseeds bottom out immediately after harvest and arrival of produce in the agricultural goods markets. Once the season is over, the price goes up as there's a mismatch between demand and supply. This is commonly seen in the supply and demand of crude oil across the globe, driven by OPEC (The Organization of the Petroleum Exporting Countries). In case of crude oil, there could be limits to buying large volumes in advance and hence strategies like buying forward and annual contract price options would help.

4. Inventory is a hedge against uncertainties in demand and lead times. It provides a measure of safety to keep operations running when demand levels and lead times cannot be known with certainty. For example, in the engineering industry, capacity has to be added in lumps because of economies of scale, but demand maybe sporadic and uncertain. There could be a period of shortage in capacity and sudden spurt in demand due to temporary economic upswing or trigger by an event. For example, Olympics 2008 in Beijing generated a huge demand for steel and iron ore across countries including India. Those who wanted to benefit out of this had to necessarily carry inventory.

5. Inventory acts as a hedge against contingencies that one experiences because of events like strikes, fires, terrorist attacks, and natural calamities and disruptions like a tsunami, swine flu, and so on. Such triggers affect supply, and the inventory management policy must factor the same. For example, in mid 2000, even expected disruptions in port operations at Mumbai and Chennai created a huge challenge for foreign trade-dependent businesses to receive and move goods.

Thus, inventory plays a major role in supply chain effectiveness and efficiency, and is important for achieving a competitive advantage. Inventory management is a strategic area in logistics operation and has an impact on the efficiency and effectiveness of the overall supply chain system. As the cycle of production and consumption never matches, products need to be kept in stock to get over the uncertainties in demand and supply. However, higher inventory levels will affect the bottomline of the company. This is a high risk and high impact area, which has to strike a balance between two divergent goals of lower cost and higher levels of customer service.

10.2.3 Types of Inventory

To accommodate the functions of inventory, firms maintain four types of inventories: (1) raw material inventory, (2) work-in-process inventory, (3) finished goods inventory, and (4) maintenance/repair/overhauling (MRO) supply inventory.

Raw material inventory is that which has been purchased but not processed. This inventory can be used to ensure material availability for the production process and decouple suppliers from a defined production run. However, the approach would be to eliminate supplier variability in quality, quantity, or delivery time so that the focal firm is insulated from the risk of stoppage of a production run.

Work-in-process (WIP) inventory is made up of components or raw material that have undergone value addition but have not formed the final product. WIP inventory reduces the time it takes for a product to be made, which is referred to as production cycle time. Reducing production cycle time reduces inventory. WIP is critical in the engineering industry where components from vendors and subcontractors are scheduled in assembly, and at times sequencing of components may require value addition on the arrival of sequenced material. So based on the requirement of a business, work-in-process needs to be addressed.

Finished goods inventory is that which is ready to be delivered to distribution centres, retailers, and wholesalers, or directly to the customers. Finished inventory is waiting for a demand pull or movement in the supply network based on a push system. The point is that it is waiting for a customer order to be serviced. For example, printers that are configured at a dealer's warehouse or with the focal firm's warehouse are part of finished inventory.

Maintenance/repair/overhauling (MRO) supply inventory refers to supplies consumed in the production process but would not be a part of the end product or primary value-adding activity or component. MRO items support the main activity or production process. MRO items include consumables (such as plant upkeep items), lubricants, tools and gaskets, and office supplies (such as stationery, computers, and furniture). In a sugar plant, due to the acidic nature of the material which is processed, the milling and processing section requires cleaning and overhauling of mills and process sections during season. So the availability of MRO items would be crucial in such a case. Though by and large maintenance activity can be planned, there is an inherent operational requirement for stock operational maintenance items such as spare motors, pumps, crushing rollers, hopper pins, and so on.

10.3 CLASSIFICATION OF INVENTORY

10.3.1 Cycle Inventory

Cycle inventory is the average inventory that builds up in the supply chain because a supply chain stage either produces or purchases in lots that are larger than those demanded by the customer. Raw materials, components, and parts are required for production. The cycle plays a crucial role in keeping the production process continuous. Raw materials and work-in-process inventory are a major part of production-related inventory.

Lot or batch size refers to quantity that a supply chain stage either produces or orders at a given time. Determining how frequently to order and in what quantity is called lot sizing. If Q = lot or batch size of an order and d = demand per unit time, then:

Cycle inventory = $Q/2$ (depends directly on lot size)
Average flow time = Average inventory/Average flow rate
Average flow time from cycle inventory = $Q/2d$

Typically, in a coal-based captive power plant of 500 MW capacity, coal is prepared for use by crushing the rough coal to small pieces. The coal is then transported from the storage yard to in-plant storage silos by rubberized conveyor belts. The plant consumes 250 tonnes of coal per hour under full load and about 6,000 tonnes of coal per day if there's a continuous run. A shipload of 50,000 tons is imported in a lot. Based on this data, cycle inventory of coal is 25,000 tonnes. Since unit of time is a day and consumption per day is 6,000 tonnes, average flow time would be 8.33 days and average flow time from cycle inventory would be 3.125 days.

Cycle inventory is held primarily to take advantage of economies of scale in the supply chain. Supply chain costs are influenced by lot sizes. The primary role of cycle inventory is to allow different stages to purchase products in lot sizes that minimize the sum of material, ordering, and holding costs. Ideally, cycle inventory decisions should consider costs across the entire supply chain, but in practice, each stage generally makes its own supply chain decisions—this increases total cycle inventory and total costs in the supply chain.

10.3.2 Safety Inventory

Safety inventory is the inventory carried for the purpose of satisfying demand that exceeds the amount forecasted in a given period. Inventory is carried based on the forecast of demand and forecasts are rarely completely accurate. If the average demand is 1,000 units per week, there could be times when the actual demand is greater than 1,000 and times when the actual demand is less than 1,000. In such times when demand is higher, there is a lost sale. In order to avoid customer service problems and the hidden costs of unavailable components, companies hold something called as safety stock. This gives a cushion against uncertainties in demand, lead-time, and supply, thereby ensuring that operations aren't disrupted.

10.3.3 Seasonal Inventory

Seasonal inventory refers to the inventory that is used to absorb uneven rates of demand or supply that businesses face. Manufacturers of consumer electronics in India experience seasonality in sale, which is around the festive time, between October and the first week of January. If there is no stock of SKUs during this period, the focal firm may lose market share. Hence holding of seasonal inventory helps meet the volatility in demand and supply. A focal firm may stock up SKUs to meet seasonality.

10.3.4 Pipeline Inventory or Inventory in Transit

Inventory moving from one node to another in the materials flow system is called pipeline inventory. Materials move from suppliers to a plant, from the plant to a distribution centre or customer, and from the distribution centre to a retailer. Inventory in transit across partners in network is referred to as pipeline inventory. Pipeline inventory consists of orders that have been placed but have not yet been served. This can be reduced by reducing stocking locations, improving materials handling, and avoiding delays in distribution.

10.4 COSTS TO BE RECKONED WHILE HOLDING INVENTORY

Like any asset or economic activity, especially in business, there would be direct (explicit) and indirect (implicit) costs associated with managing inventory. A supply chain manager must have a clear understanding and evaluation of costs while arriving at such decisions. Such decisions could be on deciding the inventory level, lot sizing, and practices relating to inventory management or on drivers such as transportation, facilities, pricing, and sourcing.

1. **Inventory holding (or carrying) cost:** It is a variable cost on items such as storage and handling, taxes, insurance, interest on capital, and shrinkage cost. The annual cost to maintain one unit in inventory typically ranges from 20 to 25 per cent of its value, depending upon the cost of capital and cost of storage, which are two key elements here. In a developing country, the cost of capital could be high as it is scarce, and cost of storage could be higher in populous locations because of pressure on land. A country like India has the disadvantage of both and hence inventory holding cost plays a crucial element in managing inventory across a supply chain network.

   For example, a fertilizer company in India has a stand-alone revenue of around Rs 2,400 crore and would have an inventory of a different nature averaging Rs 240 crore. Taking holding cost at 15 per cent, which would include cost of capital and other elements as mentioned above, absolute inventory holding costs would be Rs 36 crore. If the stand-alone business makes about 12 per cent return on sales, its profit would be Rs 288 crore. Since this is a regulated business, the profit margin is decent. There are many businesses where the gross operating margin is less than 10 per cent and inventory turnover matters, or else holding cost is significant in terms of gross profit margins.

   One may note that the cost of capital could direct costs, like the cost of borrowed capital for inventory. The more appropriate cost is the opportunity of cost of investment, as the total capital invested in inventory must get the market rate of return.

2. **Storage and handling costs:** These costs are incurred when a firm rents out space. There is also an opportunity cost if one is going to use own space, as the firm can utilize the storage space alternatively.

3. **Taxes, insurance, and shrinkage related costs:** Insurance is a direct cost outflow and is required to manage risks, and is mandatory when it is on borrowed capital. When inventory is high, the insurance on the inventory also increases. Shrinkage takes place in three forms.

   (a) Obsolescence occurs when inventory cannot be used or sold to the full value due to change in model, engineering modifications, or low demand.

   (b) Deterioration through physical spoilage or damage results in lost value.

   (c) Pilferage, or theft of inventory from the warehouses.

4. **Ordering cost:** This refers to the cost involved in the ordering process. These are all administrative costs involved in order generation. With proliferation of

technology application, this has been marginalized. But it is important to be cognizant of the same.

5. **Carrying cost:** Also called holding cost, carrying cost is the cost associated with having inventory on hand. It is primarily made up of the costs associated with the inventory investment and storage cost. For the purpose of the Economic Order Quantity (EOQ) calculation, if the cost does not change based upon the quantity of inventory on hand, it should not be included in carrying cost. In the EOQ formula, carrying cost is represented as the annual cost per average, on-hand inventory unit. Though carrying cost is the cost of money tied up in inventory, it also includes obsolescence, insurance, personal property taxes, and storage costs.

Thus, these are the major costs associated with inventory management. There would be other costs that would be relevant but those are derived out of options in a decision situation.

10.5 INVENTORY MANAGEMENT

Supply chain managers along with functional managers in production and operations management, marketing, and finance establish systems for managing inventory, as service level and cost are the key supply chain objectives that need to be addressed. In this section, we briefly examine two ingredients of such systems: (1) how inventory items can be classified (using ABC analysis) and (2) how accurate inventory records can be maintained.

10.5.1 ABC Analysis

ABC analysis divides on-hand inventory into three categories on the basis of annual monetary value. This classification is based on the Pareto principle for inventory management. The Pareto principle states that there are a 'critical few and trivial many'. The idea is to establish inventory policies that focus resources on the few critical inventory parts and not the many trivial ones. It is not realistic to monitor inexpensive items with the same intensity as very expensive items.

To determine annual dollar volume for ABC analysis, one must measure the annual demand of each inventory item times the cost per unit. Class A items are those on which the monetary value (Quantity X price per unit) is high. Although such items may represent only about 15 per cent of the total inventory items, they represent 70 to 80 per cent of the total monetary commitment. Class B items are the inventory items of medium annual monetary value. These items may represent about 30 per cent of inventory items and 15 to 25 per cent of the total value. Those with low annual dollar volume are Class C, which may represent only 5 per cent of the annual monetary value but about 55 per cent of the total inventory items.

Chennai Electronics Ltd, makers of electronic components for industrial applications, has reviewed its ten inventory items on a volume and rate basis as shown in Figure 10.2. The supply chain analyst grouped these ten items into ABC classifications as shown in Table 10.1 and Figure 10.2.

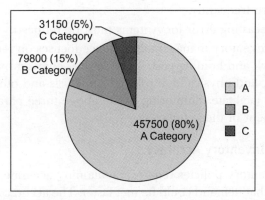

Figure 10.2 ABC classification of ten select items at Chennai Electronics Ltd

In the above case, since unit price variation is high, ABC analysis makes sense rather than Fast-Slow-Normal (FSN) moving inventory analysis. Table 10.2, which shows the ABC and the FSN analysis of stocks in three warehouses of the Chennai-based chemical business, leads to the same conclusions. Still, at SKU level, it could be different.

Criteria other than monetary value can also determine item classification. For instance, anticipated engineering changes, delivery problems, quality problems, or high unit cost may lead to upgrading items to a higher classification. The advantage of dividing inventory items into classes allows policies and controls to be established for each class.

Policies that may be based on ABC analysis include the following:

1. Supplier development should be much higher for individual A items than of C items.

Table 10.1 Chennai Electronics Ltd—ABC classification of ten select items

Stock code	Volume	Unit price	Monetary value	%	Cum %	Classification
#10605	2,700	125	337,500	59	59	A
#11245	600	200	120,000	21	80	A
#10252	1,500	21	31,500	6	86	B
#12245	1,150	42	48,300	8	95	B
#12050	600	24	14,400	3	97	C
#10751	100	60	6,000	1	98	C
#12758	1,200	2.5	3,000	1	99	C
#01048	850	6	5,100	1	100	C
#01450	1,750	1.2	2,100	0	100	C
#14751	550	1	550	0	100	C

2. A-class items, as opposed to B and C items, should have tighter physical inventory control. The accuracy of inventory records for A items should be verified more frequently.

3. Forecasting error for A items must be reduced.

Good inventory management practice focuses on reducing inventory, especially of safety stock and holding cost. This can be achieved by effective forecasting, supplier reliability, and physical control. ABC analysis and other methods of classification of inventory facilitate monitoring of the above three parameters and thereby guide the development of those policies.

10.5.2 Inventory Accuracy

Good inventory policies require maintaining accurate records and proper storage of goods so that demand could be met faster. The accuracy of records is a critical ingredient in production and inventory systems. Record accuracy allows organizations to focus on those items that are needed, rather than assuming that 'on an average everything is available'. Only when an organization can determine accurately what it has on hand can it make precise decisions about ordering, scheduling, and shipping. To ensure accuracy, incoming and outgoing record keeping must be good, as must be stores/warehouse security. A well-organized store/warehouse will have limited access, good housekeeping, and storage areas that hold fixed amounts of inventory. Bins, shelf space, and parts will be labelled accurately.

Cycle Counting

With the deployment of ERP and specialized software for inventory management, accuracy has improved. So has also the ease of maintaining stocks! However, these records must be verified through a continuing audit. Such audits are known as cycle counting. Historically, many firms performed annual physical inventories. This practice often meant shutting down the facility and having not-so-experienced people count parts and material. Later, cycle counting was established as an effective way of verifying inventory records. Cycle counting uses inventory classifications developed through ABC analysis. With cycle counting procedures, items are counted, records are verified, and inaccuracies are periodically documented. The cause of inaccuracies

Table 10.2   ABC and FMS analysis of stock

Warehouse	A (70%)	B (20%)	C (10%)	Total products	F (70%)	N (20%)	S (10%)	Total products
Delhi	24	33	112	169	24	34	111	169
	14% of 169	20% of 169	66% of 169		14% of 169	20% of 169	66% of 169	
Bangalore	17	29	122	168	16	28	124	168
	10% of 168	17% of 168	73% of 168		10% of 168	17% of 168	74% of 168	
Chennai	21	33	118	172	16	24	132	172
	12% of 172	19% of 172	69% of 172		9% of 172	14% of 172	77% of 172	

Table 10.3 Cycle-count calculation

Item classification	Quantity	Policy	Number of items to be counted each day
A	1000	Every 20 working days	1,000/20 = 50
B	3000	Every 60 working days	3,000/60 = 50
C	16000	Every 160 working days	16,000/160 = 100

is then traced and appropriate remedial action taken to ensure integrity of the inventory system. A-class items are counted frequently, perhaps once a month; B-class items are counted less frequently, perhaps once a quarter; and C-class items are counted perhaps once every six months. The time window must be determined depending upon the nature of the business and the importance of the inventory to the total business. For example, retail business is based on inventory at display and inventory at back store space. It would be difficult to frequently count inventory in retail business. On the other hand, high-value fashion business such as watches may require much shorter window for physical stock counting.

Ahmedabad Antique and Home Furniture Corporation, a high-quality home interior design showroom, has about 20,000 items in its inventory. After hiring Nimesh Shah, a supply chain analyst for the summer, the firm determined that it has 1,000 A items, 3,000 B items, and 16,000 C items. The company policy is to count all A items every twenty working days, all B items every sixty working days, and all C items every 160 working days. He recommends the following calculation (shown in Table 10.3) on the number of items to be counted on each day.

So 200 items are to be counted each day in the above example. One may follow the policy of counting the particular number of items either sequentially or randomly. Another option is to cycle-count items when they are reordered.

Cycle counting also has the following advantages:

1. It eliminates the shut down and interruption of production necessary for annual physical inventories.
2. It eliminates annual inventory adjustments as adjustments are finished as and when counting is completed on a day.
3. It allows the cause of the errors to be identified and remedial action to be taken.
4. It maintains accurate inventory records.
5. It improves the effectiveness of the audit personnel because of limited and routine action.

10.6 CONTROL OF INVENTORIES IN RETAIL AND SERVICES

The management of service inventories deserves special attention. For example, in the food business, especially in restaurants, the ability to offer variety and cost, and balancing of both becomes critical. Also, there are certain choices that need to be offered 24×7. Forecasting has its own challenges and customer loyalty must be rewarded with appropriate service, which would decide the success of the business. Two macro processes, namely CRM and internal supply chain management, must be interfaced effectively in order to manage within stocks available.

This is true of hotel reservation, which is a part of the service business. Unoccupied rooms are inventory and price realizations using discount must balance arrival and service. This is again true in air ticketing, which is a perishable inventory as an unfilled seat is an inventory and revenue lost. Hence, lots of sensitivities are attached in managing retail and service inventories. Learning from past experiences and professionalizing operations with the integration of back-end and front-end support would determine the success of the business.

The following techniques could be useful in managing retail and perishable service-level inventory:

1. Good personnel selection, training, and discipline. This is important in food-service, wholesale, and retail operations, where employees have access to directly consumable merchandise and the end customer.

2. Demand estimation and revisions on a near dynamic state and reworking pricing to enhance product movement and realizations. This would reduce the risk of opportunity loss.

3. Tight control of incoming shipments. This task is being addressed by many firms through the use of bar code and radio frequency ID systems that read every incoming shipment and automatically check tallies against purchase orders. When properly designed, these systems are very hard to defeat. Each item has its own stock-keeping unit (SKU).

4. Effective control of all goods leaving the facility. This job is done with bar codes on items being shipped, magnetic strips on merchandise, or via direct observation.

5. Deployment of right analytics to understand customer choices, preferences and feedback, and improve on loyalty programme. Although inventory is important for a company to satisfy its customers, unsold or piled up inventory can add to the total operational costs and become a weak link in the network. The quality of inventory has to be continuously monitored and the decision about when to make it live is critical for the success of the supply chain.

Thus, the application of the above techniques helps a company adopt best industry practices.

10.7 INVENTORY MODELS

There are a number of models that help determine the inventory level, reordering point, cost, and so on. Since numerous business situations such as static, comparative static, and dynamic have to be considered for decision-making, different models are propounded and practised. Here, some of the models involving fewer complications are explained.

10.7.1 Independent Versus Dependent Demand

Inventory control models assume that the demand for an item is either independent of or dependent on the demand for other items. For example, the demand for mobile phones is independent of the demand for any other item whereas demand for battery used in phones is a derived demand.

Working on inventory control models requires understanding of the following costs relating to inventory, which are explained earlier. The holding, ordering, and set-up costs are the costs associated with holding or 'carrying' inventory over time. Therefore, holding costs also include obsolescence and costs related to storage, such as insurance and cost of capital employed in inventory build. Table 10.4 shows the kinds of costs that need to be evaluated to determine holding costs. Many firms fail to include the entire inventory holding costs as some of these are hidden or opportunity costs in nature. Consequently, inventory-holding costs are often understated. This was observed in a case where the company ignored holding costs in managerial decision-making. When restructuring of warehouses was considered for purposes of inventory aggregation, it was observed that when inventory-holding cost was considered, the decision dynamics changed. This is quite common, especially in the small and medium industries segments. All numbers are approximate, as they vary substantially depending on the nature of the business, location, and current interest rates. Any inventory-holding cost of less than 15 per cent is suspect, but annual inventory holding costs often approach 40 per cent of the value of the inventory. (Refer to Table 10.4)

Ordering cost includes cost of supplies, forms, order processing, clerical support, and so forth. Set-up cost is the cost to prepare a machine or process for manufacturing an order. This includes time and labour to clean and change tools or holders. Supply chain operations managers can lower ordering costs by reducing set-up costs, and set-up costs can be reduced by using such efficient procedures as electronic ordering and payment.

In many environments, set-up cost is highly correlated with set-up time. Set-ups usually require a substantial amount of work prior to the set-up actually being performed at the work centre. With proper planning, much of the preparation required by a set-up can be done prior to shutting down the machine or process, thus reducing set-up time substantially. Machines and processes that traditionally took hours to set-up are now being set-up in less than a minute by the more imaginative world-class manufacturers. One may note that reducing set-up times is an excellent way to reduce inventory investment and to improve productivity.

Table 10.4 Inventory-related costs

Cost factor	Cost range as % of value
Storage cost	2–4
Holding cost (Cost of capital—function of inventory turnover and capital employed)	6–12
Material handling cost	1–3
Labour cost	2–4
Insurance, pilferage, and obsolescence cost	1–5

10.7.2   Inventory Models for Independent Demand

There are two important questions that need to be addressed: when to order and how much to order. The following independent demand models are discussed here:

1. Basic economic order quantity (EOQ) model
2. Production order quantity model
3. Quantity discount model

The Basic Economic Order Quantity (EOQ) Model

The economic order quantity (EOQ) model is one of the oldest and most commonly known inventory control techniques. This technique is relatively easy to use but is based on several assumptions:

1. Demand is known, constant, and independent.
2. Lead time—that is, the time between placement and receipt of the order—is known and constant.
3. Receipt of inventory is instantaneous and complete. In other words, the inventory from an order arrives in one batch at one time.
4. There are no quantity discounts.
5. The only variable costs are the cost of setting up (set-up cost) and the cost of holding or storing inventory over time (holding or carrying cost).
6. Stock-outs (shortages) can be completely avoided if orders are placed at the right time.

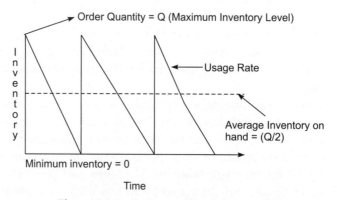

Figure 10.3   Inventory fixed time model

With these assumptions, the graph of inventory usage over time has a saw-tooth shape, as in Figure 10.3. In the figure, Q represents the amount that is ordered. If Q = 1,000 units, then all 1,000 units arrive at one time (when an order is received). Thus, the inventory level jumps from 0 to 1,000 units.

In general, an inventory level increases from 0 to Q units when an order arrives. Because demand is constant over time, inventory drops at a uniform rate over time. When the inventory level reaches 0 each time, the new order is placed and received, and the inventory level again jumps to Q units (represented by the vertical lines). This process continues indefinitely over time.

Minimizing Costs

The objective of most inventory models is to minimize total costs. With the assumptions just given, significant costs are set-up cost and holding (or carrying) cost. All other costs, such as the cost of the inventory itself, are constant. Thus, if we minimize the sum of set-up and holding costs, we will also be minimizing total costs.

Figure 10.4 shows total costs as a function of the order quantity, Q. The optimal order size, Q*, will be the quantity that minimizes the total costs. As the quantity ordered increases, the total number of orders placed per year will decrease. Thus, as the quantity ordered increases, the annual set-up or ordering cost will decrease. But as the order quantity increases, the holding cost will increase due to the larger average inventories that are maintained.

As we can see in Figure 10.4, a reduction in either holding or set-up cost will reduce the total cost curve. A reduction in the set-up cost curve also reduces the optimal order quantity or lot size. In addition, smaller lot sizes have a positive impact on quality and production flexibility.

As it could be seen in Figure 10.4, the optimal order quantity occurs at the point where the ordering-cost curve and the carrying-cost curve intersect. With the EOQ model, the optimal order quantity will occur at a point where the total set-up cost is equal to the total holding cost. This is the case when holding costs are linear and begin at the origin—that is, when inventory costs do not decline (or increase) as inventory volume increases and all holding costs are in small increments. Additionally, there is probably some learning each time a set-up (or order) is executed—a fact that lowers subsequent set-up costs. Consequently, the EOQ model is probably a special case. However, by conventional wisdom, this model is a reasonable approximation.

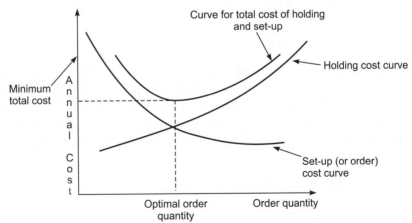

Figure 10.4   Total cost as a function of order quantity

To arrive at Q*, the following may be used:

1. Set-up or ordering cost equation to be arrived at
2. Holding cost equation
3. Solve for set-up cost equal to holding cost and arrive at optimal order quantity.

Using the following variables, we can determine set-up and holding costs and solve for Q*:

$$Q = \text{Number of pieces per order}$$
$$Q^* = \text{Optimum number of pieces per order (EOQ)}$$
$$D = \text{Annual demand in units for the inventory item}$$
$$S = \text{Set-up or ordering cost for each order}$$
$$H = \text{Holding or carrying cost per unit per year}$$

1. Annual set-up cost = (Number of orders placed per year) × (Set-up or order cost

$$\text{per order}) = \left(\frac{\text{Annual demand}}{\text{Number of units in each order}}\right) \times (\text{Set-up or per order})$$

$$= (D/Q)\,(S) \tag{10.1}$$

2. Annual holding cost = (Average inventory level) × (Holding cost per unit per

$$\text{year}) = \left(\frac{\text{Order Quantity}}{2}\right) \times (\text{Holding cost per unit per year})$$

$$= (Q/2)\,(H) \tag{10.2}$$

3. Optimal order quantity is found when annual set-up cost equals annual holding cost, namely,

$$(D/Q)\,S = (Q/2)\,H \tag{10.3}$$

4. To solve for Q*, simply cross-multiply terms and isolate Q on the left of the equal sign.

$$2DS = Q^2H$$
$$Q^2 = 2DS/H$$
$$Q^* = \sqrt{2DS/H} \tag{10.4}$$

A company, say ABC Ltd, is in the assembly operation of electrical components. It purchases a component from a vendor and proposes to reduce its inventory cost by determining the optimal number of units to obtain per order. The annual demand is 7,000 units; the set-up or ordering cost is Rs 210 per order; and the holding cost per unit per year is Rs 6. Using these figures, we can calculate the optimal number of units per order:

$$Q^* = \sqrt{2}\,DS/H$$

$$Q^* = \sqrt{2}\,(7,000)\,(210)/6 = 700 \text{ units}$$

Expected number of orders = N = Demand/Order Quantity = D/Q*

Expected time between orders = T = Number of working days per year/N
$$= 7,000/700 = 10 \text{ orders per year}$$

T = Number of working days per year/Expected number of orders
$$= 300 \text{ working days per year}/10 \text{ orders} = 30 \text{ days between orders}$$

Total annual cost = Set-up Cost + Holding Cost $\tag{10.5}$

In terms of the variables in the model, we can express the total cost TC as

$$TC = (D/Q) \times S + (Q/2) \times H$$
$$= (7,000/700) \times 210 + (700 / 2) \times 6$$
$$= 2,100 + 350 \times 6$$
$$= 2,100 + 2,100 = 4,200$$

The total inventory cost expression may also be written to include the actual cost of the material purchased. If we assume that the annual demand and the price per unit are known values (for example, 7,000 hypodermics per year at P = 60) and total annual cost should include purchase cost, then Equation 10.5 becomes:

$$TC = (D/Q) \times S + (Q/2) \times H + PD$$

Because material cost does not depend on the particular order policy, we still incur an annual material cost of $D \times P = (7,000) (60) =$ Rs 420,000.

Reorder Points

After deciding on how much to order, one would look at the second inventory question, when to order. Simple inventory models assume that receipt of an order is instantaneous. In other words, they assume (1) that a firm will place an order when the inventory level for that particular item reaches zero, and (2) that it will receive the ordered items immediately. However, the time between placement and receipt of an order, called lead time, or delivery time, can be as short as a few hours or as long as months. Thus, the when-to-order decision is usually expressed in terms of a reorder point (ROP)-the inventory level at which an order should be placed (see Figure 10.5).

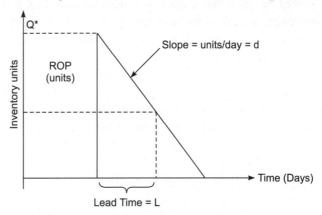

Figure 10.5 The Reorder Point (ROP) curve

The reorder point (ROP) is given as

ROP = (Demand per day) (Lead time for a new order in days)
$$= d \times L \qquad (10.6)$$

This equation for ROP assumes that demand during lead time and the lead time are constant. When this is not the case, extra stock, often called safety stock, should be added.

The demand per day, d, is found by dividing the annual demand, D, by the number of working days in a year.

$$d = D/\text{Number of working days in a year}$$

Computing the reorder point is demonstrated in the example below:

EXAMPLE 1   ABC Cycle Ltd, a manufacturer of sports bikes, has an annual demand of 240,000 units in a year. The firm operates 300 days in a year. On an average, delivery of an order takes seven working days. We calculate the reorder point as:

$$d = D/\text{Number of working days in a year} = 240{,}000/300 = 800 \text{ units}$$
$$\text{ROP} = \text{Reorder point} = d \times L = 800 \text{ units per day} \times 7 \text{ days} = 5{,}600 \text{ units}$$

Thus, when inventory stock drops to 5,600, an order should be placed. The order will arrive seven days later, just as the firm's stock is depleted.

Safety stock is especially important in firms whose raw material deliveries may be uniquely unreliable.

Production Order Quantity Model

In the previous inventory model, we assumed that the entire inventory order was received at one time. There are times, however, when the firm may receive its inventory over a period of time.

Such cases require a different model, one that does not require the instantaneous-receipt assumption. This model is applicable under two situations: (1) When inventory continuously flows or builds up over a period of time after an order has been placed or (2) when units are produced and sold simultaneously. Under these circumstances, we take into account daily production (or inventory-flow) rate and daily demand rate. Figure 10.6 shows inventory levels as a function of time.

Since this model is especially more suitable for the production environment, it is commonly called the production order quantity model. It is useful when inventory continuously builds up over time and traditional economic order quantity assumptions are valid. We derive this model by setting ordering or set-up costs equal to holding costs and solving for optimal order size, Q^*. Using the following symbols, we can determine the expression for annual inventory holding cost for the production order quantity model:

Q = Number of pieces per order
H = Holding cost per unit per year
p = Daily production rate
d = Daily demand rate, or usage rate
t = Length of the production run in days

1. Annual inventory holding cost = (Average inventory level) (Holding cost per unit per year)   (10.7)
2. Average inventory Level = Maximum inventory Level/2   (10.8)
3. Maximum Inventory Level = Total produced during the production run – Total used during the production run = $pt - dt$ (10.9)

However,   Q = total produced = pt, and thus t = Q/p.

Therefore,

Maximum inventory level = p (Q/P) – d (Q/P)

= Q – (d/p)Q

= Q (1 – d/p   (10.10)

4. Annual inventory holding cost = (Maximum inventory/2) X (H)

= Q/2 [1 – (d/p)] H   (10.11)

Figure 10.6 shows the change in Inventory levels over time for the production model.

A major difference between the production order model and the basic EOQ model is the annual holding cost, which is reduced in the production quantity model.

Using this expression for holding cost and the expression for set-up cost developed in the basic EOQ model, we solve for the optimal number of pieces per order by equating set-up cost and holding cost:

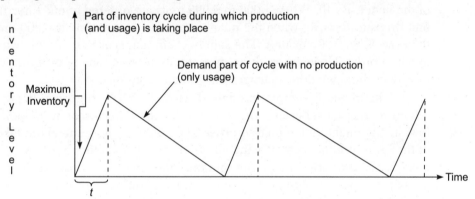

Figure 10.6   Change in inventory levels over time for the production model

Set-up cost = (D/Q) S

Holding cost = ½ HQ [1 – (d / p)]

Set ordering cost equal to holding cost to obtain Q^*_p:

(D / Q) S = ½ HQ [1 - (d / p)]

Q^2 = 2DS / H [1 – (d/p)]

$Q^*_p = \sqrt{2DS/H}$ / H [1 – (d / p)]

We use the above equation, Q^*_p, to solve for the optimum order or production quantity when inventory is consumed as it is produced.

EXAMPLE 2   Chennai Cycle Corporation has the following data for its manufacture:

1. Daily production rate (p) = 1400
2. Annual demand (D) = 240,000 units; Daily demand d = 800 units
3. No. of working days = 300

4. Set-up cost (S) = Rs 450
5. Holding cost (H) = Rs 20

$$Q^*_p = \sqrt{2} \, DS / H \, [1 - (d / p)]$$

$$Q^*_p = \sqrt{2} \, (240,000) \, (450) / 20[1 - (800/1,400)] = 5,020 \text{ units (rounded off)}$$

We can also calculate Q^*_p when annual data are available. When annual data are used, we can express Q^*_p as:

$$Q^*_p = \sqrt{2} \, DS / H \, (1 - \text{annual demand rate} / \text{annual production rate})$$

Quantity Discount Models

A quantity discount is a reduced price (P) for an item when it is purchased in larger quantities, which may be for all units or for staggered quantities. It is not uncommon to have a discount schedule with several discounts for large orders. A typical quantity discount schedule appears in Table 10.5. As can be seen in the table, the normal price of the item is Rs 10. When 3,000 to 5,999 units are ordered at one time, the price per unit drops to Rs 9.30; when the quantity ordered at one time is 6,000 units or more, the price is Rs 9.00 per unit. The supply chain manager must decide when and how much to order. However, with an opportunity to save money on quantity discounts, how does the operations manager make these decisions?

As with other inventory models discussed so far, the overall objective is to minimize total cost. Because the unit cost for the third discount in Table 10.5 is the lowest, one might be tempted to order 6,000 units or more merely to take advantage of the lower product cost. Placing an order for that quantity, however, even with the greatest discount price, might not minimize total inventory cost. As discount quantity goes up, the product cost goes down. However, holding cost increases because orders are larger. Thus the major trade-off when considering quantity discounts is between reduced product cost and increased holding cost. When we include the cost of the product, the equation for the total annual inventory cost can be calculated as follows:

$$\text{Total cost} = \text{Set-up cost} + \text{Holding cost} + \text{Product cost (or)}$$
$$TC = (D/Q) \, S + (QH/2) + PD$$

where   Q = Quantity ordered
           D = Annual demand in units
           S = Ordering or set-up cost per order or per set-up
           P = Price per unit
           H = Holding cost per unit per year

Table 10.5 Impact of quantity discounts

Discount number	Discount quantity	Discount (%)	Discount price (p)
1	0 to 2,999	No Discount	Rs 10.00
2	3,000 to 5,999	7	Rs 9.30
3	6,000 and over	10	Rs 9.00

Now, we have to determine the quantity that will minimize the total annual inventory cost. Because there are several discounts, this process involves four steps:

Step 1: For each discount, calculate a value for optimal order size Q*, using the following equation:

$$Q^* = \sqrt{2} \, DS/IP$$

Note that the holding cost is IP instead of H. Because the price of the item is a factor in annual holding cost, we cannot assume that the holding cost is a constant when the price per unit changes for each quantity discount. Thus, it is common to express the holding cost (I) as a percentage of unit price (P) instead of as a constant cost per unit per year, H.

Step 2: For any discount, if the order quantity is too low to qualify for the discount, adjust the order quantity upward to the lowest quantity that will qualify for the discount. For example, if Q* for discount 2 in Table 10.6 were 2,000 units, you would adjust this value up to 3,000 units. Look at the second discount in Table 10.6. Order quantities between 3,000 and 5,999 will qualify for the 7 per cent discount. Thus, if Q* is below 3,000 units, we will adjust the order quantity up to 3,000 units.

The reasoning for Step 2 may not be obvious. If the order quantity Q* is below the range that will qualify for a discount, a quantity within this range may still result in the lower total cost.

Step 3: Using the preceding total cost equation, compute a total cost for every Q* determined in Steps 1 and 2. If you had to adjust Q* upward because it was below the allowable quantity range, be sure to use the adjusted value for Q*.

Step 4: Select the Q* that has the lowest total cost, as computed in Step 3. It will be the quantity that will minimize the total inventory cost.

EXAMPLE 3   A buyer is offered discounts on the price of his purchases based on quantity bought. This quantity schedule was shown in Table 10.5. The normal cost for the item is Rs 10 per unit. For orders between 3,000 and 5,999 units, the unit cost drops to Rs 9.30; for orders of 6,000 or more units, the unit cost is only Rs 9.00. Furthermore, ordering cost is Rs 240 per order, annual demand is 24,000 units, and inventory carrying charge, as a percentage of cost, I, is 20 per cent. What order quantity will minimize the total inventory cost?

The first step is to compute Q* for every discount in Table 10.6. This is done as follows:

$$Q^*_1 = \sqrt{2} \ (24,000) \ (240)/(.2) \ (10.00) = 2,400 \text{ units}$$

$$Q^*_2 = \sqrt{2} \ (24,000) \ (240)/(.2) \ (9.30) = 2,489 \text{ units}$$

$$Q^*_3 = \sqrt{2} \ (24,000) \ (240)/(.2) \ (9.00) = 2,530 \text{ units}$$

The second step is to adjust upward those values of Q* that are below the allowable discount range. Since Q^*_1 is between 0 and 2,999, it need not be adjusted. Because

Q^*_2 is below the allowable range of 3,000 to 5,999, it must be adjusted to 3,000 units. The same is true for Q^*_3. It must be adjusted to 6,000 units.

After this step, the following order quantities must be tested in the total cost equation:

$$Q^*_1 = 2,400$$
$$Q^*_2 = 3,000\text{–adjusted}$$
$$Q^*_3 = 6,000\text{–adjusted}$$

The third step is to use the total cost equation and compute a total cost for each order quantity. This step is taken with the aid of Table 10.5, which presents the computations for each level of discount introduced in Table 10.6.

The fourth step is to select that order quantity with the lowest total cost. Looking at Table 10.6, one can see that an order quantity of 6,000 units will minimize the total cost. One may note that factors like price, quantity, and holding costs would be critical.

10.7.3 Probability Models with Constant Lead Time

Inventory models discussed so far make the assumption that the demand for a product is constant and certain. When product demand is not known but can be specified by means of a probability distribution, the following models are applied. These types of models are called probabilistic models.

An important concern of management is maintaining an adequate service level in the face of uncertain demand. The service level is the complement of the probability of a stockout. For instance, if the probability of a stockout is 0.05, then the service level is 0.95. Uncertain demand raises the possibility of a stockout. One method of reducing stockouts is to hold extra units in inventory. As mentioned earlier, such inventory is usually referred to as safety stock. It involves adding a number of units as a buffer to the reorder point.

$$\text{Reorder point} = \text{ROP} = d \times L$$

where d = Daily demand

          L = Order lead time, or number of working days it takes to deliver an order

The inclusion of safety stock (ss) changes the expression to

$$\text{ROP} = d \times L + \text{ss} \ldots \tag{10.12}$$

Table 10.6 Total cost computations for quantity discounts

Discount number	Unit price	Order quantity	Annual product cost (in Rs)	Annual ordering cost (in Rs)	Annual holding cost (in Rs)	Total (in Rs)
1	10	2,400	240,000	2,400	2,400	244,800
2	9.30	3,000	223,200	1,920	2,790	227,910
3	9.00	6,000	216,000	960	5,400	222,360

The amount of safety stock maintained depends on the cost of incurring a stockout and the cost of holding the extra inventory. Annual stockout cost is computed as follows:

Annual stockout costs = the sum of the units short × the probability × the stockout cost/unit × the number of orders per year

EXAMPLE 4 Tanjore Paints (P) Ltd has determined that its reorder point for paints is 80 ($d \times L$) units. Its carrying cost per frame per year is Rs 400, and stockout (or lost sale) cost is Rs 3,000 per unit. The store has experienced the following probability distribution (Table 10.7) for inventory demand during the reorder period. The optimum number of orders per year is six.

How much safety stock should Tanjore Paintings keep on hand?

The objective is to find the amount of safety stock that minimizes the sum of the additional inventory holding costs and stockout costs. The annual holding cost is the holding cost per unit multiplied by the units added to the ROP. For example, a safety stock of 20 paintings, which implies that the new ROP, with safety stock, is 100 (= 80 + 20), raises the annual carrying cost by Rs 400 (20) = Rs 8,000 (see Table 10.8).

For any level of safety stock, stockout cost is the expected cost of stocking out. We can compute it, as in Eqn 10.12, by multiplying the number of frames short by the probability of demand at that level, by the stockout cost, by the number of times per year the stockout can occur (which in our case is the number of orders per year). Then we add stockout costs for each possible stockout level for a given ROP. For zero safety stock, for example, a shortage of ten paintings will occur if the demand is ninety, and a shortage of twenty frames will occur if the demand is 100. Thus the stockout costs for zero safety stock are:

(10 paintings short) (.2) (Rs 3,000 per stockout) (6 possible stockouts per year)
+ (20 paintings short) (.1) (Rs 3,000) (6) = Rs 72,000.

The safety stock with the lowest total cost is twenty paintings. Therefore, this safety stock changes the reorder point to 80 + 20 = 100 paintings.

When it is difficult or impossible to determine the cost of being out of stock, a manager may decide to follow a policy of keeping enough safety stock on hand to meet a prescribed customer-service level. In such instances, the use of safety stock is

Table 10.7 Probability of lead time demand

Number of units	Probability
60	0.2
70	0.2
80	0.3
90	0.2
100	0.1

Table 10.8 Stockout and likely impact on inventory

Safety Stock	Additional Holding Cost	Stockout Cost	Total Cost
20	(20) (400) = Rs 8,000	Rs 0	Rs. 8,000
10	(10) (Rs 400) = Rs 4,000	(10)(.1)(Rs 3,000)(6) = Rs 18,000	Rs. 22,000
0	Rs 0	(10)(.2)(Rs 3,000)(6) + (20)(.1)(Rs 3,000)(6) = Rs 72,000	Rs. 72,000

when demand is probabilistic. The manager may want to define the service level as meeting 95 per cent of the demand (or, conversely, having stockouts only 5 per cent of the time). Assuming that demand during lead time (the reorder period) follows a normal curve, only the mean and standard deviation are needed to define the inventory requirements for any given service level. Sales data are usually adequate for computing the mean and standard deviation. In the following example we use a normal curve with a known mean (μ) and standard deviation (σ) to determine the reorder point and safety stock necessary for a 95 per cent service level.

We use the following formula:

$$ROP = \text{Expected demand during lead time} + Z\sigma \qquad (10.13)$$

where Z = Number of standard deviations

σ = standard deviation of lead time demand

EXAMPLE 5 Gujarat Chemicals (P) Ltd (GCPL) stocks a chemical that has a normally distributed demand during the reorder period. The mean (average) demand during the reorder period is 350 tonnes, and the standard deviation is 15 tonnes. The supply chain strategist wants to follow a policy that results in stockouts occurring only 5 per cent of the time.

(a) What is the appropriate value of Z?

(b) How much safety stock should the hospital maintain?

(c) What reorder point should be used?

Figure 10.7 may help you visualize the example.

μ = Mean demand = 350 tonnes

σ = Standard deviation = 10 tonnes

Z = Number of standard normal deviates

The solution is approached as follows:

(a) We use the properties of a standardized normal curve to get a Z value for an area under the normal curve of .95 (or 1 – 0.5). Using a normal table (or MS Excel formula =NORMDIST()), we find a Z value of 1.65 standard deviations from the mean.

(b) Safety Stock = $x - \mu$

Because $Z = x - \mu / \sigma$

Then Safety Stock = $Z\sigma$ \qquad (10.14)

Solving for safety stock, as in Eqn 10.14, gives

Safety stock = 1.65 (10) = 16.5 tonnes

(c) The reorder point is ROP = expected demand during lead time + safety stock = 350 tonnes + 16.5 tonnes of safety stock = 366.5, or 367 tonnes

Equations 10.13 and 10.14 assume that an estimate of expected demand during lead times and its standard deviation are available. When data on lead time demand are not at hand, these formulae cannot be applied and we need to determine if: (a) demand is variable and lead time is constant: or (b) only lead time is variable; or (c) both demand and lead time are variable. For each of these situations, a different formula is needed to compute ROP.

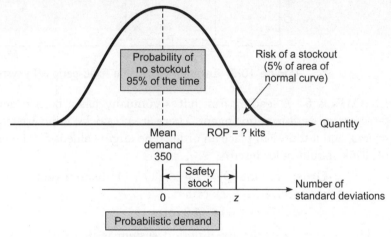

Figure 10.7   Probability of stockout

10.7.4   Fixed-Period (P) System

The inventory models that have considered so far are fixed-quantity, or Q systems. That is, the same fixed amount is added to inventory every time an order for an item is placed. We saw that orders are event-triggered. When inventory decreases to the reorder point (ROP), a new order for Q units is placed.

To use the fixed-quantity model, inventory must be continuously monitored. This is called a perpetual inventory system. Every time an item is added to or withdrawn from inventory, records must be updated to make sure the ROP has not been reached.

In a fixed-period, or P system, on the other hand, inventory is ordered at the end of a given period. Only the amount necessary to bring total inventory up to a pre-specified target level is ordered. Figure 10.8 illustrates this concept.

Fixed-period systems have several of the same assumptions as the basic EOQ fixed-quantity system:
- The only relevant costs are the ordering and holding costs
- Lead times are known and constant
- Items are independent of one another

The downward-sloped line again represents on-hand inventory. When the time between orders (P) lapses, we place an order to raise inventory up to the target value

(T). The amount ordered during the first period may be Q_1, the second period Q_2, and so on. The Q_1 value is the difference between current on-hand inventory and the target inventory level.

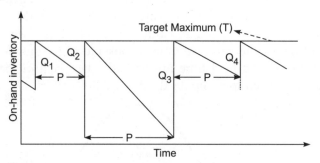

Figure 10.8 Inventory level in a fixed-period (P) system

EXAMPLE 6 A leading fruit juices company has a back order for 60 cases in a territory for its distribution agent. There are no stocks, none are expected from earlier orders, and it is time to place an order. The target value is 500 cases. How many cases of drink should be ordered?

Order amount (Q) = Target (T) – On-hand inventory – Earlier orders not yet received + back orders

$= 500 – 0 – 0 + 60 = 560$ cases

The advantage of the fixed-period system is that there is no physical count of inventory items after an item is withdrawn—this occurs only when the time for the next review comes up. This procedure is also convenient administratively, especially if inventory control is only one of the several duties of an employee.

A fixed-period system is appropriate when vendors make routine (that is, at fixed-time interval) visits to customers to take fresh orders or when purchasers want to combine orders to save ordering and transportation costs (therefore, they will have the same review period for similar inventory items). For example, a vending machine company may come to refill its machines every Tuesday.

The disadvantage of the P system is that because there is no tally of inventory during the review period, there is the possibility of a stockout during this time. This scenario is possible if a large order draws the inventory level down to zero right after an order is placed. Therefore, a higher level of safety stock (as compared to a fixed-quantity system) needs to be maintained to provide protection against stockout during both the time between reviews and the lead time.

10.8 INVENTORY IN SUPPLY CHAIN—EFFICIENCY AND EFFECTIVENESS

Any reduction of inventory would substantially decrease working capital needs. The drive for working capital is dependent on changes in customer demand, with shorter order-to-delivery cycle times. Such a demand for a responsive supply chain is challenging to many manufacturers. Earlier when competition was not severely intense, manufacturers would stockpile large quantities of raw materials, load up the shop floor with work-in-process, and pack warehouses with finished goods. But now information flow has replaced the need for inventory.

The pressures to reduce inventories, and therefore working capital requirements, are increasing, even in times of relatively low interest rates. The opportunity to use a finite source of capital in alternate deployment for higher return is always there in business. For example, reducing inventories could provide the necessary capital to finance new product development, expand marketing and sales, introduce modernization, redesign business processes, improve supply chain management, plan an expansion, and so on.

Inventory control requires the tracking of all parts and materials purchased—work-in-process and finished goods at various places in the channel of distribution. Having a sophisticated tracking system alone does not improve your bottomline; it is how you use the information that your system provides.

From a financial perspective, inventory control is no small matter. Often, inventory is the largest asset item on a manufacturer or distributor's balance sheet. As a result, there is a lot of management emphasis on keeping inventories down so that they do not consume too much cash. The objectives of inventory reduction and minimization are more easily accomplished with modern inventory management processes that are working effectively.

10.9 INVENTORY CONTROL PROBLEMS

In actual practice, the vast majority of manufacturing and distribution companies suffer from lower customer service, higher costs, and excessive inventories than are necessary. Inventory control problems are usually the result of using poor processes, practices, and antiquated support systems. The inventory management process is much more complex than the uninitiated understand. In fact, in many companies, the inventory control department is perceived as a little more than a clerical function and pushed lower down the hierarchy. Inventory managers are also caught in cross-team conflicts mainly among production, marketing, and finance. Such practice towards inventory control leads to material shortages, excessive inventories, high costs, and poor customer service. For example, if a customer orders a product that requires a manufacturer to acquire 30 part numbers to assemble a product and only 27 of the 30 part numbers are available, there are 27 part numbers that are excess inventory . This typically happens in project engineering and capital machinery manufacture.

Generally, the following control tools and measures facilitate good control on inventory:

- ABC analysis of the assortment categorized by stock value/volume
- Variance in throughput time of the product group in totality
- The number of damages/claim
- Mean throughput time of the product group/vendor-wise/location-wise
- Reliability of the inventory regarding quantity and correct place

Thus, inventory management decisions involve trade-offs among the conflicting objectives of low inventory, high resource utilization, and good customer service. For making supply chain leaner, firms are using selective control techniques such as EOQ, ABC, and so on, and other inventory control models. Therefore, inventory should be held only when the benefits of holding it exceed the cost of carrying the inventory.

SUMMARY

Inventory in supply chain plays a crucial role in balancing divergent supply chain objectives, namely cost and responsiveness. Inventory management should facilitate to offer variants of models at competitive costs to customers. In internal supply chain process and supplier relations management, inventory is important to manage production plan and schedule at optimal cost.

Inventory improves customer service by providing product availability. It helps to achieve production, purchase, and transportation economies. Inventory would act as a hedge against price changes as well as a hedge against uncertainties in demand and lead times. Inventory management is a strategic area in logistics operation and has an impact on the efficiency and effectiveness of the overall supply chain system.

Firms maintain four types of inventories: (1) raw material inventory, (2) work-in-process inventory, (3) finished goods inventory, and (4) maintenance/repair/overhauling (MRO) supply inventory.

Inventory can be held as cycle inventory, which is the average of inventory between two lots, safety inventory (to meet variability in demand during lead time), seasonal inventory (to meet predicted seasonality in demand), and finally, pipeline inventory, which would be inventory in transit.

Inventory managers are concerned with: (1) how inventory items can be classified and (2) how accurately inventory records can be maintained. ABC analysis divides on-hand inventory into three categories (A, B, and C) on the basis of annual monetary value. This analysis is based on Pareto hypothesis and companies would save substantially if they focus on Category A items, which are of high value, are low in volume, but form nearly 80 per cent of total pecuniary value of the inventory.

A decision maker in inventory would address two fundamental questions: 'How much to order?' and 'When to order?' Different models are used to address these two questions. Inventory control models assume that demand for an item is either independent of or dependent on the demand for other items. Most commonly used independent demand models in situations are: basic economic order quantity (EOQ) model, production order quantity model, and quantity discount model. These models make the assumption that demand for a product is constant and certain.

There are inventory models that apply when product demand is not known but can be specified by means of a probability distribution. These types of models are called probabilistic models. An important concern of management is maintaining an adequate service level in the face of uncertain demand. The service level is the complement of the probability of a stock-out.

In actual practice the vast majority of manufacturing and distribution companies suffer from lower customer service, higher costs, and excessive inventories than are necessary. Inventory control problems are usually the result of using poor processes, practices, and antiquated support systems. The tendency to hold inventory in case there is an unexpected demand must be replaced by scientific management practices.

KEY TERMS

ABC analysis: A category is high-value, low volume items, B is important but less important than A, and C is of marginal significance. The goal is to categorize items that would be prioritized, managed, or controlled in different ways. ABC analysis is also called 'usage-value analysis'.

Cycle counting: A cycle count is an inventory management procedure where a small subset of inventory is counted on any given day. Cycle counts contrast with traditional physical inventory in that physical inventory stops operation at a facility and all items are counted, audited, and recounted at one time. Cycle counts are less disruptive to daily operations, provide an ongoing measure of inventory accuracy and procedure execution, and can be tuned to focus on items with higher value or higher movement.

Economic order quantity (EOQ): EOQ is the level of inventory that minimizes the total inventory holding costs and ordering costs.

Finished goods inventory: Finished goods inventory is that which is ready to be delivered to distribution centres, retailers, and wholesalers, or directly to the customers. Finished inventory is waiting for a demand pull or movement in the supply network based on a push system. The point is that it is waiting for a customer order to be served.

Holding cost: Holding cost is money spent to keep and maintain a stock of goods in storage. The most obvious holding costs include rent for the required space; equipment, materials, and labour to operate the space; insurance; security; interest on money invested in the inventory and space; and other direct expenses.

Lead time: It is the period of time between the initiation of any process of production and the completion of that process.

Maintenance/repair/overhauling supply (MRO) inventory: It refers to supplies consumed in the production process but would not be part of the end product or primary value-adding activity or component.

Ordering cost: It is the total of expenses incurred in placing an order.

Perpetual inventory system: Perpetual inventory or continuous inventory describes systems of inventory where information on inventory quantity and availability is updated on a continuous basis as a function of doing business.

Pilferage: Pilferage is the theft of part of the contents of a package. It may also include the theft of the contents where the package is left, perhaps resealed with bogus contents. Small packages can be pilfered from a larger package such as a shipping container. Broader aspects of theft may include taking the entire package, pallet load, truck load, shoplifting, and so on .

Probabilistic models: A statistical model is a set of mathematical equations that describe the behaviour of an object of study in terms of random variables and their associated probability distributions.

Quantity discount: It is the incentive offered by a seller to a buyer for purchasing or ordering greater than usual or normal quantity of goods or materials, to be delivered at one time or over a specified period.

Raw material inventory: It refers to goods on hand for direct use in manufacturing or further processing of goods for sale.

Reorder point (ROP): ROP is the level of inventory when a fresh order should be made with suppliers to bring the inventory up by the economic order quantity (EOQ).

Safety stock: It is a term used by inventory specialists to describe a level of extra stock that is maintained below the cycle stock to buffer against stockouts.

Service level: Service level measures the performance of a system. Certain goals are defined and the service level gives the percentage to which they should be achieved.

Set-up cost: These are the expenses incurred in setting up a machine, work centre, or assembly line, to switch from one production job to the next.

Set-up time: It is the period required to prepare a device, machine, process, or system for it to be ready to function or accept a job. It is a subset of cycle time.

Shrinkage: Inventory recorded on a company's books but not on hand, due to theft, loss or accounting error.

Work-in-process inventory: It refers to partially completed goods, parts, or sub-assemblies that are no longer part of the raw materials inventory and not yet part of the finished products inventory. Work-in-process inventory forms a part of the working or current assets of a firm and is valued usually at a lower cost and realizable value.

CONCEPT REVIEW QUESTIONS

1. Describe the role of inventory in supply chain and its relationship with supply chain objectives with examples.
2. Define types of inventory with examples.
3. What are the classifications of inventory in supply chain management? Explain their purpose.
4. Explain ABC analysis. What is the purpose of the ABC classification system?
5. Explain the FNS inventory policy. Is it different from ABC analysis?
6. What is cycle counting? How is it advantageous in inventory management?
7. Identify and explain the types of costs that are involved in an inventory system.
8. Explain the basic EOQ model. What is the relationship of the economic order quantity to demand, the holding cost, and set-up cost?
9. Explain the quantity discount model. When quantity discounts are offered, why is it not necessary to check discount points that are below the EOQ or points above the EOQ that are not discount points?
10. Explain why it is not necessary to include product cost (price or price times quantity) in the EOQ model, but the quantity discount model requires this information.
11. What impact does a decrease in set-up time have on EOQ?
12. What is meant by service level? How does it influence inventory management?
13. Describe the difference between a fixed-quantity (Q) and a fixed-period (P) inventory system.
14. What is 'safety stock'? What does safety stock provide safety against?
15. When demand is not constant, which are the parameters that determine reorder point?
16. State a major advantage, and a disadvantage, of a fixed-period (P) system.

CRITICAL THINKING QUESTIONS

1. Kishore Sharma gathered the following data on 12 items in inventory along with unit cost and annual demand.
   Using ABC analysis, classify items into different categories and draw a graph for the same.
2. Natural Fruit Juice Ltd sells apple juices in 1-litre tetra packs in boxes of 12. Demand for Natural Apple juice is 500 boxes per week in a territory. Natural Juice Ltd has a holding cost of 30 per cent and incurs a fixed cost of Rs 5,000 for each replenishment order it places. Given that cost is Rs 1,000 per box of apple juice, how much should the order be in each replenishment lot? If a trade promotion lowers the price of a juice box to Rs 950 for a month, how much should a firm order given the short-term price reduction?
3. A scientific lab equipment company has approximately 9,000 SKUs for different branches of sciences. Elizabeth, a management graduate from a premier institute specializing in Operations management, is in charge of inventory. She finds out that 10 per cent of inventory is A category, 25 per cent is B category, and the balance 65 per cent consists of C-category items. She hires part-timers at the rate of Rs 5.00 for counting the A category items, Rs 4.00 for the B category items, and Rs 2.00 for the C category items per day. Category A items are counted once in 10 working days, Category B items once in 25 working days, and Category C items once in 150 working days. What is her daily counting number and labour rate for each category?

Code	A1234	B2345	C3456	D4567	E5678	F6789	G7890	H8901
Unit cost (in Rs)	20	12	3.5	275	600	42	8	54
Annual Demand (in units)	3,000	2,400	4,500	1,800	1,200	900	2,000	800

4. An auto accessories unit stocks seat covers for supply to two-wheelers across a distribution network in a territory. The demand is for 96,000 units per year. The order cost (S) is Rs 8,000. The holding cost per unit is Rs 32.00. Calculate EOQ, annual holding costs, and annual ordering costs.

5. Appealing Furniture showroom sells cots along with mattresses as a set. Its best-selling cot and mattress has an annual demand of 600 units. The ordering cost (S) is Rs 4,000 and the holding cost is Rs 200 per unit, per year. To minimize the total cost, how many units should be ordered each time an order is placed? If the holding cost per unit were Rs 240 per unit, per year instead of Rs 200 per unit, per year, what would the optimal order quantity be?

6. The annual demand for a micro-nutrients supplement in a pharmaceutical chain in a territory within a city is for 12,000 units. The firm works for 300 days in a year and the delivery on an order takes 3 days to be replenished. Calculate the reorder point.

7. The XYZ Company has an assembly plant in Pune, India and its parts plant in Aurangabad, India. The parts are transported from Aurangabad to Pune using trucks. The total shipment cost for approximately 250 km—including loading, unloading, and empty return charges—is Rs 3,000. The Pune plant assembles and sells 500 finished products each day and operates 50 weeks a year. Part #9630 costs Rs 1,000 and XYZ Company incurs a holding cost of 20 per cent per year. How many of part #9630 should XYZ Company put in each shipment? What is the cycle inventory of part #9630 at XYZ Company?

8. A factory in-house machine shop uses 5,000 pieces during a year. The holding cost per piece is Rs 40 per piece per year and the order cost (S) is Rs 1,000. The lead time is 2 days and the workshop functions for 300 days in a year.
   (a) Calculate EOQ.
   (b) Given EOQ, what is the average inventory? What would be the annual inventory holding cost?
   (c) Given EOQ, how many orders would be made each year? Calculate the annual order cost.
   (d) What is time between two orders?
   (e) What is the reorder point (ROP)?

9. The weekly demand for a particular style of dress in a boutique called Raaga is normally distributed with a mean of 280 and a standard deviation of 140. The store manager continuously monitors inventory and currently orders 1,400 units of a style each time the inventory drops to 700 units. The manufacturer currently takes two weeks to fill an order. How much safety inventory does the store carry?

10. An emergency light equipment manufacturer, Bright Light (P) Ltd, in Noida near Delhi makes emergency lamps used in home segment. The firm operates its production facility 300 days per year. It has orders for 30,000 lamps in a year and a production capacity of 200 units per day of operation. Setting up lamp production costs Rs 5,000. The cost of each lamp is Rs 250 and the holding cost is Rs 12.50 per lamp per year.
   (a) What is the optimal size of the production run?
   (b) What is the average holding cost per year?
   (c) What is the average set-up cost per year?
   (d) What is the total cost per year, including cost of lamps?

11. A Baroda-based chemicals manufacturing plant has a demand for 400 pumps in a year. The cost of a pump is Rs 12,000. It costs Rs 8,000 to place an order and the carrying cost is 25 per cent of the unit cost. If pumps are ordered in quantities of 100, the firm gets a discount of 5 per cent. Evaluate the offer of discount and advise the company.

12. A health equipment store sells 50 units on an average of a top-end treadmill model. The demand is normally distributed with a standard deviation of 5 units. The management wants a service level of 97 per cent. What value of Z should be applied? How many units must be carried as safety stock? What would be the reorder point?

13. Jai Ho Engineering (P) Ltd (JHPL) stocks steel that has a normally distributed demand during the reorder period. The mean (average) demand during the reorder period is 3,000 tonnes, and the standard deviation is 750 tonnes. The supply chain strategist wants to follow a policy that results in stockouts occurring only 5 per cent of the time. What is the appropriate value of Z? (b) How much safety stock should the hospital maintain? (c) What reorder point should be used?

14. Mysore Construction Equipments orders a supply of heavy-duty chains on the first day of each month from its supplier in Chennai. The target value is 40 units in P-system. It is time to order and there are 5 units on hand. Because of delayed shipment during last month, 18 units ordered earlier should arrive shortly. How many units must be ordered now?

15. Reliable Electricals sells electrical mixers/grinders (dry) for the home segment. The reorder point, without safety stock, is 200 units. The carrying cost is Rs 200 per unit, per year and the stock cost is Rs 2,400 per unit, per year. Given the following demand probabilities during the reorder period, how much safety stock should be carried?

16. An auto component company has an inventory turnover of 24 in a year. The company wants to

Demand during reorder period	0	100	200	300	400
Probability	.2	.25	.3	.15	.1

progress to an ITR of 36. It is looking at both the supply chain objectives of cost efficiency and responsiveness. You may suggest an approach to achieve the same. The company operates an ERP for its production planning and scheduling, and has a good internal information flow for its operations.

PROJECT ASSIGNMENTS

1. Visit an engineering firm that uses yard as a stocking point. Analyse their physical inventory handling and control plan. You may suggest improvements and/or capture key learning and benchmarks with what is available in open source.

2. You may visit a nearest large retail store in your city and analyse their inventory classification, reordering points, and model used.

3. Visit a perishable market, say, vegetable and fruits, and find out their inventory management practice. Do they deploy quantity discount models and how effective are they?

REFERENCES

Ballou, Ronald H. and Samir K. Srivastava, *Business Logistics/Supply Chain Management*, Pearson, 2007

Bowersox, Donald J. and David J. Closs, *Logistical Management: The Integrated Supply Chain Process*, Tata McGraw-Hill, India 2000

Chopra, Sunil and Peter Meindl, *Supply Chain Management: Strategy, Planning and Operation*, Pearson, 2004

Heizer, Jay and Barry Render, *Principles of Operations Management*, 5th Edition, Pearson, 2004

Inman, R. Anthony, 'The Impact of Lot-Size Reduction on Quality,' *Production and Inventory Management Journal* 35(1) (first quarter 1994): 5–8; and *International Journal of Production Economics* (1 August 1996): 37–46.

Raman, A., N. DeHoratius and Z. Ton, 'Execution: The Missing Link in Retail Operations,' *California Management Review* 43(3) (Spring 2001): 136–141.

Russell, Roberta and Bernard W. Taylor, *Operations Management: Quality and Competitiveness in Global Environment*, 5th edition, Wiley India Edition, 2005

www.cio.in

CASE STUDY: POWER HOME ELECTRONICS INDIA LTD

Power Home Electronics India Ltd (PHEIL) is a leading multinational company in home electronics goods manufacture, operating in different segments and factories across the four regions of India. The President of the company, Shyam Lal, presided over an event of Supply Chain Excellence award instituted by a leading industry body and academic institute. There, Shyam Lal heard the jury head present different metrics. He understood from the programme that measuring and reducing the end-to-end supply chain cycle time is imperative for survival and gives substantial competitive edge to the company. He learnt that there are two components of cycle time—'horizontal time', which is the time taken for movement from one place to another and 'vertical cycle time', which is the time the material stays in one place without movement. Managing both has their own challenges.

Shyam Lal called his internal audit firm, a leading firm in management audit and consulting business across the globe, to advise him on implementing cycle time in his company. Peter was the team leader in the audit firm who wanted to facilitate Lal. Peter collected relevant information and summarized as below:

Present Ordering and Stocking Policies

1. Factory to Supplier: Order Quantity = Two weeks' consumption of RM

   ROL = Two weeks' requirement + 25% Safety stock
2. Wholesaler to Factory: Ordering policy = Monthly ordering

   Order quantity each month = Maximum stock level–Stock balance

   Maximum stock level = Monthly demand from Retailers + Leadtime demand + 1 week safety stock
3. Retailer to Wholesaler: Order quantity = 2 weeks' demand from consumers

   ROL: = Two weeks demand + 25% safety stock
4. Manufacturing cycle time = 2 weeks

Actual figures based on six months' average

Sl. No.	Item	Sales/consumption per month (Rs Lakh)	Inventory Turnover based on monthly sales
1	At supplier end	45	4.0
2	At Factory		
	RM (Consumption)	80	1.33
	WIP (Production value)	120	1.2
	FG (Sales value)	160	2.0
3	Wholesaler	40	0.6
4	Retailer	25	1.33

5. Transport time from Supplier to Factory, Factory to wholesaler. and from Wholesaler to Retailer = One week each.

Transportation time: Average: 7 days, Range: 5–10 days

Peter found from his practice guidance that the total cycle time would exceed 120 days and offers a gold mine for containing costs and improving customer service.

Questions

1. Map the supply chain nodes and movement of PHEIL. How would you go about collecting information?
2. Present a checklist on conducting management audit of their inventory system and procedures for data gathering.
3. Compute the total supply chain cycle time based on their policies and the actual end-to-end cycle time.
4. Estimate the average funds blocked up in the system.
5. Mention the contributory factors for the long actual cycle time and suggestions for reducing them.

Acknowledgement: Thanks to D. t, T.V. Subramaniam, Management Consultant Chennai for sharing the above.

11

Key Operational Aspects in Supply Chain

Learning Objectives

After studying this chapter, you will be able to:

◆ Understand the key operational aspects that would influence supply chain operations, such as
   (a) Just-in-Time (JIT)
   (b) Kanban
   (c) Vendor-managed Inventory (VMI)
   (d) Quality improvement programmes
   (e) Green supply chain
   (f) Ethical supply chain management practices
   (g) Supply chain security

11.1 OPERATIONAL PRACTICES IN SUPPLY CHAIN

It is important for supply chain managers to understand diverse operational practices across industries and geographies, and emulate most of them to their benefit. These practices include just-in-time (JIT), vendor-managed inventory (VMI), kanban, improvement in in-plant logistics through deployment of lean production and quality improvement programmes, green supply chain, and ethical supply management. JIT and most of the other practices are often used in the industry by production and operations management teams of companies. A lot of literature on successful cases, challenges of implementation, and methods to overcome the same are available in the public domain. Supply chain managers must keep themselves informed about the latest developments in this area and learn to coordinate effectively across supply chain network partners for the successful implementation of these practices. For example, a successful JIT, VMI, or kanban operation requires the support of suppliers, service providers such as transport operators, and distribution centres and warehouses.

11.2 JUST-IN-TIME

Just-in-time (JIT), which is more commonly referred to as Toyota Production System (TPS), was initially aimed at improving the manufacturing process and was considered as one of the important production management tools. To achieve this, it required interfacing with sourcing and distribution strategies and partners. Actually, JIT consists of three main parts—JIT purchasing, JIT manufacturing, and JIT distribution. A key philosophy of lean management, JIT focuses on waste reduction and continuous improvement. The aim of lean production is to ensure that the customers receive exactly what and when they want, without any wastage, through continuous improvement. For this reason, JIT is fundamentally dependent on demand and the enabler of the pull strategy in a supply chain.

JIT reduces wastes and ensures that no undesired inventory is carried. Since there is no excess inventory, it reduces holding cost and obsolescence cost. A logical question here would be how it improves the response time. That would be the challenge as JIT requires sharing of production schedule or distribution plan, and synchronizing accordingly. Prima facie, JIT operations are based on thorough planning and scheduling, and variations at that stage are feasible. Thus, if implemented carefully, JIT works in such a way that at scheduling level both efficiency and responsiveness can be achieved. One such success story is given in Exhibit 11.1.

Exhibit 11.1 Chennai Plant Becomes the Hub of Nokia's Production Centres

Nokia is consistently a leading brand name in mobile phones as well as across products and services that are rated annually. Nokia has implemented world-class manufacturing systems like best-in-class quality, lowest cost production, and just-in-time delivery for the manufacture of mobile handsets.

The Nokia plant (known as the Nokia Telecom Park), located in Chennai, achieved a volume of 125 million handsets within two years of its establishment. Having started from a small town called Sriperumbudur, near Chennai, this facility and has become a hub for manufacturing mobile phones for the company, with a scope for exports. According to a senior management member, Nokia has reached a production volume of 125 million handsets because of the world-class manufacturing facility and its just-in-time delivery. The two sections of the plant, which consists of 100 board assembly and final assembly, take care of these factors. Board assembly is where the motherboard is assembled with components and the final assembly is where the customization takes place. In the Nokia Telecom Park, which is a special economic zone, there are seven global component manufac-turers, namely Salcomp, Aspocomp, Foxconn, Perlos, Jabil, Laird, and Wintek.

Nokia is already well respected in Chennai for taking care of its employees and for sticking to their stringent environmental standards. The Japanese management practice of continuous improvement, Kaizen, has been implemented to improve employee awareness of global aspects and improve productivity.

The Chennai plant plays an integral role in Nokia's global production network for mobile devices and is the tenth mobile device manufacturing facility globally. Today, Nokia India is exporting 'made-in-India' mobiles to more than fifty countries. About 50 per cent of the production from the plant is consumed domestically and the balance is exported to countries across West Asia, Africa, Asia, Australia, and New Zealand.

Excellence in manufacturing and just-in-time delivery of components are key to the success of leading brands, which could be as complex as Nokia, where one would have new brands being regularly introduced, old ones being cannibalized, and markets spread worldwide that require multiple-level customization.

Source: http://www.hindu.com/2008/05/14/stories/2008051456181600.htm

11.2.1 JIT Efforts

The following are the various JIT efforts, mainly in manufacturing and sourcing:

1. **Cellular manufacturing:** Cellular manufacturing is a design of workplace as part of the lean production system, facilitating the reduction of waste. Cellular manufacturing arranges factory-floor labour into semi-autonomous and multi-skilled teams, or work cells, who manufacture complete products or complex components. The workers are multi-skilled to implement flexible and more number of activities rather than specializing in one activity under traditional mass manufacturing.

2. **Multi-skilled workforce:** A skilled worker is specialized and trained in a particular function or activity. This practice was prevalent in traditional manufacturing where specialization was important to improve productivity and quality. Under the current system, especially in businesses where flexibility and responsiveness are required, the workforce must be multi-skilled, able to perform an array of activities or functions. For example, in developed nations where labour is expensive and scarce, a truck driver would also function as delivery staff and document processor.

3. **Kaizen/Continuous improvement:** Kaizen, a Japanese philosophy of continuous improvement, is a daily activity, the purpose of which goes beyond just productivity improvement. It is about bringing in a scientific method of production focused on the elimination of waste. It is also a process which, when performed correctly, humanizes the workplace, eliminates overly hard work, and teaches people how to spot and eliminate waste in business processes. The philosophy can be defined as bringing back the thought process into the automated production environment dominated by repetitive tasks that traditionally required little mental participation from the employees. Kaizen requires employee involvement and management commitment for continuous marginal improvements at the workplace.

4. **Set-up time reduction:** Set-up time reduction is a powerful manufacturing improvement tool. It requires change in manufacturing practices, methods, attitudes, and sometimes culture. Set-up time reduction can help improve flexibility, reliability, and consistency in the production methods under a competitive environment. It allows small-lot production, which in turn cuts throughput time and gives faster customer response. Simultaneously, work-in-process inventory is decreased and workflow is improved. This technique can be applied to most equipment and processes. One must work with the set-up time reduction team to develop improved techniques, specialized equipment, and the integration of the set-up into the lean production plan.

5. **Small-lot sizing:** Small-lot production is an important component of lean manufacturing system. Since the lot size directly affects inventory and scheduling, small lot is recommended where variability is limited. It further reduces variability in the system and streamlines production with high quality focus.

6. **Stable production schedules:** Production scheduling facilitates deployment of resources for achieving a production plan and a stable schedule is one that has least variance in input/output schedules. In manufacturing, the scheduling function coordinates the flow of parts and products through the system, and balances the workload on machines and personnel, departments, and the entire plant.

7. **Total Productive Maintenance (TPM):** It is a maintenance philosophy designed to integrate equipment maintenance into the manufacturing process. The goal of any TPM programme is to eliminate losses tied to equipment maintenance, or, in other words, keep equipment producing only good products, as fast as possible, with no unplanned downtime. This helps for synchronized operations of a supply chain network.

8. **Total Quality Management (TQM):** TQM is a management approach that aims for long-term success by focusing on customer satisfaction. TQM is based on the participation of all members of an organization in improving processes, products, services, and the culture in which they work.

9. **Vendor development:** Vendor development is one of the popular techniques of strategic sourcing, which improves the value we receive from suppliers. Vendor development can be defined as any activity that a buying firm undertakes to improve a supplier's performance and capabilities to meet the buying firm's supply needs.

10. **Kanban:** An inventory control system for tracking the flow of in-process materials through the various operations of a just-in-time production process that improves supply chain efficiency through a reduction in costs.

11. **Standard containers:** These are common-sized containers that are used to efficiently move, store, and count inventory.

12. **Quality circles:** Quality circle is a group of volunteers composed of workers, usually under the leadership of their supervisor (but they can elect a team leader), who are trained to identify, analyse, and solve work-related problems and present their solutions to the management in order to improve the performance of the organization, and motivate and enrich the work of the employees.

11.2.2 Reasons for JIT Efforts

The reasons for JIT efforts are the following:

1. **Simplifying, stable production plan, or minimum variability:** To achieve just-in-time material movement, managers reduce variability caused by both internal and external factors. Variability is any deviation from the optimum process that delivers perfect product on time, every time. The less variability in the system, the less waste in the system. Variability occurs because:

   • Employees, machines, and suppliers produce units that do not conform to standards, are late, or are not the proper quantity.

- Engineering drawings or specifications are inaccurate.
- Customer demands are unknown.
- Excess stock has to be maintained to meet unexpected demand.

2. **High volume repetitive manufacturing:**   High volume repetitive manufacturing makes JIT workable as the process is standardized.

3. **Proximity of suppliers:**   The proximity of suppliers is an advantage for JIT as vendors can supply on time.

4. **Rising inventory levels:**   When one considers waste in the production of goods or services, one will have to count anything that does not add value as waste. Although products that are stored, inspected, or delayed, products waiting in queues, and defective products are part of inventory in the asset book, they do not add value and are 100 per cent waste. JIT speeds up throughput, allowing faster delivery times and reducing work-in-process. Reducing work-in-process releases assets in inventory for other, more productive purposes.

5. **To gain competitive advantage in the market:**   JIT deployment in a firm helps in reaping the benefits of waste and variability reduction, and thereby risk, and improving responsiveness, thereby increasing revenue and profitability. Table 11.1 shows JIT focus and benefits to a firm. Thus, it would be a source of competitive advantage.

Let us look at the case of a consumer electronics products manufacturer, say, a television manufacturer. The company in India has a market size of 1.2 million and runs the plant for 300 days in a year. The average production rate is 4,000 units per

Table 11.1   JIT focus and benefits to a firm

JIT focus	Benefits
Reduced number of vendors; supportive supplier relationships; quality deliveries on time	Simplification of procurement process and focus on vendor development
Small lot sizes; low set-up time; specialized bins for holding set number of parts	Quick change over of production, reduction of wastes and thereby cost
Work-cell layouts with testing at each step of the process; group technology; movable, changeable, flexible machinery; high level of workplace organization and neatness; reduced space for inventory; delivery directly to work areas	Quick response, flexibility, and waste reduction
Zero deviation from schedules; level schedules; suppliers informed of schedules; kanban techniques	Variability reduction in the workplace reduces wastes; kanban improves supplier participation and hence no requirement for safety stock
Statistical process control; quality suppliers; quality within the firm	Quality improvement and better value
Empowered and cross-trained employees; training support; few job classifications to ensure flexibility of employees	Employee involvement and empowerment
Support of management, employees, and suppliers	Key stakeholders involvement

day. The firm manufactures televisions in three shifts a day of eight hours each. The first and second shifts of the day, from 6 a.m. to 10 p.m., produce 1,600 sets each, and the third shift produces 800 sets. Generally, the night shift would predominantly produce basic models. The company is basically in assembly operations and major suppliers include manufacturers of circuits, boards, control panels, glass screens, electrical, and so on. The company has its own colour tube manufacturing facility that synchronizes to production schedule requirement with a lag for two days. Hence, there is a little uncertainty with a day's production schedule. Other component suppliers are on two hours JIT and night shift is on four hours JIT. This drastically reduces the complication of in-plant stores and management of stock. Also, there is no issue of misplaced parts or joint parts missing. Because there is a JIT, supply problems associated with kitting and sub assembly are also avoided. Thus, implementation of rigorous JIT and world class manufacturing practice helped the firm to be a leading brand in India. The company has all its major suppliers in close vicinity and those who are far away have consortium JIT services by a third-party logistics service provider.

JIT partnerships exist when the supplier and purchaser work together with a mutual goal of removing waste and driving down costs. Such relationships are critical for successful JIT. Every moment material is held, some process that adds value should be occurring.

11.2.3 Mission of JIT

1. **Elimination of in-transit inventory:** Many a time in-transit inventory is high for a firm. This could be mainly because of supplier location, formalities involved in transfer, and speed at which goods could be moved. This adds up to the inventory cost and hence is a focus area in JIT. Firms that practice JIT are addressing in-transit inventory reduction by encouraging suppliers and prospective suppliers to locate nearby manufacturing plants and provide frequent small shipments. The shorter the flow of material in the resource pipeline, the lesser the inventory. There are cases where the supplier is encouraged to hold stores within the production facility of the focal firm and supply on production line. It is not that such practices would work in all situations. Inventory with suppliers also has a cost and gets added to the material cost. Hence it is not cost-effective and efficient to ask suppliers to hold inventory. It is thus important to study the feasibility of JIT in each case before implementation.

2. **Elimination of in-plant inventory:** JIT delivers materials where and when needed. Raw material inventory is necessary only if there is reason to believe that suppliers are undependable. Likewise, parts or components would be delivered in small lots directly to the using department as needed. Practically, in-plant store and activities towards the same are limited to the JIT window of service.

3. **Elimination of unnecessary activities:** JIT suppliers are pre-approved vendors whose quality is certified through inspection and pre-approval activities.

Once they are on board for supplies, they supply on self certification, and random checks are done. Thus, in JIT, receiving activity and incoming-inspection activity are unnecessary and eliminated.

4. **Elimination of redundant suppliers:** JIT focuses on reducing the number of suppliers and working with a few committed suppliers on a long-term contract. This facilitates improvement in quality and building mutual understanding between the firm and supplier. On such a platform, it is easier to work on zero defects and continuous improvements.

5. **Reduce inventory:** JIT drives operations managers to move towards eliminating inventory. Reducing inventory helps to handle problems of variability and other problems in the manufacturing process. With reduced inventory, the management can do away with the exposed problems until the process is clear. This goes on till there is virtually no inventory and no problems of variability. Shigeo Shingo, co-developer of the Toyota JIT system, says, 'Inventory is evil.' It is evil because it skirts cost as many firms fail to impute right holding costs in operating decisions.

6. **Reduce lot sizes:** The focus of JIT is to reduce wastes, and small lots help in a big way for achieving this objective. Reducing the size of batches can be a major help in reducing inventory and inventory costs. When inventory usage is constant, the average inventory level is the sum of the maximum inventory plus the minimum inventory divided by two. Lowering the order size increases the number of orders but drops inventory levels. The trade-off is between ordering costs and inventory costs. With advancement in technology and application of order management system, ordering cost is reduced drastically and ease of ordering is improved dramatically.

Ideally, in a JIT environment, order size is one and single units are being pulled from one adjacent process to another. More realistically, analysis of the process, transportation time, and containers used for transport are considered when determining lot size. Such analysis typically results in a small lot size larger than one. Once a lot size has been determined, the EOQ production order quantity model can be modified to determine the desired set-up time. This can be arrived at using the following:

$$Q^* = \sqrt{2DS/H\,[1-(d/p)]},$$

where   D = annual demand, S = set-up cost, H = holding cost, d = daily demand, and p = daily production

11.3 KANBAN

Kanban helps to achieve small lot sizes by moving inventory through the shop only as needed rather than pushing it on to the next workstation independent of demand. This is typical of a pull system and the ideal lot size is one. The approach would be to schedule products to a time window, provided set-up times are lowered. Also, 'pull' inventory system through work centres should be ensured. A 'card' is often used to signal the need for another container of material—hence the name kanban. The card is the authorization for the next container of material to be produced. Typically, a kanban signal exists for each container of items to be obtained. An order for the container is then initiated by each kanban and 'pulled' from the producing department or supplier. A sequence of kanbans 'pulls' the material through the plant.

The system has been modified in many facilities so that, even though it is called a kanban, the card itself does not exist. In some cases, an empty position on the floor is sufficient indication that the next container is needed. In other cases, some sort of signal, such as a flag or rag alerts that it is time for the next container. Electronic kanban (e-kanban) is now in vogue.

When there is visual contact between producer and user, the process works like this:

1. The user removes a standard size container of parts from a small storage area.
2. The signal at the storage area is seen by the producing department as authorization to replenish the using department or storage area. Because there is an optimum lot size, the producing department may make several containers at a time.

There are certain issues to be addressed in a manufacturing environment while implementing kanban. These would include:

1. Use of lights or flag or empty space or web technologies instead of a card when there is no physical contact.
2. In an MRP system, the schedule can be thought of as a 'build' authorization and the kanban as a type of 'pull' system that initiates the actual production.
3. The kanban cards provide a direct control (limit) on the amount of work-in-process between cells.
4. If there is an immediate storage area, a two-card system may be used—one card circulates between the user and the storage area, and the other circulates between the storage area and the producing area.
5. Depending upon work centre requirement, each item in kanban may deploy appropriate technique for the 'pull', and specifications and terms could be different. It is more important on the spirit of kanban rather than standardization of all supplies, though, ideally, standardization is welcome.

11.3.1 Arriving at Order Size While Using Kanban Cards or Containers

In a JIT system, while using kanban, it may be important to arrive at order size and the number of kanban cards, or containers. To determine the number of containers moving back and forth between the using area and the producing areas, one may first set the size of each container. This is done by computing the lot size by using a model such as the production order quantity model. To arrive at the number of containers, one may need to know: (a) lead time needed to produce a container of parts and (b) the amount of safety stock needed to account for variability or uncertainty in the system.

Kanban size can be arrived at using the following equation:

$$Q_p = (2DS)/H(1 - p/d)$$

where Q_p is order quantity, D = annual demand, S = set-up cost, H = holding cost, p = daily usage rate, and d is daily production rate

The number of kanban cards is computed as follows:

Number of kanbans (containers) = (Demand during lead time + Safety stock)/ Size of container.

The following example illustrates how to calculate the number of kanbans needed.

EXAMPLE: Mysore Auto Component Ltd, which manufactures an assembly item, gets a component—a casting shell—from its vendor. The supply chain manager of Mysore Auto Component Ltd wants to move to kanban as the vendor is within the same industrial district. He approaches a production management consultant to implement the kanban system. The consultant collects the following data to arrive at the number of kanban containers required for transporting casting shells.

Daily demand = 5,400 units
Production lead time = 2 days
Safety stock = ½ day
Container size (determined on a production order size, EOQ basis) = 2,700 units

Solution:

Demand during lead time = lead time × daily demand = 2 days × 5,400 = 10,800
Safety stock = (5,400/2) = 2,700
Number of kanbans (containers) needed = (Demand during lead time + Safety stock)/Container size
(10,800 + 2,700)/2,700 = 5

Since containers are designed for few hours of production, adherence to the production schedule without variability is important. Any change must be planned with adequate time for adjustments. Kanban places added emphasis on meeting schedules, reducing the time and cost required by set-ups, and economical material handling. The supply chain manager must sensitize the same among partners, or else the system could collapse.

In-plant kanban systems often use standardized, reusable containers that protect the specific quantities to be moved. Such containers are also desirable in the supply chain. Standardized containers reduce weight and disposal costs, generate less wasted space in trailers, and require less labour to pack, unpack, and prepare items. Green supply chain also focuses on reuse of containers and elimination of degradable items in packing and containers which could be a challenge for kanban. For example, components may have to be sent in pallets and not in wooden containers. Kanban brings value for green supply chain as containers are usually reusable.

11.4 VENDOR-MANAGED INVENTORY

Vendor-managed inventory (VMI) can be defined as a mechanism where the supplier creates the purchase orders based on the demand information exchanged by the focal firm—manufacturer, retailer, or customer. VMI is a backward-replenishment model where the supplier does the demand creation and demand fulfilment. In this model, instead of the focal firm managing its inventory and deciding how much to fulfil and when, the supplier does. One may be interested in knowing how and why VMI is effective.

VMI helps manufacturers, suppliers, and all partners in the supply chain network to improve inventory turnover by reducing inventory and thereby achieving supply chain cost effectiveness. One may consider VMI as part of JIT where the onus of supply is with the supplier. Hence, like in JIT, VMI also requires a committed production schedule and advance sharing of production schedule, plan, and communication of changes. Otherwise, VMI might collapse.

11.4.1 Advantages of VMI

The advantages of VMI are as follows:

1. Vendors are responsible for the fulfilment of supply at the manufacturing line. This relieves the focal firm of holding the stock as inventory and the responsibility for effective and efficient management of the same. When the vendor is made responsible, the vendor ensures that the production schedule is followed based on the plan released and also tries to fill the production line as per the requirement. Overheads of the focal firm could be higher and the supplier with less overheads may be able achieve a cost advantage. There could be a counter argument stating that the supplier's capital cost is going to be higher and unless the supply chain network reduces inventory, there could not be a real advantage.

2. Another advantage could be that the inventory that would have been carried in the books of the focal firm is now off the books and with the suppliers. To that extent, capital deployment reduces and ratios reflect well. This is a real advantage only when the comparative capital cost of carrying reflects in the vendor's books instead of the focal firm's. For example, ABC Auto Components Ltd carries inventory for fifteen days of its stock worth Rs 150 million, and its cost of carrying including capital cost is 15 per cent, that is Rs 22.5 million. If it implements VMI and is able to save a portion of the holding cost, then it is an advantage. However, at times the cost of implementing VMI goes beyond Rs.22.5 million, resulting in the vendor's capital and holding cost becoming higher than 15 per cent. In such cases, it is not worth to implement VMI.

3. VMI allows outsourcing of processes like stores function as this activity becomes minimal. Since stores would be limited to essential and mainly for a short time window, the focal firm can reduce managerial efforts on the same and outsource it to a third-party logistics service provider who would bring efficiency on opera-

tion at a lower cost. In case of ABC Auto Components Ltd, where it gets inventory for every 4 hours window, the stores function is outsourced to the main third-party logistics service provider who handles the milk run for VMI. It becomes easy as they try to consolidate processes and take ownership for feeding to the line. This also helps in intermediate value addition like sub-assembly, kitting, and in some cases repacking and labelling. Again, such activities could have a cost focus because of outsourcing.

4. One of the key advantages of VMI implementation could be savings on human and physical resources as vendors and service providers would bring higher productivity compared to focal firm employees. The focal firm's employees become protected and at times pampered, covering low skill functions under the ambit of large employee benevolent schemes. Though these are 'welcome and feel good' initiatives, these do not add value to customers in a majority of the cases. With a larger objective of value enhancement, VMI helps in allowing vendor and buyers to concentrate on the core areas and maximize value creation.

5. Another possible advantage is that VMI, especially when done through third-party service providers, facilitates enjoying benefits of shared costs of activities. This is widely prevalent in the auto components manufacturing industry. For example, a Pune-based auto major is serviced by a third-party logistics provider, who maintains a small warehouse and receives stock from multiple vendors and supplies for the firm's production line. The vendors located within Pune facilitate the VMI for the focal firm by doing milk runs. So the responsibility of serving the production line is with the vendors who have a back-to-back contract with the third party logistics service provider.

It is not that VMI is not without issues. Commonly faced issues include a tendency of the vendors to overstock for 'in case' demand, leading to inaccurate and poor housekeeping. Second, tax laws in India make it slightly complicated with respect to ownership and stocking in focal firm stores. Finally, focal firms are not realistic in establishing contractual relationships and pricing. This trust-based relationship often results in the buyer raising questions about the viability of VMI operations.

Here, a VMI experience of an auto component company in Chennai with a logistics service provider is discussed for better understanding. ABC Auto Component Ltd, located in Chennai, is a tier 1 supplier and receives material from a number of vendors through Chennai Logistics Service Ltd, a logistics service provider. Chennai Logistics Service Ltd has a leased warehouse and has invested in assets. Vendors have an agreement with Chennai Logistics Service Ltd for delivering through them at the production line. About twenty vendors are grouped under VMI, and all of them are from Tamil Nadu and Karnataka with a maximum distance of about 600 km. Chennai Logistics Service Ltd also does milk runs within Chennai for delivery to ABC Auto Components Ltd from fifteen different vendors. It has a scheduled milk run for pick-up from its warehouse and local collections and shift-wise single delivery to the production line. It maintains a cleared stock of five days and an inventory of two days under inspection, which is by self-declaration. Chennai Logistics Service Ltd handles all physical aspects of products such as inspection, stores, and movement, including inbound and outbound transportation of off-the-city material that moves in and out of its warehouse to ABC Auto Component Ltd. The value it brings is inspection facilitation, stacking and storage, and intermediate value addition in a few components. Also, Chennai Logistics Service Ltd takes care of documentation for movement and delivery and reporting to ABC Auto Components Ltd and the vendors. It also takes care of vendors' invoicing activity as well as following up of receivables for supplies. Thus, VMI benefits both the vendors and the focal firm.

VMI is commonly used in the retail industry and in many packaged consumer goods. This works well where the end-user's demand for products is relatively stable with short-term fluctuations in the supply chain. With the ability of supply-chain applications to manage inventories at retailer locations, VMI concepts are being applied at both the distribution centre level and the store level. VMI is a continuous replenishment programme that uses the exchange of information between the retailer and the supplier to allow the supplier to manage and replenish merchandise at the store or warehouse level. This also enables the supplier to make better projections and anticipate the number of products it needs to produce or supply.

VMI is a strategic initiative that must be well understood and structured among retailer, supplier, and trading partners. It requires establishing good information transaction system and contracts defining roles and responsibilities, without which the system could collapse. Also, there must be enough thoughts on allowing variability in demand and supply, and addressing failure. Instead of the system being highly rigid, there must be adequate scope for being structured and pragmatic about market needs.

The benefits of VMI to the retailer and supplier are discussed in Table 11.2.

Table 11.2 Benefits of VMI to retailer and supplier

Retailer benefits	Supplier benefits	Requirement
Reduced inventory as there is control on lead time and safety stock is reduced due to visibility.	Encourages supply chain cooperation. Partnering and support in strategic initiatives are possible through collaboration.	Partnering approach.
Reduced stockout as it is the responsibility of the supplier to fill on time.	Effective cost management as there is reduction in errors.	Information exchange.
Increased sales as a natural outcome of higher availability and customer satisfaction.	Reduces purchase order (PO) errors and potential returns.	Effective contracts and guidance.
Reduced forecasting and purchasing activities as the supplier does the same and shares with the retailer.	Improved visibility results in better forecasting.	An understanding between both parties and involvement of trade partners.

11.5 QUALITY

Quality is one of the operations issues in supply chain management. Quality is significant from the perspective of the internal supply chain, which is primarily manufacturing, and of external players of the supply chain, namely suppliers, dealers/distributors and intermediaries such as transport operators, third-party warehouses, and so on. The orientation on quality establishes a strong relationship in the implementation of JIT as well. When a quality process is set with suppliers and when the supplier is pre-approved, quality checking need not be done in every transaction of the supply. Random quality checks would be sufficient. This reduces the turnaround time of the material from order to receipt and the onus of quality is heavily on the supplier. Since these processes are documented and established after a thorough interactive process, failure to adherence assumes a high penalty. Hence, quality is important in a supplier relationship.

Similarly, when JIT is implemented, it focuses on reducing the cost by obtaining good quality. This saving occurs because scrap, rework, inventory investment, and damage costs are eliminated. Secondly, JIT improves quality. As JIT limits queues and lead time, it can keep a close watch on quality deviations and alerts can be quick whenever a quality deviation occurs. This drastically reduces volume of losses of production and rework. Moreover, as a philosophy, JIT encourages a quality-oriented culture. Thus, the quality focus improves the efficiency of internal operations of the supply chain where there are limited disturbances in network operation.

Contemporary practices of quality can be seen in the reference given at the end of the chapter. It is important to note that most of the contemporary models on excellence in business and quality certification include supply chain process evaluation as a key parameter. Quality as a culture thus would not only improve internal operations but also transactions with suppliers and other network partners.

Let us focus on the operational aspect of quality management in a supply chain network. For example, an auto component tier 1 vendor, while supplying to an auto major, may have different levels of a quality validation process. Being a quality-focused company and winner of quality awards, ABC Auto Components Ltd has a rigid quality standard and culture built among employees. The internal supply chain, which includes in-plant logistics like movement inside the plant, stores management, buying, and manufacture, has clearly defined procedures. The company has implemented 5S and also adheres to TQM practices. Operations management takes care of every facet of processes that excel in quality. All these efforts would bring value to the customers only when quality standards in supply chain activities are implemented. Looking at three macro processes, namely supplier relations management, internal supply chain, and customer relations management, we note that internal supply chain activities are well taken care of.

With respect to supplier relationship management, ABC Auto Component Ltd has a rigid supplier selection process. Suppliers are screened for the track record and qualification on important parameters such as quality adherence in purchasing, process adherence in manufacture, employee awareness, and all support activities such as stores and movement. After this, the supplier goes through training and surveillance of rigid implementation of quality standards till the products reach the shop production line of ABC Auto Component Ltd. Thus, supplier relations management process ensures thorough quality management in supply.

As mentioned, in manufacturing, ABC Auto Component Ltd has implemented various quality management methodologies and won quality awards. Moreover, such implementation is mandatory for this company to be a tier 1 supplier to the auto major. There are a number of Indian auto components companies who have won quality awards, which are mentioned in Appendix 11.1. Thus, the internal supply chain process takes care of quality issues in supply chain management. This covers all facets such as receiving, manufacture, stores, in-plant movement, finished goods stock, and final despatch. In fact, companies engage logistics services providers who have explicit quality standards and practices.

Finally, ABC Auto Component Ltd follows established quality standards in its customer relations management process also. Again, being a tier 1 supplier of the auto major who is its main customer and has declared certain quality standards, ABC Auto Component Ltd needs to adhere to a strict quality framework. A substantial portion of such initiatives requires self declaration and monitoring by the supplier. Hence ABC Auto Component Ltd engages intensive quality processes such as maintaining pre-approved standards for materials, reducing rejections, quality processes such as documentation and explicit policy statements, and so on. Thus, in the customer relations management function, ABC Auto Component Ltd is bound by quality management in its supply chain.

Quality orientation and management is an integral part of supply chain management and professionals involved in quality standards also ensure that the supply management functions take complete onus of maintaining quality standards. Hence, it is important to build this perspective in all operational aspects of supply chain management.

11.6 GREEN SCM

Green supply chain management (GSCM) practice is gaining importance and acceptance across the globe, especially in developed nations since mid-2000. Increasingly, recommendatory practices are being adapted and some areas are becoming a mandatory requirement. Here, a brief understanding of issues in green supply chain management is given.

Green supply chain management involves traditional supply chain management practices that integrate environmental aspects such as natural resource conservation, limiting of pollution, and so on. With increased awareness across the globe and prevalence of statutory bodies and rules, companies are under pressure to consider environmental issues while designing a supply chain network. Social pressure is subtly increasing as the world's environmental problems such as global warming, toxic substance usage, and decrease in non-replenishable resources are increasingly catching the attention of the society through a proliferation of reports in media and the adverse impact on pockets of society is being opposed publicly. World over various governments have launched campaigns to promote awareness to manage this problem.

Several organizations responded to this by applying green principles to their company, such as using environment-friendly raw material, reducing the usage of petroleum power, and using recycled papers for packaging. It is believed that Pepsi-Cola saved $44 million by switching from corrugated to reusable plastic shipping containers for 1 litre and 20-ounce bottles, conserving 196 million pounds of corrugated material. In India, Pepsi water business replaced cartons with plastic material, thereby reducing adverse impact on the environment. (Refer to Exhibit 11.2.)

Exhibit 11.3 on the green initiative by a multinational company operating in India is an example of GSCM practices. The corporate board of many companies has taken up this issue and proactive declarations on green practices are being encouraged. This drives the adoption of green principles by many departments within an organization, including supply chain. This idea covers every stage in manufacturing, from the first to the last stage of the lifecycle of a product, that is, from product design to recycling. Though green supply chain is believed to be impacting manufacturing, it is also implemented in service industries such as education, hospitals and healthcare, and government. Consciously, services and governments have initiated numerous green activities that would be in the ambit of the supply chain. Governments have reduced paperwork consciously, encouraging electronic work process in support of green initiatives. In contemporary practices, returns filing for duties and taxes, which is one of the key business processes for transfer and movement of goods, is electronic now. This is in trend with the recent emergence of GSCM, which provides the opportunity to review processes, materials, and operational concepts from a different perspective. It incorporates the role of environment in supply chain value creation.

Basically, the business system, in order to conserve energy and prevent the dissipation of harmful materials into the environment, would like to promote a green supply chain. This leads to cost savings or at times increased cost as activities are niche and social cost benefit analysis promotes green initiatives. In order to design a green supply chain, the entire inputs and outputs in the product lifecycle need to be

---

Exhibit 11.2   Aquafina: Eco-friendly Packing

PepsiCo's Aquafina, the nation's bestselling brand of bottled water, is launching the Eco-Fina Bottle, the lightest half-litre bottle of any nationally distributed bottled water brand in the market. The Eco-Fina Bottle is the latest evolution of Aquafina's ongoing efforts, which began in 2002, to develop the lightest and one of the most environment-friendly bottles in the market. The Eco-Fina Bottle will be available in 24-packs and begins shipping to retail outlets nationwide.

At a weight of just 10.9 grams, the Eco-Fina Bottle is made with 50 per cent less plastic than the half-litre Aquafina bottles produced in 2002, eliminating an estimated 75 million pounds of plastic annually. In addition to making the half-litre bottle lightweight, Aquafina is driving additional environmental benefits by producing the Eco-Fina Bottle right at Aquafina purification centres where filling occurs and by eliminating cardboard base pads from Eco-Fina Bottle 24-packs, which will contribute to saving 20 million pounds of corrugate by 2010.

Source: http://phx.corporate-ir.net/phoenix.zhtml?c=78265&p=irol-newsArticle&ID=1270013&highlight.

Exhibit 11.3   Green Supply Chain Initiatives

Indian companies are going green in line with many of their Western counterparts who are building environmental sustainability into their business practices. There is also subtle pressure from international buyers to go green. It is believed that Walmart, which annually imports over $3 billion in goods from Indian suppliers, have advised them to adopt green practices or risk losing the retail giant as a customer.

For Indian companies, there are other compelling reasons to develop environmentally conscious practices. Mounting electricity costs, which were adversely impacting the profits of Tulsi Tanti's textile business, forced them to develop a wind energy system. Today, his company, Suzlon Energy, is one of the largest wind-turbine makers in the world. A number of sugar companies like E.I.D. Parry have gone for cogeneration of power to improve economics of sugar business and thereby following green initiatives. Bajaj Auto set up a wind-power generation system that provides substantial energy needs of its plant realizing savings of $5 million annually.

In order to go green, a company's senior management and employees must believe in the philosophy, and commit themselves to implementing it. For example, at Cisco, CEO John Chambers and team are pushing in various green initiatives such as 'let's talk Cisco green', bike-to-work day, preferred parking for hybrid cars, educational videos, and green websites. These programmes have helped Cisco build a sustainable culture and formulate a strong green policy.

Leading companies in India are also committing themselves to the green cause. For example, Wipro recently launched Eco Eye, an ecological sustainability initiative that, among other things, ensures that the firm does not do business at the cost of ecology. Wipro is increasingly focusing on energy efficiency and effective e-waste management.

For a company wanting to develop greener products, it's important to put on a 'green cap' during idea generation and conception. These decisions affect the carbon footprint of an entire product lifecycle. Such an approach is far more efficient and cost-effective than making incremental improvements later. Nokia is an example. It is making eco-friendly phones with biodegradable phone covers and recyclable batteries. The company is also working towards reducing up to 50 per cent of the energy consumed by mobile chargers. MRF, one of India's largest tyre manufacturers, has created an eco-friendly tubeless rubber tyre that reduces rolling resistance and fuel consumption.

Green Supply Chain

For many companies, the supply chain is likely to be the operational area that impacts the environment. And that provides many opportunities for improvement. Recently, two-thirds of the 300 organizations that responded to the Global Supply Chain Trends 2008–10 survey have put environmental sustainability as a key factor in their global supply chain strategy.

There are many ways to 'greenify' a supply chain. Companies can reconfigure parts of the physical network to locate suppliers, manufacturing and customers near each other to reduce fuel consumption and other environmental costs. For greener sourcing, they can select suppliers with a green mindset. When it comes to manufacturing, these companies must know that lean often means green, since eliminating waste can also lead to reduced material usage and energy bills. For end-use and disposal, companies can develop after-life product recycling and take-back programmes. Nokia, for example, has set up 'green boxes' across all Nokia dealers in India, where customers can deposit old mobile phones for recycling.

All these instances point to a green movement emerging in the country. And the right approach can turn this into a sustainable source of competitive advantage.

Source: Mark Hermans and Biswajit Das, 'A Green Evolution'.

http://business.outlookindia.com/inner.aspx?articleid=2783&editionid=76&catgid=12&subcatgid=1079

holistically considered. Inputs include energy, materials, and other resources. Outputs include products, waste, and revenues generated. Unnecessary inputs can be eliminated and outputs can be re-used. Material conservation, energy savings, and waste reduction would reduce cost and make the firm competitive. On the other hand, adoption of rigorous practices and systems, and sustained investment in design may increase cost. Finally, balancing of these factors and achieving reduction in socio-economic costs would be the advantage of a green supply chain.

One may state that external environmental aspects may guide business decisions of a firm but could not be among its chief concerns. This is no longer relevant as there is an increasing pressure due to recommendatory regulatory guidelines in developed nations and various certifying and award agencies. Managers are starting to look at environmental problems as business issues where many can gain sustained competitive advantage. For example, customer service businesses such as food, oil, and gas for automobiles, toys, and packaging are placing a lot of importance in going green. Firms charting green supply chain strategies are finding that both the buyer and the seller can benefit through shared cost savings, among other things. Successful strategies consider the entire lifecycle of a product where opportunities for improvement are noted at each stage of the lifecycle, from raw material sourcing through manufacturing, use, and product end-of-life. GSCM is defined as integrating environment thinking into supply chain management, including product design, material sourcing and selection, manufacturing processes, delivery of the final product to the consumers, and end-of-life management of the product after its useful life (Srivastava 2007). According to this definition, GSCM relates to a wide range of production from product design to recycle or incineration or any form of destruction.

One may look at the impact of going green on supply chain management. It begins with the factors that influence the company to adopt the GSCM. These factors can be categorized according to the forces that drive them, such as government, market, industry, competition, and internal reasons. Boks and Stevels (2007) categorized green into three types, depending on the different perceptions of the environment among different stakeholders involved: scientific green, government green, and customer green. In scientific green, Life Cycle Assessment (LCA) is used to determine the environmental impact of products, processes, and systems. However, it concerns only the emissions, not other aspects. In government green, several factors are considered, such as population density, geographical position, and the availability of energy sources. These factors affect the government agenda to maintain or improve the quality of life. In customer green, the focus is on the impact of products, processes, and systems on people, especially their health and safety, than on resources or emissions. Thus, a green supply chain works towards reducing wastages, recovering material for saving non-renewable substances, controlling emissions and improving the quality of air and water, and adopting green culture in the work environment. Table 11.3 provides areas where green initiatives and supply chain perspectives can go together.

Table 11.3 Green perspective vis-à-vis SCM perspective

Green perspective	SCM perspective
Reducing wastages	• Product design and functionality • Efficiency of facilities: both production and distribution centre • Inventory reduction moving towards zero stock • Sourcing: constantly endeavouring for alternate sources of material and uses • Pricing: using mark down, especially in perishables and non-reusable material to avoid wastages and spoilages. • Information efficiency could reduce wastages. • Transportation as per standards may reduce wastages by avoiding situations such as vehicle breakdown, under-utilization of vehicles, and so on.
Recovering material for saving non-renewable substances	• Product design facilitating efficient reverse logistics process and recovery of substances such as batteries, electronics parts, and so on. • Use of pallets with recycled material, reducing packaging material consumption. • Controlling emissions, and improving the quality of air and water. • Transportation is a major activity that involves emissions. The focal firm should adopt an aggressive stance with transportation service providers to control emissions. • The focal firm should adopt stringent measures to control emissions in facilities. • Pollution control regulatory authorities should constantly monitor if emission standards are being followed. • Apart from these, cost-saving measures such as improving air cooling and using natural lighting control emissions.
Green culture in work environment	• Adopting green culture in the work environment of supply chain functional areas is important. Some of the trucking companies, logistics service providers, and corporates have consciously promoted the same so that the emotional aspects of a green supply chain are taken care of.

11.6.1 Benefits of GSCM

More and more companies are incorporating green initiatives in the supply chain domain as they find unique value opportunities in GSCM. Some of the benefits are:

1. It helps to reduce cost and contributes towards increase in profitability. A common understanding of sustainability concepts, goals, and objectives provides a platform for continuous improvements through green initiatives, which further reduce the cost of operations. Similarly, a green focus helps in implementing best sustainable practices within the supply chain that will standardize operations and allow for improving customer service. This facilitates increase in top line and thereby profitability. Thus, GSCM enables the achievement of the supply chain objectives of cost efficiency and customer responsiveness.

2. Asset utilization efficiency is achieved through the implementation of green initiatives, especially in transportation and inventory management. Also, adopting business sustainability policies with suppliers and customers will promote alignment across the supply chain assets and help in managing contingencies. As a plan for total approach towards managing financials of business and mitigation of risks, some of these initiatives would be helpful. Promoting greater understanding of sustainability within the company's supply chain will mitigate environmental, social, and market risks. There are cases of sugar companies, leather processing, and chemicals and pesticides companies being affected in India when there had been some stringent implementation of regulation by authorities. As a twined area of operation of compliance and asset management, green initiatives in supply chain are productive.

3. Competitive advantage could be reaped because of focus on green, leading to innovation, product differentiation, and brand building. There is a segment in the market that is willing to pay premium to green practices as it is conscious of future generation needs and encourages companies to focus on the same.

The following guidelines, which focus on supplier-based learning, can help companies get ahead of the green curve and transform GSCM into a business value driver, rather than a cost centre:

1. The focal firm must determine the levels of integration with its suppliers and practise on-site raw material management. Some joint improvement activities may be developed over time. Suppliers can be transformed into cost-cutting partners if one focuses on developing long-lasting effective relationship rather than negotiating the transaction cost. Suppliers may be encouraged to cut waste and reduce resources needed by per unit of production. The suppliers can also be educated on how to realize new revenue streams from the sale of recycled materials.

2. Learning from suppliers on redesign of processes in ways that deliver enormous savings, which is a cross-learning of suppliers from their multi-customer base. It is often possible to make excellent products using simple manufacturing techniques. One can also modify processes, substitute materials, and utilize the high availability of low cost labour or other resources to re-design processes that previously produced large amounts of waste in the overall system. A typical example is the cogeneration of power using bio masses and wastes, and the efficiency in operating cycle for producing power in India.

Often, companies can improve their performance by green efforts that lead to higher profitability—both in the short term (by reducing waste) and in the long term (by improving customer loyalty). The companies should consider the following questions:

- What is the impact on the carbon footprint if one were to off-shore or change business processes?
- Where should one locate a manufacturing site, given different environmental concerns and requirement of statutory compliance?

- How does one schedule plant operations to minimize waste and emissions and conserve energy?
- How does one minimize the carbon footprint of the distribution network without significantly impacting customer service or profitability?

Profit levels will depend on the supply chain expertise at the strategic, tactical, and execution levels of green initiatives. Though all time horizon initiatives are under focus, this is discussed under operations because finally green lives through operations or actual implementation.

A sustainable supply chain must take into account all business requirements, including environmental issues that may crop up in the years to come. To optimize an operational green supply plan, supply chain managers must understand the company's growth strategy and the logistical challenges that the organization faces. Then they should deploy and monitor green initiatives as part of supply chain domain or orchestrate through quality programmes.

11.7 ETHICAL SCM

As discussed above, during the past decade firms have come under increasing pressure to consider the environmental and social aspects of supply chain relationships. Ethical practices are widely discussed in sourcing and procurement functions. There is a tendency to relate ethical practices on fair procedures for buying. However, such demands have been there for many decades, which were initially forced by lenders, especially of multilateral agencies, and the same format is now being followed by domestic lending institutions as well. One would want to explore the relationship between a focal firm and its suppliers in order to find out how such a relationship works in practice.

Supply relationships can be extremely complex and ethical considerations would be not only in procurement but also in internal supply chain processes and in customer relationship management functions as well. Ethical practices could be related to a substantial heritage of environmental and social aspects of supply chain management.

The ethical supply chain issues and the key drivers are shown in Figure 11.1. Some of the observations are as follows:

1. Ethical footprints in supply chain refer to fair and just supply chain operations in day-to-day activities, which would be legal, economical, and socially acceptable and of high esteem to the corporate as an entity. Such measures are to be clearly mapped and declared. The implementation of ethical practices would be monitored by day-to-day measurements that get triggered by any deviations.

2. The drivers of ethical practices are societal factors, including cultural issues. There are societies that are paranoid about environmental issues and values on fairness. Such societies naturally drive ethics in business. Different surveys point out the same, and also bring out societies that are lagging in cultural issues because of varied pressures and require reorientation of ethical standards by implementing statutory regulations and rigorously addressing the same.

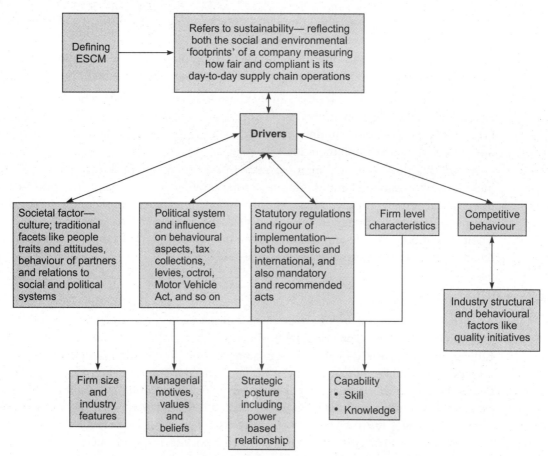

Figure 11.1 Ethical supply chain and its drivers

3. Firm-level characteristics—for example, the size of a firm (measured by the number of employees), revenue and geographical spread, strategic posture, managerial values, bargaining power with stakeholders, basic skill levels, and knowledge and industry factors (such as the level of maturity and standards as explained by group behaviour)—would influence ethical standards. For example, auto components from India that export to developed markets must demonstrate high ethical standards as required by trade practices and declarations with respect to the same. Similarly, transparency and openness of the healthcare or the financial services sectors require high standards of ethical practices. Power inequality tends to lead to the exploitation of one player over the other. This may lead to a slide in the ethical standards as one player may use its bargaining power to gain unfair returns or any other economic gain. Managers are agents of investors and these agents are trustees of the values and beliefs of the system. In case managers delink trusteeship and act in their collusive power driven by motives of gains in compensation or stature, there could be slips in ethical standards. A number of scams consistently surface in the supply chain

domain of the corporate landscape. There is a need to monitor this and boards are expected to play an active role in bridging the trustee's responsibilities and aspirations by fair and ethical means. There are mandatory requirements to declare 'interested parties' dealings in purchases and outsourcing or any other commercial transactions, and these interested parties must be outside the ambit of such supply chain domain decision making. The basic skill and knowledge of operators involved plays a significant role in ethical standards. Inadequate skill and knowledge may lead to passive slippages, which is not a welcome approach to ethical behaviour. Finally, the size of a firm, as measured by number of employees, turnover, and/or asset deployment, could influence ethical standards though there could be divergent views on the same. Generally, large, multi-location businesses may have greater pressure to follow ethical standards, and surveillance could be higher in these businesses as different statutory bodies may be involved.

4. Competitive behaviour stems from the rivalry among firms to garner market share, or originates from the evolution of a common code of behaviour or standards for common purpose, or is caused by the sheer compulsions of the market. Some of the classic examples are quality-led practices in Indian companies, mainly in automotives and automotive components, engineering, manufacturing, and services businesses. Sometimes ethical moves by leading players necessarily force smaller players to adopt the same standards. For instance, ancillaries maybe compelled to adhere to high ethical standards because of the ancillary development programme initiated by a parent company in the region. The cases of Maruti Suzuki and BHEL in India are proof of competitive behaviour leading to high ethical practices. Traditional industries, which are fragmented and unstructured, and represented by large number of players with high dispersion of revenue and profits, do not always implement ethical practices because of cutting of corners by some firms for survival. Thus, competitive factors play a critical role in establishing ethical supply chain management practices.

There are a few hypotheses on ethical behaviour in supply chain that are discussed here. An ethical index is developed and tested against drivers measured through ordinal responses from practising managers.

1. There is a positive association between a firm's managerial decision and ESCM.
2. There is a positive association between a firm's capability and ESCM.
3. There is a positive association between a firm's nature of supply relationship, power-dependency and ESCM.
4. There is a positive association between a firm's culture and its managerial decision.
5. There is a positive association between a firm's external pressures and its managerial decision.
6. There is a positive association between firm size/industry structure and its managerial decision.

7. There is a positive association between a firm's managerial values and strategic posture and its managerial decision.

8. There is a positive association between a firm's culture and external pressures.

It may be thus noted that ethical standards are emerging as a key operational issue in supply chain management. There are international standards and institutions like ISO 14001, SA 8000, Ethical Trade Initiative, International Labour Organization, Fair Labour Association, and UN Global Compact driving ethical standards, especially on supply chain management function, which a supply chain manager must take cognizance of. Some of these are briefly mentioned in Appendix 11.2.

11.8 SUPPLY CHAIN SECURITY MANAGEMENT

Supply chain security refers to the efforts to enhance the security of the supply chain, especially of the transport and logistics system for the world's cargo. It combines traditional practices of supply chain management with the security requirements of the system, which are driven by threats such as terrorism, piracy, and theft. Typical supply chain security activities include:

- Credentialing of participants in the supply chain
- Screening and validating of the contents of cargo being shipped
- Advance notification of the contents to the destination country
- Ensuring the security of cargo in-transit via the use of locks and tamper-proof seals
- Inspecting cargo on entry

The following are typical questions relating to supply chain security that would be addressed by a supply chain manager:

1. How are the recent supply chain security programmes or certification initiatives impacting a company and its operations?

2. How are the new/upcoming requirements in 'security compliance data' impacting a company's operations management?

3. What is the contemporary quotient of a company's latest 'supply chain security' technologies/hardware?

4. Is the company's supply chain vulnerable to 'supply chain security' and can have a related impact on performance? If so, does the company have organized a 'supply chain security management' policy?

11.8.1 Contemporary Initiatives

There are a number of supply chain security initiatives in the United States and around the world today. These include:

1. The Customs Trade Partnership against Terrorism (C-TPAT), a voluntary compliance programme for companies to improve the security of their corporate supply chains. This supply chain security programme is led by US Customs and Border Protection (CBP) and focused on improving the security of private com-

panies' supply chains with respect to terrorism. Group bargaining power could also tilt ethical balance as monitoring and surveillance become difficult and enforcement is random and through self declarations. Standards in such cases are improved through cultural intervention. Types of participants in C-TPAT include:

- US importers of record
- US/Canada and US/Mexico highway carriers
- Rail, sea, and air carriers
- US marine port authority and terminal operators
- US air freight consolidators, ocean transportation intermediaries, and non-vessel operating common carriers
- Mexican manufacturers
- Certain invited foreign manufacturers
- Licensed US customs brokers

Some benefits to the C-TPAT partners include:

- Reduced customs inspections
- Reduced border delays
- Entitlement to a CBP account manager
- Eligibility for account-based processes
- Participation in the war against terrorism
- Need certification to proceed with Importer Self Assessment (ISA) programme

The Green Lane Maritime Cargo Security Act would enhance these potential benefits for companies at the highest level of security within C-TPAT.

2. The Authorized Economic Operator as part of the World Customs Organization SAFE framework of standards. The Security and Accountability For Every Port Act (or SAFE Port Act), an Act of Congress in the United States covering port security, was passed in October 2006. The SAFE Port Act codified into a number of programmes to improve the security of US ports, such as:

- Additional requirements for maritime facilities
- Creation of the Transportation Worker Identification Credential
- Establishment of inter-agency operational centres for port security
- Port Security Grant Programme
- Container Security Initiative
- Foreign port assessments
- Customs Trade Partnership against Terrorism

3. The Container Security Initiative, a programme led by US Customs and Border Protection in the Department of Homeland Security, focused on screening containers at foreign ports. The Container Security Initiative (CSI) was launched in 2002 by the US Bureau of Customs and Border Protection (CBP), an agency of

the Department of Homeland Security. Its purpose was to increase security for container cargo shipped to the United States. As the CBP puts it, the intent is to 'extend [the] zone of security outward so that American borders are the last line of defence, not the first.'

CSI consists of four core elements:
- Using intelligence and automated information to identify and target containers that pose a risk for terrorism
- Pre-screening those containers that pose a risk at the port of departure before they arrive at US ports
- Using detection technology to quickly pre-screen containers that pose a risk
- Using smarter, tamper-evident containers

The CSI programme offers its participant countries the reciprocal opportunity to enhance their own incoming shipment security. CSI has also inspired and informed global measures to improve shipping security. In June 2002, the World Customs Organization unanimously passed a resolution that will enable ports in all 161 of the member nations to begin to develop programmes along the CSI model.

4. Efforts for countries around the world to implement and enforce the International Ship and Port Facility Security Code (ISPS Code), an agreement of 148 countries that are members of the International Maritime Organization (IMO).

5. Pilot initiatives by companies in the private sector to track and monitor the integrity of cargo containers moving around the world using technologies such as RFID and GPS.

6. The International Organization for Standardization has released a series of standards for the establishment and management of supply chain security. ISO/PAS 28000 Specification for security management systems for the supply chain offers public and private enterprises an international high-level management standard that enables organizations to utilize a globally consistent management approach to applying supply chain security initiatives.

SCM security needs across industries vary widely depending upon a number of factors, which are listed below:
- Consumer protection as in case of pharmaceuticals and perishables
- Transport safety/dangerous goods, that is, chemicals
- Import protection extended to traditional goods and services, that is, textiles, agricultural produce, and agro-based goods
- Export controls for high technology and essential commodities
- Critical infrastructure for spare parts/utilities networks, international trade, logistics, and automation service providers

Hence a supply chain manager must analyse relevant security issues and address the same under the broad framework practised across industries.

There is a paradigm shift in supply chain management security and controls. Typically, container movement can be depicted as in Figure 11.2. Traditional customs control typically begins at port of unloading, which is a single-point intervention. There is a practice for early single-point intervention wherein custom control can be pushed back to a location where containers are loaded for the last leg of the voyage. Then, further advanced maritime security covers the entire maritime portion of goods movement. Further advanced practices currently adopted include securing the supply chain from end-to-end. Supply chain managers must be sensitive to such developments and operationally equip for a security cover for the entire supply chain.

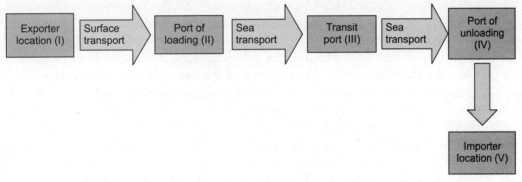

Figure 11.2   Movement of cargo from export to import location

On the role of customs, one may note that no two customs administrations necessarily look alike. While developing and less developed countries focus on revenue collection, developed countries focus on border protection with emphasis on the enforcement of import and export prohibitions and restrictions, including those arising from Free Trade Agreements (FTA). However, the current trend is due to FTA, and the recent increase in international terrorism concerns has seen border security emerge as a priority across all economies.

For centuries, the customs role has been one of 'gatekeeper', with customs authorities representing a barrier through which international trade must pass, in an effort to protect the interests of the nation. Today, the catch-cry is 'intervention by exception'—that is, intervention when there is a legitimate need to do so—and intervention is based on identified risk. The result is the outcome of Customs Blueprint. The Revised Kyoto Convention entered into force on 3 February 2006, and as of 10 January 2007, fifty-two economies were contracting parties to the convention. It is designed to provide the underlying conditions and instruments to help contracting parties to achieve a modern customs administration and to make a major contribution to the facilitation of international trade. The Revised Kyoto Convention incorporates important concepts of contemporary compliance management. These include the application of new technology, the implementation of new philosophies on customs control, and the willingness of private sector partners to engage with customs authorities in mutually beneficial alliances.

In order to facilitate trade, after extensive consultation with commerce and industry, the WTO identified the following broad areas of concern at the international level, namely excessive government documentation requirements, lack of automation and insignificant use of information technology, lack of transparency, unclear and unspecified import and export requirements, inadequate customs procedures, particularly audit-based controls and risk assessment techniques, and lack of co-operation and modernization amongst customs and other government agencies, which impedes efforts to deal effectively with increased trade flows.

Security imperative after 9/11, drawing heavily on the US C-TPAT initiative, the World Customs Organization (WCO) released its Framework of Standards to Secure and Facilitate Global Trade. According to the WCO, the Framework aims to establish standards that provide supply chain security and facilitation at a global level to promote certainty and predictability; enable integrated supply chain management for all modes of transport; enhance the role, functions, and capabilities of Customs to meet the challenges and opportunities of the twenty-first century; strengthen co-operation between Customs administrations to improve their capability to detect high risk consignments; strengthen Customs/Business co-operation, and promote the seamless movement of goods through secure international trade supply chains.

Customs and supply chain issues are interwoven, especially if a company is part of global business either as an importer or exporter or any of its constituents in supply network have a role in such business. As goods and materials move across national frontiers, managing the customs function is a key factor to success within the efforts of supply chain management. Within each of the supply chain functions, which include procurement, manufacture, marketing, and distribution, customs consideration can have a significant impact. One may note that customs law is not static. Rules and regulations are constantly reviewed and businesses need to be aware of developments and changes and their interpretations. Many customs regimes may exist that could give an international supply chain similar competitive advantages.

These are to be treated as operational aspects as every transaction must consider the impact of these and supply chain risk and security elements.

SUMMARY

Some of the key operations aspects that would influence supply chain operations are: JIT, VMI, kanban, improvement in in-plant logistics through deployment of lean production and quality improvement programmes, green supply chain, ethical supply management, and supply chain security.

Just in Time (JIT), which is more commonly referred to as Toyota Production System (TPS), is the backbone of the lean manufacturing system that requires interfacing with sourcing and distribution strategies and partners. Actually JIT consists of three main parts, namely JIT purchasing, JIT manufacturing, and JIT distribution. JIT is a key philosophy of lean management, focused on waste reduction and continuous improvement. Once JIT is implemented, it

takes care of a number of operating efficiencies as it requires a regimented approach. Some of the matured industries like automotives, consumer electronics, and services deploy JIT effectively.

Another tool, namely kanban, a typical pull system, helps to achieve small lot sizes by moving inventory through the shop only as needed rather than pushing it on to the next workstation independent of demand. Mature industries deploy kanban effectively in production line inventory management. Vendor-managed Inventory (VMI) is another technique where the onus of managing inventory is passed to the vendors and the focal firm provides support for the same. VMI effectiveness and participation depends upon the vendor's strengths and ability to supply on production line. These techniques along with quality management perspectives are found to be effective in managing supply chain operations.

With increased awareness across the globe and prevalence of statutory bodies and rules, companies are under pressure to consider environmental issues while designing a supply chain network. More and more companies are adopting green supply chain practices. During the past decade firms have come under increasing pressure to consider the environmental and social aspects of supply chain relationships. Ethical practices are widely discussed in sourcing and procurement functions. There is a tendency to relate ethical practices on fair procedures for buying. Now it spans across all supply chain activities. With the proliferation of technology and strict adherence to various statutory needs, ethical practices are gaining importance. A related aspect here is supply chain risk management and security, especially in movement of cargo. This is gaining importance because of increased threat of terror and disruptions due to natural calamities and epidemics wherein supply chain network is interrupted. Supply chain operations must initiate risk mitigation strategies and practices to meet any such untoward happening.

Thus, supply chain operations would be influenced by policies, systems, procedures, and new generation practices, which a supply chain manager must be sensitive to and quick to absorb.

KEY TERMS

Ethical supply chain management (ESCM): Ethical footprint in supply chain refers to fair and just supply chain operations in day-to-day activities, which would be legal, economical, and socially acceptable and of high esteem to the corporate as an entity.

Green supply chain: Green supply chain management involves traditional supply chain management practices which integrate environmental aspects such as natural resource conservation, limiting air, water, and noise pollution in deployment of supply chain drivers and using more electronic documents, and so on.

JIT partnerships: JIT partnerships exist when the supplier and purchaser work together with a mutual goal of removing waste and driving down costs. Such relationships are critical for successful JIT.

Just-in-time (JIT): JIT is aimed at manufacturing process improvement and considered as one of the important production management tools. To achieve this, it requires interfacing with sourcing and distribution strategies and partners. JIT consists of three main parts, namely JIT purchasing, JIT manufacturing, and JIT distribution. JIT is a key philosophy of lean management, focused on waste reduction and continuous improvement.

Just-in-time inventory: Just-in-time inventory is an inventory management strategy that is aimed at monitoring the inventory process in such a manner as to minimize the costs associated with inventory control and maintenance wherein the inventory process relies on the efficient monitoring of the usage of materials in the production of goods and ordering replacement goods that arrive shortly before they are needed.

Kaizen: Kaizen, a Japanese philosophy of continuous improvement, is a daily activity, the purpose of which goes beyond just productivity improvement. It is about bringing in a scientific method of production focused on elimination of waste.

Lean production: Lean production is an assembly-line methodology developed originally for Toyota and the manufacturing of automobiles. It is also known as the Toyota Production System or just-in-time production. Lean production philosophy is focused on eliminating waste and empowering workers, reducing inventory, and improving productivity.

Level schedules: It is a manufacturing technique that aims to create a smooth flow of production over a period. Its objective is to minimize disruptions caused by sudden changes in demand levels by matching the product family schedules with product-by-product schedules. Both sales and production departments would agree for fixed volume and output duration.

Manufacturing cycle time: The manufacturing cycle time, also known as throughput time, is the time required to turn raw materials into completed products.

Pull system: Pull/Kanban is a method of controlling the flow of production through the factory based on a customer's demand. Pull systems control the flow of resources in a production process by replacing only what has been consumed. They are customer order driven production schedules based on actual demand and consumption rather than forecasting.

Push system: Push system refers to ordering of goods or components in anticipation of demand. It is driven by fixed rate schedules or volume schedules determined by lead time estimates.

Supply chain risk: Supply chain risk refers to challenges in achieving supply chain objectives of overall supply network profit optimization and responsiveness. Many of the key risk factors have developed from a pressure to enhance productivity, eliminate waste, remove supply chain duplication, and drive for cost improvement, external factors like disruptions in operations due to terror, natural calamities, and strikes.

Supply chain security: Supply chain security refers to efforts which enhance the security of the supply chain: the transport and logistics system for the world's cargo. It combines traditional practices of supply chain management with the security requirements of the system, which are driven by threats such as terrorism, piracy, and theft.

Variability: Variability is any deviation from the optimum process that delivers perfect product on time, every time. The less variability in the system, the less waste in the system.

Vendor-managed inventory (VMI): It is a mechanism where the supplier creates the purchase orders based on the demand information exchanged by the focal firm: manufacturer, retailer, or customer. VMI is a backward replenishment model where the supplier does the demand creation and demand fulfilment.

CONCEPT REVIEW QUESTIONS

1. Define just-in-time system and how it improves supply chain operating efficiency in manufacturing and service business. Use examples for the same.

2. Explain the advantages and disadvantages of the JIT system.

3. Describe the kanban system and its application for supply chain operating efficiency with examples.

4. Explain e-kanban and its advantages.

5. Explain the concept of vendor-managed inventory and its deployment in manufacturing and retail environment.

6. Describe the importance of quality management in improving the efficiency of supply chain operations with examples.

7. What is a green supply chain? Explain key drivers of green supply chain with examples.

8. 'Ethical supply chain management is a far cry and makes no business sense. A supply chain manager must focus on economics rather than feel good ethical values.' Do you agree or disagree? Elucidate with examples.

9. What do you understand by supply chain risk and security management? Explain various standards and institutions that facilitate supply chain security in global business.

CRITICAL THINKING QUESTIONS

1. Smart Electronics Home Products Ltd is trying to reduce inventory and wants you to install a kanban system for agitators in washing machines on one of its assembly lines. Determine the size of the kanban and the number of kanbans (containers) needed.

Set-up cost = Rs 10,000

Annual holding cost per washing machine = Rs 2,250

Daily production = 1,000 units

Annual usage = 225,000 (50 weeks × 5 days each × daily usage of 900 agitators)

Lead time = 3 days

Safety stock = ½ day's production

2. Currently a consumer products company sells its products by packing in cartons made of paperboards and straps made of metal strips. The cost of carton packing is Rs 100 and metal strip is about Rs 20. Their SCM manager who recently attended a conference on Green Supply Chain wanted to initiate a proposal to replace cartons with thick plastic foils, which would have rough finish for handling and stamping around, to do away with the need for metal straps. The material cost of plastic foil is about Rs 80, labour cost is Rs 15, and energy cost is about Rs 5 per pack. The total number of units packed in a year is roughly about 600,000 units. You may advise with a report on the advantages and disadvantages of this proposal.

3. 'JIT and VMI shift inventory cost from focal firm's cost sheet to vendors and complicate further the process of material delivery and handling. It also gives behavioural stress to vendors who may have to work among them and third-party service provider.' Elucidate.

4. 'Quality culture in Indian auto industry has enhanced supply chain operations' efficiency.' Elucidate with examples from auto majors—Tier I and tier II.

5. 'Ethical behaviour of firms in procurement and sourcing is driven by managerial values and beliefs and local country cultural values.' Discuss with examples.

PROJECT ASSIGNMENTS

1. Visit a nearby large engineering or automotive component plant where JIT is deployed and prepare a report on the effectiveness of the JIT system. Map supplier category covered under the same. Also probe whether kanban and VMI are deployed and how they achieve efficiency in supply chain operations.

2. Probe VMI application in retail industry and how it helps supply chain partners in delivering value to customers in your city.

3. Based on your analysis, prepare a report for quality initiatives supporting supply chain operations' efficiency in a business which you have studied closely.

4. Visit a large-scale manufacturing plant and map green initiatives deployed by them in logistical drivers such as facilities management, transportation, and inventory handling.

5. Prepare a report based on your discussions with the Head of Sourcing of a large manufacturing unit on challenges and opportunities in deploying ethical standards in procurement.

REFERENCES

Boks, C. and A. Stevels, 'Essential Perspectives for Design for Environment: Experiences from the Electronics Industry,' *International Journal of Production Research*, 45 (18–19), 2007, 4021-4039

Khiewnavawongsa, S. and E.K. Schmidt, 'Green' Power to the Supply Chain, http://www.tech.purdue.edu/it/GreenSupplyChainManagement.cfm

Kumar, Phani and Muthu Kumar, 'Vendor Managed Inventory in Retail Industry,' Tata Consultancy Services, February 2003

Kumar, V. Rishi, 'Just Get Lean and Mean,' Business Line, 17 January 2005, http://www.thehindubusinessline.com/bline/ew/2005/01/17/stories/2005011700180300.htm

Mahadevan, B., 'Are Indian Companies Ready for

Just-In-Time?,' *Management Review*, April–June, July–September, 1997, pp. 85–92

Millington, Andrew, 'Responsibility in the Supply Chain,' Andrew Crane, Abagail McWilliams, Dirk Matten, Jeremy Moon and Donald S. Siegel (eds), *The Oxford Handbook on Corporate Social Responsibility*, March 2008

Russell, Roberta and Bernard W. Taylor, *Operations Management: Quality and Competitiveness in Global Environment*, 5th edition, Wiley India Edition, 2005

Srivastava, S. K., 'Green Supply-Chain Management: A State-of-the-Art Literature Review,' *International Journal of Management Reviews*, 9 (1), 53–80, 2007

Stauffer, David, 'Supply Chain Risk: Deal With It;' http://hbswk.hbs.edu/cgi-bin/print?id=3442, 28 April 2003

Stevels, A., Green Supply Chain Management Much More Than Questionnaires and ISO 14.001 IEEE, 96–100, 2002

Womack, James, 'Best Time to Junk Old-fashioned Mass Production,' *The Economic Times*, 22 August 2008

http://business.outlookindia.com/inner.aspx?articleid=2783&editionid=76&catgid=12&subcatgid=1079

http://mastergroup.tradeindia.com/Exporters_Suppliers/Exporter12362.175758/SA8000-Certification.html

http://phx.corporate-ir.net/phoenix.zhtml?c=78265&p=irol-newsArticle&ID=1270013&highlight

www.ethicaltrade.org/about-eti

www.fairlabor.org/about_us_history_a1.html

www.hindu.com/2008/05/14/stories/2008051456181600.htm

www.iso14000-iso14001-environmental-management.com/iso14001.htm

www.isqnet.org/deming-prize/

www.unglobalcompact.org/AbouttheGC/TheTENPrinciples/index.html

Appendix 11.1   Leading Quality Award Winners in India

Deming Application Prize

Sundaram-Clayton Ltd, Brakes Division	1998
Sundaram Brake Linings Ltd	2001
TVS Motor Company Ltd	2002
Brakes India Ltd, Foundry Divison	2003
Mahindra and Mahindra Ltd, Farm Equipment Sector	2003
Rane Brake Linings Ltd	2003
Sona Koyo Steering Systems Ltd	2003
SRF Limited, Industrial Synthetics Business	2004
Lucas-TVS Limited	2004
Indo Gulf Fertilizer Limited	2004
Krishna Maruti Limited, Seat Divison	2005
Rane Engine Valves Ltd	2005
Rane TRW Steering Systems Ltd, Steering Gear Division	2005
TATA Steel Ltd	2008

Quality Control Award for Operations Business Units

Hi-Tech Carbon GMPD	2002
Birla Cellousic, Kharach: A unit of Grasim Industries Ltd	2003
Reliance Industries Ltd	2007

Japan Quality Medal

Sundaram-Clayton Ltd, Brakes Division	2002
Mahindra & Mahindra Ltd Farm Equipment sector	2007

Source: www.isqnet.org/deming-prize/.
*The List is Representative and Not Exhaustive.

Appendix 11.2	**International Institutions and Standards Facilitating Ethical Supply Chain Practices**

ISO 14001 Environmental Management: BS EN ISO 14001

ISO 14001 was first published in 1996 and specifies the actual requirements for an environmental management system. It applies to those environmental aspects over which the organization has control and can be expected to modify.

ISO 14001 is often seen as the cornerstone standard of the ISO 14000 series. This standard is applicable to any organization that wishes to:

- Implement, maintain, and improve an environmental management system
- Assure itself of its conformance with its own stated environmental policy (those policy commitments of course must be made)
- Demonstrate conformance
- Ensure compliance with environmental laws and regulations
- Seek certification of its environmental management system by an external third-party organization
- Make a self-determination of conformance

Source: http://www.iso14000-iso14001 enviromental-management.com/iso14001.htm

SA 8000

SA 8000 (Social Accountability 8000) is the first international certification on social responsibility. Its main objective is to guarantee workers' rights in such a way that everyone involved wins— companies, workers, trade unions, government.

SA 8000 standard was launched in 1997 by CEPAA (Council on Economics Priorities Accreditation Agency), an NGO, later renamed SAI (Social Accountability International). SA 8000 is the first global standard for corporate social responsibility. It is based on both international human rights conventions (International Labour Organization, the International Declaration of Human Rights, and the UN Convention on the Rights of the Child) and satisfying relevant local legislation. It aims to guarantee basic rights of workers involved in the production processes. SA 8000 Standard is composed of the following nine requirements:

1. Child labour is not permitted.
2. Forced labour is not permitted
3. Health and safety have to be assured
4. Freedom to organize and collective bargaining have to be guaranteed
5. Discrimination is not permitted
6. Disciplinary practices are not permitted
7. Working hours shall not exceed 48 hours a week, with a maximum of 12 hours overtime
8. Remuneration shall be sufficient
9. Management systems shall guarantee that the requirements are effectively satisfied

SA 8000 certification follows the structures of both the Quality Management Standards ISO 9000 and the Environment Management Standard ISO 14000, and emphasizes the importance of an ongoing improvement process. Development and ongoing oversight of the standard is addressed by a multi-sector Advisory Board with experts from business, trade unions, government, and NGOs from around the world and across industries. Facilities seeking certification of compliance to the standard must have robust management systems in place and undergo an audit by an independent, accredited certification body. SAI and its Advisory Board oversee the accreditation of certification bodies, which are required to demonstrate extensive background in systems auditing, intensive training in SA 8000, and the institutional capacity to assure quality and responsiveness. There are currently nine accredited certification bodies that have certified facilities in thirty countries. SAI regularly consults with international experts on ways to strengthen certification audits and the SA 8000 guidance documents.

The highlights include:

- Companies seeking to independently verify their own social record and that of their contractors
- Contractors that produce goods for US and European companies and wish to demonstrate to companies and consumers that they are treating workers fairly.
- Development or multilateral organizations seeking to ensure that they procure from companies that are not exploitative.

There are two options for companies to implement SA 8000:

1. **Certification to SA 8000:** Companies that operate production facilities can seek to have individual facilities certified to SA 8000 through audits by one of the accredited certification bodies. Since the SA 8000 system became fully operational in 1998, there are certified facilities in thirty countries on five continents and across twenty-two industries.

2. **Involvement in the Corporate Involvement Programme (CIP):** Companies that focus on selling goods or that combine production and selling can join the SA 8000 Corporate Involvement Programme (CIP). The CIP is a two-level programme that helps companies evaluate SA 8000, implement the standard, and report publicly on implementation progress. The features of the two levels of CIP are:

1. **SA 8000 Explorer (CIP Level One):** Evaluate SA 8000 as an ethical sourcing tool via pilot audits

2. **SA 8000 Signatory (CIP Level Two):**
   - Implement SA 8000 over time in some or all of the supply chain through certification
   - Communicate implementation progress to stakeholders via SAI-verified public reporting

Source: http://mastergroup.tradeindia.com/ Exporters_Suppliers/Exporter12362.175758/ SA8000-Certification.html.

ETHICAL TRADE INITIATIVE

Ethical trade means that retailers, brands, and their suppliers take responsibility for improving the working conditions of the people who make the products they sell. Most of these workers are employed by supplier companies around the world, many of them based in poor countries where laws designed to protect workers' rights are inadequate or not enforced.

Companies with a commitment to ethical trade adopt a code of labour practice that they expect all their suppliers to work towards. Such codes address issues such as wages, hours of work, health and safety, and the right to join free trade unions.

Why is ETI Needed?

'Doing' ethical trade is much harder than it sounds. Modern supply chains are vast, complex, and span the globe. Labour issues are themselves challenging. For example, what exactly is 'a living wage'? What should a company do if it finds children working in a supplier's worksite? Evicting children from the workplace can, paradoxically, make their lives worse.

Ethical Trade Initiative (ETI) brings corporate, trade union, and voluntary sector members together in a unique alliance that enables them to collectively tackle many thorny issues that cannot be addressed by individual companies working alone.

The ETI is a ground-breaking alliance of companies, trade unions, and voluntary organizations. They work in partnership to improve the lives of workers across the globe that make or grow consumer goods—everything from tea to T-shirts, from flowers to footballs.

Source: http://www.ethicaltrade.org/about-eti.

INTERNATIONAL LABOUR ORGANIZATION

The International Labour Organization (ILO) was created in 1919 by Part XIII of the Versailles Peace Treaty ending World War I. It grew out of nine teenth-century labour and social movements that culminated in widespread demands for social justice and higher living standards for the world's working people. In 1946, after the demise of the League of Nations, the ILO became the first specialized agency associated with the United Nations. The original membership of forty-five countries in 1919 has grown to 121 in 1971.

In structure, the ILO is unique among world organizations in that the representatives of the workers and of the employers have an equal voice with those of governments in formulating its policies. The annual International Labour Conference, the ILO's supreme deliberative body, is composed of four representatives from each member country— two government delegates, one worker, and one employer delegate, each of whom may speak and vote independently. Between conferences, the work of the ILO is guided by the governing body, comprising twenty-four governments, twelve workers, and twelve employer members, plus twelve deputy members from each of these three groups. The International Labour Office in Geneva, Switzerland, is the organization's secretariat, operational headquarters, research centre, and publishing house. Its operations are staffed at headquarters and around the world by more than 3,000 people of some 100 nationalities. The activities are decentralized to regional, area, and branch offices in over forty countries.

The ILO has three major tasks, the first of which is the adoption of international labour standards, called Conventions and Recommendations, for implementation by member states. The Conventions and Recommendations contain guidelines on child labour, protection of women workers, hours of work, rest and holidays with pay, labour inspection, vocational guidance, and training, social security protection, workers' housing, occupational health and safety, conditions of work at sea, and protection of migrant workers.

They also cover questions of basic human rights, among them, freedom of association, collective bargaining, the abolition of forced labour, the elimination of discrimination in employment, and the promotion of full employment. By 1970, 134 Conventions and 142 Recommendations had been adopted by the ILO. Each of them is a stimulus, as well as a model, for national legislation and for practical application in member countries.

A second major task, which has steadily expanded for the past two decades, is that of technical cooperation to assist developing nations. More than half of ILO's resources are devoted to technical cooperation programmes, carried out in close association with the United Nations Development Programme and often with other UN-specialized agencies. These activities are concentrated in four major areas: development of human resources, thorough vocational training and management development; employment planning and promotion; the development of social institutions in such fields as labour administration, labour relations, cooperatives, and rural development; conditions of work and life—for example, occupational safety and health, social security, remuneration, hours of work, welfare, etc.

Marking the beginning of its second half-century, the ILO has launched the World Employment Programme, designed to help countries provide employment and training opportunities for their swelling populations. The World Employment Programme will be the ILO's main contribution to the United Nations Second Development Decade.

Third, standard-setting and technical cooperation are bolstered by an extensive research, training, education, and publications programme. The ILO is a major source of publications and documentation on labour and social matters. It has established two specialized educational institutions: the International Institute for Labour Studies in Geneva, and the International Centre for Advanced Technical and Vocational Training in Turin, Italy.

FAIR LABOUR ASSOCIATION (FLA)

History

Today's agreement on fighting sweatshop practices is an historic step toward reducing sweatshop labour around the world and will give American consumers confidence that the clothes they buy are made under decent and humane working conditions.

–President Bill Clinton
3 November 1998

With these words, President Clinton recognized the extraordinary commitment and efforts of the Apparel Industry Partnership (AIP), a unique new coalition of apparel and footwear companies, human rights, labour rights, and consumer advocates, which had been working for more than two years to draft a common Code of Conduct and Principles of Monitoring. On 3 November 1998, the AIP presented its agreement on the Code of Conduct and the Principles of Monitoring to the President, and the Fair Labor Association (FLA) was formed. In short order, the coalition would add colleges and universities to its roster and formally commence its historic mission to end sweatshop labour and improve working conditions worldwide.

Few who had gathered at the White House in 1996 for a meeting convened by President Clinton would have thought so much could be accomplished in such a short span of time. At that meeting, the President challenged leading apparel and footwear companies and representatives of labour, consumer, religious, and human rights groups to take steps to improve working conditions around the world and to provide the public with information it could use to make informed purchasing decisions. The AIP took up the challenge and helped to create an organization that required affiliated companies to abide by a code of conduct and monitoring requirements, established an accreditation programme to determine whether company obligations were met, and instituted a public reporting mechanism to inform consumers about company participation and compliance.

Out of those beginnings, the FLA was born. Officially incorporated in May 1999, the non-profit organization is a collaboration of companies, civil society organizations, and colleges and universities. It monitors factories in the supply chains of affiliated companies to assess compliance with FLA standards and requirements. In this process, special attention is given to whether affiliates have put policies and procedures in place to detect and correct instances of non-compliance. The FLA reports the results of individual independent external monitoring audits and issues annual reports as part of its commitment to transparency.

As the FLA has matured, it has continued to strengthen its structure, broaden its oversight, and increase its reach. Today, there is equal representation of its three constituencies on FLA's policy-making Board of Directors, increased accountability for affiliate companies and licensees, and oversight of product areas that reach beyond the apparel and footwear industries. As it enters its second decade, the FLA is working to fulfil its mission in more innovative and comprehensive ways, putting even greater emphasis on sustainable compliance—identifying the root causes of non-compliance and creating approaches that address those root causes—and on collaboration among companies and with local civil society organizations, to increase the likelihood that compliance efforts will be effective and sustained over the long term.

Source: http://www.fairlabor.org/about_us_history_a1.html.

UN GLOBAL COMPACT

The Ten Principles

The UN Global Compact's ten principles in the areas of human rights, labour, the environment and anti-corruption enjoy universal consensus and are derived from:

- The Universal Declaration of Human Rights
- The International Labour Organization's Declaration on Fundamental Principles and Rights at Work
- The Rio Declaration on Environment and Development
- The United Nations Convention Against Corruption

The Global Compact asks companies to embrace, support and enact, within their sphere of influence, a set of core values in the areas of human rights, labour standards, the environment, and anti-corruption.

Human Rights

- **Principle 1:** Businesses should support and respect the protection of internationally proclaimed human rights; and
- **Principle 2:** Make sure that they are not complicit in human rights abuses.

Labour Standards

- **Principle 3:** Businesses should uphold the freedom of association and the effective recognition of the right to collective bargaining;
- **Principle 4:** The elimination of all forms of forced and compulsory labour;
- **Principle 5:** The effective abolition of child labour; and
- **Principle 6:** The elimination of discrimination in respect of employment and occupation.

Environment

- **Principle 7:** Businesses should support a precautionary approach to environmental challenges;
- **Principle 8:** Undertake initiatives to promote greater environmental responsibility; and
- **Principle 9:** Encourage the development and diffusion of environmentally friendly technologies.

Anti-Corruption

- **Principle 10:** Businesses should work against corruption in all its forms, including extortion and bribery.

Source: http://www.unglobalcompact.org/AbouttheGC/TheTENPrinciples/index.html.

12

Managing Obstacles and Enabling Coordination in Supply Chain

Learning Objectives

After studying this chapter, you will be able to:

♦ Understand the importance of financial flows and how it is to be managed with basic parameters being explained

♦ Describe supply chain coordination, the Bullwhip Effect, and their impact on performance

♦ Identify causes of the obstacles in coordination in a supply chain

♦ Discuss approach to improve coordination

Supply chain coordination happens only when physical flow, information flow, and financial flow are synchronized. One would have observed that supply chain operations adequately power physical flow management—from receiving of order to supply of goods and services to a customer. This integrates order management with distribution manufacturing and procurement functions. Information flow is critical as order capture needs to be transmitted to upward linkages for effective manufacturing and on-time delivery. The different aspects of information flow are discussed in Chapters 15 and 16 wherein tools and techniques are illustrated.

12.1 FINANCIAL FLOW MANAGEMENT

Financial flow management is the third important aspect in enabling coordination and supply chain. Though obstacles in supply chain occur due to disruptions in the three flows mentioned above, it is important to understand some of the critical aspects of financial flow. This is explained with the example of an export supply chain—from manufacture to the delivery of garments—from Tirupur. Typically, banks fund export units against order and inventory. A normal operating cycle is about 90–120 days and inventory turnover would be three to four times a year. On the receipt of an order, a company estimates the production schedule and prepares cash flow requirements. It is commonly found that 50 per cent of the total order value may be required to start with—for buying of material and booking capacity wherever required through one's outsourcing partners. The promoter is expected to bring 25 per cent of the value of the order/inventory and the balance 75 per cent is funded by the banker. The order processing thus starts with own funds and funds released by the bank. On the completion of the order and on the receipt of Letter of Credit (LC), the company despatches goods. Depending on the type and nature of the LC and acknowledgement by the buyer or buyer bank, the focal firm's banker releases the balance money.

It is observed that sundry debtors go up to 120 days in this export business. Export Credit Guarantee Corporation (ECGC) advises the company and the banker about the creditworthiness of the buyer based on its information on defaulters and intelligence. There have been, however, cases when the company assumes greater risk and takes more contracts. Such companies get into financial trouble within a few deals, which again dwindles their ability to fund other orders. For smooth realization of funds against an order, it is important that all items and volume are delivered as per the order. More importantly, quality must be as per the agreed terms. These factors are critical for streamlined financial operation.

Banks have got certain procedures and practices set over the years in order to facilitate the growth of the export business. One of the key processes is KYC (Know Your Customer) norms. As per their norms, banks verify the registration of the company, the quality of its auditors, accounting practices, and composition of board of directors in case of companies. State Bank of India, a leading public sector bank, enjoys nearly 27 per cent of market share in the export cluster. They have a competitive advantage in helping their customers through their network of overseas branches. This becomes very important whenever a buyer defaults and a recourse is required to recover the value of supplies. Moreover, forewarning signals are possible if a bank has a network of branches across countries. A bank also does regular stock audits and management evaluation while funding a business. There is a separate credit risk appraisal process which starts with self appraisal by the applicant, followed by industry and business risk, management risk, and environmental risk evaluation at regular intervals to ensure quality of funds deployed. This helps the company to have a detailed risk appraisal and work on a combat strategy.

In the small export economy the pressure on the financial system is high. There are sixty-two branches of forty-six banks operating in this economy, and State Bank alone has seven branches with a market share of 27 per cent. Normally the ownerships of these businesses range from proprietary, partnership, and companies both private and public limited. The distribution of manufacturing units is as follows:

Knitting of fabrics	1,500
Bleaching, dyeing, and printing	1,200
Compacting	300
Embroidery	250
Garments	2,500
Other ancillaries	500
Total	**6,250**

The value of total export is about Rs 10,000 crore.

The importance of financial flow can be understood from the above distribution of manufacturing processes that are vertically and backwardly dependent on the order and the garment manufacturing firm. Any obstacle arising in financial transfer will lead to jeopardizing the supply network. If an order is rejected for quality, it is not just the vendor who gets hurt but those who are part of the supply chain indirectly are also hurt. It is important that the financial credibility of buyers and the partnering organization in the supply network be understood and shared for a healthy operation. To some extent, ECGC and the bank facilitate this information sharing. Manufacturers have their own network and share such information among their own community. Tirupur Exporters Association plays a key role in information sharing. However, despite such information bridges, financial performance failure by the buyer or by the banker is common in this business.

So the key learning for managing financial flows is that, for processing of an order, units in downward stream require release of funds and final honour of invoice after delivery. Whenever the system fails to capture such sensitive information or there is siphoning of money for personal needs, financial obstacles prop up. This is true for any business. It may be clear that the integration of financial flow with information flow and physical flow is critical. Unless the information system captures product movement and confirms the same to the funder, fund releases cannot be done on time. A financial flow cycle is shown in Figure 12.1.

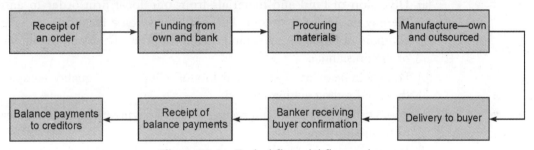

Figure 12.1 Typical financial flow cycle

12.1.1 Problems in Financial Flow Synchronization

1. Financial bankruptcy or failure of the customer organization and supplies not being paid for. The company in such cases goes for recovery mechanism, which is arduous and time consuming.

2. Sudden change or reduction in the order size, and the customer getting away with marginal penalty and the manufacturing unit being saddled with huge inventory involving costs and poor realization.

3. Quality variance observed at customer end and lot rejection. Though it is a physical flow management issue, it has got a serious impact on financial flow management as the goods are rejected and not paid for, the customer needs to reverse logistic operation and liquidate stock at huge discounts. Thus cash flow and credibility are affected and future funding becomes difficult.

4. From the manufacturing end, financial obstacles may happen if:
   (a) Financial solvency of the firm is affected by poor management of funding and diversion of funds from operations to capital account or any personal account.

    (b) Overexposure to risk and aggressive order booking without adequate cover. There have been times when a focal firm booked the order on trust and faith, which are at times misplaced, and got into a financial mess.

    (c) Overexposure to purchase of material and booking of capacity of outsourced partners not matching to orders, thereby outflow of cash leading to financial imbalance.

    (d) Over inventory policy, leading to blockage of funds

    (e) Poor fund management and improper funding sources, leading to high cost of funds under loss of financial balance.

    (f) Poor checks and controls for receivables and payables management and thereby lack of trust among partners, leading to strain on physical and financial flows.

    (g) Inability to provide documentation for banks to fund on time and thereby getting into financial stress.

5. Financial flow obstacles could arise at the supplier end, jeopardizing the supply network, if there is:

    (a) Diversion of fund and materials from one focal firm order to another, thereby choking the system. This happens when a focal firm order in the component grouping schedule gets into disarray. This could be intentional or circumstantial.

    (b) Poor management of stock and loss of value due to quality erosion, and thereby funding getting choked.

    (c) Poor cost management and receivables and payment management, leading to financial strain.

    (d) Improper source of funding and use of private funding sources at high cost, leading to loss of economics of operation and thereby stretching financial deployment.

    (e) Misappropriation of funds for temporary use to cover up certain violation or personal needs, and thereby getting into financial stress.

    (f) Inability to provide documentation for banks to fund on time and thereby getting into financial stress.

One of the financial aspects that influence operating decisions and thereby could prop up as an obstacle is the fiscal factor, comprising taxes, duties, and direct controls. Document handling is one of the elements of fiscal requirements wherein for purposes of clearance and movement of goods documents must be properly presented and validated. There are third-party service providers who enable this function. Secondly, duties, especially of sales tax, in India are different for movement within states and outside states. To take advantage of sales tax, earlier companies used to locate warehouses in major states where demand was substantial. This could come up as an obstacle, especially due to obsolescence of inventory and behavioural factors of warehouse operators and so on. With the implementation of General Sales Tax, which may lead to a uniform sales tax structure across the country, this might change.

Another important element of the fiscal aspect is direct physical checking at fiscal borders, which leads to delays. Implementation of technology solutions such as whole truck scanning, and so on, might improve this.

12.1.2 Role of Technology in Financial Flows

Technology plays an important role in managing financial flows as the implementation of ERP provides visibility across departments and allows the partnering organization to monitor critical financial choking points and escalate across decision hierarchy to streamline the flow. Creditors and debtors no longer need to do excessive follow up as ERP enables a smooth flow of financial resources and physical goods.

The level of openness and transparency with which an organization operates determines its information and financial flow efficiency. For example, when a vendor completes an order delivery, the vendor becomes eligible for payment on the twenty-first day of delivering the goods against the 'goods received' note raised at the time of supply. A trigger is automatically generated for cash flow planning and any gap is highlighted so that the concerned parties can plan accordingly to adjust financials links for making the supply network still effective. However, one comes across a number of cases that in real life where such synchronization does not take place. Now this baffles an analyst as to how and why process and technology fail to streamline the financial flow.

Let us take the case of a consultant delivering a knowledge input for redesigning a supply chain network for a large corporate and raising an invoice for payment as per the agreed terms. ERP would start the trigger based on whether it is a planned or non-planned expenditure. If it is a non-planned expenditure, it will need to be authorized to trigger the initialization of the payment process. What would be normally paid in three weeks' time will take months if authorization fails to happen! In supply chain financial flow, mismanagement happens mainly because of aberration in practice compared to what is defined in the system, which is rigid. People who are in decision making must regularly participate in process and technology refinement and also authorize variations for synchronization management.

ERP must be linked to backward and forward linkages and partners in the system. The system must be transparent and provide access to partners to check their status using Internet technologies for their relevant portion. Any aberration in schedule must be openly discussed among partners instead of taking recourse to activities that may lead to break up or strain of the network relationship. It is common that a focal firm has some cash flow crunch and request the buyer for early payment. Such intervention and rescheduling cannot be captured by technology. It can only be shared orally, through a trust-based relationship, rather than through a technology process. Hence, supply chain financial flows must be sensitive of such occurrences and take cognizance of long-term supply chain goals of establishing shared normal profits.

Appendix 12.1 gives a typical financial analysis reckoner that supply chain partners may use for monitoring the financial performance of network partners.

12.2   BULLWHIP EFFECT IN SUPPLY CHAIN

The Bullwhip Effect is now a well-documented and researched anomaly of distribution channel communication, which is either based on lack of trust or habituated padding of forecasts to beat rationing, and so on. Forrester, in his work on industrial organization and competition (1961), studied about the dynamics of competitive forces impacting variability in the system. This was the genius who did further studies on the Bullwhip Effect. Hence this is also known as the Forrester Effect. This is called Bullwhip Effect because a small variation on one end, which is controlled, shows up a large variation on the other end because of a spiralling effect resembling a bullwhip. It is also called as Whiplash Effect or Whipsaw Effect.

Bullwhip Effect, in a study by Proctor & Gamble (P&G) established that wherein babies used diapers at a steady rate, the demand order variability in the supply chain were amplified as they move up the supply chain. Similarly, Hewlett-Packard (HP) observed that though the sales of one of its printers had a variation, orders from resellers and printer division to the company's integrated circuit division had even greater fluctuations reflecting Bullwhip Effect (Lee et al. 1997, and Chopra et al. 2007). Typically, Bullwhip Effect works in downstream where a small variation at the customer end leads to a wide variation at manufacturing as shown in Figure 12.2.

Bullwhip Effect is due to distorted information from one to other, leading to inefficiencies. Inefficiencies may erupt as excessive inventory, blocking of investments, lost sales for lack of synchronization, misguided capacity plans, poor scheduling, and dissatisfaction among customers. Such inefficiencies also lead to poor cost management, thereby causing erosion in profits and dissatisfaction among partners in the network.

Assume that the summer demand for fruit juices by the customer goes up by 7 per cent. Retailers assume that it is likely to rise by 10 per cent, and hence, to avoid short supplies, they transmit orders at 12 per cent increase. Dealers/agents for the region assume it is likely to touch 15 per cent and may go up to 20 per cent. The brand owner assumes that 20 per cent would not be truly reflective and provides for 25 per cent increase in production. Thus, there is 18 per cent higher production compared to release and stocks pile up at each level based on releases, leading to inefficiencies. By the time estimates are corrected, the season is over. Many a time the brand owner comes back with stock liquidation and every player in the network is forced to book a loss for inefficiencies, which is the cost of Bullwhip Effect.

According to Lee et al (1997), four major causes of Bullwhip Effect are: demand forecast updating, order batching, price fluctuation, and rationing and shortening. Each of these individually or jointly may lead to Bullwhip Effect. One would also wonder how such variations could happen if information technology and process improvements are enabled throughout the network. This is where the fifth factor, namely behavioural factor, as choice of an action of a player in the network would be more induced by his/her own appreciation of the situation, risk perception, and the ability to position in the network.

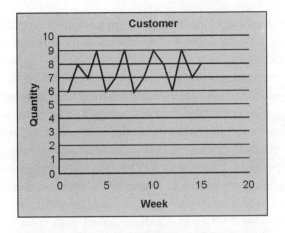
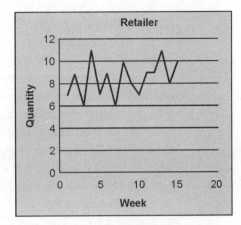
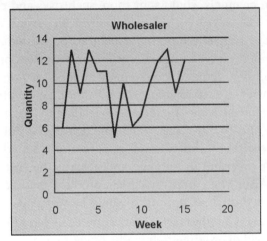
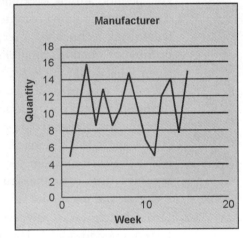

Figure 12.2 Bullwhip effect across channel

1. **Demand forecasting:** People see a shortage and intuitively they forecast higher. Salespeople don't want to be caught without supply, so they make sure they have supply by forecasting more sales than they expect. Procurement needs 100 pieces of a part, but they know if they ask for 100, they'll get 80. So they ask for 120 to get 100. Demand forecasting is an art and a science. Reports from sales personnel and inventory managers, based on anything from partners' data to opinions are gathered along with actual sales data and historical trends and put into systems that use statistical algorithms to generate numbers. But there's no way for all the supply chain software to know from actual, perceived, and jacked up figures in anticipation of rationing for arriving at a validated forecast.

Further, there is a tendency to err for more rather than for shortage. So they forecast a high demand. A high demand forecast leads to excess inventory. In the third fiscal quarter of 2001, CISCO experienced a sales drop of 30 per cent and wrote off a $2.2 billion high mountain of inventory and 8,500 people were laid off (Berinato 2001). Thus, Bullwhip Effect stems from customer demand forecast being stepped at every level, leading to wider variations and loss of efficiency in the supply network.

Demand forecast updating is explained above. The question would be how one could handle the same. Typically, this can be handled by transparent systems and sharing of information. One will have to see how it would work under different markets and competitive conditions. For example, in the FMCG business where there are multiple channel operators, it is difficult to precisely estimate demand forecasts of every player. The system will have to tolerate or average out inconsistencies so that the aberration is limited to a small variance. Apart from intentions, skill and ability to deploy tools are limited at this level and hence a focal firm manufacturing FMCG goods must expect such volatility. Competition among distribution channels would spur more such risks and demand errors could be common. The ways by which a focal firm can cover it up is by using technology to capture near real-time movement at the secondary distribution channel, multiple sources forecasting, interacting on estimates, and so on. This would mean a high cost of demand forecasting with increased time, effort, and cost involvement. However, such an approach is better than creating inefficiencies and paying a price for the same. Inefficiencies leading to cost and poor responsiveness would also hurt brand value, which is expensive to build. Hence appropriate demand forecasting techniques are important. In a market where the customer can pay for precision in estimate and absorbs the cost, it becomes easier to do the same. Also, when there are certain products that are of high cost and cannot be stock piled, such an approach would be welcome.

2. **Order batching:** Order batching is another factor that causes Bullwhip Effect. It is common to stock items. Instead of ordering frequently, buyer may order bi-weekly, monthly, or any other longer time bucket. This may be practised to reduce time, effort, and cost of ordering. Such ordering process leads to wrong perceptions among suppliers, leading to improper coordination. Also, orders may get bunched and again production inefficiencies happen as there is peak and trough instead of steady state of quantities for manufacturing. Another common reason for order batching is for exploiting transportation economies, especially which may arise due to full truck load despatches. This leads to moderate high order cycle times, leading to obstacles in the system. This is again common in case of FMCG, consumer products group, and replacement markets of spares and components across industries, and so on.

3. **Price fluctuation:** Price fluctuations as a factor leads to obstacles. There are certain products that are close to being commodities that face such severe problems. These include seasonal products that are based on natural factors. Grocery items such as grains, spices, beverages, sugar, and edible oils have clear seasons. Market arrivals are high during production/harvest times whereas demand need not materialize during the same period. Production points and focal firms will have to off-load produce during season. They sell lesser quantities

during off season. In order to increase off take, focal firms provide discounts on volume of goods bought during the peak arrival time. Thus, pricing obstacles arise when the pricing policies for a product lead to an increase in variability of orders placed as buyers are not sure of quantity that would be available during a time window.

Price obstacles could arise because of lot-based discounts. Lot of size-based quantity discounts increase the lot size of orders placed within the supply chain. For example, if a dealer places twenty-four units of an item in a category, his or her price is Rs 100 per unit whereas if the order is of thirty-two units, the price would be Rs 98, and if 36 units, it would be Rs 95. Such lot-based pricing leads to aggregation of orders. The buyer brings a skew in the ordering pattern and it lacks a definite pattern when this is coupled with promotions and seasonal variability, which is inherent in product characteristics. Such instances lead to obstacles with failure of forecasts and inability to adjust to variations. Here, this is lead by lot quantity discount pricing factor.

Another aspect of pricing obstacles is triggered by trade promotions and other short-term discounts offered by a manufacturer. This results in forward buying. Typically, a wholesaler or retailer purchases large lots during the discount period to cover demand during future periods. Forward buying results in large orders during the promotion period followed by very small orders later on. For example, three retailers can choose to behave in different patterns assuming that there should be a minimum lot of twenty-four units and all demand must be met. If one relaxes this further, one may observe many more combinations of ordering pattern arising. As it can be seen, Table 12.1 shows a uniform ordering and pricing factor and steady state demand. Table 12.2 shows the tendency to exploit the maximum out of lot-based discounts and achieves least-price realization at Rs 97 per unit. However, there is a carrying cost and risk associated with the same. Table 12.3 shows a mid-path behaviour and price realized is also Rs 98.13, higher than scenario 1 and 2. In scenarios 2 and 3, one may observe forward buying distorting the demand pattern. This illustration is too much simplification of real life wherein many traders and retailers interact and group behaviour is dynamic and fluid without facilitating easily a scientific analysis for forecasting managers with manufacturing units. This is where, more than often, errors happen, leading to distortions. After a while, instead of managing forecast, the effort goes for managing distortions, which is a less-desired situation in supply chain management.

The above illustration is a regular promotion feature. There are situations of seasonal promotions and the impact would be that the shipments during the peak period are higher than the sales during the peak period because of a promotion offered. The peak shipment period is followed by a period of very low shipments from the manufacturer, indicating significant forward buying by distributors. The promotion thus results in a variability in manufacturer shipments that is significantly higher than the variability in retailer sales.

4. **Incentives:** Incentives may also cause obstacles. In our system, incentives work in supply chain network operations at different levels. This becomes especially true if partner firms are operating and pricing/distribution cost structure is based on incentives. For example, Exhibit 12.1 reflects one such incentive structure in the services supply chain.

If one looks at the case below, individual profits and constraints drive supply chain performance, especially in case of services like this one, and it is perishable because it is time-based. Such situations arise in manufacturing as well when a demand is seasonal and incentives must be used to achieve maximum profits during the period. What is important here is how such situations truly

Table 12.1   Uniform order pattern—scenario 1

Time	Quantity demand	Ordered quantity	Price per unit	Value (Rs)
1	24	24	100	2,400
2	24	24	100	2,400
3	24	24	100	2,400
4	24	24	100	2,400
5	24	24	100	2,400
	120	120		12,000
	Price per unit			100

Table 12.2   Lot-based pricing—scenario 2

Time	Quantity demand	Ordered quantity	Price per unit	Value Rs
1	24	36	95	3,420
2	24	24	100	2,400
3	24	36	95	3,420
4	24	24	100	2,400
5	24	0	100	0
	120	120		11,640
	Price per unit			97

Table 12.3   Lot-based pricing—scenario 3

Time	Quantity demand	Ordered quantity	Price per unit	Value Rs
1	24	32	98	3,136
2	24	24	100	2,400
3	24	32	95	3,040
4	24	32	100	3,200
5	24	0	100	0
	120	120		11,776
	Price per unit			98.13

Exhibit 12.1 Supply Chain Challenges in Clinical Services Management

Madras Diabetic Management Centre (MDMC) is a leading 50 years plus clinical brand in Chennai that is currently operated by second generation promoters in serving the community to manage increasing incidence of diabetes in the city. Though the chief physician and promoter has a huge brand value in running the clinic, he takes on board doctors who are attached to the clinic and serve on time windows as service expands.

Typically, a diabetic patient who arrives at the clinic for a master health check up at 7.00 a.m. goes through a number of tests based on the health quotient, which would include haematology, cardiac, liver function, eye, wound management, foot management, dental, abdominal functions, and so on. Though a diabetic management clinic must have such specialization, the scheduling of services is based on patients' arrival. All patients cannot be scheduled serially and at the same time demand would not be uniform. At 8.30 a.m., the front office freezes the schedule for expert services and informs doctors on call to extend the same. These doctors on call assess at a lot size for them on a day in a clinic and call from a number of clinics to decide on the time window. If it is a peak demand day like Saturday or a day on which the chief doctor visits, the demand for service is high and the system would get disrupted. Similarly, on days of low demand, specialists would not make a visit leading to disruption. Patients who are blissfully unaware of supply chain issues get irritated and choke the system. It becomes quite a challenge because of the need to work on partner service model and varying volume and the inability to predict and commit level of service. Doctors on call are driven by incentives to serve a clinic on a particular day based on the number of patients to be served by them in different locations and travel time. Patients are also drawn by fee-based incentives as clubbing demand for services gives economy in test and monitoring costs. Thus one comes across such scheduling services problem in services supply chain which is quite common but for which a solution is evasive.

---

intend to maximize supply chain profits instead of one silo. For example, if the compensation of a transportation manager at a firm is linked to the average transportation cost per unit, the manager is likely to take actions that lower transportation costs even if they increase inventory costs or hurt customer service. It is natural for any participant in the supply chain to take actions that optimize performance measures along which they are evaluated. This becomes one of the key obstacles in supply chain.

Another significant incentive-based obstacle is sales force incentive. An improperly structured and managed sales force incentive can lead to clubbing and falsification of orders, which creates obstacles in the system. In many firms, sales force incentives are based on the amount the sales force sells during a time window, which could be a week, a fortnight, or a month. The sales are measured as order booked in and quantity sold to distributors or retailers (sell-in). Measuring performance based on sell-in is often justified on the grounds that the manufacturer's sales force does not control performance to deliver, which is a function of the manufacturing and service departments. Unfortunately, sales forces push sales and sometimes even falsify the selling process where sales are booked at the end of a period and despatch is committed to the next period. This hurts manufacturing and service as they carry sizable back orders and face the risk of order cancellations. Such practice also leads to unevenness in the ordering pattern, which brings high variability.

Figure 12.3 shows a sales skew as 10:28:62 within the month wherein maximum sales happen towards the end of the month. This was for a successful brand when integration of supply chain activities was not fully complete. During the same time, its monthly sales pattern was also skewed as shown in Figure 12.4. It was a challenge how this company achieved coordination and is now able to synchronize the supply chain function. It is important here to note that sales force and system has a tendency to aggregate orders towards the end of a month, which is common in distribution-intense businesses such as FMCG, consumer products group like electronics, mobile phones, white goods, and in industries like pharmaceuticals and commodities.

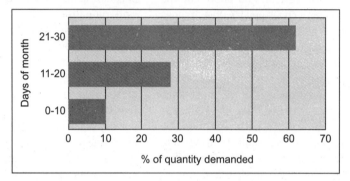

Figure 12.3   Ordering pattern for a leading FMCG brand in India

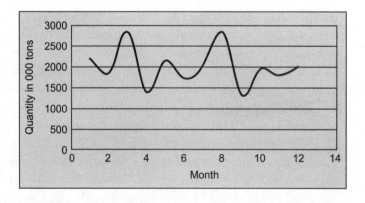

Figure 12.4   Monthly sales of a leading FMCG brand in India

Incentives based on volume movement from primary distribution channel or supply network lead to falsification of demand. Goods are moved and there could be excess stock built down the channel. This could be because of incentives or fear of short supply and rationing, leading to excess demand allocation. When demand is severe , the intermediary involves in push strategy to move goods down the channel. Here, you may note information asymmetry as there is no visibility and tracking.

In a later section, approaches to manage these obstacles are discussed.

5. **Information asymmetry:** Information-processing obstacles occur in situations when demand and service information is distorted as it moves between different stages of the supply chain, leading to increased variability in orders and delivery function within the supply chain. Exhibit 12.2 illustrates such information asymmetry in real life affecting supply chain effectiveness and efficiency.

This is common in supply chain structuring, especially when it links up with multiple partners and a service component is involved. The ability to link databases and coordinate for delivery is what is critical. Information obstacles are critical in supply chain functions such as airline or financial services, where if one in thousand customers is negatively impacted, it leads to long-term negative publicity.

Another reason for information-led obstacles is when forecasting is based on orders and not actual demand, especially in situations where order to demand is not a full or near-full conversion. When stages within a supply chain make forecasts that are based on orders they receive, any variability in customer demand is magnified as orders move up the supply chain to manufacturers and suppliers, which is what is demonstrated by the Bullwhip Effect. Each stage views its primary role within the supply chain as one of filling orders placed by its downstream partner and looks at its operation in silo. In the system, the manufacturing firm, which is the focal firm here, views its demand as the stream of orders received and produces a forecast based on this information. As information is distorted, inaccuracies of the Bullwhip Effect come into play.

The lack of information sharing between stages of the supply chain magnifies the Bullwhip Effect. For example, the lack of information sharing between the

---

Exhibit 12.2 Information Asymmetry in Manufacturing Leading to Inefficiency

A leading automotive company in business of tier I manufacture (ABCL) is a supplier to a car manufacturer in Chennai on JIT basis. The car manufacturer has a production plan and schedule, based on its marketing team's input. Marketing team generally forecasts a steady rate uniform demand and the production schedule is drawn accordingly. As the month progresses, marketing would realize that demand variations are happening and would change demand estimates, leaving a constraint with manufacturing to be flexible.

Manufacturing, through its sourcing team, coordinates with tier I vendors including ABCL on a close time window. ABCL supplies through a 3PL service that runs a milk run for every shift for a few vendors including ABCL. ABCL receives through e-mail notifications the change in supplies and in turn informs 3PL, who is in turn expected to coordinate with the transport service. Information flow is not looped up to that point where distortions impact performance. The transport operator makes empty runs or has more loaded capacity which imbalances the system. When the contract is based on standard rates, deviations become difficult to handle.

Information asymmetry happens because of frequent change in schedule and inability to link up till last mile for delivery. The result is inefficient trips, increase in costs, conflicts in managing contracts, and dissatisfaction among network partners.

retailer, stockist, and manufacturer leads to a large fluctuation in the manufacturer's orders.

12.3 BEHAVIOURAL OBSTACLES

Behavioural obstacles are those activities, deeds, and conduct of actions or responses to actions or in anticipation of actions in a supply chain network, which cause disruptions in the network.

These problems are related to the way the supply chain is structured, the communications between different stages and players' attitude and approach. Some of the behavioural obstacles are as follows:

1. Each stage of the supply chain views its actions locally and is unable to see the impact of its actions on other stages. This is seen in an earlier illustration of diabetic clinic management where doctors on call are more concerned about their own revenue rather than servicing the patients at the clinic on time.

2. Different stages of the supply chain react to the current local situations rather than trying to identify the root causes. This is quite common as supply chain operations take priority over long-term perspective and until the supply chain network gets choked or the supply chain manager of the focal firm initiates a global network perspective, it would not surface automatically.

3. Based on local analysis, different stages of the supply chain blame each other for the fluctuations, with successive stages in the supply chain becoming enemies rather than partners. This is explained with an example in Exhibit 12.3 where the retailer coordinates with multiple players for the customer to receive a branded plasma TV. The failure of action leads to blame game rather than holistically looking at solution. Practically, the retailer fails to estimate correctly resources for delivery during such promotional initiatives and tolerates slack in delivery performance. Customers and brand owners are at a disadvantage in such efforts.

4. A lack of trust among supply chain partners cause them to be opportunistic at the expense of overall supply chain performance. The lack of trust also results in significant duplication of effort. More importantly, information available at different stages is either not shared or is ignored because it is not trusted. A typical example of lack of trust is rationing and gaming practice followed by focal firms.

   When there's a big order from retailers, manufacturers would allocate limited production capacity and thereby there would be a short supply. Such short volume needs to be shared among many prospective buyers and rationing is enforced. This can occur for a high-demand product, especially on introduction, when market making and strategic focus for the brand are in short supply. Maruti Suzuki, for example, has faced this situation when it introduced Swift Dzire. There are a number of consumer products, especially those that are of possession value such as high-end mobiles, entertainment gadgets, and so on, that go through this. A part of their problem is demand estimation and the other

---

Exhibit 12.3 Role of Partners in Supply Chain Network Performance

In India, International Consumer Exhibition (ICE) Mega Expo has grown in size ever since it began in 1999, with 20 exhibitions under one roof. Spread over 2 lakh square feet, the fully air-conditioned hall offers products ranging from consumer electronics, home furniture, automobiles, IT products, carpets, garments, sofas, massage chairs, handloom and handicrafts, shoes, toys, watches, and jewellery. It is reported that more than 300 firms take part in the fair, and everyone competes with others to woo the consumers. Some of the products are being offered at 60 per cent discount. One would expect to do business worth Rs 10 crore (*The Hindu*, 9 August 2009).

Typically a customer books a purchase of plasma TV of a leading brand with a regional retailer whose price is lower than that of the brand owner because the retailer is sharing the channel discounts with the customer. However, supply chain activities get completed only when the plasma TV is delivered, installed, and the warranty is provided with assurance of post-sales service.

The retailer informs his/her distribution centre (DC) to deliver to the customer location. The DC aggregates the order, draws up a delivery schedule,

and accordingly coordinates the same. Hence, this is a delivery milk run, where the customer will have to accept the time window given by the DC. After delivery, the DC informs, and the retailer in turn coordinates with the service department for installation. On installation, the brand owner is informed for certifying installation and triggering the warranty process. On customer's choice, an annual maintenance contract is entered into, which would be managed by a third-party service provider. If one tracks these links, one would appreciate the role of each player and information flow on time which is critical for a satisfying customer experience. Alternatively, if the customer buys from the brand owner or at full price from the retailer at the showroom, coordination is taken care of by the vendor with greater comfort and on an exclusive basis.

Thus, when supply chain involves multiple role agents to accomplish certain activities to provide a satisfying customer experience, the performance of the role players in executing the different tasks and effective communication are vital for streamlining the supply chain function.

---

is a sudden spurt in demand. One commonly used rationing scheme is to allocate the available supply of products based on orders placed. Under this rationing scheme, if the supply available is 75 per cent of the total orders received, each retailer receives 75 per cent of its order. Such a policy spurs a behaviour attitude of jacking up demand in anticipation of sizing down the same for a lower quantum of supply. Thus, a rationing scheme results in a game in which retailers try to increase the size of their orders to increase the amount supplied to them. Such behavioural aspect hampers demand estimation and also results in improper distribution based on positioning taken by different players in the network.

5. Another important behavioural aspect is the ability to learn and quickly work on improvements in a supply chain network. This requires learning skills, culture, and commitment among players. This would happen only when there is a lead campaign in driving overall supply chain profit sharing and visibility to all players on costs and benefits. Whenever learning aptitude is missing, network obstacles go up.

Thus, obstacles in supply chain happen because of poor commitment of partners, improper processes, inadequate technology, and behavioural constraints among partners with inability to match individual goals and objectives with that of group in the network.

12.4   APPROACHES TO IMPROVE COORDINATION

Here some of the common approaches to improve coordination are discussed. The list is not comprehensive and these solutions are recommended for application based on the situation.

1. A manufacturer can use lot size-based quantity discounts to achieve coordination for commodity products if the manufacturer has large fixed costs associated with each lot. The manufacturer may use two-part tariffs and volume discounts to help achieve coordination. Given demand uncertainty, manufacturers can use buy-back, revenue-sharing, and quantity flexibility contracts to spur retailers to provide levels of product availability that maximize supply chain profits. All these approaches require sharing of information across the network and that all players are transparent to take advantage of production economies and work on a coordinated mode. This is commonly possible in a mature industry where there is an evolved supply chain system.

2. Managers can devise pricing strategies that encourage retailers to order in smaller lots and reduce forward buying. This would require relationship and experience building. Instead of lot-based discounts, volume-based discounts over a planning horizon would help. Volume-based quantity discounts result in smaller lot sizes, thus reducing order variability in the supply chain. Volume-based discounts with a fixed end date at which discounts will be evaluated may lead to large lots close to the end date. Offering the discounts over a rolling time horizon helps dampen this effect.

3. Managers can improve coordination within the supply chain by aligning goals and incentives so that every participant in supply chain activities works to maximize total supply chain profits. One key to coordinated decisions within a firm is to ensure that the objective any function uses to evaluate a decision is aligned with the firm's overall objective. All facility, transportation, and inventory decisions should be evaluated based on their effect on profitability. The focal firm must lead such initiatives and use an approach that is normally done through regulatory price mechanism where normative costs and capital costs are considered for arriving at a normal profit. Inefficiencies are to be borne by those who deviate from norms. Business must constantly look at it and update cost and profitability. When such an open approach is not there, there is a tendency to sway away from common goal of optimizing overall profits. For example, we saw in lot-based pricing that the buyer gets an advantage over seller. Somewhere in the system, this must be shared between them so that it normalizes over a period of time. Similarly, sales force incentives are structured in a way that pushing sales in the month end improves incentives but chokes the system.

One of the approaches would be to insist on delivery only on receipt of actual order. Establishing an even flow of material could be an advantage.

4. Managers can achieve coordination by improving the accuracy of information available to different stages in the supply chain. Capturing sale in secondary distribution is important to eliminate the Bullwhip Effect. If secondary distribution sale is captured, then sell in (push) of goods in the network could be difficult. Technology and process are available at a reasonable cost enabling this. One may start with sharing point-of-sale (POS) data across the supply chain. This would not work in case of retail where competing brands are being sold and need to do cleansing of data before being shared. More importantly, such effort must infuse confidence among competition. In reality, the only demand that the supply chain needs to satisfy is from the final customer. If retailers share POS data with other supply chain stages, all supply chain stages can forecast future demand based on customer demand. When it is not economical for the retailer to share this, an initiative is required. This was discussed in Collaborative Planning, Forecasting and Replenishment (CPFR) and Efficient Consumer Response (ECR) in Chapter 9 where such industry-wide approach is being attempted.

However, there are other solutions available to improve coordination. Firms link secondary distribution through technology solutions that are available. This is discussed in a later chapter. To give an idea, today software tools in supply chain domain help for linking up with secondary distribution. Last-mile deliverymen also update data through handheld equipments. This may be the way ahead. Retail could still be left out which needs to be worked on. Companies link their ERP, Advanced Planning Module, Business Intelligence tools, and distributors' network with a common platform which extracts information and uses for operating and planning decisions across the supply chain network. Further advancements would enable much more dependable networking of database, computer, and field-level operations through handheld mobile communication for coordinating supply chain function.

Process improvements happen as technology applications are enabled. Only drawback could be that process improvements would also bring rigidity and escalations and deviations are to be addressed. Over a period, such requirements must be incorporated into the technology system framework. Interfacing of process improvement and technology upgrade must be continued exercises as supply chain decision environment must be constantly changing with a spiral effect.

5. A reduction of lot sizes decreases the amount of fluctuation that can happen between any pair of stages of a supply chain, thus decreasing the chances of obstacles. To reduce lot sizes, managers must take actions that help reduce the fixed costs associated with ordering, transporting, and receiving each lot.

Order processing costs are reduced in engineering and auto industries with implementation of information systems. In case of transportation, FTL (full truck load) costs are lower than LTL (less than truck load) and reduced lot size transportation cost may go up. This is managed through moving together varied products, use of third-party logistics service providers at reasonable costs and being part of milk runs that combine shipments for several retailers on a single truck. Technologies help handling varied lot sizes for shipping, booking transport, and receiving complex orders with small orders of many products.

6. Behavioural obstacles can be countered by sharing information to limit gaming. Managers can design rationing schemes that discourage retailers from artificially boosting their orders. One approach would be to implement turn-and-earn, wherein the available supply is based on past retailer sales rather than current retailer orders. Tying allocation to past sales removes any incentive a retailer may have to artificially increasing orders, as a result dampening the Bullwhip Effect. Other firms have tried to share information across the supply chain to minimize shortage situations. A focal firm can also initiate a fair allotment of capacities. Once capacity has been allocated appropriately across different products, it is less likely that shortage situations will arise. The availability of flexible capacity can also help to balance for shifting capacities for products on demand.

Focal firms must strive to achieve coordination through building of trust and strategic partnerships within the supply chain. A better relationship also tends to lower the transaction cost between supply chain stages. For example, a supplier can eliminate its forecasting effort if it trusts orders and forecast information received from the retailer. Similarly, the retailer can lessen the receiving effort by decreasing counting and inspections if it trusts the supplier's quality and delivery. In general, stages in a supply chain can eliminate duplicated effort on the basis of improved trust and a better relationship. Auto industry, consumer products group, engineering, organized retail, and so on are currently working on this with varying levels of success. What happens is that whenever a business cycle turns a downside, focal firms drop their transparency level. Whenever there is pressure of delivery, suppliers and channel partners drop trust levels. Thus, in both situations building trust is becoming a challenge.

Finally, systems and initiatives like supplier development, green supply chain, ethical supply chain practices, and corporate governance improve trust as these initiatives are involving partner network on value-based relationships. Supplier development involves sharing of technical know-how, support in process and at times with volume and financial commitment. In case of a green supply chain, environmental concerns and value for future generation are the driving factors. In the process, it is natural to be attitudinally more transparent and be viable. Ethical supply chain practices involve structuring of policies and procedures across the supply chain so that there is fair and just approach in transacting and hence more transparency. Finally, current corporate governance standards seek a lot of good practices in various facets of management, including supply chain management, to be followed rigorously.

To sum up, better coordination in supply chain could be achieved with technology adaptation, process improvements, information sharing, changing of incentives, operational improvements, and stabilization of pricing. These would become meaningful only when building of cooperation and trust within the supply chain. People and partners in network and their roles and responsibilities are critical for managing the three flows—namely, physical, financial, and information, in a synchronized way so that the system benefits. That is the only way a firm can be competitive in the long run unless it is a monopoly.

SUMMARY

Supply chain coordination happens only when physical flow, information flow, and financial flow are synchronized. Financial flow management is critical in supply chain. Proper physical flow and endorsement of the same and right capture is what would enable financial flow. Unless the information system captures product movement and confirms the same to funder, fund releases cannot be done on time.

Technology plays an important role in managing financial flows as the implementation of ERP provides visibility across departments and allows the partnering organization to monitor critical financial choking points and escalate across decision hierarchy to streamline the flow.

The Bullwhip Effect is now a well-documented and researched anomaly of distribution channel communication. This is called Bullwhip Effect because a small variation on one end, which is controlled, shows up a large variation on the other end because of a spiralling effect resembling a bullwhip.

Bullwhip Effect is due to distorted information from one to other, leading to inefficiencies. Inefficiencies may be in the form of excessive inventory, blocking of investments, lost sales for lack of synchronization, misguided capacity plans, poor scheduling, and dissatisfaction among customers. Such inefficiencies also lead to poor cost management, thereby resulting in erosion of profits and dissatisfaction among partners in the network.

Four major causes of Bullwhip Effect are: demand forecast updating, order batching, price fluctuation, and rationing and shortening. Each of these individually or jointly may lead to a Bullwhip Effect. Over and above, the fifth factor, namely behavioural factors as choice of an action of a player in the network would be more induced by his own appreciation of situation, risk perception, and ability to position in the network.

Better coordination in supply chain could be achieved with technology adoption, process improvements, information sharing, changing of incentives, operational improvements, and stabilization of pricing. These would become meaningful only with building of cooperation and trust within the supply chain.

KEY TERMS

Backward integration: A form of vertical integration that involves the purchase of suppliers in order to reduce dependency.

Bullwhip effect: A small variation at one end that is controlled shows up a large variation on the other end because of spiralling effect resembling a bullwhip. It is also known as Whiplash Effect or Whipsaw Effect.

Business risk: A business risk is a circumstance or factor that may have a negative impact on the operation or profitability of a given company. Risk can be the result of internal conditions, as well as some external factors that may be evident in the wider business community.

Channel distribution: A chain of intermediaries, each passing the product down the chain to the next organization, before it finally reaches the consumer or end-user is referred to as 'distribution chain' or the 'channel of distribution'.

Clearing & forwarding (C&F) agents: The C&F or shipping agents are the companies that have been authorized and issued licence by Customs and Airport Authority of India to get the goods inspected at the customs warehouse. These shipping and clearing agents only prepare the export documents for our shipments. In trade, C&F agents are also involved in domestic trade, where they serve as intermediaries by linking the primary and secondary member in a distribution channel.

Demand forecasting: Demand forecasting is the process of trying to predict the future demand for a product or service in units or in revenue.

Ethical supply chain management: Ethical footprint in supply chain refers to fair and just supply chain operations in day-to-day activities which would be legal, economical, and socially acceptable and of high esteem to the corporate as an entity.

Forward integration: A form of vertical integration that involves the purchase of channels of distribution or players in forward linkages in order to reduce dependency.

Full truck load (FTL): FTL refers to full load to a vehicle capacity and normally moves from origin to destination.

Green supply chain: Green supply chain management involves traditional supply chain management practices that integrate environmental aspects like natural resource conservation, limiting air, water and noise pollution in deployment of supply chain drivers, using more electronic documents, and so on.

Industry risk: Industry risk refers to the dangers to a particular business that stem from far more wide ranging issues involving the entire industry that the company belongs to.

Just-in-time (JIT): JIT is aimed at improving the manufacturing process and is considered as one of the important production management tools. To achieve this, it requires interfacing with sourcing and distribution strategies and partners. JIT consists of three main parts, namely JIT purchasing, JIT manufacturing, and JIT distribution. JIT is a key philosophy of lean management, focused on waste reduction and continuous improvement.

Know your customer norms: As part of Know Your Customer (KYC) principle, RBI has issued several guidelines relating to identification of depositors and advised the banks to put in place systems and procedures to help control financial frauds, identify money laundering and suspicious activities, and for scrutiny/monitoring of large value cash transactions.

Less than truck load (LTL): LTL is less than truck load and may have multiple points of pick-up and drop.

Letter of credit: A standard, commercial letter of credit is a document issued mostly by a financial institution, used primarily in trade finance, which usually provides an irrevocable payment undertaking. Letters of credit are used primarily in international trade transactions of significant value, for deals between a supplier in one country and a customer in another.

Lot-based discounts: Price discounts offered on lots of goods purchased by a buyer and discounts are staggered based on lot size.

Management risk: Management risk refers to the dangers to a particular business that stem from far more wide ranging issues involving the quality, competence, and practices of management who are trustees of investors in the company.

Milk run: In a milk run, vehicle stops are on different nodes/dates wherein a scheduler may attempt to consolidate pick-ups or drops on a route by tightening days of a week.

Primary distribution: The distribution of goods from manufacturing to mother warehouses and dealers and CFAs till the goods reflect on the stock of the nodal organization and move out from its book finally to the channel players.

Rationing: Rationing is the controlled distribution of goods or services demanded across channels as demand is higher than supply on a particular time window.

Secondary distribution: The movement of goods from dealers to retailers and ultimate customers.

Variability: Variability is any deviation from the optimum process that delivers perfect product on time, every time. The less variability in the system, the less waste in the system.

Vendor-managed inventory: It is a mechanism where the supplier creates the purchase orders based on the demand information exchanged by the focal firm (manufacturer) or retailer or customer. VMI is a backward replenishment model where the supplier does the demand creation and demand fulfilment.

CONCEPT REVIEW QUESTIONS

1. Explain the importance of financial flow management in a supply chain network. Elucidate with an example where financial flows are choked due to some constraints in the system.

2. What is Bullwhip Effect and how does it relate to lack of coordination in a supply chain?

3. What are the different obstacles in a supply chain that a manager needs to focus on for achieving proper coordination? Also, explain the causes of each of the supply chain obstacles with examples.

4. In what way can improper incentives lead to a lack of coordination in a supply chain? What counter measures can be used to offset this effect?

5. Explain the role of information efficiency for achieving coordination in a supply chain. How can firms overcome such obstacles?

6. Which are the factors that lead to a batching of orders within a supply chain? How does this affect coordination? Which are the actions that can minimize large batches and improve coordination?

7. Elucidate with an example that application of technology and process improvements can improve coordination across supply chain network.

8. 'Establishing trust and relationship is critical for achieving coordination across supply chain network.' Discuss.

CRITICAL THINKING QUESTIONS

1. Analyse the following data and suggest what actions are likely in a supply chain network that may support or hinder in the system:

   a. There is a uniform demand of 120 units in a time window for 8 periods; and replenishment is also 120 units at price per unit at a steady rate of Rs 500 per unit.

   b. Focal firm is giving a discount of 5 per cent on the price if retailers buy in lots of 140 and another 2 per cent if quantity bought is 150 units.

   c. If there is a lost sale opportunity for want of stock, the imputed cost per unit is Rs 50.

2. An FMCG company observes month-wise order for production as shown here:

Month	Units in 00s
1	1,200
2	950

3	1,650
4	800
5	1,150
6	830
7	1,000
8	1,600
9	800
10	1,050
11	1,000
12	1,100

The supply chain head wants to discuss with the production head and distribution head on streamlining production and optimizing the production capacity of 140,000 units per month. In case of spare capacity he would like to deploy for another category. You may advise on this thought process of supply chain manager.

3. A leading shoe manufacturing and marketing company based in New Delhi has its production base 70 km away. It is a national brand and has export volume aggregating to 25 per cent of its turnover. Customer-service levels are important for its sustained growth in a highly competitive market. Its estimated monthly production is Rs 80 crore in terms of sales value. The marketing department has given a demand schedule as below:

Week	1	2	3	4
% Demand	42	28	18	12

Though production department is currently able to balance with export orders for balancing production system, it gets into trouble when there is a spike in the export schedule. It demands smoothening of local demand pattern through improved coordination. It is of the opinion that marketing department is pushing more than what is really reflective of the market. The Chairman and Managing Director call in the supply analyst to study this problem. You may advise issues to be probed and suggest an approach to do the same.

4. A leading manufacturer of dairy products is selling ghee through a marketing and distribution agent across India under the brand name 'Gomatha'. The arrangement is that the dairy processor would manufacture ghee in bulk and hand over to marketing agent Shyam Ghee Marketing and Distributors based out of Coimbatore. The selling price (MRP) of ghee is Rs 320 per kg. Dairy processors transfer to Shyam at 70 per cent of MRP. Shyam gives retailers 5 per cent of MRP assuming that stock clearance is 15 days. Shyam accounts for 25 per cent of MRP for packing in SKUs, promoting, and distributing the product. According to one estimate, Shyam has a margin of nearly 12 per cent in the business whereas dairy processor has about 5 per cent. With increasing procurement price and pressure on other dairy products, the processor wants to negotiate with Shyam the realization value across the network. The dairy processor's Chairman proposes to his strategic team to get into marketing and distribution business through acquisition. What are the issues that need resolution here? How would you approach a solution to this issue?

5. Assume that you are the head of vendor management in a manufacturing company. One of your key strategic suppliers is facing problem in managing supplies on time for the last six weeks. Your competitive intelligence sourcing gets you information that this vendor is defaulting payments of statutory liabilities to government, accounts payable is mounting, banks are alerting on balances for honouring of cheques and salary is being delayed. You want to assess and facilitate him back to proper financial health. How would you approach the recovery?

PROJECT ASSIGNMENTS

1. Visit a supply chain manager in a manufacturing firm and understand mapping of financial flows for synchronized supply chain operation.

2. Visit a freight forwarding company and discuss about document handling in international trade. Prepare a report on structure of the three flows, their interface, and how it is managing such transactions.

3. Discuss with a retail major the obstacles to its supply chain for different categories. Find out for each class of categories, namely branded, private label, and own brand type of obstacles, and initiatives taken to manage the same.

REFERENCES

Berinato, Scott, 'What Went Wrong at Cisco in 2001,' 1 August 2001 http://www.cio.com/article/ 30413 What_Went_Wrong_at_Cisco_in_2001

Chopra, Sunil, Peter Meindl and D.V. Kalra, *Supply Chain Management*, Pearson, 2007

Lee, Hau L. Padmanabhan V. and Whang Seungjin, 'The Bullwhip effect in Supply Chains,' *MIT Sloan Management Review*, April 1997

Simchi-Levi, David, Philip Kaminsky, and Edith Simchi-Levi, *Designing and Managing the Supply Chain*, Tata McGraw Hill , 2004

Thompson, Arthur A. and A.J. Strickland, *Strategic Management: Concepts and Cases*, 12th Edition, McGraw-Hill International, 2001

http://burnyourfuel.com/2009/02/04/cars/maru-ti-dzire-reduced-waiting-period-to-three-months/, 12 August 2009

www.hindu.com/2008/08/09/stories/ 2008080960191200.htm, 11 August 2009

Key Financial Ratios for Reference of Supply Chain Professionals

Activity Ratios

1. Inventory turnover = Sales / Inventory of finished goods

   When compared to industry averages, it provides an indication of whether a company has excessive or perhaps inadequate finished goods inventory.

2. Fixed assets turnover = Sales / Fixed assets

   This is a measure of the sales productivity and utilization of plant and equipment.

3. Total assets turnover = Sales / Total assets

   This is a measure of the utilization of all the firm's assets; a ratio below the industry average indicates the company is not generating a sufficient volume of business, given the size of its asset investment.

4. Accounts receivable turnover = Annual credit sales / Accounts receivable

   This is a measure of the average length of time it takes the firm to collect the sales made on credit.

5. Average collection period = 365 × (Accounts receivable/Total sales)

   This indicates the average length of time the firm must wait after making a sale before it receives payment. This has implications for financial management and quality of customers (marketing).

Liquidity Ratios

1. Current ratio = Current assets / Current liabilities

   This indicates the extent to which the claims of short-term creditors are covered by assets that are expected to be converted to cash in a period roughly corresponding to the maturity of the liabilities.

2. Quick ratio (or acid – test ratio) = (Current assets – Inventory)/Current Liabilities

   This is a measure of the firm's ability to pay off short-term obligations without relying on the sale of its inventories.

3. Inventory to net working capital = Inventory/ (Current assets – Current liabilities)

   This is a measure of the extent to which the firm's working capital is tied up in inventory.

Profitability Ratios

1. Gross profit margin = (Sales – Cost of goods sold) / Sales

   This is an indication of the total margin available to cover operating expenses and yield a profit.

2. Operating profit margin (Return on Sales) = Profits before taxes and interest / Sales

   This is an indication of the firm's profitability from current operations without regard to the interest charges accruing from the capital structure.

   Average collection period = 365 × (Accounts receivable/Total sales)

3. Net profit margin (or net return on sales) = Profits after taxes Net sales

   This shows after tax profits per rupee of sales. Low profit margins indicate that the firm's sales prices are relatively low or that costs are relatively high, or both.

4. Return on total assets = Profits after taxes/ Total assets

   Also, (Profits after taxes + interest) / Total assets

   It measures the return on total investment of the firm. It is sometimes desirable to add interest to after tax profits to form the numerator of the ratio since total assets are financed by creditors as well as by stockholders; hence, it is accurate to measure the productivity of assets by the returns provided to both debt and equity capital.

5. Return on stockholder's equity (or return on net worth) = Profits after taxes/Total stockholders' equity

This is a measure of the rate of return on stockholders' investment in the enterprise.

6. Return on common equity = (Profits after taxes–Preferred stock dividends)/(Total stockholders' equity – Par value of preferred stock)

This is a measure of the rate of return on the investment the owners of the common stock have made in the enterprise. More commonly referred to as 'return on equity' (or ROE).

7. Earnings per share = (Profits after taxes – Preferred stock dividends) / Number of shares of common stock outstanding

This shows the earnings available to the owners of each share of common stock.

8. Cash flow from operations = Profit after tax + Depreciation

Leverage Ratios

1. Debt-to-assets ratio = Total debt / Total assets

This measures the extent to which borrowed funds have been used to finance the firm's operations.

2. Debt-to-equity ratio = Total debt / Total stockholders' equity

This provides another measure of the fund provided by creditors versus the funds provided by owners.

3. Long-term debt-to equity ratio = Long-term debt / Total shareholders' equity

This is a widely used measure of the balance between debt and equity in the firm's long-term capital structure.

4. Times-interest-earned ratio = Profits before interest and taxes / Total interest charges

This measures the extent to which earnings can decline without the firm becoming unable to meet its annual interest costs. This is also referred to as coverage ratio.

5. Fixed-charge coverage = (Profits before taxes and interest + Lease obligations) / (Total interest charges + Lease obligations)

This is a more inclusive indication of the firm's ability to meet all of its fixed-charge obligations.

13 Global Supply Chain Perspectives

Learning Objectives

After studying this chapter, you will be able to:
- Gain an insight into the various aspects of global supply chain
- Understand the cost drivers and impact on global supply chain configuration
- Comprehend the responsiveness-based global supply chain configuration
- Appreciate the challenges in establishing a global supply chain
- Understand supply chain risks and approach for effective global supply chain
- Gain an insight into changing perspectives of logistics infrastructure

13.1 GLOBAL SUPPLY CHAIN

According to Mabert and Venkataramanan (1998), 'a supply chain is a network of facilities and activities that perform the functions of product development, procurement of material from suppliers, the movement of materials between facilities, the manufacturing of products, the distribution of finished goods to customers, and after-market support for sustainment.' With increased globalization and offshore sourcing, global supply chain management is becoming an important issue for many businesses. Establishing global facilities to serve customers across the globe and also serving domestic customers of large markets from global low-cost resources are a part of global supply chain management.

Global supply chain management involves managing the underlying factors behind the trend and reducing the costs of procurement of components or goods and services. This would require decreasing the risks related to purchasing activities while achieving cost efficiency. The big difference is that global supply chain management involves a lot of complexity in managing a company's global interests and suppliers while local supply chain management is less complex as information is easily traceable.

While managing global supply chain management across countries, cost and responsiveness are the supply chain objectives that drive the entire process. Many a time, cost could be a factor for low-value, mass-production-based goods. For example, in case of manufacturing of components for automobiles or consumer functional goods such as shoes, cost of production or conversion is a driving factor. Brand owners look for labour and other resources in low-cost economies as they are cheap there. In case of high value and less predictable demand, goods are set up for responsiveness. For example, high precision electronics capital equipments will have facilities, which like the distribution centre, would be located across the globe for achieving responsiveness. Singapore or any competitive location that is well connected by air transportation could be a hub for such a facility.

However, both cost efficiency and responsiveness are important in establishing global supply chain network. Moreover, the ability to assess complexities such as cost of space, finance, infrastructure including communication network, regulatory conditions, tariffs, and other factors related to doing business are essential for success too. Additionally, companies need to keep in mind the factors in the exchange rate. Global supply chain managers must analyse these factors continuously so as to establish effective supply chain goals of cost efficiency and responsiveness.

While discussing aspects of global supply chain, an analyst must consider time as an important element. Time as an element in global supply chain assumes importance in balancing cost efficiency and responsiveness. Goods produced in one location are shipped from one country to another. The productivity of the overseas employees and the extended shipping times can either positively or negatively affect the company's lead time, but either way this time needs to be included into the overall plan. International logistics like transferring of shipping consignments involves time of movements and handling through customs under international regulatory requirements. Thus, the setting up of an international supply chain network requires understanding lead time of goods and cost of distribution vis-à-vis balance between cost efficiency and responsiveness.

It may be observed from Exhibit 13.1 on India and China in the global pharmaceuticals supply chain that locating facilities in low-cost countries and supplying to MNCs for marketing in developed markets explains the aspects of facilities' location, transportation, sourcing, information management, and so on in global supply chain in the API market in supply chain. One may note that countries like China, India, and a host of Asian countries dominate markets, and the role of a supply chain manager is increasingly becoming important for the success of such businesses.

13.2 GLOBAL SUPPLY CHAIN AND UTILITIES

As mentioned in Chapter 1, time, place, and possession utilities play a significant role in a global supply chain. Because of varying climatic conditions across global markets, product demand and supply are skewed over time. Such skews facilitate marketers and they take advantage and serve large customer groups. Most of the agricultural products are seasonal but demand is even throughout the year as the season varies across the globe. But supply chain integrators in agricultural and agriculture-based goods even out supply by processing, grading, storing, and marketing at demand centres over time.

The place utility plays a significant role in global supply chain too. Trade is justified because demand centres are starved of production and supplies happen through

---

Exhibit 13.1   India and China in the Global Pharmaceuticals Supply Chain

As of 2005, China continues to be mostly a supplier of older, off-patent molecules, while Indian Active Pharmaceutical Ingredients (API) manufacturers often focus on newer, still-patented molecules. As a result of the introduction of product patents in India in January 2005, one may see increased interest in older molecules by Indian API manufacturers, though the full impact of this change is difficult to determine at this time.

While India still has more established companies than China, China has been aggressively increasing its number as of 2005. More interesting fact is that these companies export for generic markets both in developed and developing nations such as South American countries and Africa. Hence API advantage is low-cost manufacture in India or China and supplies to established MNCs in foreign countries or through their own brand in the same market. A number of the fast-growing Indian generic companies and API manufacturers entered into alliances with generics in the US, with an increasing number of the Indians focusing on supplying the finished dosage form as opposed to just the active ingredient. Supply chain integration happens through facilities' location and serving customers in different locations using extensively global logistics through well-developed third-party logistics service providers.

Another interesting strategic initiative is acquisitions of US companies by Indian companies. For example, in April 2005, Indian company Jubilant Organosys announced its intent to buy out over 75 per cent stake in an undisclosed US generics company. And in May 2005, Chennai-based Malladi Drugs announced the acquisition of Novus Fine Chemicals, which is believed to be the first such cross-border acquisition by an Indian pharmaceutical company in the API segment. There is also much activity in the reverse direction, with US and Western European generics continuing to acquire or take ownership of stakes in Indian manufacturers.

Source: Adapted from 'Where India and China fit in Global Supply Chain,' Kate Kuhrt, Thomson Scientific, June 2005, http://scientific.thomsonreuters.com/news/2005-06/8279854/.

---

global imports. Alternatively, a supply country is a large producer and has comparative advantage in selling to another country. For example, Brazil is currently the largest sugar-producing nation in the world. In 2006 it produced 30 million tonnes of sugar, which made up 20 per cent of the world's total sugar production. Of the 30 million tonnes of sugar, Brazil exported 17.7 million tonnes of sugar to other nations, which comprised almost 40 per cent of the sugar traded in the world that year. One needs to get into the place of demand centre.

There are intermediaries who buy and sell raw sugar and others who process raw sugar as refined sugar and sell it in demand centres. A global supply chain of sugar requires networking of supply companies, traders linking up with facilities processors near or in demand centres, and then the sugar being sold to either large intermediaries who manufacture sugar-based products or the end customer through the distribution channel.

Similarly, in the roses market, Amsterdam is the world's leading rose auction market. Roses come from different parts of the globe and they are graded, sorted, and auctioned in the market. The goal in a production centre is to exploit natural endowments to optimize production that would far exceed demand. Also, demand may not be an exact match for local production but could be different for different locations. Hence roses move towards demand centres and logistics plays a key role in global supply network of roses in the market. It is expensive because of air transportation, and then there is a dwelling time in the Netherlands before it is shipped to the demand centres. The roles of intermediaries such as transport operators, controlled temperature warehouse operators, and traders are critical in ensuring cost effectiveness and responsiveness in a supply chain. Thus, creating and fulfilling place utility is one of the key aspects of a global supply chain.

The possession utility in a global supply chain becomes significant when a focal organization wants to have controlled ownership of a vendor or a resource. For example, in 2001, the US-based Emerson Corporation acquired Avansys Power, a unit of Shenzhen-based Huawei Technologies of China. Emerson Electric, the biggest player in manufacturing telecom power equipment, thus identified a low-cost production base for its products. Similarly, Huawei realized that Avansys was a non-core business for the company. Also, Huawei needed cash to expand throughout China. 'With the emerging trend of globalization, it's important that we focus resources on our core business—designing, producing, and selling the highest quality telecommunications and data communications equipment,' said Huawei's spokesman (Moon, et al. 2004). Hence, ownership control for cost efficiency becomes an important factor for smooth functioning of a global supply chain network.

Thus, time, place, and possession utilities drive the configuration of a global supply chain network. Aspects of global supply chain can be better understood if one could take one of the cross-functional drivers, namely sourcing across countries to achieve supply chain goals (Figure 13.1).

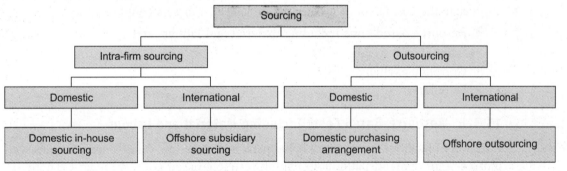

Figure 13.1 Sourcing choices for a firm

One may note that a company may either outsource, that is buy-out material, components, and goods for adding value before it moves up to customers or produce all these internally. These options of manufacturing or outsourcing could either be done domestically or globally, based on techno economics of the sourcing decision. A number of factors that drive such decisions are strategic in nature. It is pertinent to note here that global supply chain decisions rely on decision inputs from a supply chain manager.

One approach that a company can pursue is to go with market trends, which have established a buying pattern in a mature industry. However, if a company has to be a cost or product differentiator, then it may take an aggressive approach by soliciting low-cost partners in countries that have a cost advantage or a technology lead. For example, a number of electronic manufacturing companies have been set up in China because of cost advantage as they could provide more to leading manufacturing firms. According to Society of Manufacturing Engineers (August 2005), multinational companies are increasing their purchase of hi-tech parts and components from Chinese vendors. Exports of technology products from China formed nearly 8 per cent of total exports as of 2005. Low cost and high productivity of Chinese resources would increasingly push multinationals either to set up facilities or alliances with firms to act as sourcing agents. Companies have also set up international procurement offices in China.

Similarly, multinationals like Nokia, Dell, Siemens, and a host of auto and auto component manufacturers have set up facilities in India considering cost advantages for the firm. It helps to increase a customer base in India as it is a large market. It also helps to meet local demand with local cost advantages, which helps to garner a large size of the market. This could be one of the strong reasons why Nokia is successful in India.

Thus, a firm may globally buy or manufacture given certain cost advantages or improve responsiveness as the service level increases phenomenally.

13.3   COST DRIVERS AND IMPACT ON GLOBAL SUPPLY CHAIN CONFIGURATION

It was mentioned earlier that global supply chain network configuration is driven by cost drivers. It is again emphasized here that a supply chain manager should appreciate the cost factor in greater depth. The cost factors could be as follows:

- Resource-based costs including material and labour rates
- International freight tariffs
- Currency exchange rates
- Duty rates

13.3.1   Resource-Based Costs Including Material and Labour

Location of facilities across borders happens in case of low-value, mass products with more certain demand patterns to exploit resource-based cost advantages. There are instances where raw material cost may be cheaper because of the place of origin, which may attract converters to set up facilities. A number of minerals and mines-based products such as aluminium, cement, copper and steel, natural resources-based products such as tea, coffee, rubber, and large chemical plants, and so on get located at the place of origin. Another important factor which is mobile but still tends to be localized is labour. Labour-intensive manufacturing such as manufacture of apparel, footwear, jewellery, and auto components again tend to attract facilities or sourcing opportunities in places where labour costs are cheaper.

For example, if one were to look at Nike's supply chain, it provides a clear view of the extent of the global supply chain links of the company. Nike is a major market share holder in the footwear industry with players like Reebok, Adidas, Converse, and New Balance as competitors. Nike is far ahead of its competitors. Nike, which is headquartered in America, has manufacturing units throughout the Asian region. The company deploys outsourcing strategy using subcontractors. Their subcontractors are located in China, Indonesia, and Vietnam. Their factories are in Italy, Philippines, Taiwan, and South Korea. These factories are 100 per cent owned by the subcontractors who are solely dedicated for manufacture of Nike products. Nike's supply chain upstream begins with purchasing the materials that will be used in the production of its products. Many of these materials used in production are available in the locations where the manufacturing takes place, but some specialized materials have to be imported to the manufacturing company. The rationale is reduced costs of production and focus on core competence of marketing by Nike and manufacturing by contract manufacturers.

Like Nike, Reebok also has manufacturing base through outsourcing strategy wherein manufacturers from Asia supply finished goods. As economies grew and skills were enhanced and standardized, production base shifted to less developed regions around the world. Nike and Reebok compete on brand. Their reach in the domestic market and their ability to focus on cost reduction matter the most. However, one must get into greater depth of success of global outsourcing strategy as it is only one of the key success factors of this business.

One may note that resource-based cost factors could be drivers favourably impacting the configuration of a global supply chain.

13.3.2 International Freight Tariffs

Another important cost factor is international freight tariffs. International freight movements are mainly through ships that handle nearly 95 per cent of the volume of goods traded, which may be around 65 per cent of value traded. This clearly establishes that shipping would be the least-cost modal choice available in international logistics. Air transportation is one of the costliest modes, which is used for responsiveness. The other multimodal choices could be available only within a region, say like in Europe or North America.

Though cost of manufacturing may be advantageous, one will have to look at the final landed cost at the place of consumption. While outsourcing, a firm may establish a low cost of manufacture. But the landed cost will depend on the mode of shipping and the efficiency of the movement. When one discusses the choice of the mode of transportation, one may notice it is not shipping charges alone where logistics matter but also the impact of mode options on inventory costs, including impacts cycle, safety, and in-transit inventories.

For example, in case of Nike, long lead times associated with Nike's order service is a major vulnerability to manage demand. The lead time for orders placed by Nike with its manufacturers is around four months. In addition, Nike pre-orders four months in advance because its manufacturers cannot meet demand. Hence, Nike must optimize mode of transportation so that freight cost and inventory costs are optimized and be profitable with choice of global supply chain configuration. This is quite normally expected for such kind of mass production.

13.3.3 Currency Exchange Rates

Another important cost driver could be exchange rate and its parity. When a firm engages in global sourcing of material or components or goods, it carefully looks at landed cost which means that there must be parity in exchange rates. A firm may use its bargaining power and use strong currency as basis for cost fixation and payments. At an intrinsic level, transactions are driven by economic rationale and both partners would like to see exchange rate parity. Exchange rate fluctuations are driven by market forces and regulatory reactions in certain cases which are influenced by a number of factors. It is important that a supply chain manager understands such nuances of commercial implications while designing a supply chain network. As mentioned elsewhere, though there would be a cross-functional team which would be working on these parameters, it is important that a supply chain manager is cognizant of the dynamics.

For example, the Asian financial crisis affected five countries—Thailand, Indonesia, Malaysia, South Korea, and the Philippines—which were playing a significant role as partners of supply chain for many MNCs located in developed nations. The crisis created an immediate economic turmoil and these currencies were devalued against major currencies. Trade balances, foreign currency reserves, corporate governance, depth of financial markets, and quality of government regulation, were all affected in 1997. There was an intervention by regional and global development banks and political system to revive these economies. Though buyers who had pegged to dollar value would not have been adversely affected, the fact remained that currency fluctuations brought in difficulty.

It is important to note here that currency exchange rate and its stable position would give cost advantage and parity during transactions.

Another related issue in cost drivers is again of financial costs per se. Production units deploy capital which has a significant cost. The cost of capital across countries varies like less developed regions have high cost of capital. One way by which global supply network addresses this is by allowing free flow of capital across regions. However, it may not be a right decision to assume landed cost at prevailing capital cost in the country. Macro factors such as inflation, lending rates, and cost of capital would also reflect in currency rates by play of market factors. Still it is directly relevant while deciding on location of units, and when one looks at cost drivers such capital costs along with foreign currency cover costs must be looked into. It may be noted that global supply chain networks are widening because these factors are favourable in reducing the overall cost and increasing the efficiency.

13.3.4 Duty Rates

Looking at cost drivers while establishing a global supply chain network, one would necessarily have to look at the customs rate. For example, if one were to import materials into a country and convert using local cheap labour and reach out to the global market by exporting from there, it means that the firm would be paying huge amount of customs and other duties for achieving economies in conversion cost. For example, if a firm decides to use Bangladesh labour cost for achieving economies in conversion of cotton into garments wherein it imports Egyptian fine quality cotton, then one will have to check the total cost of transaction. To exploit these advantages one should look only at countries that have established Special Economic Zones wherein conversion can happen at the cost of no duties and the local country can earn in strong international currencies, thus facilitating the growth of the trade.

As mentioned earlier, as an economic need to combat inflation and foreign currency reserves, Mexico established the maquiladora regime for foreign manufacturers, which allowed them to establish export processing operations in Mexico without requiring local ownership. The maquiladora regime allowed foreign companies to bring in machinery, equipment, components, and raw materials for use by the Mexican maquiladora plant without having to pay duties. All transactions could be denominated in US dollars. Maquiladoras operated on a cost-plus basis, charging enough to meet their payrolls and related operating costs plus a nominal profit. Proximity to the US border, lower labour rates at Mexico, and access to lower US duty rates for raw materials and components helped the maquiladora regime players to enjoy cost economies in establishing effective global supply chains (Goetz and Gossett PLLC).

Thus, cost drivers emanating from resource-based factors including labour rates, international freight tariffs, exchange rate stability, and duties play a significant role in the configuration of a global supply chain.

13.4 RESPONSIVENESS-BASED GLOBAL SUPPLY CHAIN CONFIGURATION

Responsiveness refers to speed at which a customer's demand can be served and the level of service which could be achieved. The following parameters on responsiveness are the key requirements for establishing effective global supply chain network.

- Response Time—Lead time or cycle time; and also export license approval cycle and customs clearance
- Product variety
- Product availability
- Customer experience
- Order visibility
- Post sale service and returns management

13.4.1 Response Time

While designing a global supply chain network, a focal organization will have to probe lead time or order cycle time and also a related concept, namely in-transit time. The time between the placing of the order and arrival of the shipment is called the lead time or order cycle time. This would decide key logistical drivers such as facilities location and allocation, inventory management policy, and choice of transportation mode. In case of consumer products group, if size justifies, the focal organization would locate its facilities in demand centres so that the response time would be quick.

However, for reasons of availability and cost, one may have to have locations in multiple countries. Large manufacturing companies are increasingly adopting global supply chain management. Even retail customers based businesses such as Li & Fung are reported to be involved in global supply chain networks. As mentioned earlier, auto manufacturers especially import components from low-cost locations. Obviously in such conditions lead time or order cycle time is going to be a critical success factor.

It is important to note that focal organizations or any partner across supply network would like to carry excess inventory to reduce cycle time or improve responsiveness beyond a point. This leads to the fundamental issue of supply chain wherein one would like to reduce product delivery cycles and at the same time reduce time and cost of delivery. Moreover, this becomes more complex in businesses where the product becomes obsolete faster and uncertainty on demand is high. Time becomes a sensitive factor. This is common in retailing, especially in fashion garments, electronic goods, and the computer industry.

In such cases whether it is own manufacture or outsourcing, one will have to be involved in upstream production of dispersed manufacturing. Though it would be an easier option to place the firm's order and allow upstream manufacturer to plan, manufacture, and deliver to the focal organization, such an option would involve longer cycle time. With long-haul movements in global scenario, such options increase risk and cost. Alternatively, such focal organizations may choose an option of building trust and moving on to interact more closely with upstream vendors and develop basic requirements in place and confirm order closure to order fulfilment time. For example, if it is a garment business, the focal organization can ensure that the vendor buys basic yarn and material including dye colours and block capacity to fill order on a shorter cycle time. Similarly, in the case of auto components, common parts can be manufactured in advance to combat challenges of cycle time.

13.4.2   Product Variety

While configuring a global supply chain network, product variety is also an important parameter. This is again driven both by the demand and the supply side. For example, in a country, demand product variety could be an important factor because of product preference, customer segments and culture, and so on. Japan and a few other developed nations demand high variants in consumer electronics goods and in motorcycles, which are driven by trend in demand factors of local preference. Alternatively, in countries like India and many other developing nations, the large markets prefer functional products that meet the requirement of basic needs of a customer. For example, in case of the two-wheeler market, the developing nations look more at the economy factor than performance or style.

While setting up a global network, such factors must be considered. Wherever demand is substantial and basic, setting up a local facility is always helpful. On the other hand, if market requires responsive supply chain with product variants, postponement and quick response as discussed above would have to be necessarily worked into. Buyers must work closely with upstream to ensure that product variants and response time are fulfilled for developed markets.

13.4.3 Product Availability

While analysing global supply chain dimensions, product availability could be viewed from perspectives of the focal organization receiving supplies from global sources, that is, demand centre being served from global source, and being present in major world markets such as USA, EU, and Asia. The key parameter on product availability is customer service level. The focal organization would have to have a target customer service level and then configure the global supply chain network. The complexity of this parameter is less when one considers a product that has a stable demand and is standardized. This would be common for many functional goods and a global network is established more for cost factors. For example, for the leather industry, which deals with standard products like protective shoes, accessories, and functional products, the demand is by and large stable and predictable. Product availability on time for various SKUs is more critical and determines the success of a focal organization.

In case of high-value products with an unpredictable demand, availability is going to be a critical factor for effectiveness of the supply chain. For example, for medical equipments, especially spares whose demand may not follow a stable demand pattern, availability is critical as down time may not be permitted. For such products, availability is ensured through increased inventory and quick transit using high cost and efficient mode of transportation like air.

On a wider geographical demand, availability can be managed by different strategic options which would include setting up facilities like manufacture or distribution centres that would help to reach large demand points. Product availability again is a function of demand preferences and the ability to set up facilities to manage the same. For example, Singapore and Hong Kong are preferred locations for setting up regional distribution centres for high-value goods and enable a shorter cycle time. By this, the focal organization is able to reach the Asian markets easily. Hong Kong can be an ideal Regional Distribution Centre (RDC) location for easy and lower-cost movement and management of a number of high-value cargo or product groups, which may include specialized or high-value spare parts, electronic components, semiconductors, LCD/Plasma TVs, and luxury fashion goods and accessories. Similarly, every region has such nodal ports or centres which facilitate establishing regional distribution centres to reach those markets.

For example, Belgium and the Netherlands play a crucial role in Europe. Dubai and Gulf economies play the role of a nodal centre for reaching Gulf and North African economies and also parts of Russian economies. It is important to note that while establishing a global supply chain network, a focal organization must ensure that product reach is planned through a network of facilities to ensure product availability.

13.4.4 Customer Experience

Customer experience would include all aspects related to ease of buying, completing transaction, and experiencing of a product or service. Customer experience is what a customer would measure cardinally or as ordinal value to price paid. Especially, experience of a product or service has been very critical in the success of a global supply chain. In the auto sector, one can find a model to be successful in one region but not so well accepted in another region. Such experiences are common for the electronics and fashion goods such as garments, jewellery, and accessories. Hence, it is important to understand the customer experience and match it reasonably with expectations and configure the global supply network accordingly.

13.4.5 Order Visibility

Order visibility relates to the ability of customers to track the order from placement to delivery to have the comfort of fair response to order placement. With the advent and proliferation of technology applications in customer relationship management, which is one of the three macro processes of supply chain management, there has been a heightened expectation from customers on order response efficiency. Order visibility is demanded and focal organizations are keen to provide the same. However, establishing order visibility is not just about plugging technology. It requires tremendous synchronization with the ground-level capability of supply chain partners like transportation intermediaries, warehouse operators, and integration with vendors' systems, and so on. When a global link moves across less-developed countries, this becomes a challenge as infrastructure, culture, capability, and communication are not homogeneous across countries.

13.4.6 Post-sales Service and Returns Management

Post-sales service is one of the key primary activities of a value chain and is an important aspect of supply chain, linking the customer with the focal organization in any commercial transaction. The ability of focal organizations to sell a product or service and provide continued value on agreed terms as part of the contract at the time of sale is critical for the success of the supply chain in a global scenario. Typically, a focal organization links up post-sales service through authorized agents who are trained on the product and provide access to spare parts for enhancing value to customers. Success of some international brands such as Canon, Sony, and a host of other MNC brands explains the relevance of post-sales service and provision warranty commitments. Unless international customers have access to such assured experience, customers would not support the success of a global supply chain network.

Similarly, returns management is another related feature which is an important aspect of supply chain process. Certain products by international standards require managing returns because of hazardous material used in product configuration. There are certain products where recovery process may also be involved. Batteries, computers, and electronics products, communication sets including mobile phones are under such clauses. It is understood that Nokia manages returns well and ensures safe disposal of recovered hazardous material. Corporate social responsibility and ethical behaviour of focal organizations require integration of supply chain accordingly. In global operations, this becomes critical if the nodal organization does not have the facility but is obligated to provide such a commitment.

Thus, responsiveness-based global supply chain requires addressing the important features mentioned above like response time management, product variety, product availability, customer experience, order visibility, post-sales service, and returns management.

13.5 CHALLENGES IN ESTABLISHING A GLOBAL SUPPLY CHAIN

It is understood that while establishing a global supply chain, a number of macro, industry, and competitive factors influence the configuration. This has been discussed in Chapter 6. A recap of these factors is given below:

Macro-economic factors such as competitive conditions, exchange rate, demand risks, tariffs and duties, tax incentives, and fiscal support are likely to influence the configuration of a global supply chain. Competitive conditions play a significant role as entry and exit barriers with respect to a business supported by economic factors and policy of local government are critical. For example, in countries like India and other developing countries, the government still holds a substantial regulation on foreign investment and disinvestments. Apart from these, competitive factors would also include factor endowments impacting production economies, number of players, and rivalry among firms and development of related and support industries. Factor endowments impact cost of production, extent of rivalry of firms impact level of entry barrier, and price-setting strategies and maturity of related and support industries impact the cost of operation with respect to support activities such as procurement and primary activities like inbound and outbound transportation, and so on.

Exchange rates are again determined by the administrative mechanism in some countries either fully or partially and play the role of market forces in major developed economies. This would have an impact on the global supply chain. Financial flows are influenced by the exchange rate. For example, US dollar to Indian rupee was Rs 43.8918 for one US dollar in April 2004, went as low as Rs 39.2704 for one US dollar in January 2008, and peaked again to Rs 51.2062 for one US dollar in March 2009. This gives an idea of fluctuations and impact it can have on export and import of goods and services. When a currency appreciates, exporting is less attractive and importing becomes attractive. On the other hand, when it depreciates, exports become attractive and importing becomes less attractive. However, there are ways to handle this. Financial flows can be covered with financial instruments and techniques like using forwards, options, futures, derivatives, and hedging. It would be beyond the scope of this book to get into the details of each of these.

A supply chain manager would involve financial experts to handle the same. Another way to handle this is to manage physical flows in creating capacities in multiple locations and using the capacity as a hedge against unfavourable movements in exchange rates by swapping production plans to locations where it works out to be more economical.

Demand risk is another challenge in establishing a global supply chain. This is especially significant if global reach is driven by market expansion and reach to Triad markets, namely US, Europe, and Asia. Any fluctuation measured by variability in demand would affect readjustment of allocation of facilities to the market and thereby total supply chain profits. For example, for a glass manufacturing company, which has facilities in Asia, Europe, and the US, supplying glass to commercial properties and automotives could be affected directly by economic trends. In a situation like the global economic crisis of 2008–09, which started off in the US and engulfed Asia, the demand fluctuations are likely to immensely affect manufacture of glass in different locations. The management must reallocate capacity to minimize costs, avoiding redundant inventories and unviable transportation costs, and at the same time ensure that group profits across the network are optimized. On the other hand, if one looks at the Asian tigers' crisis in 1997, it was limited to the Asian economies and adjustment was necessary but was fairly less complex compared to the current crisis.

Tariff, duties, tax incentives, and fiscal support play a significant challenge in establishing a global supply chain network. As mentioned earlier, tariff, duties and fiscal support are determined by the domestic country's economic focus and regional cooperation among the consortium of nations. This has been also discussed in detail in Chapter 6. The government initiates a number of fiscal supports like setting up of special economic zones, export processing centres, liberalized capital equipment imports for priority industries or where technology is lagging, tax holidays for promoting investments in less developed zones, and so on. Such incentives improve viability and improve supply chain profits. To cite an example in India, some of the key fiscal incentives provided for setting up facilities in an SEZ include:

- 100 per cent income tax exemption for a block of five years, 50 per cent tax exemptions for two years, and up to 50 per cent of the profits ploughed back for next three years and allow carrying forward of losses
- Exemption from Central Excise duty on procurement of capital goods, raw materials, consumable spares, and so on from the domestic market
- Reimbursement of Central Sales Tax paid on domestic purchases
- Supplies from Domestic Trade Area to SEZ to be treated as exports

A number of such features can be looked into to gain an insight into how these features facilitate setting up a global supply chain. It is important to note here that fiscal policy could be a challenge or facilitator for setting up a global supply chain and a supply chain manager must familiarize with the same to ensure an efficient and effective supply chain.

13.5.1 Political, Legal, Societal, and Technological Factors

Any focal organization when it links up its supply chain in a country would like to evaluate political stability and the risks associated with political factors. World Bank published governance indicators in 2004: Voice & Accountability (VA), Political Stability (PS), Government Effectiveness (GE), Regulatory Quality (RQ), Rule of Law (RL), Control of Corruption (CC). A country like India scored percentile ranks in

2004 on VA, PS, GE, RQ, RL, and CC at 54, 24, 56, 27, 51, and 47 respectively. These are single-point data and no inference is attempted here. However, one may note that when countries are ranking low on corruption and high on being politically biased in encouraging commercial bias, then a focal organization may find it difficult; this is because the transaction costs, which are also not fully accounted for, would increase the cost of operation and decrease supply chain profits.

More importantly, such locations would be a drain on the efficiency of resources as significant time and effort would go into lobbying for action. The legal factor is important as it depends upon the efficiency of judiciary and the ability of the judiciary to be unbiased and objective. It is closely linked to the maturity of the political system the country adapts and the quality of its judiciary. One may also relate societal factors here in same accordance. Societal maturity depends on sentiments and group dynamics of a society. Long standing traditions and belief system largely influence such behaviour. While setting up a global supply chain network, the same must be treated as one of the challenges and the approach must be tuned to societal behaviour. In India, MNCs like Cargill and food retail faced initial trouble because of societal factors.

13.5.2 Infrastructure and Support System

Infrastructure refers to communication, roads, ports, and airports. Transportation including railroad and development of financial network, apart from other things, would be important for setting up effective global supply chain network. China, South Korea, and a few other Asian countries could attract MNCs to set up operations because of their focus in developing their infrastructure and support system for trade-driven growth. Any focal organization would evaluate these factors with higher importance as the efficiency of supply chain drivers depends upon these factors. In countries like India, the governments has are now focusing on these factors to be a part of global supply chain network. Development of roads, airports, sea ports and cargo rail movement in public-private partnership mode is a step towards this direction.

13.6 MICRO FACTORS THAT INFLUENCE DESIGNING OF A GLOBAL SUPPLY CHAIN NETWORK

There are certain micro or firm-level factors that are to be considered while establishing a global supply chain network.

1. Establishing **compatibility** among partners is a key to the success of a global supply chain network. When a focal organization stretches out globally, linking up partners along the supply chain, it must ensure that they are like-minded and work for benefits across the chain rather than looking at silos of their own operation. This would break harmony among players and result in inefficiency and avoidable cost and effort in terms of money and time. Though one may study many of these factors from a macro point of view, it is important to go in for a due diligence on partners on a fixed interval to ensure compatibility. Many

relationships have fallen through for lack of similar approach or change in behaviour pattern.

2. **Configuration** is again another important firm-level factor that a focal organization must decide while structuring a global supply chain. The pattern of arranging relationships across supply chain partners need not necessarily be stereotyped or fixated. For example, in one location, the vendor could be a strategic partner with fixed commitment, transfer of technology, or even financial support, and in another country it could be a commercial dealing as preferred supplier. This could be the result of macro factors or even player-specific factors and comfort zones in relationships. Though macro factors could be pointers for configuration, specific concerns must be raised before linking up each player and structure a format for relationship to be a partner in global supply chain.

3. **Coordination** among partners across a supply chain is critical for the success of a global supply chain network. This could be achieved by the focal organization only when it deploys an effective information system to encourage free flow of information and achieve transparency and openness in the system. Apart from information flow, physical and financial flows must be well established. A financial flow is harmonized only when documents of possession and ownership are clarified, transacted, and transferred effectively among parties so that physical flow happens. Though trust may be important and gained over years after observing a consistent track record of transactions, the ability to put through a policy and procedures for effective coordination is important. The onus for structuring a coordinated relationship across partners in a global supply chain network lies with a focal organization. There are a number of intermediaries who facilitate such transactions.

4. Finally, level of **control** over operations and effectiveness of global supply chain determines the success of such configuration. When one measures control, it is reflected in the degree of power and command over partners in achieving synchronization for three flows, namely physical, financial, and information. A focal organization is one which ultimately owns up a global supply chain network and is responsible for a span of control. It must set up policy, system, and hierarchy to ensure compatibility, effective configuration, and coordination among all partners. Though negotiating power and level of interdependence may influence de facto effectiveness of control, it is important that a focal organization in the long run drives its global supply chain network. Regular audit and review mechanism would facilitate for effective control mechanism.

Thus, apart from macro factors, firm-level factors do influence global supply chains. The following strategic initiatives could be useful for putting through a global supply chain (Kotabe and Helsen 2001):

1. Identify the components or processes like planning, product development, sourcing, manufacturing, distribution and logistics of focal organization in reaching global markets.

2. Determine the global location of the company's competitive advantages, considering both economies of scale and scope. While economies of scale would help in reducing per unit cost of manufacture, economies of scope would facilitate to exploit resources with excess capacity to be utilized effectively for achieving cost efficiency in reach.

3. Do a thorough analysis of transaction costs including cost of negotiation, formal contracts, and hidden costs between links in the global supply chain and select the lowest cost mode that provides the most value or higher responsiveness for which the customer is willing to pay.

4. Determine the comparative advantages of countries relevant to each link in the supply chain and of relevant transaction costs and order them on cost efficiency for exercising a choice.

5. Provide flexibility in corporate decision making and organizational design to respond to changes in scenario and firm-specific requirements.

Thus, a firm must evaluate macro and micro factors and design strategies to meet challenges for achieving success in establishing a global supply chain network.

13.7 GLOBAL SUPPLY CHAIN INTENSE BUSINESS—AN ANALYSIS

It may be useful to understand aspects of global supply chain by analysing supply chain perspectives of a global business wherein India plays a significant role. The leather industry is one such business and a number of small and medium organizations are involved in regional clusters in promoting this business. There are large groups that actively trade in this business. India Trade Promotion Council and a host of other industry organizations like Council for Leather Exports, Central Leather Research Institute, Footwear Design and Development Institute, Indian Shoe Federation and Indian Finished Leather Manufacturers' & Exporters' Association, and national bodies like Confederation of Indian Industry (CII) and Federation of Indian Chamber of Commerce and Industry (FICCI) facilitate growth of this business.

Some of the prominent clusters of this industry in South India include Chennai, Ambur, Ranipet, Vaniyambadi, Trichy, Dindigul, Hyderabad, and Bangalore; Jallandhar and Kanpur in North India; West Mumbai; and Kolkata in the East. One may observe that conversion centres are close to the metropolises of India for reasons of local consumption and convenience of exports. The industry depends on the availability of raw material such as skin and hides, and processing of the same. Support industries include leather machinery and chemicals. This industry is extremely dependent upon availability of skilled labour, designers, technical consultants, and managerial professionals, especially those who could be experts in marketing, and negotiating with international buyers and logistics operators. Logistics plays a significant role in this industry, and specialized services like use of hangers and special packaging and movement are required.

It may be observed from Figure 13.2 that leather footwear and footwear components like shoe uppers, soles, and so on constitute nearly 40 per cent of exports.

Leather goods like accessories, harnesses, saddles, leather gloves, and so on constitute nearly 24 per cent of exports. Finished leather is again another significant product which is an intermediary and gets finished by buyers. Leather garments constitute about 11 per cent of exports.

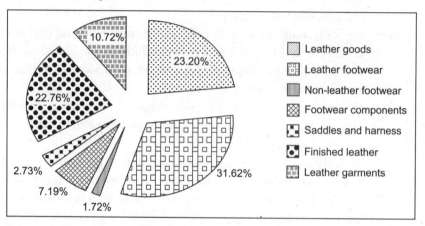

Source: http://www.iilfleatherfair.com/info_overview.html.

Figure 13.2 Percentage share of leather products exported from India in 2003–04

Supply chain issues including sourcing and buying raw material at best of prices and processing the same before conversion into products is one of the important supply chain drivers in this industry. From a global perspective, sourcing efficiency is critical since price efficiency in trade can be achieved only then. There is also involvement of international buyers in sourcing at two levels: one, ensuring that ecological and statutory complaints including non-involvement of child labour are adhered to, and two, quality of finished leather is such so as to ensure there are no rejections at the buyer end on receiving consignments.

Location of facilities is another important supply chain driver. If one may observe from the kind of products traded, it is more labour intensive and involves handling of effluents as most of the process materials produce significant waste and the ability to manage the same is vital for success in this business. Indian leather industry's key market includes world's leading importers who are in the USA, UK, Germany, Italy, and other developed nations in Europe. These countries may process finished leather in a mechanized environment with less labour and low waste generation as cost of handling both is high. Facilities equipment is imported from developed nations for achieving high standards of productivity. Also, facilities location is driven by the availability of raw skin and hides, which is very high in India. India has developed the capability of handling warehouses/distribution centres for storing, packing, and exporting of leather and leather products. There are intermediaries which are third-party logistics companies that specialize in handling leather industry.

Transportation is another supply chain driver, and as seen earlier, leather clusters are located close to airports and seaports. International players in intermediary operation of leather goods movement facilitate transportation. As mentioned above, third-party logistics service providers take care of warehousing and transportation. This brings up the role of another critical driver, namely inventory. There is a certain amount of seasonality in the leather industry as conversion of the raw leather into leather goods establishes peaks and troughs of the buying pattern. The industry evens out with normal operation of capacity with finished leather and converts close-to-order situations. Raw material would also have some seasonal factors which are again managed through better forecasts and planning. Being a traditional industry in India, there is enough expertise available.

Thus, most of the players in the leather industry in India would have a role in the global supply chain network, mainly in the supplier relations management process, and there would be few strong players in manufacturing and conversion; and some key personnel in marketing and customer relationship management. There has been increased focus on improving supply chain effectiveness of this business with induction of professionals as India has the scope of moving up in the value chain.

13.8   SUPPLY CHAIN RISK

Supply chain risk refers to an uncertainty or unpredictable event affecting one or more of the parties within the supply chain network. It can also emanate from external sources like macro or industry factors, which adversely influence supply chain effectiveness and efficiency. This affects cost and responsiveness, leaving a longer-term impact rather than just transactional setback. Risks can be triggered by a wide variety of factors like political instability, terror attack leading to disruption of movement, natural calamities, economic uncertainties like exchange rate fluctuations, inflation, demand risks, and product-led factors like shelf life and short lifecycle demanding product improvements.

13.9   SUPPLY CHAIN RISK MANAGEMENT

Supply chain risk management is a structured and synergetic process throughout the supply chain, which seeks to optimize the totality of strategy, processes, human resources, technology, and knowledge for managing supply chain risks. The aim is to control, monitor, and evaluate supply chain risk, which will serve to safeguard continuity and maximize profitability. Traditionally, focal organizations would build inventory to combat such risks. In contemporary business, excess inventory means huge costs and companies are expected to learn to avoid wastages. Obsolescence of inventory is an avoidable cost and companies are building capabilities to manage supply chain risks. Also one may note that risk cannot be limited to logistical drivers like delay in movement or lost demand for want of inventory. Hence a comprehensive risk management strategy in global supply chain is required to be in place.

Terror attacks like 9/11 in the US, which resulted in near embargo of trade for a short period, shake up the global supply chain network. There are many such disruptions like wars in the Middle East, SARS, Bird Flu, tsunami, and other natural calamities in different regions. India faced terror attacks and natural calamities like floods and earthquakes of high magnitudes which impacted trade. Many a time these are treated as sporadic events or as outliers and the system adjusts itself over a period of time with regulations and combat plans from all nations and entities. However, it is important in a global supply chain that such risks are evaluated and disruption management is strategized and made actionable when such incidents occur.

Risk management can be done by initiating the following combat measures:

1. It is important to estimate risks in global supply chain network and put strategic thoughts in place. Unless risks are perceived and covered, one may respond with knee-jerk reaction on incidence of disruption. The cover does not necessarily limit to financial flow cover, namely insurance. One should also look at aspects like physical flow management as loss of customer faith is difficult to restore. In situations of major disruptions like 9/11, customers do understand and there is a certain demand adjustment happening. What is more critical is the ability to respond quickly and restore normal operations across the supply chain. It is important to handle minor or localized disruptions effectively as such repeated disruptions may hamper all partners, right from the customer to the supplier across the network.

2. Greater mutual understanding of the interests and problems of all supply chain partners is another aspect which would improve the scope of reducing global supply chain risk. This can be managed through contracts and documentation wherein the roles and responsibilities of the partners can be clearly spelt out and deviations can be penalized or compensated by the failing partner. Another approach is to develop a process based on experience and handle exceptions as defined in the process or through mutual consent. It is important here to note that the focal organization and its partners must consciously strive to coordinate effectively and anticipate risks. Many a time even the best of players move ahead with transactions and relationships without a formal plan to mitigate risks.

3. Global supply chain risk assumes greater significance if the management focuses only on the cost factor. At times, operating managers, being cost-focused, fail to evaluate risks appropriately. Also, certain risks are not quantifiable for want of adequate reliable data points and the operating managers fail to capture risk. There are also tendencies wherein supply chain managers give more than required levels of responsiveness for global supply chain partners and assume greater risk. If one analyses all these, it is lack of right sense and application of appropriate tools and techniques which increase risk. The best way to handle the same is to involve professional support for the same.

4. A related feature in global supply chain management is establishing a competitive edge through the acceptance of controlled risks. Many a time there could be a tendency to assume the position of being an aggressive risk taker or the exactly opposite position of risk aversion. It may be useful to be risk neutral which comes through seasoned risk analysis and deployment of appropriate tools and

techniques. An overview of such tools and techniques is out of scope here. One may look into aspects of using variance analysis, deployment of statistical distribution functions for estimating risk, use of portfolio management techniques and involving in futures and derivatives to cover risk. It is only appropriate that a supply chain manager involves an inter-disciplinary team for estimating and managing global supply chain risks.

13.9.1 Benefits of Effective Supply Chain Risk Management

Risk management provides a number of direct benefits as follows:

1. It provides the ability to anticipate and respond promptly to external trends and developments. Response time to manage disruptions is faster and effective. All partners would benefit out of such an effort.
2. When a focal organization estimates global supply chain risks and involves its partners, it automatically builds relationship and trust among partners, giving more visibility and transparency. This would have a trickledown effect on overall supply chain effectiveness and profitability.
3. When a focal organization resolves to combat global supply chain risks, it naturally focuses on likely triggers of uncertainties and improves risk management. Knowledge initiatives systematically build capability and culture for handling disruptions. It helps to draw on analytics of data and information and also from experience of others, which is critical in such situations. It builds professionalism in managing supply chain risk instead of initiating one-off activities. Involvement of multidisciplinary professional expertise like statisticians, economists, finance experts, logisticians, and others would help to build robust systems.
4. Finally, broad-based application of IT tools in all areas involving supply chain partners and linking up would reduce the scope of risk and provide transparency and visibility. It may involve spending and convincing partners to participate in information network. This may carry its own trigger of risks. However, today expertise is available to optimize investment in creating collaborative IT tools for global supply chain network and risks can be minimized.

13.10 CHANGING PERSPECTIVE OF LOGISTICS INFRASTRUCTURE

Global supply chain is increasingly influenced by changes that are happening in the structure of logistics infrastructure across the globe. One of the key logistics drivers is transportation, and one may observe some key changes that are likely to impact future trends in supply chain.

There has been a robust growth in the sea-borne container trade over the past three decades. The total container traffic handled across the globe in the year 1991 was 93.65 million twenty-foot equivalent unit TEUs and it went up to 208.09 million TEUs by 2002, registering a 7.5 per cent growth. The following significant factors have led to the growth of containerization globally:

1. Savings in total transport cost
    (a) Reduction of freight rates
    (b) Savings in packing charges
    (c) Reduction of marine cargo insurance premiums
    (d) Saving in storage in port warehouses
2. Reduction of inventory cost
    (a) Assured transit times
    (b) Faster turnaround and quick delivery of merchandise
    (c) Improved services to customers
    (d) Reduction of cargo claims
3. Large-size vessels and bringing more economies
4. Consolidation of liners bringing value to trade
5. Advancement of technology, especially IT application, facilitating trade and equipment handling facilities at quay and yards bringing economies.

It can be observed from Exhibit 13.2 that there are certain parts of the globe where there is high growth in containerization. These ports have been modernized or have established sizeable operations in container terminals to match trade demands. More importantly, these ports have good primary hinterland, which contributes to the trade. This means that there is a realigned global supply chain with China (as seen from the number of Chinese ports figuring in the list), which is gaining importance as a manufacturing base. Apart from Asian ports, Rotterdam, Los Angeles, Hamburg, Antwerp, Long Beach, and Felixstowe have registered high growth rates.

The growth in the world container trade and a focus on transportation cost and time considerations in the past decade have brought about marked changes in the liner shipping industry, the notable ones being:

1. Ships and ports/handling facilities have increased in size and capacity
2. Emergence of a new economic global service pattern
3. Creation of direct feeder services network
4. Changes in ship to shore transfer
5. Inter-modal expansions via land bridges, and so on

The global trend of using larger ships—which incorporates the concept of 'hub and spoke' and 'relay', all oriented towards freight optimization—has a direct impact on the development of port infrastructure in terms of port location and its sizing—water depths, channel dimensions, berths and cargo handling methods. The shipping industry is set to witness the ship-sizes of the second generation of Post Panamax vessels attain a capacity of 10,000 + TEUs from the present size of 8,000 TEUs. Due to the economy in terms of the overall transportation cost, fourth generation/Post-Panamax vessels are already operational on inter-continental routes which would again redefine shipping cost and supply chain network. The higher growth rate and technological development in shipping may force a port to provide facilities in accordance with the planned/realized logistic trends.

Further on transportation efficiency, air cargo handling is also experiencing changes. China and some of the Asian countries including India have attracted large investments. In India, Mumbai and Delhi are the two major hubs for international air cargo. With public-private partnership, the Bangalore and Hyderabad airports have invested significantly on air cargo facilities which would favourably impact increased cargo handling. Such investments would impact global supply chain linkages positively. As mentioned earlier, while establishing a global supply chain for perishables and for high-value goods, it is important that the air cargo facilities are modern and attract international linkages so that lead time can be reduced. Also, with direct links, one can reduce multiple handling and thereby the cost of shipment. Hence, economies would necessarily work on the modernization and expansion of cargo facilities to be actively participating in trade. A focal organization will have to plug in such data and information while establishing a global supply chain network.

Exhibit 13.2 Trends in Container Traffic in Major Ports

Port	Country	1991	1995	2000	2007	Growth %	CAGR as on 2007	Rank CAGR
Singapore	Singapore	6,354	12,529	17,040	27,935	9.2	9.10%	9
Shanghai	China		2,844	5,613	26,150	19	20.31%	2
Hong Kong	China	6,162	11,830	18,100	23,999	10.6	8.33%	12
Shenzhen	China			3,994	21,099	38.1	26.84%	1
Busan	South Korea	2,694	4,789	7,540	13,254	12.1	9.83%	6
Rotterdam	Netherlands	3,766	4,503	6,275	10,790	5.1	6.39%	16
Dubai	UAE	1,255	1,924	3,059	10,650	11.6	13.40%	3
Kaohisung	Taiwan	3,913	5,053	7,426	10,256	7.3	5.83%	18
Hamburg	Germany	2,189	2,340	4,248	9,917	8.5	9.29%	8
Los Angeles	USA	2,038	2,555	4,879	8,355	10.5	8.65%	11
Antwerp	Belgium	1,761	1,527	4,082	8,175	9.5	9.45%	7
Long Beach	USA	1,768	2,740	4,601	7,312	8.9	8.71%	10
Port Klang	Malaysia		2,757	3,207	7,118	7.4	8.22%	13
All Major Ports	India	681	1,257	2,185	5,412	15.6	12.97%	4
New York/New Jersey	USA	1,865	2,070	3,006	5,299	6.4	6.34%	17
Bremen/Bremenhaven	Germany	1,277		2,714	4,892	8.1	8.22%	14
Tokyo	Japan	1,784	2,178	2,889	3,720	4.5	4.42%	20
Gioia Tauro	Italy		1,345	2,653	3,445	11.9	8.15%	15
Colombo	Sri Lanka	596	1,005	1,704	3,382	10.2	10.75%	5
Felixstowe	UK	1,434	2,219	2,800	3,341	6.1	5.10%	19
Global Total			93,646	134,460	187,857	216,508	7.5	7.23%	

SUMMARY

Global supply chain management is about taking the supply chain function across boundaries of nationality, wherein the focal organization by itself or through its partners brings enhanced value to all the players in the network. Establishing global facilities to serve customers across the globe and also to serve domestic customers of large markets from global low-cost resources are part of global supply chain management.

It may be interesting to note that it is not one factor but a number of factors such as the ability to assess complexity in terms of cost of space, finance, infrastructure including communication network, regulatory conditions, tariffs, and other factors related to doing business that are essential for the success of a global supply chain network.

While setting up an international supply chain network, one may have to clearly understand lead time of goods and cost of distribution depending upon the balance between cost efficiency and responsiveness. Ultimately, fundamental goals of supply chain in terms of cost and service level have to be met.

To cite an example, low cost and high productivity of Chinese resources would increasingly push multinationals either to set up facilities or enter into alliances with firms to act as sourcing agents. Companies have also set up international procurement offices in China.

Cost drivers emanating from resource-based factors including labour rates, international freight tariffs, exchange rate stability, and duties play a sig-

nificant role in the configuration of a global supply chain.

Responsiveness-based global supply chain requires addressing important features like response-time management, product variety, product availability, customer experience, order visibility, post-sales service, and returns management.

A firm must evaluate macro and micro factors and design strategies to meet challenges for achieving success in establishing a global supply chain network.

Supply chain risk refers to an uncertainty or unpredictable event affecting one or more of the parties within the supply chain network or emanating from external sources which could be macro or industry factors that adversely influence supply chain effectiveness and efficiency.

Risks can be triggered by a wide variety of factors like political instability, terror attack leading to disruption of movement, natural calamities, economic uncertainties like exchange rate fluctuations, inflation, demand risks and product-led factors like shelf life and short life cycle demanding product improvements.

Global supply chain is increasingly being influenced by changes that are happening in the structure of logistics infrastructure across globe. One of the key logistics drivers is transportation and one may observe some key changes that are likely to impact future trends in supply chain.

KEY TERMS

Asian Tigers: Asian Tigers refers to the highly industrialized economies of Hong Kong, South Korea, Singapore, and Taiwan. These regions were noted for maintaining exceptionally high growth rates and rapid industrialization between the early 1960s and 1990s. Indonesia was also considered to be one among the fast growing economies during this period. However, the crisis in 1997 in Asia leading to currency risk gave a setback for a short period.

Cost drivers: Cost drivers include those factors that influence decisions while establishing global supply chain links based on cost parameters. These could be relating to labour, other resources, and distribution costs.

Currency exchange rates: The rate or price of one country's currency expressed in another country's currency. For example, one USD would be exchanged for, say, 50.2823 INR. The higher the exchange rate for one USD in terms of INR, the lower the relative value of the INR. Exchange rates are determined by market forces and few cases by a national monetary regulatory body.

International freight tariff: International freight tariff relates to rates, duties, and charges to be paid for movement of goods and services from one country to another. International freight economics play a deterministic role in establishing a global supply chain network.

Intra-firm sourcing: Intra-firm sourcing refers to the process of manufacturing a component or a part within the entity through one of its subsidiaries or group firms or a different strategic business unit so that the core competency of a different group within the firm can be used effectively. For example, an auto major that may be using a number of castings and forgings may in-source it from its subsidiary.

Outsourcing: Outsourcing is a process, such as product design or manufacture, involving a third-party vendor. The decision to outsource is often made in the interest of lowering cost or making better use of time and effort relating to cost, based on the core competency of the firm that outsources and the firm to which the process is outsourced. In manufacturing, certain components are outsourced to vendors because the vendor can achieve economies and being standardized, product cost savings could be a key factor.

Regional cluster: A regional cluster is a geographic concentration of interconnected firms, suppliers, and associated institutions in a particular field. For example, the diamond industry cluster is located in India at Surat, Gujarat, which is one of the largest diamond clusters in the world. More than 10,000 units are operating closely in promoting the business. There are more than 300 clusters in India. Clusters are considered to increase the productivity with which companies can compete, nationally and globally.

Regional distribution centre (RDC): Regional distribution centre refers to the place or facility where goods or stocks, components and/or finished goods are stored temporarily for servicing a requirement quickly. In global business, RDCs play a significant role in serving regional demand centres quickly as lead time from plants could be high.

Resource-based costs: Resource-based costs refer to those costs that are determined by natural endowments of resources or the ability to exploit resources for a cost advantage. For example, a labourer from China or Far East is highly productive in precision works like electronics assembly. These costs are driven by certain natural and skill orientation factors leading to competitive advantages.

Third-party logistics service providers: These firms are either asset- or non-asset-based who own and operate transportation equipment and warehousing buildings and provide service to nodal organizations.

CONCEPT REVIEW QUESTIONS

1. Explain the various aspects of a global supply chain with examples. How would supply chain goals be aligned in global approach to satisfy a customer?

2. What are the cost drivers that would impact the global supply chain configuration? Explain with suitable examples the role of drivers on global supply chain effectiveness.

3. Describe responsiveness-based global supply chain configuration with examples of a product group you are familiar with.

4. Analyse the various macro factors that could hamper establishing an effective global supply chain. Give suitable examples on various factors.

5. What are the various industry, competition, and firm specific factors that could affect a global supply chain? What are the managerial levers available in handling the same?

6. Explain your understanding of supply chain risks in the global context and how you would propose to manage the same. Elucidate with examples.

7. 'Supply chain risk requires a multidisciplinary approach to assess and manage contingencies.' Elucidate. What are the benefits of being prepared to face a global supply chain risk?

8. Explain the role of supply chain drivers for establishing a global network. Describe the impact of advancements/improvements in transportation on global supply chain.

9. What are the key aspects impacting the dynamics of a global supply chain:

- A manufacturing firm with multiple sourcing
- A manufacturing firm with markets across regions and chooses to supply from low-cost region
- Industry setting up a cluster and promoting supply chain initiatives for development
- For a service provider like third-party logistics company involved in facilitation of global business

CRITICAL THINKING QUESTIONS

1. Based on web research on the diamond processing industry in Surat, in Gujarat, India, analyse how a supply chain analyst can improve the competitiveness of the operators.

2. 'A trading organization like MMTC in India plays a significant role in promoting trade and its key success depends upon supply chain efficiency.' Elucidate.

3. Describe foreign currency risk on global supply chain network and explain how it can hurt financial flows. Choose to illustrate with a few currencies like USD vs Euro, USD vs Japanese Yen. Base your discussion on data on exchange rate and illustrative transactions on any business of your choice.

PROJECT ASSIGNMENTS

1. Choose a company that is an active partner in a global supply chain link. Probe on key success factors of the company in its global business. Discuss the likely incidence or incidences of supply chain risk and how the company has faced or is prepared to face the same.

2. Visit a nearest container port and understand the efficiency it has brought in supply chain for the manufacturing industry port users. Use a case study approach to substantiate your findings.

3. Choose a leading supply chain integrator who is closely associated with trade, industry, or a firm. Probe the role of the integrator in improving the efficiency of the global supply chain network.

REFERENCES

Goetz, Richard G. and Dykema Gossett PLLC, 'Perspectives on Establishing Manufacturing Operations in China, India, and Mexico,' http://www.dykema.com/publications/docs/Goetz.pdf, accessed on 9 April 2009

Kate Kuhrt, 'Where India and China fit in Global Supply Chain,' Thomson Scientific, June 2005, http://scientific.thomsonreuters.com/news/2005-06/8279854/, accessed on 5 April 2009

Kotabe, Masskai and Kristiaan Helsen, *Global Marketing Management* , John Wiley & Sons Inc (sea) Pte Ltd, 2001

Mabert, Vincent A. and M.A. Venkataramanan, 'Special Research Focus on Supply Chain Linkages: Challenges for Design and Management in the 21st Century,' *Decision Sciences*, 29 (3), 537–552, 1998

Magretta, Joan, 'Fast, Global, and Entrepreneurial: Supply Chain Management, Hong Kong Style, An Interview with Victor Fung,' 30 November 1999, *Harvard Business Review*, 23 August 2006

Moon, Hwy-Chang, Hee-Kyung Kim and Dong-Hyun Lee, 'Cross Border Mergers & Acquisitions: Case studies of Korea; China; and Hong Kong,' Asia Pacific Economic Cooperation, 2004

'The Future Position of Hong Kong as a Regional Distribution Centre,' Hong Kong Trade Development Council, http://info.hktdc.com/econforum/tdc/tdc060802.htm#, accessed on 13 April 2009

http://findarticles.com/p/articles/mi_qa3618/is_200508/ai_n14880665/?tag=content;col1, 'China's Cost Advantage,' Manufacturing Engineering, August 2005

www.highseasugar.com/, accessed on 5 April 2009

www.iilfleatherfair.com/info_overview.html

www.worldbank.org/wbi/governance/pdf/Governance_Indicators_eng.pdf, accessed on 14 April 2009

www.worldbank.org/wbi/governance/pdf/Governance_Indicators_eng.pdf.

14

New Business Models with Technology and Process Integration

Learning Objectives

After studying this chapter, you will be able to:

- ◆ Understand the definition of business model
- ◆ Gain an insight into supply chain and business models
- ◆ Understand the technology applications for recreating business through reconfiguration of supply chain
- ◆ Understand the role of supply chain in success of e-business models
- ◆ Comprehend pure technology applications in supply chain
- ◆ Understand the process improvements, technology, and new business models
- ◆ Gain an insight into the challenges and learning in designing and deploying new business models through new supply chain initiatives

---

14.1 BUSINESS MODELS

A 'business model' is simply the way an enterprise organizes itself to acquire customers, create revenue streams, and make profits. It is fundamental to the existence of a business wherein an organization aligns its resources for making a product or services for realizing value from its operations in the market. Various stakeholders commit factors of production and engage in the product and resources market for the purpose of establishing a business. A business model is thus a framework wherein resources and capabilities are churned to attract, retain, and grow customers, and thereby make money for distribution of money among stakeholders.

The simple business model explained here is of a knowledge-based supply chain professional services firm named Alpha Supply Chain Services (P) Ltd, which provides consulting and evaluates supply chain business processes for businesses located in India. The objective here is not to discuss how to set up and manage business but to highlight the major elements of a business model.

Alpha is set up by a group of academicians, industry experts, and technology experts to provide supply/distribution network evaluation, business process studies for technology implementation, evaluation of technology options, and recommend a vendor or product and sourcing options. It also provides supplier evaluation, supply chain organization structuring and framework of roles and responsibilities, and addresses strategic issues in supply chain such as facilities choice, transport options, ethical audit, green initiatives, and so on.

Alpha has four principal consultants with a specific area of specialization with a team of two senior consultants in each team (a total of eight) and about twenty-four associate consultants across four locations in India. Resources are swapped across locations based on capability demand of assignments. Each location markets all range of services and resources move on to their respective assignments. The consultants cost Alpha annually Rs 48 million as compensation and the company has to bill more than Rs 120 million to be attractive in this business. The company has 1,200, 2,400, and 7,200 available man days among principal, senior, and associate consultants and per diem charges for each of these would vary. The utilization factor could be anywhere between 25–40 per cent as it takes time to deploy marketing, establishing proof of concept, learning technology advancement, competitive intelligence, and brand building initiatives. The company has to deploy in technology since services must have technology orientation to be successful in this business.

The business model would work only if Alpha could market its services for at least 40 assignments and charge a professional fee of Rs 3 million per assignment. To bill such revenue, the company must have the capability to offer innovative solutions and offer clients value that far exceeds the professional fees. First, a component of the business model should be dedicated to identifying Alpha's potential clients and providing a boutique of services. Second, the focus should be on resources and capability management. In this business, human resources, namely experienced, committed, and qualified professionals, is an investment. Attracting and retaining could be the next challenge, which is also an element of the business model. Third, profitability of the assignments depends on billing scope, solution capability, and customer attitude to work with Alpha.

Though supply chain advisory services are a recent trend, any business model, whether it is manufacturing or services, would have similar elements such as robust product/services offering, product/services market, resources availability, and financial viability including price and cost, and so on. In a competitive market, any successful model is likely to be imitated and attractiveness would stabilize at normal rates of return, limiting the attractiveness. If one has to hold on to the top position, one has to necessarily differentiate the business model with new approach. Supply chain domain offers such scope.

14.2 SUPPLY CHAIN AND BUSINESS MODELS

Supply chain focuses on managing three flows, namely physical, financial, and informational. Any business model would address managing all these three using supply drivers, namely facilities management, transportation, inventory, sourcing, pricing, and information structure. Business models reorganize these innovatively to create new models and thereby a competitive advantage. One of the cases of such supply chain driven business models is discussed in Exhibit 14.1.

Exhibit 14.1   Aravind Eye Hospitals

Aravind Eye Hospitals began in 1976 at Madurai with eleven beds. Today, in addition to the hospital in Madurai, there are four other Aravind Eye Hospitals in Theni, Tirunelveli, Coimbatore, and Puducherry, with a combined total of nearly 3,590 beds. It handles close to 2.4 million patients and about 270,000 surgeries in a year (data as of 2006). The model provides quality care at a price point affordable to the poor as well. A core principle of the Aravind System is that the hospital must provide services to the rich and poor alike, yet be financially self-supporting. This principle is achieved through high quality, large volume care, and a well-organized system. Shah and Murthy (2004) in their interview with Dr G. Venkataswamy and R.D. Thulasiraj bring out the various facets of managing such a hospital and highlight the role of leadership.

Here, one may note some key initiatives which make the model different from others:

1. Prior to the establishment of Aravind Eye Hospital, any community outreach programme was mainly meant for creating awareness and was largely supported and funded by the government. Aravind Eye Hospital made this a part of its initiative and business model as it wanted to create service mobility by reaching out to patients at their locations. An integral part of Aravind is its community outreach programmes such as screening eye camps, school eye health programme, village volunteer programme, and so on, all of which provide different strategies for taking eye care service to the doorstep of the community. They provide curative, preventive, and rehabilitative care to the community along with IEC (information, education, and communication) programmes to improve service delivery to potential patients in the community. Facilities deployed to reach patients include a mobile van with a VSAT antenna provided by Indian Space Research Organization (ISRO), used for voice, data transmission, and video conferencing. Add to this, an efficient utilization of resources differentiates Aravind from other hospitals.

2. Aravind Hospitals have implemented advanced IT systems and provide online support for doctors and patients and other role players in the network. IT applications include: Hospital Management Systems, Financial Accounting, Materials Management, Community Outreach, Personnel Management, Office automation, GIS, and Tele-medicine. It is at an advanced stage of implementing 'EyesTalk' software in other hospitals, which will enable ophthalmologists/physician/eye care providers in any part of the globe to consult with Aravind Eye Hospital's ophthalmologists. This would mean IT as a business service. They have also set up Aravind Virtual University—a facility to conduct classes, discussions, and share thoughts over the Internet. They have introduced Electronic Medical Record and Wireless PDA applications in patient care and facility maintenance. This early application of IT in its services turned out to be a key competitive differentiator for Aravind Hospitals and helped them to build a successful business model.

3. Aravind Eye Hospitals have started tele-ophthalmology, which is a techno-savvy method by which the medical facility is taken to rural or remote areas by using computers, video conferencing, and the Internet. It enables a doctor to interact with the patients sitting at a remote end in a faraway place through video conferencing, share data through computers, and diagnose the patient with the help of the local doctor who uses ophthalmic diagnostic equipments to transfer the images. Also, ophthalmology is one field of medicine where imaging plays a major role and many a diagnosis can be made by viewing the images. So it becomes apt to use IT in ophthalmology for reducing the urban-rural divide. The advantages of tele-ophthalmology are:

(a) Service accessible and affordable by reducing travel cost and time for the patients

(b) Service to remote markets with specialized eye care

Aravind Tele-Ophthalmology Network (ATN) is linked through the Aravind Eye Hospital Madurai

IT network, which is connected with its other hospitals in Coimbatore, Theni, Puducherry, Tirunelveli and eye camps. It is linked to remote centres through Internet wherein they partner with hospitals, Internet eye care practitioners, rural Internet service centres, eye care and associate eye care institutions. Thus, information as driver has helped the hospital to deploy innovative business models in remote areas.

4. On the sourcing and alliance spectrum, the hospital has moved to set up manufacturing the intraocular lens. Manufacturing is a non-profit entity established with a technology partner to provide value to the patients.

Thus, Aravind Eye Hospitals have established an innovative business model with supply chain drivers enabling creation of an extended value system for all players in the network.

Source: www.aravind.org.

There are more such cases wherein the supply chain is an important element of business models. Such interventions happen through reworking the three flows or by reconfiguring supply chain drivers or by combining both.

14.3 TECHNOLOGY APPLICATIONS FOR RECREATING BUSINESS THROUGH RECONFIGURATION OF SUPPLY CHAIN

Technology explosion in the last two decades has transformed many companies' fortunes and created a new competitive horizon where some traditional companies had to give space for new generation companies which had a strong technology network and business models in place. Few traditional companies were able to quickly reposition themselves and compete. In this section, we would look at a few such cases and draw some inferences.

First, one may look at the services supply chain of retail investors of stocks in companies listed in the capital market in India. Before 2002, trading was primarily physical transfer when a retail investor had to sell or buy a share. A stock broker played an important role in the physical transfer of stock. The retail investor not only depended on information but also on physical handling of shares. The Securities and Exchange Board of India (SEBI) mandates a demat account for share trading above 500 shares. As of April 2006, it became mandatory that any person holding a demat account should possess a Permanent Account Number (PAN). The advantages of demat account include:

- A safe and convenient way to hold securities
- Immediate transfer of securities
- No stamp duty on transfer of securities
- Elimination of risks associated with physical certificates such as bad delivery, fake securities, delays, thefts, and so on
- Reduction in transaction cost
- No odd lot problem, even one share can be sold
- Automatic credit into demat account of shares, arising out of bonus/split/consolidation/merger, and so on

It changed the role of brokers in the financial services supply chain wherein instead of handling physical flows, they had to become information- and research-driven or else had to change their scope of business. Retail investors benefited as this community of investors could deal with investments with confidence and this changed the characteristics of the market, which became more transparent with regard to information. This is the real benefit of technology adoption in capital market as the volume of transactions increased and all the players in the network gained in the process. It is important to note here that technology is the driver for the reconfiguration of the processes of trading, and supply chain processes of retail investment in shares changed from physical to virtual using an electronic platform. Financial services are meant for investing in ownership of a company and trading for profit, and earlier physical instruments such as share certificates, which were proof of a transaction, have now become virtual. The experience of ownership is still there without the rigour of physical handling and risks associated with it. Similar opportunities exist in many other areas, especially in the financial services supply chain. A host of applications have come up in the banking and insurance business wherein one can issue a virtual check, demand services of banks by account holders, and purchase insurance on cyber space through portals.

Secondly, there are areas of IT implementation that span from the supplier end to the ultimate customer as in the case of Sony and Godrej products in India. (Refer to Exhibit 14.2.)

Companies look at deploying technologies like radio frequency identification (RFID) and using connectivity to reach to the distributor and retailer level in secondary distribution, which was not earlier possible in a traditional supply chain network.

Thus, technology applications have opened up new vistas of market and business. One can look at the following cases in India from services and non-profit organizations:

1. Logistics of conducting elections in India is a huge challenge. Earlier, elections in India were conducted through physical ballot papers through which voters exercised their choice in different polling booths. These ballot papers were later aggregated in counting centres, sorted, and counted. This process was simplified with the application of technology in the form of voting machines that are compact and facilitate counting electronically. Now, the whole process is transparent, cost effective, quick, and less expensive. This is shown in Exhibit 14.3.

   Education is widely imparted through deployment of technology in India. This is commonly increasing seen in executive management education wherein premier institutions are tying up with organizations such as Reliance Communications, NIIT, and Everonn Systems to deliver content through their studios, making the courses available to participants on scheduled time slots in a receiving station of the partner organizations. This provides scope for a long-term, continuing learning, and professionals can learn during weekends without a need to travel. Technology adoption has reconfigured this supply chain management learning services wherein all players in the network benefit.

Exhibit 14.2 IT for Unblemished Supply Chain Performance

There is a proliferation of SKUs as product variants are increasing and customers are becoming choosy about product features. A focal organization must align its supply chain to satisfy such customers. Take cars for instance. While a car manufacturer makes some key components like the body and the engine, a lot else comes from auto ancillary providers—everything from tyres to plastic components to brakes to batteries and several other parts that go into a typical car. In fact, now a customer can select many parts of the car as per his/her liking except the basic body and engine. In developed countries, such configuration is happening in the light commercial vehicles segment where vehicles are customized according to buyers' demands.

Tony Murphy, Solutions Head—Manufacturing, Datacraft, explains, 'Supply chain management as we know it today is driven by information. The Internet has driven connectivity across the supply chain right down to the customer.' This is being firmed up by Mani Mulki, VP, Information Systems, Godrej Industries. He mentions that 'the most challenging part of implementing supply chain management for us was the last segment, which involved integration of our huge number of retail outlets across India.' He views that challenge would be to make the technology backend robust and ensure that the backend architecture services the distributors' supply chain, suppliers, and production units at a much more efficient level wherein the network could connect close to 90,000 retailers. According to Drew Martin, SVP and CIO, Information Systems and Solutions of America, Sony Electronics, 'At Sony, where a lot of products are produced by third-party manufacturers like Flextronics, we have to really think end-to-end when it comes to managing the supply chain as we do not control it in its entirety.' This is what drives their IT system configuration for managing SCM.

Four important areas where technology in business can be implemented are:

1. Organizations now manage limited resources, so technology deployment must be carefully chosen. Skill sets and competencies that are core to the business should be enabled by technology.

2. The second area is supply chain connectivity. India is faced with tremendous challenges because there is distributed manufacturing all over the country. Unless connectivity is available across all corners of the country, supply chain efficiency cannot be achieved.

3. The third area which arises out of connectivity is a real-time or near real time management of supply chain network using technologies like RFID.

4. The fourth area is regarding security. Many global companies, who wish to do business with Indian manufacturers and trading partners, will insist upon compliance to international standards.

Certain verticals like the automobiles sector have been the most forward looking, and emerging verticals like FMCG and pharmaceuticals are catching up. According to Murphy, 'Many automotive companies in India have opted for a lean manufacturing process. They are adopting global technologies that embrace enterprise systems, resource planning, and supply chain connectivity. They are at par with the best practices in the world. We are also seeing innovation in FMCG and pharma. I think over time you'll start to see more of an extended supply chain emerging. RFID will be a technology that will be deployed at various points along the supply chain. It could be used for asset tracking, asset utilization, or IT security, and eventually, there will be a ubiquitous deployment of these types of solutions that offer the ability to understand what is happening in real-time.'

Source: Birnur, Esha, 'Flawless Supply Chain Performance Depends on CIO,' 11 June 2008, http://biztech2.in.com/india/features/scm/flawless-supply-chain-performance-depends-on-cio/27431/0, accessed on 2 August 2009.

Exhibit 14.3 'An Event of Such Magnitude Never Seen in the World'

Election Commissioner S.Y. Quarishi's take on Election 2009 (As told to Sheela Bhatt)

India's election is not just an electoral exercise, but an event of such a magnitude that has no parallel in the world. A large electorate, 714 million voters; more than 8 lakh (800,000) polling booths, each polling booth with a team of five members expresses size of operation. There are almost 8.28 lakh booth-level officers. Additionally, about 8–9 million people are appointed to run the elections, which includes the security forces. They are trained at various levels. Each booth has to have a mode of communication so that the Election Commission would get to know within 10 minutes if anything goes wrong. This is something we tried for the first time in 2009. The Election Commission's regular budget is just Rs 20 crore (Rs 200 million) for this election. The Commission with 300 people is a very small organization conducting one of the biggest exercises in the world.

Logistics

Bharat Electronics Ltd and Electronic Corporation of India Ltd, both government undertakings, manufacture the electronic voting machines (EVMs) under the Election Commission's guidance and that of a technical committee headed by a professor of IIT, Madras. This committee of experts has been constituted by the Parliament. The EVM is a cheap machine; it costs about Rs 8,000 to Rs 10,000. The machine has two units: the control unit, and the other is the ballot unit. The control unit preserves all the data. One unit can handle 16 candidates. So, if the number of candidates is more than 16, then we need two machines. If there are 33, then we need three machines, and if there are up to 64 candidates, four machines can handle this. Beyond that, one will have to go for old style ballot paper. An EVM is a stand-alone machine; it does not communicate with anyone outside. The fairness of this stand-alone machine will be lost if there is a remote control.

To highlight the logistical challenges, in the last phase of polling, the Election Commission (EC) spent three or four days on just two polling stations in Kashmir, and in Ladakh, which were at the altitude of 13,000 feet, and where Indian Air Force helicopters could not land with EVMs. The EC despatched twelve people in two parties by foot, in knee-deep snow, to carry the machines a distance of 40 km. They walked for two days and two nights and then conducted the poll. They had taken along with them satellite phones. There were just thirty-seven voters. They were as important to us as the rest of the 700 million. Special arrangement for counting was made. The EC authorized one of the two senior officers and declared him an Assistant Returning Officer (ARO) legally. He counted the votes and conveyed through the satellite phone. That result was announced first before the rest of the counting began. There were re-polls in just 660 booths out of the total 838,000 booths.

One could imagine the complexity of doing this with physical ballot papers where logistics and cost of operation would have been phenomenal and time and resources deployed for completing the process could have been more.

Source: http://election.rediff.com/special/2009/may/18/loksabhapoll-election-commissioner-s-y-quarishi-on-election-2009.htm, accessed on 2 August 2009.

---

2. Another example would be asset utilization of religious endowments. One such instance is Tirumala Tirupati Devasthanam (TTD), which manages temples, medical facilities, education, and a number of other social activities that are run economically through self-generated funds. Millions of people pay a visit to the shrine, which is situated in a range of hills. Add to this, arrival variability increases the problem of managing number of visits on weekends and certain popular dates. The endowment also has the onerous task of protecting the environment and balancing the asset creation for the convenience of people. It

achieves all of this by using technology to limit the number of people visiting the shrine.

TTD has applied technology for managing its operations. It has a queue system that is effectively managed to achieve the constant flow factor. Queues are formed using differential pricing mechanism with varied time windows. A queue is formed with sale of tickets through electronic media where one can book visits in a planned manner. This reduces sudden variations in queue size. Nearly 40,000 pilgrims visit the shrine daily to offer their prayers. To reduce the waiting time in the queues, TTD has introduced the e-Darshan facility wherein the pilgrim is provided with a darshan (view of the shrine) slot remotely before actually reaching Tirumala. This system was started with a token system and later replaced with the biometric system, which is now under operation. These e-Darshan counters are in almost all TTD community centres, which are places of worship and social activities, and information centres in and outside Andhra Pradesh. Pilgrims are permitted to enter the Vikuntam Queue Complex-I according to the time slot provided to them.

It is not just the arrival and service that matter but also asset utilization. Availability of transport, accommodation, and support facilities like food are stressed with increased patronage. Apart from reducing customer disappointment, TTD has the challenge of making people happier and hence technology application eases the pressure. In order to manage assets, visibility of traffic is critical. Technology enables the same. Since TTD is self-financed, receipts by way of offering from devotees are important. Hence customer patronage and satisfaction are important. TTD has created TTD local offices in different districts that originally were points of selling services and have now become places of worship and social activity. Apart from streamlining main temple visits, this approach helps to improve faithfulness and commitment.

TTD has enabled electronic offerings. Innovations, integration with logistics, supply chain partners, e-procurement, and managing the three flows, namely physical, financial, and informational, are success factors brought about through technology applications. The key learning is that even a complex supply chain service that is faith-driven can be managed with electronic application as transparency enables to build customer faith and loyalty.

3. Another important public intervention of technology in transport in India is railway booking through the Internet and other related technologies. India is a vast country and Indians in general depend upon Indian Railways for movement of people and cargo. It is one of the largest organizations in the country with millions of employees and complex systems. The railway services also face the problem of peak traffic and heavy customer dissatisfaction. Indian Railways was once less popular for its varied time schedule and improper allocation of seats for travel. This was because most of the facilities were managed manually. During the last ten years, the railways have implemented technology solutions where ticket booking is through the Internet, ATMs of banks, and other digital

versions, including through approved vendors. Apart from issuing tickets, the railways have introduced e-procurement, online cargo booking, tracking of rail movements (www.indianrailways.gov.in). Thus, even large commercial government organizations involving masses are able to apply technology for improvements and benefits of different stakeholders in the system.

4. Coal auction enabled by the portal www.coaljunction.com, a sales division of metaljunction.com, has successfully applied technology in order to improve sourcing decisions of coal by industrial and other users in India using the Internet. coaljunction conducts eSales on behalf of Coal India Limited (CIL) and its subsidiaries, the largest coal conglomerate in the world. coaljunction has made the entire buying process not only simple but also transparent. Transparency improves price efficiency as information is available on a real-time basis and improves the confidence of all the stakeholders in the network. This also brings about a fair market price realization for Coal India Limited and its subsidiaries. coaljunction has managed to break many barriers, especially of intermediaries and unstructured funding organizations, and created many changes in the coal market.

Technology brings some of the smallest buyers of coal in direct touch with a giant conglomerate like Coal India Limited. In a country where 70 per cent of the energy requirement is fuelled by coal and supplies usually mired with red-tapism and rampant black marketing, coaljunction has initiated a process where a consumer can avail of an order as small as 9 tonnes. Technology applications and in-depth market know-how are critical factors for its success.

To conclude, technology applications help re-create business values through transparency and visibility, online negotiation wherever applicable, price discovery with better information efficiency, and structure logistical drivers effectively due to the above advantages.

14.4   ROLE OF SUPPLY CHAIN IN E-BUSINESS MODELS

E-business enables execution of business transactions over the Internet, which improves efficiency and impacts responsiveness, which are the two supply chain objectives. There are two different important models of e-business, namely business to business (B2B) and business to customer (B2C). B2B depicts transactions between the focal firm and other partner firms in supply chain through the Internet. One can think e-procurement of goods wherein the focal firm gives the tender electronically and prospective vendors participate and negotiation takes place. Finally, a vendor is finalized through such interactions. Thus, e-procurement is an Internet-based, value-added application of e-commerce to facilitate, integrate, and streamline the entire procurement process, from the buyer to the supplier and back. There is no substitute for Digital Certificate/Signature in e-commerce. This is approved by the IT Act and has a legal sanctity.

E-procurement brings advantages of transparency in the procurement process, reduces the opportunities for abuse of power, improves competition without geographical limitation, reduces cycle time of procurement, and provides cost efficiency. Exhibit 14.4 gives the e-procurement process of IFFCO, a leading fertilizer manufacturer in India.

In e-procurement, it is possible that the vendor has the scope to take advantage of the customer by having more information about the customer than they would have if the customer was in a normal supply chain management structure. Also, vendors participating in bids may not be serious, which could lead to failure in executing the contract after winning the same. Hence, the focal firm needs to do pre-bidding evaluation more rigorously so that it gets scrutinized prospects for the bid. This is where metaljunction.com and other platforms offer tie up with scrutinizing agencies that could validate the parties for enabling the success of any transaction.

Apart from e-procurement, which is information intense, there are also other B2B transactions like collaborative initiatives for product development, production information and product and market research, testing and analysis of results, literature development, and so on. One may note that providing information across the supply chain, negotiating prices and contracts, allowing customers to place orders and track the same, and managing financial flows, are primary aspects of B2B e-business models. From a supply chain perspective, these constitute effective information flow, flawless financial flow, and streamlined physical flow. B2B is more of sourcing and pricing, and information and logistical drivers like warehousing, inventory, and transportation enable the same. New business models evolve around these drivers and management of flows.

B2C e-business models are of two types. The first model is the one in which the brand owner or the corporate directly sells to the customer across locations and is directly responsible for the sale. For example, the Asian Paints 'home solutions' enables a person to directly book for a retail paint solution. There are B2C models that provide information across the supply chain, especially on products, and facilitate

---

Exhibit 14.4   IFFCO E-procurement system

Step-wise IFFCO e-procurement system is given below:

- Vendors submit their bids online using digital signature.
- Vendors can upload/update/delete uploaded files.
- Vendors can take printout of quotations for their reference.
- Vendors can give advance intimations about despatch.

- Vendors can see the history of Purchase Orders placed and can make queries on it.
- Opening and evaluation of bids is in a secured and legal environment using Public Key Infrastructure (PKI), encryption, and digital certificates.
- Summary of technical and priced bids quoted by different vendors has been provided on the e-procurement website for limited access to the vendors who participated in the bidding process for that particular enquiry.

Source: www.iffcoindia.com/Static_Files/eprocurementguide.html, accessed on 3 August 2009.

product evaluation, price comparison, and a few even allow the customer to place the order, track it, and pay online.

The second type is portals like Rediff Shopping and ebay, which are platforms and facilitate brand owners and customers to interact and retail merchandise online. For example, Rediff Shopping includes clauses like:

- It does not sell or retail any products and does not ensure that the users shall perform their obligations in respect of the transaction concluded on this site and further expressly disclaims any warranties or representations expressed or implied in respect of quality, safety, merchantability, fitness for a particular purpose, or legality of the products listed and transacted on Rediff Shopping.
- Rediff Shopping shall neither be liable nor responsible for any actions or inactions of vendors and/or sellers or any breach of conditions, representations, or warranties by the vendor or manufacturer of the products.

In both the models, it is important to note that logistical drivers need to be well organized if it is to involve completion of transaction with physical and financial flows.

Both in the case of B2B and B2C models, all players in the supply chain network look for responsiveness and cost efficiency. There are cases where there is efficiency but responsiveness is low. For example, if one order is on Flipkart.com, a unit of WS Retail Services Pvt Ltd, Bangalore, India, the book may reach a buyer in two or three days and payment is made instantaneously through the financial partner. This requires managing stock (inventory), warehousing, and transportation of outbound material for fulfilling the order. This reduces the transaction cost but probably increases service time compared to a brick and mortar store of books.

Thus, e-business models depend upon an effective supply chain. The services supply chain has moved up in maturity level in using Internet-enabled customer experience in business transactions. Manufacturing- and distribution-driven networks are in the process of evolving e-business models as there are conflicts arising between traditional and contemporary business models.

14.5   PURE TECHNOLOGY APPLICATIONS IN SUPPLY CHAIN

Pure technology applications are advancing in logistical drivers, namely warehouse/distribution centres, inventory management, and transportation management. Here only a mention is made on such developments and readers may read reference material given at the end of this chapter and from other sources.

Warehousing is one such area where pure technology applications are picking up. In a country like India where labour is cheap, such advancements would be slow except in cases where the volume of transactions is high and accuracy levels required are high as well. Warehousing/distribution centre operations include receipts, putaway, storage, retrieval, and value-added services. Fully or semi-automated warehouses/distribution centres may incorporate automated unloading and putaway, automated retrieval, hanging garment systems, auto-sorting systems and automated load-building. For customers with suitable volumes and product profiles, a firm could design, build, and operate automated warehouses, creating efficient, fast throughput of cased, hanging, and palletized products across single or multi-temperature regimes. Exhibit 14.5 illustrates the Redington plan to invest in such an automated distribution centre (ADC).

Thus pure technology application in distribution centres could lead to efficiencies in operations. One will have to optimize such investments in India where labour costs are low and land costs are high. It would still make sense to deploy such technology solutions for high-value, accuracy-deterministic, and high-volume businesses.

Another technology application would be RFID. There are several ways in which RFID technology can be utilized in warehouses and distribution centres, both in existing warehouse systems and other ADC technologies. In receiving, items, cases, and/or pallets are read by a portal-reading unit placed at the dock door as they are unloaded from the truck. Data are transferred into the warehouse management system (WMS), updating its database. The system reconciles its orders and sends back information that will allow some items to be cross-docked for immediate transport, while others can be staged and stored. If bar codes were being used here, all received items would have to be scanned, their labels clearly visible by workers, making the process much more labour-intensive. When stored on shelves with readers, the items are automatically recorded by the readers; when they are removed, the action is also automatically recorded. All of this happens without human hands ever touching a scanner, keyboard, or clipboard. If cases are broken up and items repacked, each item is reassigned to a tagged case by scanning the item's bar code or RFID tag and the case/Pallet tag. That information transfer initiates an assignment of the pallet or case to a truck or dock. Cases/Pallets are moved along conveyor belts, triggering readers along the way that track the movement and also adjust conveyors as needed to redirect the cases/pallets. Thus, technology helps in managing a distribution centre.

RFID is useful in managing inventories especially of finished goods and work-in-process for high-value and sensitive products like human organs or precise parts and components for high-risk and technology equipments. Effective inventory

---

Exhibit 14.5 Automated Distribution Centres by Redington

Redington India Ltd intends to set up four automated distribution centres (ADCs) in four metros at a total cost of Rs 150–200 crore, which would provide better utilization of warehouse space and improved operational efficiencies. It distributes products for companies such as Nokia, LG, Whirlpool, Microsoft (Xbox) and Apple (iPod). It recently added Imate (mobile phones) and Belkin (accessories for Apple range of products). It distributes products of varying weights from 6 g (Belkin) to 6 tonnes (digital printing machine) per unit and the size also varies widely. The company handles 100 tonnes of products a month out of Chennai and 600 tonnes across the country. Redington has fifty-eight warehouses across the country.

Redington incurs an expenditure of Rs 14 crore on rents in 2008. It expects to save substantially because of the ADC. The ADCs will feature a 'Very Narrow Aisle' pallet rack system. The racks will go up 40 ft, with not more than a metre separating two racks.

Source: http://www.thehindubusinessline.com/2008/08/06/stories/2008080650910700.htm.

management depends upon consolidating, integrating, and analysing data collected from many sources, such as distribution centres and warehouses. Conventional tracking systems require manual intervention, which is labour intensive, time consuming, and error-prone. On the other hand, the use of RFID technology has significant advantages over conventional methods. In a replenishment-based system, whenever the total inventory at a warehouse or distribution centre drops below a certain level, the RFID-enabled system could place an automatic order. RFID-tagged products will allow stores to track the location and count of inventories in real time. This will better monitor the demand for certain products and place orders to prevent an out-of-stock situation. The high levels of inventory monitoring obtained using RFID can particularly benefit FMCG industries. On the retailing side, RFID technology at the point-of-sale (POS) can be used to monitor demand trends or to build a probabilistic pattern of demand. This application could be useful for the apparel industry or products exhibiting high levels of dynamism in trends.

Similarly in transportation, RFID helps tracking goods while on the move. RFID systems give a total visibility of product movement in the supply chain. This may help to make early decisions about inventory control in case there is any interruption in the supply. It partially or completely eliminates the time and effort required for counting while loading/unloading the items. This results in reduction of total lead-time for the arrival of an order. The pharmaceutical industry and perishable products industry could use RFID systems for reducing lead-times that will help to increase total useful shelf life of items. Since transportation and inventory trade-off are related to lead time efficiency, RFID helps in reducing the lead time through transportation and inventory efficiency.

Similarly in railroad, technology upgrades are initiated. Railways are setting multimodal logistics parks through public-private partnership. Dedicated freight corridors (DFCs) are being developed, entailing construction of approximately 3300 km of mostly double, electrified, high-axle load tracks, with a liberal space envelope, fit for high-capacity wagons and heavy haul freight trains at cruising speeds of 75 km/hr and top speeds of 100 km/hr, between Jawaharlal Nehru Port Trust (JNPT), Mumbai, and Tughlakabad to Rewari (western route) and Kolkata to Ludhiana (eastern route). A number of industrial nodes are also being planned as a part of a related initiative by Government of India (Delhi–Mumbai Industrial Corridor) alongside the western route of the DFC or Delhi–Mumbai Industrial Corridor (DMIC).

There are a number of other pure technological applications in the transportation sector such as efficiency of vehicle in carrying loads and movement across locations. New generation vehicles fitted with electronics components reduce the failure rate and time and hence improve transportation cycle time efficiency. In India now Volvo and Hino trucks are being marketed by leading commercial vehicle players (see Exhibit 14.6).

All such technology advancement along with infrastructure development and improved business horizon necessarily leads to building of new business models driven by dynamic supply chain drivers.

14.6 PROCESS IMPROVEMENTS, TECHNOLOGY ADOPTION, AND BUSINESS MODELS

There are a number of business processes that interface with the supply chain domain and a business constantly strives to improve such processes with technology as the enabler. These processes include:

- Product development and commercialization
- Sourcing and procurement
- Supplier management
- Materials and production planning
- Logistics and inventory management
- Demand management
- Order fulfilment
- Customer service management

Business process improvements in the above processes are enabled because of the scope technology advancements offer today. Process improvements are important in the learning curve of an organization. These are relevant across organizations and industries because of standardization of frameworks and certifications offered by various institutions involved in the implementation of technological solutions or products.

With increased implementation of lean supply chain, agile supply chain, responsive supply chain, resilient supply chain, and smart supply chain, companies are committed to process improvements that bring supply chain efficiency. For example, those who implement lean supply chain focus on eliminating waste in the system by avoiding processes leading to waste. With technology, this can be captured better. On the other hand, an agile supply chain focuses on flexibility. A key characteristic of an agile organization is flexibility, which lies partially in flexible manufacturing systems (FMS). Initially it was thought that the route to manufacturing flexibility was through automation to enable rapid changeovers (that is, reduced set-up times) and thus enable a greater responsiveness to changes in product mix or volume. Thus, agile supply chains are highly competitive, capable of winning in a volatile and cost-conscious environment. This again requires process improvements and with technology enablement could lead to better efficiency levels. Likewise,

---

Exhibit 14.6 New Generation Trucks by Volvo in India

Volvo has launched a new generation of its Volvo FH and Volvo FM trucks in the Indian market. The products include an entirely new 13-litre engine that improves upon various aspects affecting transport economy. The new trucks have high performance engines with the FH model being fitted with the Volvo D13A. With the introduction of these new engines, the power levels have also been increased and the FH will have 520 hp, while the FM will have up to 400 hp. The company has started production of the new truck models at its Hoskote (Karnataka) plant. No additional investments have been planned.

Source: www.hinduonnet.com/thehindu/thscrip/print.pl?file=2006061704421800.htm&date= 2006/06/17/&prd=th&, accessed on 3 August 2009.

adoption of any framework for efficiency and responsiveness, including in contingency, leads to process improvements. Such process improvements are embedded with technology for better results.

14.7   PEOPLE-LED SUPPLY CHAIN CHANGES AND NEW BUSINESS MODELS

New business models are new and often innovative ways of organizing the enterprise to generate profits. People, namely managers and entrepreneurs, are key initiators of innovation. New business models are emerging in a multitude of different formats in different industries around the world. In particular, new business solutions in financial services, insurance, education, healthcare and hospitality, and travel exist today. New business models in supply chains were first seriously considered in 1996 when Accenture trademarked the fourth party logistics concept namely 4PL. Accenture defined the 4PL model 'as a supply chain integrator that assembles and manages the resources, capabilities, and technology of its own organization, with those of complementary service providers, to deliver a comprehensive supply chain solution'. A 4PL integrator is a solutions expert who depended upon intellectual capability and technology deployment for offering hybrid solutions to customers.

There are a few companies who have specialized professionals-based supply chain solutions that are people driven. Companies like Cargomen Logistics offer export-import document handling and getting clearance based on their knowledge and people network. This qualifies as a 4PL service because they offer end-to-end solutions for handling international trade. Although as an organization they handle only a limited portion of all the processes, the rest of the processes are enabled through partnering vendors. Similarly companies like Expeditor offer a whole range of 3PL and 4PL offering for different industry groups based on their international exposure and knowledge transfer across locations. According to Expeditors, people, systems, and culture are critical elements in offering best of breed solutions. As a company it strives to offer the same. Any people-based supply chain organization must be able to organize these three elements for achieving efficiency and responsiveness.

Thus, people skills along with process improvements and technology could help to create new business models and be leaders in competition. Companies have gone through these and achieved success. Such companies in India include: metaljunction.com, ITC, Britannia, Hindustan Unilever Ltd, Ford, Hyundai, Maruti, Mahindra, to list a few.

14.8   CHALLENGES AND LEARNING

Though there are a number of cases that prove that new business models are enabled with innovative approaches in technology application, business process improvement, and people efficiency, it is important to note the following observations:

1. There is no standard formula which assures success; neither does the success of one guarantees the success of another company. Each company has its own

requirements and arrives at a solution to meet those requirements. Though companies have a tendency to imitate successful models, such imitation cannot work well with partnering organizations. The contrary is also true. At times, first movers fail and followers are more successful.

2. There is a tendency to overinvest in or underplay technology. It is important to understand the requirement of technology, and if required, it could be better to stagger investments as players in the network understand and appreciate visibility and transparency, which bring value to all players in the network.

3. Process adoption needs to be gauged for its effectiveness. There is a tendency to make process changes of technology upgrade because of standard bodies and award institutions. However, one would realize that such initiatives require a strong cultural fit and support from all players in the system. Change management while working on the process of improvements is one of the risk elements that may affect supply chain objectives.

4. The skills and kind of leadership used in supply chain domain is still not adequate. Instead of one assuming expertise, a company may invest in constant upgradation through training and research and associations with centres of excellence in the domain. Supply chain lead position depends upon quality of personnel, especially of senior management team. If new business models through reconfiguration need to be initiated, then the company must invest on building human resource capability.

5. Finally, a successful business model is one in which the customer pays preferably a premium and every player in the network system shares the benefits and pride of challenges of establishing a path-breaking model, which is not easily imitable and provides sustainable competitive advantage.

SUMMARY

A business model is a framework, wherein resources and capabilities are churned to attract, retain, and grow a customer base and thereby make money for distribution among stakeholders. Any business model, whether it is manufacturing or services, would have elements like robust product/services offering, market, resources availability and financial viability including price and cost, and so on to be successful.

Technology explosion in the last two decades has transformed many companies' fortunes and created a new competitive horizon where some traditional companies had to give space for new generation companies that had a strong technology network and business model in place.

Technology applications help in recreating business values through transparency and visibility, online negotiation wherever applicable, price discovery with better information efficiency, and structuring of logistical drivers effectively due to the above advantages.

E-business enables execution of business transactions over the Internet, which improves efficiency and impacts responsiveness, which are the two supply chain objectives. There are two important models of e-business, namely business to business (B2B) and business to customer (B2C).

Providing information across the supply chain, negotiating prices and contracts, allowing customers to place orders and track the same, and managing financial flows, are the primary aspects of B2B e-business models. B2B is more of sourcing, pricing, and information. Logistical drivers like warehousing, inventory, and transportation enable the same. New business models evolve around these drivers and management of flows.

Business to consumer e-business models are of two types. In one model, the brand owner or the corporate directly sells to the customer across locations and is directly responsible for the sale. In the other model, there are portals that are platforms and facilitate brand owners and customers to interact and retail merchandise online.

Pure technology application in distribution centres could lead to efficiencies in operations. One will have to optimize such investments in India where labour costs are low and land costs are high. It would still make sense to deploy such technology solutions for high-value, accuracy-deterministic, and high-volume businesses.

All such technology advancements along with in-frastructure development and improved business horizon necessarily lead to building of new business models driven by dynamic supply chain drivers.

There are a number of business processes that interface with supply chain domain and a business constantly strives on improving such processes with technology as enabler. New standards and certification processes cover supply chain domain areas as well and process refinements leading to new opportunities. Similarly, people skills along with process improvements and technology could help to create new business models and be leaders in competition.

It is important that companies set up new business opportunities by carefully integrating technology, processes, and people unique to each of the major supply chain networks instead of imitating success from elsewhere. Also, it is important to ensure sustainability in edges carved out through new business models.

KEY TERMS

Automated distribution centres (ADCs): ADCs are those that use computerized vehicles to store, select, and move pallets around a large warehouse.

Business model: Business model defines the operations of a business including the components of the business, the functions of the business, and the revenues and expenses that the business generates.

Business to business: Business to business (B2B) describes commerce transactions between businesses, such as between a manufacturer and a wholesaler, or between a wholesaler and a retailer.

Business to customer: Business-to-consumer (B2C) describes activities of businesses serving end consumers with products and/or services.

Cycle time: Cycle time is a metric for continuous improvement with the aim of driving down the deviations in the time it takes to produce successive units on a production line.

Digital certificate/signature: A digital certificate is an electronic 'credit card' that establishes one's credentials when doing business or other transactions on the web. It is issued by a certification authority (CA). It contains a name, a serial number, expiration dates, a copy of the certificate holder's public key (used for encrypting messages and digital signatures), and the digital signature of the certificate-issuing authority so that a recipient can verify that the certificate is real.

E-commerce: E-commerce consists of the buying and selling of products or services over electronic systems such as the Internet and other computer networks.

E-procurement: E-procurement is done through websites that allow qualified and registered users to look for buyers or sellers of goods and services. Depending on the approach, buyers or sellers may specify costs or invite bids. Transactions can be initiated and completed between buyer and seller.

Ethical audit: This refers to neutral, third-party verifiable process to understand, measure, report on, and help improve an organization's social and environmental activities and effectiveness.

Flexible manufacturing system: A flexible manufacturing system (FMS) is a manufacturing system in which there is some amount of flexibility that allows the system to react in case of changes, whether predicted or unpredicted.

Green supply chain: A green supply chain is the process of using environment-friendly inputs and transforming these inputs through change agents, whose by-products can improve or be recycled within the existing environment. This process develops outputs that can be reclaimed and re-used at the end of their lifecycle, thus creating a sustainable supply chain.

Information efficiency: This refers to free flow of information for players in the system for arriving at market-determined demand and supply at a price.

Point of sale: A point-of-sale (POS) terminal is a computerized replacement for a cash register.

The POS system can include the ability to record and track customer orders, process credit and debit cards, connect to other systems in a network, and manage inventory.

Radio-frequency identification (RFID): RFID is the use of an object which is normally an RFID tag applied to or incorporated into a product, or person for the purpose of identification and tracking using radio waves. Tags could be active or passive tags depending upon value as the former are expensive.

Supplier evaluation: An assessment of existing or new suppliers on the basis of their delivery, prices, production capacity, quality of management, technical capabilities, and service is supplier evaluation.

Warehouse management system: Warehouse management system is computer software designed specifically for managing the movement and storage of materials throughout the warehouse.

CONCEPT REVIEW QUESTIONS

1. Describe a business model. What are the key aspects of a successful business model? Elucidate with an example.
2. Explain the role of supply chain drivers in new generation business models that you may choose to discuss here.
3. Analyse technology intervention for business reconfiguration of supply chain with an example.
4. 'Pure technology interventions through automated distribution centres provide new business opportunities.' Elucidate. What are the advantages and disadvantages of ADCs?
5. 'Process improvements and people expertise along with technology provide new business opportunities.' Explain with examples.
6. What are the challenges in creating and sustaining new business models through supply chain initiatives? How can a firm handle the same?

CRITICAL THINKING QUESTIONS

1. Map the processes of a large retail mom-and-pop store called Select & Buy Store (SBS) which is likely to face competition from organized retail chain. SBS has about 1,500 regular customers who contribute 90 per cent of sale and the monthly turnover of SBS is about Rs 15 lakh. It experiences 40 per cent of sale in the first week and 20 per cent each in the next three weeks. SBS has a Point-of-Sale (POS) billing system and carries 21 days stock by experience. Peter's son Sam, who has done his MBA from a local school, learns about retail supply chain and wants to introduce a new model by integrating CRM, internal processes, and SRM with vendor-managed inventory in store. He believes tying up with e-payment and credit card company would help as it can generate orders whenever convenient to the customers and the delivery personnel can deliver the goods to the customer at a pre-appointed time window. He also feels such set up would help better demand forecasting and

could help them overcome the challenge they were about to face from the organized retail sector. He draws Peter's attention to a recent cover story published in *Business Today*, which tells that mom-and-pop stores are still lords of the trade. Prepare a detailed report on how Sam can transform this change and what would be his key success factors?

2. Ram Singh is recruited by a Hong Kong based integrated logistics company that has 3PL services and has moved into technology and knowledge-based (TKB) logistics solutions company. Considering Ram Singh's success in managing a 3PL company in India and the potential of TKB logistics services in India, he was appointed as Country Head. Imagine that you are Ram Singh and prepare a business plan for parent company to invest further on this.

PROJECT ASSIGNMENTS

1. Visit a nearby document storage facilities management centre which is a warehouse services business for a business process of document storage, retrieval, and management. Map its processes, technology, and people capability in establishing this business model.

2. Visit an auto or engineering product manufacturing company and analyse its product development initiative using technology. Explain in terms of turnaround time for product development.

REFERENCES

Birnur, Esha, 'Flawless Supply Chain Performance Depends On CIO,' 11 June 2008, http://biztech2.in.com/india/features/scm/flawless-supply-chain-performance-depends-on-cio/27431/0, accessed on 2 August 2009

Gattorna, John, *Living Supply Chains: How to Mobilize the Enterprise Around Delivering What Your Customer Wants*, Dorling Kindersley (India) Pty Ltd, Pearson Power, 2008

Harrison, Terry P., Hau Leung Lee, John J. Neale, 'The Practice of Supply Chain Management: Where Theory and Application Converge,' *International Series in Operations Research & Management Science*, Vol. 62, 2005

http://election.rediff.com/special/2009/may/18/loksabhapoll-election-commissioner-s-y-quarishi-on-election-2009.htm, accessed on 2 August 2009

Rushton, Alan, John Oxley and Phil Croucher, *The Handbook of Logistics and Distribution Management*, Kogan Page, 2000

Shah, Janat and L.S. Murthy, 'Compassionate, High Quality Health Care at Low Cost: The Aravind Model,' In conversation with Dr G. Venkataswamy and R.D. Thulasiraj, *IIMB Management Review*, September, 2004

www.aravind.org

www.asianpaints.com/homesolutions/what_is_unique.aspx

www.coaljunction.com

www.hinduonnet.com/thehindu/thscrip/print.pl?file=2006061704421800.htm&date=2006/06/17/&prd=th&, accessed on 3 August 2009

www.iffcoindia.com/Static_Files/eprocurement guide.html, accessed on 3 August 2009

www.indianrailways.gov.in

www.tirumala.org

www.thehindubusinessline.com/2008/08/06/stories/2008080650910700.htm

Avon Solutions & Logistics (P) Ltd—An Integration of People, Process, and Technology for a New Range of Services

It was in December 2006 when investors were scheduled to meet K. Krishnakumar (KK) to evaluate his business and invest in the same. According to KK, when Avon Solutions & Logistics (P) Ltd started, it was aimed as a mailroom outsourcing solutions, which was primarily focused on manpower staffing services for a business process of handling mails of a company. KK now has the satisfaction of professionalizing a new range of niche services wherein people, process, and technology integration has led him to the position of being the first mover in that sector while being successful at the same time. Based on his experience in the logistics domain, KK started the company in 2001 with a small team of people who came along with him. His core strengths have been leadership, people management, and appreciation of document handling and its role in supply chain.

BUSINESS

Avon is a pioneer in India, which started offering integrated mailroom management solution with clients across diverse industries such as banking, insurance, consulting, technology, and manufacturing. Its processes, training methodologies, software, technology integration, mail management expertise, and quality rigours, all are proprietary in nature. Customers have saved costs and realized substantial value addition. Mailroom became cost efficient and responsive, and customers were delighted to grow with them across locations. The mission of Avon is to be the first choice among providers of mailroom management solution by offering substantial competitive advantage to the clients.

The genesis of business is based on the fact that a mailroom is one which connects stakeholders in the system with the company, and employees' productivity depends upon the efficiency of a mailroom. Hence, Avon decided to provide a completely enhanced mailroom management solution that streamlines and accelerates corporate communication, by interspersing technology, processes, increasing productivity, improving service quality, and creating total customer delight. The product is based on the foundation of a typical onsite mailroom unit indulging in sorting, mail rounds, vendor interaction and management, inbound and outbound mail management, and so on., topping it up with value add-ons like MIS generation, customer service, cost management, vendor management, and even pre-processing of mails. Typically, its solution encompasses well-trained manpower, highly defined proficient processes, complete automation of mailroom operations with proprietary software, and authentication using up-to-date technology.

For example, for industries such as banking and insurance, Avon offers back-end mailrooms, a highly automated and well-designed solution resembling a miniature courier operation with enhanced pre-processing capabilities and a matching manpower profile. Similarly, it offers front-end mailroom solutions that aptly integrate up-to-date-technologies and highly skilled manpower to offer a truly world-class mailroom solution.

CUSTOMER BENEFITS

According to KK, with a customer, vendor management practices have not only reduced the vendor base drastically, but also posted 15 to 20 per cent savings. This has been true of many other customers. Similarly, through a combination of technology solutions, Avon has reduced mailroom queuing time from 20 minutes on an average to almost instantaneous. Since one loses productive time due to mailroom queuing, Avon has combined supply chain objectives of efficiency by way of cost reduction and responsiveness in a business process like handling of mails in a corporate. Avon's customers include: Accenture, Deloitte, Deutsche Bank, Standard Chartered Bank, Indian School of Business, Microsoft, Tata Life, MediAssist, and so on. These are the best of corporates/brands in business.

SOFTWARE AND SOLUTIONS

1. People are key to this business. MailPRO has a systematic approach towards prudent manpower management right from hiring, training, placing, rotating, motivating, till rewarding. There are in-house training sessions and they also ensure uninterrupted manning of mailroom activities every time, efficiently.

2. Process deployment through Avon's I-MAP, which decides the kind of manpower required, extent of technology and automation, mailing schedules, mail round schedules, and so on, and redesigns the entire workflow, the complete layout of inbound mail management, outbound mail management, vendor management, and other value-added services as it would deem fit. I-MAP also ensures that every activity of the processes achieves maximum efficiency for the client at every stage.

3. Technology: MailIT of Avon endeavours to elevate any mailroom with up-to-date technology and automation, and thus improve business communication speed and create a competitive advantage in the long run. The software captures every mailroom activity, till high-level reports such as department-wise mail usage pattern, customer communication tracking, timely reply reminders, and cost allocation. The software spans the entire breadth of possible management information.

Avon offers a range of technology solutions, some of which are first of its kind even on an international scale. These include:

1. **TrackIN:** Uses authentication technologies such as Biometric, RFID tags, HID/Access cards, Signature Pads for inbound mail management and electronic storage of proof of delivery. This enables secure handling and thereby results in enormous reduction in frauds and misuse, and also reduction in turnaround time.

2. **Mailkiosk:** Mailroom information at common areas through touch screens for employee use. This is useful for a corporate with a high employee base, such as IT and BPO companies, where there is a high volume of personal mails.

3. **Mailnet:** Inter-branch mailroom networking for corporates with large branch network is the focus of this product. This is useful for banks, insurance companies, telecom, and so on, and aims at coordinating and synchronizing independent mailrooms of multiple branches to work in unison. One can get instant updates on inter-branch mails which facilitate automatic cross verification.

The advantages of mailroom software include:

Total process management and automation, establishing central repository for all mailroom data, tracking vendor performance, rates and time management, prompting user's reply, forward, or take action, in effect prioritize/advise on course of action, managing resources management and allocation, productivity monitoring and management, activity-based profitability tracking and establishing quality in services, and so on.

SCOPE OF SERVICES

Module	Range of services
Inbound mail management	• Customized inbound mail management process • Complete Electronic data capture and systems driven control and monitoring • Immense significance given to TAT to minimize errors and misuse • Instant capture of proof of delivery within the organization through variety of options such as PDA, Signature Pads, RFID technologies • Archiving, and destroying in case of incoming mails
Outbound mail management	• Collection of outbound mails at pre-defined collection points • Vendor management, contract negotiation, cost management • All round monitoring and efficiency management in terms of synchronization of courier cut off times with internal work time, data capture of all outbound mailing and content verification • Consolidation, bulk mailing, franking • Track deliveries alongside third party courier tracking mechanisms • Instant/Automatic feedback to the senders on mail status • Mail rounds such as inter-office shuttle, time bound intra-office messenger services
Vendor management	• Vendor contract management • Maintenance of standard vendor base

Module	Range of services
	• Transparent dealings with vendors through tripartite arrangement on parameters such as price, routes covered, geographic areas, service levels, proof of delivery, reducing turnaround time, and so on
Value added services	• MIS and report generation • Pre processing of mails like checking contents for insurance claims or Letters of Credit are routine and can easily be coded into a basic set of rules which can be followed at the mailroom stage

According to KK, while in pursuit to offer excellence to customers, Avon systems and procedures had discovered a whole new way of offering the solution. The results such as cost reduction, increase in mailroom productivity, increase in corporate productivity and even employee morale though were incidental at the beginning, have now become benchmark. Companies are outsourcing this process as it's a non-core activity. Avon considers accountability, higher efficiencies, contingencies, and near-zero error in business process as the challenges. The model could be imitated or pirated. According to KK, managing senior management and customers has helped him to be a leader and attract venture capitalists to be interested in his business. His philosophy is that 'be it the trained and well-motivated manpower, or the highly streamlined processes, or interspersing of latest technologies for authentication such as PDAs, RFID, and so on, we endeavour to bring in total user delight and empowerment and make work as passion'.

15

Information Technology in SCM

Learning Objectives

After studying this chapter, you will be able to:
- Understand the application of IT in SCM
- Understand the capital investment perspective in SCM systems
- Understand the requirement analysis process for SCM systems
- Identify enterprise applications domains and their relevance to business, e-SCM
- Understand the classification of SCM systems
- Gain an insight into the key challenges in executing SCM systems projects

A supply chain network consists of many players, right from the customer to any vendor who contributes in fulfilling the customer's demand. It includes various parties who directly or indirectly enable such a network. For example, a tier 1 auto component vendor, who supplies engine parts like pistons and piston rings, will have an important role in the network of the auto Original Equipment Manufacturers (OEM) where information visibility on near/real time is critical for achieving effectiveness. Given this situation, application of information technology highlights the importance of 3As in achieving seamless integration along the supply chain. They are *Accuracy*, *Accessibility*, and *Appropriateness* of information.

In decision-making, *accuracy* of information is very vital. One must ideally have absolutely accurate information for tracking, consolidating, and/or mining data from historical transactions. In the absence of this, one could use past patterns for projecting the future. In either case, a reliable and consistent IT system would play a key role. Disparate systems shall be integrated to avoid redundant data creation/ transfer at multiple points.

A second important characteristic is *accessibility* of information which should be timely and should flow upwards in the hierarchy for decision-making. This is important especially in a multi-location, multi-level organization, where there are a number of external players. Security considerations and a conservative outlook add another dimension to an already complex situation. To achieve efficient supply chain integration, there is a need to evolve a system that provides accessibility at the right level.

A third important characteristic related closely to accessibility is the *appropriateness* of information. This relates to structuring and defining the hierarchy of information.

15.1 IT APPLICATIONS AND THE SCM HORIZON

Supply chain activities can be categorized into three areas, namely planning, execution, and collaboration. Supply chain planning tools take care of demand planning, production planning, sourcing, sales and planning, inventory and warehousing planning, transportation planning, and aggregate planning. Information technology is applied in each of the planning components and integrated. Data points for these activities come from disparate sources or from the enterprise system. The enterprise system enables mainly transactions of internal supply chain and functional aspects such as production, finance, human relations, and marketing. Supply chain IT draws transactions processing, which is important for establishing linkages with three flows, namely: physical, financial, and information. Once internal processes are captured for supply chain decisions, a supply chain manager must ensure linkages with external partners, namely vendors, services providers, channel partners, and customers, for which collaboration tools are required.

Here, it is important to understand important to understand the company's stand on IT expenditure—how much it will invest in IT for its supply chain and also for its partners.

15.2 SUPPLY CHAIN INFORMATION SYSTEMS AND CAPITAL INVESTMENT

There are three underlying trend currents that influence the way businesses respond to demand and supply.

1. The industry trends
2. The telecom technology trends
3. The applications trends

With suppliers, logistics service providers, alliances, and new entrants into markets from various parts of the globe, industries across sectors are becoming increasingly competitive. Adapting to models of off-shoring and outsourcing, global manufactures are realizing many cost advantages. Innovations in telecom technologies such as optical fibre and wireless communications are changing the business landscapes with digital transactions and convergence of voice, data, and images. Applications of telecom technologies are leading businesses to adapt e-business and e-commerce models and take advantage of global business opportunities. With application of telecom technologies in the global business scenario, today's businesses are overcoming traditional barriers with ease.

The Telecom Genie's Magic

1. To overcome geographic barriers for say, instant sharing of designs for product development, one can use high-speed Internet.

2. To remove time barriers for the ease of document transfer and handling using Electronic Data Interface (EDI), one can use many Internet-based options.

3. Cost barriers, such as cost of transactions, drop steeply when compared to the brick and mortar model.

4. Transaction support for the ease of workflows and financial transactions smoothens financial flows.

Using the potential of telecom technologies, Internet-based information systems are redefining the business landscape. More detailed analysis of this is covered in Chapter 14. Rapidly evolving from traditional client server systems to web-based information systems, Internet technologies have become today's de facto standard for enterprise information systems. Business executives are realizing the importance of investments in supply chain information systems.

15.2.1 Calculation of ROI on Supply Chain Information Systems' IT Infrastructure

Like any other capital investment decisions, executives are rationalizing investments in supply chain information systems. For this purpose, a fundamental financial calculation is used as a method to rationalize investment:

Investment Rationale on IT for SCM

Return on Investment (ROI) can be calculated using the following formula:

$$ROI = \frac{(\text{Monetary Benefits [Tangible and Intangible]} - \text{Cost of using Technology})}{\text{Cost of Using Technology}} \times 100$$

*Both tangible and intangible benefits shall be considered for quantifying monetary benefits.

It is important to quantify costs and benefits along with risk under the categories mentioned in Table 15.1.

ROI Calculation

1. Project costs including capital expenses, implementation labour, management and support, operations and contract expenses = A
2. Project benefits including net tangible benefits = B
3. Project risks quantified as potential expenses = C

$$\text{ROI for IT infrastructure} = \frac{(B - A - C)}{(A + C)} \times 100$$

It is important to note here that both tangible and intangible = net tangible benefits have to be considered and project risks must be factored. Project costing is a specialized subject and a professional accountant's involvement is necessary for rationalizing investments in information systems.

Table 15.1 Costs, benefits, and risks

Technical benefits	Business benefits
1. Software development, automation 2. Integration with applications and business processes	1. End-user productivity 2. Participation in dynamic business 3. Collaborative business activities 4. Better and cheaper customer service 5. Other benefits
Costs and expenses	**Risks associated with technology**
1. Hardware requirements 2. Software requirements 3. Training requirements 4. Network bandwidth requirements 5. Monitoring tools 6. Operational costs and vendor consulting	1. New technology 2. Standards not matured or finalized 3. Software development tools and servers 4. Quality of third party software 5. Security

15.3 REQUIREMENTS ANALYSIS OF IT FOR SCM

One of the key perspectives of supply chain information systems is to understand their classification. There are many software products available in the market that could be purchased and deployed. On the other hand, there is no scarcity of talented manpower that can understand the business requirement and build an appropriate information system. There are five simple steps to identify what type of information system is required for business as shown in Figure 15.1. As one notices, these steps are made to facilitate 'buy or build' decision making.

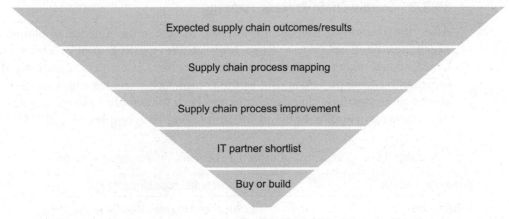

Figure 15.1 Five simple steps to identify information systems requirement

15.3.1 Expected Outcomes/Results List

Supply chain planning is done with a well-defined result/outcome in focus. Without such focus, success would be only accidental. As practiced for financial budgeting, marketing planning, and any other functional objectives in business, the CIO (Chief Information Officer) shall also define expected results/outcome of the information systems. One important lesson is hidden in this paragraph. If one observes, information systems have to serve the purpose of business; otherwise they become superfluous. Successful companies would always be customer-centric and their processes would be crafted to let multi-functional teams stay focused on customer requirements and yet coordinate among themselves. Any supply chain planning session normally would have participation from key stakeholders:

- Sales and Marketing personnel
- Accounts and Finance personnel
- Production and Logistics personnel
- Supply Chain and Customer Relationship personnel
- Administration and Human Resources personnel
- Electronic data processing and information systems personnel

While the first five sets of personnel identify and set the expectations of supply chain results/outcomes, the sixth set of personnel would enable the rest of the five sets of functions to achieve the expected results (Table 15.2). That's how successful cross-functional teams set expected supply chain results/outcome targets, and achieve them together. Conventionally, this is a typical end result of strategy meetings in board rooms. The expected supply chain results/outcomes are like dots on a canvas, which reveal a two-dimensional image when connected. When this image is compared with competitors' image, the strategies of market players unfold.

15.3.2 Supply Chain Process Mapping

After the business expectations are set by the cross-functional planning team, executives have to take a fresh look at the existing supply chain processes. Conventional process mapping tools like flow charts and process charts could be used to depict business processes. But as the complexity increases with interdependencies among processes, flow charts and process charts may not be easier to organize. A very useful process mapping notation for simplifying the complexity is BPMN (Business

Table 15.2 Sample list of expected outcomes/results for an enterprise

Business function	Expected outcome/result (YoY)
1. Marketing	70 per cent increase in customer satisfaction
2. Logistics	10 per cent reduction in transportation cost
3. Supply chain	40 per cent reduction in total cost of supply chain
4. Electronic Data Processing (EDP) and information systems	To be identified after planning and study of existing supply chain processes

Process Management Notation). However, it's very useful to add some more shapes to the BPMN notation to meet the enterprise requirements.

Following are the steps to draw process maps:

1. Identify persons and organizations involved in business processes (example, customers and sales organization, engineers and production organization, accountants and accounting organization, managers, and supply chain organization)

2. Identify related events that each of the persons or organizations may experience (example, a customer makes a purchase, enquires, complains to the sales organization)

3. Identify processes that may be triggered with each of the events (example, purchase may trigger an order management process, complaint may trigger a call centre process)

4. Identify the interconnectivity among processes and connect them as and when required

The advantages of following this notation are as follows:

1. Any change in one process will not affect the rest of the processes in the map.

2. It becomes very easy to change individual processes as it decouples roles and activities.

3. Integration points with any interfaces like printers, devices, and other information systems would be clearly revealed.

15.3.3 Supply Chain Process Improvement

With the drafts of existing supply chain process maps on one hand and expected results/outcomes on the other, one can now use years of functional expertise to identify process improvements to achieve results. Some of the generic improvements could be:

- Adding or deleting a person or organization to the business
- Adding or deleting an event to the person or organization
- Adding or deleting a process related to events
- Adding or deleting interconnections between processes

15.3.4 Identifying an IT Partner

Now, with the final supply chain process maps drawn to achieve business results/outcomes, start looking for an appropriate IT partner. An IT partner could be a services provider or a product vendor. ROI approach would help one identify an appropriate IT partner.

15.3.5 Buy or Build

Depending on the rationale, decide whether to buy a product to enable improved business processes or hire an IT team to build the system. One of the generic guidelines that may help in making this decision is the classification of enterprise information systems before evaluating IT vendors. Enterprise information systems could be classified into three generic types:

1. No management principles (NMP)
2. Basic management principles (BMP)
3. Shared management principles (SMP)

Enterprise information systems built with no management principles generally tend to provide basic transaction support like recording buy and sell transactions with stock and cash balances.

Enterprise information systems built on basic management principles were skewed mostly towards internal efficiencies. Three management principles drive these systems architectures:

1. Accounting principles
2. Value chain principles
3. Management accounting and production management principles

When basic management principles are shared and practised by trade partners, shared management principles emerge. Supply chain management and customer relationship management were two such practices that share basic management principles with trade partners. Enterprise information systems built on shared management principles generally tend to extend efficiencies outside the organization to trade partners.

During evaluation of IT partners, one shall look at the expected business results/ outcomes and classify the business requirements into any of the three types: NMP, BMP, or SMP. This would help one to search and shortlist appropriate IT companies for partnering.

15.4 E-COMMERCE, E-BUSINESS, AND SCM

One may note that technology applications in business have changed the landscape of many businesses where electronic business network works as a medium in the market. This requires physical delivery for which supply chain drivers play a crucial role and financial transactions again need to be linked through financial network enabled by cyber space. This is where linkages of e-commerce, e-business, and supply chain figure.

For example, let us look at two dimensions as illustrated in Figure 15.2:

• Horizontally across competition
• Vertically through suppliers

Economics tells that wherever a business is successful and makes profits, competition naturally evolves. Competition is generally viewed from the customer's dimension of business. However, it is equally important in a competitive market to take into account the supplier's side. While the customer dimension would make the enterprise think about ways to capture market share, the supplier dimension would make the enterprise think about ways to capture the supplier share. Lang et al. (2002) attempted to show the similarities and advantages of such approach in their work.

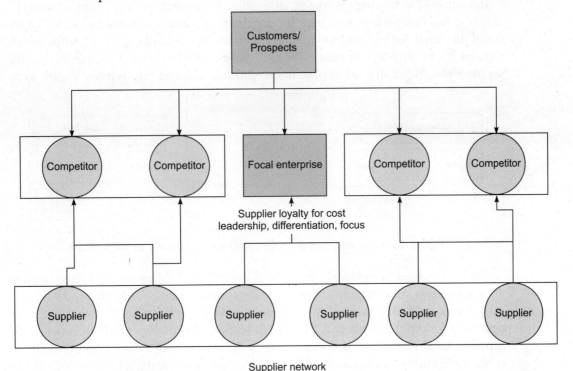

Figure 15.2 Competitive advantages with supplier management

An organization would look at customer strategies before considering strategies to control and channelize a supplier's bargaining power. Global enterprises realized the importance of prioritizing customer strategies and executing supplier strategies, and encouraged comprehensive supplier management practices. As shared management practices increased, suppliers were invited to participate in enterprise business strategy meets at very early stages of business cycles. Nations also realized the importance of creating clusters to support global enterprises and increase the competitiveness of industries. As a result, the special economic zones and supplier clusters were established. With the customer's demand on one side and the suppliers cooperating and coordinating with enterprises on the other side, industrial ecosystems started flourishing in the global economy. A few examples of ecosystems that were very successful in India are textile and auto components clusters in Tamil Nadu, and the electronics and IT cluster in Karnataka.

With ecosystems thriving for growth, competition has been clearly redefined. In addition to competing with cost, quality and product differentiation, enterprises have increasingly started using supply chains as competitive weapons. Distribution networks and supplier networks are becoming very critical in business strategy formulation. The classic paradox though continues and the enterprises are continuously learning new ways for balancing responsiveness and effectiveness in supply chains in changing economic conditions.

Information technology works as an enabler for executing supply chain strategies in this global competitive scenario. Supply chain operations reference model (SCOR) could be used as an outline to comprehend the strategic role of information technology in strategy execution. SCOR categorizes business processes across the supply chain under five titles: plan, source, make, sell, and return (refer Figure 15.3).

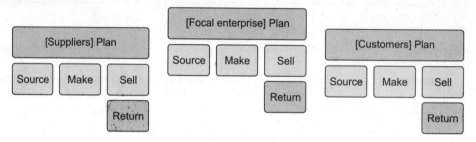

Figure 15.3   Generic supply chain processes according to SCOR model

The value chain of the focal enterprise is directly dependent on the value chains of the participants in its supply chain to create a value system. Smooth product flows, cash flows, and information flows keep the value system healthy and are very necessary for rapid growth. SCOR helps to identify the interconnectivity between the supplier, focal enterprise, and customers' business processes that would facilitate to create blueprints of information system components for making informed decisions in the following areas:

- Location
- Sourcing and procurement
- Production
- Inventory (warehousing)
- Transportation (distribution)

While SCOR helps to create blueprints of supply chain processes, information technology enabled business processes would transform business by facilitating e-commerce and e-business models.

O'Brien (2006) defines e-Business as 'the use of Internet technologies to internetwork and empower business processes, electronic commerce, and enterprise communication and collaboration within a company and with its customers, suppliers, and other business stakeholders'; e-Commerce as 'the buying and selling, and marketing and servicing of products, services, and information over a variety of computer networks'.

Table 15.3 indicates various e-SCM tools and their applications across supply chain functions:

Table 15.3 Application of e-business tools

Supply chain functions	e-SCM tools	Applications
Supplier development	WWW-assisted supplier selection, communication using Internet (e-mails), research on suppliers and products with WWW and intelligent agents	Partnership, supplier development
Purchasing	EDI, Internet-purchasing, EFT	Ordering, fund transfer, supplier selection
Warehousing	EDI, EFT, web-based integrated inventory management, WWW-distribution management	Inventory management, forecasting, scheduling of workforce
Sales and distribution	EFT, Online TPS, Bar coding system, ERP, internet delivery of products and services	Internet sales, selection of distribution channels, transportation, scheduling, third-party logistics

Source: Adapted from Gunasekaran et al. (2002).

To enable e-SCM models, Figure 15.4 mentions generic infrastructure layers.

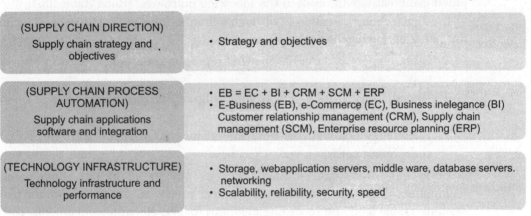

Figure 15.4 Generic e-SCM infrastructure layers

15.4.1 Supply Chain Process Automation

E-commerce

The main elements of e-commerce include:

1. Consumer shopping on the web, called B2C (business to consumer)
2. Transactions conducted between businesses on the web, called B2B (business to business)

3. Transactions and business processes that support selling and purchasing activities on the web, like supplier management, inventory management, distribution management, and information management.

The general processes of e-commerce can be sequenced as follows:

1. Attract customers through advertising, marketing
2. Interact with customers through catalogues, negotiations
3. Handle and manage orders by following activities
4. Order capture
5. Payment
6. Transaction
7. Fulfilment (physical good, service good, digital good)
8. React to customer inquiries through customer service and order tracking

Business Intelligence Systems

Business Intelligence is the ability to learn about, learn from, understand, and interact with one's business environment. Business intelligence as a concept when applied to functional areas would result in the following outcomes. (Refer Table 15.4.)

Intelligence may be gathered through a number of means. The general techniques for gathering intelligence are:

1. Using human resources to provide reporting on a target function of investigation.
2. Directed surveillance (that is, following and/or observing target function, secondary data analysis).
3. Technology enabled real time surveillance (Transaction software, RFID, Bar code, Smart cards).

Every enterprise gathers intelligence by any or all of the above-mentioned techniques. While the platforms (periodical review meetings, corporate planning sessions, casual talk) and recording mediums (paper, electronic documents, corporate intranets, and private blogs) may differ across business functions, in general gathered intelligence is shared across the executives periodically. Many applied mathematics and statistical analysis methods (known as quantitative methods) are conventionally used to analyse intelligence data. Apart from quantitative methods, qualitative methods and pictorial representations are also used for analysis. Some of the most commonly used quantitative methods are as follows:

1. Frequency tabulation
2. Time series analysis
3. Variance analysis
4. Measures of central tendency
5. Linear programming
6. Regression analysis
7. Rank correlation

Table 15.4 Applications and results of business intelligence

Business function	Type of intelligence	Outcome
Sales	Sales intelligence/Competitive intelligence	Comprehend competitor products features, positioning, customer requirements, pricing changes, near future demand, sales executives performance
Marketing	Marketing intelligence/Customer intelligence	Comprehend market environment, regulatory changes, new entrants, substitute products, channel behaviour, customers bargaining power, customer experience, customer satisfaction, new business opportunities
Production	Production intelligence	Comprehend production cycles, root causes for production variances, engineers' performance, machine performance, material requirements, inventory performance, quality variances
Distribution and logistics	Distribution and Logistics intelligence	Comprehend channel performance, transportation performance, warehouse performance
Purchase	Supplier intelligence	Comprehend costs, quality variance, supplier performance, substitute material options
Finance	Financial intelligence	Comprehend share performance, key ratios performance, currency performance, cost variance, budget variance, business valuation
Human resources	HR intelligence	Comprehend employee satisfaction, complementary skills, employee behaviour, attrition root causes

8. Probability theory
9. Statistical distributions
10. Differential calculus and integral calculus

The analysis outputs are in general considered by management teams for making informed decisions in business. When the data is small in size, managers apply any or few of the quantitative methods to analyse the data gathered for a well-defined purpose and interpret the results. For large volumes of data, iterative and complex quantitative computations, many software tools with predefined executable algorithms are used.

While software programming languages like C, C++, MS DOT Net, Java, and so on are used to create such software tools to automate quantitative algorithms, relational database management systems (RDBMS) are used to organize fundamental data in an optimized format. There are two more concepts that support execution of complex quantitative algorithms:

- Data warehousing
- Data mining

The concepts of data warehousing, when applied on multiple databases, would result in purpose-specific data cubes, also known as data marts, which feed the base data to various algorithms for analysis. This is also called as knowledge discovery in databases (KDD).

Data mining is the process of analysing data from different perspectives and summarizing it into useful information. Data mining involves various algorithms that sweep through relational databases, data warehouses, and data marts to perform four types of actions that would result in information for making better decisions:

1. Data visualization
2. Data summarization
3. Data analysis
4. Data modelling

Brio, Business Objects, Cognos, Data Channel, Plumtree, Portera, and Viador are some of the companies that provide various BI tools.

Customer Relationship Management Systems (CRM)

Customer-centric organizations comprise teams that continuously focus on customer requirements to extend services, creating memorable customer experiences. Following are the three outcomes of customer relationship management:

- Customer retention
- Customer acquisition
- Customer enhancement through cross selling and upselling

Generally, for achieving the above-mentioned outcomes, cross-functional teams led by sales and marketing executives work together to formulate and execute marketing strategies such as discount offers, loyalty programmes, gifts, lotteries, exchange offers, instalment schemes, events, periodical maintenance checkups, and free service camps.

Creating a memorable customer experience involves streamlined and well-coordinated business processes that extend across three phases: presales, sales, and post sales (shown in Figure 15.5).

Many times these phases would involve people and processes from sales and marketing, delivery, customer support, and customer service functions. This creates a major challenge in terms of synchronized response to create a memorable customer experience as there may be various customer touch points (point-of-sales, delivery, service, telephone, e-mail, website, and direct mail). For example, the sales team may have the first-hand information about customer requirements and contact details, the marketing team may have demographic details of the customer, and the customer support team may have history of customer requests, and so on. Maintaining paper records across functions and sharing them to provide customer service is certainly not an appropriate idea in case of a large customer base. The customer relationship management software enables enterprise teams to create such memorable customer experiences.

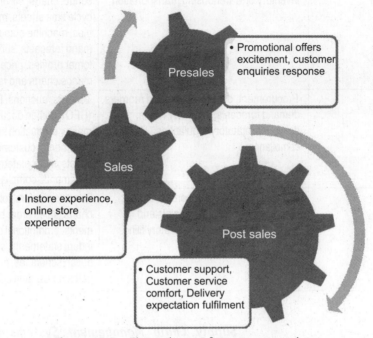

Figure 15.5 Three phases of customer experience

The Customer Relationship Management (CRM) software enables a single instance of customer records so that every executive at various customer touch points can access updated customer information at any given point of time. This empowers teams interfacing customers at various touch points to understand customer transaction history and provide better service.

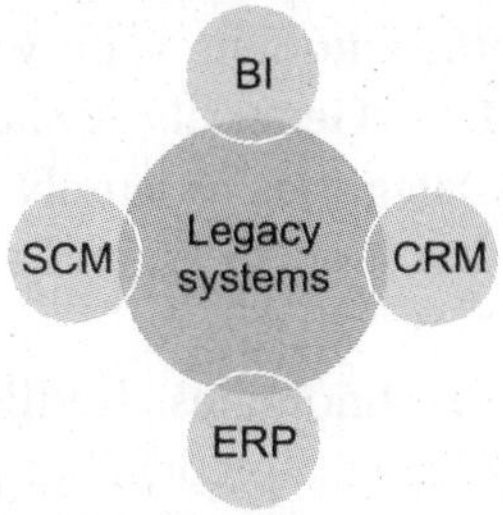

The full potential of the CRM software would be unleashed when it is integrated with operations, accounts, human resources, and purchasing information systems; or in other words, to legacy systems, ERP, or supply chain systems. Figure 15.6 below shows the integrated enterprise system outline.

Figure 15.6 Integrated enterprise systems outline

Amdocs, Avidian, Centraview, CRIXP Corp., Database Systems Corp., Epicor, FrontRange Solutions, IBM, Microsoft, NetSuite, Onyx Software Corporation, Oracle, PeopleSoft, Pivotal Corporation, RightNow Technologies, Sage, Salesforce.com, SAP, Siebel Systems, SSA Global, SugarCRM (commercial distribution), SuperOffice are some of the companies that sell proprietary CRM software.

Table 15.5 SCM activity layers, activities, and tools

SCM activity layers	SCM activities	SCM tools
Planning	Sourcing, materials, sales and marketing, inventory or warehousing, transportation	Supplier directories, financial ratios, quality control charts, bill of material, production cycle time sheets, master production schedules, machine output charts, customer demand forecasts, survey questionnaires, customer profiles, price histories, stock performance charts and ratios, trip sheets
Collaboration	Procurement, design, claims and reorders, demand forecasts, inventory levels, deliveries, statutory regulations, compliance	Tenders, auctions, Request for Quotation (RFQ), design documents, bill of material, master production schedules, settlement statements, customer demand forecast sheets, stock statements, movement statements, compliance filing statements
Execution	Purchasing, production, orders and promotions, indenting, receipts and dispatches, fulfilments, regulatory filings	Purchase orders, job sheets, quality control charts, sales order books, invoice statements, promotional offer materials, pricelists, indent statements, stock statements, distribution schedules, goods receipts and despatch notes, delivery notes, reports

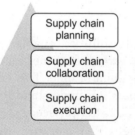

Figure 15.7 Three layers of supply chain management tools

Supply Chain Management Systems (SCM)

By nature, supply chain systems automate business processes across organizations both on the supply and demand side of the focal enterprise. As mentioned earlier, enterprises building information systems based on shared management principles tend to manage processes and relationships in three basic activity layers as mentioned in Figure 15.7.

Supply chain information systems automate supply chain activities as mentioned in Table 15.5. Generally it classifies the SCM activity layer into three categories as supply chain planning tools, supply chain collaboration tools, and supply chain execution tools.

SAP, Oracle, JDA Software, Manhattan Associates, i2 Technologies, RedPrairie, Infor, CDC Software, IBS, Aldata, Sterling Commerce, Swisslog, Epicor, HighJump, Brooks Software (Applied Materials), Microsoft, Click Commerce, QAD, IFS, ILOG are some of the software companies that provide supply chain planning, collaboration, and execution solutions.

Enterprise Resource Planning Systems (ERP)

Better resources planning would enable enterprises to execute and manage internal business processes. Enterprises that build information systems with basic management principles to improve internal process efficiencies tend to have architectures built on any of the three below-mentioned principle sets:

1. Accounting principles
2. Value chain principles
3. Management accounting and production management principles

In general ERP revolves around managing three types of resources—men, material, and money. Resources are used to manage functions and execute processes to achieve business objectives. Managing these resources for a small enterprise is relatively easier. But enterprises face many challenges when the size of resources increases along with business. While some of the successful enterprises have managed resources using legacy software like manufacturing execution systems, material resource planning systems, and accounting systems, many were faced with the challenge of integrating multiple legacy systems. Two important challenges were as follows:

1. To facilitate a causal connection between a visual model of business processes and the software implementation of those processes
2. To ensure a level of integration, data integrity, and security that is not easily achievable with multiple software platforms

Enterprise resource planning (ERP) systems were adopted widely by enterprises as they successfully addressed the two challenges mentioned above. ERP is a framework of various applications that were built around a central database as illustrated in Figure 15.8.

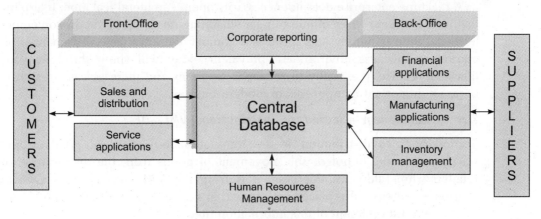

Figure 15.8 ERP applications framework

Source: Adapted from Davenport, T. H., 'Putting the enterprise into the enterprise system,' *Harvard Business Review*, 76(4), 121–131, 1998.

Some of the ERP applications are ACCPAC, Adonix, e-intelliprise, BusinessWorks, MAS 500, Carillon ERP/EMS, Comiere, EMS-Framework, Costpoint, Vantage, JobBOSS, Macola Progression, MAX, Expandable ERP, Flexi Financial Enterprise Suite, SEIBAN, IFS Applications, TRANS4M, NewVision,

Movex, Intuitive ERP, EnterpriseIQ, OpS-SQL, Lawson, VISUAL Enterprise, MAPICS, Solomon, Great Plains Dynamics, eEnterprise, Navision, Elliott, NetSuite, TRAVERSE, OpenPro ERP, Oracle Applications, PeopleSoft, JD Edwards, QAD, Ramco e.Applications, INFIMACS, MANAGE 2000, iRenaissance, SAP, Fourth Shift, BPCS, BAAN, Protean, and PRISM, Infinium, IMPACT Encore, SYSPRO.

Real Time Enterprise

Organizations globally have spent heavily over the past decade and find themselves with countless disparate applications and information islands. What most organizations desire is an end-to-end integrated solution, which will meet their needs as they attempt to expand into new business opportunities, improve market share in segments that they are already active, increase revenue inflows, cut operating costs, build on relationships with customers and partners. This requires a high level of business visibility, which only an integration of systems and business processes will bring.

The current trend seems to indicate an investment in ERP software in a bid to acquire an integrated end-to-end solution. However, these organizations have found that ERP functions only across their organization, and that to have external connectivity they have to purchase the value additions that the ERP vendor offers. The current business environment demands that organizations require accurate real-time information from systems that are possibly disparate. There is also a need for business process management tools not only within the organization but across its network of stakeholders as well.

A real time enterprise does not necessarily operate in literal real time. It also means that near real time wherein one can get when one needs the same. In contemporary business, time is money and speed is a competitive advantage. An analysis of the market or business environment prevalent today will show shrinking product lifecycles. Hence, the ability to reduce cycle times and increase cash-to-cash cycle times are important components of modern business.

Tier I Component—Secondary Distribution—VMI—OEs

Secondary sales distribution is the transaction/movement of goods from the warehouse to the depot or the movement of goods from the distributors to the retailers/wholesalers. In this case, it is from the VMI facilitator to OEs or to distributors in case of replacement market, in case of replacement market. It is the capture and transmission of this information that one should focus on.

Importance of Capture and Transmission of Secondary Sales Information

Organizations have gradually shifted from a push strategy, where production was done based on experience and goods were dumped onto distributors, to a pull strategy where production and replenishment of distributor stock levels are based on information and market feedback. The capture and transmission of distributor sales or secondary sales information in real time becomes vital. It is here that the importance of downstream supply chain management solution comes into play.

In case of a company which has global presence, it then requires visibility of movement on actual versus planned goods from the VMI facilitator and preferably the OEs production plan as well. Also, this needs to be synchronized with domestic distribution with local OEs and the replacement market.

Limitations of IT when it comes to capturing sales data at a secondary distribution level

The larger the distribution networks of the organization, the greater the number of distributors, warehouses depots, and so on, which means tracking a product downstream becomes more complicated. In this specific case of auto components supply, the focus is on one chain of the network, namely VMIs at the international market, but it is closely tied up with other parts of the chain in the domestic market as well. Hence the complication and need for right information on supply chain network of the focal organization would become critical for success.

ERP attempts to integrate all the departments and functions across an organization onto a single computer system. All these can be provided to the component supplier through one window. But ERP by itself is limited to the four walls of one's organization. An organization that wants end-to-end integrated software has to buy all the add-ons and the extensions that these ERP vendors offer.

When it comes to choosing an IT solution to effectively track and receive real-time information from downstream distributors, it revolves around four factors as follows:

1. Cost
2. Availability of infrastructure
3. Need Competence of implementation personnel

15.5 CHALLENGES IN IMPLEMENTING SUPPLY CHAIN INFORMATION SYSTEMS

Supply chain information systems are part of the infrastructure fabric and so are recorded into the capital expenses accounts. Since it's a capital investment decision, the following steps are followed by management teams in general before making decisions:

1. Strong business case highlighting the need for information systems and benefits
2. Creating a blueprint of supply chain information systems that includes comprehensive study and documentation of existing technology infrastructure
3. Budget allocation
4. Returns-on-investment calculation or total-cost-of-ownership calculation using cost, benefits, and risk parameters
5. Build or Buy decision
6. Vendor analysis to shortlist and initiate strategic relationship
7. Project plan (resources, time, and effort)

Three major challenges that surface during the implementation of supply chain information systems:

1. **Project communication:** Many a time when it comes to implementing supply chain systems projects, communication becomes the biggest barrier to overcome.

   Functional teams, technology development teams, and cross-functional project coordination teams generally tend to have different styles of communication. Functional teams would generally be used to the communication styles of the enterprise, technology development teams would communicate in standard notations, and project coordination teams tend to have their own templates of communication. This barrier has to be comprehended well ahead of the project implementation and a common communication framework has to be established to ensure a single voice across teams.

2. **Leadership:** Change management is critical for reaping the benefits of implementing supply chain information systems. To facilitate the expected change at various levels of the organization, enterprise demands leaders who can share the enterprise vision, project objectives, and lead changes by being part of teams creating champions. Identifying leaders and creating champions is an art and has to be spearheaded by the executive team.

3. **Supply chain network partner involvement:** Apart from convincing and getting the buy-in from internal stakeholders, a robust supply chain management system can be in place only when external partners of a multi-level supply chain such as vendors, service providers, channel partners, and customers get hooked to the system. The level of linkages and hierarchy of information rights, visibility and transaction enablement are to be clearly defined. More critical aspect would be convincing partners to invest on both necessary IT infrastructure and support systems. Appendix 15.1 elucidates a case on these lines.

SUMMARY

Three key flows are to be noted in the SCM domain: the product flow, the finance flow, and the information flow. To enable seamless information flow across supply chain partners, information systems have to be integrated. Integrated SCM systems would enable enterprises to overcome geographic, time, cost, and transaction barriers.

Supply chain information systems would require large amount of budgets and long hours of key management time for successful deployment. Capital budgeting approach is one of the methods to rationalize investments into an SCM systems investment. Conventional ROI approach provides appropriate rationale for management teams to make an appropriate business case for budget approvals.

SCM systems requirement analysis is a simple, five-step process:

1. Define business objectives as expected outcomes/results
2. Create supply chain process maps
3. Improve supply chain processes to fulfil business objectives
4. Select appropriate IT partner
5. Make a decision to build or buy

Enterprise applications are generally classified into five categories:

1. Ecommerce (EC) applications that facilitate electronic financial transactions
2. Business intelligence (BI) applications that provide insight into huge volumes of transaction data available across enterprise databases
3. Customer relationship management (CRM) systems that provide comprehensive customer experience by providing customer profiles across various touch points
4. Supply chain management (SCM) systems that facilitate supply chain planning, collaboration, and execution
5. Enterprise resource planning (ERP) systems that manage centralized database and integrate various functions inside enterprises and could be extended across other domains, Electronic Commerce, BI, CRM, and SCM

Supply chain information systems could be classified into three generic categories:

1. Supply chain planning tools
2. Supply chain collaboration tools
3. Supply chain execution tools

Supply chain information project teams would face three key challenges:

1. Project communication across multiple teams (internal and external)
2. Leadership availability to drive change
3. Ensuring partner involvement to enable seamless flow of information across supply chain

KEY TERMS

Business intelligence (BI): As a practice, BI refers to skills, technologies, applications, and practices used to help a business acquire a better understanding of its commercial context. BI applications provide historical, current, and predictive views of business operations to support better business decision making and are also called as decision support systems (DSS).

Business process modeling notation (BPMN): BPMN is a graphical representation for specifying business processes in a workflow. BPMN was developed by Business Process Management Initiative (BPMI), and is currently maintained by the Object Management Group since the two organizations merged in 2005. As of January 2009, the current version of BPMN is 1.2, with a major revision process for BPMN 2.0 in progress.

Customer relationship management (CRM): CRM consists of the processes a company uses to track and organize its contacts with its current and prospective customers. Typical CRM goals are to retain customers, acquire new customers, and improve cross selling and up-selling opportunities.

Electronic commerce (e-commerce): As a practice, e-commerce consists of the buying and selling of products or services over electronic systems such as the Internet and other computer networks. Electronic funds transfer, Internet marketing, online transaction processing, electronic data interchange (EDI), inventory management systems, and automated data collection systems are some of the innovative applications of e-commerce systems.

Electronic supply chain management (e-SCM): An approach where information technology is used to enable seamless information flow across supply chain partners.

Enterprise resource planning (ERP): ERP is a company-wide information system used to manage and coordinate all the resources, information, and functions of a business from shared data stores.

ROI: A performance measure used to evaluate the efficiency of an investment or to compare the efficiency of a number of different investments. To calculate ROI, the benefit (return) of an investment is divided by the cost of the investment; the result is expressed as a percentage or a ratio.

CONCEPT REVIEW QUESTIONS

1. How are information systems helpful in supply chain management?
2. How does a management team rationalize capital investment to configure supply chain information system?
3. How does an enterprise arrive at a decision to build or buy supply chain information systems?
4. How can a manager identify the requirements for automation in an enterprise supply chain?
5. Classify supply chain management activities. List the various management tools used to perform supply chain activities.
6. What are the three key challenges that enterprise teams face during the implementation of supply chain information systems?

CRITICAL THINKING QUESTIONS

1. An apparel manufacturer, APM, has 350 retailers who sell more than 30 SKUs across India. APM's distribution network contains ten key distributors who are located in the following cities: Mumbai, Chennai, Hyderabad, Cochin, Bangalore, Bhubaneswar, Kolkata, Delhi, Jaipur, and Ahmedabad. APM receives orders and stock information from distributors via e-mail and it takes approximately two days to respond. However, the stock information across retail outlets is not visible to APM. As there is extreme competition in the apparel sector, end customers have a wide range of choices of brands. APM is unable to decrease its price as it would affect its bottom line directly. On the other hand, the raw material for APM is supplied by two suppliers who are located in Ahmedabad and Surat. The suppliers follow the conventional method to accept orders and payments and have no computers for recording transactions. The management at APM was thinking of alternatives to increase profitability and reduce time to respond. If you were the supply chain manager at APM, what would be your next steps?

PROJECTS/ASSIGNMENTS

1. Choose any of the following supply chain execution activities:
   (a) Warehouse
   (b) Transportation
   (c) Sourcing
   You may use any of the process mapping tools that illustrate supply chain processes for an enterprise that has the following supply chain structure:

Tier 1 suppliers—Production plant—Dealers—Distributors—Retailers

REFERENCES

Lang, André, Daniel Paravicini, Linkom SA, Yves Pigneur and Eric Revaz, 'From Customer Relationship Management (CRM) to Supplier Relationship management (SRM),' HEC Lausanne, 2002

O' Brien, James, *Management Information Systems* 7th Edition, MHHE, 2006

Davenport, T. H., 'Putting the Enterprise into the Enterprise System,' *Harvard Business Review*, 76(4), 121–131, 1998.

| Appendix 15.1 | IT Tool Enablement for Global Supply Chain |

Here one may look at the issues relevant for this tier I engine parts (pistons and rings) supplier from India, referred here as IPRC. IPRC business is structured as below:

IPRC makes pistons and piston rings for domestic automotive companies, international auto manufacturing companies, and replacement markets. Typically, these companies supply to international market leaders through VMI facilitators located at different locations. Here, the two hypothetical customers are car manufacturers Ford and GM. (Refer Figure 15.9)

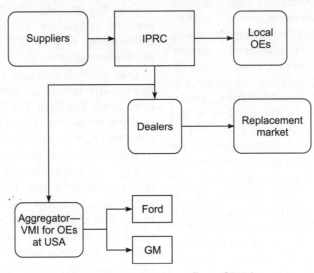

Figure 15.9   Business flow of IPRC

The key objectives of this manufacturer are as follows:

1. Though exports serve only about 22 per cent of their revenue, a presence in the international market and supply to international giants is important to IPRC.

2. International supply has to be managed through a vendor-managed inventory system, which means stock and information connectivity at the facilitator's point is critical.

3. International supplies would require better planning and carrying of inventory for a longer time than domestic because of lot sizes, scheduling, and optimization of shipping costs.

4. Optimal mix of domestic and international production with favourable bias towards international markets for margin and brand building.

Here is a case where information at VMI stock points is going to be critical both for OEs of car manufacturers, and more importantly, to the focal manufacturer like IPRC whose supply chain issue is discussed. One of the effective options is to trace the business process here of the networked organizations, namely IPRC, VMI facilitator, and the OEs that are on disparate systems across the supply chain network. Real Time Enterprise fits in such cases to link systems and streamline information flow.

Tool Implemented by IPRC: Real Time Enterprise (RTE)

With the objective of linking up various constituents in the supply chain network, IPRC has linked up the various players with a tool called Real Time Enterprise developed and executed by an organization called Take Solutions Ltd. Here the tool and significance of the solution are described.

Take RTE

Take RTE is a rapid RTE framework with a process-centric approach. The framework aims to transform an organization into a 'Real Time Enterprise' rapidly, at a cost-effective price. The framework is process-centric and allows the organization to use its existing business processes instead of adhering to rigid business processes like ERP systems, making the organization nimble and flexible. This in turn allows the organization to rapidly respond to changes in the organization's environment and the changes in the market. Changes in the business processes and business rules are easily dealt with rapidly while using the RTE tool. The critical advantage that Take RTE brings to an organization is its ability to deploy solutions and do away with latency. ERP systems seem to face problems when it comes to integration with the organization's existing applications and systems (Figure 15.10).

The most serious problems related to integration with existing applications are as follows:

1. A number of companies did not manage to integrate their ERP solution with existing systems.
2. Another set of companies have stated that the integration procedure was unsuccessful.
3. A majority of companies do not attempt to incorporate their applications as integration is a complex, costly, and time-consuming process.

Take RTE on the other hand allows for easy, seamless integration. The solution is an offline/online model. Take-ipoint is the offline downstream distribution system.

Take-ipoint is installed at the distributor/VMI location. All ipoints are integrated at the process level using the Take RTE framework along with workflow and data warehousing. The central server is also integrated to back-end ERP.

The solution has proved itself to be the ideal downstream distribution solution. The advantages are cost effectiveness, easy configuration, and adaptability to change in business processes, and so on. Any change forced by any of the network operators can be easily implemented through this software, especially considering the fact that the component manufacturer depends heavily on the OE's process structuring and efficiency.

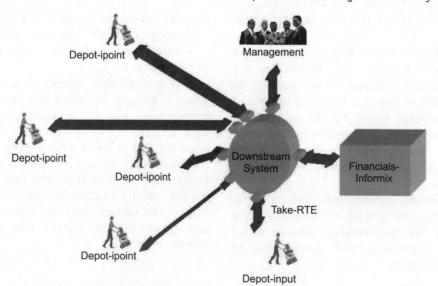

Figure 15.10 Applications of system

ipoint makes use of global growing infrastructure and the growing access to the Internet even in remote areas via dial-up access. The ipoint or the offline component transfers the required information to the hub via FTP (file transfer protocol), which is part of the TCP/IP protocol suite that the Internet utilizes. This makes it a feasible, low-cost solution. The ipoint part of the solution is a simple functional option which is extremely user friendly when compared to complex ERP systems. Take solutions have taken into account the level of expertise available to distributors in rural India when designing their solution.

The solution brings several value propositions to organizations implementing it across their downstream distribution network. Let's look at the value proposition brought to IPRC.

IT Systems and Value Propositions for IPRC

IPRC has implemented a leading ERP solution and its financial and manufacturing modules. The manufacturing module was deployed in all its factories while the financial module was implemented at its corporate office and its zonal offices.

RTE-Value Proposition 1

- It reduces inventory through enhanced planning and forecasting processes, since up-to-date secondary sales information is available from its distribution network. This data can be used with demand forecasting software tools to effectively forecast future sales.
- It helps in better control over cash flow.

Business Problem Faced by IPRC

Accurate information on stock positions in warehouses was unavailable to the manufacturing side of the operations. This affected the production scheduling, which in turn led to incorrect inventory levels in the warehouses, thus affecting the cash flow. These drawbacks led to cost escalation due to incorrect inventory levels and thereby the profitability moved southwards.

Impact after Implementation

Due to the availability of accurate stock positions, there was a marked improvement in production planning. There were savings in inventory costs due to better inventory control, resulting in improved cash flow and profitability. IPRC has indicated that their order service especially to the OEs in overseas markets improved with reduced stock levels.

RTE-Value Proposition 1

The availability of up-to-date secondary sales data makes this product an effective tool to gather data for market research purposes and planning.

Business Problem 1 Faced by IPRC

Accurate real time data is unavailable to IPRC to apply product performance measurement and apply their metrics.

Impact 1 after Implementation

After deploying the Take RTE based solution, the organization is able to enforce sales forecast and analyse the impact of any event. This is due to the reduction in the average time taken to gather secondary sales and stock data from seven days to two hours or less.

RTE-Value Proposition 2

Improved service for downstream stakeholders.

Business Problem 2 Faced by IPRC

Damaged/dead and non-saleable stocks were creating operational issues. Manual processes were employed to handle reverse logistics from retailers and distributors. Tracking claims and their statuses was a problem, time taken to process claims was far from acceptable, and there was a lack of consistency in the quality of work.

Impact 2 after Implementation

The work flow engine allows the tracking and monitoring of activities like claims processing, returns from retailers and distributors (reverse logistics), distributors' order processing, stock transfers, and payment processing. VMI facilitators, distributors, and other channel partners were able to track the status of their claims and came to know where their claims are in the processing cycle.

RTE-Value Proposition 3

- Reduces order processing cycle time and helps move towards continuous fulfilment.
- No opportunity loss

Business Problem 3 Faced by IPRC

The distributors were placing the order manually. This was time-consuming and led to incorrect shipments to retailers and heavy opportunity losses.

Impact 3 after Implementation

Orders were placed on the web. Those orders got routed to the appropriate fulfilment centre almost instantly. There was a reduction in the time taken in the ordering, processing, and execution process, which came down from an average of six days to two hours.

There is a reduction in the time taken to inform distributors of the launch of a new product with product details or of a revision in price from a period of five days to ten minutes post implementation.

RTE-Value Proposition 4

Flexibility

Business Problem 4 Faced by IPRC

Business processes across the distributors were not uniform. The customer wanted to make critical processes uniform and standardized across the distribution network while retaining those locally unique processes which were necessary to be retained.

Impact 4 after Implementation

A local distribution system (ipoint) was installed at the distributor's location. This was customized to implement local processes that were unique to the distributor. The critical business processes were centralized by installing the hub and the points were integrated with the hub. This let the IPRC to impose uniform rules and processes across its distribution network while still being able to retain locally unique processes at the distributor's end.

To conclude, IPRC's business model depends a lot on international business, which is critically dependent on the VMI facilitator. This business influenced local market margin, availability, and production planning for this auto components company. By better configuration of IT and supply chain network, the company could achieve efficiency in a cost-effective way.

16 CHAPTER

Application of Technology in SCM

Learning Objectives

After studying this chapter, you will be able to:
- ♦ Understand the classification of supply chain management information systems
- ♦ Learn about technology devices in supply chain management
- ♦ Understand risks in supply chain information systems projects
- ♦ Comprehend benefits of supply chain information systems

16.1 SCM INFORMATION SYSTEM CLASSIFICATION

In the previous chapter, we have noticed that there are three layers of supply chain management tools, namely supply chain planning tools, supply chain collaboration tools, and supply chain execution tools. However, from the enterprise information system's dimension, these automated tools could be classified based on their purpose as shown in Figure 16.1.

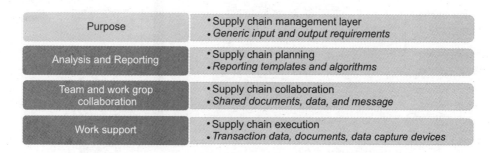

Purpose	• Supply chain management layer • *Generic input and output requirements*
Analysis and Reporting	• Supply chain planning • *Reporting templates and algorithms*
Team and work grop collaboration	• Supply chain collaboration • *Shared documents, data, and message*
Work support	• Supply chain execution • *Transaction data, documents, data capture devices*

Figure 16.1 Purpose-based classification of supply chain management layers

There are many information system vendors who offer a wide range of supply chain management solutions using different information technology frameworks. However, the purpose of the frameworks would remain the same (as mentioned in Figure 16.1) to enable the tools to function across three supply chain management layers.

Each of the supply chain management activities rely on supply chain processes that span across various functions inside and outside the enterprise boundaries. Since the application of technology varies from enterprise to enterprise, we would follow a standard hypothetical enterprise case for better understanding (as illustrated in Figure 16.2).

The hypothetical enterprise makes ten different product categories. The enterprise has a corporate office located away from the factory. The raw material required to make finished products is determined by the factory team and is procured by the corporate sourcing team. The raw material and finished products are stored in the factory warehouse for further movement. The enterprise follows a distributor–retailer channel sales model. Sales for the enterprise are managed by two regional offices. Apart from the factory warehouse, the enterprise also operates two different warehouses located at regional offices to ensure customer responsiveness. The enterprise manages all transactions related to sales, production, human resources, accounts, and finance with ERP application software.

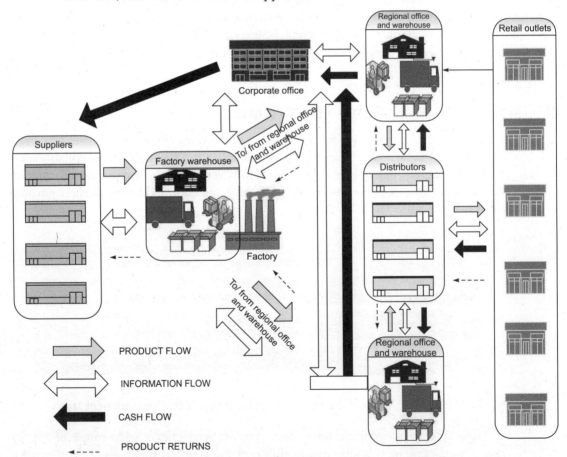

Figure 16.2   Hypothetical enterprise supply chain map

If we recollect the SCOR model from the previous chapter, the supply chain activities in the hypothetical enterprise could be organized under five processes as shown in Table 16.1:

Table 16.1 Supply chain processes, activities, and layers

SCOR process	Enterprise supply chain activity	Relevant supply chain management layer
Plan	Sourcing, materials, distribution (warehouse, transportation, and channel), returns	• Supply chain planning
Source	Identify and evaluate potential suppliers, organize suppliers, procure materials, monitor supplier relationships	• Supply chain collaboration for identifying, evaluating, organizing, and monitoring suppliers • Supply chain execution for procurement
Manufacture	Primarily manufacturing activity for value creating to a product or service	• Predominantly covered in ERP and integrated with SCM layers
Sell / Distribute	Organize storage locations, manage storage locations, organize transportation mode, manage transportation mode, organize distribution channel, manage distribution channel	• Supply chain collaboration for organizing and managing distribution channel • Supply chain execution for organizing and managing storage and transportation
Return	Organize sales returns, organize purchase returns	• Supply chain collaboration for organizing sales and purchase returns

*This table is applicable only for the hypothetical enterprise supply chain model. One may rework on the table template based on the supply chain map of the enterprise.

Each layer identified above comprises various processes that span across the enterprise and extend beyond the enterprise to suppliers and channel partners (distributors and retailers). The integrated process snapshot is illustrated in Figure 16.3.

As also discussed in the previous chapter, the five steps that the hypothetical enterprise has to follow are:

1. Set expected supply chain outcomes/results
2. Map supply chain processes
3. Improve supply chain process
4. Shortlist an IT partner
5. Decide to buy or build

If the expected supply chain outcome is a seamless flow of customer order information across multiple nodes in the enterprise supply chain, then Figure 16.3 is a rough supply chain process map outline to achieve this outcome. Figure 16.3 is an abstract model as it only illustrates the sequential flow of activities at various nodal points in the enterprise supply chain. Since the enterprise follows two-tier distribution models, it may also be called an extended supply chain connecting distributors and retailers to the enterprise supply chain. The nodal points include retailers, distributors, warehouses, factory, and the suppliers. A single event at the retailer point, namely customer order, triggers a possible sequence of related events based on business rules across other nodal points in the supply chain. The sequence of processes may change based on the event and the nodal point that triggers it. For example, if the end consumer returns a product to the retailer, a whole new set of

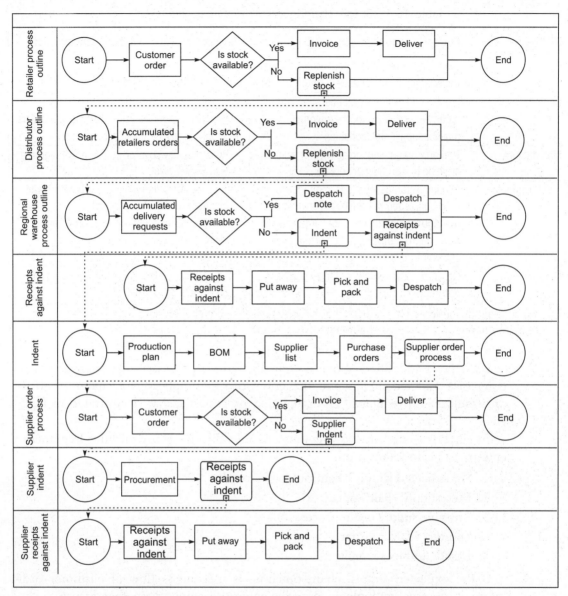

Figure 16.3 Sample integrated supply chain process snapshot

events are triggered across the related nodes, namely distributors, warehouses, and the factory. The advantage of illustrating supply chain processes using Business Process Model and Notation (BPMN) is that it reduces the complexity and highlights the integration points with existing enterprise systems, mandatory human actions, and other process-related activities such as physical movement of goods and delivery of services.

On improvement of supply chain process maps, the necessary application software requirements could be drafted and further used for identification and evaluation of IT partners/vendors. Refer Appendix 16.1 for a list of leading supply chain software suppliers.

On rearranging Table 16.1 with the information technology framework dimension, the following supply chain data flow and related application software requirement evolves (shown in Table 16.2).

16.1.1 Supply Chain Planning Software Solutions

Supply chain planning solutions enable enterprises to model supply chains involving suppliers and outsourced manufacturers, factories, warehouses, and distribution centres. These models allow enterprises to optimize inventories, production, distribution, and transportation. In general, supply chain planning solutions designs may include master planning, allocation planning, distribution planning, as well as inventory planning.

A well-structured supply chain planning solution would give an enterprise the ability to represent multi-tiered supply chains with items, operations, routings, resources, suppliers, distribution modes, and raw materials. It would support for build-to-stock, build-to-order, or configure-to-order business models and empower

Table 16.2 Supply chain data flow and application software requirement

Supply chain management layer	Supply chain management tools	Supply chain data flow	Aapplication software
Supply chain planning (Analysis and reports)	Supplier directories, financial ratios, quality control charts, supplier score cards, bill of materials, warehouse performance measures and charts, transportation performance measures and charts, customer demand forecasts, survey results and charts, customer profiles, price histories (summaries and charts), stock performance charts and ratios	Data flows from ERP application software, supply chain collaboration and execution application software	Reporting and analytics
Supply chain collaboration (Team and work group collaboration)	Tenders, auctions, RFQ, design documents, bill of materials, master production schedules, settlement statements, and customer demand forecast sheets, stock statements, movement statements, compliance filing statements	Data flows from ERP application software, supply chain execution application software and supply chain collaboration user interfaces	Supplier management, channel management, returns management
Supply chain execution (Work support)	Purchase orders, job sheets, quality control charts, sales order books, invoice statements, promotional offer materials, pricelists, indent statements, stock statements, distribution schedules, goods receipts and despatch notes, delivery notes	Data flows from ERP application software and supply chain execution user interfaces	Procurement management, warehouse management, transportation management

executives to evaluate complex supply chain alternatives, including parts, suppliers, routes, resources, modes, and capacity.

The accumulated transaction data across the supply chain could be consolidated and shared across the ecosystem/supply-network for advanced analytics and optimization. Supply chain intelligence solutions in general work on primary data or in conjunction with data warehouses and data marts that may be summarized as action-oriented, role-based dashboards.

Exhibit 16.1 comprises a list of supply chain planning software products offered by a supply chain solutions vendor.

16.1.2 Supply Chain Collaboration Software Solutions

Supply chain collaboration solutions provide application software designed to plan replenishment, manage orders, and provide visibility to lower fulfilment costs, improve on-time delivery performance, and enhance customer satisfaction. Collaboration solutions can be oriented to the supply side or demand side of the

---

Exhibit 16.1 Supply Chain Planning Software Applications from TAKE Solutions Ltd

TAKE Cameo does demand forecasting for an enterprise that owns and manages brands. It reconciles environmental factors that influence demand and provides the ability to use artificial neural networks to learn and combine parameterized historical sales data with other information pertaining to trend change triggers, competitor moves, new product introductions, planned promotions, and so on, and the sensitivity of demand to these influences, in order to generate demand item/category-wide forecasts of increasing accuracy. TAKE Cameo's Forecasting engine uses an artificial neural network by sigmoid function employing a feed-forward ANN with the error back-propagation (EBP) learning algorithm. The values of monthly sales and special actions such as promotion schemes are used as inputs to the system. The lagged values of sales of at least a business cycle (or financial year) should be available.

TAKE BizAxis is a data warehousing foundation that uses pre-defined, reconfigurable, purpose-centric cubes and facilitates an information supermarket that consolidates all information shared across the ecosystem/supply-network for advanced analytics and optimization. The sales and distribution modules cover the primary and secondary sales related data.

TAKE Insight is a business intelligence tool that works on primary data or in conjunction with TAKE BizAxis and uses pre-defined, reconfigurable, business process-centric metrics reflecting the health of the supply network, which are summarized as role-based dashboards—say for the Business Head, Functional Head, Managers, and so on, with a view to facilitating intervention where required. The primary sales and secondary sales modules address the requirement of putting the status of a multitude of such transactions into a complete business context using metrics based on the SCOR model.

TAKE Optima—Inventory Optimization is an optimization engine that works on primary data or in conjunction with TAKE BizAxis and uses the genetic engineering algorithm to facilitate inventory deployment in the distribution chain. It optimizes freshness, cost of transportation, and product availability at the demand nodes while considering the options of modes of transportation, unit load assumptions for each mode, capacity of each mode of transportation, statutory requirements of inventory deployment, capacity of storage nodes, and so on.

Source: TAKE Solutions Limited.

enterprise. Exhibit 16.2 shows supply chain collaboration software solutions by TAKE Solutions.

Supply side-oriented collaboration solutions would allow enterprises to plan collaboration around forecast and capacity coordination, short-term order execution, shipment, and inventory tracking. Some solutions also enable lean supply processes such as vendor-managed inventory (VMI), pull-based (kanban) replenishment, and other just-in-time (JIT) programmes.

A well-structured supplier collaboration solution would give an enterprise long- and short-term collaboration on forecasts, schedules, inventory, and orders, and enforce process discipline through business rules.

Demand side-oriented collaboration solutions would link every phase of order management, from capture to invoice and settlement, and with close integration to the demand management and order planning loops, creating a single face to the customer across disparate processes, nodal points, and enterprise systems.

A well-structured customer collaboration solution would give an enterprise the ability to capture orders from EDI (electronic data interchange), mobile, web, call centre, planning, and other sources, would configure build-to-order (BTO) and engineer-to-order (ETO) processes, would enable real-time order promising, would enable integrated pricing, and would manage returns. Enhancing customer collaboration, collaborative replenishment solutions would enable companies to manage various aspects of their replenishment programmes like collaborative forecast

---

Exhibit 16.2 Supply Chain Collaboration Software Application from TAKE Solutions Ltd

Xtended Process Control (X.PC) for contract manufacturing provides advanced functionality to enable the user to control the activities of contract manufacturers and other third-party partners who manufacture, store, and ship goods on behalf of the focal organization. By deploying Internet, bar code, RFID and RF scanning technology at key process points within the trading partners' facilities, X.PC applications eliminate the errors that are typically introduced when the organization outsources contract manufacturing and logistics to third parties.

A key element in the X.PC Suite is the ability to 'drop ship' items from the contract manufacturer's or 3PL's facility directly to the end customer. By placing certain controls on the shipping processes of the trading partners, the user can have them ship directly to the customers with confidence. Since all the information is driven from the ERP, last minute order changes or cancellations are caught before the shipment is finalized, ensuring accuracy. In addition, X.PC provides fully compliant bar code labels and shipping documentation printed at the user supplier's shipping dock, pulled directly from the user's system.

X.PC currently consists of two separate modules, configurable based on the shipment signal (Purchase Order or Sales Order) and when the transfer of ownership occurs.

PO Drop Shipment (POD)

POD allows manufacturers and distributors to drop ship items based on purchase orders within the ERP. These are generally build-to-order or ship-to-order items produced by contract manufacturers on the user's behalf.

SO Drop Shipment (SOD)

SOD allows manufacturers and distributors to drop ship items based on sales orders within the ERP.

Source: TAKE Solutions Ltd.

adjustments, customer demand changes, and performance management. Replenishment solutions in general tend to enable forecast analysis, promotions collaboration, demand change liability/flexibility management, replenishment, and monitoring.

A generic characteristic of the collaboration solution is to allow the user to better understand the operations and coordinate the business activity with partners, suppliers, and customers. As there would be multiple stakeholders in an enterprise supply chain, a supply chain collaboration solution also should empower trading partners to improve their inventory positions at stores and distribution centres. In short, a supply chain collaboration solution should support full-scale collaborative planning, forecasting, and replenishment (CPFR) programmes.

Innovative supply chain collaboration solutions enable a network of private exchanges, which can be defined as a hybrid of the public and private marketplace models based on the enterprise supply chain strategy. Typically, such solutions connect trading partners to private marketplaces and provide content and community to the trading partners participating in the site. We will discuss more about such exchange models in the next chapter.

16.1.3 Supply Chain Execution Software Solutions

Supply chain execution solutions provide application software designed to automate the procurement, transportation, and warehousing business processes. When implemented systematically, these solutions would provide a single, accurate view of the entire supply chain execution process and related information from the point of origin to the point of consumption in order to meet customer requirements. Exhibit 16.2 details supply chain execution software solutions by TAKE Solutions.

Warehouse Process Execution

A warehouse management solution (WMS) helps in executing the daily operations of a warehouse or distribution centre. While original warehouse systems were initially used only for warehouses, the emergence of specialized supply chain practices in enterprises has expanded the application to include areas such as manufacturing, transportation management, slotting, labour management, accounting, and order management.

As warehouses are at the convergence of the demand and supply in a supply chain, a good WMS should be able to adapt quickly and easily to any changes in the complex warehouse operations. The basic function of a WMS is to improve the efficiency of warehouse operations by simplifying and optimizing operations of a warehouse, especially with focus on men and material.

Traditional warehouse management systems focused on supporting the basic functions within the four walls of a warehouse classified under receiving, put away, storing, picking, issue, value addition, and documentation. However, the additional competitive pressures imposed by today's supply chain have resulted in software vendors integrating warehouse processes with multi-modal transportation. The result is the introduction of yard management, dock scheduling/dock management, slotting, compliance, automated replenishment as part of the WMS solution. Some of the important warehouse functions that are supported by a WMS are explained below:

1. **Scheduling:** Scheduling of appointments to receive the material.
2. **Receiving:** Acceptance of goods from an outside transportation or an attached factory.
3. **Put away:** The movement of received goods to a storage area can involve intermediate staging.
4. **Material routing:** The problem of selecting the best suitable and shortest order picking route.
5. **Yard management:** Deals with the overseeing and administration of a warehouse yard.
6. **Dock management:** Navigation of trucks into the dock bays, monitoring and servicing of the loading bays for smooth operation, and controlling of the dock door opening and dock levellers.
7. **Marshalling:** Buying all goods for an order together.
8. **Cross-docking:** In its purest form, cross-docking is the action of unloading materials from an incoming trailer or rail car and immediately loading these materials in outbound trailers or rail cars, thus eliminating the need for warehousing (storage). In reality, pure cross-docking is rare outside of transportation hubs and hub-and-spoke type distribution networks. Many cross-docking operations require large staging areas where inbound materials are sorted, consolidated, and stored until the outbound shipment is complete and ready to ship. This staging may take hours, days, or even weeks in which case the staging area is essentially a warehouse.
9. **Storing:** The actual storing of the material in the warehouse bins, shelves, racks, and so on.
10. **Slotting:** The activities associated with optimizing product placement in pick locations.
11. **Interleaving:** Functionality of WMS to mix tasks to reduce travel time. Sending a forklift driver to put away a pallet on his way to his next pick is an example of task interleaving.
12. **Cartonization:** It is the process that suggests a container for packing items based on packing constraints such as cubic volume of items and container volume.
13. **Packing and Repacking:** The packing process generates packing lists and shipping labels (if required). The format and information included in the packing list and shipping labels are adapted per case according to customer's requirements.
14. **Kitting:** Process in which individual items are separate, but related items are grouped, packaged, and supplied together as one unit. For example, in ordering a PC online, a customer may select memory, drives, peripherals, and soft-

ware from several alternatives. The supplier then creates a customized kit that is assembled and shipped as one unit.

The most important characteristic of a WMS is its ability to support the integration of technological advancements such as RFID, automated material handling equipments, and the ability to support the touch points with other supply chain applications. The detailed set up and processing within a WMS can vary significantly from one software application to another. However, the basic logic will use a combination of item, location, quantity, unit of measure, and order information to determine where to stock, where to pick, and in what sequence to perform this operation.

Use of web-based applications allows transaction processing using EDI or portals for transmission of advanced shipment notices, inventory details, and so on between supply chain participants providing real-time access to data. This improves visibility, and enables practices such as merge-in-transit, cross-company sharing of warehouse space, freight consolidation, and complimentary commodities.

Transportation Process Execution

Transportation Management Solutions (TMS) automate operations involved in moving raw materials and finished goods from one point to the other in a supply chain. Traditional TMS functions include freight audit and payment, transportation procurement, carrier management, and transportation order capture. The expanded footprint includes fleet management, global trade management, and business intelligence capabilities.

Some common functions of TMS are explained below:

1. **Transportation procurement:** From single lanes to entire networks, it helps in managing the bid process entirely online to obtain the right carriers, right modes, at the best price.

2. **Transportation execution:** Provides different options for consolidating deliveries and orders as shipments. It is possible to combine orders based on rules and strategies, using integrated optimization tools. It is also possible to combine orders using collaboration over the Internet.

   Different types of shipment documents could be defined to reflect various transportation forms used in the system. The shipment documents could be used to:
   - Specify shipment stages, legs, border crossing points, and load transfer points
   - Assign service agents and means of transport
   - Define the packaging for goods (Handling Unit Management)
   - Specify planned transportation deadlines
   - Record actual transportation deadlines and statuses
   - Specify output required for transportation (such as shipping papers, XML, and EDI messages)

- Define transport-relevant texts
- Separate document types deal with inbound and outbound shipments

3. **Fleet management:** Manage and optimize all assets of both private and dedicated fleet operations including drivers, tractors, and trailers.

4. **Audit payment and claims:** Pay for only the services you used at the price contracted. Identify overcharges, duplicate bills, and other errors immediately. Manage both cargo and detention claims with carriers and suppliers.

5. **Appointment scheduling:** Avoid charge-backs from hours-of-service violations and staff your warehouse appropriately by encouraging carriers to schedule deliveries online.

6. **Yard management:** Know trailer positions and status instantly. Schedule arrivals by dock and reduce loading and unloading time.

7. **Transportation visibility:** Transportation visibility covers transportation and customs issues for inbound and outbound processes. It allows monitoring and controlling of the transportation process from the creation of the delivery to the delivery receipt at the customer site, including arrival, proper loading (keeping in view the unloading sequence), and unloading events as well as customs-related entries. It provides input for analysing the adherence to the planned duration of the entire shipment, including the duration of customs processing and the arrival of customs documentation.

Enterprises link to their trading partners and transportation service providers using web-based EDI and XML to get shipping, contract, and service information real time. Since many of the factors such as fuel rates, carrier availability, road and weather conditions, routes affecting transportation, are dynamic in nature, this type of data is managed in a centralized web-based environment where it can be updated in real-time to support in-transit decision making.

Inventory Management Process Execution

Inventory Management Solutions (IMS) enable monitoring, management, and optimization of inventory performance at every stage of the supply chain by reducing safety stocks to the level that balances risk against cost at the desired level. It also helps in determining the optimal storage locations and recommends a stocking policy for each inventory item. IMS can be used wherever there is an inventory, for example, in manufacturing facilities, distribution centres, warehouses, or retail outlets. Modern inventory control systems rely upon bar code systems and RFID tags to provide automatic identification of inventory items.

The following are the key processes that are controlled by any IMS:

1. **Inventory planning and ordering:** This is often accomplished with material requirements planning, often referred to by its acronym MRP, or in a lean manufacturing environment with kanban ordering to affect deliveries of material.

2. **Inventory optimization:** This process involves mathematical tools to calculate where inventory should be deployed to satisfy predetermined supply chain management objectives.
3. **Physical inventory control:** This involves receiving, movement, stocking, and overall physical control of inventories.

Sourcing and Procurement Process Execution

Sourcing and procurement solutions allow enterprises to make and enforce sourcing decisions. Modern sourcing and procurement applications automate spend analysis and compliance management to support sourcing strategy.

Sourcing software application helps managers to differentiate suppliers based on their performance records and provide exception reporting for fast issue resolution. It also includes special functions such as global sourcing taxation and law, hazardous material management, reuse, and recycling. It provides a set of negotiation tools such as Request for Quotations (RFQs) to purchasing contracts.

While procurement/e-procurement software applications facilitate direct and indirect material purchases, they focus on automating and recording the transaction processing of the purchasing activity (typically understood as the procure-to-pay cycle). The e-sourcing software applications target strategic sourcing processes, such as supplier selection, spend analysis, contract management, proposal creation, bidding, auctioning, supplier risk analysis, and raw material/component optimization (typically understood as the source-to-settle cycle).

In general sourcing or e-sourcing applications would support the following functions:

- Obtaining materials and services
- Identifying and evaluating potential suppliers to meet those needs
- Negotiating and implementing contracts with selected suppliers
- Monitoring and improving ongoing supplier relationships

The procurement applications would support the following functions:

- Recognize the need for purchase and provide electronic catalogues
- Generate an order in electronic format and communicate the order to the supplier using automated workflows
- Record received goods/material data from supplier
- Provide the ability to make payments against the received goods

16.2 TECHNOLOGY DEVICES IN SCM

Device interfaces form an extension of technology infrastructure and play a very important role in the data collection of a product's position and movement in the supply chain. There are many devices that serve the purpose of printing and reading product data in the supply chain. Some of the widely used devices are: bar code, radio frequency identification devices (RFID), handheld terminals, printers, and pocket PCs. Exhibit 16.3 shows the software applications used in TAKE Solutions Ltd.

Exhibit 16.3 Supply Chain Execution Software Applications from TAKE Solutions Ltd

TAKE Hub automates business processes involved in managing a network of hubs/warehouses. It can support a scenario of a network of single-user hubs for an enterprise as well as that of a network of multi-user hubs for a third-party logistics service provider. Functional coverage includes arrival management, receipt, put-away, preserve, pick, pack, and ship processes. Custom configurable value-addition processes like labelling, kitting, and product conversion are also supported. Other features include batch control/serial no. control, location management, resource management (MHE, human resources, and other assets).

TAKE Best automates procurement business processes, that is, scheduling and managing the execution of the individual deliveries of items from suppliers against contract, based on a variety of product pull signals, including back-to-back orders, electronic kanbans, and discrete user indents. Functional coverage includes the process and associated activities of purchasing, receiving product to contract requirements, determining product conformance to requirements/acceptance criteria, processing returns, authorizing payments, and paying suppliers for product or services.

TAKE Forward automates the transportation business processes. It can support a scenario of managing transportation for an enterprise as well as that of carrier providing third-party logistics services. It facilitates the process of defining and maintaining the information that characterizes the product, containerization, mode of transportation, vehicle, route, terminals, regulations, rates/tariffs, and backhaul opportunities. Functional coverage includes the process of contract management (3PLSP), route planning, consignment creation, shipment scheduling, mode and carrier selection (captive fleet and/or outsourced service provider options) and consignment/delivery tracking.

TAKE Inforis is an ERP for an SME involved in manufacturing. It automates the planning and scheduling of production activities (includes sequencing, and, depending on the factory layout, any norms for set up and run) as well as the physical execution. Functional coverage includes materials planning, acquisition of input materials, staging and release of work product/staged product/finished product based on procurement/production/delivery signals. Enabling the manufacturing processes through other functions such as sales, accounting and finance, and HR are also facilitated.

TAKE iPOINT is a comprehensive trading and accounting process automation system for distributors/stockists/VARs who engage in trading operations to service multiple principals (brand owners) and their end-customers. It automates the VARs' supply chain business processes, both on the buy-side as well as sell-side of their business. Functional coverage includes the ability to handle order-based sales, beat sales, and OTC sales processes with discounts/promotions. Other features include ATP-based order promising, order fulfilment, life cycle management, manual and automated procurement/replenishment, batch control, FIFO inventory rotation policy, credit policy administration, collections and remittances management, journals, ledgers, trial balance, P&L, and the ability to provide information pertaining to secondary sales to the principal.

TAKE Mobitranz: The Van sales module for distributors/stockists/VARs who engage in trading operations to service multiple principals (brand owners) and their end-customers using hand-held terminals (HHTs). Functional coverage includes route management, sales force allocation, trip planning, sales and collections management, inventory control, and merchandizing. The warehousing module for 3PLSPs facilitates management of a warehouse, inclusive of the receipt, put-away, preserve, pick, pack, and ship processes.

Source: TAKE Solutions Ltd.

The technology used in each of the device types mentioned in Figure 16.4 may differ; however, their functions could be classified into two types: printing and reading.

(SUPPLY CHAIN DIRECTION) Supply chain strategy and objectives	• Strategy and objectives
(SUPPLY CHAIN PROCESS AUTOMATION) Supply chain applications software and integration	• EB = EC + CRM + SCM + ERP • e-Business (EB), e-Commerce (EC), Business intelligence (BI), Customers relationship management (CRM), Supply chain management (SCM), Enterprise resource planning (ERP)
(TEHNOLOGY INFRASTRUCTURE) Technology infrastructure and performance	• Storage, web application servers, middle ware database servers, networking • Scalability, reliability, security, speed
(DEVICE INTERFACE) Data capture devices—printers and readers	• Bar code, RFID, pocket PC, Handheld terminals, GSM/GPRS, printers, others

Figure 16.4 Supply chain device interfaces

Some of the applications of these devices in supply chain are illustrated in Figures 16.5 and 16.6.

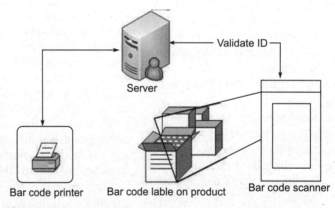

Figure 16.5 Bar code applications in product identification

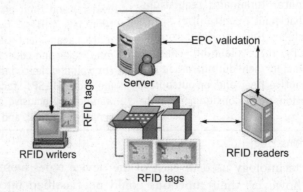

Figure 16.6 RFID applications in product identification

The above illustrations have been simplified (Castro and Wamba 2007) for easy understanding as we confine the discussion to applications. Handheld terminals are used in many areas as readers and data input interfaces. GSM and GPRS technologies have been used in the transportation domain to track and trace the movement of goods in transportation vehicles.

Some of the RFID applications in the supply chain management domain across industries are shown in Table 16.3.

Bar-coding and RFID have emerged from the same roots—Auto Identification. This is a broad category of technologies that are used to identify objects, humans, and animals. Other technologies linked to Auto-ID include optical character recognition systems, biometric systems, and smart cards (Wyld 2006).

Even though RFID and bar-coding come from the same technology family they are different in many ways (Wyld 2006). Table 16.4 shows that RFID has many benefits over traditional bar-coding systems.

Table 16.3 Examples of RFID applications in supply chain management

Enterprise	Applications	Source
Toyota (South Africa)	• Transporters tagged to streamline manufacturing and vehicle tracking • The tags are intended to remain with the vehicle throughout its life and hold its maintenance history	Baudin and Rao (2005)
Harley Davidson (USA)	• Process automation through tagging bins carrying parts to provide instructions to employees at each stage of the process	Baudin and Rao (2005)
Jonson controls (USA)	• Tracking of car and truck seats through the assembly process	Baudin and Rao (2005)
HP (Brazil)	• Printers tagged at a Brazilian factory to track them through shipping and reverse logistics	Roberti (2006)
Nissan (North America)	• Using active RFID tags to track auto parts, manufacturing processes, and finished vehicles	Bacheldor (2006)

Table 16.4 Comparison between bar code and RFID (adapted from Wyld 2006)

Bar code	RFID
• Require line of sight to be read	• Can be read without line of sight
• Can only be read individually	• Multiple tags can be read simultaneously
• Cannot be read if damaged or dirty	• Can cope with harsh or dirty environments
• Can only identify the type of item	• Can identify a specific item
• Cannot be updated	• New information can be over-written
• Require manual tracking and therefore are susceptible to human error	• Can be automatically tracked, removing human error

16.3 RISKS IN SUPPLY CHAIN INFORMATION SYSTEM PROJECTS

As in the project execution of any enterprise information system, the execution of supply chain information systems projects also contains risk factors. In general, supply chain information projects involve more than one enterprise and business line, and tend to be influenced by more risk factors.

Before we get into the risk perspective of supply chain information systems, let us take a quick look at how to classify enterprise and supply chain risk factors. Enterprise risk management and supply chain risk management are two evolving areas of research. When considered from the enterprise and supply chain risk perspectives, risks could be both from external factors such as competitors, legal, regulatory, catastrophes, and customer expectations, and internal factors such as business strategies, policies, business process execution, employees, analysis, and financial reporting, technology, and data.

With the broad context of enterprise risk management, if one looks from the perspective of supply chain information systems projects, the following risk factors may be taken into consideration:

1. **Supply chain process design:** In the world of extreme competition, critical factors such as cost, quality, and differentiation among offerings may not give the enterprise the required competitive edge. In the extreme competitive market environment, business processes complement critical factors (cost, quality, and differentiation). With the growing criticality of business processes, enterprises tend to design and improve supply chain processes that involve modelling, automation, and improvement. Since processes would be automated, any incomplete or non-comprehensive supply chain process design tends to be detrimental to the enterprise.

2. **Technology infrastructure/architecture/design:** As automated supply chain processes tend to complement competitive factors for enterprises, technology infrastructure/architecture/design determines the quality of process output. With technology explosion, technology obsolesce would become a big challenge. Envisaging future technology developments and building necessary technology foundation are critical factors in competitive environments.

3. **Enterprise application integration:** Enterprises with a global outlook are all working towards capturing transactions and other business-critical data in real-time, and correlate information across applications. The complexity of supply chain systems may increase with changes and additions of features to existing systems over a period of time. This may contribute to increased costs and expose to risks of failure for many enterprises. With more than one enterprise participating in supply chain information systems, enterprise application integration becomes a necessary solution for successful implementation. The essential supply chain objectives of enterprise application integration (EAI) are to connect systems across supply chain processes, and integrate applications and

business partners. A well-engineered EAI solution makes maximum re-use of existing applications and resources without requiring extensive rework. EAI deployments often start small with an initial pilot project, but may run into problems while scaling up to supply chain-wide transformation.

4. **Data relevance and integrity:** As the supply chain processes are executed, there would be invariably records that have no value in either business process or analytics. Saving such records in databases can affect the system's ability to accurately analyse information, continue to deflate confidence in data, and cause problems in performance, and may result in added maintenance. Developing an archival strategy as part of your data quality practice is a significant component that should not be overlooked. Poor data relevance would affect trust in data, disables processes, reduces accuracy of analysis, and results in sub-optimal databases.

   Data integrity refers to maintaining the correctness and consistency of the data. For example, if an identification number is specified to be 16 digits, the database management system may reject an update attempting to assign a value with more or fewer digits or one including an alphabetic character. Most database management systems do not support such constraints but leave them to the domain of the supply chain application software.

5. **Technology reliability and recovery:** Technology reliability can be defined as the probability that an information system will continue to perform its intended function without failure for a specified period of time under stated conditions. Unreliable technology may affect an enterprise's reputation, customer satisfaction, management cost, and competitive advantage. For any information systems project, reliability analysis has to be performed and recovery plans have to be in place from day one of operations.

6. **Technology execution and continuity:** With unexpected catastrophes and unrest in national borders and internal security, enterprises with a global outlook are creating reactive and comprehensive business continuity plans. Integrated information systems enabling the business processes and the resultant databases shall contain a backup mechanism to quickly reinitiate business processes and recover databases to support business activities. Many enterprises maintain a backup of databases and enterprise/supply chain information systems servers in appropriate locations to support disaster recovery and business continuity.

7. **Vendor/partner reliance:** Given the significance of information technology in business and supply chain strategy, relationship with technology vendors/partners is generally considered to be strategic in nature. For this purpose, a vendor/partner has to be evaluated across various parameters before forging any relationship to avoid any possibility of future support services, which becomes very critical for maintenance of supply chain information systems.

8. **Legal and regulatory compliance:** Enterprises with global business outlook cannot ignore legal and regulatory compliance areas in international business. Supply chain information systems shall address legal and regulatory compliance for web applications. This would be achieved with a combination of comprehensive application security assessments, customizable security policies, and detailed compliance reporting designed for specific laws and regulations. Few laws and regulations are listed below:

1. 21CFR11
2. Basel II
3. California Online Privacy Protection Act
4. California SB1386
5. Canada Personal Information Protection and Electronic Documents Act (PIPEDA)
6. Children's Online Privacy Protection Act (COPPA)
7. EU Directive on Data Protection (Directive 1995/46/EC)
8. EU Directive on Privacy and Electronic Communications (Directive 2002/58/EC)
9. Director of Central Intelligence Directive 6/3 (DCID)
10. Federal Information Security Management Act (FISMA)
11. Gramm-Leach Bliley Act (GLBA)
12. Health Insurance Portability & Accountability Act (HIPAA)
13. ISO 17799
14. Japan Personal Information Protection Act (JPIPA)
15. NIST 800–53
16. North America Electric Reliability Council (NERC)
17. Open Web Application Security Project (OWASP) Top Ten
18. Payment Card Industry (PCI) Data Security Standard (DSS)
19. Safe Harbor
20. Sarbanes-Oxley Act (SOX)
21. U.K. Data Protection Act

9. **Change management:** With new technology being deployed and existing processes being automated, many of the enterprises users tend to exhibit resistance to change. Sometimes this kind of resistance to using new information systems by end users may put an entire project to risk. Change management is a set of processes that is employed to ensure that significant changes are implemented in an orderly, controlled, and systematic fashion to effect organizational change. In case of supply chain management it is more than one organization. Leadership and communication would play a major role in transforming people who are one of the key components of an information system.

10. **People:** Activation of supply chain information systems would cause a ripple effect on the people who could be assuming the role of end users, managers, or

leaders in the enterprise supply chain. The ROI on the information systems would be realized only when people skills, competencies, and performance improve. Managing people from the information systems perspective deals with leadership, skills/competency, change readiness, communication, performance incentives, accountability, fraud, and abuse.

Risk management of supply chain information systems projects includes the following generic steps:

1. Implement a framework for supply chain information systems risk assessment and mapping.
2. Outline the responsibilities of risk managers with their respective domains.
3. Identify and define the risks to which the supply chain is exposed and how to map incidents.
4. Determine the threat level and focus on the risk that has the greatest potential to affect supply chain performance.
5. Establish levels of controls for processes corresponding with the perceived threat.
6. Conduct periodic risk assessments to determine changes in supply chain risk profile and assess performance.

16.4 BENEFITS OF SUPPLY CHAIN INFORMATION SYSTEMS

Following are a few benefits that enterprises can derive after implementing supply chain information systems:

- Reduced Bullwhip Effect in inventory because of information sharing
- Increased profits across supply chain partners because of faster cycle times and reduced inventory costs
- Improved customer satisfaction because of consistent quality and service responsiveness
- Improved customer service with real-time information because of product track and trace functions
- Ease of documentation with automated, paperless customs transactions
- Improved supplier relationship because of advanced information sharing
- Improved planning capabilities because of comprehensive information about supply chain participants' performance
- Increased forecast accuracy because of collaborative forecasting across supply chain partners
- Improved coordination with third-party service providers because of information sharing and process integration
- Increased supply chain profits by replacing inventory with information in supply chain

SUMMARY

Supply chain information systems can be classified based on three key business purposes: planning and analysis, team and work group collaboration, and work support. Supply chain information systems have been designed to fulfil these purposes and further classified under three types: supply chain planning systems, supply chain collaboration systems, and supply chain execution systems. While business process automation enables enterprise business strategy execution, supply chain device interfaces enable data collection. Some of the widely used device interfaces are bar code and RFID. These device interfaces are enabled with technology that can print and read necessary information to and from devices.

Supply chain information system projects involve risks as listed below:

- Supply chain process design
- Technology/infrastructure/architecture design
- Enterprise application integration
- Data relevance and integrity
- Technology reliability and recovery
- Technology execution and continuity
- Vendor/partner reliance
- Legal and regulatory compliance
- Change management and people management

KEY TERMS

Build-to-order (BTO): Build-to-order, also referred as make-to-order, is a production approach where once a confirmed order for products is received, products are built. BTO is the oldest style of order fulfilment and is the most appropriate approach used for highly customized or low-volume products.

Collaborative planning, forecasting, and replenishment (CPFR): CPFR is a concept that aims to enhance supply chain integration by supporting and assisting joint practices. CPFR seeks cooperative management of inventory through joint visibility and replenishment of products throughout the supply chain. Information shared between suppliers and retailers aids in planning and satisfying customer demands through a supportive system of shared information. This allows for continuous updating of inventory and upcoming requirements, making the end-to-end supply chain process more efficient. Efficiency is created through reduced expenditures for merchandising, inventory, logistics, and transportation across all trading partners.

Electronic data interchange (EDI): EDI refers to the structured transmission of data between organizations by electronic means. It is used to transfer electronic documents from one computer system to another or from one trading partner to another trading partner.

Electronic product code (EPC): EPC is a family of coding schemes created as an eventual successor to the bar code. The EPC was created as a low-cost method of tracking goods using RFID technology. It is designed to meet the needs of various industries, while guaranteeing uniqueness for all EPC-compliant tags. EPC tags were designed to identify each item manufactured, as opposed to just the manufacturer and class of products, as bar codes do today. The EPC accommodates existing coding schemes and defines new schemes where necessary.

Engineering-to-order (ETO): In ETO, also called project-based manufacturing, the product is designed specially for one customer.

GPRS: General packet radio service (GPRS) is a packet-oriented mobile data service available to users of the 2G cellular communication systems global system for mobile communications (GSM), as well as in the 3G systems.

GSM: GSM (Global System for Mobile communications) is the most popular standard for mobile phones in the world.

Just-in-time (JIT): JIT is an inventory strategy implemented to improve the return on investment of a business by reducing in-process inventory and its associated carrying costs. In order to achieve JIT the process must have signals of what is going on elsewhere within the process. This means that the process is often driven by a series of signals, which can be kanban, that tell production processes when to make the next part.

Kanban: Kanban is a signalling system to trigger action. As its name suggests, kanban historically uses cards to signal the need for an item.

Radio-frequency identification (RFID): RFID is the use of an object (typically referred to as an RFID tag) applied to or incorporated into a product, animal, or person for the purpose of identification and tracking using radio waves. Some tags can be read from several metres away and beyond the line of sight of the reader.

Supply chain operations reference (SCOR) model: SCOR is a process reference model developed by the management consulting firm PRTM and AMR Research and endorsed by the Supply Chain Council (SCC) as the cross-industry de facto standard diagnostic tool for supply chain management. SCOR enables users to address, improve, and communicate supply chain management practices within and between all interested parties in the extended enterprise.

CONCEPT REVIEW QUESTIONS

1. Briefly explain how supply chain solutions are classified.
2. Discuss the importance of the following solutions with an example:
   (a) Supply chain planning
   (b) Supply chain collaboration
   (c) Supply chain execution
3. Discuss about current developments in devices used to capture supply chain data.
4. What are the risks associated with supply chain information systems projects and what steps should one take to manage risks?
5. What are the benefits of supply chain information systems to an enterprise?

CRITICAL THINKING QUESTIONS

1. A biscuit manufacturing company wanted to increase its market share with increased focus on secondary distribution network. The company's supply chain managers found that there is 20 per cent excess inventory in their warehouses every month to meet uncertain levels of orders from distributors. The distributors too maintain a 5 per cent buffer stock to meet uncertain demand from retailers. They also found that it took fifteen to twenty days for the biscuit manufacturer to settle claims as documents from every region have to be processed and approved by the marketing team. The company uses state-of-the-art ERP to manage its transaction.

   As a supply chain analyst what would be your next steps to increase focus on secondary distribution network, reduce supply chain cost, and increase responsiveness?

PROJECT ASSIGNMENTS

1. Visit a nearby manufacturing enterprise, seek permission, and study about the following:
   (a) How does the enterprise organize information systems?
   (b) What are the purposes of using enterprise information systems?
   (c) How does the enterprise manage supply chain information?
   (d) How does the enterprise map the enterprise supply chain processes?
   (e) Identify enterprise supply chain information systems needs and suggest appropriate solutions.

REFERENCES

Bacheldor, B., 'Nissan North America Installs RFID-based Real Time Location System,' http://www.refidjournal.com/article/articleview/2866, 2006

Baudin, M. and A. Rao, 'RFID Applications in Manufacturing,' http://www.mmtinst.com/RFID$20applications%20in%20manufacturing%20_Draft%207.pdf, 2005

Castro, Linda and Samuel Fosso Wamba, 'An Inside Look at RFID technology,' *Journal of Technology Management and Innovation*, Jotmi Research Group, 128141, 2007

Roberti, M., 'HP Takes RFID End to End,' http://www.rfidjournal.com/article/articleview/2172/1/8, 2006

Wyld, D., 'RFID 101: The Next Big Thing in Management,' *Management Research News*, 29(4), 154–173, 2006

www.takesolutions.com

Appendix 16.1   **List of Leading Supply Chain Software Suppliers**

Supplier	Website	SCP	WMS	MES/MRP	TMS
SAP	www.sap.com	✓	✓	✓	✓
Oracle	www.oracle.com	✓	✓	✓	✓
JDA Software	www.jda.com	✓			✓
Manhattan Associates	www.manh.com	✓	✓		✓
i2 Technologies	www.i2.com	✓			✓
RedPrairie	www.redprairie.com		✓	✓	✓
Infor	www.ibsus.com	✓	✓	✓	✓
CDC Software	www.cdcsupplychain.com	✓	✓	✓	✓
IBS	www.ibsus.com	✓	✓	✓	✓
Aldata	www.aldata-solution.com	✓	✓	✓	✓
Sterling Commerce	www.sterlingcommerce.com		✓		✓
Seisslog	www.swisslog.com	✓	✓		✓
Epicor	www.epicor.com	✓	✓		✓
HighJump	www.highjumpsoftware.com		✓	✓	✓
Brooks software (Applied Materials)	www.brookssoftware.com			✓	
Microsoft	www.microsoft.com	✓		✓	
ClickCommerce	www.clickcommerce.com		✓		✓
QAD	www.qad.com	✓	✓	✓	✓
IFS	www.ifsworld.com/us	✓		✓	
ILOG	www.ilog.com	✓			
TAKE	www.takesolutions.com	✓	✓		✓

* SCP: Supply chain planning
* WMS: Warehouse management solution
* MES/MRP: Manufacturing execution system/Manufacturing resource planning
* TMS: Transportation management solution

17

Approach to Supply Chain Assessment and Excellence

Learning Objectives

After studying this chapter, you will be able to:
- Understand the definition of supply chain assessment
- Comprehend the need for assessment of supply chain
- Understand the importance of validating current processes and their effectiveness, measuring efficiencies of resources, and eliminating redundancies
- Understand the stages of supply chain assessment and improvement mechanism
- Appreciate the barriers to audit and improvement
- Comprehend the approach towards excellence, management philosophies, and tools
- Gain an insight into supply chain assessment services and service providers in India

---

Supply chain design and management would be sensitive to business situations that are dynamic. Any set process is a static situation expected to accommodate dynamic trends. In reality, such movements would not fit in the band. Even when it is within the band, one may have to understand sensitivities. Hence, an assessment at regular intervals through audit for evaluating current process validation and identifying areas for improvement would be important. Audit would mean systematic validation by experts who are trained in the domain and the audit mechanism, and who could detail and probe, if necessary. Originally, these were functions of the internal management audit team. With increasing trends of specialized audit expertise, certification processes and awards, these services are now provided by a new generation of experts. They also bring advantages of peer evaluation, benchmarking within the industry, and are best in class across industries.

Recently, assessment initiatives involving audit and improvements have begun to include other management functions and systems. For example, quality, environment, and safety are to name a few. Assessment of logistics and supply chain management is becoming increasingly necessary for validating the functional effectiveness of an organization.

17.1 ASSESSMENT OF SUPPLY CHAIN

Supply chain assessment is the process of systematic examination of a supply chain network. It is carried out by an internal or external team of qualified members to ensure adherence to standards, achievement of performance parameters, and identification of areas of improvements. It is an important part of organization's initiative to ensure synchronized flow of goods and services, finance, and information to achieve desired results through integrating various external and internal stakeholders for serving the ultimate customers of the focal organization at the least cost. Figure 17.1 shows the supply chain assessment model.

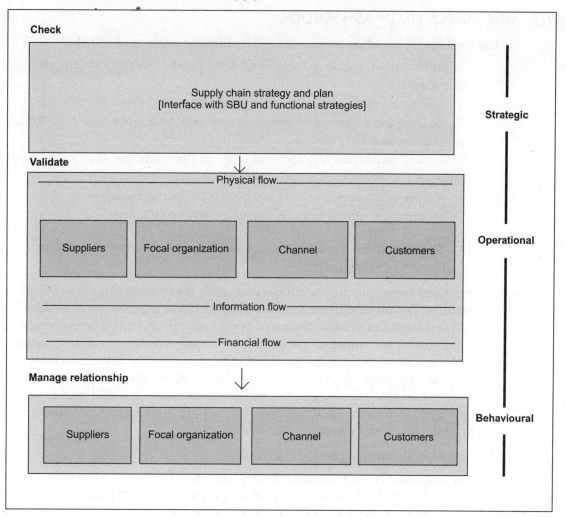

Figure 17.1 Supply chain assessment model

Till recently, supply chain assessment had been part of special audit initiatives by the internal audit team of an organization. Special internal audits were also carried out when the management had to resolve a backward or forward linkage partner relationship, or when an initiative demanded to structure a relationship as a part of alliance or joint venture initiative.

However, supply chain assessment is to be performed at predefined time intervals to ensure that the institution has a clearly defined supply chain strategy, and that goals and policies are implemented for effective and efficient results. This can help to determine if the organization could achieve high standards with respect to customer efficiency, cost optimization, and sharing of benefits across the link. Audit is a preliminary step to identify issues, and assessment gets into more critical aspects for identifying areas for improvements.

17.2 WHY SUPPLY CHAIN ASSESSMENT?

The need for supply chain assessment can be broadly categorized as below:

- To understand dynamic changes in demand parameters and changing demand characteristics
- To validate current process, roles, responsibilities, and their effectiveness
- To measure the efficiency of resources deployed and probe the scope for improving the same
- To identify redundant activities and roles and to study the elimination of the same
- To comply with internal control mechanism as part of management audit
- To strategize growth plans as part of improvement initiatives

17.2.1 To Understand Dynamic Changes in Demand Parameters and Changing Demand Characteristics

As mentioned earlier, supply chain focus is to satisfy the ultimate customer of the focal organization. The product or service offered by the focal organization faces dynamic demand characteristics in some cases, and in some situations it could be evolving with slow changes. The strategic orientation of supply chain establishes logistics perspectives such as facilities set up, distribution network, transportation choices, or inventory policy based on certain demand characteristics that could be forecasted over a time horizon. The changes or volatility of competition would lead to certain changes in characteristics and pattern of demand that may require reassessment of resources deployed and a logistics framework.

The following scenario explains the concept:

A retail pharmacy chain was established in an urban location with forty-five stores across the city serving a population of about 8 million. The chain was the first of its kind and had tremendous advantage in its service capability and customer satisfaction. However, some of the best-in-class stores of this chain had a problem in serving during peak demand times, which necessitated some initiatives by way of incremental service counters, billing section, and so on. In response to the threat posed by the retail pharmacy chain, small players reassembled under a new brand and structured an alliance relationship, which challenged the current format of the first mover.

This is the kind of situation that calls for an assessment to evaluate the efficiency and effectiveness of resource deployment. Based on an assumption, a resource deployment plan must be strengthened. The management may even initiate competitive actions before it is too late to revive the market leadership position or woo back customers. This clearly establishes the need for an assessment to bring the logistics system in line with the inherent demand characteristics. More proactive organizations regularly do such assessment of demand perspectives for mapping market characteristics and parameters.

17.2.2 To Validate Current Process, Roles, Responsibilities, and Their Effectiveness

A process is where there's value addition to the input in the form of new material or restructured activities. This results in a value-addition to the output as well. The value creation could be due to the time, form, and place utility that goes into the input during the process. Supply chain activities involve deployment of processes to accomplish goals and objectives with respect to operations, be it receiving, manufacturing, storing, or distribution. Apart from these, a number of processes are involved with respect to customers, suppliers, and various role agents such as logistics service providers. As one may observe, this multiplicity of processes and role agents are changing in a dynamic environment which would need reassessment and assurance for supply chain effectiveness and responsiveness. The reverse, namely dynamic and competitive business environment, leads to changes in processes and roles of agents in the supply chain.

A common occurrence in an FMCG company that sells different product categories of personal care products, hair care products, and facial (beauty) care products is being considered. The company was giving distributors credit limit for off-take of stock based on product category, which would be managed by each product family managers. In such a situation, even the same distributor who wants to alter credit limits to utilize sales opportunity during a season had to reach out to more than one category manager to change the limits. This was limiting products sale and hence distribution management software was to be installed. When the sales and distribution software was linked, the role and process changes were possible through the click of a button. Then, the limits could be changed temporarily and the warehouse is intimated for revised limits and lost sales are reduced. There could be many such opportunities across the supply chain network.

17.2.3 To Measure the Efficiency of Resources Deployed and Probe the Scope for Improving the Same

Supply chain drivers, namely facilities, inventory, transportation, information, and sourcing, and so on require resources to be deployed for process execution. Resources could be physical, financial, and human. For example, a warehouse involves physical space and equipment, financial resources in the form of rental or investment in assets, and human resources in terms of employees at warehouse both at the execution and supervisory levels. Similarly, buying may involve a team of buyers (human), material being bought (physical) and financial transaction. Any change in the supply chain network configuration, which may be change in volume and character of resources and supply chain driver deployed, would require revisiting the supply chain strategy and plan, for which an assessment is essential. The following scenario from a large engineering yard elucidates this.

A large engineering yard contracts its movement, loading, and maintenance of goods in the yard through a third party. However, there are complaints about delay, especially with respect to the release of material for value addition at the ancillaries. On probing, it was found out that equipment operators work in collusion with the transport operators and randomly prioritize rather than going according to the release schedule.

Such aberrations in operations surface only when an assessment is performed. There could be many such aberrations in supply chain resource deployment and productivity leading to inefficiency in the supply chain.

17.2.4 To Identify Redundant Activities and Roles and Study the Elimination of the Same

There could be a number of redundant activities and roles in a supply chain network. This might have been due to improper configuration or due to dynamic changes impacting the configuration. Typically, supply chain configuration involves multiple layers and role players in the system, which is established for operational conveniences. As systems evolve and operations stabilize, some of these activities or role agents become redundant. Many a time, these go unnoticed because there could be no stoppages or strain to chain the activities. However, such redundancies provide scope for cost savings and potential impairment of the flow at a later stage.

In a transportation network operated for a milk run, there may be a possibility that the operator is informed about skipping a call of service both by the nodal organization (who could be the manufacturer) and the supplier for assuring the information flow. This may be acceptable till the system settles but needs to be established as a singular accountability. The worst situation would be when both of them fail to inform and the operator makes a call for a pickup or drop which gets billed as an unproductive call. It is pertinent to check for such vulnerabilities in the supply network. Therefore, assessment of the supply chain network is very important.

17.2.5 To Comply with Internal Control Mechanism as Part of Management Audit

A management audit is done in a scientific manner. Productivity and effectiveness of management are key determinants of an organization's success. A good management aims to maximize management performance by focusing on improving processes within the organization. Supply chain activities and its main component, internal supply chain, require adherence to proper processes and systems for achieving effectiveness and efficiency. The management audit team generally carries out some standard audits and some special audits by rotation on various aspects, which are important for the internal performance of the firm and its constituents. Few areas such as inventory management policy, activity-based costing, and information technologies for managing flows are covered in routine management audits. However, a firm may inquire specifically about some cases such as transfer pricing of logistics functions across product groups, and so on, which can be done through special audits. Supply chain assessment thus supports internal management audit.

Similarly, there could be times when a specific assessment may be needed. It may be needed to evaluate any part of the system or role played in the system, and to redefine the same or structure new relationships. There could be a possibility that in an alliance spectrum a supplier is moving up from being an alliance partner to a joint venture relationship or a subsidiary. Apart from regular due diligence that may be required from a financial perspective to consummate a transaction, a supply chain assessment may be important to make the best value out of the transaction by structuring the relationship based on value chain and synchronize the value system. Though this could be important to validate the value system even as an alliance partner, it is all the more pertinent when an investment is envisaged. When such transition in a strategic alliance spectrum happens, an assertion on value gains further tightens the bond.

17.2.6 To Strategize Growth Plans as Part of Improvement Initiatives

One may revisit strategy in order to achieve certain goals and objectives. These would have an impact on the supply chain domain. Such situations would require a supply chain assessment and evaluation of whether strategic reorientation requires redesigning of supply chain configuration, which may include either adjustment or reorganization of resources and capabilities, or any other such initiatives. For example, a new product introduction would facilitate competitive scope by way of using existing distribution for the new range of products. This might require assessing current spare capacity along the network and the capability to handle additional products in the channel. Similarly, an existing distribution centre facility can handle more product categories and even different groups of products that can be evaluated through an assessment programme.

One can evaluate many such growth strategies like the ones cited here.

As an entry strategy, one MNC cement company bought out a small 200,000 tonnes of production per annum cement plant and converted into a 3 million tonnes output per annum grinding plant. Simultaneously, it set up a clinker plant about 500 km from the acquired unit, and transported through rail to utilize the advantage of split location to sell at nearby deficit markets in India.

Such strategies need a lot of support through supply chain assessment at different stages to validate growth plans. Thus, it is important to carry out supply chain assessments for various reasons to drive advantage to the all partners in the system. The assessments help to evaluate various elements like customer service levels, transportation cost, inventory costs, demand levels, and asset utilization factors. The reasons for assessment could be to bring the logistics system in line with the inherent demand characteristics, identify opportunities for improvement, understand the nature of logistics in the firm and its relative costs, determine if logistics meets its performance goals, and so on.

Supply chain should be continuously measured and improved in order to ensure the effectiveness and efficiency while meeting the customer demands on time. If firms don't measure, they can't improve; if they can't improve, they can't be competitive and can't be the customer's first choice. Hence, supply chain assessment is critical and essential for the firms to tap the potential areas such as planning, sourcing, manufacturing, delivery, and returns in supply chain to accelerate growth, competitiveness, and sustainability.

17.3 MECHANICS OF SUPPLY CHAIN ASSESSMENT

Supply chain assessment begins with audit by way of understanding the strategy, current supply chain initiatives, and measures on supply chain parameters such as cost, efficiency, reliability, asset utilization, and productivity. Assume a situation where an organization has not developed a conscious supply chain network, but allowed it to evolve based on a series of processes and activities that are made independently. It would be worse with the below-mentioned symptoms, especially when there is no link between the strategy and supply chain:

1. Inadequate response to customer request and unhappy customers
2. Long cycle time
3. Sub-optimal costs
4. Lack of coordination
5. Less reliability among partners
6. More rigidity in system
7. Mismatch in inventory
8. Sub-optimal resource deployment
9. Supply chain profits being sub-optimal and relationship among partners being strained

An audit mechanism shall be able to diagnose the prevalence of such symptoms or parameters. Improvement initiatives would be able to inquire deep into the design and structure of the supply chain network. Together, these constitute an assessment initiative. Figure 17.2 shows the various stages of supply chain assessment and improvement mechanism.

Stage 1: As-is basis study

Initially, the assessment team must get a broad picture of the business and the supply chain strategy. The team must capture the linkages of other corporate/strategic business unit level strategies and functional strategies. This would help to map key deliverables of the supply chain function. Then it would clearly map supply chain processes, all activities and role agents, and their roles as it is. This is core to the purpose of assessment. Once these are clearly on an as-is basis, then performance data, which is historical, needs to be collected. The time period for such analysis must be decided by the type of the issue to be addressed and its scope. Anywhere between 18 months to 60 months could be relevant. However, certain issues that could be predominantly operational would require shorter time buckets. The audit team should not be tempted to probe too much into operational issues, which would defocus the purpose of supply chain assessment.

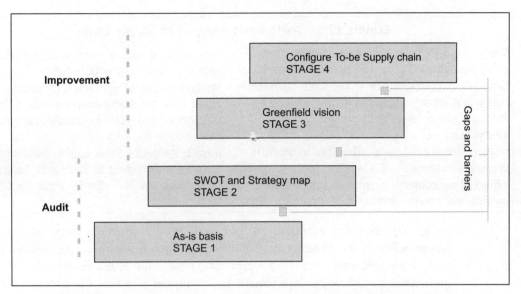

Figure 17.2 Stages of supply chain assessment and improvement mechanism

Source: Adapted from Ayer B. James, *Handbook of SCM*, 2000.

During the audit, it is important first to understand the supply network of the focal organization product/service groups and any specific focus area of assessment to avoid losing value. If the problem is not visible, then it must be driven by the key area concept that contributes significantly to supply chain effectiveness and efficiency. Secondly, the assessment team must get the process maps, supply chain hierarchy, people skills, resources, and financials. Thirdly, the assessment team must get the metrics if it is already deployed or else quickly develop a data sheet of performance indicators and capture the same. Fourthly, the audit team must understand the roles and responsibilities of all the players in the supply chain network that is being probed and capture the expectations and current sense of value.

One of the important stakeholders at this stage is the customer. Supply chain mapping shall go backwards from value to customers and contribution made by each stakeholder, process, and role agent. This would give a deep understanding of the critical issues that need focus. It may be observed that this stage of the process is more of a description and snapshots of the situation rather than being analytical or recommendatory on processes or role agents. The assessment team must avoid influencing any role agent or stakeholder at this stage so that one may not jeopardize information gathering. (Refer Exhibit 17.1)

Stage 2: Assessment of Strengths, Weaknesses, Opportunity, and Threat (SWOT)

The as-is basis analysis would throw clear lights on the strengths and weaknesses of the existing supply chain system, processes, and functions. These are again mapped along with the strategic focus. Independently, a functional aspect would be attractive. For example, the supply chain network may have an excellent, state-of-the-art warehouse. But the cost of warehousing may not be in sympathy with the strategy of cost

---

Exhibit 17.1   As-is Basis Analysis of Supply Chain

Study: Strategic focus and linkage between supply chain and SBU and other functional strategies.

Expected outcome: Arrive at key strategic issues that would impact supply chain structure and performance which needs to be probed.

Study: Supply chain processes, owners' roles and responsibilities, and perspectives like network, inventory, and so on.

Expected outcome: A deep understanding of activities and main points in structuring, and organizing of supply chain perspectives in tune with strategic focus would emerge then.

Study: Analysis of performance indicators on the above on a timeframe covering aspects like asset utilization, productivity, flexibility, responsiveness, and so on.

Result: Analytics show gap in performance and variance with respect to standards. Relating strategic focus one can identify areas for addressing resolution.

---

leadership that the company is pursuing in the product class. Moreover, the functionality of the product may not require such a warehousing facility. In which case, this would turn out to be a weakness. There could a similar case of an overkill on information technology deployment by a supplier whereas the product could be a stable-demand item that has less significance in terms of value and vitality. In this case, if the information system is a part of the overall supply chain system of OEM (original equipment manufacturer) at an incremental cost, could it be advantageous? If not, and if the supplier has independently deployed information systems to improve supplier rating score, probably it could be a weakness adding to the supply chain cost. Hence, one may note that the strengths and weaknesses are contextual and must be mapped to the purpose of the analysis. One may look at a number of such strengths and weaknesses and reduce to four to six of each for an issue to be addressed.

Similarly, the assessment team must look at the external environment at which the supply chain network is operating to explore possible opportunities and threats in the system and their links to the supply chain network being probed. There are a number of opportunities that are thrown open by political, economic, legal, environmental, and societal factors for enhancing supply network efficiency. Let us assume a situation where for political reasons, a state economy reduces duties and taxes to encourage investments. Obviously, this might lead to review of the facilities location decision and reconfiguring the supply chain network. This commonly happens in international trade when trade blocks and countries announce sops for attracting investments. A supply network cannot be rigid and ignore such opportunities. Similarly, tightening of environmental acts would require a different approach in packaging and handling at the distribution centres, with recyclable crates, and so on. This may impact cost and time efficiency adversely but still may be a requirement as per the standards set by the focal organization in the supply chain network.

Changes in security-related rules in the international arena would require more transparent disclosure of information and increased need for information system and data structuring. If any of the partners in the network fails to adhere to the same, it may result in delay or stoppage of flow of goods and services. Again, this may be looked at as adversely affecting the time and cost parameters. However, it must be viewed as a system requirement and demand by conditions relating to trade and security policy impacting uniformly all organizations. Similarly, societal factors like demonstration effect for certain factors strongly influence the distribution pattern of certain goods and services, which has an impact on the role played by certain agents in the supply network. Interestingly, one can observe that transport operators in and around a particular large manufacturing/engineering facility behave in a certain fashion more because of societal pressure rather than an individual economic choice. There is a need to capture these critical factors which would impact supply chain effectiveness and efficiency.

Once the SWOT analysis is done one may draw a solutions matrix, which would be as shown in Table 17.1.

Stage 3: Greenfield Vision

After completing the situation analysis matrix with the strategic focus orientation, the supply chain assessment team would have to look at possible gaps and opportunities for improvements and develop the to-be process. Ideally, one may look at the Greenfield vision of this and envisage benefits and costs for a newer horizon on supply chain improvements. However, for an existing network, there could be a number of barriers, which is because of the baggage carried. It may be still important for the assessment team to understand the Greenfield vision to know how the best of the latest players would emerge in this field. Greenfield vision helps to develop 'out of the box' thinking, breaking conventional thought processes. Also, it captures the latest development in the area probed whether it is in the system, function, or perspective. The assessment team would ideally be looking into:

1. A fresh thinking on process flow, which would be an improvement over the current process flow
2. Resources deployment including physical, human, systems, and intellectual
3. Organization's hierarchy for decision making where focus could be on standardization of routines and taking up strategic focus to higher levels of management
4. Development of metrics if it were to be applied

Table 17.1 Situational matrix template

	Strengths	Weakness
Opportunities	Identify Strength, Opportunities (SO) strategies to bolster strengths and opportunities for significant impact	Identify Weakness, Opportunities (WO) strategies which would help to map opportunities and note the weakness which do not adequately help to reap benefits. Focus on overcoming the weakness through resources deployment and productivity improvements
Threats	Identify Strengths, Threat (ST) strategies which would be based on using strengths to overcome threats and/or look at de-risking the threats.	Identify Weakness, Threat (WT) strategies which would be tough situation where one may have to look at weakness and possible threats as well.

5. Cost and benefits analysis of this Greenfield approach

On completion of this, the assessment team may get into analysis of impediments to adapt the Greenfield vision due to organizational and structural constraints. However, critical inputs are carried on tweaking a solution for the current supply chain network, which would be implemented in the next stage.

Stage 4: Configure 'To-be Supply Chain'

The Greenfield vision gives an idea about how to approach the configuration of a supply chain network based on the gaps and contemporary developments. As mentioned earlier, constraints in the existing structure may lead to certain trade-offs that the audit team has to arrive at. However, it is important to discuss trade-offs and the rationale of those with the key players in the system to ensure buy-in of the recommendation. Otherwise, the recommendation could not be implemented successfully. It is also important to map here how the supply chain assessment team must qualify the trade-off. One of the key aspects of the trade-off could be cost and benefit of the proposed Greenfield solution versus the recommended solution. The Greenfield solution may lead to a state-of-the-art distribution centre with high level of automation and self-guided handling equipment. Though such an option would standardize the operation and ensure a well-defined productivity level, the given distribution layout, people attributes, and cost of severance of contract may not fit in.

Hence, the assessment team must embark on the progressive deployment of a solution and leave a road map rather than harping on a best of breed solution. Such trade-off and recommendation could be arrived at after an evaluation of options based on the framework, contemporary development, discussions with key decision makers, scenario building, and carefully evaluating options.

The assessment team must clearly keep the client interest and feasibility as the top priority rather than being revolutionary in approach. It is important to note that revolutionary thought and action that may reconfigure not only the supply chain network but even the competitive situation need not be avoided by decision makers. To cite an example, certain networks in trade like commodities and securities driven by technology, policies, and systems have changed phenomenally, rather with creativity and convenience of all players. This has increased volume of transactions at a low cost. Similarly, in India dairy products and edible oil have changed character and quality of competition to the benefits of customers and all other players by the reconfiguration of supply chain. One can also cite examples of companies such as Marico, Asian Paints, and Metal Junction, who have led through a revolutionary supply chain structure.

17.4 BARRIERS TO AUDIT AND IMPROVEMENT

It may be interesting to note what could be impediments to an assessment on supply chain for improvements. The assessment team shall recognize that it is by nature of human mindset there would be resistance to probing or validation of existing processes, roles, and resource deployment. Any such effort for inquiry could be perceived to be top-driven and viewed to be challenging the existing network. If the assessment team appreciates the concerns of different stakeholders, it may engage with them meaningfully to solicit right involvement and work on the improvement of the supply chain network. Based on experience, the concerns and suggestion to handle the same are discussed here. The list is only indicative and suggestions are more recommendatory.

17.4.1 Lack of Commitment from Top Management

Many a time, assessment is initiated by the top management, which continuously looks for improvement or takes initiatives based on external environmental factors. They may show excitement to engage the services of the assessment team for improving the supply chain. Unless the spirit is communicated down below, the study may lose its significance. Also, the top management shall have a mechanism to ensure fair outcome of the study and implement the recommendations. Any policy shift or strategic decision involved for going ahead with the recommended supply chain structure shall be supported with the resource commitment. There could be a situation wherein supply chain reconfiguration would require aligning or readjustment of alignment with key players for which top management involvement may be required. These are fundamental to the success of supply chain reconfiguration for which the assessment team shall ensure buy-in of top management throughout the study.

17.4.2 People

People are key to supply chain efficiency and effectiveness. For example, a yard operation involves a number of equipment operators who are important to ensure efficient movement of goods on a schedule. Similarly in transport operations, space booking and route scheduling may still have some manual components. People play a key role in supply chain planning and operations, rather in execution of strategy in supply chain. Any assessment of such supply chain functions will involve evaluating productivity of people resources. On such evaluation, one may analyse the relevance of each resource for the supply chain structure. An assessment process on as-is basis would require evaluating resources on a sample basis or on enumeration based on number of people engaged in supply chain processes. Many of such people resources could be collusive and protected through formal or informal structures like unions and federations. They may have fear of loss of jobs when an assessment is triggered. Such fear may lead to resistance for studying their job roles and productivity. The assessment team must convince the importance of the study and how system improvement would improve people skills and productivity, and thereby benefit everyone in the supply chain network. The assessment team must focus on assuring their support at the initiation stage of the study itself.

17.4.3 Role Agents

Similar to the behaviour pattern of people in the supply chain network, a number of agents who have different roles in the network tend to behave differently to the assessment mechanism depending upon the bargaining power they hold on the focal organization. Suppose, if the role agents have more power—and have been able to exploit their position to their advantage—but it leads to sub-optimal supply chain profits, they are unlikely to be supportive for any probing of their functions and effectiveness. For example, let us look at a situation where in an engineering manufacturing location, transport operators who are shipping over-dimension cargo in specialized vehicles may not be placing vehicle for improved time efficiency. However, the focal organization may not be able to streamline the same as these are niche services. Assessment team may have the onerous task of probing into the same and recommending an acceptable solution, which would require involvement of such operators in the assessment process. One can come across such conflicts in the internal supply chain, which is quite common between the marketing team that captures orders and the manufacturing team that services the orders. Hence, it is important for the assessment team to appreciate such ticklish issues and capture clearly for adding value to the supply chain structure.

17.4.4   Fear of Unknown and Resistance to Change

Many a time in an assessment process, the middle and senior management do not extend the required support because of agency problems and fear of unknown. The management working on behalf of the owners assumes too much of importance and gets carried away with the complexity of the issue, enjoys managerial powers and importance, and loses focus on effectiveness and efficiency. Like the bottom strata of employees in the structure, these managers are also driven by fear of employment, power, need to deskill, and acquire new skills. Hence, they have motives to hinder a probe into operations and relevance of structure. They are biased with a few role agents and employees in the system to protect their own interests. A classic situation may arise, power struggle could already be making the system ineffective as the sourcing team may not be in sync with the production team, which in turn may not be aligned to the marketing and services teams. An assessment team shall identify such power groups and address their concerns in order to get the clear picture and recommend best of solutions.

17.4.5   Behavioural Constraints

One can commonly come across behavioural attitudes like 'know-as-much' attitude and looking for 'drastic initiatives' and missing incremental changes, and so on. There is a likely tendency that could be observed in the finalization of the assessment report wherein the assessment team would be interacting with the key decision makers for finalizing the recommendation based on scenario building. Many a time, the tendency, especially from critics of the study, would be negative for not being pragmatic or for lack of dramatic outcomes. This is again a behavioural issue, which needs to be addressed effectively by the assessment team to achieve desired results. Without any bias, the team shall first evaluate the critical comments and counter the arguments scientifically. Many a time an unbiased and objective approach brings in value and helps to convince most of the decision makers. To avoid hitting a bottleneck in the closing stage, it may be good to involve key decision makers in the advanced stages of study by consultation process.

Supply chain assessment may cut across different impediments to the study from various sources. It must be prepared to counter all these in a meaningful way and contribute to the purpose of engagement. It is also important to keep in mind the timeframe of the study and the implementation plan while countering such impediments. There is a likely tendency of getting into protracted arguments and probing and losing time focus. Also, the critics may facilitate closure of the study but stall implementation, which again does not serve the purpose of engagement. Hence, negotiation of the issues positively is critical to the success of the assessment mechanism and eventual improvement of the supply chain network.

17.5 APPROACH TOWARDS EXCELLENCE

Leaders in any business today have achieved this position after having conceived a vision and toiled hard to achieve the same through rigorous implementation of strategies. The best practice that a company adopts today is not the ultimate as one knows by observation that leading positions cannot be sustained for a long period unless one consistently works on improving the current state of affairs. Hence identifying and implementing best practices is a journey, not a destination.

There are different approaches to achieve excellence, which have been articulated by many visionaries or management gurus over the decades. These philosophies have emanated from quality movements that impact supply chain activities dramatically. There are management approaches such as business process reengineering, Total Quality Management, and benchmarking, which are amenable for structuring a framework to work on supply chain excellence. Similarly, quality award frameworks—such as European Foundation for Quality Management, Deming award, and Malcolm Baldrige—award companies for giving due credence to supply chain activities in their assessment framework. Moreover, institutions like Supply Chain Council with its SCOR model and Lean Enterprise Institute (LEI) forum facilitate validation and approaches to supply chain excellence. Refer to Figure 17.3.

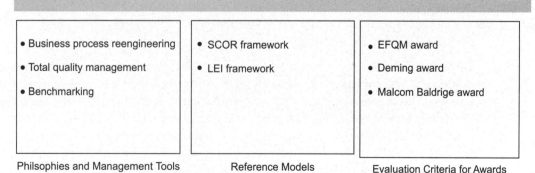

Figure 17.3   Approach to excellence

Each organization and its key functions, processes, and system must benchmark 'over time'; and against 'best in class in industry', and 'best in class in World' for performing the value chain activities effectively and efficiently. The value chain activities encompass supply chain activities like facilities management, inbound and outbound transportation, inventory, sourcing, and post sales management, and so on. There is a likely tendency that some of these supply chain activities, which may not be a key component to value chain management, may get lesser importance. However, it is the responsibility of supply chain authority to ensure that all activities are taken care of.

17.5.1 Benchmarking for Excellence

Benchmarking is how well a company performs its particular activities and processes over time and against the best in industry and best in world performers for continuously striving towards excellence. However, it happens only if there is a strategy and policy towards improving the quality of that specific process or activity. Hence, it is pertinent to bring supply chain issues over here. Many times internal supply chain and policies such as inventory management are part of benchmarking study in manufacturing companies as production cost and efficiency are key to survival. Many intermediaries adopt benchmarking, as it is a competitive pressure or a demand from a downstream buyer. It is to be noted that quality initiatives are not a one-time or standard activity. The same quality practices cannot be adopted across organizations as each organization has its unique requirements. Having said that, benchmarking is a spirit and passion with which one would drive change for improvement. Supply chain managers must inculcate the same in their systems to achieve excellence. Though organizational excellence is a macro goal, it is important to pursue the sub goal, such as supply chain excellence, for achieving the macro-level objectives and professional demands of supply chain managers.

The benchmarking initiatives have stimulated managerial awareness for more than two decades on business process reengineering, Total Quality Management (TQM), and other continuous improvement techniques, including excellence models. Within each of these, new philosophy and methodology frameworks have emerged. One may find any of these approaches meaningful and contributory for achieving supply chain excellence.

17.5.2 TQM for Excellence

TQM is a philosophy of managing a set of business practices that emphasize continuous improvement in all operations, 100 per cent accuracy in performing activities, involvement and empowerment of employees at all levels, team-based work design, benchmarking, and fully satisfying customer expectations. Management interest in TQM has generally originated from engineering and manufacturing, service businesses such as banking and finance, and customer-facing activities. Usually managers have quality and customer satisfaction problems as common in their competitive arena and apply TQM for achieving competitive advantage.

While TQM originally started by concentrating on the production of quality goods and services and the delivery of excellent customer service, it is now being applied to all facets of management for achieving corporate excellence. It can be observed from Exhibit 17.2 that TQM reforms corporate culture and adopts continuous improvement as business philosophy.

TQM focuses on creating a continuous approach for being ahead in competition on parameters such as product design, cycle time, cost, product quality and reliability, service, and customer satisfaction. These little improvement steps are called kaizen by the Japanese. These are applicable in logistics and supply chain domain as well, demonstrated by Toyota and being practised in India by Toyota Kirloskar and a large number of automotive companies and their components companies in India. Hence, the concept is well grained in the quality circles. But it is important to drive home the fact that TQM needs to applied to all facets of supply chain activities, which is currently not being practised as it is beyond the control of the focal organization and the power of relationship decides the level of adoption. This shall truly change the culture of supply chain environment.

17.5.3 Supply Chain Reengineering for Excellence

Many a time the management has a tendency to initiate supply chain reengineering (applied business process reengineering) to accomplish certain short-term goals with respect to quality, cost, or customer acquisition. The essential difference between supply chain reengineering and adoption of TQM culture in supply chain is that the former provides for a quantum jump in benefits much more as one-time static intervention whereas the latter works on continuous improvements and being dynamic. The supply chain authority needs to work on both as the organization would have to look for opportunities for drastic improvements in the configuration of the supply chain network and achieve innovativeness and competitive advantage. This could be more on the strategic level of supply chain and its interface with other functions, SBU level strategy, and corporate strategy.

At the same time, a number of supply chain activities and processes at the planning and operational level need continuous improvements and hence quality initiatives must be sustained. It may be interesting to note that the reengineering initiative could be top down, triggered by the top management, while continuous improvement could be part of a quality movement, wherein the bottom and middle levels

---

Exhibit 17.2   Twelve Aspects Common to TQM and Continuous Improvement Programmes

1. Committed leadership
2. Adoption and communication of TQM using mission statements, slogans, and so on
3. Closer customer relationships
4. Closer supplier relationships
5. Benchmarking
6. Increased training
7. Open organization
8. Employee empowerment
9. Zero defects mentality
10. Flexible manufacturing
11. Process improvement
12. Measurement

Source: Powel, Thomas C., 'Total Quality Management as Competitive Advantage,' *Strategic Management Journal,* no.1, pp. 19, January 1995.

participate with leadership from within. This is where supply chain managers could lead in a big way.

17.5.4 Aiming Awards for Excellence

Quality and excellence awards help in supply chain improvements. The criteria for excellence awards is efficiency in supply chain functions. One may observe that the Deming award and Malcolm Baldrige award companies in their assessment of business excellence consider the supply chain component as well. To substantiate, the Baldrige criteria of performance excellence framework includes customer, market focus, and process management, which includes manufacture and supply management as well. EFQM (European Foundation for Quality Management, founded in 1988) in its approach looks at enablers (which include leadership, policy and strategy, people, partnership, and resources and processes); results on people (including customers and society), and performance measures which could be financial. It portrays the RADAR approach, which has Results, Approach, Deployment, Assessment, and Review as the elements.

Even in EFQM model, supply chain activities are substantially evaluated in partnership and process, and in result areas. In India, CII institute of Quality has an award instituted for business excellence, named as CII-EXIM Award for Business Excellence, which would be a useful reference on these initiatives. A supply chain manager must get involved in such model assessment to focus on improvements in the supply chain and look for opportunities for benchmarking. The philosophy and framework of these models can be customized for supply chain excellence by the companies or a group of them to benchmark the industry-wide approach. The EFQM model is especially amenable to this, and with the involvement of the CII centres of excellence, one can move ahead with more meaningful industry-wide application. CII Institute of Logistics and S.P. Jain institute of Management have independently and along with partnering organizations instituted an excellence award in supply chain for Indian companies.

17.5.5 Reference Models for Excellence

It is important to mention here that at the international arena, Supply Chain Council (SCC) with its Supply Chain Operations Reference Model (SCOR) is facilitating its members in benchmarking supply chain and provides support for supply chain improvements (www.supply-chain.org). The model is based on standardized terminology and processes provided by SCC. Configuring these processes, supply chain entities are evaluated either for part of supply chain network or any focused role agent, and so on. SCC defines a supply chain from the supplier's suppliers to the customer's customers' perspective, which is commonly referred to as an extended supply chain. There are five processes in Level 1 of SCC. These include plan, source, make, deliver, and return. There were four processes originally and return was later added in 2002. The directional movement of the first four are from suppliers to the customer, while the last is on reverse. The model as described envisages a predominantly physical flow though informational and financial flows are important as well.

The five process types of Level 1 are divided into twenty-two process categories, including 'enable process' categories of each process type. This level is used for mapping redundancies of businesses and processes. Each process category is mapped as one of the types, namely: planning, execution, and enabling. Planning processes support the allocation of resources to the expected demand. They are on a planning horizon and generally executed periodically in short time buckets. They could be influencing flexibility in supply chain with respect to changes in demand and supply. The executing processes could be relating to current or planned demand. These relate to nature of orders, their scheduling and movements. Enabling processes are those that support planning and executing. They support flow of information and relations among other processes. In SCOR Level 3, process categories are further divided into process elements. Most elements provide an input stream and output stream on material and information. Metrics and best practices for these are part of the SCOR model. The metrics are divided into five categories, namely, reliability, flexibility, responsiveness, cost, and assets. The first three of these are external and customer-driven, whereas the last two, cost and assets, are internal and financial in perspective. The model deals with these at appropriate levels, which are not covered in this book.

One may observe that the approach has been analysing the business and competition; configuring the supply chain of the focal organization, mapping performance metrics, evaluating and recommending practice and systems; and implementing the recommended system. SCOR mainly facilitates such probing and mapping through its framework, expertise, and professionals.

Another philosophy and framework which directly facilitates achieving excellence in supply chain is lean management (www.lean.org). Srinivasan (2004) describes the importance of lean principles and framework as a basis for achieving supply chain excellence. A value stream map is designed by developing a systems perspective and understanding a customer's expectations. Using the value stream map and benchmarking best practices, the supply chain flow should be configured. Such a supply chain can be managed using metrics related to the benchmarks and designed configuration.

17.6 SUPPLY CHAIN ASSESSMENT SERVICES IN INDIA

In India, there are organizations that provide supply chain assessment services. CII Institute of Logistics, a Centre of Excellence of CII, offers this service to its members. CII Institute of Logistics has been doing pioneering work in supply chain and logistics through knowledge sharing and industry initiatives by holding bi-annual conferences on topical issues of the domain. Its members and international speakers share a number of new initiatives, which could be adopted across industries. The members describe how they were earlier and how they transformed their supply chain through innovations. CII Institute of Logistics thus enjoys a platform through which it can offer audit services with its expertise.

Apart from CII, a number of consulting organizations such as KPMG, E&Y, Accenture, and Deloitte tend to offer such assessment services through their services division. Also, a number of logistics service providers and specialist organizations such as DHL, GATI, SAFEXPRESS, and TVS Logistics, tend to provide audit and solutions to improve supply chain effectiveness and efficiency. Academic institutions such as Indian Institute of Management at different locations and premier schools such as Indian School of Business, NITIE, and Loyola Institute of Business Administration, to name a few, have Centres of Excellence in Logistics and Supply Chain Management, which could offer such services.

The reason why this has been discussed here is that the current offering is niche and the potential is huge. Also many corporate and entities who are part of various supply chain networks need to focus on improvements and deploy more of audit services in order to make Indian business competitive in the international arena. Fortunately, the growth of information technology companies in India who may be in product development or unit of product MNCs, IT service companies, and integrators have great implicit knowledge through their experience in global business in the logistics and manufacturing domain. Professional knowledge sharing through forums would help supply chain assessment services in India to mature.

To give a flavour of supply chain audit, one of the experiences is shared here. The problem is real but the name and instance are illustrative.

Smart Engineering Limited (SEL) has approached consultants to study their supply chain strategy, practices, and processes, and find the areas of improvement. The reason they want to identify the areas of improvement is because they want to cater to the huge surge in demand for their engineering components and also meet their customers' demands on time by ensuring availability of products at the project site in a sequential order at an optimal cost.

The objectives of the study were to measure SEL supply chain's effectiveness, efficiency, and identify the key focus areas for further improvements. The following methodology was deployed to study the SEL's supply chain strategies, practices, and processes.

- Studying department procedures and department instructions
- Interviewing the key supply chain process owners, executors, and systems personnel
- Data collating and analysis
- Process mapping and analysis

Supply Chain Operations Reference Model (SCOR) has been taken as a reference for standard measurement such as inventory days of supply, cash to cash cycle, and logistics cost in the assessment. The model is the product of Supply-Chain Council (SCC), an independent, non-profit, global corporation advancing the state-of-the-art in supply chain management systems and practices.

The supply chain assessment covered the following deliverables to accomplish the objective of the assessment.

- Demand growth and financial performance analysis at SEL
- SEL material flow mapping and analysis

- SEL information and workflow mapping and analysis
- Key focus areas for continuous improvements to cater to the huge demand surge in supply chain while ensuring that the products are reaching the project site on time and in a sequential order.

During the study it came up that SEL should adopt certain corrective measures. These measures included an efficient, effective, and integrated supply chain planning and process aligned with technology (planning lead time), collaborative planning with suppliers (sourcing lead time), and setting up metrics and incentives for role agents. In addition, by concentrating on R&D and outsourcing manufacturing activities (manufacturing lead time) as well as non-core activities (delivery lead), the SEL supply chain could be highly competitive by ensuring time to market at the best cost.

SEL has been experiencing a great pressure from customers for delivering a customized product with a shorter lead time in the sequence order at a low cost. However, SEL was challenged by growing material costs, which went up from 50 per cent to 60 per cent over successive years. This obviously reduces the profit margin, which alerts any financial stakeholder. SEL has been facing a greater challenge on delivering the products on time in a sequence order to the customer site, which in turn delays the erection and commissioning process at the site. Consequently, it affects the customer service level and also increases the total cycle time and opportunity costs.

SEL supply chain is an engineer-to-order chain because SEL designs, manufactures, and delivers each product based on its customer's unique requirements and specifications. Hence, customer-specific orders would trigger the entire supply chain process from engineering document, material planning, manufacturing, and delivering to the customer site.

To meet this challenge strategically, SEL has been working on the standardization of the designing process to reduce designing lead time. Hence, engineering design document is the trigger for the entire supply chain planning and operations process. The value engineering concepts have been adopted to reduce the material cost. SEL's inventory strategy was to keep a high inventory to cater to a customer's demand on time. Outsourcing non-core activities and being proactive to the customer's needs are some of the supply chain strategies that have been adopted by SEL.

The above discussion gives an idea of complexity of supply chain for SEL. If SEL's turnover is Rs 500 crore and its SCM cost is about 4 per cent of the revenue, the SCM cost should be around Rs 20 crore. Any supply chain improvement impacting reduction of SCM cost to 3.5 per cent of the total revenue would mean that the SCM cost would be Rs 17.5 crore. This is a saving of Rs 2.5 crore, which must be shared among the various stakeholders across the supply chain network.

This would sound like a miniscule impact on the task and efforts. Also, it may mean that a lot of compromise needs to be made. But on the other hand, it may improve service levels, which would mean increased turnover, capacity, and long-term benefits. Hence, it is recommended that an organization have a larger perspective on supply chain audit initiatives.

SUMMARY

Supply chain assessment is the process of systematic examination of a supply chain network carried out by an internal or external quality assessor or an assessment team. It is an important part of an organization's initiative to ensure a synchronized flow of goods and services, finance, and information. This is achieved through integrating various external and internal stakeholders for serving the ultimate customer of the focal organization at the best-defined cost.

Supply chain assessments are conducted in order to:

- bring the supply chain system in line with the inherent demand characteristics
- reassess supply chain effectiveness and responsiveness
- validate current processes and roles and responsibilities and their effectiveness
- measure the efficiency of resources deployed and probe scope for improving the same
- identify and eliminate redundant activities
- comply with internal control mechanism as part of the management audit

Supply chain assessment is important when a management proposes to strategize growth plans. It then needs to synchronize with the overall strategy of growth for avoiding any bottleneck in the organizational/business growth plans.

The assessment team would arrive at a process flow, which would be an improvement over the current system. They would also look into deployment of resources, organization hierarchy for decision making, development of metrics if it were to be applied, and the cost and benefits analysis of this Greenfield approach.

The impediments to assessment may encompass lack of commitment from the top management, people, role agents, fear of unknown, and resistance to change management.

Companies may choose to follow supply chain excellence using any of the management philosophies or tools such as benchmarking, best practice analysis, business process reengineering, TQM, or aiming at awards such as Deming, Malcom Baldridge, and EFQM, or adapting to reference models such as SCOR or LEI.

KEY TERMS

Audit: Audit is an assessment of systems, processes, transactions, or any such activities to conform on validity and reliability of framework, structure, policy and procedures. This is predominantly done for the purpose of internal control from a management perspective. Such audits ensure validation and verification of conformity of standards.

Benchmarking: Benchmarking is how well a company performs its particular activities and processes over time and against the best-in-industry and best-in-world performers for continuously gauging itself for improvement.

Focal organization: An organization in which supply chain assessment is being done for the purpose of improvements.

Greenfield vision: A way of visualizing the advantages of a new entrant in an industry.

Milk run: A typical method of transportation used to optimally plan the pick-up and delivery of goods in a selected route.

Role agent: A company in the supply chain of a focal organization that influences the physical, information, and financial flows.

Supply chain assessment: Supply chain assessment is the process of systematic examination of a supply chain network carried out by an internal or external team of qualified members to ensure adherence to standards, achievement of performance parameters, and identification of areas of improvements. It is an important part of an organization's initiative to ensure synchronized flow of goods and services, finance, and information to achieve desired results through integrating various external and internal stakeholders for serving the ultimate customers of the focal organization at the least cost.

Total quality management (TQM): TQM is a philosophy of managing a set of business practices that emphasize continuous improvement in all operations, 100 per cent accuracy in performing activities, involvement and empowerment of employees at all levels, team-based work design, benchmarking, and fully satisfying customer expectations.

CONCEPT REVIEW QUESTIONS

1. Define supply chain assessment.
2. Explain the importance of supply chain assessment with an example.
3. Give scenarios that require assessment to evaluate resource deployment efficiency and effectiveness.
4. How would identification and elimination of redundancies help in supply chain assessment?
5. What are the four stages of supply chain assessment? Explain each stage briefly.
6. What are the impediments to supply chain assessment?
7. What are the management philosophies and tools for supply chain excellence?

CRITICAL THINKING QUESTIONS

1. Identify an operating unit with which you are familiar. Develop a critical assessment of its supply chain configuration.
2. A traditional audit team opines that there is no need for conducting specific audits on supply chain processes and work on improvement. You are in charge of a consulting firm wanting to convince the prospective client on a supply chain audit. The prospect is in the business of tier I auto component manufacture. Detail your arguments in favour of supply chain audit service.
3. Use the SCOR model for mapping the supply chain of a product you are familiar with.

REFERENCES

Powel, C. Tomas, 'Total Quality Management as Competitive Advantage,' *Strategic Management Journal*, no. 1, pp. 19, 16 January 1995

Srinivasan, M. Mandyam, 14 *Principles for Building & Managing Lean Supply Chain*, Thompson, 2004

Wheelen, L. Thomas and L. David Hunger, *Strategic Management and Business Policy*, Pearson, 2002

www.lean.org, accessed on 12 January 2009

www.supply-chain.org, accessed on 12 January 2009

www.cii-iq.in/pdfs/excelance.pdf, accessed on 12 January 2009

www.ciilogistics.com/, accessed on 12 January 2009

www.efqm.org/Default.aspx?tabid=35, accessed on 12 January 2009

18

Supply Chain Organizational Issues

Learning Objectives

After studying this chapter, you will be able to:

♦ Understand the role of a supply chain manager
♦ Comprehend the corporate size, business complexity, ownership pattern, and level of decision making in a supply chain
♦ Gain an insight into intra-organizational decision making versus outsourced supply chain
♦ Understand the inter-disciplinary approach to decision making
♦ Understand the importance of empowering professionals in supply chain decision making
♦ Gain an insight into technology applications for supply chain organization decisions

It is important to properly understand and recognize supply chain organization structure, role, and performance for effective supply chain management. Like any other function or domain area, results to be achieved are clear and well defined in structuring. What matters is how much of overall organizational focus is there on this function. Are there differences among firms in an industry and across market that make structuring for each firm unique? If so, one may like to appreciate the key focus areas for doing the right things at the right cost and right productivity levels.

One may note that the triad of supply chain management includes technology, processes, and people. All these are interlinked. One would here look at people-related issues in greater detail, and aspects of inter-linkages with the other two, namely technology and processes, would also be highlighted. People management in the supply chain domain is well facilitated if there is appropriate technology adoption, and processes are well defined. However, one should take cognizance of the numerous people-related issues in the supply chain domain that are discussed here.

There are certain myths about people capability requirement for supply chain management function, which is generally believed to be execution-focused with limited scope for planning. It is also believed that logistics drivers, namely warehouse, transportation, and inventory management, are transactional and involve working with low-end resources, while management time and effort are required only for setting policies and operational guidelines. One must understand that supply chain activities are focused on immediate results, which explains such an approach.

However, in today's context, the scope of logistical drivers is changing with wider application of technology in business and needs a reassessment.

Contrary to popular belief, supply chain management is highly plan-oriented and requires a deep understanding of business processes and manoeuvrability to synchronize these processes for delivering customer satisfaction. In the global business, one could mention corporates such as Dell Computers, Walmart, and Zara Clothing for achieving phenomenal success by creating supply chain-centric organizations. In India, the success of companies such as Amul, Asian Paints, and Metal Junction would emphasize the role of planning and strategy in driving success. Hence, in contemporary business, supply chain is critical and an organization must have fundamentally strong policy and strategy orientation. This happens only when leadership is committed.

There is a common approach, especially in conventional businesses, to keep the supply chain domain limited to the ambit of middle and junior echelons of the hierarchy. This was reasonably true till recently when logistics functions were treated more as execution-oriented and delivery-centric. In today's context, this has changed significantly. Now there is a need to involve the senior and top management in supply chain decisions. This could easily be explained by the concept of 'economies of scope', which Michael Porter advocated for better utilization of resources. This kind of application could be thought of at the middle and junior management levels. However, its successful implementation and the drive to be constantly up in a competitive arena needs to come from the top management. Similarly, one could think of many innovations in configuring a new supply chain, roles for partners, and exciting relationships for optimizing resources and revenues.

Hence, an organization must have strong leadership commitment and involvement of senior management in deciding most of the supply chain functions. Obviously, systems, policies, and procedures must be structured to make the best use of such involvement.

18.1 ROLE OF SUPPLY CHAIN MANAGERS

Supply chain managers are engaged in different facets of a business—from identifying material source, to procuring, moving, storing, manufacturing, distributing, and engaging customers in completion of sale and post-sales management. Supply chain managers have a tremendous impact on the success of an organization. They are represented at all hierarchies of management decisions, namely planning, strategizing, and operating levels. In short, these managers are across the organization and connect with external entities to satisfy the organization's ultimate customers.

Since supply chain managers have a role in facilitation and collaboration, apart from execution, they are in a unique position to help other functions execute their strategies. A supply chain manager performs cross-functional roles involving multiple departments. For example, for the sourcing function, the operations, quality, commercial, and legal departments are involved. For the planning function, marketing, customer service, production, systems, and finance are involved.

Similarly, delivery management involves coordinating with marketing, operations, and finance for credit limits and with logisticians. Truly, a supply chain manager's role is multi-functional, relationship intense, and customer focused.

A supply chain manager must be able to link up all relevant operational and support functions in order to fulfil a customer's demand. Depending upon the nature of the industry, this role would vary. In a business where production economies are high, sourcing and manufacturing could be critical, and typically, an operations manager would be the key role player in managing the firm's supply chain. There may not be an identified supply chain manager. Even if there's one, the focus would be more on execution of logistical drivers of the supply chain. For example, in a heavy engineering company, order procurement and management would be done by the marketing department, which would pass on the order to production, which would then coordinate with other functional managers for supply chain aspects. The production department does vendor coordination and production functions of adding value to material and components. It is dependent on the transportation manager and yard managers for logistical support. Such an approach would lack supply chain orientation as the thought process is driven by a silo approach.

Similarly, in an FMCG company, the role of a supply chain manager would mostly be that of managing distribution network and all strategic and planning decisions would be driven by the marketing manager. In case of inventory-driven companies, supply chain strategic decisions would be driven by the finance department and the logistician would run the support function. These are not comprehensive approaches to manage a supply chain in today's business because the customer is the key in most of the businesses. Like firms benefiting out of proliferation of information technology, customers are exploiting information and communication to their advantage. Hence, the role of a supply chain manager is at the higher echelons of management rather than just supporting the execution of functional aspects.

Figure 18.1 explains the interface of supply chain decisions with other functions such as marketing, finance, operations, technology, and so on. Though supply chain involves a high degree of logistical functions that are primarily execution focused, the planning and strategy aspects of supply chain are multi-disciplinary and have to involve a group approach. Realizing the importance of supply chain for the success of the focal firm, organizations are increasingly structuring a supply chain command at the top-level management to ensure coordination with all the functions

18.2   VARIETY OF ROLES IN SUPPLY CHAIN

It may be observed from the above that a supply chain manager has different roles under his command and builds a team accordingly. Each role presents a different aspect of supply chain, which might require different skill sets, capabilities, and experience to handle decision situations. So a supply chain manager would have a combination of human resources to achieve tangible results, develop processes to improve performance, or apply technology to analyse data. All these skills in combination lead to effective supply chain. One may again find the role of a supply chain manager across a variety of organizations—manufacturers, retailers, transportation companies, third-party logistics firms, government agencies, and service firms—having a commonality in function, and yet being unique to the industry. The array of decision situations needing supply chain expertise is nearly endless and challenging.

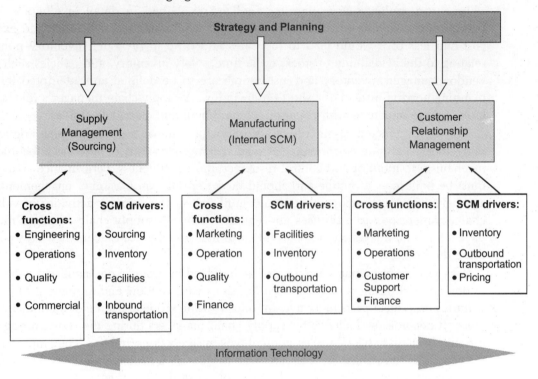

Figure 18.1 Interface of supply chain decisions with functions

One may note that from the decision hierarchy level, a large number of supply chain managers focus on transactional-level operating decisions. These roles would involve managing product flows from the vendor or warehousing facilities, conversion, managing distribution work, and order management. There is an active involvement in the information flow due to the demand of transparency and visibility by partners across the chain. The operating-level roles are primarily seen in logistics enablers such as third-party logistics service providers, integrators, port terminals, distribution centres, railroad and other transport operators, and so on. The skill sets of each of these functions are different and require specialized training for fulfilling requirements of the function.

The next level of decision-making hierarchy would be at the planning level. These roles focus on supply management, demand forecasting, inventory policies, performance analysis, or customer engagements. Supply chain management involves coordinating with vendors, understanding their viability, working on product development and quality aspects, and so on. Demand forecasting is one of the key planning tools. It is a vital input across all supply chain functions. Unless the forecast is reliable, a supply chain manager cannot commit resources and effort across partners in a supply chain. The quality of demand estimate is an important factor which determines supply chain effectiveness. Hence a supply chain manager must work on this function in a focused manner.

Inventory policies as a planning tool are explained in detail in Chapter 10. Inventory is a double-edged sword: more of it would lead to inefficiency and extra cost and less of it would lead to lost sales and drop in revenue. Inventory policy relating to the availability of stock, cycle time, safety inventory, and policies such as vendor managed inventory and just-in-time are to be defined and attempted for a planning horizon instead of a short-time window. A supply chain manager's role is to look at these initiatives with resources commitment and clear deliverables.

The performance analysis role of a supply chain manager goes with planning and budgeting. Analysing performance at regular time intervals is required as a feedback mechanism to monitor and control resources and effectiveness. Performance analysis must be built-in as a routine and should be system driven. Customer engagement is another important function that would fulfil one of the primary activities of value chain, namely post-sale services and enhancements. A supply chain manager must have a focus on this function as current customers and their satisfaction is what would drive the business.

A supply chain manager would also be involved in strategic decisions with respect to domain and business unit. Alliance decisions with vendors and formations of joint ventures on critical parts that have an industry-wide scope are some of the indicative areas. It becomes a challenge for supply chain managers during the restructuring of the supply chain network and creation of new business opportunities. They must have the capability to establish its feasibility with key decision makers. Board-level strategic decisions in areas relating to supply chain or those that are triggered by the supply chain domain require a supply chain manager to handle such issues with ease. For example, expansion into a new territory would require setting up facilities and all other logistics and cross-functional drivers to be coordinated. A supply chain manager should be competent to lead such a decision team and develop such initiatives.

Supply chain function requires a core team approach. It is generally believed that a core team is created where the requirement for management bandwidth is high, and many times under such conditions, complexity and criticality would also be high. In a traditional approach, a core team is deployed for the SCM domain for handling last-week delivery requirement or handling contingencies. This is typically an operations team on a specific, short-term agenda.

However, creating a core team for managing supply chain strategies and planning framework is vital in contemporary business. This is mainly because of the complexity in planning, strategizing, and operationalizing varied tasks of different processes and finally managing key relationships. Unless there is a core team which builds beneath those managerial talents for execution, the scope to create a hybrid supply network is limited.

18.3 HORIZON OF PEOPLE AND ORGANIZATIONAL ISSUES IN SCM

Refer to Figure 18.2 to understand the concept of the organizational issues in supply chain management and how people excel in the supply chain structure.

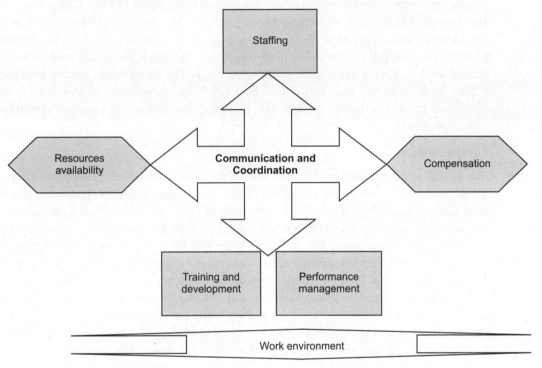

Figure 18.2 People processes in supply chain organization

Source: Adapted from PCMM.

Staffing

The staffing function per se requires estimating requirements and ensuring that resources are deployed at all levels. In the operational aspects of logistics functions, employees are classified as semi-skilled or skilled employees. Sometimes staffing in skilled functions such as operators in container terminals, special purpose vehicles, document handlers, and so on poses a challenge. So a correct estimation of such requirement is important to facilitate the staffing function. Most of the key industries have their own technical training institutes from where resources are picked up.

Staffing for planning and strategic supply chain functions has always been a challenge. The combination of academic credentials and experience is an issue. Generally, firms are able to get resources with experience and academic credentials may have to be improved. This is mainly because of the importance given to this function earlier. Once on the job, supply chain executives do not get the required time for learning and upscaling. So staffing knowledge resources proves to be a challenge.

Resource Availability

For any staffing function, resource availability is one of the key factors. There is a concern with respect to the availability of skilled manpower, and especially manpower with the right orientation. According to a report (2006), China has a big shortage of skilled and experienced logistics and SCM managers. The strong demand for experienced logistics staff has led to high staff turnover levels. This imposes continuous training overheads on the logistics suppliers. Sourcing and retaining skilled staff in China will be an ongoing issue for the foreseeable future. However, China and countries like India and Singapore are conscious of this factor, and government and industry bodies are constantly working on resource capability enhancement.

Compensation

Till recently, the logistics sector was not on demand. Though there had been supply gaps, compensation was not reflective of this and hence market adjustments did not take place, especially in India. However, with growth in the IT industry, especially in the solutions and services components for USA and Europe, there is an increased demand for logistics and supply chain domain specialists for developing solutions for auto, consumer products group, retail, manufacturing and hi-tech industries. Apart from this, they also focus on pure domain industry solutions for service providers. Due to the inadequate availability of trained manpower in this sector, domain specialists from local industries and management and engineering graduates started taking training in this function. The demand and supply of supply chain domain experts for the IT industry pegged up salary levels for knowledge resources. Globally, there is a need to understand the market dynamics of resource requirement and allow interplay of market forces for fixation of compensation for healthy trends.

Training and Development

Skill development in this domain is possible with training and development as the gap between the supply and demand is vast. Also, incremental demand for skill upgrading for existing professionals and employees is being constantly felt because of changes in business processes and application of technology. Training and development need has to be also seen across levels. The lower rung consists more of operators who need technical skills. The middle rung would be executives involved in policy administration and operation decision support environment who would require training on developments in domain, new applications, and technology adaptation. The senior layer consists of decision makers who require training on model building, decision evaluation criteria, and strategic inputs for improving quality of decisions.

In India, a paper titled 'Skill gaps in the Indian logistics sector: A white paper' was presented by KPMG in 2007 in the CII-organized Logistics Summit 2007. In line with recommendations made therein, one could think of:

1. Creation of a grading/certification process through a common industry platform. Indian Institute of Materials Management and CII Institute of Logistics are some professional bodies which could competently handle this in India.

2. Innovative training practices and visible benefits including career development. This is being consciously practised in the IT industry. Since employees are attracted by on-site positions and recognize that certification in domain, especially from APICS (Advancing Productivity, Innovation and Competitive Success), The Association of Operations Management (http://www.apics.org/Certification/), help career development, there has been a trend for such initiatives. Also, IT companies provide a lot of internal training opportunities through planned initiatives—they usually tie up with professionals and institutions to improve the domain skills of their employees. Manufacturing and supply chain service providers may also adopt some of these practices. Many leading multinational companies are already doing this. What is left are the large portion of SMEs and unorganized service providers who are dependent on open programmes offered by institutions and academia.

3. Incentives and reward recognizing training and development initiatives taken by employees. This is a common people-related practice. In India, when the quality movement was spearheaded by manufacturing companies, they successfully adopted the practice of providing rewards and incentives. It would encourage employees to inculcate a spirit and culture of learning and compete for acquiring latest skills, knowledge, and technology for achieving better competitive advantage in the supply chain domain.

Thus, training and development are important for capability development of an organization in the supply chain domain. Individual employees must also look at training and development opportunities for personal career development and move up in the hierarchy of supply chain domain managers.

Performance Management

The objective of performance management is to objectively assess the work accomplished, understand the capability, resources, and environment, and facilitate for improving performance so that both the organization and the individual employee would benefit. Wherever the organization comes across group or individual constraints either by way of resources or behavioural issues, such constraints are broken. Also, it requires competent mentors who would work with groups and individuals for performance enhancement. The availability of internal resources and specialized external experts is a continued problem in this industry. Even though internal resources could be available, both the mentor and the protégé do not get the required time window for effectiveness of such initiatives as they are heavily into operational issues, and planned programmes like the mentoring process go down on the priority list.

There is a need for organizations and industry players to work consciously to create a structure that would facilitate inter-organizational performance-related issues and develop resources, expertise, and programmes for improving effectiveness.

Communication and Coordination

This is another important people-related function for effective supply chain organization. Effective communication and coordination skills among players including employees in such domain are important. This would help for better sharing of information, roles, and responsibilities of actors in the internal and external supply chain and within and inter-group relations. As mentioned earlier in this chapter, a number of inter-departmental activities are involved in supply chain organization and such activities would require strong and effective communication and coordination. For example, a marketing team member may have important information on the pattern of a demand that is being adjusted downward due to customer behaviour even on a shorter window. If this is not communicated effectively to the supply chain manager and operations, regular production would run according to the planned schedule, which would temporarily lead to a glut in stock with distribution centres and may require even readjustments. If there is an effective communication hierarchy and coordination, such an impasse can be avoided.

Thus people processing in supply chain must focus on setting systems and practice of effective communication and coordinating among employees involved in the domain and culture. It must involve striking such a balance with external stakeholders as well.

Work Environment

Work environment relates to establishing and maintaining physical and emotional work conditions in which domain employees operate to deliver results. There must be conscious efforts to maintain hygiene and high spirits of environment for improving productivity. There are studies which highlight that work environment in the logistics domain is a concern and recommend improvements. New generation companies in manufacturing and service sector, and also traditional companies that are following quality processes, are addressing this adequately.

The softer issue is more about a psychological impression about working in this environment. It is popularly believed that people with tough physique and temperament can work in this domain because of demanding work conditions and timelines. The chances for attracting high calibre resources for planning and strategic functions of the domain are dismal unless it is in the IT industry and in high-end consulting and service providers business. There is a need to consciously work on these aspects so that the best of resources are attracted and they are productive to a world-class level in any comparable domain. The industry experiences wide variations in resource and environment aspects, which needs to be addressed.

If one may look at organizational issues discussed, this may limit to only certain selected and largely rudimentary people processes. However, the focus of a firm would be to continuously improve and align employees, workgroup or function-level teams, organizational capability, and that of supply chain partners.

18.4 CORPORATE SIZE, BUSINESS COMPLEXITY, OWNERSHIP PATTERN, AND IMPACT ON DECISION MAKING

The size of a firm, measured by revenue, number of strategic business units, locations, and employees, is indicative of the complexity of supply chain organizational issues. Large-size firms face higher challenges in terms of people capability, hierarchy, and managing people processes as they become complex. Large organizations have large revenue because of the huge volume of transactions requiring intense logistical operations, supply chain planning, and deployment of support functions. Similarly, firms with a number of strategic business units either by location or by diversity of business would also have intense supply chain organizational issues. Exhibit 18.1 exemplifies the challenges faced by supply chain logistics.

In case of closely held private companies that are run by families, supply chain complexity could still be there. But the organizational approach would be based on a decision taken by few top management team members and/or outsourced consultant viewpoints. The level of professionalism in the domain could be limited because of this approach. Such companies' ownership-driven management style may not be amenable to bringing a professional approach in the ambit of supply chain decisions. This has been observed in India in a number of family-owned textiles, sugar, chemical, food processing, and other businesses. Progressive companies in this group either themselves or through industry-led initiatives bring in improved organizational support for decision making.

One may also note that at times small businesses face severe supply chain challenges, many of which are organizational issues such as skills and people required, as shown in Exhibit 15.4. It is important to note how a few SMEs could counter this and grow. There are a number of cases in India who have handled such challenges effectively. Rex Fashions in Chennai, a regional retail brand, started as a tailoring shop and is today a brand with two large stores of readymade garments, enjoying a strong brand loyalty. Rex Fashions gives a range of choices with good customer service and personalized customer relationship management in place. The stores have extremely well-set practices such as data analysis, tracking of stock, in-store inventory management, pricing strategies, and order management process with brand

---

Exhibit 18.1   Indian Oil Company Ltd—Supply Chain Logistics Challenges

Indian Oil Corporation Ltd (IOCL) is currently India's largest company by sales with a turnover of Rs 247,479 crore (US $59.22 billion), and profit of Rs 6,963 crore (US $1.67 billion) for the fiscal 2007. Indian Oil is also the highest-ranked Indian company in the Fortune 'Global 500' listing, having moved up to the 116th position in 2008. It is also the 18th largest petroleum company in the world.

Indian Oil in the fiscal year 2006–07 increased the refineries and pipelines network capacity beyond 60 MMTPA and achieved record growth in handling throughputs. New investments worth Rs 10,000 crore were put on stream during the year 2006–07. It has investments plan close to Rs 43,250 crore in the next five years. By 2011–12, the Indian Oil group, with 80 MMTPA refining capacity in its fold, would be playing a key role by emerging as an export-oriented hub. The pipelines network which provides strategic logistics advantage to the

Contd.

marketing operations are also set to cross 10,000 km in two years' time. Indian Oil has about 32,000 marketing outlets which would focus on tapping rural markets, non-fuel revenues, and pure retailing business. Indian Oil is into petrochemical industry with plants at Panipat and Paradip. In the natural gas business, it is attempting quantum growth in LNG imports, infrastructure and marketing, besides city gas distribution. In the high-risk business of oil exploration and production, Indian Oil is with a consortium of established players. These provide adequate window on complexity of its logistics and supply chain.

Challenges

As a leading oil supplier, IOCL has many roles to fill. Apart from the corporate-level challenge of maintaining leadership with being diversified and integrated in the energy sector, it must fulfil its responsibility of providing national security, public distribution, and being environment conscious.

Around 2005, IOCL selected Honeywell to provide and implement its supply chain solution. As the company looked for ways to maximize profits, one thing was clear: it needed more visibility into the supply chain and optimize the same. Like many large companies, IOCL managed its disparate projects within different departments or divisions across the organization, and ran into communication issues between those divisions. As a result, decisions were sometimes based on incomplete data, or they couldn't be applied across the entire corporation. Their challenge was how to plan for the various possible breaks that could occur in the supply chain and how to best optimize each specific point to increase their profitability and link activities of their five separate refineries.

To put Honeywell's project's size in perspective, IOCL needed to integrate, view, and make decisions based on eighty crudes sourced from South America to South East Asia, ten refineries and five detailed models, along with a large network of 200 depots, forty terminals, seventeen pipelines and six transportation modes. After an extensive study of the problem, the company evaluated different supply chain management solutions to address the issues it had identified, and then researched how best to implement a solution that would be required to integrate the refineries' supply chains.

Solution Implementation

The supply chain management solution consists of an integrated suite of advanced forecasting, planning, and scheduling tools to more effectively manage the broader supply chain. An integrated framework throughout the solution supports various modules and state-of-the-art tools for a broad range of business decisions. These enable the company to monitor the condition of the supply chain in real-time or near real-time and provide immediate feedback and exception notices. Building on and extending several of the system's core features, the solution finally allowed IOCL to 'get its arms around' a very complex business. The models developed with the supply chain management solution covered IOCL's entire supply chain, from crude purchase to finished product distribution, including demand, refinery process models, blending models, and distribution system models.

It is important to note here that the solution could be successfully implemented because of change management initiatives taken which include:

- Support from top management and high-level sponsors who believed in the end goal and could help make it happen
- Employee buy-in, which is critical for a project as daunting as this one
- Identification of process champions and early involvement of end users
- Establishment of a good foundation, performing 'as-is' and 'to-be' analysis
- Ensuring all processes had owners

If one observes the list above, it is mainly people processes and people who are key to this integration.

Source: http://www.iocl.com/Aboutus/ and Stephen Clark, Supply Chain Logistics Challenges, http://hpsweb.honeywell.com/NR/rdonlyres/73CFB6B7-DDC8-4731-A325-5F5F568A228E/16347/PTQ_Q405_SupplyChainLogisticsChallenges3.pdf.

owners. The ability of entrepreneurs to get involved personally in building business processes, especially supply chain orientation, has been responsible for its success.

Thus, though large firms are well suited to deploying professional organizational efforts and people process in supply chain organizations, business complexity and entrepreneurial drive would drive SMEs as well to adopt similar practices.

18.5 INTRA-ORGANIZATION DECISION MAKING VERSUS OUTSOURCED SUPPLY CHAIN

Decision making on whether an activity is to be intra-firm or outsourced is discussed elsewhere. In general there is a myth about supply chain function as a contractual outsourced activity and that contract drives delivery and hence there is limited scope for partnering approach. Most commonly, the user organizations contract transportation and warehousing activities. Earlier most of these contracts were informal and understanding driven and formalized at a convenient pace. However, the recent trends are towards establishing detailed execution agreements. Most of the service-level agreements are more of annual rate contracts with reasonable coverage for cost escalations, especially for energy prices at various trigger points, which result in percentage increase in costs. Since most of these contracts are for short durations, they are not comprehensive and biased towards operations. Hence monitoring and delivery is more through managing the rate and delivering the agreed services. The user typically monitors and reviews delivery performance. Since the services are routinely contracted, there is limited or no organizational learning. The supply chain organization would be thinly staffed for managing outsourced contracts by evaluating on constant intervals the parameters agreed upon at the time of entering into an agreement. Unfortunately, such an approach would work reasonably if the service provider provides niche services and is professionally mature. Since many times the user industry is not demanding and is unwilling to pay for such quality and service-level initiatives, service providers also do not build on organizational capabilities. This would be a serious limitation as the service providers would not be able to move up the value curve and thus user industry would lose out on competitiveness. Exhibit 18.2 discussed the challenges faced by SEMs.

Exhibit 18.2   UPS Asia Business Survey and Challenges of Supply Chain for SMEs

SME leaders in India cite a lack of supply chain efficiency and transportation infrastructure as a bottleneck for achieving competitiveness. Across Asia, top three business concerns of SME include: quality of services (50 per cent), customers loyalty (48 per cent), and retention of quality manpower (47 per cent), and this is valid for India as well. Indian SMEs highlight the problems faced in supply chain performance, which include: difficulty in demand forecasting (42 per cent), lack of knowledge and expertise in supply chain management, and fragmented service providers.

The UPS ABM 2007 survey was conducted based on interviews with 1,200 business executives of SMEs across twelve markets in the Asia Pacific region.

Source: UPS Asia biz monitor: Indian SMEs still bullish: Majority of Asian SME Leaders see India rise as beneficial; Announcement/Mumbai 11 April 2007.

http://www.business-standard.com/india/storypage.php?autono=280816

In reality, evolved supply chain network would require focal organizations to be on a partnering mode with service providers. The service-level parameters must be well defined, and at the same time, commitment in terms of revenue target, investment, and quality needs to be established by the parties involved. More importantly, such agreements need to be meticulously implemented for creating value across the supply chain. Sharing value across the chain is the fundamental philosophy of creating an effective supply chain organization.

18.6 EMPOWERING PROFESSIONALS IN SUPPLY CHAIN DECISION MAKING

Traditionally, supply chain managers who are mainly involved in procurement, warehousing and transportation management functions, are relatively in lower and middle level of management with limited span of control. In contemporary business, supply chain management (SCM) has assumed a lot of significance. SCM has truly been multi-disciplinary and requires high demand of managerial skill sets rather than execution capabilities. SCM domain capability relies on planning and strategizing management of people, processes, partner relations, and technology. During the last decade, one might have observed new successful corporates who have gained industry leadership positions and gained high valuations in the market because they came up with new models of managing business. Such companies have redefined the industry value chains and in the process their own. In such changing phase of business, the ability of the focal organization to empower supply chain managers with greater span of control and authority matter the most.

Advantages of empowerment of supply chain managers would be:

1. Ability to network and gather more competitive intelligence.
2. Move from operational mind framework to inter-disciplinary framework so that a number of behavioural obstacles in supply chain can be knocked off.
3. Reduce risk of Bullwhip effect as empowerment facilitates working closely with network partners.
4. Provide critical inputs like developments and opportunities in sourcing, new initiatives, and for any other strategic initiatives on the supply chain domain.

Over the years, corporate organizations have empowered professionals in supply chain organization to fuel growth opportunities. Also, a number of inorganic initiatives such as mergers, acquisitions, and joint ventures have facilitated focal organizations to empower supply chain professionals. In one of the cases, an electrical components company, which is a part of a global group, was operating on a multi-domestic company model where the domestic entity took care of local markets even though there could be some imports for local manufacture. After the parent company decided to amalgamate neighbouring markets and create common resources for supply chain, it required necessarily to empower supply chain professionals for procuring material and develop vendors for product mix of multi-country plants in the region.

Thus, empowering supply chain professionals facilitates improvement of efficiency and effectiveness through better span of control and authority among players in the network.

18.7 TECHNOLOGY APPLICATIONS FOR SUPPLY CHAIN ORGANIZATION DECISIONS

There is a myth that technology must be supportive for logistics and supply chain functions, but the primary focus should be on production planning and scheduling of production. Before enterprise resources planning (ERP) was introduced, supply chain managers used to work with office tools and hook up with decision support systems for decision making. This approach was mainly driven by the rationality of business process mapping, which viewed supply chain again as a support function. Planning and collaboration components were missing, and by and large execution components were well covered.

Such an approach works in mature traditional businesses where processes and relationships were established clearly and conflict resolution through deterrence or relationship was comfortable. But as business complexity intensified, supply chain professionals were supposed to participate in analytics, planning, and collaborative initiatives. This required them to work with technology on data mining and analytics and use sophisticated modelling and forecasting techniques for decision making. The next generation ERP and domain-specific software provide such enhanced opportunities. Unless a focal organization is keen to bring such an orientation with its supply chain organization, such requirements would be outsourced and advantage of using own resources with implicit knowledge could be missing. Even if an organization involved outsourced expertise, it must have their own supply chain managers who could interact with such experts with their implicit knowledge on markets, players, and business for value enhancement.

It was observed in one of the re-engineering of distribution network, external experts came up with consolidation of facilities and use of third-party services for delivery to dealers. Since most of these demands are for products that are 'Made-to-stocks', consolidation proved to be effective. The technology for linking with dealers directly helped to capture demand information more effectively than sales. Supply chain managers were earlier operating more with inputs from C & F agents managing distribution centres and had limited scope of analytics. With the change in structure and extension of technology to the next level of primary distribution, which is the last leg in primary distribution and source link for secondary distribution, mapping of demand there helped in improving supply chain efficiencies.

Hence, it is important to use appropriate technology in the supply chain domain for organizational effectiveness.

To conclude, an effective supply chain organization is critical for any corporate to be competitive and dynamic in the environment of business and to proactively hold on to its leadership position. There are a number of myths about logistics and supply chain functions as being rudimentary and execution focused. A focal organization must write off such myths. It would take a conscious effort and commitment towards creating and sustaining competitive assets through supply chain design, planning and operations. The adoption of best practices and the deployment of high-quality managerial talent and contemporary asset creation for business are vital. The ability to work on partnering relationships with the user industry and a network model on support service providers are critical for niche creation.

SUMMARY

Supply chain people resources must be inter-linked with appropriate technology adoption and well-defined processes. One would appreciate that a number of people-related aspects in the supply chain domain require special attention on people processes as this function is interdisciplinary in nature and cuts across the organization.

In contemporary businesses, supply chain is critical and the organization must have fundamentally strong policy and strategy orientation. This happens only when leadership is committed.

Supply chain managers are engaged in the different facets of business—from identifying material source, to procuring, moving, storing, manufacturing, distributing and engaging customers in completion of sale and post-sales management. Supply chain managers are represented at all hierarchies of management decisions, namely planning, strategizing, and operating levels. In short, these managers are across the organization and connect with external entities to satisfy the organization's ultimate customers.

Though supply chain involves a high degree of logistical functions that are primarily execution focused, the planning and strategy aspects of supply chain are multi-disciplinary and have to involve a group approach. Realizing the importance of supply chain for the success of the focal firm, organizations are increasingly structuring a supply chain command at the top-level management to ensure coordination with all the functions

People processes in the supply chain organization must focus on setting systems, and the practice of effective communication and coordination among employees involved in the domain and culture must involve striking such balance with external stakeholders as well.

Though large firms are well suited to deploying professional organizational efforts and people processes in supply chain organizations, business complexity and entrepreneurial drive would demand SMEs as well to adopt similar practices.

Though outsourced organization in logistics brings core value of such firms in cost efficiency and service improvements, it is important for the internal supply chain department to work closely with them.

Empowering supply chain professionals facilitates improvement in efficiency and effectiveness through better span of control and authority among players in the network.

It is important to use appropriate technology in the supply chain domain for organizational effectiveness.

KEY TERMS

Career development: Career development is commonly understood as career progression opportunities for an employee through a sequence of jobs, involving continually more advanced or diverse activities and resulting in wider or improved skills, greater responsibility, and pecuniary benefits.

Competitive intelligence: Data and information gathered by a firm to analyse and understand the market and competition in order to effectively run its business is described as competitive intelligence.

Cross-functional roles: It refers to the responsibility an employee would have in order to work with different functional expertise towards a common goal. It may include people/skill from operations, logistics, finance, marketing, operations, and human resources.

Data mining: Data mining is the process of extracting patterns from data and using such patterns for managerial decisions. A number of tools and techniques are available for facilitating the same.

Demand forecasting: Demand Forecasting is the activity of estimating the quantity of a product or service that a firm would require, to achieve sales revenue. Demand forecasting involves techniques including both informal methods, such as educated guesses, and quantitative methods, such as the use of historical sales data or data based on surveys and estimates.

Economies of scope: Economies of scope is a term

that refers to the reduction of per-unit costs through the production of a wider variety of goods or services. Economies of scope refer to efficiencies primarily associated with demand-side changes, such as increasing or decreasing the scope of marketing and distribution, of different types of products.

Empowerment: Empowerment refers to the practice of power with employees so that they can take initiatives and make decisions to solve problems and improve service and performance. It is based on the concept of giving employees the skills, resources, authority, opportunity, motivation, as well as holding them responsible and accountable for outcomes of their actions.

Enterprise resources planning (ERP): ERP refers to multi-module application software that integrates activities across functional departments such as finance, accounting, marketing, and human resources, and also from product planning, parts purchasing, inventory control, product distribution, to order tracking.

Mentor and protégé: A mentor is a well-respected expert in a domain or function who has experience and implicit knowledge on the subject and shall be a coach or guide or counsellor to the protégé. Protégé are those who could be under a mentor for receiving from deep and intimate understanding of the subject.

Silo approach: Silo approach in decision making is an approach where professionals approach a problem from stand-alone perspectives of a domain instead of settling for a cross-functional approach.

Span of control: Span of control is the number of people/subordinates that can be effectively managed by one manager. It is an organizational theory term that refers to how relationships are structured between leaders and subordinates in organizations.

Staffing: Staffing refers to the process of selecting and training individuals for specific job functions and defining responsibilities. It also refers to the number of employed personnel in an organization or programme.

CONCEPT REVIEW QUESTIONS

1. Describe the role of supply chain managers. How would you see the role being influenced by nature of business, ownership and size? Explain with examples you are familiar with.
2. Explain the horizon of supply chain people processes with examples.
3. Explain the role of supply chain managers in managing the outsourced logistics function with an example.
4. Technology application improves supply chain organizational effectiveness. Discuss.

CRITICAL THINKING QUESTIONS

1. 'Setting up a knowledge management practice in a supply chain domain either internally or encouraging the supply chain manager to be a part of an external knowledge network is critical for enhancing supply chain value.' Elucidate.
2. 'Empowering supply chain professionals in contemporary business helps in fostering growth.' Analyse. Give some examples.

PROJECT ASSIGNMENTS

1. Choose a company you are familiar with. Probe the role of a supply chain manager. Describe people processes of the supply chain organization of the company studied.
2. Visit an engineering company, preferably either in the auto or consumer durable goods industry. Map the roles of inter-disciplinary functions for effective supply chain.
3. Using web research, analyse various job descriptions of supply chain managers and also training, development, and professional learning opportunities.

REFERENCES

'China Logistics—Challenges and Opportunities,' EFT Research Service, March 2006

'Skill gaps in the Indian logistics Sector: A White paper,' presented by KPMG in 2007 in the CII organized Logistics Summit 2007.

Clark, Stephen, 'Supply Chain Logistics Challenges,' http://hpsweb.honeywell.com/NR/rdonlyres/ 73CFB6B7-DDC8-4731-A325-5F5F568A228E/ 16347PTQ_Q405_SupplyChainLogisticsChallenges3. pdf

www.apics.org/Certification/

www.business-standard.com/india/storypage. php?autono=280816

www.iocl.com/Aboutus/

19

Supply Chain Performance Management

Learning Objectives

After studying this chapter, you will be able to:

- Understand the importance of measuring performance
- Gain an insight into performance measures and perspectives
- Comprehend the performance areas and measures with both traditional and contemporary approaches
- Understand the application of frameworks and tools from management accountant perspective

19.1 IMPORTANCE OF SUPPLY CHAIN PERFORMANCE MEASUREMENT

In contemporary business, supply chain management is a key strategic factor for increasing organizational effectiveness and for achieving organizational goals such as improved competitiveness, better customer care, and increased profitability. One of the definitions of supply chain is: 'A system whose constituent parts include material suppliers, production facilities, distribution services and customers linked together via the feed forward flow of materials and the feedback flow of information' (Stevens 1989). This may need to include financial flows too, making supply chain management the management of three flows—physical goods/services, information, and financial.

Apart from the core supply chain function, organization strategies like outsourcing and globalization would have an impact on supply chain management. It is becoming increasingly difficult and less economical for companies to produce their needs on their own if they are beyond their area of expertise. In such cases, outsourcing becomes one of their main production strategic initiatives. Also, the ever-increasing trend in globalization and customer orientation requires a logistics sensitive organization. Supply chain management (SCM) is an approach that has evolved out of the integration of these considerations with the primary objective of satisfying the ultimate customer through the optimization of resources and better management of relationships, transcending beyond the nucleus organization, thereby synchronizing the supplier, channel partners, and customers for enhancing value.

Supply chain cannot be optimized in isolation. It requires a complete alignment of the organization, from planning to execution to operations, towards adding value for the end customer. It is important that strategic and tactical aspects of a supply chain are well integrated so that the synchronization of demand and supply can be ensured. Supply chain metrics should be aligned from the top-level corporate strategy to the frontline tactical operations. Strategic issues in supply chain would include redesigning of both manufacturing facilities and distribution centres to achieve optimization of sales, and product innovations to meet customer needs. Such strategic initiatives impact supply chain nodes and improve competitive advantage usually through cost cutting, cycle time reduction, or supplier relationships. A responsible top management would set up a process of continuous improvement for which strategic metrics are important to ascertain the progress. On the other hand, tactical or operations aspects in supply chain management include the day-to-day management of the supply-demand conditions. For example, the assessment of whether the inventory for a given order is available or a demand can be met if the order is placed within certain lead time could be an operational measure. Moreover, the standard process and technology would enable an organization to act uniformly and predictably to this ever-changing market demand and needs.

A firm would have to align its supply chain function with other functional strategy, SBU level strategy, and corporate level strategy to achieve competitive edge. If quality was an important emerging issue two decades back in India, today supply chain is an emerging issue at the corporate level to ensure growth. Hence, setting up right supply chain performance metrics is going to be important for a firm.

While developing appropriate performance measures, one must keep in perspective the issues of scope, such as whether the performance measure (or measurement system) should include a single organization or all the partners in the network? Is the performance measurement to include one product line or many? Lee and Billington (1992) draw attention to the lack of supply chain metrics as a pitfall in managing supply chain inventories. They argue that discrete sites in a supply chain do not lead to an improved productivity if each is to pursue its goals independently, which has been the traditional practice.

19.2 PERFORMANCE MEASURES

As supply chain is vital in business management, it is important to monitor and measure the performance of supply chain. The objectives of supply chain performance measurement are as follows:

1. There are a number of operational aspects of supply chain, such as movement of goods, storage efficiency, facility operations, inventory parameters, supplier efficiency, and so on. There is a need to track performance against operating plans and to identify opportunities for enhanced efficiency and effectiveness. Also, a number of alerts must be set to raise alarm in operating deficiencies so that timely actions could be taken to avoid jamming of production processes.

2. Supply chain activities can be viewed from the functional perspective of accomplishing demands of logistics and cross-functional drivers, namely, facilities, inventory, transportation, sourcing, pricing, and information technology. Operational measures would cover a large part of the functional measures. Apart from this, supply chain process orientation, that is, process linkages enabled towards serving the demand of the ultimate customer, could be improved by mapping time, effort, and resource efficiencies.

3. Supply chain management involves a number of inward facing activities as well as outward facing activities. The internal and external categorization makes it easier to measure and analyse functions, and address issues for improvements.

4. Supply chain performance measurement system must facilitate benchmarking across peers, best of the industry, and across industries. Temporal benchmarking would also help in constantly striving for improvements. Since supply chain management is a cross-functional approach, the progress in management, thought, and practice can be adopted easily.

5. Finally, the objective of supply chain performance measures must be to consolidate and not focus on isolated issues of logistical drivers. This is where the contemporary approach to performance management as viewed by management accountants is helpful.

Thus, the objectives of supply chain performance measures require a well-designed management information system for monitoring and controlling operations, plans, and strategies, and directing resources for the optimization of skills and facilities in supply chain. Monitoring would help to report service levels and cost components to the management, partners, and customers. Controlling facilitates in tracking and resolving problems, and ensuring compliance with standards. Finally, directing resources to deal with people-related issues help in motivating personnel in their function areas.

19.3 APPROACHES TO PERFORMANCE MEASURES

The supply chain performance measures are classified based on traditional approach and contemporary approach as explained in Chapter 17. The traditional measures are based on the approach to specific deliverables and resource efficiency. These measures cover areas like customer service, cost, productivity, asset utilization, and quality. Thus they are directed towards responsiveness and cost goals of supply chain as well as physical, financial, and informational flows. On the other hand, contemporary measures are based on frameworks and practices driven largely by management accountant practice, to bring more comprehensiveness and better range of techniques for relating causes and effects of decision situations. This approach is better suited to the purpose of reporting to the top management and getting resources allocated for achieving efficiency and effectiveness. Comprehensive measures bring a multi-disciplinary approach to decision making in supply chain domain.

19.3.1 Traditional Approach

The customary approach to measure any performance is to focus on financial and operating parameters. So the traditional approach to measuring supply chain performance is based on the following operational and financial issues:

1. Productivity, which is measured as a ratio of output to input.
2. Quality, as reflected in adherence to standards, percentage of returns and rejects, damages, and so on
3. Customer service parameters, such as product availability, reliability, time, fill rate, can be classified as:
   - Marketing–logistics interface, which would include product, pricing, promotions, and other facets of marketing
   - Customer service and retention, leading to repeat purchases and upgrades.
4. Cost factors, which include total amount spent on each logistical and cross-functional drivers to fulfil customer orders.
5. Asset management, which covers the productivity of capital investments and current assets including inventory and management of current liabilities.

Productivity Measures

Productivity is measured as a ratio of output to input. The output can be measured by way of the amount of revenue earned and the volume of goods produced. Inputs could be factors of production like man-hours, number of persons employed, cost of labour, capital employed, and so on. To measure productivity, one should first define the time window and unit of measurement. Once the unit of measurement has been decided, it is important to ensure that the numerator and denominator are defined appropriately and relevant for a metrics. For example, while measuring shipping efficiency, numerator would be quantity or value shipped, which must be related to the number of shipping employees, hours spent, or amount spent as wages. Some commonly used productivity measures in supply chain include:

1. **Units shipped per employee:** Employee productivity is one of the key measures as it captures employee efficiency and effective span of operation. For example, in a regional distribution centre, the productivity of an employee gains importance with respect to meeting peak demand. The efficiency of employees in the delivery of goods in retail formats, such as pharmaceuticals, grocery, and general retail stores, also counts.
2. **Units to labour cost:** Similarly, employee cost efficiency could be an important factor. The difference between productivity per employee and employee cost efficiency is that while the former is the number of units produced or served per employee, the latter is a measure of productivity vis-à-vis employee costs, which include salaries, rentals, and running costs. It is important to keep employee costs low as they are passed on as cost of products. For example, company X may have higher productivity in terms of units shipped per employee at a location in Mumbai, but its employee cost efficiency could be unfavourable

compared to another location as its employee cost is higher. So the company's warehouse operator productivity could be higher in Mumbai, but the cost of employee is also higher. There is a need to balance both to achieve employee cost efficiency.

3. **Equipment downtime:** Equipment downtime refers to the loss of time due to machinery breakdown or the failure of a component. This could critically affect supply chain productivity both directly and indirectly. For example, the failure of material handling equipment in regional distribution centres could affect turnaround time. Similarly, a fault in transportation vehicles and material handling equipment fitted at vehicles could lead to inefficiency. An indirect impact would be when production equipment fails, leading to a failure of successive stages, causing an overall slowdown in supply chain. For example, when a hopper in a sugar plant fails, material loading in milling section would also halt, leading to stoppages in the supply chain, and this would require a readjustment of the sourcing plan. More serious mechanical problems could lead to further serious impediment in supply chain. Hence, this is an important measure for supply chain efficiency.

4. **Capacity utilization:** According to Wild (1995), 'All the operations planning takes place within the framework set by capacity decisions.' From the above statement, the role of 'capacity' in determining the level of all supply chain activities is clear. This highlights the importance of measuring and controlling capacity utilization, which directly affects the speed of response to customers' demands. Hence, by measuring capacity, gains in flexibility, lead-time, and deliverability will be achieved.

5. **Order per sales person:** Order per sales person is another employee productivity measure that measures the productivity of order management team. Though this may reflect the efficiency of sales personnel, this inter-disciplinary parameter is important to estimate the probability of order and relate it to supply chain planning function. A supply chain manager coordinates between the sales team and operations team for planning and scheduling the production function.

6. **Order entry efficiency:** This is a measure of both productivity and quality. Order entry efficiency measures the ability to capture a customer order quickly and delight the customer on order capture. This is related to service level efficiency and shows the productivity of order management function too. Order entry efficiency is critical in case of e-business model and other businesses where an impersonal mode of order capture is involved.

The above list of productivity measures is indicative and not exhaustive. An analyst can work on a number of parameters relating output to input, and find ways to increase efficiency over time and across firms and product groups. As an important part of SCM, the performance of the production process also needs to be measured, managed, improved, and suitable metrics for it should be established.

Quality Measures

A quality indicator refers to an attribute of a logistical or cross-functional driver that can be used to gauge the quality of supply chain performance in a specific area. For example, an improvement in shipping accuracy is a quality indicator or construct that can reflect the shipping accuracy, and as it focuses on improvement, it must be over time or across locations or competition. Thus, the term 'shipping accuracy' is a broad overarching construct, while the term 'quality indicator' refers to a more specific construct which deals with a particular dimension of quality, usually represented by a number or proportion. The term 'quality indicator' is used in practice in a manner distinct from the term 'quality measure', whereas some practitioners use it interchangeably.

A quality measure is in effect a rule (or the result of a rule) that assigns numeric values to a specific quality indicator. The essential distinction between quality indicators and quality measures is that quality measures take on numeric values, while quality indicators refer only to unquantified attributes of the supply chain function. For example, an improvement in shipping efficiency, which could be a perceptional factor, is a quality indicator, while shipping accuracy, quantitatively reflected by a numeric value based on wrong deliveries or returns, is a quality measure. The time period over which an outcome measure is defined is the outcome interval or time window of analysis.

Some of the commonly used quality measures in supply chain are as follows:

1. **Number of faultless notes invoiced:** An invoice shows the delivery date, time, and the condition under which goods were received. This is also referred to as document/invoice accuracy. By comparing these with the previous agreement, it can be determined whether a perfect delivery has taken place or not. Also, the areas of discrepancy can be identified so that improvements in delivery performance can be made.

2. **Order entry accuracy:** This is an important measure for order management at the warehouse level. With increased automation, this error is being addressed largely. Yet the scope of order entry error is high because of manual feed and improper understanding of product features. A wrong order entry triggers a whole range of unwanted activities across the supply chain. For example, a motorcycle wrongly booked with exterior colour choice of 'Neptune blue' instead of 'blue' would lead to problem at the delivery time when the customer would refuse to take possession of the vehicle due to non-compliance of his colour choice. The probability of this error increases with the number of product variants and SKUs.

3. **Picking/Shipping accuracy:** This is again an important measure in order management or customer service and warehouse management. Picking accuracy is a warehouse-level picking efficiency measure. It refers to the number of orders that are picked accurately as per order fill requirement. This is important because picking accuracy captures the service level at picking activity level. This can be commonly seen in component stores and warehouses, pharmaceutical

stores, and finished goods warehouses where customer order needs to be picked for delivery. Shipping accuracy is a measure of correct despatches to the customer as per the order. This is generally measured by subtracting the number of returns, which could be due to wrong addresses, from the total number of despatches.

4. **Number of customer returns:** The number of customer returns as a quality measure is important from the perspective of customer acceptance of products and despatch efficiency, that is, the product is delivered without being damaged. In countries like India, it is generally not in practice to encourage customer returns on perceived dissatisfaction with product performance. The replacement of products under warranty is a better indicator.

5. **Damage frequency:** This is a related measure of quality. Damages can occur while at manufacture, warehousing, transportation, and in delivery process. Any supply chain manager would focus on achieving zero damages. One of the cases where this kind of measure can be critical is where customer requirement is unique and customer service is hampered for want of proper care. For example, a customer in Patna orders for a beige colour, 300 litres, single door, traditional refrigerator of a brand that is manufactured in Mumbai. The normal lead time for such a product could be fifteen days. While shipping in a truck, this SKU is damaged to the extent of rework which would delay the delivery by another three weeks. One can imagine the extent of customer dissatisfaction in such orders. Hence damages must be carefully analysed by category and order, and it must be ensured that supply chain performance is sensitive to this factor.

6. **Number of credit claims:** This is again a related measure of customer returns. This could be a sensitive measure as the normal practice is that when there is a return, the customer is provided a replacement or an alternate SKU. The number of credit claims is a surrogate indicator of lost sales.

7. **Information availability:** Another important quality parameter is the level of information available for tracking to the customer or any of the supply chain partners in the system. This is typically important in e-business where the customer deals through cyberspace and there is no physical interaction. Supply chain partners such as suppliers, after completing their physical flow, wait for financial flow and keenly track information on financial transactions. Hence it is a critical quality measure which a focal organization must provide to its stakeholders.

Similarly, one can look at a number of quality measures which reflect efficiency in terms of promise versus delivery and satisfaction levels.

Customer Service Measures

Customer service measures are some of the critical performance measures of supply chain effectiveness. A supply chain network is organized for serving an ultimate customer and hence measures around availability, reliability, and operating parameters towards customer needs would be important to understand supply chain effectiveness.

1. **Order lead-time:** The total order cycle time, which is also called 'order lead-time', refers to the time that elapses between the receipt of the customer's order and the delivery of the goods. This includes the following time elements:

   Total order cycle time = Order entry time (through forecasts/direct order from the customer) + Order planning time (design + communication + scheduling time) + Order sourcing, assembly and follow-up time + Finished goods delivery time.

   A reduction in the order cycle time leads to a reduction in the supply chain response time. Equally important is the reliability and consistency of lead-time. Because of bottlenecks, inefficient processes, and fluctuations in the volume of orders handled, there will be variations in activity completion times. The overall effect of this may lead to a substantial reduction in delivery reliability and customer service level.

   To deal with these, for example, the concept of 'manufacturing cell' can be applied, in which well-integrated actions are performed in parallel by cross-functional teams to effectively decrease the order lead-time and reduce the redundancies.

2. **The order entry method:** The order entry method determines the way and the extent to which the customer specifications are converted into useful information, and are passed down along the supply chain. Such information connects all levels of supply chain and affects the scheduling of all activities. A proper control of the order is possible, provided that the order entry method is capable of providing timely, accurate, and usable data at various entry levels, and hence, can be used as a metric of performance measure.

3. **The customer order path:** The path that the orders traverse is yet another important measure whereby the time spent in different routes and non-value adding activities can be identified and suitable steps can be taken to eliminate them.

4. **Delivery metrics:** This refers to the flexibility of delivery systems to meet particular customer needs. Flexibility, which is seldom used in supply chain analysis, can measure a system's ability to accommodate volume and schedule fluctuations from suppliers, manufacturers, and customers. Indeed, flexibility is vital to the success of a supply chain, as supply chains exist in an uncertain environment. Slack (1991) identifies two types of flexibility: range flexibility and response flexibility.

   Range flexibility is a band on variance of higher and lower limits with which an operation can be allowed to change. On the other hand, response flexibility is understood to be comfortable in terms of cost and time or both with which a firm can accommodate changes in supply chain change requirements. In design phase, a supply chain architect would work on this flexibility to facilitate the supply chain to respond to shocks in environment. For example, a 20 per cent reduction in demand may force to cut down production and also absorb inefficiencies in inventory and transportation cost. Also pressure would build across distribution channels. Another typical situation would be when a main component supplier fails to deliver because of external factors. This could disrupt the supply chain, which could be salvaged if it is within the flexibility range and response levels. It is an important aspect of supply chain planning to provide such flexibility under normal circumstances in order to absorb variances.

Being flexible refers to making available the products/services to meet the individual demand of customers. This has become possible as a result of the development of such technologies as flexible manufacturing systems (FMS), group technology (GT), and computer-integrated manufacturing (CIM). The flexibility that these systems impart has a high impact on winning customers. Manufacturers have started adopting the strategy of postponing assembly/product completion close to the customer to improve the flexibility.

Availability is typically measured by fill rate. Fill rates could be item wise, line wise, value wise, and order wise. In order to measure how effectively a focal organization is fulfilling a customer's orders, one of the following measures may be used.

For example, a customer orders ten items, out of which nine are delivered, which means that item fill rate is 0.9 or 90 per cent.

Case fill rate is measured as the amount of cases shipped on the initial shipment versus the amount of cases ordered. For instance, a company orders ten products that total to 400 cases. The manufacturer ships out 360 cases in the first instance and the remaining forty cases later. The fill rate for this purchase order is 90 per cent. It is calculated once the initial shipment takes place. The number of order lines is not considered in this calculation. This fill rate measure gives 'weight' to the order lines that are shipped out. On the other hand, if the value of the order shipped is Rs 90,000 on total value of customer orders worth Rs100,000, then the value fill rate is 90 per cent. Similarly, if a customer has

---

Key Delivery Metrics

$$\text{Item fill rate} = \frac{\text{Number of items delivered to customers}}{\text{Number of items ordered by customers}}$$

$$\text{Case fill rate} = \frac{\text{Number of cases delivered complete to customers}}{\text{Number of cases ordered by customers}}$$

$$\text{Value fill rate} = \frac{\text{Total pecuniary value delivered to complete to customers}}{\text{Total pecuniary value of customer orders}}$$

$$\text{Order fill rate} = \frac{\text{Number of orders delivered complete}}{\text{Number of customer orders}}$$

placed 10 orders for a period of fifteen days, out of which nine are served, then order fill rate is 90 per cent.

A related measure in this delivery metrics category is 'backorder' which is an unfilled customer order. A backorder is a demand (immediate or due in the past) for an item whose current stock level is insufficient to satisfy demand. Some companies count items that are not confirmed (not allocated) and past the requested delivery date (or requested ship date). Other companies may also count those items with stock confirmed, but past the due date. Backorders may be expressed in 'pieces', 'SKUs' or in 'value'. Backorder calculations are often tracked at a variety of levels which could be customer, product group, SBU, or company wise. Backorder is measured as backorders in past due time buckets based on the Requested Delivery Date/Requested Ship Date.

Stock-outs are another related measure of customer service. Stock-out refers to the inability to serve a customer order due to the non-availability of stock. This could also be a failure to produce for want of raw material or component (work-in-progress) during production, resulting in failure to serve a customer order. This could be (1-fill rate) if the failure is mainly for want of stock availability, which cannot be assumed as a failure to serve, and could be due to other factors as well such as the failure of other logistical drivers like transportation. For example, if the fill rate is 90 per cent, stock-outs is (1–90%) which is 10 per cent. Thus customer service measures relate to efficiency in fulfilling customer orders.

5. **Customer service and satisfaction metrics:** The whole exercise of applying the supply chain strategy could be costly and futile, if supply chain metrics are not linked to customer satisfaction (Lee and Billington 1992). This measurement is needed to integrate the customer specification in design, to set the dimensions of quality, for cost control, and as a feedback for the efficiency of process.

6. **The customer query time:** The customer query time refers to the time it takes for a firm to respond to a customer inquiry with the required information. On several occasions, a customer enquires or needs to be informed about the status of an order, and the stock availability of the goods ordered. It is important for the focal organization to analyse its service level as compared to competition. To be competitive, an organization must measure how well its service performance compares against the competitors.

7. **Measuring customer perception of service:** This is done primarily through direct interviews with customers. What are their needs? What is the service level they receive versus what are their expectations? These are the questions firms should ask the customers to improve their products/services, and to increase their confidence in the firm's supply chain.

Cost Measures

The most important efficiency measure is the cost factor as it is direct and simple to calculate and easy to interpret.

1. **Total inventory costs:** Though it was traditionally perceived as a buffer in production to cope with uncertainties, inventory actually emerged to be one of the reasons for the increase in lead-time (Slack et al. 1995). Every firm today realizes that customers are demanding more in terms of SKU variants, reduction in time to serve, and so on. Effective inventory management would be essential for achieving the same as one cannot be insensitive to cost while providing responsiveness. The balancing of responsiveness and cost should be evaluated continuously and trade-off between two opposing supply chain objectives with proper performance measures must be tracked.

In a supply chain, the total cost associated with inventory consists of the following:

- Opportunity cost consisting of warehousing, capital and storage.
- Cost associated with inventory as incoming stock level, work in progress.
- Service costs, consisting of cost associated with stock management and insurance.
- Cost held up as finished goods in transit.
- Risk costs, consisting of cost associated with pilferage, deterioration, and damage.
- Cost associated with scrap and rework.
- Cost associated with shortage of inventory, accounting for lost sales/lost production.

In dealing with these costs, consideration should also be given to part/material size. A low cost part may have a large size, and consequently, a large space requirement. Also, in deciding which cost should be tackled first, Pareto analysis can be used to prioritize the options. In addition, proper trade-offs should be considered in dealing with inventory at various levels in a supply chain.

2. **Total distribution cost:** Perhaps the most important ongoing research concerning logistics is in the area of designing efficient and cost-effective distribution systems. Therefore, a thorough understanding and a good performance evaluation of total distribution costs are essential. A profile consisting of various distribution cost elements should be developed so that appropriate trade-offs can be applied as a basis for planning and reassessment of distribution systems, and thus, the overall cost effectiveness can be achieved. For example, an increase in the number of depots and its effects on other distribution costs can be estimated. Using economies of scale, the optimal number of depots that corresponds to minimum total distribution cost can be obtained.

The distribution cost would include:

1. Inbound cost to regional distribution centres and any stock point.

2. Outbound cost from a distribution centre to the next stage and from every stage to the ultimate customer.
3. Cost of managing regional distribution centres, which will include wages and salaries, rent, insurance, and so on.
4. Stock holding cost, which is inventory holding cost.

3. **Finance and logistics cost:** The financial performance of a supply chain can be assessed by determining the total logistics cost. Since logistics cut across functional boundaries, care must be taken during decision-making as the cost in one area affects the cost in other areas. For example, a change in capacity has a major impact on costs associated with inventory and order processing. What is needed is a trade-off based on a logistics-oriented cost accounting system which will uniquely identify the cost associated with each activity as well as its impact on others. This can readily be combined with customer profitability to make the approach a powerful one.

The other cost measures include the cost of goods returned, wastages, and lost sales—which is an opportunity lost—and must be imputed as percentage of loss. An attempt must be made to capture the total supply chain cost and relate the same to supply chain profits. It is difficult to map lost sales as this measure is spread across organizations of the supply chain network. But this could impact the ultimate cost measure.

4. **Asset measure:** Supply chain assets include plant, equipment, and current assets such as accounts receivable and inventories (Stewart 1995). It is common that firms do their best to make the most of capital assets they have deployed in business. This would be more focused during times of downtrend in business as margins would be under pressure and contribution towards capital cost would get reduced. Total cash-to-cash cycle time would be a critical measure of capital invested towards revenue generation. This is typically expressed as the average number of days required to transform the cash invested in assets into the cash collected from a customer. Another important measure would be towards providing an insight into the rate of return on investment (ROI). This determines the performance of business in generating profits on the total capital invested. On analysing variances, one can study the impact of logistics/supply chain management policies on ROI.

Some key asset management measures:

$$\text{Inventory turnover} = \frac{\text{Unites sold during a time period}}{\text{Average units inventory during the time period}}$$

$$\text{Inventory turnover} = \frac{\text{Cost of goods sold during a time period}}{\text{Average inventory valued at selling price during the time period}}$$

(If average inventory is valued at cost, then numerator must be at cost of goods sold)

Inventory levels and number of days supply: Average inventory/average sales per day:

Thus, days of supply is measured as the total inventory in the supply chain—which is inbound, at plant and all stocking locations in the channel—and expressed as calendar days of sales available based on recent sales activity (or forecasted rate of sales). For example, in food flavours segment, it is believed that over 120 days of supply is being held by manufacturers, depot operated by CFAs, wholesalers, and retailers, whereas in intermediary segment it would be about sixty-five days.

Cash-to-cash cycle: The length of time between the purchase of raw materials, conversion into product, marketing of the same, and the collection of accounts receivable generated in the sale of the final product is referred to as cash-to-cash cycle. This is a critical measure as the efficiency of this cycle improves profitability.

Assume a company which invests on fixed capital and provides a variable capital of Rs 100 crore to use fixed capital to produce goods. Cash-to-cash cycle is twelve in a year, meaning that it is turning around Rs 1,200 crore, and if it makes 10 per cent margin, profits would be Rs 120 crore. By effective management of cash-to-cash cycle, through improved credit terms and receivables management, the firm achieves a ratio of 18, which means that it would achieve a turnover of Rs 1,800 crore and the profit would go up to Rs 180 crore, which is a 50 per cent increase. Supply chain managers must understand the nitty-gritty of this measure and apply in business.

Du Pont chart analysis: This shows the relationship among key ratios to understand asset performance measures. The original DuPont measure is as follows:

Net income/Capital employed = (Net income/Sales) × (Sales/Capital employed)

where Net income / Capital employed is return on Capital employed;

Net income/Sales is return on Sales; and;

Sales/Capital employed is Asset turnover ratio

This measure relates to sales efficiency, which is a function of price and cost management, and asset efficiency, which relates sales as a function of asset turnover, and both together determine the efficiency of capital employed. This financial measure has a significant relevance to supply chain managers as quite a few aspects are in their ambit of control.

The later version of DuPont chart related return on capital employed, which is also referred as return on investment, to financial leverage and cost of capital and measured value it can create to stakeholders. It is important to note that operating drivers of this measure include cost factors, responsiveness, receivables management, sourcing, and asset utilization efficiency.

Thus, asset utilization measures are key parameters of supply chain and ratios are to be defined more to measure performance across supply chain or relate performance across the chain.

19.3.2 Drawbacks of Traditional Measures

Traditional approaches of measuring supply chain performance have the following shortcomings:

1. They are not linked to strategy. Mostly measures lack a clear distinction between metrics at strategic, tactical, and operational levels. Metrics that are used in performance measurement influence the decisions at strategic, tactical, and operational levels. Using a classification based on these three levels, each metric can be assigned to a level where it would be most appropriate. For example, in dealing with inventory, it would be most suitable to assess it from an operational point of view where day-to-day inventory level can be measured and monitored. Therefore, it is clear that for effective management in a supply chain, measurement goals must consider the overall supply chain goals and the metrics to be used. These should represent a balanced approach and should be classified as strategic, tactical, and operational metrics, and be financial and non-financial measures as well. With these perspectives, the authors approach the subsequent sections to answer the pertinent question about balanced scored card tool as a supply chain measure.

2. They have a silo approach. Most often, supply chain metrics bring out the performance of individual departments, such as cost per unit purchased, percentage of on-time supplier shipment for the procurement department, or set-up times, capacity utilization, and percentage of scrap for the plant. However, this type of silo approach sacrifices the overall process and end goals in the interest of improving the performance of an individual department. As a result, functional silos are reinforced within the organization.

3. Many companies have realized the importance of financial and non-financial performance measures. However, they have failed to understand them in a balanced framework. According to Kaplan and Norton (1992), while some managers and researchers have concentrated on financial performance measures, others have concentrated on operational measures. Such an inequality does not lead to metrics that can present a clear picture of the organizational performance. As suggested by Maskell (1991), for a balanced approach, companies should bear in mind that while financial performance metrics are important for strategic decisions and external reporting, one may note that day-to-day control of operations, whether it is manufacturing or distribution, is better handled with physical and non-financial metrics like capacity utilization, downtime, labour utilization, and so on. Many a times operating measures are overlooked in the interest of overall business performance measures. To achieve this, next-generation supply chain performance management systems will need to do more than show departmental metrics—they need to have a process orientation.

4. Traditional metrics lack hierarchical approach. The metrics that help one to measure the overall performance of supply chain are not standalone. They are related to each other, sometimes in a hierarchical structure. When one captures through hierarchy, one may get to understand the root cause more effectively. For example, if a hierarchical relationship were developed between outbound shipment cost metric and those metrics that affect shipment costs, one may note

that outbound shipment costs are moving up despite the carrier rates trending down due to lower fuel costs. This could be because one of the divisions or branches must be using express cargo shipments significantly and hence costs could be up. However, the traditional supply chain measurement approach has no way to define such relationships. Contemporary supply chain performance management systems would define and show relationships between metrics.

Thus, traditional measures suffer from deficiencies of prejudice towards cost and traditional customer service. Also, metric parameters are isolated and cannot easily be related to cause and effect. Since these metrics reflect average values over a period of time, these could be misleading as absolute values at times become important.

19.3.3 Contemporary Approach

The contemporary supply chain measurement approach must have three capabilities: an analytical framework; a process orientation; and linkages. The measurement must facilitate root cause analysis, suggest approach for improvement areas, and monitor action implemented for validation of corrective actions. The contemporary approach involves the application of following frameworks and tools from management accountant perspective:

1. Balanced score card
2. Activity Based Management and costing
3. Economic Value added
4. Process driven metrics—SCOR framework

Analytical Framework

A framework is one which brings structure to an analysis and would work if certain fundamentals are well laid out. These include:

- Explicit statement of supply chain objectives;
- Identification of key metrics that affect the objectives;
- The description, targets, and acceptable range for each metric; and
- List of reports where the metric can be found.

Process Orientation

As supply chain management has deep-rooted process orientation, performance measurement system must capture the same. Also, since supply chain management cuts across functions, it is important to capture these inter-relations. When there is a delink among departments, there is a tendency to observe local optimization at the cost of overall process orientation. Typically, a supply chain analyst must enable all round process-based metrics with a focus on current and future requirements. Also, metrics must be continuously evaluated as a firm grows.

Linkages

An ideal system should use the analytical framework to define linkages between two metrics that are related to the business process but associated with different departments. In addition, the system should be able to show linkages of any metric with different hierarchies within the same department.

These inter- and intra-department linkages help users do a better job at root cause analysis and identify the key issues/metrics affecting objectives and targets. As a result, an organization's ability to perform operational analysis is significantly enhanced.

In addition, most measurement systems offer a window into the past but have no way of showing how a related metric would be affected if one moved up or down by certain units. Without this capability, managers can't easily tell how to change a process (and related metric) or what kind of trade-off to make to improve the supply chain performance. The contemporary supply chain performance management systems should facilitate proactive actions and, if possible, enable predictive modelling capabilities.

Firms usually depend upon traditional performance management approach, which provides role-based dashboards and scorecards. These are primarily developed in-house by the IT department using Business Intelligence (BI) tools. However, to address the dynamic business requirements listed above, firms must deploy new generation supply chain measurement tools such as TAKE Insight, Balanced Scorecard and SCOR, some of which discussed in Chapter 16, which are in the market. With all these new capabilities, an organization will be able to measure the effectiveness and efficiency of its supply chain, and make better decisions to streamline the supply chain and align it with the organization's overall objectives. Such supply chain performance management systems will enable supply chain executives to move from a mode where they are managing crisis with intense focus on operations to one where they are managing opportunities.

19.4 EVALUATION OF PERFORMANCE METRICS

Beamon (1996) presents a number of characteristics that are found in effective performance measurement systems, and hence can be used in evaluating the measurement systems. The basic characteristics of these systems are inclusiveness (measurement of all pertinent aspects), universality (allow for comparison under various operating conditions), measurability (data required is measurable), and consistency (is consistent with organization goals). Benchmarking is an important method which is used in performance measure evaluation. It is useful as it can serve as a means of identifying improvement opportunities.

19.4.1 Balanced Scorecard and Supply Chain Metrics

In the previous sections, a review of various issues of competitiveness that are currently in vogue for improving the efficiency and effectiveness of a supply chain were presented. These performance measures and metrics have to be illustrated with help of a framework so that a cohesive picture can easily be obtained to address what needs to be measured, and how it can be dealt with. Balanced scorecard is one such framework (shown in Figure 19.1).

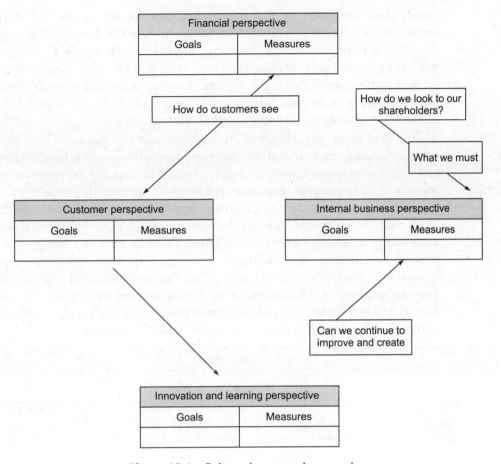

Figure 19.1 Balanced scorecard approaches

Source: Adapted from Robert Kaplan.

Developed at the Harvard Business School, the balanced scorecard is a comprehensive, top-down view of organizational performance with a strong focus on vision and strategy. The balanced scorecard was developed as it was felt that financial measurements, while an important indicator of corporate performance, tend to be somewhat retrospective. Financial metrics typically show how an enterprise has performed, but gives little indication as to how it will perform. A true balanced scorecard must include metrics that provide both historical and future insights. Thus, a scorecard must comprise both leading and lagging indicators. Leading indicators drive performance, whereas lagging indicators are actually results of past performance. For example, in a logistics analysis system, 'customer complaints' is a lagging indicator, while 'on-time delivery' is a leading indicator. To achieve 'balance', the methodology prescribes the strategic assessment of four perspectives: financial, customer, internal, and innovation and growth.

The effectiveness of the balanced scorecard has convinced supply chain managers that traditional financial and operational measures are not sufficient for strategic supply chain analysis. The first step towards developing an effective scorecard is to define the organization's vision and goals. Next, while keeping the organizational structure in mind, the management must decide which supply chain strategies will lead to successful goal attainment. These strategies are then translated into specific tactical performance driving activities. Finally, metrics are established for each activity. Once a vision and subsequent strategy have been developed, the individual metrics—or vital signs—are integrated at relevant places.

The four main key elements in supply chain management are: supply chain operational efficiency, the optimization of supply chain cost, customer satisfaction, and continuous improvement of supply chain. The four key perspectives in balanced scorecard are internal business perspective, financial perspective, customer perspective, and learning and growth perspective. The four key elements of supply chain may be measured through the four perspectives of balanced scorecard, thus establishing a linkage between both. Also, this tool provides framework approach, process orientation, and linkages. For example, the ability of supply chain operational efficiency can be assessed via the measures that equate with internal business perspective. The linking of balanced scorecard and supply chain can be seen Figure 19.2 and Figure 19.3, where supply chain goals and supply chain performance parameters are discussed in relation to the balanced scorecard.

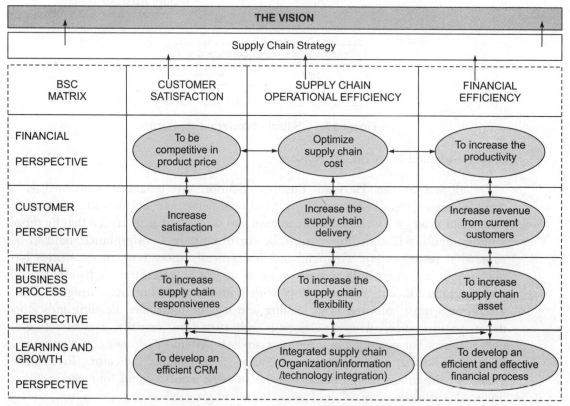

Figure 19.2 Balanced scorecard vis-à-vis supply chain goals

There are many advantages of applying balanced scorecard approach to supply chain performance management system. The main advantages are listed below.

1. It emphasizes the inter-functional and inter-firm nature of supply chains and recognizes the need to ascertain the extent to which firms effectively work together and the extent to which functions are coordinated and integrated.

2. The framework will increase the chance that a 'balanced' management approach is indeed practised within firms and among the supply chain partners.

3. The measures relating supply chain strategic perspectives and four balanced scorecard perspectives provide cross-functional and process linkages. The cited measures in Figure 17.3 are suggestions that may stimulate the management to create more appropriate measures to match their unique circumstances.

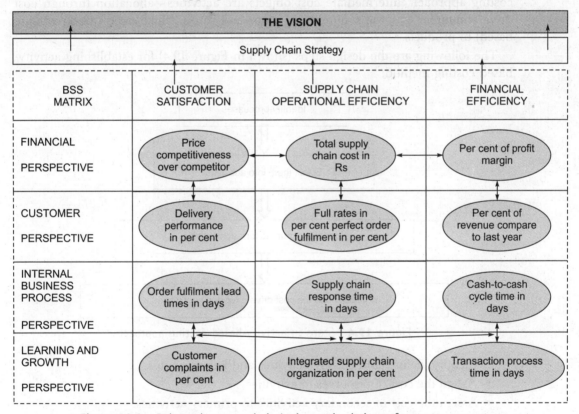

Figure 19.3   Balanced scorecard vis-à-vis supply chain performance parameters

4. The use of this approach should help supply chain managers focus attention on achieving goals that are beyond the typical measures of performances used within firms.

19.4.2   Activity-based Management and Costing

Activity-based management (ABM) is a systematic method of planning, controlling, and improving labour and overhead cost. ABM is based on the principle 'activities consume costs'. While traditional cost systems focus on the arbitrary approach based on volumes or values, ABM systems focus on the 'cost drivers'. Activity-based costing (ABC) is a systematic cause-and-effect method of assigning the cost of activities to products, services, customers, or any cost object. ABC is based on the principle that 'products consume activities'. Traditional cost systems allocate costs based on direct labour, material cost, revenue, or other simplistic methods. As a result, traditional systems tend to over-cost high volume products, services, and customers, and under-cost low volume.

In traditional costing systems, intermediate cost objects are typically departments—indirect costs are generally allocated through volume-based drivers (number of units, direct labour hours, and so on) to products. On the other hand, in activity-based costing approach, intermediate cost objects are activities—allocation through cost drivers (number of set-ups, number of parts, and so on, which need not be volume based) to products.

The following are the design steps (shown in Figure 19.4) for establishing activity-based costing method:

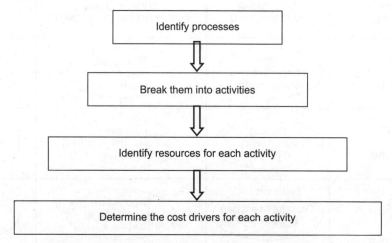

Figure 19.4 Steps in activity-based costing approach

- Identify, define, and classify activities and key attributes.
- Assign the cost of resources to activities.
- Assign the cost of secondary activities to primary activities.
- Identify cost objects and specify the amount of each activity consumed by specific cost objects.
- Calculate primary activity rates.
- Assign activity costs to cost objects.

ABC would suit the firms that have high overhead costs, with a diverse set of operating activities, a diverse range of products, and wide variation in the number of production runs and high cost set-ups. In supply chain management, one would come across many such situations, such as managing the distribution centre of a wide product range, which would include transportation to different customer segments and inventory management with varying demands of activities and purchase functions. The application of ABC in such situations help in appropriate pricing and establishing optimal profit mix for any given set of activities with varying degree of demand.

19.4.3   Economic Value Added (EVA)

Economic value added (EVA) is an estimate of true economic profit after making corrective adjustments to accounting like calculating notional or book charges on capital after deducting the opportunity cost of equity capital. EVA can be measured as net operating profit after taxes (NOPAT) less the money cost of capital. EVA is similar in nature to that of calculating another financial performance measure—residual income (RI). In both cases, money cost of capital refers to the amount of money rather than the proportional rate (per cent cost of capital). The amortization of goodwill or capitalization of brand advertising and other similar adjustments are the translations that occur to economic profit to make it EVA. This concept assumes higher relevance because the account cost of capital may not be truly reflective of opportunity cost.

This has significant application in supply chain functions where there are intangibles involved or in cases such as transport operations and warehouses where

Table 19.1 Performance attributes and definition

Performance attribute	Performance attribute definition	Level 1 metric	Classification
Supply chain delivery reliability	The performance of the supply chain in delivering: the correct product, to the correct place, at the correct time, in the correct condition and packaging, in the correct quantity, with correct documentation, to the correct customer.	• Delivery performance • Fill rate • Perfect order fulfilment	Customer facing
Supply chain responsiveness	The speed at which a supply chain provides products to the customer	• Order fulfilment lead time	Customer facing
Supply chain flexibility	The agility of a supply chain in responding to marketplace changes to gain or maintain competitive advantage time	• Supply chain response • Production flexibility	Customer facing
Supply chain costs	The costs associated with operating supply chain	• Cost of goods sold • Total supply chain management costs • Value-added productivity • Warranty/returns processing costs	Internal facing
Supply chain asset management efficiency	The effectiveness of an organization in managing assets (fixed and working capital) to meet demand.	• Cash-to-cash cycle time • Inventory days of supply • Asset turns	Internal facing

Source: Supply Chain Council.

book depreciation and capital charges make less significance as they are driven by accounting standards and may have accelerated charging system. In reality, economic profit is arrived at after considering realistic charges on capital employed.

19.4.4 Process Driven Metrics

Supply Chain Operations Reference (SCOR) framework, which currently runs version 9.0, is a framework based on process orientation which is developed and endorsed by Supply Chain Council as a diagnostic tool. SCOR classifies supply chain metrics broadly into two groups: customer facing and internal facing.

SCOR defines the performance attributes (shown in Table 19.1) as critical to success in supply chain performance:

- Delivery reliability
- Order flexibility
- Responsiveness
- Supply chain cost
- Asset management

SCOR framework is a paid service of Supply Chain Council. There are practising professionals who enable the deployment of this diagnostic tool.

The integrated corporate and supply chain strategies, with an alignment of key performance metrics, would ensure that an organization reacts faster to the maker's demands at an optimal cost by adding value to the end customer. Moreover, the key performance metrics should be balanced across the organization in order to achieve a common goal in the supply chain. Though traditional measures give substantial ex post metrics, it is important to have a mix of contemporary and traditional measures deployed, and analysts must be able to effectively use this mix for decision making.

SUMMARY

The ever-increasing trend in globalization and customer orientation requires a logistics sensitive organization. The strategic and tactical elements should be integrated and managed to achieve a balance between supply and demand in the supply chain network. Supply chain metrics should be aligned from the top-level corporate strategy to the frontline tactical operations.

Aligning the supply chain strategy and associated metrics with corporate strategy is the key to achieving competitiveness. Supply chain performance metrics would be important for monitoring and evaluating competitiveness among firms. The objectives of supply chain performance measurement system would include a need to track performance against operating plans and to identify opportunities for enhanced efficiency and effectiveness. The validation time, effort, and resource efficiencies would help to initiate process improvements and help in benchmarking performance among peers, industry, and best in class.

Supply chain performance measures are classified as traditional and contemporary measures. Traditional measures are based on approach to specific deliverable and resource efficiency. This covers areas such as customer service, cost, productivity, asset utilization, and quality. These measures cover responsiveness and cost goals of supply chain as well as physical, financial, and informational flows.

On the other hand, contemporary measures are based on frameworks and practices driven largely by management accountant practice to bring more comprehensiveness and better range of techniques for relating cause and effects of decision situations. Such approach is more beneficial, especially for reporting to top management and getting resources allocated for achieving efficiency and effectiveness. Comprehensive measures ensure multi-disciplinary approach to decision making in supply chain domain. Contemporary measures include: application of activity-based management and costing; using economic profit method; and employing process-based metrics, such as SCOR model and balanced scorecard method.

The deficiencies of traditional measures are that they are not linked to strategy, have a silo approach, and lack hierarchical approach. The metrics that help one to measure the overall performance of supply chain are not standalone. Traditional measures suffer from deficiencies of bias toward cost and traditional customer service. Also, metric parameters are isolated and cannot easily be related to cause and effect. Since these metrics reflect average values over a period of time, these could be misleading as absolute values at times become important.

The contemporary supply chain measurement approach must have three capabilities: an analytical framework; a process orientation; and linkages. The measurement must facilitate root cause analysis, suggest approach for improvement areas, and monitor action implemented for validation of corrective actions. Contemporary measures include deploying balance scorecard, using activity-based management and costing, economic value added principle, and using process-centric framework, namely SCOR model.

The integrated corporate and supply chain strategies, with an alignment of key performance metrics, would ensure that an organization reacts faster to the maker demands at an optimal cost by adding value to the end customer. Moreover, the key performance metrics should be balanced across the organization in order to achieve a common goal in the supply chain.

KEY TERMS

Activity-based costing (ABC): Activity-based costing is a costing model that identifies activities in an organization and assigns the cost of each activity resource to all products and services according to the actual consumption by each product. It assigns indirect costs (overhead) into direct costs.

Balanced scorecard: It is a strategic planning and management system that is used extensively to align business activities to the vision and strategy of the organization, improve internal and external factors, and monitor organization performance against strategic goals. Robert Kaplan of Harvard Business School and David Norton developed the balanced scorecard as a performance measurement framework that combined non-financial performance measures to traditional financial metrics to give managers and executives a more 'balanced' view of organizational performance. This can be applied for measuring supply chain effectiveness as well.

Benchmarking: It is a process in which organizations evaluate various aspects of their processes in relation to best practice, usually within a peer group defined for the purposes of comparison. This allows organizations to develop plans on how to make improvements or adopt best practices, usually with the aim of increasing some aspect of performance. Benchmarking may be a one-off event, but is often treated as a continuous process in which organizations continually seek to challenge their practices. This can be applied for measuring and analysing supply chain effectiveness.

Business intelligence (BI): It refers to skills, technologies, applications, and practices used to help a business acquire a better understanding of its commercial context. BI may also refer to the collected information itself. BI applications provide historical, current, and predictive views of business operations.

Cellular manufacturing: The group of similar parts is known as part family and the group of machineries used to process an individual part family is known as machine cell. It is not necessary for each part of a part family to be processed by every machine of corresponding machine cell. This type of manufacturing in which a part family is produced by a machine cell is known as cellular manufacturing.

Computer integrated manufacturing (CIM): The term is used for a method of manufacturing in which individual engineering, production, marketing, and support functions of a manufacturing enterprise are linked through a computer-automated system. In a CIM system, functional areas such as design, analysis, planning, purchasing, cost accounting, inventory control, and distribution are linked through the computer with factory floor functions such as materials handling and management, providing direct control, and monitoring of all process operations.

Economic value added (EVA): It is an estimate of true economic profit after making corrective adjustments to accounting provisions and charges on capital, including deducting the opportunity cost of equity capital. EVA can be measured as Net Operating Profit After Taxes (or NOPAT) less the money cost of capital. This can be applied to supply chain function and assets.

Flexible manufacturing system (FMS): A flexible manufacturing system is a manufacturing system in which there is some amount of flexibility that allows the system to react in the case of changes, whether predicted or unpredicted.

Group technology (GT): It is a manufacturing philosophy in which the parts having similarities are grouped together to achieve higher level of integration between the design and manufacturing functions of a firm. The aim is to reduce work-in-progress and improve delivery performance by reducing lead times.

Lagging indicators: Lagging indicators follow an event or are results of past performance. An example is a customer compliant.

Leading indicators: Leading indicators drive performance and signal future events. An example is 'on-time delivery'.

SCOR framework: The Supply-Chain Operations Reference-model (SCOR) is a process reference model that has been developed and endorsed by the Supply-Chain Council as the cross-industry standard diagnostic tool for supply-chain management. It is a process reference model for supply-chain management, spanning from the supplier's supplier to the customer's customer. The SCOR-model has been developed to describe the business activities associated with all phases of satisfying a customer's demand.

DISCUSSION QUESTIONS

1. Discuss objectives of setting up a supply chain performance measurement system.
2. Explain the traditional measures of supply chain performance measurement system. What are the different categories of measures? How are they useful in managing supply chain effectiveness and efficiency?
3. 'Cost based measures are fundamental to managing supply chain efficiency.' Elucidate with examples.
4. 'Asset utilization is an important element of supply chain goal. Cash and cash equivalent is one of the key current assets, especially in downturn, for managing supply chain.' Discuss.
5. 'Customer-related measures are those which marketing and customer functional managers are paranoid about. In reality it is also one of the features of measurement.' Discuss with examples.
6. What are the deficiencies of traditional measures? Explain in detail with examples.
7. Discuss contemporary measures of supply chain performance and how they can be useful in managing supply chain effectiveness.
8. Discuss the scope of activity-based costing for improving supply chain profitability. Give example where it can be applied.
9. Explain balanced scorecard and its deployment for managing the supply chain of a division or logistical driver.

CRITICAL THINKING QUESTIONS

1. Analyse different productivity, quality, customer service, cost and asset utilization measures of a transport service provider and shipper. How could the same parameter be viewed by two role players differently?
2. Describe a facility centre where warehousing activity takes place as per traditional and activity based costing method.
3. The company ABC Ltd collected the following data for three of its divisions:

	A	B	C
Inventory days of supply	30	45	24
Days sales outstanding	15	20	14
Days payables outstanding	10	24	10

Calculate cash-to-cash cycle time. If monetary terms are as follows, what would be your recommendations for the company?

	A	B	C
Inventory (in Rs lakh)	300	100	180
Sales receivables outstanding (in Rs lakh)	200	50	80
Payables outstanding (in Rs lakh)	225	36	90

4. Read the data given below of company XYZ Ltd and analyse the same.

Attribute	XYZ Ltd class	Competition PQR same in	Best of industry
Fill rate Delivery performance	75%	82%	98%
Perfect order	70%	78%	99%
fulfilment	40%	60%	94%
Supply chain response time in days	27	21	5
Production flexibility in days	15	11	2
Total supply chain costs as % total costs	20%	15%	6%
Inventory days	45	36	15
Cash-to-cash cycle in days	60	48	18

PROJECT ASSIGNMENTS

1. Choose a company that you are familiar with. Discuss its key supply chain strategy and relate with its vision. Develop a balanced scorecard measure on supply chain performance for a SBU or division, and also for a few key supply chain managers.

2. Visit a regional distribution centre and develop a set of traditional measures on productivity, quality, customer service, cost, and asset utilization. Do a temporal analysis and analyse performance of the regional distribution centre and make your recommendations.

REFERENCES

Beamon, B.M., 'Performance Measures in Supply Chain Management,' Proceedings of the 1996 Conference on Agile and Intelligent Manufacturing Systems, Rensselaer Polytechnic Institute, Troy, New York, NY, 1996

Camp, R.C., 'Benchmarking the Search for Industry Best Practices that Lead to Superior Performance,' ASQS Quality, 1989, Cohen, M.A. and H.L. Lee, 'Strategic Analysis of Integrated Production-distribution Systems: models and methods,' Operations Research, Vol. 36, No. 2, pp. 216–28, 1998

Christopher, M., *Logistics and Supply Chain Management*, Pearson Education Limited, 1998

Cohen, M.A. and H.L. Lee, 'Resource Deployment Analysis of Global Manufacturing and Distribution Networks,' *Journal of Manufacturing and Operations Management*, Vol. 2, pp. 81–104, 1989

Cohen, M.A. and S. Moon, 'Impact of Production Scale Economies, Manufacturing Complexity, and Transportation Costs on Supply Chain Facility Networks,' *Journal of Manufacturing and Operations Management*, Vol. 3, pp. 269–92. ress, Milwaukee, WI, 1990

Kaplan, Roher S. and David P. Norton, 'The Balanced Scorecard: Measures that Drive Performance,' *Harvard Business Review*, January–February 1992, pp. 71–79

Lee, H.L. and C. Billington, 'Managing Supply Chain Inventory: Pitfalls and Opportunities,' *Sloan Management Review*, Vol. 33, pp. 65–73, 1992

Lee, H.L. and C. Billington, 'Material Management in Decentralized Supply Chains,' *Operations Research*, Vol. 41, No. 5, pp. 835–47, 1993

Mapes, J., C. New and M. Szwejczewski, 'Performance Trade-offs in Manufacturing Plants,' *International Journal of Operations and Production Management*, Vol. 17, No. 10, pp. 197–208, pp. 1020–33, 1997

Maskell, B.H., Performance Measurement for World Class Manufacturing, Productivity Press, Cambridge, Massachusetts, 1991

Neely, A., M. Gregory and K. Platts, 'Performance Measurement System Design,' *International Journal of Operations & Production Management*, Vol. 15, No. 4, pp. 80-116, 1995

Slack, N., 'Flexibility as a Manufacturing Objective,' *International Journal of Operations Production Management*, Vol. 3, No. 3, pp. 4–13, 1983

Slack, N., S. Chambers, C. Harland, A. Harrison, and R. Johnston, *Operations Management*, Pitman Publishing, London, 1995

Slack, N., *The Manufacturing Advantage*, Mercury Books, London, 1991

Stevens, J, 'Integrating the Supply Chain', International Journal of Physical Distribution and Materials Management, 19(8), pp. 3–8, 1989

Stewart, G., 'Supply Chain Performance Benchmarking Study Reveals Keys to Supply Chain Excellence,' *Logistics Information Management*, Vol. 8 No. 2, pp. 38-44, 1995

Towill, D.R., 'Supply Chain Dynamics,' *International Journal of Computer Integrated Manufacturing*, Vol. 4, 1991

Towill, D.R., 'The Seamless Supply Chain—the Predator's Strategic Advantage,' *International Journal of Technology Management*, Vol. 14, pp. 37–55. Research, Vol. 94, No. 3, pp. 1–15, 1997

Wild, R., Production and Operations Management, London: Cassell Educational Limited.

www.supply-chain.org

Case Studies

1. Challenges of Wind Turbine Generator Component Manufacturers in Meeting Demand
2. Transportation Options and Challenges for a Fertilizer Manufacturing Firm
3. Perishables Supply Chain Operation of Hyderabad Food and General Merchandise Chain Stores
4. Retail Supply Chain—Challenges of Mobile Phone Retail Brand
5. Time Sensitive Supply Chain Operations in Fruits and Vegetables Market at Koyambedu in Chennai
6. Sambandam Spinning Mills Ltd—Capacity Growth and Managing of Inventory
7. SME Cluster—Processing of Coconut Kernel and Extraction of Oil: A Case Study on Kangeyan at Tirupur District
8. Redington (India) Limited—An End-to-End SCM Solutions Company
9. Auto Components—Supply Chain Issues in Perspective: An Interview
10. Cargomen Logistics (India) Pvt. Ltd—Transforming from Advisory to Operations
11. Pollachi Lorry Owners' Association—Woes of Being an Owner and Still Being Profitable
12. Facilities and Information Technology as Key Competitive Forces in Export Garments Growth
13. Dilkhush Products Ltd
14. Sourcing Intelligence as Way Forward
15. Scheduling of Transport Services for Employees in a Financial Services BPO in Pune

Challenges of Wind Turbine Generator Component Manufacturers in Meeting Demand

Spares management and alliance relationship

Ashitosh Sharma, head of supply chain management of one of the India's leading wind turbine generator manufacturer, is preparing for a meeting with Champak Lal, Chairman and Managing Director (CMD) of the company. Lal justifies his stock of components and yearly write-offs due to the obsolescence the company is forced into. Sharma understands that his CMD's concerns are fair and reasonable from the investor perspective. However, Sharma presents an industry perspective based on the pre-budget meeting held in January 2009.

India needs energy for its future development and sustainability. It is estimated that India will be power hungry for 100,000 MW by 2010. To meet this demand, government is initiating lots of power projects. There are multiple ways to produce power—various fuels like coal, gas, water, sunlight, wind, or uranium may be used. However, each type of power generation has environmental impact in the form of CO_2 emissions. Figure 1 illustrates the CO_2 emissions with each type of fuel used in power generation.

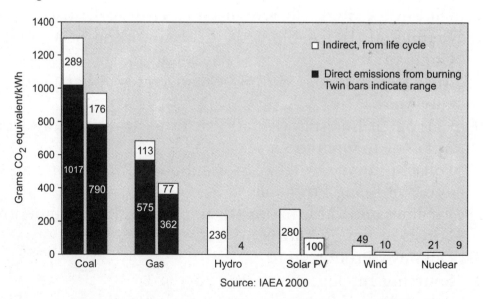

Source: IAEA 2000

Figure 1 Greenhouse gas emissions from electricity production

As CO_2 emissions accelerate global warming, hydro, solar and wind based power generation is being encouraged. The recent deal with USA on nuclear technology for power generation would enable India to generate more clean power with reduced CO_2 emissions.

As Indian government started encouraging clean power generation in the late 1990s, many entrepreneurs started installing 250 kW range wind turbines. A governing body called Ministry of New and Renewable Energy (MNRE) was formed to regulate and encourage technological partnership from overseas companies. As the efficiency of wind turbine generators (WTG) depends on its parts, MNRE persuaded Finance Ministry to offer concessional duties for importing parts of WTGs.

In India, a target of 10,500 MW has been fixed for Eleventh Five Year Plan for wind power capacity addition through commercial projects with private sector investments. However, state-wise targets have not been fixed for power generation from wind. The overall target vis-à-vis achievement during the last three years is given in Table 1:

Table 1 The overall target vis-à-vis achievement

Year	Target (MW)	Achievement (MW)
2005–06	450	1,716
2006–07	1,000	1,742
2007–08	1,500	1,663

The state-wise detail of achievement during the last three years is given in Table 2:

Table 2 State-wise detail of achievement

State	2005–06	2006–07	2007–08
Andhra Pradesh	0.5	0.8	0.0
Gujarat	84.5	284	617
Karnataka	144	266	190
Kerala	0.0	0.0	8.5
Madhya Pradesh	11	16	130
Maharashtra	545	485	268
Rajasthan	73	112	69
Tamil Nadu	858	578	381
Total	**1716**	**1741.8**	**1663.5**

Source: mnre.gov.in/press-releases/press-release-15122008-1.pdf http://mnes.nic.in.

The installation of WTG is based on potential sites. Centre for Wind energy technology (CWET), an autonomous research body of Government of India, is involved in approving the feasibility of WTG and the transfer of technology from technology partners in India. CWET estimated that India has potential sites to generate power of around 45,000 MW. As on March 2008, companies tapped only 8,500 MW. The major potential for wind power generation is in Tamil Nadu, Gujarat, Rajasthan, Maharashtra, and some parts of Karnataka.

The cost of a typical wind power generation project is approximately Rs 5 crore/ MW. The installation and generation takes about three months from the date of order and there is an estimated guaranteed return of 30 per cent on the installed capacity. The client expects the project to be completed in six months' time from the date of order. This involves site erection and component configuration. As income tax benefits are available for wind energy, early completion helps to take advantage in improving accounting profits. In addition, the government gives incentives on WTG through power banking, depreciation, and regulated tariff.

Normally, WTG operate with wind speed between 3 m/sec to 12 m/sec, and high efficiency is obtained in the wind speed range of 4 to 6 m/sec. The parts of WTG include: tower, blades, hub, base frame, couplings, gear box, alternator, electrical controls, and brakes. Figure 2 indicates the proportionate cost of each part to the total cost.

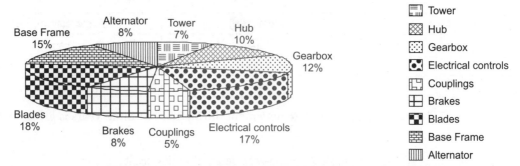

Figure 2   Proportionate cost of WTG parts to total cost

A major challenge is faced by the producer when the generation capacity has to be increased by optimizing space and infrastructure while maintaining the same wind speed. Technology plays a major role in identifying the correct combination of material and process for better returns. The parts of WTG may be sourced from India or overseas technology partners.

Major players in WTG technology are the following:

Company	Country
Kennersys	India
Global Wind Power	India
Suzlon	India
GE	USA
Vestas	Denmark
Gamesa	Spain

Norwind	Norway
Repower	Germany
Siemens	Germany
Winwind	Finland

Denmark is the pioneer and leader in wind energy generation, followed by Netherlands and Germany. Many power production units source components from Germany and other parts of Europe, and so face the challenge of higher costs when it comes to increasing capacity and efficiency. A possible alternative is to manufacture components in India or import from China.

The total cost of WTG includes 75 per cent of material costs and 25 per cent of other costs. Indian WTG component manufacturers have many concerns in meeting the demand and accelerating growth. According to Sharma, the key concerns include:

1. Rising fuel prices and the threat of carbon emissions would increase demand for wind energy projects. Energy intense companies would establish wind farms and generate power using wind energy and wheel it through state electricity board distribution system after paying necessary wheeling charges. However, wind energy generators are affected by rising fuel prices as it increases their manufacturing cost. Though these costs could be transferred, it still remains a concern.

2. There is a new trend in post sales service as project clients are demanding four years warranty. Since the configuration of parts could be specific to each site, parts and components must be accordingly stored and maintained. This increases post sales service costs. Though it is required that each unit sold must be serviced, the difference between warranty maintenance and normal maintenance is that the former requires a higher level of service and leads to more inventory holding.

3. It may be noted that average lead time is about eighteen months for raw materials because of unique customized design requirements. Generally, as mentioned earlier, project promoters would expect the project to be completed in six months. Hence, it requires rigorous demand planning exercise and schedule availability of common parts in advance. There may be at times crashing supply of specific components as per site demand.

4. Since customer order to delivery time is only six months, there is little scope for controlling the raw material costs. Actually, this contradicts normal logical approach. Shorter the duration better must be the control on raw material prices. But in this business, as explained earlier, components are at times stocked eighteen months in advance and thus purchased at the price prevalent at that time. When a project promoter negotiates price, he is guided by current cost factors and this many a times adversely affects the component vendors.

5. Technology is critical to this business and so supplier development becomes a strategic decision as vendors need to be trusted partners in supply chain net-

work. Multinational companies, which are starting operations in India, have to make major investment in infrastructure and transfer of technology. Industry experts estimate that there could be more than 25 per cent savings when the components are sourced from domestic manufacturers. So the multinational companies develop local vendor partners to produce required parts. In a few years, Indian WTG manufacturers would be able to meet international quality standards and would compete for export opportunities to international wind energy markets.

Sharma thus feels that industry characteristics currently lead to mismatch between supply lead time and demand for project completion, and that stocking is essential. One of the alternatives could be to transfer technology to Indian vendors and source from them. But this has the risk of seeding competition. Sharma revisits the spectrum of alliance relationship and considers setting up of joint ventures or subsidiaries.

DISCUSSION QUESTIONS

1. Based on web research, comment on the scope of wind energy projects in India and study specific locations state wise. Is there a scope for inter-state investments and power being wheeled to a different location? If so, what are the risks?

2. What are the issues with respect to stocking of parts and components of WTG? How could this affect business if stocks are increased or alternatively, reduced?

3. What do you understand by post sales service and mapping related costs of the same? How does the demand for four years warranty translate to high post sales service costs?

4. What it means to a WTG component manufacturer if the average lead time is eighteen months for raw materials with limited protection of raw material costs and the expected customer order to delivery time is only six months? How increasing common parts would help to improve stock related issues in this business?

5. When technology is critical, how does supplier development become a strategic decision? Explain alliance spectrum. What are the advantages and disadvantages of both options considered by Sharma?

Transportation Options and Challenges for a Fertilizer Manufacturing Firm

Vehicle deployment for outbound transportation

It is June 2009, the beginning of southwest monsoon in India. J.L. Narasimha Rao, General Manager, XYZ Fertilizer Ltd, is firming up his SBU level plans, committed earlier to the corporate office in Chennai, about the sale of fertilizers from his Kakinada plant in Andhra Pradesh in India. Rao is a firm believer of efficient operational management, making the product of the right quality reach the right customer at the right time, at the right cost, and through the right mode. He believes that his logistics management team is one of the best and wants to have a discussion with Sunil Kumar, his outbound transportation manager.

Indian Fertilizer Industry

India has been an agriculture-based economy—the agriculture sector and its associated industries contribute to nearly one-fourth of the country's GDP. The fertilizer industry is one such associated sector which has shown significant growth since the last decade. This industry in particular has been instrumental in achieving self-sufficiency of food grain production. The Government of India has also created an environment conducive for fertilizer business by way of subsidies/concessions to farmers and compensations to manufacturers. The Department of Fertilizers is responsible for policy formulation, promotion and development of fertilizer industry. The government participation in the industry has ensured success in addressing the capacity requirements, though the efficiency of the sector has taken a beating. However, recent changes in government policies are aimed at improving the efficiency of the sector. The government policies are oriented more towards deregulating the sector and less on policy parameters and long-term goals. India, however, is one of the largest producer and consumer of fertilizers in the world.

In 2008–09, India became the second largest consumer of fertilizers in the world after China. The total consumption of various nutrients was estimated at about 25.3 million tonnes in that year. The total production in that year was estimated at 32.8 million tonnes of urea, phosphatic, and SSP combined, while the demand exceeded 46.7 million tonnes.

The production of urea is almost nearing self-sufficiency, while the demand for nitrogenous fertilizers is wholly met through indigenous industry. The raw materials needed for the production of phosphatic fertilizers are imported in large scales.

Indian fertilizer industry is however not completely devoid of challenges. The policy parameters are not lucid, especially for nitrogenous and phosphatic fertilizers, which slows down the domestic capacity building process. The limited availability of feedstock is also forcing companies to look into joint venture options; fluctuations in gas pricing are also posing a significant challenge for fertilizer companies. The combined cost of feedstock and fuel accounts to anywhere between 60 and 80 per cent of the total production cost, making the efficiency improvement process an immediate necessity for the sector.

The Indian fertilizer industry earlier was dominated by public enterprises, which still hold a major share; however, now the private sector is also fast emerging and has high installed capacity for phosphatic fertilizers. The sector as a whole is looking at bridging the demand–supply gap in the country and the major players are striving towards achieving this objective. The surge in demand in the Indian fertilizer industry on one hand and supply uncertainty on the other makes decision making on utilization of production units a difficult task for all the companies; cost benefit ratio becomes a crucial factor. The fertilizer companies are hard pressed to take difficult decisions with respect to capacity utilization in a short period.

Freight Rate Management by Government

The fertilizer industry has been regulated for long in India because of the dynamics of agrarian economic issues faced by the country. Freight equalization policy is essentially concerned with the equalization of freight charges where the short distance charges subsidize the long distance movement. It is essentially applicable to rail fare, but road fare is also included wherever railhead is not available. In such cases of rail and road combined movement, rail freight up to the closest railhead point is taken and then road transport charges up to the terminal point are adjusted and equalized. Typically, the way the freight equalization scheme works is by estimating the weighted average expenditure on freight in advance (based on the expected lead distances and the corresponding tariffs) and adding it to ex-factory price. This provides the basis for the allocation of freight equalization fund. In the case of fertilizer industry, not only freight but also the total production cost is equalized by means of a subsidy resulting through a price equalization account based on normative costs and assured rate of return. Rao is constantly worried of operating in such a regulated environment because if the plant fails to achieve normative basis of costs both in production and distribution, then it could be a loser.

Company Background

Company XYZ is a leading fertilizer company in India, manufacturing a wide range of fertilizers, pesticides, and specialty nutrients. XYZ has multi-locational production facilities and markets its products all over India and exports pesticides to various countries across the globe. The company has eight manufacturing units located in the states of Andhra Pradesh, Tamil Nadu, Maharashtra, Gujarat, and Jammu & Kashmir. The company is also engaged in rural retail business in Andhra Pradesh through its outlets 'Mana Gromor Centres'.

XYZ is among the largest phosphatic fertilizer players in India. The company also markets phosphogypsum and sulphur pastilles. The company's fertilizers are sold under well-established brand names, viz. Gromor, Godavari, Paramfos, XYZ Gold and XYZ Super. XYZ has four fertilizer plants, of which two plants are located in Viskhapatnam and Kakinada in Andhra Pradesh, and two are in and around Chennai in Tamil Nadu. XYZ produces and sells phosphatic fertilizers of various grades, including Di-Ammonium Phosphate (DAP) and Single Super Phosphate (SSP), and has a combined installed capacity of 22 lakh tonnes of DAP/complex fertilizers and 1.32 lakh tonnes of SSP. The company's fertilizer products are also extensively marketed and sold through a network of dealers or Mana Gromor Centres.

Demand and Distribution Pattern

The company's sales volume in the year that ended on March 2009 was 21.62 lakhs MT, which included 1.19 lakhs MT of imported DAP and 0.55 lakhs MT of imported MOP, compared to 21.71 lakhs MT sold during the previous year. The company has been marketing its fertilizers in eleven states, including Andhra Pradesh, Karnataka, Maharashtra, and Tamil Nadu. The production and sales of the company's fertilizers are highly dependent on and regulated by the availability of phosphoric acid and other raw materials.

The movement of fertilizers is strictly governed by the movement orders issued by the Indian government, entailing higher distribution cost because of multiple destination points. XYZ has a dominant presence in Andhra Pradesh, Tamil Nadu, Karnataka, Chattisgarh, and Maharashtra, and is a significant player in West Bengal and Orissa.

XYZ continues to invest in infrastructural facilities, including raw material godowns, bagging and distribution facilities. This helps the company in improving its capacity to handle higher volumes of raw materials as well as finished goods. The company has also made sizeable investments at its Vishakapatnam and Kakinada plants to increase production capacity and enhance operational efficiencies. The research and development facility at Vishakapatnam enables the company to develop new grades of fertilizers, including water soluble fertilizers, SulphoZinc, and so on.

The setting up of 407 Mana Gromor Centres across Andhra Pradesh has enabled the company to sell its products directly to farmers, thereby reducing its dependence on intermediaries, which has benefitted both the company as well as the farmer community. This has triggered direct interaction with farmers, which has helped the company in developing customized products to meet the farmers' specific needs.

Transportation Challenges

Sunil Kumar, the logistics and distribution manager at Kakinada plant, is posed with various operational problems and constraints. He is primarily concerned about the time and mode by which his company's products would reach the end user, including the remote markets. As mentioned above, XYZ follows a multi-tier distribution system. Kumar has to ensure the products reach two categories of intermediaries— dealers/stockists as well as village retail centres (Mana Gromor Centres).

The planning for the distribution of fertilizers each season is handled by the government to meet the seasonal demand. The manufacturer has to keep stock in readiness at intermediate points such as dealers and retail centres so that it can satisfy the demand quickly. XYZ also has its individual market strategy to align its sales objective with that of the macro level policies, resulting in mutually beneficial outputs.

Table 3 shows the month-wise sale of ammonium phosphatic fertilizers during the year 2008–09. As mentioned in the table, the total sale of ammonium phosphatic fertilizers for the year was 1.4 metric tonnes. The demand goes up in the months of July to September and November to January, and therefore the sale is higher in these periods. During the months of July to September, the demand stems primarily from Kharif season, and the demand in the months of November to January is due to the Rabi season. It is advisable to have buffer stock in the months preceding and following the peak season to accommodate a sudden upsurge in demand.

The fertilizer is transported from Kakinada to various places that fall within the 800 km radius. Table 3 shows the road and rail movement statistics—approximately 67 to 71 per cent of the fertilizer is transported by truck, and 30 to 33 per cent by train. Every district within the 800 km radius has at least one stocking point. The practice has been to transport the fertilizer by road if the distance from Kakinada is within 400 km and by rail if the distance is beyond 400 km. The loading factor varies significantly with road and rail. A normal truck by road can carry up to 9 tonnes. In rail transportation, each wagon can carry up to 58 tonnes and the available capacity is fifty-six wagons per train. A rail rake also could be booked, which has a capacity of 1,600 tonnes. These are the current operation conditions based on which Kumar has to make his transportation decision.

Table 3 Sale of ammonium phosphatic fertilizer

Month	Quantity (in tonnes)	% of quantity sold	Truck load	Rail load	% by rail
Apr	29	2	19	9.744	33%
May	29	2	19	9.744	33%
June	44	3	31	12.992	30%
Jul	146	10	104	42.224	29%
Aug	190	13	131	58.464	31%
Sep	219	15	154	64.96	30%
Oct	88	6	62	25.984	30%
Nov	219	15	154	64.96	30%
Dec	219	15	154	64.96	30%
Jan	175	12	123	51.968	30%
Feb	73	5	50	22.736	31%
Mar	29	2	19	9.744	33%
Total	1,460		1021.52	438.48	

Movement by Rail

Sunil has to liaise with the railway officials on a continuous basis to ensure rake and wagon availability, and he also needs to address full load requirements so as to truly benefit from the nominal cost of rail transportation. The production capacity in Kakinada plant needs to be matched with the demand of the districts within 800 km radius of Kakinada. While the road transportation is faster, more efficient, and easily accessible, the trucking industry in general poses certain challenges such as complex documentation procedures and a higher cost per tonne for transportation compared to rail transport. For covering the same distance, the difference in the transportation cost could be anywhere between Rs 300 to Rs 350 per tonne, favouring the rail transportation. The demand uncertainty needs to be met by opting for road transportation even when distances are greater than 400 km. This is because the wagon availability needs to be checked and booked two weeks prior to the date of loading. Full wagon load conditions also need to be considered; thereby making road transport more viable for smaller shipments to be delivered on a short notice period. The road transport service providers, however, operate in an unorganized environment. So Kumar needs to choose an appropriate transporter who will provide high quality service at a nominal cost.

The time taken for supply of wagons is between ten and fifteen days after placing request with the railways, while rakes are supplied in a shorter period of one to ten days. The transit time for wagon loads is between twenty and thirty days, while that of rake load is between ten and twenty days. The same distance while covered by road transport takes only five to seven days. During the peak season, both road and rail capacities are fully utilized. Kumar needs to manage loading at the frequency of one train every thirty-six hours and nearly eighty-five trucks every day. In case of delay, backup storage needs to be arranged with the warehouse manager, since the stocking of other finished products such as pesticides and specialty nutrients also increase during the same period. The loading of products is possible only between 6 a.m. and 9 p.m. daily from the factory warehouse.

Trade Offs

While the reliability of supply is a crucial factor in the distribution of fertilizers, inventory transportation balance needs to be maintained at an optimal level so as to ensure operation efficiency of the company. Kumar is faced with the challenge of revisiting his company's existing transportation plan and schedule and reduce the cost of operations while maintaining an on-time delivery schedule to all the accessible districts from Kakinada. The demand information is given to the factory on a weekly basis; the loading can be consolidated on a fortnightly or monthly basis depending on the distribution pattern, availability of road and rail capacity, and cost of operations.

Kumar should also address the manpower requirements for loading of trucks directly for despatch and for transportation to the railway station. Labourers work in eight-hour shifts, and during peak season they work in two consecutive shifts. Two labourers are needed to load a 9-tonne truck. Kumar needs to tie up with road transporters to transport his cargo to the railway station. On an average, twenty-five labourers are available to work in each shift for loading operations.

Kumar is also given an option of outsourcing his transportation requirements to a third party logistics service provider. The service provider has capabilities to provide packaging, scheduling, booking appropriate mode of transport, and delivering goods as requested by Kumar. However, cost of outsourcing these services will be higher than carrying out the operations in-house. By developing a long-term relationship with the service provider, cost benefit could be accrued over the years to come.

The transportation trade-off problem described above is a common challenge in any manufacturing set up, which has to market its products to the interior parts of the country. The reliability of the supply of fertilizers is highly critical since the agricultural products are seasonal. Rail is generally the preferred mode of transport for bulk commodities like fertilizers. The cost of rail transportation is lower but it has constraints such as access to specific destinations and loading problems. Road transportation is more flexible and less time consuming than rail, but it has a higher cost. Therefore, while making a decision with regard to the transportation of fertilizers, one has to consider various possibilities—rake versus wagon loads, as well as road versus rail transport.

Kumar's responsibility is to meticulously evaluate the various options available for transportation, including outsourcing to a 3PL service provider, deriving a cost benefit analysis and then making a model choice decision. He also needs to take into account the storage considerations during peak season. The costs of primary and secondary movement versus storage costs need to be carefully evaluated, and the decision should be made accordingly. The decision should most importantly take into account the seasonal nature of demand and an optimum solution for the entire year should be scheduled. There are also considerations of a sudden upsurge in demand in specific locations, hence buffer stock is needed at certain storage points and retail outlets. All these costs should be taken into account while deciding from the available outbound transportation options.

In the case of XYZ, the transportation cost plays a very significant role in the profitability of the firm. Coupled with the warehouse and inventory costs, the logistical trade-off needs to be achieved for improving operational efficiency. The result of this valuation of transportation options would also have considerable impact on the procurement process.

DISCUSSION QUESTIONS

1. What is the cost comparison of transporting the finished product from Kakinada to the districts within 800 km radius by road and by rail?

2. How much spillover of stock is possible during the peak period? What is the associated cost?

3. What is the cost benefit analysis of performing the operation in-house versus outsourcing it to 3PL service provider?

4. What is the impact of fuel prices in choosing the mode of transportation?

5. What are the costs of transportation for the same load and same distance through rake versus wagon?

6. What is the optimal transportation plan of a company based on—cost or benefit of services?

Perishables Supply Chain Operation of Hyderabad Food and General Merchandise Chain Stores

Supply chain processes and role of drivers in perishables business

Hyderabad Food & General Merchandise Chain Stores (HFGM) is a part of the national retail stores established by one of the largest industrial groups in India in the year 2000. The premise on which the group has embarked on this business is that consumerism in India is growing. Fast urbanization, especially the growth of metros, and trends in consumer spend on brands and private labels among many fast moving consumer goods (FMCG) justified the investment. People are getting conscious of quality, price, and the experience of buying, and these factors work against the erstwhile pop and mom stores (kirana shops). However, what remains as a challenge today is the level of inventory, especially private labels and perishables which contribute to supply chain efficiency and cost management.

1 SOURCING

Sourcing activity is a primary function in the retail industry and it decides the success and failure of a business. HFGM handles this function in-house. For sourcing FMCG commodities, prices are negotiated with manufacturers and contracts are drawn up. However, a similar practice in the fruits and vegetables market is a Herculean task, which the Hyderabad Super Market executives have mastered. Hyderabad Super Market has consolidation points (CP) at six different locations across Andhra Pradesh—Vadlapudi, Amalapuram, Bhimavaram, Narsapalem, Khammam, and Tekkali. The teams at these points source the produce from the farmers and *mandis* directly and supply to three distribution centres (DC). The indent is given two days prior to the actual consolidation. The supplies are sourced from *mandis* or local markets only when the produce from the farmers is not sufficient to meet the indent from the DCs. The shortages at the CPs are handled in the following ways, in the same order or preference as listed:

   (a) Procure from other CPs, within state
   (b) Procure from *mandis*
   (c) Procure from nation-wide CPs
   (d) Shutout notice to the DC

2 PRICING

The pricing is set by the HFGM executives who are educated and trained in the agriculture sector. They ascertain the rates based on the following factors:

(a) Price at the market

(b) Maximum price, minimum price and model or average price offered to farmers

(c) Required quantity and quality

Once the price is set, it is announced to the farmers. The farmers are given proper registration numbers and are registered with Hyderabad Super Market. They can sell their produce for the whole day at the fixed price, despite any fluctuations in the local market. This is advantageous to the farmer also, as he is certain about the revenue at the end of the day, and is protected from market fluctuations. Also, since Hyderabad Super Market always uses standardized weights, the farmers are very loyal to the firm.

3 SORTING AND GRADING: THE DAILY ACTIVITY

Sorting and grading was a major activity of the City Processing Centre (CPC), which was later handed over to DCs. The farmers produce has to be graded as per Hyderabad Super Market's quality norms. There are two levels of grading:

1. iStandard Quality: Standards set by Hyderabad Super Market

2. oStandard Quality: Non Hyderabad Super Market standards

The executives at DC can reject the produce that does not meet the HFGM quality standards. However, they sometimes accept the produce to maintain the relationship with farmers and sell it at a subsidized price. Once the produce is graded and sorted, it is packed in separate crates and loaded on the trucks. The procurement manager is the backbone of this entire operation. There are procurement associates working under his leadership, who in turn lead the labourers.

4 PACKING

Packing is always done in crates for better handling. Be it FMCG goods or fruits and vegetables, they are all packed in crates. Colour coding is followed strictly for the Wet and Dry DC. All the FMCG products are packed in Colour A crates, whereas all the fruits and vegetables are packed in Colour B crates. The fruits and vegetables are further provided some special protective packing to enhance visual appeal as well as to safeguard the items.

5 WAREHOUSE MANAGEMENT

The HFGM warehouse which is commonly known as the Distribution Centre or DC is located far from the city limits. It's about 30,000 sq. ft and is the biggest DC of HFGM. The choice of location is based on the following factors:

(a) The area is situated outside the city limits, so that the problem of traffic congestion can be avoided.

(b) It is well-connected by road to the city and to highways.

(c) Typical benefits from locating at a town instead of a city, such as less restrictions and constraints for movement.

The DC follows strict discipline in people management. Every employee is required to take an oath of adherence to rules and responsibilities, and to maintain discipline in his dealings within the DC. The DC also follows its own philosophy of management.

The entry and exit to DC are guarded and the entrants are thoroughly checked. The DC functions all 365 days with three shifts per day. The DC is fully operational in 3PL mode. The staff comprises mainly contract employees. There are only fifteen Hyderabad Super Market direct employees who run the show. Several factors such as cost, volume of transactions, dynamism of operations, and increased retail sales of SKUs push the decision to remain in a 3PL mode rather than opting for 4PL.

5.1 Design of the Warehouse or DC

The warehouse or DC is a neat rectangle. There are multiple entries and exits for the DC called docks. The rationale behind such a move is that the nature of delivery of goods in this industry is highly time-sensitive and product availability is a crucial factor in deciding survival rather than profitability of the business, necessitating simultaneous loads/unloads via multiple docks.

The staging area is a mini-warehouse in itself where all the sorting, grading, and tagging happens. The inbound and outbound cargo are brought to the staging area, verified, tagged, and then only sent for distribution. The inbound and outbound docks are separated in such a way that there is no overlap to avoid confusion.

The DC has adequate parking space both at the sides and in the front. It is high and wide to accommodate as much goods as possible. There are multiple storage practices:

1. **Racking system:** Racking system is used for storing goods in bulk quantities. For example, a carton consisting of 10 boxes of 50×200g Colgate toothpaste boxes each is a bulk item. This will be stored in the rack.

2. **Storage bins:** Storage bins are used only for loose quantities storage. When the toothpaste carton (from the above example) is opened for supplying 25×200g boxes to a particular store, the entire box is shifted to the storage bin and the twenty-five pieces are moved to the staging area for loading on the truck.

3. **Cold storage:** Cold storage is used for fruits and vegetables. Onions and potatoes need to be stored in a particular temperature so as to retain their freshness. Also, mangoes are stored in gas chambers to facilitate faster ripening.

5.2 DC Classification

The DC is classified into Wet DC or Dry DC based on the nature of commodities handled. This is necessary because the transportation function is distinctly different for FMCGs and fruits and vegetables.

(a) Though HFGM handles both types of commodities, they are differentiated to facilitate handling—classification helps avoid confusion and mismanagement to a large extent. Moreover, it is important to classify commodities for legal reasons. The Wet DC is registered under the Industries Act and the Dry DC under the Shops and Establishments Act. Fruits and vegetables need to be processed and require special protective packing, so they are registered under the Industries Act. However, FMCG products don't have processing and special packing requirements. Since the major activity is trading, the registration is under Shops and Establishments Act.

5.3 Operations in Dry DC

HFGM warehouses are very advanced and the daily operations of the DC are as described below.

Indent to the Vendor

The indent is automatically generated by Warehouse Management System (WMS) based on the quantity remaining in the bins and racks as applicable. The vendor details are stored in the WMS database. Once the reorder point for a particular commodity is reached, WMS automatically triggers the indent to the registered vendor based on the data available. The indent is basically a purchase order. An advance shipping notice is given to the vendor to facilitate faster response time.

The Vendor

Based on the indent from the DC, the vendor sends his supply to the DC. The vendor has to ensure the following for the supply:

(a) The quantity and quality of the material to be supplied based on the indent received from the DC
(b) Fix up an appointment with the shift executive (at the DC) to know the time of delivery at the DC
(c) Prompt delivery at the DC

The Shift Executive

On hearing from the vendor, the shift executive finds a free slot in the dock and fixes up a time for the vendor to unload the supply at the DC. The materials received from the vendor are left in the staging area. Then samples are checked for quality. Once the shift executive is satisfied, he generates bar codes (from WMS) and pastes them on the inbound cartons. The bar codes are used to indicate the location, quantity, and description of inventory in the DC. Once the bar codes are pasted, the items are ready to be put away to particular locations. The items are placed on a palette for better handling. Each handling unit/palette is assigned a bar code too.

The Stacker

The function of a stacker is to find bar-coded location in racks and place the palettes. He has to ensure that he places the palettes in the correct position by a manual checklist. Each location has a check digit which is unique. The stacker enters the particular digit in the manual checklist. Stacking is done by fork lifts, stackers, and reach-trucks.

Indent to the DC

The DC will receive indents from stores when the reorder point is reached for a particular SKU. The reorder point is ascertained by the Minimum Bin Quantity (MBQ). If the SKU's quantity levels reach below MBQ, an indent is generated to the DC.

Pick List

A pick list is automatically generated once the indent is received. In case the indent is for a quantity greater than the quantity available at DC, the available quantity is supplied, and an indent for replenishment to the vendor is initiated for rest of the quantity. A pick list is generated with the following details:

(a) Name and address of the store
(b) Product description with code
(c) Location of product in the rack
(d) Quantity required
(e) The check digit-for manual verification by the loader
(f) Signature of the supervisor

The pick list is sorted based upon the store and rack to facilitate optimized picking. It is optimized such that the loader need not go in to the same passageway more than once for a particular store. The loader has to just pick the items in the pick list, and leave them in the staging area in a palette/handling unit.

Despatch

Once all the items have been picked from the racks, they are ready to be despatched to the store. The items are stacked neatly on the palette and are positioned near the dock, waiting to be loaded into a vehicle. The despatches are given to transportation department which takes care of both inbound and outbound transportation for Dry DC.

Operations in Wet DC

The Wet DC, as discussed above, deals only in fruits and vegetables. The operations of the Wet DC are not divided in as many stages as the Dry DC because there is a problem of storage. Mostly the items are just cross-docked. The vehicles from collection centres arrive at the DC, where the supplies are received by the CPC (City Processing Centre). The CPC receives supplies till 3 a.m. in the morning. Once the supplies have been received, the CPC allocates stock, based on the stores indents, up to 10:30 a.m. The bar codes are scanned and allocated to the stores. The loading is done in crates. Each crate has a carrying capacity of 10 kg. For items that are not to be cross docked, the bar codes are scanned and fed in to WMS. The non-cross-docked items are mostly put away in cold storage for storage at standardized temperatures or special handling, for example, mangoes are ripened at a particular temperature. The transfers are initiated and despatches are given to the transportation department, which takes care of the outbound activities of the Wet DC.

Network Design

The HFGM DCs are situated at three prime places inside the state—Hyderabad, Vijayawada, and Vishakhapatnam.

The network was designed keeping the following factors in mind:

(a) Proximity to the city that the DC is catering to
(b) Easier access to the collection centres
(c) Connectivity to other facilities

IT in Warehouse Management

As discussed above, technology is used at each and every stage of warehouse management. Be it for bar codes or fork lifts, the equipment used is state of the art. Every aspect is thoughtfully interwoven with the rest of the system.

Every shift executive has a handheld device, with which every item is identified. He generates a bar code for each of the items in the inbound lot by entering the description, expiry date, and the maximum retail price of the item. The handheld device transmits data to the repository. This information is used to pick a particular item. First-in-First-out (FIFO) method is used to pick items to retain the freshness of goods. The bar coded locations are linked via WMS to the handheld devices. The stock audits reveal that there is only 0.04 per cent leakage in the system, which should soon be curbed.

Every store in the HFGM supply chain is linked to the DC with leased line connectivity. It is connected to the ERP and every indent from the store to the DC is managed electronically. The complete order management process is simplified with minimal manual intervention. Periodical audits and regular statistics collection keep the system in check. The following numbers reveal the actual performance of the HFGM DC:

(a) DC fill rate: 70% to 80%.

(b) DC efficiency: 95%

(c) Stock accuracy: 99%

(d) Despatch accuracy: 99%

(e) Damage and expiry: 0.04%

6 TRANSPORTATION MANAGEMENT

Transportation management is a specialized function in itself which is separately managed by a trained set of executives in HFGM. The function is highly dynamic and involves several on-the-fly decisions. However, these decisions are taken by professionals who have not less than eight years of experience in the same field.

The transport manager in HFGM has the following responsibilities:

(a) Outbound operations in Dry DC. The inbound operations are handled by the vendors themselves.

(b) Inbound and outbound operations in Wet DC.

All the operations in the DC are time-bound and transportation is no exception. The transport manager adheres to strict schedules. He plans the routes, the number of vehicles plying on those routes, the sequence of stores to be catered and the contingency plan in case there is a mishap. Transportation is mostly outsourced. However, HFGM also maintains own vehicles.

6.1 Types of Movement

(a) Primary Movement

The primary movement of fruits and vegetables is from sourcing locations such as farms, mandis or any wholesaler/trader or CC to CPC. The transportation happens mostly in full truck-loads. This movement is mostly undertaken by the vendors themselves. Based on the indents from the DC, the vendors themselves arrange transport and supply to the DC.

(b) Secondary Movement

The secondary movement involves moving the supplies from the DC to stores. While the secondary movement of fruits and vegetables happens in cold vehicles, FMCGs, staples, and other general merchandise are moved in closed containers. It is also used for movement of fruits and vegetables from sourcing locations like farms, *mandis*, or any wholesaler/trader to DC. The transportation happens in less-than-truck-loads or part loads. The movement is primarily through milk runs to different retail stores across the city.

6.2 Types of Vehicles

- Dry vehicle: For FMCG products and fruits and vegetables that do not require refrigeration
- Refrigerated vehicle: For fruits and vegetables that require refrigeration
- Frozen vehicle: For frozen products—they are commonly known as chiller vehicles.

6.3 Routing and Scheduling

The inbound operations at the Wet DC have to be finished before 4:00 a.m. So all the trucks from the CCs should reach the DC before this time. In case a truck misses the schedule, the transport manager is responsible for routing the truck. There are three schedules which are shown below in Table 4:

Table 4 Schedules

Delivery	Wet DC	Dry DC
I Delivery	Morning delivery (6 a.m.)	Afternoon delivery (2 p.m.)
II Delivery	Afternoon delivery (2 p.m.)	Evening delivery (8 p.m.)
III Delivery	Evening delivery (4 p.m.)	Night delivery (4 a.m.)

Though the schedules do not vary by time, they vary by the number of vehicles plying on the routes. The routes are all fixed and they follow the simple algorithm of nearest-store-next. The number of vehicles on weekdays are considerably lesser in number than on weekends, when the demand soars. However, the chiller vehicles are not altered in schedule because the demand is almost constant.

6.4 Fixed Routes

Every truck plies on a predetermined route. The driver is given a specific time to reach each destination. If he doesn't reach a particular destination as per the schedule, he has to contact the DC to intimate the whereabouts of his present location and the reason for his delay. The next stop of the driver is planned accordingly.

6.5 Security measures

Several security measures are taken to curb the possibility of theft during transit. Self-locking tapes, which are numbered sequentially, are used in addition to locks to enforce security. The store manager at each store is responsible for the following:

(a) Checking whether the self locking tape is intact
(b) Acceptance of cargo
(c) Affixing the next tape for the driver to proceed to the next stop

The last store manager also needs to perform the additional function of ensuring that the crates are brought back to the DC. The drivers are not supposed to enter or exit the DC without swiping their smart cards. A new system is being evolved, in which the driver would be required to swipe his smart card at the time of entry, parking at the dock, stuffing beginning, stuffing ending, and exit from the DC. This will be used to collect statistics on the turn around time of every request. Also, it will reduce security vulnerabilities.

6.6 Issues in Transportation

Transportation is the most used as well as abused function. The people involved in transportation represent the front face of operations in any supply chain management function. The most common problems are:

(a) Dealing with RTOs and the local traffic police: Though these problems are generally managed by the transporters themselves, statistics reveal sometimes these complaints are handled by transport executives at HFGM.
(b) Internal problems of coordination: Since the departments in the HFGM are recognized as individual cost centres, the executives try to maximize profitability for their own cost centres. This results in higher profits but in the long run leads to lack of coordination between the departments.

HFGM has devised many innovative ways to solve the problems in their transportation function, but, as a transport manager at HFGM puts it, ' ... there is still room for improvement.'

6.7 IT in Transportation

There are a lot of ways in which IT can be used in the transportation function. HFGM uses IT only in the transaction portion and not for the tracking of vehicles. HFGM does not require the tracking function due to the following reasons:

(a) The distances are short.
(b) Communication with drivers via mobile phones dilutes the need for GPS tracking.

However, HFGM has employed a lot of automation in the transaction portion. The drivers are given a vehicle load plan, which specifies the pattern in which the crates are to be stacked inside the vehicle. The driver has to ensure that the crates are loaded exactly in the same way. The load plan is generated with the route and the order of the stores to be serviced by the vehicle.

To conclude, in perishables business, it is important to ensure right sourcing, stocking in right temperature and hygienic conditions, and transporting at efficient cost so that goods are available at the right price, right quality, right quantity to the right customer at the right time. Price management is another important aspect as freshness and price are to be balanced and mark down has to be managed effectively.

DISCUSSION QUESTIONS

1. Map supply chain drivers of HFGM perishables and their key factors for the success of HFGM operations.

2. Discuss in detail warehouse operations of perishables and how it is different from dry goods stores management.

3. Explain the role of transportation, sourcing, IT and pricing on managing perishables supply chain objectives of HFGM.

Retail Supply Chain—Challenges of Mobile Phone Retail Brand

Retail supply chain issues on inventory and order planning and management

Indian mobile phone retail market is fundamentally different from other countries' mobile phone markets because of highly price-sensitive consumers, complex consumer buying patterns, and huge geography. The penetration of Internet and television into rural areas has increased awareness and thus demand for mobile phones. The growth in telecom network has resulted in more than 340 million mobile subscribers. India has the fastest-growing mobile phone market. Here, handsets are cheaper than anywhere else in the world. As compared to television, the penetration of mobile phones has been much faster. BSNL and Reliance Communications pushed the envelope of mobile phone usage with irresistible promotional offers. Changing consumer buying patterns, improved consumer literacy, and increased competition have led to the emergence of a new sector called fast moving consumer durables. Major brands such as Motorola, Samsung, Nokia, LG, Virgin, Fly, and HTC have been extending their reach from urban areas to rural areas with the conventional consumer durable distribution model. However, mobile phone retailing is becoming increasingly organized, in keeping with the developments in the retail sector. The supply chain of a cell phone retailer is shown in Figure 3.

Unlike the early days of mobile phones, today consumers have a broad product range, and more importantly, global brands to choose from. Along with a wide product choice, the consumer wants shopping experience and service expectations, thus setting the rules for mobile phone retailers in India. Chennai Phones is one such smart mobile phone retailers in Tamil Nadu. With more than 120 staff across twenty stores in and around Chennai city, Chennai Phones has emerged as south India's leading mobile retail chain. As in any other business, Chennai Phones also faces tough competition from four exclusive mobile phone retail chains in the region. During the month of August 2008, the Managing Director called on a meeting for identifying next steps in growth plans. After few hours of discussions, four senior executives—CEO, Head of Marketing, Head of Sales, and Head of Purchase—and the MD arrived at the list of challenges in executing its growth strategy:

1. Price
2. Product and technology knowledge
3. Customer experience and promotions

4. Post-sales support
5. Inventory replenishment and purchasing
6. Real estate price

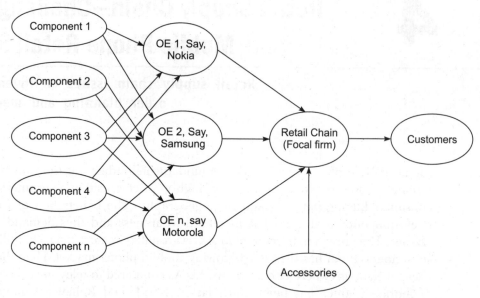

Figure 3 Supply chain network of mobile phone retail chain stores

Price

With steady increase in new mobile phones models, prices have declined steeply and reached a level where the average price of a mobile phone is around Rs 3,500. On one hand, the reduced prices motivate consumers to maintain more than one mobile phone; on the other hand, they are forcing retailers to sacrifice profit margins for cash flows. Chennai Phones maintains three to five high end models ranging between Rs 30,000 and Rs 50,000 with 2 to 4 per cent profit margin and twenty to fifty models ranging between Rs 1,200 and Rs 3,000 with 4 per cent profit margin. Please refer to sales summary in Table 5.

The Head of Sales pointed that when compared with competitors' profit margins towards the end of the year, Chennai Phones found that there is no significant difference. Head of Purchase supported him saying that 'manufacturers have maintained moderate transparency in providing profit margins across retailers in the city'. He also pointed that three new mobile phone OEMs have approached him with a proposition of 5 to 7 per cent margins and a strategic decision has to be taken regarding the agreement as it may affect Chennai Phones' relationship with premium brand owners.

The Head of Marketing cited his latest primary survey results and highlighted a point that many of the Chennai Phones customers have enquired about prices at competitors' stores before buying at Chennai Phones. This gesture indicates that prices at Chennai Phones were less than competitors, yet consumers bargain for better prices. However, he also highlighted that many customers felt that experience at competitors' stores is much better than at Chennai Phones' stores.

The CEO quickly surfed through the financial statements and highlighted a critical point saying, 'net profit margin has been decreasing steadily', and he was investigating to identify reasons for the same. Table 5 on Sales summary highlights the need to sell high end models which contribute 20 per cent of sales volume and would be 80 per cent in terms of value whereas low end would be 80 per cent in terms in volume and 20 per cent by value. Unfortunately, high end models seem to have low margins as seen in the table.

Table 5   Sales summary

Model	Price range (Rs)	Profit margin (%)	Number of models	Sales per month (Units)
High end	30,000 to 50,000	2% to 4%	3 to 5	3,000
Low end	1,200 to 3,000	4%	20 to 50	12,000

Product and Technology Knowledge

The explosion of new technologies, shorter product life cycles, and increasing consumer knowledge have set unwritten rules in mobile phones sales. Before purchase, many consumers surf through the Internet for information on latest technology advancements and innovative features, and compare the models of their choice across multiple criteria. Web technologies have helped retailers to make their presence in ever expanding cyber world and support consumers in making better choices. But the problem Chennai Phones was facing was a little different. Consumers who walk into the store expected the same product information, and in many cases, little more than available on the Internet.

The Head of Sales pressed this point and expressed his concern for customer satisfaction as the attrition rates at senior sales executives' level touched an alarming rate of 10 per cent. Attrition has a direct impact on the customer satisfaction level as new recruits take time to gain product and technology knowledge. You may refer to the attrition effect in Table 6.

Table 6   Attrition effect

Number of staff	Per employee cost company (INR)	Attrition rate (per month)	Number of training sessions (per month)	Cost of training
120	9,000	10%	2	10% of per employee cost to company

He also expressed his concern on the availability of talent pool as product and technology knowledge demands certain education level. Many of the new recruits have only high school certificates and sometimes not even high school, as graduates mostly reject offers for sales executive positions because they get more lucrative offers from other sectors. He suggested that human resource management and development should be treated as separate functions.

Customer Experience and Promotions

The Head of Marketing touched upon an important point. He said that competition is easily matching Chennai Phones' product, price, people, place, and promotions. There is only one in which Chennai Phones can make an impact—by creating memorable customer experience. He said that given the situation, 'creating memorable customer experience only can differentiate Chennai Phones from other store chains and he is working on the customer strategy with the help of a professional services firm'. This being the long-term challenge, he shifted emphasis from customer experience to promotions that would quickly increase sales. He suggested that as other me too brands, the conventional media should be used for promotions-newspapers, local television, and radio channels—and budget should be allocated for the same.

Post-Sales Support

The Head of Sales pointed to an emerging pattern in consumer expectations about post-sales service. Consumers expect the highest levels of service irrespective of brands or models from the retailer. He said this aspect of consumer behaviour opens new opportunities with high margins (20 to 50 per cent) to retailers, but throws a challenge of competent workforce to meet the demand. In response, the CEO made a quick comment, saying 'so far there has been very minimal support from manufacturers to initiate authorized service centres as they demanded adherence to standards'.

Inventory Replenishment, Rotation, and Purchasing

Retailers in consumer durable industry have been witnessing the tight connection between inventory replenishment, rotation, and performance. The shelf space management has been a continuous challenge, and unlike perishable products, durables suffer from a different problem—technology or model obsolescence. Manufacturers tend to support retailers with price protection for an agreed period. Chennai Phones has been steadily growing in and around Chennai as the manufacturer ensures the availability of stock to retailers. Inventory replenishment from the manufacturer or at the store level has been almost less than twenty-four hours. The purchase department at Chennai Phones uses home-grown ERP for real time stock status and placing purchase orders online.

The Head of Sales showed the inventory numbers as in Table 7.

Chennai Phones enjoys a credit period of forty days from its suppliers and so was able meet the expectations of manufacturers. However, the challenge lies ahead as in the growth strategy the MD has set the target of expanding Chennai Phones' stores from twenty to thirty-five across Andhra Pradesh, Kerala, and Karnataka and increasing sales by 150 per cent in a span of one year.

Table 7 Inventory overview

Model	Price range (INR)	Profit margin (%)	Number of models	Sales per month (Units)	Monthly inventory (Units)
High end	30,000 to 50,000	2% to 4%	3 to 5	3,000	3,500
Low end	1,200 to 3,000	4%	20 to 50	12,000	13,000

Real Estate Rentals

Real estate rentals range from Rs 60 to Rs 300 per sq. ft based on the location of the store. Operating small stores at various locations, Chennai Phones has managed to maintain the average rental expense at Rs 100 per sq ft. Its average store size being 250 sq. ft, Chennai Phones plans to open bigger stores in tier 2 towns as part of its growth strategy.

DISCUSSION QUESTIONS

1. Explain the supply chain network of a retail mobile phone brand and give the role of every node in the network. State the value propositions of each node and how value system from the focal firm, that is retail chain store, is staged.
2. How can Chennai Phones increase profit margins while meeting the challenges? Prepare a worksheet with the available data.
3. What can the manufacturers do to support the retail chains without reducing retailers' profit margins?
4. Make a projection of inventory in line with MD's expansion plans and sales target.
5. How should Chennai Phones structure the inventory replenishment policy to meet the growth objectives and avoid stock outs?
6. Do a quick research on the following:
   (a) Does any consumer durable retailer in India have established authorized service centres for post-sales support?
   (b) How do manufacturers provide post-sales support in consumer durables?
7. How can Chennai Phones create memorable customer experience to differentiate from competition?
8. With increasing cost of promotions in conventional media, do you agree with the Head of Marketing to increase promotions budget?
9. What could have been the reasons for reduced overall profit margins at Chennai Phones? Can Chennai Phones reduce prices on mobile phone further?
10. Do you suggest Chennai Phones to focus on post-sales support? What would be the advantages for Chennai Phones?

Time Sensitive Supply Chain Operations in Fruits and Vegetables Market at Koyambedu in Chennai

Supply chain mapping and role of drivers for perishables wholesale market and trade

Koyambedu market serves as the centralized distribution centre for perishables such as flowers, greens, and vegetables and the fruits (both inland and imported fruits). Established by the State Government of Tamil Nadu under the jurisdiction of Chennai Metropolitan Development Authority (CMDA), Koyambedu market is located at the Chennai city limit with road facility and proximity to the Chennai Mofusil Bus Terminal and Private Bus Terminals. This makes transportation easy without causing disturbance to the city traffic by utilizing the by-pass road.

The entire market premises are divided into three parts/blocks:

1. Vegetable market known as Periyar Vegetable Market
2. Fruits Market known as Anna Fruits Market, and
3. Flower Market

In each block, many shops with variable space were allotted and were sold to wholesale merchants/dealers/commission agents by the CMDA of Chennai. Cold Storage facility is provided by TANFED (State Government of Tamil Nadu undertaken cold storage depot) within the market premises for merchants/dealers and the public. All common amenities are made available for merchants/dealers and public within the premises.

There is sufficient space in the market premises for transportation vehicles carrying goods to move in and out of the market. Also, there is ample parking space for vehicles handling vegetables/fruits/flowers. Most of the perishable goods arrive at the market at night by trucks and are parked at one end of the market-adjacent to the Anna Vegetable Market.

Shops are either self-occupied or occupied on lease/rent. The shops are categorized into five types on the basis of size as listed in Table 8.

Apart from the above, some vegetable retail shopkeepers run their own shops on the pavements and in the open space within the market premises with permission from the Vegetable Merchants Association in the market. The association structure is shown in Figure 4. The Periyar Vegetable Market Association and the Anna Fruits Market are headed by President.

Table 8 Categorization of shops

Type	Space (in sq ft)	No. of shops
A1	2,400	50
A2	1,200	25
A3	600	175
A4	300	400
A5	150	450

As per the association's market guidelines, the traders of fruit markets can trade only in fruits of any variety, and similarly, the vegetable traders/merchants can trade in vegetables. Similar guidelines are provided to the traders in flowers.

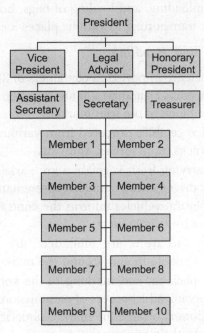

Figure 4 The structure of vegetables/fruit merchant association

Supply/Procurement

Vegetables

- Vegetables are procured and also supplied from and to various places of Tamil Nadu, Kerala, Karnataka, Andhra Pradesh, Maharashtra, Gujarat, and Delhi.
- Fresh garlic is also imported from China
- Cinnamon is imported from Sri Lanka
- Fresh vegetables are also exported to Singapore, Malaysia, and Canada by some of the exporters who own/trade at Koyambedu markets.
- Small retailers and large retailers, and the public wanting to purchase a large quantity of vegetables and fruits visit the market for procuring them.

Fruits

- Fruits are procured from and also supplied to various places in Tamil Nadu, Karnataka, Andhra Pradesh, Maharashtra, Himachal Pradesh, and Delhi.
- Apples are imported from USA, Austria, and Australia.
- Mangoes are exported to Singapore, Malaysia, Sri Lanka, Mauritius, and Dubai.
- Fruits and vegetables are imported/exported using air transportation.
- The exporters of vegetable and fruits collect them at the market and get them packed at the market premises before moving them to air cargo for exports by air.
- Commission agents and contract labourers provide the service of handling, packing, unloading, and loading of bags, boxes, and baskets of fruits and vegetables for transporting to various places locally as well as for export purpose.

Transportation and Handling

- Fruits, which are imported in containers of 20'/40', are brought to the fruit market after customs clearance and are stored in the cold storage at the first floor of the middle block in the fruit market.
- Fruits and vegetables procured from various states arrive at the market late at night by trucks, mini lorries, and vans.
- Vehicles carrying fresh vegetables are parked in the parking area on arrival at night. The driver/cleaner/trader/representative of the trader who accompanies the goods in the vehicles informs the contract merchant is about the arrival of the vehicles by telephone.
- Vegetables and fruits are unloaded by the unorganized and contracted labourers available in and around the market premises.
- Handling, packing, and marking of the consignments for exports are undertaken by organized labourers of commission agents at the market. This is done for the exporters outside the market association, while the exporters within the market make their own arrangements.
- Retailers make their own arrangement for procuring their needs and transporting them to their destination by pre-arranged mini-vans, vehicles, autos, and so on. They make this arrangement collectively and share the transportation cost.

Storage/Warehousing

There are two cold storage facilities maintained at the premises of the Koyambedu market. One is at the Anna Fruit Market—exclusively for the storage of fruits—and the other is next to Periyar Vegetable Market by TANFED for vegetables/fruits or any other commodity from the public on specified rates.

Distribution

The Koyambedu market at Chennai functions as the largest distribution centre for vegetables, fruits, and flowers in Tamil Nadu. The vegetables, fruits, and flowers are supplied to the market by wholesale dealers and commission agents from farmers in various places. The wholesale merchants sell directly or indirectly through their representatives, and the exporters of vegetables/fruits/flowers, large retailers, small retailers, and individual customers visit the market everyday for good deals.

The distribution/transactions begin early morning at about 3 a.m. The peak time for wholesale transaction/distribution is between 3 a.m. to 8 a.m. everyday. Thereafter retail sales continue till 6 p.m. All transactions are dealt in cash on the spot. In some cases, retailer customers, who are regular and trusted by traders, may be given goods on credit by Koyambedu merchants.

Exporters of Perishables (Vegetables and Fruits)

The exporters listed below are the traders/merchants who have their shops in the Periyar Vegetable Market, Koyambedu.

M/S Aishwarya Traders	M/S Sri Padmavathi Traders
M/S Jeeva Ganesh Impex	M/S Sri Rajalakshmi Exports
M/S N.B.B. Traders	M/S Shakti Agengy
M/S Lakshmi Impex	M/S Kutty and Co

Importers of Fruits

The importers listed below are the traders/merchants who have their shops in the Anna Fruit Market, Koyambedu, to whom purchase orders can be placed by email.

M/S Hasmukhlal Rajnikant & Company	M/S Eden Fruits
M/S Em Pee Bee International	M/S M. Peddi Raju & Co
M/S Vinayak Imports & Exports	M/S M.P. Babu
M/S Sri Rajalakshmi Exports	M/S N.C. Alexander
M/S R.S.M. International	M/S N.P.M. International
M/S Santhosh Narayan Shinde	M/S Salmaa Fruits
M/S Shree Ganesh Fruit Company	M/S M.R.M. International

Pricing

- Price per unit of vegetables is fixed by a group of merchants on competitive methods based on the freshness of goods and information collected by the representative of the traders/merchants of the Koyambedu markets from the transport drivers/representative of the commission agents who arrive with the truck during late night.
- Higher the quantity of goods, lesser the unit price fixed. Lesser the quantity of goods, higher the unit price fixed. For fresh vegetables, a higher unit price is fixed.
- Vegetables and fruits brought in trucks should be sold only to the traders/merchants of the Koyambedu and not to any other person who does not own a shop in the market.
- The entire wholesale transaction/distribution ends by 8 a.m. everyday.

- During the distribution, if the demand for a particular vegetable is higher than the available quantity, the per unit sale price of that vegetable is increased, sometime even doubled, at later hours of the distribution.
- Price per unit of the vegetable sold to retailers also varies based on the quantity, that is, larger the quantity lesser the unit price.

Competitive Markets in Chennai

Similar vegetable markets are available at T. Nagar, Mylapore, and Kothawal Chawadi. The markets at T. Nagar and Mylapore receive their supply of vegetables every day from rural areas outside Chennai and neighbouring districts. Fresh vegetables are available in the afternoon or evening in the vegetable markets of T. Nagar, Mylapore, and Kothawal Chawadi. Mostly the fresh vegetables from the T. Nagar market are supplied to Kothawal Chawadi and other places. T. Nagar market is located close to Mambalam Railway station, and most of the people who commute by local trains buy vegetables from T. Nagar market. But these markets are very small and can be treated as retail vegetable shops serving direct individual customers.

One may note that a substantial portion of fruits and vegetables in India is wasted for lack of poor infrastructure, improper handling, and lack of sensitivity to pricing. Generally, information inefficiency is high, which is relates to availability at source, at market, and demand patterns. There are too many intermediaries causing market inefficiencies and wastages. Government initiative like Koyambedu market provides necessary infrastructure and cooperative framework to improve supply chain operations.

DISCUSSION QUESTIONS

1. Map supply chain network and explain the role of supply chain drivers for the fruits and vegetable market operations.

2. 'Intermediary cooperative like merchant association can lead to supply chain efficiencies.' Elucidate.

3. What are the key logistical perspectives for export and import operations of merchants from Koyembedu market? Would they be doing better if they procure directly from source for export? Justify their operations from a market like the one in Koyembedu.

4. What kind of information management system

would you propose for merchants association to improve supply chain efficiency and customer satisfaction?

5. The presidents of fruits and vegetables associations are considering a plan to set up retail chain stores in Chennai under their cooperative brand. How would you advise them to go ahead?

6. Alternatively, one of the office bearers is suggesting tie up with major local market vendors and daily delivery through a network of milk runs. How would you approach the same? Use Google Chennai map.

Sambandam Spinning Mills Ltd— Capacity Growth and Managing of Inventory

Inventory management and procurement planning

It was February 2009 when Saravanan, Head of Production Planning, was called for a meeting with Ramesh Cotton Buyer for a discussion on corporate budget preparation for the year April 2009–March 2010. Though finance department is responsible for treasury operations and generally do not have any problem in arranging funds, it has been facing questions constantly from promoters on efficiency of deployment of working capital. They feel that there is a need for enough justification for inventory holding and stock levels, and procurement prices must be benchmarked among the best in class. In line with this, Saravanan wanted the procurement policy, especially of purchase of cotton, to be reviewed before the budget. He expects Ramesh to gather industry intelligence and relate to past performance before recommending broad approaches to buying initiatives.

Industry background

The Indian textile industry is one of the largest in the world with a massive raw material and textiles manufacturing base. Traditionally, Indian economy is largely dependent on the textile manufacturing and trade in addition to other major industries. Today, the Indian apparel and textile industry that employs around 35 million people (and is the second largest employer), yields 1/5th of the total export earnings and contributes 4 per cent to the GDP, thereby making it the largest industrial sector of the economy. The sector aims to grow its revenue to US $85 billion, its export figures to US $50 billion, and employment to 12 million by the year 2010 (Texmin 2005).

In the post quota period, the size of industry has expanded from US $37 billion in 2004-05 to US $49 billion in 2006-07. During this period, while the domestic market has grown from US $23 billion to US $30 billion, exports have increased from around US $14 billion to US $19 billion. India's share in world clothing export is about 3 per cent. The major export market is Europe, with 22 per cent share in textiles and 43 per cent share in apparel from India. The single largest buyer is US with 10 per cent share in textiles and nearly 33 per cent share in apparel. The other major export markets include UAE, Saudi, Canada, Bangladesh, China, Turkey, and Japan. The largest export segment in textiles and apparels is readymade garments, which has 45 per cent share in textile exports and 8.25 per cent share in India's total exports. Readymade garments sector has benefited significantly with the termination of Multi-Fiber Arrangement (MFA) in January 2005. Exports of readymade garments are expected to touch US $14.5 billion with a cumulative annual growth rate of 18–20 per cent (Apparel export Promotion Council). Table 9 gives product-wise exports in textiles sector.

Table 9 Product-wise export share

Commodities	2005-06 (million US $)
Readymade garments	6,038.69
Cotton textiles	3,290.31
Man-made textiles	1,948.72
Wool and woollen textiles	66.57
Silk textile	406.82
Total	11,751.11
Add handicraft, coir and jute	
Total	**13,065.24**

Source: http://www.india-exports.com/apparel.html.

This industry is poised to meet the increased global competition in the post-2005 trade regime under WTO. The likely challenges would be a flood of imported textiles into India and also making the export markets far more competitive. The pressure would be from export led economies such as China. The textile industry in India has a strong multi-fibre raw material production base, vast pool of skilled personnel, entrepreneurial talent, good export potential, and low import content. Production systems are flexible, dynamic, and vibrant. However, the industry's above strengths get substantially diluted on account of certain production process disadvantages in terms of technology and supply-chain management deficiencies. It is high time that adequate corrective measures are taken to prepare a technology savvy industry to meet the challenges ahead. Initiatives will have to be from government, industry bodies, research institutions, and individual corporate and firms. Given the nature and extent of the fragmentation and technology obsolescence in the decentralized sector, it calls for a focused action plan and programmes to accelerate and sustain the growth level of the different segments of the industry.

The National Textile Policy 2000 has envisaged a foreign exchange earning to the tune of US $50 billion by the year 2010. Besides, many important measures have been spelt out in the policy document. Before formulating the textile policy, the Government of India had set up a committee under the chairmanship of Satyam to examine and draw up action points on various sectors of the textile industry. Accordingly, the committee in its report had outlined critical issues for development and growth.

In the textile industry, the weaving sector has been identified as one of the poorest technological links in the value chain. What makes the problem more serious is that the decentralized sector, both the power looms and the handlooms, which are accounting for the production of 76 per cent of our fabrics needs, is marked by an overabundance. The textile industry can be broadly classified into two categories: the organized mill sector and the unorganized decentralized sector. Being a controlled sector, the organized mill sector has a complete information base on the organizational set-up, machinery installation, production pattern, employment, and so on. However, information-base on the decentralized sector on the above parameters is inadequate and policy planning has so far been based on hearsay and rough indirect estimates.

The organized sector of the textile industry represents the mills. It could be a spinning mill or a composite mill. Composite mill is one where the spinning, weaving, and processing facilities are carried out under one roof. Alternatively, the decentralized sector has been found to be engaged mainly in the weaving activity, which makes it heavily dependent on the organized sector for their yarn requirements. This decentralized sector comprises three major segments-power loom, handloom, and hosiery. In addition to the above, there are readymade garments, khadi as well as carpet manufacturing units in the decentralized sector.

In India, because of poor agrarian structure, where labour is abundant and the unemployment poses a serious threat to the economic growth of the country, the production technology adopted is labour intensive and with low productivity. The mill sector's competitiveness is at stake given the mushrooming of a large powerloom sector which has production-function advantages. The powerlooms and mills are able to go for mass production with better quality products. In spite of the fact that the industry could assimilate high technology levels for better quality production in the market, it has never adapted to the modern technology and, therefore, has remained obsolete. In the advent of globalization, the Government of India, as part of its modernization efforts, has decided to induct about 50,000 shuttleless looms and upgrade 2.5 lakh looms into automatic and semi automatic powerlooms and make it cost effective. Thus, industry is plagued by divergent production units with different vintage technologies and nearly cannibalizing one another instead of taking on global competition.

Tamil Nadu is one of the leading states in cotton textile industry in India. There has been veritable explosion of capacity in cotton-based complexes in the Tamil Nadu textile clusters. This has been a many sided revolution: (1) the 1990s have seen phenomenal growth of cotton spinning in Tamil Nadu and, thereafter, the mushrooming of powerlooms. (2) Tamil Nadu has been in the forefront in the Indian powerloom industry. The state ranks third only after Maharashtra and Gujarat as regards the number of textile manufacturing units in organized and decentralized sector of the textile industry. These powerloom units cater to the fabric needs of the export manufacturing units located in Delhi, Mumbai, Chennai, Bangalore, and other centres. The powerloom sector in Tamil Nadu is in various stages of textiles manufacture, right from ginning of cotton, followed by spinning to the finishing/garmenting of the end product. The powerlooms in Tamil Nadu are mainly concentrated in the three districts of Salem, Erode, and Coimbatore, accounting together for 83 per cent of the looms.

Given this background on industry and opportunities and challenges for textile units in Tamil Nadu, Saravanan would be keen to understand his problems, especially since he is located in a prime textile cluster, Salem district.

Sambandam Spinning Mills Ltd

The company produces cotton yarn in India. Its products include single/multiply, carded/combed weaving and knitting, ring doubled wet spliced, and gassed yarns. The company was founded in 1973 and is based in Salem, India. With a modest beginning in 1973, by M/s S.P. Sambandam, S.P. Ratnam and S.P. Rajendiram with 2,000 spindles, in 2009 the company had five mills with 110,000 spindlage capacity. The company produces and markets only 100 per cent cotton yarn.

The product related information is as follows:

- The company produces yarn in counts of 20 to 100. The yarn count expresses the thickness of the yarn, and must be known before calculating the quantity of yarns for a known length of fabric. The yarn count number indicates the length of yarn in relation to the weight. Based on tex system, if 50 m of yarn weighs 2 g, 1,000 m will weigh 40 g, and the count is 40 Tex.
- 100 per cent cotton auto coned/SIRO cleared
- Single/multiply yarn
- Carded/Combed weaving and knitting yarns
- Ring-doubled wet spliced/TFO yarns
- Value added products: Gassed yarn

Production and Technology of Sambandam Spinning Mills

The company manufactures 100 per cent cotton combed and blended auto coned, single and TFO double ring spun yarn for knitting as well as weaving. The company manufactures auto coned SIRO cleared cotton yarns for weaving and hosiery applications using sophisticated machinery from Truzschler, Zinser, Suessen, Schlafhorst, and so on. The installation of a high capacity yarn conditioning machine (Welker make) has enabled them to compete with international standards. The spinning mills have a combination of at least two sets of production machineries due to expansion in recent years. It has adopted the latest technology and has procured most modern machines to spin the finest quality cotton yarn conforming to global standards. The latest machinery from Europe has been imported, which gives the company an edge to achieve the best quality. Currently mills have a combined capacity of about 115,000 spindles. The entire spinning process is carried out in a computer controlled environment with online monitoring systems such as Sliverdata, Ringdata, and so on. The entire workforce, from topmost engineers to workmen, is well qualified and trained.

Blow room, carding, combing, Lap preparing machines, drawings, speed frames, winding, TFO, and yard conditioning plant are well laid out with optimal level technology deployment. Processes are highly capital intensive. According to Devarajan, Chairman and Managing Director, it would cost about Rs 50,000 of capital cost for each spindle if one were to establish a similar plant.

Technology and production processes have helped the company to achieve a productivity ranking among the top ten mills in India. The company has its own power generating capacity, which fulfils its 100 per cent power requirement. It has wind mills and other power generation facilities at Coimbatore and Tirunelveli districts and avails benefits of government policy for promoting wind power energy generation.

Quality Management

Sambandam Spinning Mills Ltd has quality classified under 5–10 per cent USTER International Standards. The company is equipped with latest generation instruments of USTER—the world's leading supplier of total quality solutions. The lab has automated technology as 25 per cent of their yarn production is exported to high quality conscious customer base in over thirty countries, including USA, England, Canada, Belgium, Italy, Spain, Turkey, and South Korea. The spinning mills have a combination of at least two sets of production machineries due to expansion in recent years. It has adopted the latest technology and has procured most modern machines to spin the finest quality cotton yarn conforming to global standards. USTER is a unique control system that provides information on yarn behaviour for further processing.

The company's yarn conforms to USTER 5–10 per cent standards. The quality control exercise starts right from the selection of raw material stage. Each and every bale of cotton is tested, based upon its parameters; it is laid down for mixing. The company emphasizes 100 per cent bale management and uses good quality raw material for further processing. Contamination control process starts at the mixing stage—first of all hand sorting of cotton and then vision shield at blow room stage to wipe out contaminations. Final control is at auto coner stage where there are SIRO cleaners and UPC 200 contamination clearers. A regular system of testing of yarn at the bobbin stage and final testing at the packaged cone stage is followed for daily production in each count and quality. The company follows stringent quality control measures-each and every employee and worker at Sambandam brings out the optimum quality through performance. The company has been certified for ISO 9001:2000 as a testimony to its quality process adherence.

Capacity, Revenue, and Markets

The company has been increasing its installed capacity of spindles-it rose from 52,580 in 2002 to 73,452 and above 100,000 by 2009. The revenue has increased from Rs 72.86 crore in 2002 to Rs 124.38 crore. There was a small drop of Rs 4 crores revenue in 2008 over 2007. The company sells nearly 75–80 per cent of its output in domestic markets and balance in overseas market. According to Devarajan, Chairman and Managing Director, yarn market is attractive both in domestic and overseas market. There is a good potential for the company to sell at same realization in domestic market to run new capacity optimally, and 20 per cent of the volume could be exported comfortably.

Cotton Procurement and Inventories

1. It may be observed from Annexure 1 the application of bio technology and new farming practices has led to an increase in area, production, and yield per hectare.

2. The output has doubled over ten years. The main contribution is from medium long (26.0 to 27.5 mm) and long (28.0 to 33.5 mm). It can be observed from Annexure 2 that long consumption by non-SSI mills has increased from 48 lakh bales to 72 lakh bales in a period of eight years.

3. It can be observed from Annexure 3 on cotton balance sheet that though supply has increased the demand has been for exports and mill consumption.

4. It may be observed from Annexure 4 that Gujarat, Maharashtra, and Andhra Pradesh are leading producers of cotton in India whereas Tamil Nadu consumes maximum.

5. As shown in Annexure 5, price of cotton has firmed up over the years. Typically, companies like Sambandam Spinning Mills carry on an average four months stock as shown in Annexure 6, which gives company level financial data.

6. Cotton is mainly kharif crop and produce arrives in market by November and prices start firming up at bottom. This trend continues till February and March. Buyers can typically stock for three to four months. One will have to necessarily work on price versus holding cost trade off. Given 10–15 per cent variation in price over a period of four months and holding financial cost at 15 per cent per annum, it may be worth holding stock provided additional factors such as storage and cost of risks are supportive.

7. The company buys about 17 million kg of 100 per cent cotton yarn per annum or about 1 lakh bales of cotton for production.

Saravanan is informed by top management that he must plan production run of the plants for 24×7 in all twelve months. According to Devarajan, a plant must utilize 92–94 per cent of its capacity. Ramesh has to discuss the purchasing plan with buying agents located at Coimbatore. Typically, Sambandam Mills buys stock in the middle of November for four months. And again replenishes every four months. It is important that the purchasing manager has a good relationship with buying agents who get samples from ginning factories. Ginning factories bale cotton and sell through agents. It is important to note that cotton cannot be held as stock by farmers, and that ginning factories, spinning mills, and other intermediaries carry stock during off season. Given the company information, Ramesh may prepare purchase plan.

DISCUSSION QUESTIONS

1. Map the supply chain and three macro supply chain processes, namely supplier relations, internal supply chain, and customer relationship management, of Sambandam Mills.

2. Present a detailed analysis of purchase function of Sambandam Spinning Mills Ltd and key success factors of effective functioning.

3. Build a production plan (capacity utilization at 98 per cent) for Sambandam Spinning Mills operation and present a purchase plan with month-wise utilization.

ANNEXURE 1

Area, Production and Productivity of Cotton in India during Last Six Decades

State	2005–06			2006–07			2007–08			2008–09*		
	Area	Prod	Yield	Area	Prod	Yield	Area	Prod	Yield	Area	Prod	Yield
Punjab	4.49	21.00	610	6.07	24.00	672	6.04	22.00	619	5.37	17.50	554
Haryana	5.19	14.00	379	5.30	15.00	481	4.83	16.00	563	4.55	14.00	523
Rajasthan	3.86	11.00	397	3.50	9.00	437	3.39	9.00	451	2.23	7.50	572
North Total	13.54	46.00	464	14.87	48.00	549	14.26	47.00	560	12.15	39.00	546
Gujarat	16.34	89.00	794	23.90	103.00	733	24.22	112.00	786	24.17	90.00	633
Maharashtra	28.00	36.00	213	31.07	50.00	274	31.94	62.00	330	31.33	62.00	336
Madhya Pradesh	5.45	18.00	494	6.39	19.00	505	6.30	21.00	567	6.55	18.00	467
Central Total	49.79	143.00	450	61.36	172.00	477	62.46	195.00	531	62.05	170.00	466
Andhra Pradesh	8.03	30.00	527	9.72	36.00	630	11.38	46.00	687	13.45	53.00	670
Karnataka	3.93	6.50	268	3.78	6.00	270	4.02	8.00	338	3.90	9.00	392
Tamil Nadu	0.85	5.50	668	1.00	5.00	850	1.19	5.00	714	1.20	5.00	708
South Total	12.81	42.00	472	14.50	47.00	551	16.59	59.00	605	18.55	67.00	614
Others	0.53	1.00	215	0.71	1.00	239	1.08	2.00	315	0.98	2.00	347
Total		232.00			268.00			303.00			278.00	
Loose Lint		12.00			12.00			12.00			12.00	
Grand Total	76.67	244.00	478	91.44	280.00	521	94.39	315.00	567	93.73	290.00	526

*Estimate

Source: Cotton Advisory Board.

ANNEXURE 2

Staple-wise Mill Consumption of Cotton (non-SSI) for the Cotton Year (Oct to Sept)

Figures in lakh bales of 170 kg each

	96–97	97–98	98–99	99–00	00–01	01–02	02–03	03–04	04–05
SHORT (below	11.3	8.2	6.13	7.27	9.71	6.96	5.99	5.93	5.16
20.0 mm)	(7.51)	(5.72)	(4.21)	(4.83)	(6.50)	(4.73)	(4.20)	(3.94)	(3.15)
MEDIUM (20.5 to	53.79	45.04	42.19	47.83	46.05	38.57	38.05	36.29	50.4
25.5 mm)	(35.76)	(31.44)	(28.99)	(31.76)	(30.83)	(26.24)	(26.72)	(24.13)	(30.80)
MEDIUM LONG	29.62	27.64	25.77	25.82	24.44	23.46	25.1	22.96	22.43
(26.0 to 27.5 mm)	(19.69)	(19.30)	(17.71)	(17.15)	(16.37)	(15.96)	(17.62)	(15.27)	(13.71)
LONG (28.0 to	47.63	53.68	58.18	47.31	43.79	47.67	53.02	70.3	71.57
33.5 mm)	(31.67)	(37.48)	(39.98)	(31.43)	(29.32)	(32.43)	(37.23)	(46.74)	(43.74)
EXTRA LONG	7.24	6.07	5.78	4.28	3.86	4.09	4.17	4.42	4.02
(34 mm & above)	(4.82)	(4.24)	(3.97)	(2.84)	(2.58)	(2.78)	(2.93)	(2.94)	(2.46)
TOTAL INDIAN	149.58	140.63	138.05	132.51	127.85	120.75	126.33	139.9	153.58
COTTON	(99.45)	(98.18)	(94.86)	(87.99)	(85.60)	(82.14)	(88.70)	(93.02)	(93.86)
FOREIGN	0.83	2.61	7.48	18.08	21.51	26.25	16.09	10.49	10.05
COTTON	(0.55)	(1.82)	(5.14)	(12.01)	(14.40)	(17.86)	(11.30)	(6.98)	(6.14)
GRAND TOTAL	150.41	143.24	145.53	150.59	149.36	147.00	142.42	150.39	163.63
	(100%)	(100%)	(100%)	(100%)	(100%)	(100%)	(100%)	(100%)	(100%)
SSI Mills	7.50	6.54	6.24	8.37	10.97	11.70	11.63	12.99	16.38

Note : Figures in bracket indicate percentage to the total.
Source : Office of the Textile Commissioner, Mumbai.

ANNEXURE 3

Cotton Balance Sheet (as drawn by the Cotton Advisory Board)

Cotton year from October to September	99–00	00–01	01–02	02–03	03–04	04–05	05–06	06–07	07–08	Quantity in lakh bales of 170 kgs 08–09
SUPPLY										
Opening stock	36.50	40.50	29.00	40.00	24.00	21.00	72.00	52.00	47.50	43.00
Crop size	156.00	140.00	158.00	136.00	179.00	243.00	244.00	280.00	315.00	290.00
Imports	22.01	22.13	25.26	17.67	7.21	12.17	4.00	5.53	6.50	7.00
Total Availability	214.51	202.63	212.26	193.67	210.21	276.17	320.00	337.53	369.00	340.00
DEMAND										
Mill consumption	150.60	149.36	147.00	142.42	150.39	163.98	182.00	194.89	203.00	195.00
Small Mill consumption	8.37	10.97	11.70	11.63	13.00	16.57	20.00	21.26	23.00	20.00
Non-Mill consumption	14.39	12.70	13.06	14.78	13.71	14.48	15.00	15.88	15.00	15.00
Total consumption	173.36	173.03	171.76	168.83	177.10	195.03	217.00	232.03	241.00	230.00
Export	0.65	0.60	0.50	0.84	12.11	9.14	47.00	58.00	85.00	50.00
Total disappearance	174.01	173.63	172.26	169.67	189.21	204.17	264.00	290.03	326.00	280.00
Carry forward	40.50	29.00	40.00	24.00	21.00	72.00	56.00	47.50	43.00	60.00

Source: Cotton Advisory Board.

ANNEXURE 4

Annual Average Prices of Kapas for Important Varieties

Prices in Rs per quintal

Year	Bengal desi	J-34	LRA	H-4	S-6	DCH-32
1996–97	1,168	1,770	1,786	1,905	2,010	2,316
1997–98	1,773	2,101	2,095	2,186	2,278	2,973
1998–99	1,883	2,080	2,037	2,135	2,141	2,532
1999–00	1,443	1,836	1,835	1,909	2,067	2,732
2000–01	1,438	2,068	2,103	2,207	2,310	2,784
2001–02	1,833	1,828	1,750	1,891	1,901	--
2002–03	1,875	2,218	2,110	2,215	2,323	2,927
2003–04	1,962	2,591	2,470	2,533	2,632	3,152
2004–05	1,689	1,844	1,835	2,003	2,037	2,840
2005–06	1,738	1,999	--	2,002	2,058	4,111
2006–07	1,871	2,133	--	2,168	2,280	3,034
2007–08	2,351	2,523	--	2,483	2,613	2,827
2008–09	3,051	2,800	--	2,850	2,850	--

Source: CCI Branch Offices.

Price trends as proportion of average month wise is as below:

October	November	December	January	February	March	April	May	June	July	August	September
0.77	0.76	0.84	0.85	0.84	0.92	0.96	1.05	1.18	1.23	1.29	1.32

ANNEXURE 5

Capacity, Production, and Inventory of Sambandam Spinning Mills Ltd

Rs in 00000

Inventories	2006	2007	2008
Stores and spares	49.56	53.97	48.69
Cotton	2,519.36	2,463.10	2,055.26
Cotton-in-process	580.78	929.07	703.32
Yarn	477.15	594.94	685.04
Process waste	8.10	3.79	5.24
Total Inventories	**3,634.95**	**4,044.87**	**3,497.55**
Turnover	12,438.06	12,805.59	11,170.71
Inventory turnover ratio	3.42	3.17	3.19
Number of months	3.51	3.79	3.76

Quantitative information			2006	2007	2008
a) Capacities	Installed	Spindles	62,176	73,452	73,452
b) Production	Yarn	Kgs	5,74,0651	6,829,709	7,705,941
	Fabric	Kgs	35,280	72,939	--
	Process waste	Kgs	1,863,923	2,438,171	2,638,634
c) Consumption	Cotton	Kgs	7,500,054	9,478,159	10,520,691
	Others	Kgs	201,187	214,331	66,604
d) Sales	Yarn	Kgs	5,634,591	6,723,604	7,658,151
	Fabric	Kgs	35,280	72,939	--
	Waste	Kgs	1,858,951	2,433,237	2,638,866
f) Stocks at end yarn			2006	2007	2008
	Kgs	236,488	3,42,593	3,90,383	
	Rs	47,715,286	59,494,044	6,85,04,167	
Process waste		Kgs	10,032	14,966	14,734
	Rs	809,840	3,78,835	5,24,023	
Cotton-in-process		Rs	58,078,004	92,907,098	7,03,320,06

S. No	Particulars	2007–08	2006–07	2005–06	2004–05	2003–04	2002–03
1	Fixed Assets	14921.33	12373.09	7910.98	6364.72	5572.58	5,291.69
2	Net Current Assets	6321.19	5129.27	4960.81	3431.75	2900.43	1504.70
3	Total Capital Employed	21564.98	17856.12	13226.09	10199.46	8792.16	7007.41
4	Shareholders' Funds	3370.96	2925.60	2293.09	1970.45	1691.92	1483.95
5	No. of Share	4264600	4264600	4264600	4264600	4264600	4264600
6	Net Worth per share (Rs.)	79	69	54	46	40	35
7	Turnover—gross	12683.86	13057.76	11427.97	9372.42	9081.04	7436.66
8	Turnover—net	12438.06	12805.59	11170.71	9047.60	8437.45	7285.62
9	Gross profit—PBDIT	2604.05	3326.21	2575.87	2123.30	1871.85	1294.57
10	Profit before tax—PBT	855.76	1308.83	1230.98	1035.13	598.85	519.93
11	Profit after tax—PAT	591.76	1121.83	663.38	546.03	327.85	310.93
12	Related Earnings	1284.11	2098.59	1222.33	1054.77	904.99	620.91
13	Dividend %	25	60	65	50	35	35
14	Earnings per share (Rs)—Basic	13.88	26.31	15.56	12.80	7.69	7.29
15	Installed capacity—Spindles	73452	73452	62176	62372	53540	52580

As of March 31	2006	2007	2008
Working Capital to Sales (x)	0.38	0.32	0.35
Working Capital Days (days gross sales)	135.50	114.01	124.42
Receivables (days gross sales)	55.77	35.60	19.93
Creditors (days cost of sales)	52.48	64.92	44.77
FG Inventory (days cost of sales)	101.69	123.29	21.17
RM Inventory (days consumption)	--	--	192.88

Notes:

1. During the year 2002–03, 21,800 shares were forfeited.
2. Reduction in spindle capacity in 2005–06 is the effect of modernization.

SME Cluster—Processing of Coconut Kernel and Extraction of Oil: A Case Study on Kangeyan at Tirupur District

Cluster supply chain and information efficiency in small business

Karthekeyan is the only son of Periyaswamy Goundar, who owns 50 acres of coconut grove in Pollachi near Coimbatore and runs the business of merchandizing coconut kernels, and processing and sale of coconut oil. Karthekeyan completed his schooling from Ooty Public School and obtained a degree in mechanical engineering from a premier technology institute, after which he decided to pursue MBA. After completing his MBA from one of the best institutions in western India, Karthekeyan worked in sourcing operations of an MNC, which is in the FMCG business. Though Karthekeyan had very lofty dreams, the sudden ill health of Periyaswamy Goundar compelled him to take over trusteeship of family wealth and settle at home. Periyaswamy Goundar briefed him on nuances of coconut cluster operations, which set the tone for Karthekeyan impressing on the challenges of industry structure and supply chain for effective operations.

Sourcing of Coconut and Kernels

Known as a coconut city, Pollachi enjoys favourable agro-climatic conditions because of strategic location along the Palakkad pass, where it receives monsoon rains from both southwest and northeast monsoons. Also the temperature is pleasant throughout the year—it is neither hot nor cold, and conducive for nurturing coconut and giving best of yield. The farms at Pollachi are well irrigated and fertile. Add to this, the culture and the discipline of labourers and landlords are conducive for nurturing coconut groves. Along with coconut, farmers grow beetal palm trees as inter crops to improve their earnings.

The best of the coconut yield is between March and October which contributes almost 75 per cent of the annual yield. Coconuts from Pollachi are sold as tender coconuts for consumption, which is by and large at premium across Tamil Nadu and Kerala. Approximately 30 per cent of yield during peak season and 10 per cent during off-season is sold as tender coconuts. By and large, rest of the coconuts go in for processing.

Processed coconut can be sold directly as kernels and used for edible purpose. This contributes about 25 per cent of available coconuts for processing. The balance 75 per cent coconuts, which are predominantly used for the extraction of oil, move at two levels. One, premier FMCG companies such as Marico Industries and HUL procure kernels from vendors and process either on their own or through contract manufacturers for selling as branded oil. Two, a large portion is crushed by small processors and sold in bulk through commodity markets, which goes primarily to rural and semi-urban markets for consumption and also as intermediary to personal care product segment.

Direct Consumption Trade

The produce which moves as tender coconut from Pollachi is traded by middlemen or brokers at different consumption centres. They fix a farm gate price, and using road transport mainly, 10–16 tonne trucks are moved to urban locations like Chennai, Coimbatore, Trichy, Madurai, Cochin, Bangalore, and so on. Typically, more of tender coconut is sold during March to September when the rest of Tamil Nadu goes through summer climatic conditions. The volume of sale is generally observed to be stable, and the availability of trucks at reasonable rates has been an influencing factor. Approximately, a truck carries 10,000 units of coconuts and the cost of transportation to Chennai, including secondary distribution to tender coconuts sale points, is about Rs 1.50. The market price for a tender coconut is Rs 15. The farm gate price is about Rs 10.

Process Cluster at Kangeyan

There are about 500 units at Kangeyan that process the kernels brought from Pollachi. There about seventy units with crushing and oil extraction capacity. The average oil extraction is about 10 tonnes per day. These units buy coconuts from Pollachi and also from other locations like Theni, Uttamar Palam of Kambam district, Rajapalayam, Then Kasi, Dindigul, Vedasandu, Pudukottai, and Thanjavur districts. From Kangeyan, Pollachi is about 80 km by road and it is possible to get load at a transportation cost of Rs 2,000 per 10 tonnes load. The other locations from where about 30 per cent of the requirement is bought would average about Rs 6,000 per 10 tonnes load.

One may like to understand two aspects of this cluster. First, the climatic conditions at Kangeyan support kernel processing as it receives less rainfall and has moderate temperature. Second, entrepreneurial attitude of people, commitment of labour, and natural orientation of families towards this business has helped for development of this business in this region. Apart from processing of kernels, rice mills are also key agro business established in this location.

It may be noted that out of the 500 units only 100 process kernel throughout the year. The balance 400 units are predominantly seasonal in operation. Also, from the statistics of distribution of process activity, only seventy out of 500 units, which is about 14 per cent, are in the oil extraction business. One may have to understand the structure of this business. A large size of operation, which is sun drying of kernel and grading, is manual. These two activities are not easily amenable for automation at viable costs. Another important characteristic is that there is a limitation to sun drying and grading as it requires about ten to fifteen days of labour and can be done by only those who have acquired the skill for fast handling over years of experience. One of the major risks is exposure to rains and kernels getting wet. In such event there will be huge losses as the material balance is oil content 63 per cent to 64 per cent; oil cakes about 31 per cent to 32 per cent; vapour of 4 per cent to 6 per cent.

So the Kangeyan cluster is justified because of organizational efficiency and environmental factors.

Now let us look at the dispersion of process capacity in greater detail. The 86 per cent units, which process kernels, are typically two-tons-a-day facilities. They procure coconut and make kernels, and trade the same. They would not be able to process edible oil because of economic viability, especially due to material mix of grade of kernels. Typically, only 20 to 25 per cent of kernels would go for edible purposes. The balance 75 per cent, a mix of full graded kernels versus broken kernels, determines the ability to process. Also, the economical viability of oil processing depends on the ability to reduce wastages. Another important factor in oil processing is to ensure utilization during off-season as well.

The typical economics of coconut, kernel, and processing data are given in Table 10.

Table 10 Price per kernel (grade-wise)

Price of per kernel (grade wise)	(adjusted for wastages)	28,000	27,000	25,000
Average grade distribution of kernel		30%	30%	40%
	Yield	Market Price Rs.		
Edible oil per tonne	64%	48,000		
Oil cake per tonne	31%	4,000		
Processing cost per tonne of oil		1,000		
Coconut landed cost	Rs 10–11 per unit			
No. of coconuts for 1 tonne of kernel		2,500 units		

One may note that the economic viability of edible coconut oil processing depends on oil recovery percentage and the quality of kernels purchased. In terms of price recovery, edible kernels are sold to intermediaries who take the product to Andhra Pradesh or north India at a premium of Rs 30,000 per tonne. The next grade kernel is purchased by branded oil processors at a price of Rs 29,000 per tonne. There will be wastage of 3 to 5 per cent but selling to these two markets as shape and grade are important. The balance would go as low value kernels. The details of utilization of coconut in processing are given in Figure 5.

Processing Activity (Refer to Figure 6)

1. A coconut along with shell is received at yard and stocked in a heap covered by coconut fibre.
2. Manual separation of kernels and shell from the coconut is done, and the shell is pushed to a heap that goes for usage in boiler or sale directly.

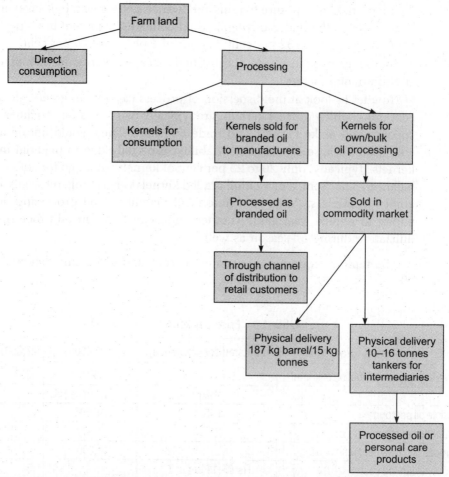

Figure 5 Options for coconut utilization across value system

3. Kernels go for sun drying in open yards at slotted locations.
4. After six to ten days of sun drying, kernels are graded manually into three lots-one, for consumption, two, for sale to processors, and three, own processing. While grading, labour uses two bins similar to kanban practice.
5. Apart from own purchases of coconuts, sun-dried kernels are also bought from process units to supplement for business. This moves to the grading stage.
6. Edible grade is aggregated and sold through intermediary. Kernels for processing are sold to processors and delivered at a mutually agreed time window from the unit.
7. The leftover kernel are moved through hoppers to crushers or an intermediate steam drying process before transferring to crushers, depending on the moisture content. Two levels of crushing takes place and oil cakes with left over oil are sold for solvent extraction process.
8. The finished oil goes to storage through tanker trucks of 10 to 15 tonne capacity.

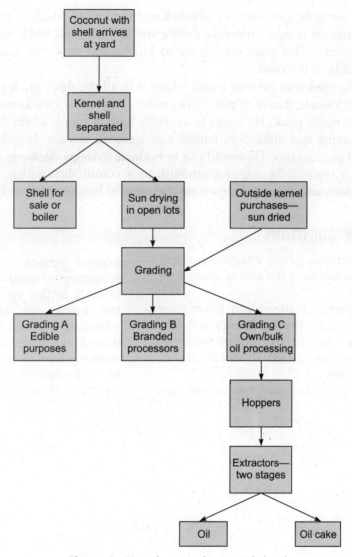

Figure 6 Kernel processing at unit level

A sizeable portion of material is also packed in 187 kg barrels, and on demand basis 15 kg tin packing is also undertaken.

9. The unit houses families who provide labour and live inside the campus. During this season, mills operate three shifts, and one production manager and promoter representative takes care of managerial demands.

Information and Price Efficiency

There is a coconut oil producers association which operates as a registered society at Kangeyan, providing necessary price and transaction information to its members. Operators like Marico Industries have promoted information and price efficiency by encouraging a community network and bidding of purchase quantity at certain price points on regular intervals during the day through SMS using mobile telephone network. This gives confidence to Millers and improves information efficiency for trading in the market.

Karthekeyan inherits a mill which is in all the three grades-it directly sells 30 per cent kernels, it sells 30 per cent to millers and 40 per cent kernels are processed from a 10 tonne plant. He wants to critically look at supply chain drivers, namely, facility planning and utilization, labour management, storage, inventory, sourcing, pricing, and product mix. He would like to evaluate strategic decisions of going bigger, setting up a regional brand, and establish as a commodity trader. You may evaluate his options and prepare a report on the same to be presented to Periyaswamy Goundar.

DISCUSSION QUESTIONS

1. Explain locational factors influencing supply chain operations as in this case of coconut oil extraction.

2. Describe impact of pricing and information drivers on supply chain efficiency and how technology adaption like dissemination of information through SMS in mobile phones helps the same.

3. If you are Karthekeyan, how would you evaluate options of growth: a. Horizontal acquisitions of similar 10 tonnes oil processing units; b. Setting up large capacity plant like 100 tonnes oil extraction and solvent extraction; c. Establish a regional label either through own processing or through buying and managing supplies from similar capacity mills. In all options, discuss supply chain issues significant for exercising the chosen option.

Redington (India) Limited—
An End-to-end
SCM Solutions Company

Success and challenges of supply chain business

Redington (India) Limited has successfully positioned itself as a focused distribution player with a significant reach across India, Middle East, and Africa. It originally started as a pure IT products distribution firm in 1993 in India, which is a typical high-value low-margin distribution-centric business. This is a role typically played by an intermediary in IT hardware distribution. Such price sensitivity and geographical spread requires well organized logistics and supply chain operations to be successful. The key success factors are believed to be risk management capability, effective supply chain infrastructure management, and efficient utilization of the Management Information Systems.

Redington India Ltd is successful as observed from their financial data given in Annexure 1 and 2. Its revenue has grown from Rs 1,528.54 crore in 2002–03 to Rs 6,071.64 crore in 2008–09, which is a fourfold growth. Profit after tax during this period has gone up from Rs 10.57 crore to Rs 80.69 crore, which is nearly an eightfold growth. One may look at the capital employed that has moved up from Rs 14.09 crore in 2002–03 to Rs 904.29 crore in 2008–09. Because of its good performance, it was able to have attractive financial returns to its equity capital investors as EPS went from Rs 3.60 in 2002–03 to Rs 10.36 in 2008–09. The consolidated turnover of the company for the financial year 2008–09 stands at Rs 12,683.14 crore with a profit after tax of Rs 159.66 crore.

Such growth would have naturally had supply chain operations challenges. Over the sixteen years, the company has transformed itself from a pure IT products distribution firm with traditional cash and carry model to a leading integrated supply chain solutions provider that includes non IT products and involves the management of inventory of greater than 7,200 SKUs while transacting business with over 21,000 channel partners. This explains the SCM complexity.

Supply Chain Solutions

Supply chain solutions form an integral part of Redington's operations. A major part of this activity is warehousing the storage of products between point of origin and point of consumption. The function also provides information on the status, condition, and disposition of items, and involves proper receipt, safe custody, preservation, issue of material to various channel partners, and physical and financial accounting. During the year, more warehouses were added to existing ones, totalling sixty warehouses in India and seventeen abroad.

The company has forayed into third party logistics in 2007, which aids optimum utilization of space in the warehouses. This, together with improved processes for ensuring prompt delivery, enables reduced cost of material handling and increased customer satisfaction. The company also has a comprehensive insurance to cover risks and hazards such as marine, fire, in-transit, burglary, earthquake, terrorism, and so on, for each class of warehouses.

According to the published information (Annual Report of Redington (India) Ltd 2008–09), the key capabilities and growth avenues are:

- Supply Chain Management—over 8 lakh sq. ft warehousing area; movement of over 1 lakh m tonnage
- Intelligent Automatic Distribution Centres
- Credit Management—21,200 channel partners
- Vendor Management—sixty-five brands
- Product Management—6000 SKUs
- Sales Acceleration—54 branches and 1,250 professionals
- Service and Support—21 brands and 258 service centres
- ISO 9001 certification for RME service centre
- Financial Services—commercial finance to Channel Partners
- Fund Management—access to multiple source of funds; P1+ rating from CRISIL
- Imports—green Channel across ports

If one looks at the above, Redington (India) Ltd supply chain activities are on physical management, financial flows management as a service, and information management. Also, it manages various supply chain role players like product brand owners, intermediaries, and its own employees playing their part in supply chain operations for their business.

In order to get an insight into their challenges and understand their future growth plan, an interview with their General Manager-Supply Chain Business Initiatives was held.

An interview with R. Arunachalam, General Manager: Supply Chain Business Initiatives, Redington (India) Ltd Chennai.

1. Could you detail the business of Redington and how do you look at competition for you to evolve in future?

Redington is into end-to-end supply chain solutions, predominantly in the IT arena. Many popular brands like HP, IBM, Microsoft, Apple etc., are being distributed by us across various countries in South Asia (including India), Middle East, and Africa.

We have started penetrating into third party logistics (3PL) domain as a logical extension of our business, as the company is already managing 60+

warehouses across various markets, deals with 4,500+ SKUs and reaches the products to 15,000+ customers across 400 cities in less than twenty-four hours. Few clients like Vodafone Essar South for Chennai circle, Cadbury for Bangalore, Kuehne and Nagel for western India, etc. are being currently serviced by us. We make certain vertical specific strategic moves to win over competition.

2. Would supply chain assets and decisions be a key differentiator? If so, highlight the same.

   Yes, assets in supply chain make a huge difference. Redington is now into setting up of automated distribution centres in many parts of India and one in Dubai. This calls for investments and such a decision will certainly be a key differentiator among the players in market.

3. Anyone would consider logistics being non-core to main business and it would get outsourced especially when it comes to warehousing and transportation centric logistics activity. What is your view on this being in distribution business? How would you rate in-house capability?

   Redington, being in distribution for over fifteen years, considers supply chain, more specifically warehousing and transportation, as important faces of distribution. One of our core competencies is supply chain management and that has given a lot of growth to Redington. On the contrary to the conventional companies, we, having consolidated our strengths in supply chain, have entered into 3PL segment too. It would be to the benefit of the brand owners to focus on manufacturing and brand building, and leave supply chain and receivables management to players like Redington. With this objective in mind, Redington has ventured in the channel financing business through its NBFC arm, Easyaccess Finance, and intends to set-up an SCM arm for 3PL services.

4. Is your business model supply chain driven? If so what are the challenges?

   Yes, as mentioned above, our current business model revolves around supply chain. Few of the challenges are availability of good warehouse infrastructure, complicated statutory norms for movement of goods between states and union territories, higher warehousing and transportation costs, high manpower costs, absence of trained manpower, etc. With an objective to convert these challenges into opportunities, we are planning huge investments into this space and provide 3PL services.

5. Is the customer willing to pay for quality, responsiveness and if so, how do you rate the same?

   To some extent yes, customers are willing to pay. But many a time an organized player who has made lots of investments for a class facility, has to compete with the local players who are very aggressive in pricing. But in our view, customer's growing preference to quality services levels at competitive cost will change the landscape in the logistics space in a few years.

6. What are the key strategic assets like distribution centre, technology including IT and deployment of third party service providers your organization has initiated on?

   Redington has announced publicly that it is setting up four automated distribution centres in four metros of India for which the work is in full speed. We have also invested in a best of breed warehouse management system in addition to having a good ERP

7. What are the current levels of application of technology in your business?

   In the distribution business, we are one of the very few companies in India who had invested a large sum for ERP about nine years back. Hence using latest technology is something Redington always aims for and we consider our IT system as the 'heart' of our business.

8. Any specific initiative required and taken to improve competitiveness?

   Yes. Particularly in the field that we are in, constantly upgrading ourselves to new ideas or initiatives makes us more competitive. Redington's path in trying to own assets, making state-of-the-art facilities, bringing in new vendors, businesses, continuously improving efficiencies, etc., can be considered as our steps towards making us more competitive.

9. What are the investments trends likely in your business?

   For the next four to five years, we will be in the investment mode to consolidate our supply chain skills and emerge as a strong player in third party logistics.

10. What is the current level of competency of logisticians in your organization and industry?

    Industry at large has to develop the competency level and same is the case at Redington, as this function has emerged as an important independent function only a few years back. However, we plan to be ahead of industry and hence the investments in that area of operation.

11. What efforts are required for building competency?

    Exposure to the better methods of handling supply chain, customer centric focus, capital investment with long gestation period, etc.

12. Do you think that presence of large unorganized sector hampers or facilitates the growth of the business? What does it take to retain the merits of unorganized sector and still drive organized growth of the industry? Please provide any other detail which would highlight strategy and SCM for your organization and industry

    Wouldn't really say that unorganized sector hampers our business. In fact clients start looking at outsourcing because next to his door step there is an unorganized player who is willing to work to the satisfaction of clients. Slowly clients, having understood the need for better service levels and access to technology, start availing the services of the organized players like Redington.

DISCUSSION QUESTIONS

1. Visit the Redington website (http://www. redingtonindia.com/pdf/Redington_ Annual_Report_2009.pdf) and download their annual report. Referring to their Profit and Loss Account and Balance Sheet, analyse financial performance indicators relevant to supply chain management like asset utilization, cost ratios, profitability ratios, and so on. Do this for over a period of five years preferably and analyse the trend. You may read management report and other relevant information and come out with a critical analysis on their performance.

2. Look at Redington's cash flow statement and analyse their funding for additions to assets and working capital needs.

3. Based on the information available in the interview and your own research, what are the key success factors for this company?

4. Prepare a detailed report on the challenges of 3/4 PL services company and how is Redington (India) Ltd equipped to handle the same?

Source: Personal interview with Mr R. Arunachalam, www.redingtonindia.com.

ANNEXURE 1

Redington (India) Ltd (Standalone) Financials

(Rs in crore)

Particulars	2008–09	2007–08	2006–07	2005–06	2004–05	2003–04	2002–03
Total Revenue	6,071.64	5,780.27	4,717.53	3,696.62	2,507.48	1,960.20	1,528.54
EBIDTA	173.87	148.25	101.76	68.90	45.00	35.90	26.87
PBT	124.25	103.57	65.63	45.33	27.21	24.54	16.57
PAT	80.69	67.11	42.42	29.14	17.26	15.49	10.57
Networth	614.39	569.56	535.02	367.63	316.34	104.98	89.49
Capital Employed	904.29	821.82	852.09	566.96	428.78	174.26	134.03
EBIDTA/Revenue	2.86%	2.56%	2.16%	1.86%	1.79%	1.83%	1.76%
PAT/Revenue	1.33%	1.16%	0.90%	0.79%	0.69%	0.79%	0.69%
Return on Average Capital Employed*	23.79%	25.87%	19.85%	20.45%	19.08%	21.37%	17.99%
Return on Average Equity*	29.76%	24.60%	17.91%	17.45%	13.71%	15.96%	12.32%
EPS (Rs)#	10.36	8.62	6.41	4.79	4.30	5.27	3.60
Book Value per Share (Rs)	78.90	73.15	68.71	58.28	52.12	35.72	30.45

ANNEXURE 2

Redington (India) Ltd (Consolidated) Financial Highlights

(Rs in crore)

Particulars	2008–09	2007–08	2006–07	2005–06	2004–05	2003–04	2002–03
Total Revenue	12.683.14	10,883.81	9,067.14	6,795.52	4,053.93	1,960.20	1,528.54
EBIDTA	329.57	259.04	198.47	131.06	83.93	35.90	26.93
PBT	219.02	177.06	127.25	92.36	53.67	24.57	16.59
PAT	159.66	136.07	101.70	74.34	42.38	15.51	10.58
Networth	1,002.20	721.49	625.61	432.86	341.29	105.60	90.10
Capital Employed	2,226.51	1,505.44	1,226.88	911.26	570.74	174.87	134.63
EBIDTA/Revenue	2.60%	2.38%	2.19%	1.93%	2.07%	1.83%	1.76%
PAT/Revenue	1.26%	1.25%	1.12%	1.09%	1.05%	0.79%	0.69%
Return on Average Capital Employed	16.98%	18.23%	17.32%	17.02%	21.52%	21.29%	17.93%
Return on Average Equity	18.53%	20.20%	19.22%	19.21%	18.97%	15.85%	12.22%
EPS(Rs)#	20.50	17.48	15.36	12.23	10.57	5.28	3.60
Book Value per Share (Rs)	128.71	92.66	80.34	68.62	56.23	35.93	30.66

#For EPS calculation, weighted average number of equity shares has been considered

Note: Financials are post acquisition of following entities—FY 05 (Redington Gulf FZE), FY 06 (Redington Distribution Pte Ltd and Cadensworth (India) Ltd) and FY 08 (Easyaccess Financial Services Ltd).

Source: www.redingtonindia.com.

ANNEXURE 3

Profit Loss Account Highlights

(Rs in crore)

	March 09	March 08	March 07	March 06	March 05
Income:					
Operating income	6,066.16	5,771.01	4,712.56	3,692.66	2,502.82
Expenses					
Material consumed	5,720.55	5,488.70	4,512.01	3,557.21	–
Manufacturing expenses	17.43	21.15	15.03	9.33	2,421.96
Personnel expenses	75.81	61.96	40.59	30.59	19.65
Selling expenses	–	–	0.71	0.12	–
Administrative expenses	83.98	60.21	43.61	27.69	22.51
Expenses capitalized	–	–	–	–	–
Cost of sales	5,897.77	5,632.02	4,611.94	3,624.95	2,464.13
Operating profit	168.38	138.99	100.62	67.71	38.7
Other recurring income	5.48	9.27	3.89	2.75	4.66
Adjusted PBDIT	173.87	148.26	104.51	70.46	43.36
Financial expenses	44.91	40.66	35.45	22.74	13.5
Depreciation	4.71	4.02	3.49	2.87	2.65
Other write offs	–	–	–	–	–
Adjusted PBT	124.25	103.57	65.57	44.85	27.21
Tax charges	43.56	36.46	23.21	16.19	9.91
Adjusted PAT	80.69	67.11	42.36	28.66	17.30
Non recurring items	–	–	0.06	0.48	–
Other non cash adjustments	–	–	–	–	–
Reported net profit	80.69	67.11	42.42	29.14	17.3
Earnings before appropriation	80.69	67.11	152.02	109.89	80.67
Equity dividend	36.44	31.88	19.47	–	–
Preference dividend	–	–	–	–	–
Dividend tax	–	–	3.31	–	–
Retained earnings	44.25	35.23	129.24	109.89	80.67

ANNEXURE 4

Redington (India) Ltd: Balance Sheet Highlights

(Rs in crore)

	March 09	March 08	March 07	March 06	March05
Sources of funds					
Owner's fund					
Equity share capital	77.87	77.87	77.87	63.08	60.7
Reserves & surplus	536.52	491.69	457.16	304.55	255.55
Loan funds					
Secured loans	156.82	117.58	124.32	80.52	37.53
Unsecured loans	133.09	134.68	192.78	119.02	74.9
Total	**904.29**	**821.82**	**852.13**	**567.16**	**428.69**
Uses of funds					
Fixed assets					
Gross block	55.2	49.87	52.18	40.04	31.53
Less : revaluation reserve	–	–	–	–	–
Less : accumulated depreciation	–	–	22.47	19.4	16.62
Net block	55.2	49.87	29.71	20.64	14.92
Capital work–in-progress	10.28	3.26	0.87	0.51	0.08
Investments	320.93	320.82	238.08	177.56	158.93
Net current assets					
Current assets, loans & advances	1,052.98	872.31	1,003.50	635.45	395.17
Less : current liabilities & provisions	535.1	424.44	420.03	266.99	140.42
Total net current assets	517.88	447.86	583.47	368.46	254.75
Miscellaneous expenses not written	–	–	–	–	–
Total	**904.29**	**821.82**	**852.13**	**567.16**	**428.69**
Notes					
Book value of unquoted investments	320.93	320.82	238.08	177.56	–
Contingent liabilities	517.27	395.63	474.81	451.35	–
Number of equity shares outstanding (Lacs)	778.66	778.66	778.66	630.82	607.01

9   Auto Components—Supply Chain Issues in Perspective: An Interview

Industry supply chain issues in perspective

In this interview, Dr Chandrasekaran has touched upon various threads of supply chain management like inventory management, capacity planning, vendor management issues and constraints at every stage in case of auto components manufacturers. He has portrayed the relationship between the manufacturers, suppliers, and OEMs. Though the interview dates back to 2005, reader may appreciate the context then and try to relate to current trends in auto components industry.

Auto components industry: the need to consolidate

Dr N. Chandrasekaran, Head, CII—*Institute of Logistics, speaks about the need for OEMs to invest in their auto components suppliers, just as the industry is increasingly getting 'tier-ized' between a few global players and a plethora of smaller ones...*
Sridhar Chari

How is the congestion at prominent Indian ports impacting auto companies?

When we discuss issues concerning the ports, the main bottleneck that emerges is containers (which handle components) compared to the Ro-Ro operation, which is still reasonably efficient. In the case of the automobile industry inbound materials are being affected. Auto component exports are also being affected. And the ones suffering the most are the small and medium enterprises, who do not have the wherewithal to manage the delays and naturally their cash-to-cash cycle is badly affected. Even if there is a delay of six to eight weeks, we are talking of a cost overrun of 15 per cent upwards on the inventory carrying cost. Apart from that there obviously are issues like loss of credibility, penalties, negotiations, congestion charges. The solution is to reduce the cycle time by possibly diverting to other ports.

This impact the inventory levels that companies need to maintain and creates variability and pressures in production. We feel that the big players are looking at alternatives. If Chennai is becoming tough, they are looking at how to go to ports like Tuticorin. Generally, at the transhipment ports in Colombo or Singapore, they check out the status of the Chennai port. If it seems difficult, then they divert operations to Tuticorin from where the goods are taken possession of. There are processes, which facilitate the same with the support freight agencies. This flexibility however attracts an incremental cost. As a natural corollary, the inventory holdings have to rise. Currently the inventory holding function is outsourced to third party logistics providers, and by and large, they are handling it well. Of course some manufacturers directly import cars at the Mumbai port, because the western region is an important market.

What solutions would you suggest?

Companies need to bring about flexibility. They need to work out an arrangement with their service providers, so that there are no breaks in production. If the current issues continue, production models and focus will be impacted, which in turn will impact customer responsiveness. There are limited options available with corporates and hence an effective coordination among various agencies is important. Moreover, the ability to bring breakthrough, long lasting solutions like expanding the approach road to the terminals in the primary hinterland, regulatory process restructuring, technology adoption like EDI, real time data sharing and increased capacity of freight stations, etc. are needed.

Take the case of JNPT. It was doing well until last year, but currently there is congestion because the peak capacity has been reached. Normally, if container terminal capacity utilization reaches 70 per cent, the strain on support resources could be felt. But we are past 100 per cent. Hence large corporates should have anticipated these problems and been prepared.

There has been a growing trend among auto companies to rely upon a handful of vendors. What do you think might be the implications of this trend?

Big players like Tata Motors, M&M, Ashok Leyland, and TVS have reduced the number of vendors by a substantial extent. The question is, is this healthier for the auto component industry? It may be good for the principal company, because they are dependent only on a fewer number of players. It may also be good for product development, because there is closer interaction between the principal and the vendors. Yet, we have to look at the broader picture.

The chain of relationships between the vendors and the principal develops in stages. What starts with a loose arrangement grows into a strategic tie-up, following which there is investment and then a JV. Globally companies like Nissan depend on Nippon steel for both critical and high quality equipment. There are few such partnerships among Indian auto companies. Currently, the focus in India is to reduce the number of vendors, for the purposes of cost reduction and growth in volumes. So far, we have only seen few Indian manufacturers and vendors progress to the second stage (strategic tie-up). Though this paves the way for likely backward integration for the OEM by either acquiring a stake in the vendor's business, or allowing the vendor to handle a part of the manufacturer's processes, this requires considerable investment, which is not happening. Though to an extent, companies like Hyundai are making an investment into vendors for seat manufacturing. One must realize that the big component manufacturers have grown big on their own steam. They look forward to investments only when there are global plans.

How are vendors being affected in the process?

Generally, among vendors there is a principal supplier and then there is a backup supplier. In this tier-ization, we need to ensure that the backup supplier survives. If a supplier is a backup supplier for one company and a principal supplier for another, he may survive. If a supplier remains small and gets squeezed in the growth phase with a few large component manufacturers emerging at the cost of many small ones, the business risk for all stakeholders may go up. This also does not augur well for a country like India, which is looking to increase employment and growth.

If Indian auto component manufacturers have to achieve global competence then a few big players need to align with global majors. What then happens to smaller players is the question. The smaller players may have to form clusters and fight their way for market share, or they even may have to look at the aftermarket.

What happens when auto manufacturers get into logistics and component manufacturing?

Take the case of TVS, which has been into logistics for a long time. When they sensed the opportunity among the professional logistics companies they made their move in a big way.

Auto component companies need to reduce costs. Prices are not going to rise suddenly, quality is a given and if companies which have been operating on cost of production so far, have to grow, they need to develop economies of scale and only then will costs come down. Economies of scope can be achieved if one can optimize and pool costs for a diverse range of activities like the TVS group has done. Component manufacturers need to look at a larger pool of manufacturers; they can no longer survive as dedicated suppliers. They would need to make their decision-making processes very transparent and scientific. The time to hide inefficiencies is long past. Even competitor information is freely available, that efficiencies are bound to improve. Resources like warehousing and transportation can even be shared among competitors.

How do you see the auto component industry in the near to medium term?

We have a large SME sector, which has some bargaining power; but everything eventually boils down to the sustainability of OE demand. The large component players are growing larger, by building capacity. And they will have to look at the global markets. The four main aspects of SCM: planning, sourcing, manufacturing, and delivery need to be looked at. We may be very good at planning and even manufacturing, despite certain inherent cost disadvantages. The issues are primarily about delivery, where we have huge cost, with respect to logistics and transport. Sourcing again is a mix of quality and pricing which is a problem.

Some component manufacturers who produce steering systems, auto castings and engine components have grown big. But you must realize that the component demand is a derived demand for the OE demand. We are already talking of a mature market for vehicles. This OE demand in turn is a derivative of economy growth and urbanization. The upgrade to the mid car segment happened because of a growth in the IT related service industries, and the resultant boosting of disposable incomes.

Future growth of the auto industry will depend on the growth in these sectors, as also a growth in the secondary car market. But one must also realize that there is a land resource constraint (issues like parking, road quality, traffic) that stymies any unlimited expansion in this industry. Even if the Rs 12 lakh car happens, it will in all likelihood be a hit only in the C class markets, which really is unknown territory. The secondary car market is affected by lack of adequate finance. Ideally we would need greater integration through information. Technology deployment should improve; we have been talking about ports and the container freight station being automated since a long time. We should be looking actively at RFID technology.

Epilogue

The main issue according to Dr Chandrasekaran is sustainability of the OE demand. He has pointed out that component demand is a derived demand for the OE demand, which is derived from economic growth and urbanization. He has spoken about the RFID technology in 2005 which is being widely spoken about even today. Though RFID has huge potential, implementation has been slow because of cost and other implementation issues associated with the same. The aspects like port congestion and approaches to handle the same may not be as serious as it was then. And yet are pointers relevant for any situation. Vendor development and partnership is the key to all times issues in case of auto components industry.

DISCUSSION QUESTIONS

1. Based on web research and interaction with auto component majors, evaluate the relevance of issues raised above.

2. Identify a company which has successfully handled these challenges and grown along with OE/component manufacturer or has faced melt down with least stress on financials.

(Acknowledgment: Published with the permission from Automonitor, Magazine).

Cargomen Logistics (India) Pvt. Ltd—Transforming from Advisory to Operations

New business opportunities in knowledge based supply chain services

It was April 2009 when two partners Kamal and Hari of Cargomen (India) Pvt. Ltd went to China to understand growth registered by peer logistics companies which are in trade facilitation with primary focus of documentation handling and establishing services around trade facilitation. Hari was bullish that SEZ is likely to progress further if the then UPA government comes back to power. They were also concerned about Andhra Pradesh elections, as they were due at the same time, and looked forward to a government that would be favourably inclined to promotion of SEZs and trade. Kamal was worried about political environment after the experience of Singur projects where Tata Motors were compelled to shift the unit. Apart from government policy on SEZs, both the promoters were also looking at the business environment due to global meltdown and its impact in India. Both partners wanted to review portfolio of their business and were looking at Chinese logistics service providers' experience and learn from them to develop their strategic plan for a couple of scenarios.

Cargomen Business

Cargomen Logistics India Pvt. Ltd is an outsourcing partner for those in the foreign trade, either as an importer or exporter or both. One of the key elements in such businesses is handling of a large number of documentation, without which business and financial flow would not happen. All the three flows, namely physical, financial, and informational flows, are to be streamlined. For this purpose, an expert handling is required, and many organizations outsource these functions to a company whose core competence is facilitation of such services. Cargomen is one such company wherein they are tuned to work as a closely associated work centre of the business concern to deal with matters relating to statutory approvals and clearances concerning exports and imports.

Established in the year 2000, Cargomen serves the exporting and importing community. It may be pertinent to state that about more than 200 software companies (fifty of them multinationals) have chosen to outsource their work concerning governmental clearances and approvals from DGFT, STPI, CEX, customs, RBI, and so on.

Cargomen Logistics India Pvt. Ltd is a professionally managed logistics consulting company and positioned between 3PL and 4PL services. Previously known as Essar

Global Logistics, Cargomen is developing innovative solutions under 'single window clearance' concept that will enhance value to importers/exporters in a way that they manage their logistics requirements in a networked environment. The company has plans to deliver services to establish and provide comprehensive solutions for all logistics requirement of the company in day-to-day requirement, which would include 3PL activities like warehousing and transportation.

Mission of the Company

The concept of the business is to provide 'single window clearance' services wherein Cargomen becomes an integral part of the company and a perfect match for the option of 'outsourcing of services' and be an extension of customers. This gives the client a clear advantage of single point information source for customer's international cargo movement and services related to DGFT, STPI, CEX, and CUSTOMS. The aim is to provide customer satisfaction at affordable cost.

Services to 100 Per Cent EOU (Export Oriented Units) Under STP Scheme

To encourage exports and to have positive balance of payment, the Government of India has implemented a scheme, popularly known as 100 per cent EOU Scheme, wherein the manufacturer can process his operations in a customs bonded warehouse. EOU/EPZ/EHTP/STP fall under this category. The manufacturer can bring in the goods duty free, subject to export obligation. The services offered by Cargomen include:

- Registration with STPI/VEPZ;
- Arranging Customs Private Bonded Warehouse license under Section 58 and 65 of Indian Customs Act 1962;
- Arranging necessary certificates for procurement of goods duty free (i.e. Import Certificates, Procurement, CT-3 form);
- Providing services in Central Sales Tax Re-imbursement;
- Providing services in softex forms clearance from STPI;
- Necessary certificates/approvals for inter unit transfers, movement of laptop computers, Re-Export of equipments imported on loan basis;
- Maintaining the Bond Registers and Bond Balance in our database.
- Providing dedicated manpower to look after the asset tracking and day to day cargo management.
- Installation of database package for statutory compliance.

SEZ Services

SEZ approval for setting up SEZ for developer with Ministry of Commerce
- Getting notification from Ministry of Commerce for SEZ
- Arranging approval under rule 9 of SEZ rules for authorized operations
- Arranging approval under rule 12 for list of goods and services
- Arranging demarcation of SEZ into processing and non processing area
- Arranging service tax exemption from SEZ office

- Arranging VAT exemption from SEZ for SEZ units
- Arranging green card from VSEZ
- Preparation of annual performance reports and quarterly performance report and submission with SEZ
- Execution of bond cum legal undertaking with authorized officer and VSEZ
- Arranging necessary approvals from authorized officer on case to case basis
- Getting import and local clearance for SEZ goods with authorized officer

DGFT Services

These are more of foreign trade regulatory services which are important for a client to export and import goods and services.

- Application for Import / Export Code No. (IEC No.);
- RCMC (Registration-cum Membership Certificates) with the concerned Export Promotion Councils;
- Applications for DEPB, DFRC, GEMREP, ADVANCE LICENCE, EPCG (for actual users) & Negative List Licenses;
- Duty Drawback Applications and DEPB verification;
- Purchase of DEPB at Application stage;
- EPCG Licenses;
- Deemed Export Drawbacks and Refund of Terminal Excise;
- Export House/Trading House, Star Trading House, Super Star Trading House Certificate;
- Identity Card;
- Fixation of Input/Output Norms (SION) and DEPB Brand Rate Fixation;
- Buying and selling Export Licenses;
- Consultancy Service for Exporters/Importers on Exim Policy, procedures and Custom matters;
- Terminal Excise Duty Refund under Deemed exports.

Other Services

Customs Brokerage

Customs brokerage service require knowledge of policy/tariff and quality of service and is a niche area to operate. The basis for efficient Customs Brokerage is 'Knowing the product, interpretation with proper classification rules as per the international standards of classification of world customs organization. Cargomen bridges good and a trusting relationship with the Customs and the customers, which is the key to success of Customs Brokerage for each Customer.'

Transportation

Cargomen operates dedicated fleet of vehicles owned and leased from different resources. This gives an additional advantage in delivering the cargo on time. The company is planning to have more number of vehicles in all the four locations of the company viz Hyderabad, Vishakhapatnam, Chennai and Bangalore as these centres are going to be key focus locations.

Warehousing

Currently the company uses space available in market on need basis. The company understands the need to have its own facilities. Kamal and Hari feel that the investment required for such operation is high and focus of business may get shifted. Annex 1 gives some working on warehouse investment and economics. This is one of such areas where they are pondering for strategic direction.

Pre & Post Shipment Consultancy

Cargomen's experience, expertise and a strong knowledge bank enables them to provide consultancy to their customers on contemporary Export Import Policy and Procedure. This is important for any customer to reduce time and optimize the logistics cost.

Pre-Shipment Consultancy

Pre-Shipment Consultancy includes Registration, Licensing, approvals and processing of application under various schemes (i.e. STP, DEPB, DFRC, ADVANCE LICENCE, EOU, EPCG, etc.) for clearance of consignment at minimal duty/exemption valuation procedures for Import transaction with related parties and advisory service on routing of consignments at competitive freight rates.

Post-Shipment Consultancy

Post-Shipment consultancy includes duty drawback, refunds and redemption of Bank Guarantee on completion of Export obligation under various schemes, and foreign exchange realization on exports and remittance on imports and advisory scheme (related scheme).

Primarily, Cargomen is in the business of customs documentation handling and focuses on facilitation of global logistics operation of a company by providing information and financial flow enablement. The company aspires to move into physical logistics with warehousing and transportation business. One may note from market understanding that in their current businesses their revenue could be Rs 6 crores on which net margin would be 40–50 per cent. Their proposed logistics operation may provide net margin only 1–2 per cent and high intensity of activity and managerial effort.

Culture and Management

Cargomen core values are common goals, customer focus, innovation, 'entrepreneurism', endurance, teamwork, respect, flexibility, integrity, honesty and openness, fun, and most importantly TRUST.

Ch.Hariharan is founder managing partner, with over seven years of experience in this field. He has developed good relation with the department people and gained good name in the market of STP clearance. He was earlier associated with   leading companies like Leap Forwarders (P) Limited and with CS Narender & Co. In that capacity he was responsible for, services improvement, consultancy, strategic planning and industry leading initiatives. He is a recognized leader in extending the role of Hyderabad Custom House Agents in the field of Central Excise which was earlier confined with Customs Clearance only. Hariharan received his Graduate degree in Arts from Osmania University, has a Masters in Management and later specialized in Foreign Trade Management from an institute associated with IIFT, New Delhi. Hariharan has also been trained with Air India on air cargo business.

Kamal Jain is Managing Partner. Kamal's experience spans over 5 years in start-up, executive management, operations, strategic management Kamal Jain was operations incharge at Jayem Impex (P) Limited, Hyderabad before starting up this venture, where his responsibilities were Customs Clearance, customer satisfaction, Consultancy in the field of DGFT and Central Excise. He was also associated with Leap Forwarders (P) Limited, Hyderabad. Kamal received his Graduate degree in Commerce and then completed Foreign Trade Management from an institute associated with IIFT, New Delhi.

The organization is managed by well-qualified professionals who have experience and domain knowledge in the target areas of the organization. Nagarajan J. Deloitte Consulting India Pvt. Ltd, customer of Cargomen Logistics, reacted mentioning that Cargomen is on the forefront of value addition activity. Not only as an effective CHA, would also advice us on various rules and regulations, suggestions on the benefits and constant updates on the circulars/notifications including but not limited to clearance of goods. He believes that it has deployed a trained manpower onsite. Most of our queries are addressed by these personnel itself and very rarely the matter is escalated. Also, it is very much responsive by mails and accessible by phones, including holidays. He also believes that Cargomen maintains at all levels in the organization and differntiator is, the value is derived to the client as an inclusive benefit—advisory, sharing of knowledge, procedures, practices etc. Cargomen has got solutions and we have had a good experience on this front.

The organization intends to further develop and sustain them through effective training and HRM practices. CARGOMEN employees 105 people in Hyderabad, five people in Vizag and twenty-five in Bangalore and twenty-five in Chennai.

Hari and Kamal look forward to bringing in capital for funding growth avenues especially in warehousing/ICD.

DISCUSSION QUESTIONS

1. Present a report on environmental analysis of trade facilitation business looking at political, societal, economic, legal, environmental and cultural factors especially in locations where Cargomen aspires to grow.
2. Analyse businesses in which Cargomen is currently operating and their future areas of growth.
3. Prepare critical analysis of warehouse/ICD investments and a report on the same.
4. What are the managerial challenges in growth of this company? If you were to recommend a future direction, what would be your advice to the promoters?
5. If you are a capital provider, how would you estimate risk and manage the same.

ANNEXURE 1

A warehouse is an important facility in logistics operations which could be a commercial building for storage of goods. It is located near and/or in industrial areas of cities which is used by manufacturers, importers, exporters, wholesalers, transport businesses, customs, etc. It is equipped with loading docks to load and unload trucks; or sometimes is loaded directly from railways, airports, or seaports. Material handling equipments like cranes and forklifts are used for moving goods, which are usually placed on ISO standard pallets. Generally, Warehouse should be located at a convenient place near highways, railway stations, airports and seaports where goods can be loaded and unloaded easily.

The following are key concerns in warehouse land finalization, construction and management:

- Land availability: city periphery, suburbs, preferably on the city entry points
- Legality of title, Reclassification of land (wherever applicable), encumberance clearance, freehold land clear of future land bank acquisition for industry/infrastructure by government
- Topography of land, minimum area required, level of landfill required, soil strength
- Absence of flood-prone areas and areas abutting roads likely for future acquisition for expansion
- Absence of power lines or any mechanical structures in the land
- Absence of residential or any constructions which may otherwise restrict warehousing operations
- Civil/Mechanical construction—size of warehouse, span of trusses, roofing height and type, flooring type, bay area, loading/unloading ramps,
- Ergonomics—light & ventilation, seamless flow of man, material and equipment, reception area
- Proximity to manufacturing location, assembling units, gateway ports
- Accessibility 365 days, 24×7—Power back-up and IT backbone
- Warehouses meant for preservation of perishable items like fruits, vegetables, eggs and butter etc. should have cold storage facilities.
- Proper arrangement should be there to protect the goods from sunlight, rain, wind, dust, moisture and pests
- Sufficient parking space should be there inside the premises to facilitate easy and quick loading and unloading of goods.
- Round the clock security arrangement should be there to avoid theft of goods.
- The building should be fitted with latest fire-fighting equipments to avoid loss of goods due to fire.
- Paved area for laden and empty containers
- Macadamised road for trailer movements

- Container destuffing area to be earmarked
- Soil strengthening to take into account five stack laden container load
- If rail based, to ensure minimum length of at least 1.6 km of levelled land
- The railway line layout should commensurate with the container stacking and equipment (reach stacker/RMG or RTG)
- Weighbridge location at entry points and tower mast lighting
- Uni-flow planning for road movement
- To ensure uninterrupted power supply and provision of reefer points

The viability of establishing warehouse must be arrived at working:

- Project cost, Break Even Point and Return on Capital Employed (ROCE)
- Funding
- Business Potential which would determine revenue stream (Income) and Unit Cost

Revenue potential is to be arrived based on the market needs, viability for a manufacturer and the terms of agreement between the lessor/lessee. Current trends in a location like Sriperumbudur which is high growth auto and electronics goods industry, it is about Rs 45/sq. ft for factory/manufacturing units which could be component assembly or accessories inside a warehouse and Rs 15/sq. ft for normal Warehouse function. Land would cost about Rs 2 crores an acre and construction cost could be Rs 1000/sq. ft for a warehouse space.

A summer internship done by a student on establishing an ICD in Chennai is as follows:

1	Activity / Area of development	UOM	Area	Unit	Rs in lakhs
A	Shrub clearing	sq. M	360,000	20	72
B	Levelling of land including earth filling and rolling	Cu. M	240,000	100	240
2	Providing of garland canal				
A	Earth work	Cu. M	9,375	110	10.31
B	RCC slab	Sq. M	15,000	100	15
C	Culverts over GC	Nos	2	1,000,000	20
3	Roads	meters	5,500		
	Gravel	Cu. M	12,375	50	6.19
	Road surface, drain pipe crossings, sidewalk pavement	Cu. M	17,600	5,000	880
	culverts for roads	Nos	6	12	72
4	Container yard				
	Sand	Cu. M	19,865	100	19.87
	Heavy duty pavement	Sq. M	35,000	2,000	700
5	Provide beam cost for RTG runways	Sq. M	6,000	5,200	Future Development

6	Warehouse areas				
	Flooring and civil works	Sq. M	13,500	2,500	337.5
	Roofing & structurals	Sq. M	13,500	8,200	1,107.00
7	Office building gate control complex,	Sq. M	4,000	7,500	300
	Canteen w/s toilets pump houses tanks etc				
8	Compound wall	M	3,500	5,000	175
9	Empty storage pavement	Sq. M	3,000	800	24
10	Landscaping others/truck pavement	Sq. M	24,000	20	4.8
	Mechanical and electrical *—on lease				
	Structured cabling	LS			100
	High mast lighting	Nos	10	4,40,000	44
	Yard lighting	Nos	6	3,60,000	21.6
	Street lighting	Nos	100	25,000	25
	Power	Nos	1	150000	50
	Reach stacker	Nos	3	145	*
	Terminal trailers	Nos	12	25	*
	Fire fighting	LS			50
	Terminal water supply & sewerage	LS			20
	Top lifter crane	Nos	2	70	*
	Scrap handler	Nos	1	60	*
	Forklifts	Nos	4	10	*
	Work shop tools & tackles	LS			30
	Railways	LS			1,000.00
	Weigh bridge	LS			30
	DGPS controls	LS			35
	Office equipment	LS			50
	Incidentals & pre operative	LS			489.53
	Total—capex				5,928.80
	Working capital				26.51
	Total project cost				5,955.30

ANNEXURE 2

List of SEZ Developers

1. L&T Phoenix Infoparks Private Limited, Gachibowli, Hyderabad
2. Indu Techzone Private Limited, Shamshabad, Hyderabad
3. Emaar Hills Township Private Limited, Gachibowli, Hyderabad
4. TSI Ventures India Private Limited, APIIC, Nanakramguda, RR District
5. DivyaSree NSL Limited, Raidurg Village, Hyderabad
6. Shyamaraju & Co., Bangalore
7. Sierra Atlantic Software Services (P) Limited, Nanakramguda, Hyderabad (Co-Developer)
8. Kennexa Technologies Private Limited, Vishakhapatnam

Clients List of SEZ Units

9. Sierra Atlantic Software Services (P) Limited, Nanakramguda, Hyderabad
10. Applabs Technologies, DLF City, Gachibowli, Hyderabad
11. Cognizant Technology Solutions India (P) Limited, DLF Cyber City, Gachibowli, Hyderabad
12. UBS Service Center India Private Limited, L&T Phoenix Infoparks (P) Limited, Gachibowli
13. Parexel International (I) Pvt. Ltd, DLF City, Gachibowli, Hyderabad
14. Rockwell Collins India Enterprises Private, Limited, SunDew Properties, Mindspace, Hyderabad
15. Accenture Services Private Limited, Chennai
16. Tech Mahindra Limited, Mahindra Ascendas SEZ, Chennai

Clients List of STP Units

17. Google Online India (P) Limited, Level-IV, RMZ Futura, Madhapur, Hyderabad
18. Computer Science Corporation, Building No. 7, Mindspace, Hyderabad
19. Accenture Services Private Limited, Building No. 2, Mindspace, Hyderabad
20. GE India Exports (P) Limited, Begumpet, Hyderabad
21. GE Motors India (P) Limited, Banjara Hills, Secunderabad
22. Hewlett Packard India Software Operation Private Limited, Bangalore
23. CA Computer Associates India (P) Limited, Plot # 17, Software Units Layout, Hyderabad
24. Deloitte Consulting India Private Limited, Plot # 17, Software Units Layout, Madhapur, Hyderabad

25. Deloitte Financial Advisory Services India Private Limited, RMZ Futura, Madhapur, Hyderabad
26. Deloitte Support Services India Private Limited, RMZ Futura, Madhapur, Hyderabad
27. Deloitte Tax Services India Private Limited, RMZ Futura, Madhapur, Hyd
28. Deloitte & Touche Audit Services India Private Limited 17, RMZ Futura, Madhapur, Hyderabad
29. Deloitte Valuation Services Company India Private Limited, RMZ Futura, Madhapur, Hyderabad
30. Lucent Technologies India Limited, Lakshmi Cyber Center, Road No. 12, Banjara Hills, Hyderabad
31. Amazon.Com, Building No. 8, Mindspace, Hyderabad
32. HSBC Electronic Data Processing India Private Limited, Hyderabad & Vishakhapatnam
33. HSBC Software Development India Private Limited, Madhapur, Hyderabad
34. Franklin Templeton International Services India (P) Limited, Cyber Towers, Madhapur, Hyderabad
35. UBS Service Center India Private Limited, Nanakramguda, Hyderabad
36. Wells Fargo India Solutions Pvt. Ltd, Building No. 2A, MindSpace, Madhapur, Hyderabad
37. Thomson Corporation International, Private Limited, Madhapur, Hyderabad
38. Qualcomm India Private Limited, Building No. 8, Mindspace, Madhapur, Hyderabad
39. Honeywell Technology Solutions Lab Pvt. Ltd, Nanakramguda, Hyderabad
40. SAP Labs India Private Limited, Begumpet, Hyderabad
41. Xilinx India Technology Services Private Limited, Cyber Pearl, Madhapur, Hyderabad
42. IGATE Global Solutions Jubilee Hills Hyderabad
43. Sonata Software Limited, Begumpet, Hyderabad
44. Cypress Semiconductor Technology India (P) Limited, Aditya Trade Center, Ameerpet, Hyderabad
45. Skyworks solutions India Private Limited, Plot # 17, Software Units Layout, Madhapur, Hyderabad
46. Austria Microsystems India Private Limited, Cyber Pearl, Madhapur, Hyderabad
47. Cognizant Technology Solutions India (P) Limited, Plot # 17, Software Units Layout, Hyderabad
48. Tech Mahindra Limited, Cyber Gateway, Madhapur, Hyderabad
49. Tata Elexi Limited, Secunderabad

50. Kanbay Software India (P) Limited, Plot # 5, Software Units Layout, Madhapur, Hyderabad

51. Hyundai Motor India Engineering Private Limited, I Labs Center, Madhapur, Hyderabad

52. Hyundai Autonet India Private Limited, I Labs Center, Madhapur, Hyderabad

53. Sierra Atlantic Software Services (P) Limited, Software Units Layout Madhapur, Hyderabad

54. Sumtotal Systems India (P) Limited, Plot # 12, Software Units Layout Madhapur, Hyderabad

55. Avaya India Private Limited, Plot No. 17, Software Units Layout Madhapur, Hyderabad

56. Quantum Corporation, Vega Towers, Plot No. 17, Vanenburg IT Park, Madhapur, Hyderabad

57. JDA Software India Private Limited, Plot # 17, Software Units Layout, Madhapur, Hyderabad

58. USi Internetworking Services Private Limited, Plot No. 17, Vanenburg IT Park, Madhapur, Hyderabad.

59. Emerson Electric Co (India) Pvt. Ltd., Vanenburg IT Park, Plot No. 17, Madhapur, Hyderabad

60. Yash Technologies Private Limited, Madhapur, Hyderabad

61. Pindar Set BPO Services Private Limited, Madhapur, Hyderabad

62. CMC Limited, CMC Center, Gachibowli, Old Bombay Highway, Hyderabad

63. Fujitsui Limited, Aditya Trade Center, Hyderabad

64. Sitel India Limited, Cyber Pearl, Madhapur, Hyderabad

65. Satyam Venture Engineering Services Limited, S.P. Road, Secunderabad

66. C3i Support Services (P) Limited, Plot # 17, Software Units Layout, Madhapur, Hyderabad

67. Cordys R&D (P) Limited, Plot # 17, Software Units Layout, Madhapur, Hyderabad

68. Conseco Data Services (India) Private Limited, Jubilee Hills, Hyderabad

69. Four Soft Private Limited, Hi-tech City, Cyber Towers, Madhapur, Hyderabad

70. Alliance IT Consulting India Private Limited, Road No. 36, Jubilee Hills, Hyderabad

71. Valuelabs, Madhapur, Hyderabad

72. SoftSol India Limited, Madhapur, Hyderabad

73. IIC Technologies Private Limited, Punjagutta, Hyderabad

74. First India Corporation Private Limited, Ameerpet, Hyderabad

75. Megasoft Limited, Madhapur, Hyderabad

76. Mars India Private Limited, Jubilee Hills, Hyderabad

Clients List of Hotels/Convention Centre

77. GMR Hyderabad International Airport Limited, NOVOTEL Hyderabad Hotel—Hotel Project
78. Cyberabad Convention Center Private Limited, Hyderabad (Managed by Accor Hotels)
79. Indus Palms Hotels & Resorts Private Limited (IVRCL Group)
80. Sunder Taj Mahal, SD Road, Secunderabad
81. Sri Laxmi Gayatri Hotels Private Limited (Khatriya Hotels)
82. Boulder Hills Private Limited, Gachibowli, Hyderabad
83. EMAAR Hills Township, Gachibowli, Hyderabad
84. Global Hospitality Services, Hyderabad
85. Sreekanya Devallu & Sons Hotels Private Limited, Vishakhapatnam
86. Hotel Nikil Sai International, Nizamabad
87. RKS Motor Private Limited, Somajiguda, Hyderabad

Clients List of Infrastructure Providers

88. L&T ECC Limited, Madhapur, Hyderabad
89. L&T Infocity Limited, Q4 1st Floor, Cyber Towers, Madhapur, Hyderabad
90. Aparna Constructions Limited, Punjagutta, Hyderabad
91. PHOENIX Teck Park Private Limited, Road No. 14, Jubilee Hills, Hyderabad
92. IVR Prime Urban Developers Limited, Banjara Hills, Hyderabad
93. Net-Net Ventures, Madhapur, Hyderabad

Clients List of Traders

94. Blue Star Limited, Secunderabad, Hyderabad
95. Interface Modern Form Company Limited, Bangalore
96. METLIFE Enterprises, Himayatnagar, Hyderabad
97. Rite Equipment, New Delhi
98. Samsung India Limited, New Delhi
99. Actis Technologies India Private Limited, Somajiguda, Hyderabad
100. Comfort Line Systems Private Limited, Erramanzil, Hyderabad
101. Consul Consolidated Pvt. Ltd, Secunderabad
102. Technigroup International Private Limited, Banjara Hills, Hyderabad
103. DATS India Private Limited, Hyderabad
104. ESCO Audio Visual India Private Limited, Mumbai
105. WOTEK Engineering, Banjara Hills, Hyderabad
106. Hospitality Solutions, New Delhi
107. Micron Electrical, Begumpet, Hyderabad

108. Elect Systems, Hyderabad

Clients List into Broadcasting

109. Associated Broadcasting Company Private Limited, Banjara Hills, Hyderabad
110. Visage Systems, Banjara Hills, Hyderabad

Clientele at Chennai

111. Thomson Corporation International, Private Limited, Mylapore, Chennai
112. ZYLOG Systems Limited, Nandanam, Chennai
113. ADITYA Auto Products & Engineering India Private Limited, Doddaballapur, Bangalore
114. CA (India) Technologies Private Limited, Tidel Park, Chennai
115. Cypress Semiconductor Technology India (P) Limited, Tidel Park, Chennai
116. Ambica Agarbathies and Aroma Industries Limited, Vadapalani, Chennai
117. ETA MELCO Engineering Pvt. Limited, Mylapore, Chennai
118. Tech Mahindra Limited, Ascendas Mahindra IT Park, Phase I, Chennai

Clientele at Bangalore

119. Augen Technologies Software Solutions Pvt. Ltd, Residency Road, Bangalore
120. Bagmane Developers Pvt. Ltd, Lakeview Bagmane Tech Park, CV Ramnagar, Bangalore
121. BLR Logistics, M-3, Manek Apartment, Shanti Colony, Jeevaratnam Nagar, Adayar Chennai
122. Chalukya Hotels Resorts Pvt. Ltd, No.1, Palace Road, Bangalore
123. Cypress Semiconductors Technology India Pvt. Ltd, Sharada Towers, Bangalore
124. Edison Semi Conductors Pvt. Ltd, Koramangala, Bangalore
125. Esco Audio Visual India Private Ltd, #348, 12th Cross, R.T. Nagar, Bangalore
126. ETA Melco Engineering Company Pvt. Ltd, North Block, 47, Dickenson Road, Bangalore
127. First Advantage Offshore Services Pvt. Ltd, Whitefield Road, Bangalore
128. Google India Pvt. Ltd, Prestige Sigma, No. 3, Vittal Mallya Road, Bangalore
129. Hinduja Holding Builders & Developers, Rich Homes, Richmond Road, Bangalore
130. Huawei Technologies India Pvt. Ltd, The Leela Palace, Airport Road, Bangalore
131. IBC Knowledge Park, Sheriff Centre, 73/1, St.Mark's Road, Bangalore
132. Igate Global Solutions Limited, EPIP Phase-II, Whitefield, Bangalore
133. Interface Modern Form Co. Ltd, G1, Pride Elite, 10 Museum Road, Bangalore
134. Mednestor Healthcare Pvt. Ltd, New BEL Road, Bangalore

135. Pindar Set BPO Service Pvt. Ltd, IIM Post, J.P. Nagar, 7th Phase, Bangalore
136. Platinum City, 5th Floor, 73/1, Sheriff Center, St Marks Road, Bangalore
137. Quality Engineering & Software Technology, Whitefield Main Road, K.R. Puram, Bangalore
138. Quinnox Consultancy Services Limited, Silk Board Junction, Next to Wipro, Bangalore
139. Satyam Venture Engineering Service. Pvt. Ltd, Vijaya Bank Cly Outer Ring Road, Bangalore
140. Search Marketing Agency Pvt. Ltd, Infantry Road, Bangalore
141. Shyamaraju & Company, Divyasree Park, SES, Kundalahalli Village, Whitefield, Bangalore
142. Softlite Luggage Pvt. Ltd, Kamalanagar Main Road, Basaveswaranagar, Bangalore
143. Tech Mahindra Ltd, 56, Amir Tech Park, Nos 23 & 24, Hosur Main Road, Bangalore

Pollachi Lorry Owners' Association —Woes of Being an Owner and Still Being Profitable

Woes of transport service providers

Pollachi is a town and a municipality in the Coimbatore district of Tamil Nadu state of India. It is located 40 km south of Coimbatore in the Coimbatore district. Pollachi is considered as 'The land of natural wealth and prosperity' because of its rich natural endowments like water resource, fertile land, Western Ghats attracting tourists and entrepreneurial culture of people. Due to its proximity to the Western Ghats, Pollachi has a pleasant climate throughout the year.

It is an important commercial area in the region and has a big market for agricultural products. Pollachi is also famed for its market, especially for jaggery and cattle. The Jaggery Market in Pollachi is Asia's biggest jaggery market. Coconuts and tender-coconuts are exported from here to all over India.

Coir-Fibre, Curled Coir Manufacturing is an important Industry in Pollachi. Pollachi has a lot of textile and coir industries. There are more than forty mills and moulding units in Pollachi: notable ones include Sakthi Mills, Modern Mills etc. Aerospace Materials Private Limited is a company that supplies carbon papers for airplanes. Their main customer is ISRO. Pollachi is a popular movie filming location for the movie industry. Hundreds of Tamil, Malayalam, Telugu and Hindi movies are filmed here.

Based on economic factors of Pollachi and its strategic location linking Tamil Nadu and Kerala with its agrarian market forces, it is natural one would expect logistics and especially transportation by road to be an important activity and vital for success of economy. On 15 July 2009, President of Pollachi Lorry Owners Association (PLOA) wanted to discuss with Mr Mohan, Management Consultant, who also hails from the town, on working with one of the big fours in Chennai on preparing a detailed note about challenges faced by lorry transport owners and threat to the local economy. Mr Mohan collates the following information and requests his Executive Assistant Karthik to prepare a report.

Size The association has about 600 members and total number of trucks in the municipality is about 3,000 which is being owned by these members. Trucks are mainly 10 tonnes, 16 tonnes and Eicher cattle movement trucks. Though average ownership is about five, a large number of members own one or two trucks only. This is intriguing as such low ownership is across India and one may like to explore reasons for the same. It was mentioned that economics of trucking business is plagued by a number of factors.

President & Secretary of PLOA

Pollachi Lorry Owners' Association

Key aspects are as follows

1. Capital investment: Cost of a vehicle on road would be about Rs 14 lakhs as of April 2009. seventy-five per cent of this capital is funded by debt capital and balance from own sources. It is believed that the operations provide reasonable rate of return for the investors. After servicing debt capital, PLOA members' makes about 15 per cent return on own capital. Generally, availability of debt capital is not an issue as banks lend under priority sector norms for this business. Then one would like to probe that if there is a reasonable return and funding is available, then why haven't they grown bigger? One also observes that most of them have one or two trucks and commonly heard is about players who had ten to twelve trucks have reduced over the years to two trucks holding and discouraging children in family to make this investment. To understand this in greater detail one must look at second sale of vehicles and economics of operating vehicles bought in second sale.

2. Availability of drivers: There has been a recent change under Motor Vehicle Act in India wherein drivers are to be qualified to have passed eighth standard to apply for a truck driving license. The government initiative is a positive move as truck drivers need to be literate and be able to handle documents, regulatory authorities and navigate intelligently using sign boards and data available through mobile phones. Trucking industry is plagued by huge corruption (MDRA, September 2006). Fairly literate drivers can fight corruption with more information and preparedness.

   This leads to an interesting question on how it affects availability of drivers at Pollachi. Typically, a person gets into this profession as a truck cleaner who supports the driver on his voyage. After a few years of experience and confidence, a cleaner graduates into a driver first on local trips and then on highways. By then, he would be twenty-five years of age. Many times such persons are illiterates. Ninety per cent of driver community is of such population and hence the new law does not encourage people taking up this profession. Already, there has been societal pressure on transport owners and operators community, as their marriages are getting postponed as women folk see this as a less preferred profession. President of PLOA repented that he has especially suffered on this and there is discouragement for people to come forward to this profession. Increasingly family size is becoming smaller with one or two male children and families are not keen in them going for trucking profession.

   Modern vehicles are technology enabled and there are more components and parts which are electronic. Contemporary drivers need to be savvy about handling such developments without which they could be stuck. While few have a flair for such challenges, timid nature of drivers is wary of such learning and adaptation. Given this trend, availability of drivers would be a challenge unless efforts are made to realize this community to be technology friendly and be literate about handling technical hiccups.

Interestingly, migration of labourers to garment and textile is increasing as such companies pay decent remuneration, provide pick up and drop and self esteem is high in such assignments as they are also highly unioinised. Tirupur and Coimbatore are within a radius of 50 kms and companies have regular pick up and drop. Such change in professional choices hurt availability of drivers to truck owners. Apart from societal preferences for a clean job, economical factors are against trucking business. Mills also recruit labourers who have failed in schools. While on eight days trip a driver may earn Rs 3,000, mills pay Rs 200 upwards based on productivity and provide transportation in cozy buses and lunch and snacks at work. The question ahead would be how to entice people to take to truck driving profession? Will it go in the same way as in the case of construction workers, security personnel and so on wherein people from low income regions like Orissa, Bihar and North East come as migrant labourers which are quite common even in Tirupur? Would PLOA seek help of corporate under corporate social responsibility programme and NGOs to intervene and project how truck drivers can become owners and traders and make money as they progress in life?

3. Asset utilization efficiency: Truck is the key asset deployed by truck owners who are members of PLOA. Asset utilization efficiency is what matters in ensuring good returns on the investment. Asset deployment by way of moving loads would be an important element. According to MDRA study (September 2006), the average distance travelled by them was over 1,900 km in the entire trip. On an average, the truck drivers make more than five trips in a month which works out to 9,000 kms per month. Considering an average of twenty-one working days in a month, a driver covers about 425 kms a day. However, things at Pollachi and believed to be common in Tamil Nadu is that the driver covers only 5,000 kms in a month on a truck with an average about 275–300 kms a day. The reasons could be more as discussed in environmental factors below. Apart from this, culturally drivers lack commitment and sense of binding on duty because of the trouble faced in Walayur check post and socio-cultural issues like being influenced by alcohol consumption and so on. This leads to truck as an asset deployed in lesser time window resulting in opportunity loss for the owners. This forces many a times owners driving the truck on certain trips and hence scalability of ownership is limited which is a key structural handicap in this business.

4. Environmental factors: Environmental factors refer here to lack or abuse of regulations leading to delays, corruption and unhealthy practices in road transportation in India (MDRA, September 2006). From Pollachi a sizeable volume of traffic moves to Kerala which needs to pass through Walayur check post on Tamil Nadu–Kerala border. This point proves to be a bottleneck and drivers are at times stuck for two days here. This irritates them and they leave the vehicle and move. Also, on most of occasions they are expected to inch-forward vehicles in traffic at check post leading to inefficiency in petrol consumption and

hurting driver psychology. A driver experiences similar hassles in many other check posts in India. However, it is believed that in the rest of India, there have been significant improvements.

Discipline among drivers is inadequate. Also, owners are less supportive of system of blacklisting drivers who are unethical. This is mainly because of owner's pressure to deploy vehicles and attitude of drivers being exploitative of demand supply mismatch. Also, there are common incidents of driver and cleaner colluding and move away with cash or misappropriate through falsifications. Especially when owners are under pressure to have cleaners from different unknown localities such incidents become common.

In India giving bribes en route is reported to be common (MDRA, September 2006). Drivers misappropriate such circumstances and at times abandon vehicle creating further problem to owners.

Another important development which is coming up is containerization of load. This is catching up in Pollachi as well especially for coir-based products and other industrial products. This would gain further importance with labour becoming difficult to handle and convenience of loading and unloading being preferred among intermediaries in the system.

Over loading is an issue which is mainly encouraged by shipper. Though transport operators charge at times by distance and trip while in some cases it is per tonne of loaded weight. This improves earnings but leads to corruption among regulatory authorities, damages to road and so on. This is an environmental issue as everyone in the system including vehicle manufacturers builds chassis keeping scope of overload in mind. The government, of late, has taken rigid measures to curb over loading. This must lead to rationalization of rates for movement or else operators would suffer.

5. Changing trends in technology: Technology applications are helpful in improving efficiency. Few simple things which PLOA members benefit are insurance service from service providers who have automatic generation of renewal notices and easy claim processes and so on. They particularly appreciated role of IRDA (Insurance Regulatory Authority in India) on its initiatives. Second, mobile phones are helpful on guiding and tracking the truck drivers along the route. Most importantly it has reduced the waiting time for return truck loads as contacts could be instantaneously established and rates can also be fixed with prospective clients immediately. Since this is a two way communication, negotiations and closure with driver on a conference call reduces the waiting time drastically and brings improved control. PLOA members are yet to take advantage of information and facilitation service of institutions like in freight for return load management. Web enabled processes could give further advantage.

Third, PLOA members are happy about advancement in vehicles and maintenance has improved with electronic devices based fault deduction and rectification processes. Possibly linking up these data through a PLOA office designated computer system and working towards proactive maintenance may reduce downtime. They are yet to progress towards the same. Four, document management through computerization has also benefited them and helps to handle regulatory authorities' requirement. PLOA members are confident these changes would benefit them well during boom period. Finally, PLOA members feel that cashless operation is becoming difficult as most of the places demand is for cash transactions and corrupt practices discourage use of prepaid cash cards.

6. Infrastructure development: PLOA members are benefiting out of the infrastructure development especially on four lane and six lane roads. They feel that turnaround times have come down drastically. In some cases, improvements are as high as 50 per cent like in case of trips to Chennai, Bangalore, and Hyderabad from Pollachi. They feel that tolls are slightly high and offset the benefits as toll is a direct cash outflow while benefits are savings. Though toll charges are direct levies relating to truck load, customers do not accept that incidence of tax and PLOA members bear the incidence and impact of such tolls and duties.

   PLOA would like infrastructure further to be advanced especially bridges and rest places as in abroad. PLOA members also acknowledge that development of infrastructure has reduced number of accidents and according to their estimate it has come down to 20 per cent of what used to be earlier.

   They feel that social infrastructure like developing driving schools, health clinics at affordable costs for drivers and children education support and so on would make things better for this community.

7. Green and quality issues: PLOA members are not much aware of green initiatives except from usage of premium quality diesel and control of emissions. Green initiatives in trucking would include better maintenance, savings on carbon by achieving higher mileage per unit of fuel, controlling of emissions and noise pollution so that air and noise pollution are within acceptable norms and maintaining vehicles in good condition through proactive maintenance plans so that non-recyclable items are not dumped frequently and so on. PLOA is aware but no programme is deployed and measurements are missing. Awareness is more among large fleet owners rather than small operators. Similarly, quality consciousness in terms of cleanliness and upkeep is just adequate and there is enough scope to improvise. The President of PLOA agrees such initiatives would lead to feel good factor in the community.

8. Ethical practices and its impact: Ethical behavioural issues are critical for success of any business in an environment. Here for PLOA quite a few challenges are confronting them. One, as mentioned earlier, at societal level this business is plagued by corrupt practices at regulatory intervention points. This could be Octori levy, state road permits, load approval and declaration for sales tax purposes, vehicle and driver related regulatory issues and so on. This is not to point

out government systems but rather society as many consignees also misuse by giving false declaration and overloading. The point is societal level ethical practices are weak in transportation in India. This affects PLOA members directly as when truck is on a Highway all face same issues.

Individual level ethical concerns also affect business. Drivers are observed to be alcoholic and drive under influence of alcohol. This is against law and lands up vehicle and load in trouble. This also leads to absenteeism and drivers fail to report to duty. Families of drivers suffer as they misuse their earnings. Also during waiting time drivers are playing cards and involve in low end betting and waste time and resources. This does not augur well for professional service.

Another ethical concern is cleaners running away with cash collected by drivers and putting drivers in trouble. It is becoming difficult to align drivers with dependable cleaners. The latter comes for a short duration builds confidence and runs away with loot. They also steal consignment in some cases. Drivers are made to do policing to cleaners as well. At times, a few drivers join this gang as well.

In some locations, drivers are blacklisted if they are found at fault and members of association disengage them for a period till they undergo change. PLOA members find it difficult to implement this practice which encourages drivers not to be loyal.

9. Corporate Social Responsibility of PLOA: Association has got some ethical practices which need to be highlighted here. One, they have two petrol bunks which provide fuel to all its members at right quantity and right price. Two, PLOA provides insurance to its members who are covered for Rs 100,000 in case of death and Rs 50,000 in case of serious impairment. It also provides Rs 10,000 on demise of a member to perform final rites to the nearest kith and kin. PLOA also disseminates information and good practices both through formal and informal channels. They have a yard for vehicles and association functions under guidance of Tamil Nadu Lorry Owners Association (Annex 1) and National Congress (Annex 2) at Delhi. The office bearers function above party political lineage and look at industry practices.

Load Traffic Related Information

- Return load down time one to two days in metros like Chennai, Bangalore, Delhi, and Hyderabad.
- On an average, number of trips to Chennai could be four in a month and average distance trucked in a month would be 5,000 kms. If it is Hyderabad, it could be three trips. Long distances like Kolkata, Delhi, and Mumbai would be only one trip a month. Drivers do not report immediately after such trips.
- Typical load distribution:
  ○ Coconuts (Daily loads): Chennai–10, Madurai–10; Trichy–5, Andhra Pradesh–20, Cochin–5; Mumbai–5, Delhi–2; and others–20.

○ Coconut fibre–50 loads for rope making mainly to Kerala

○ Coconut Pith Chennai 10, Tuticorin 10 mainly for export

○ Coconut–100 loads to Kangeyam for oil extraction

○ Vegetables–10 trucks daily to Kerala

○ Kharif season (July to September)–Groundnut to different locations and paddy similarly to different locations

○ Cattle mainly to Kerala from Pollachi market on Tuesdays and Thursdays–50 trucks on each day

○ Poultry—50—100 trucks a day depending on market forces

○ Above are indicative loads which are representative of market dynamics there at Pollachi.

Pollachi with a population of more than 100,000 is progressive with schools, colleges, hospitals and so on. People are progressive and entrepreneurial. Legends like Shri Mahalingam have contributed to the development of this community.

Mr Mohan thinks through these inputs and suggests that Karthik must work along with him in developing a plan for revitalizing PLOA member community and facilitate in bringing health of industry to a higher confidence level wherein natural endowments of Pollachi and entrepreneurial talents are nurtured and put to high economic value. Mr Mohan suggests Karthik to look at interventions from community school, counselling, socio-cultural intervention as well. He also thinks about approaching truck manufacturers and financiers to help this community through their corporate social responsibility programme to build resources and programme. He feels that this could be something similar to 'Anand Model' (Annex 3) in dairy sector which could be replicated in other locations as well.

DISCUSSION QUESTIONS

1. Describe structure of lorry ownership and trucking business in Pollachi based on size, number of operators, competition technology, forces like entry barriers for ownership, exit barriers and so on. Build a future scenario for a typical small operator and him becoming a large operator and one for large operators.

2. Do SWOT analyses of trucking business in Pollachi and recommend strategies for large truck owners and small operators.

3. Prepare a note for PLOA office bearers on green initiatives and social and ethical practices for trucking business and recommend initiatives and action plans.

4. Develop a detailed note on challenges of trucking business in Pollachi, defend why an Anand Model initiative should be launched and describe benefits to society, truck manufacturers, operators and drivers community. Your case must be strong enough to solicit support from Consortium of manufacturers.

5. Prepare a report for representation to government on hassles faced by drivers, based on web research and publicly available content and impress on actions to be initiated for a conducive regulatory environment.

6. You are in-charge of PLOA association on technology tracking. Prepare a list of recommendations on good practices for PLOA members and suggest steps to implement the same.

ANNEXURE 1

State Level Lorry Owners' Associations

There are a number of lorry owners associations which represent owners to facilitate in handling their socio-economic and cultural issues in operations of business. Namakkal is one of the leading lorry ownership societies in India. Their association takes lead in most of the activities. They are located in different cities to help its members. It serves almost like a federal unit. There is a federation of Tamil Nadu Lorry Owners' Association based out of Chennai which serves as a federation. Other agencies like CII, FICCI, and MCCI are also supportive of their issues as transportation is the backbone of business growth in any country. Exhibit 1 shows one such initiative by Tamil Nadu Lorry Owners, Association.

Exhibit 1 Tamil Nadu Lorry Owners' Association is Planning to Hike the Freight Charges

The Federation of Tamil Nadu Lorry Owners' Association is planning to increase the freight rates due to the increase in diesel price.

Lorry Freight Charges Hiked

Federation state president Mr K Palanisamy said a decision on this would be taken at the federation's meeting in Namakkal which is going to be held on 13 July. Expressing serious reservations on the fuel price hike, he said the truck owners would be severely hit by the increase of Rs 2 per litre on diesel.

He also stated, 'The transport industry is already burdened by road tax, hike in spare parts, tyre prices. Besides, the private toll gate operators on the National and State Highways are fleecing the transporters by imposing high toll fees. This hike in diesel price will cripple the already sick industry. Therefore, the truck owners feel that a 25 per cent increase in freight rates will help them tide over losses.'

Due to the increase in freight rates, it would lead to increase in prices of essential commodities, Palanisamy said that the truckers' association was conscious of the public's concern. But with no other options left, the truck owners will demand the Centre to rollback the diesel price hike. If the government heeds the plea and effects a rollback, there will be no need to increase freight.

Source: http://namakkalcity.com/tamil-nadu-lorry-owners-association-is-planned-to-hike-the-freight-charges/.

ANNEXURE 2

Anand Model

The milk cooperatives was pioneered Shri Tribhuvandas K. Patel who has won several awards. His most important contribution has been founding the Kaira District Cooperative Milk Producers' Union which processes milk purchased from local village producers for distribution in Bombay, and now also sells other dairy products under the trade name AMUL throughout India. He began this Union in 1947 with the blessing of Vallabhbhai Patel and the inspiration of former Union Finance Minister Morarji Desai.

Later Dr V. Kurien when he was appointed as General Manager firmed up the Anand Pattern (Anand Model) milk cooperatives which are based on democratic principles of cooperative led economic growth in a community. Dr Kurien nurtured the Union from a daily collection of 500 litres a day in 1948 to one million litres a day in early 1990. He helped set up similar District Cooperative Unions in six other districts of Gujarat which eventually federated to an apex body, the Gujarat Cooperative Milk Marketing Federation Limited. The Federation covers more than 1.5 million milk producer families. Later, Dr Kurien was instrumental in getting Operation Flood assistance from World Bank in 1970 and India got continued support till 1990s. Now India leads in dairy production.

The Anand Model is essentially an economic organizational pattern to benefit small producers who join hands forming an integrated approach in order to handle their produce. The whole operation is professionally managed so that the individual producers have the freedom to decide their own policies. The adoption of modern production and marketing techniques helps in providing those services that small producers individually can neither afford nor manage. The Anand Model *cooperatives* have progressively eliminated middlemen, bringing the producers in direct contact with consumers. Despite opposition to these projects by middlemen and other powerful vested interests, Dr Kurien has been able to make major breakthroughs in the dairy and oilseeds sectors supported by the highest level in the Government of India. It proves that Anand Model can be deployed wherever cooperative effort among supply chain network partners would help common goal.

Source: http://www.indiadairy.com/ind_operationflood_anandpattern.html.

ANNEXURE 3

All India Motor Transport Congress

All India Motor Transport Congress is located at 1/16 A, Asaf Ali Road, Delhi, Delhi, India. It represents transport operators and the term transport operator includes 'Anybody who runs and/or controls any of the activities in transport industry which may mean/include/ consist of truck driver, truck owner, broker, booking agent etc.'

Reference

A Report on Corruption in the Trucking Operation in India Presented to Transparency International India (TII) New Delhi Submitted by MDRA, New Delhi-110 017, September 2006

http://www.transparencyindia.org/publication/Corruption%20in%20Truck%20Industry%20Report.pdf

Facilities and Information Technology as Key Competitive Forces in Export Garments Growth

Role of facilities and information as supply chain drivers in export business

Clifton Exports is a Government of India recognized export house, specializing in manufacture and export of knitted ready made garments to the international market since 1991. Located in Tirupur, the knitwear capital of India, Clifton Exports houses a state-of-the-art composite knitwear manufacturing facility, covering knitting, processing, finishing and garmenting. The company is believed to be committed to be proactive both to their product and customer needs, thus furthering a value added relationship.

Apparel, Clothing and Garments Production Methods

Various items of clothing are a symbol of culture, fashion and convenience and also determined by climatic conditions. Apparel and Garments can be categorized based on innumerable criteria—Clothing by Fashion, Clothing by Fabrics, Men's Clothing, Women's Clothing, Kids Clothing, Industrial Clothing, Infant Wear, etc.

Seam Engineering in Apparels

The most basic unit of an apparel or garment is fibre which is further converted into yarns and threads before the final product—the fabric or the garment—comes into being. Threads used for construction and stitching of garments are vital to the Apparel Industry. Seam Engineering includes seam and stitch construction while manufacturing garments. The basic principle is that more thread a stitch consumes, the greater will be its strength. Greater seam strength can be achieved by adjusting the sewing threads tensions, threads controls, adjustment of machines and eyelets etc. Revolution in thread manufacturing has ensured the availability of thread quality as per the fabric demands. If the factors like quality parameters of threads and machine type, lubrication of machine and threads are kept in mind, it can add quality to apparels manufactured.

Garment Processing

There are four major kinds of textile processing namely fibre processing, yarn processing, fabric processing, and garment processing. Garment processing has grown to a great extent during the past few decades thanks to fashion consciousness of the consumers. Garment finishing is mainly done through wet processing. Garments are dyed for imparting colour to them. Proper finishing can provide a better look to the apparel, change the feel and texture of the fabric, and can also add value to the end-product. Various types of finishes are given to the garments which include peach finish, anti-microbial finish, wrinkle-free finish, aroma finish, UV guard finish, acid wash, enzyme wash, moisture management, laser coating etc. The factors to be considered while processing include the choice of chemicals, production limitations and types of machinery used. Usually garment processing is done on a small scale which minimizes the damage risk.

For the textile and apparel industry, product quality is calculated in terms of quality and standard of fibres, yarns, fabric construction, colour fastness, designs and the final finished garments. Quality control in terms of garment manufacturing, pre-sales and post-sales service, delivery, pricing, etc. are essential for any garment manufacturer, trader or exporter. Certain quality related problems, often seen in garment manufacturing like sewing, colour, sizing, or garment defects should be avoided as it may lead to huge penalties like rejection of consignment.

Clifton Exports' Production Divisions (Refer Figure 7)

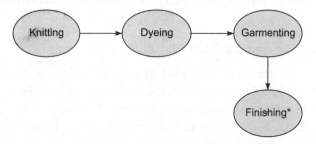

* Includes printing, embroidery and elastics and so on

Figure 7   Internal supply chain or manufacturing process of Clifton Exports

Knitting Division

Clifton Exports has state-of-the-art machinery Spandex/Lurex etc., world class circular knitting machines from Germany, Japan and Far East to produce a whole variety of fabric designs from 150 GSM in its knitting division. It produces fabrics like Fleece & Polar Fleece, Jersey, Pique, Interlock, Rib, Engineering Stripes, Single & Double Jacquards, Rib & Interlock Waffles and Rib & Interlock Pointelles and Sheared Terry (Velour) and so on. Fibers include 100 per cent Cotton, Polyester/Cotton blends, Gassed Mercerised Cotton, 100 per cent Polyester, 100 per cent Viscose/Rayon and Cotton/Viscose blends, thus, knitting provides scope for wide variety of fibres to produce wide range of fabrics. With a production capacity of 3 tonnes per day, Clifton has short production cycle time.

Dyeing Division

Clifton has a sophisticated set-up of facilities for Yarn-Dyeing, Fabric Dyeing, Garment Dyeing, Pigment Padding, Bio-Wash, Softening etc. Identifying the processing techniques is a critical area for fabric quality. Clifton has in place a well documented quality control programme, for each of its activities, which could be certified by any international labs of customer's choice. Be it shrinkage, colour fastness, pilling, laundering or dimensional stability, Clifton offers to compliment any international standard governing garments.

Dyeing is an activity which requires investments in managing effluent and systems for eliminating/reducing waste of water resources and contamination of chemicals on natural resources. One of the essential parts in the narrow fabric industry is Tape Dyeing which fulfils the apparel and home furnishing industries. Clifton has facilities for all kinds of Tape Dyeing, Cotton, Polyester, Nylon, Viscose Tapes and Laces in the imported continue dyeing and finishing machine. Clifton Knits is equipped with modern HTHP Soft flow dyeing machines, Vessel capacities ranging from 800 kgs to 50 kgs, with a capacity to dye 3.8 tonnes per day to dye all types of knitted fabrics. A well equipped lab is attached to the dyeing sector along with colour matching cabinets, and spectrophotometer for accuracy and consistency in shades. The company uses only eco-friendly dyes to maintain the international quality standards.

Garmenting

Garmenting of course is the nerve centre to Cliftons operations. With its 16,000 Polo T-Shirts a day facility, the company services its customers worldwide; with a constant strive to Total Quality Management.

Finishing

Fabric finishing is an important activity, which ensures the stability of a garment. Clifton offers Compacting, Mercerising, Stentering and Raising to provide good feel and finish of the fabrics. The garments are 100 per cent checked for international quality standards manually as well as in machines. Each and every garment is passed through needle detectors to ensure non-existence of needles staples etc. Garments are finally pressed by high technology vacuum pressing and packed to reach the destinations on time.

Clifton unit finishing ranges includes Raising, Tigering, Shearing, and Stenter. A wide variety of Fleece and regular knitted fabrics of all compositions can be brushed by raising machines. Their raising machines with the latest equipment and facilities can brush up to 5 tonnes per day. Tigering machine together with raising machine enables to produce the finest quality fleece available, with reduced pilling as well as maintaining evenness in the fabric surface. The tigering machines have an output of up to 5 tonnes per day. Clifton Knits uses most modern shearing machines, to produce specialty finishes like Velour and Terry fabrics of all compositions. Their shearing machines have the capacity to produce 3.5 Tonnes per day. Their Stenter is one of the widest finishing machines available. A workable width of up to 3.2 metres is possible. Finishing process with perfectly controlled shrinkage, and width along with intermediate processes like heat setting, and drying in open width form is possible with our Stenter. Their stenter is also equipped with weft straightening rollers for specific use of fabric with striped designs. The production capacity is up to 8 tonnes per day.

Clifton has a long and established manufacturing capability for Pigment, Plastisol, Reactive, Foam, Discharge, Non-PVC, Flock, Glitter, Sticker, Combo prints, etc. Printing quality is critical for success of business as it confirms trends, fashions, and appeal of finish. Similarly, embroidery is an area, which defines a garment presentation. Clifton is a trendsetter on embroidered garments, with its sophisticated embroidery facilities. Be it logo, chest or all over embroidery, the company has required experience to match requirement and set trends.

Another area related to finishing is that of elastics. Product ranges and descriptions in Woven Elastics, Woven Plain, Stripes Elastics, Jacquard Elastics, and Rigid Tapes. The company is equipped with a state-of-the-art high speed Woven Jacquard Needle of 384 Jacquard Hook imported from Switzerland, the first of its kind in India. This helps to produce any kind of sharp Jacquard design up to four or more colours in a fine quality. Also, it is equipped with a state-of-the-art Crochet Knitted machine of sixteen bars imported from Italy, the first of its kind in India which supports manufacture of high quality Lycra Laces and all kinds of Picot Frill Elastics in the finest quality.

This explains Clifton Exports' internal supply chain processes wherein conversion of material takes place for delivery. It is important to note here that this company has heavily invested in state-of-the-art technology in equipments instead of outsourcing intermediary processes of finishing like attaching elastics, label, printing and so on. In a cluster industry such options are available. One may note that Clifton Exports has invested on all these processes compared to outsourcing because of its advantage of its location in industrial park where space is not a constraint and establishing composite unit is advantageous. Alternatively, one can argue if there is scope for sub processes being specialized by vendors within the industrial park, then it could be advantageous to outsource. Even then scheduling and delivery risks could be high. Clifton Exports' size favours establishing a composite garment manufacturing set up. Achieving economies of scale and section wise capacity planning and utilization will be key determinants of successes as capacity mismatch across sub sections may lead to bottlenecks. Hence capacity synchronization and order plan to utilize as unitary manufacturing set up would be critical success factor.

From the Figure 8, one may note that prospective buyer first initiates a sampling generation. Typically, Clifton Exports creates in 24–36 hours and dispatches by courier and at times gets approval in a week's time. Approval triggers order generation and order can be anything from 1,000 numbers to 500,000 units. The company receives 70 per cent of orders through buying agents and balance 30 per cent are received directly from buyers. It is also important to note that buyers split orders among vendors and split mainly on styles. Direct buyers give full orders which are evolved experience over two or more years by which time the buying relationship moves from deterrence based to trust based on processes and delivery mechanism. Buying agents normally work on 5 per cent commission and delivery is always direct as manufacturers like Clifton Exports would avail duty drawback as and when determined by government policy which is currently 8.5 per cent. When Indian currency becomes strong, there are times when government has increased duty drawback to improve attractiveness of exports.

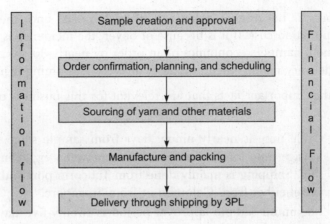

Figure 8 Clifton Exports' supply chain process

Market Segments for Apparel, Clothing, and Garments

Men's clothing   Along with the formal and casual wears for men, the market is open for variety of formal as well as designer clothes including jackets, jeans, pants, shirts, shorts, trousers, T-shirts, under wears, sports wears, beach wears etc.

Women's clothing   Fashion keeps on changing and more so for women's clothing. From formal, casual, and corporate wears to designer and exclusive wear, women's clothing doesn't know any boundaries. Ladies Frocks, tops, capris, skirts, T-shirts, tunics, jeans, nighties, shirts, shorts, trousers, swimsuits, outerwear, waistcoats, wraparound, blouses are of different types and have increasing markets.

Kids clothing   The market of children's wear includes Boy's, Girl's and Infants clothes which are expanding at a high rate like the women's apparel sales. Kids caps, dresses, jeans, jumpers, school uniforms, shirts, shorts, T-shirts are all manufactured on large scales to fulfil the demands of the market. Infant wears like bibs, diapers etc. are also in great demand.

Customers of Clifton Exports include Playboy, UK, Leclerc, France, Hema, Netherland and Gymboree, US and so on covering men's briefs, boxers, shirts, T-shirts, children, fancy gowns and be present in all segments.

When order aggregates and lumps in a same time window, Clifton Exports handles same through outsourcing maximum to an extent of 20 per cent of volume. Planning and scheduling of order is a key process. Once order is received, they begin the planning processes based on volume yarn to be ordered and received; they schedule production lines and arrange finance for managing the production. Bank funds about 50 per cent of order value on progress and once order is dispatched and LC is honoured based on the type of LC. Many a times, contract is such a way that the buyer takes CIF as he could negotiate in bulk freight rates. Buyer nominates 3PL who would handle the same and delivery could be at factory of Clifton Exports or originating sea/air port. Generally, consignments are sent by sea and from experience it is noted that 2–5 per cent of consignments are air shipped. If consignment air shipping is because of delay at Clifton Exports' end, they incur that additional transportation cost. If it is because of buyer, the incidence is borne by the buyer. Air shipment hampers economics of an order by nearly 30–40 per cent. Hence in order and delivery management, mode of delivery and timing is important.

Other important facts that are relevant for this business of Clifton Exports are as follows:

1. Cycle time is nearly ninety days from sample stage. This includes dispatch. Voyage time for Europe and U.S is between eighteen to twenty-four days by ship. Shipping is mainly done from Tuticorin port and boarded onto a mother vessel either from Colombo or from Singapore.

2. Maximum sample approval period is twenty-five days. Sample specification sheet confirms fabric, GSM and colour and so on.

3. Order dispatches could be weekly or in one lot. When the order size is huge like 500,000 pieces, dispatches are staggered in three or more stages. One may have to look at how it helps to manage production planning and scheduling.

4. Managing quality is key issue. There is a quality control team which is trained adequately in quality process which helps the management. Clifton Exports has six quality personnel and another set of quality trained personnel who are active in production floor and coordinate whenever there is an outsourced activity. Some manufacturers face problem of quality rejection which is an important risk element in producing the garments.

5. Sourcing of yarn is tied to a state-of-the-art mill in Coimbatore which is part of a large textile and textile machinery group. This is a pre approved vendor. Whenever there is more demand and this vendor finds difficult to accommodate the schedule, purchases are made from large mills in Madurai, Dindugal and Coimbatore.

6. Inventory carrying policy is as follows: twenty days of stock of yarn, ten days of dyeing and fabric about thirty days. Yarn buying is affected by price fluctuation and difficult to get into annual contract. However, because of trust based relationship Clifton Exports is able to manage this cost. Inventory cost is normally met through order based advanced realization of up to 50 per cent from banks and out of the stock value 75 per cent is funded and balance 25 per cent is brought by the company.

7. Clifton Exports which is part of seven units of a group has 236 employees. Of which two are in management grade. There are seven production supervisors, six quality supervisors, twenty-one skilled personnel in production support and about 175 skilled production personnel and twenty-five unskilled employees. Labour turnover is about 40 per cent. The company has transport pickup for labourers and provides support through canteen facilities and healthy work environment. Clifton Exports has a detailed Safety, Health and Environment policy which is driven by self actualization and also by European and USA

based buyers. Under this policy, they do not employ child labour, equal opportunity is given for employment and fair and just practices are maintained. All statutory regulations are adequately followed and filled with authorities. Pollution handling is consciously done. The company insists on its suppliers/outsourced partners wherever relevant to adapt SHE policies. Buyers do normally due diligence on SHE and quality processes regularly. The company has backup power and is highly conscious of power savings and preservation of fuel which degenerates natural resources.

8. Labour productivity is high. Labourers are driven by self-esteem and productivity is high. Concerns on labour are increasing because of absenteeism, turnover and migrant labour settlement. At Tirupur exports have grown to nearly Rs 11,000 crores which is a phenomenal growth. This has increased employment opportunities for all levels and attracted migrant labourers. It affects availability of trained manpower. Also, labourers expect to work for two shifts but less number of days in a week. If one has 200 labourers on roll, instead of being available for 1,200 days of workmen in a week, many times companies like Clifton Exports get only 900 workmen days. So it forces them adding 25 per cent spare capacity which is an issue to manage during normal conditions.

9. Finally, location at Netaji Apparel Park is of great value. Customers are impressed easily with ambience, facilities and value addition like availability of training centre, attraction of trained personnel. The park provides adequate water supply, power supply, good roads, sewage and rainwater drainage, lighting and security. Netaji Apparel Park is maintaining a high standard of Social infrastructure facilities, dust free environment and total clean atmosphere inside the park. This was not common inside Tirupur. Though cost of operations goes up by 10 per cent for the company, Clifton Exports is convinced that incremental value is realized because of the cluster location.

Information Technology

Information technology is an important supply chain driver in garments export business since there are different layers like buyer, intermediary like buying agents, focal firm in this case Clifton Exports, suppliers of materials including yarn, outsourcing partners, service providers and so on. Tirupur based garment exporters, have just finished the implementation of SAP ERP 4.7 with an aim of automating their supply chain and track inventory levels. According to one of the promoters, ERP investment is justified because, 'Since we have a business of export of garments, we are constantly expected to deliver faster, within the shortest possible order time cycle. Also the need for an ERP was felt to integrate various processes tightly, reduce inventory cycle and cost. We also needed an automatic warning system (for instance, warning that delivery schedule won't be met due to lack of stock).'

Clifton Exports has invested on a different ERP which is grown locally. IDEATEC has come out with a mini-ERP solution for Apparel Manufacturing and Exporting industry called ideaExport. This provides total solutions with Predictable Costs,

Proven Performance & Low Maintenance Costs. There are three components, namely:

- Status Tracking: Status of all Process stages is tracked so that the user is aware whether he/she is on-schedule or behind-schedule. Detailed Quantitative completion for each schedule is provided.
- Material Tracking: Reconciliation of Materials in each Process stage is maintained for better utilization and to control the process loss at various stages.
- Cost Tracking: Complete picture of the Profit & Loss statement for each order with break down in the cost projections including comparison charts & in-depth analysis reports of Pre-Production Costs & Post-Production Costs.

Clifton Exports has implemented the following modules of IDEATEC

OMS modules

Settings	Order details	Merchandising	Scheduling	Sample
Purchase	Yarn process	Yarn reprocess	Knitting	Fabric process
Fabric Reprocess	Yarn stock	Fabric stock	Accessory production issue	Accessory process
Accessory stock	Production	Piece stock	Documentation & banking	Marketing
Quality control	Work order	Supplier transactions	Accounts	General items
General transactions	Bill passing	Analysis	Reports	

In total, there are twenty-nine modules which manage business of export processing, monitoring and control of business. These modules can be accessed from remote locations. ERP takes care of planning and scheduling with minimal intervention for prioritization. Also, ERP handles all the three flows namely physical, financial and informational flows of this business.

There are certain processes still requiring manual update of data source. For example, when fabric is moved for garmenting, actual fabric taken from stock needs to be captured by way of manual entry. Supervisors are adequately trained to enter information and data on regular intervals as activity happens so that there is near real time data available for management to plan resource utilization.

Entrepreneurs and managers are technically savvy and interact with buyers on near real time basis which has improved supply chain efficiency.

DISCUSSION QUESTIONS

1. Discuss the State-of-the-art Facility management of Clifton.
2. Prepare a report on the advantages of locating in a cluster, orientation towards IT enablement and fair and ethical practices as seen in Clifton.
3. Clifton Exports' promoters are preparing for a site visit and presentation for a large order opportunity with a leading buyer in USA who is looking at 2 million pieces from this unit across four different product segments. The management must present them a SWOT analysis and convince how they can handle

such an order along with current business. This may require outsourcing 40 per cent of order to vendors and manage delivery. The other option could be to expand the plant by investing about Rs 40 crores which may have a pay back of thirty six months. But if Clifton expands in current location, it can save about Rs 10 crores. This may lead to some dislocation in current operations which has to be handled carefully to reduce risk of dislocation affecting revenue. You may advise the company on way forward.

13

Dilkhush Products Ltd

FMCG supply chain integration in forward network

(This case is authored by Dr T.V. Subramanian, Management Consultant and Advisor, Chennai)

Dilkhush Products Ltd is a typical FMCG company with an annual turnover of nearly 700 crores. It has six factories, 30 depots and 3,500 distributors spread over the entire country. It product profile comprise of ten categories such as branded coconut oil, jam, cooking oil and special flavours.

At one time, Dilkhush was faced with considerable difficulties in terms of forecasting. At the depot or the godown level, variations on some SKUs were in the range of as much as 100 per cent. There were also complexities in distribution on account of the large number (3,500) of distributors across the country. This would invariably lead to a pile up of inventories at certain places and stock-outs in others. Visibility of stocks at the distributor level was low, because after invoicing, it was impossible to determine the level of stock that distributors were holding. The only source for this was the secondary sales figure. These figures were collated manually once a month, and their accuracy was always questionable (in the FMCG industry, secondary sales calculation is the bigger challenge; primary sales are always easier to collate). Because planning cycles were fixed, decisions could not be taken online. Processes were highly individual or employee-dependent, and in the absence of an integrated approach, there was little or no communication.

The planning cycle was only 15–20 days—hardly enough to allow corrective action. Apart from the annual budget, the firm operated on a fixed 3-month cycle. Thus, once the output at the end of these three months was decided, nothing could be done in the interim. The result was that if the output for the first month were in excess, the next two months' stock would simply pile up. Invisibly therefore, there were skews towards the ends of quarters. The firm had fixed dispatch plans for the quarter—these were followed even if sales were low. There were coordination difficulties between the sales and manufacturing department, as managers were not using the same data. Typically, sales staff would complain they lost sales because of stock-outs, while the back room would say that there were excess supply lines somewhere in the system, about which they were unaware. The planning cycles for sales and manufacturing did not match. There was no system for distribution planning—one would wait for the sales person or distributor to call up and place the order. Some means of replenishment order generation was tried—however, they were on standalone systems and did not succeed. There were several 'islands' of information, inconsistencies in the MIS and no data visibility across the system. The firm had to do a lot of cleaning up before new technology could be brought in.

Mr Kelkar, the Sales and Distribution Manager recently attended a seminar on 'Supply Chain Management' organized by an Institute of Management. He realized them that Integrated SCM approach is the only way to get out of all the present ills of the company. He also saw a huge opportunity for cost savings with such an approach. However he was confused as to how to proceed since any wrong move or faulty implementation will have serious consequences to the company.

DISCUSSION QUESTIONS

1. Summarize Dilkhush's present problems in Sales and Distribution.
2. Identify the potential areas for cost savings with an integrated SCM.
3. Identify specific action plans for implementing integrated SCM including the role of IT.
4. Indicate appropriate performance metrics to measure the various aspects of Supply Chain performance in FMCG business such as Dilkhush Products Ltd.

Sourcing Intelligence as Way Forward

Scope of sourcing intelligence as a value enhancing tool

It was February 2009 when Maya, Head–HR of Beroe Inc. Chennai centre was preparing to go to campuses like IIT, Madras, National Institute of technology, Trichy and Birla Institute of Science and Technology, Pilani to recruit fifty professionals who could be good on analytics. Maya called for a meeting of Heads of product groups and Shyam Singhal is one who heads chemicals and pharmaceuticals. Shyam wanted to impress prospects with cases which they had recently done on merits of sourcing intelligence.

Procurement Trends

In the past decade, procurement of raw materials has been causing a major impact on the company profits. The cost of raw materials range anywhere between 25–45 per cent of revenue and keeping non-operating costs at around 22–25 per cent, cost of material forms substantial portion of operating cost. With pressure on markets and improved procurement practices, companies are reducing material costs.

The main problem was in having in-house procurement intelligence, which would be extremely expensive, less reliability and time taking. However, one may note that companies are outsourcing supplier intelligence in order to be competitive in this area. Beroe Inc is one of the leaders in providing procurement intelligence.

About Beroe

Beroe Inc is one of the leading procurement intelligence firms providing strategic market intelligence and decision enabling data exclusively to Fortune 500 companies. Beroe is headquartered in the Research Triangle, North Carolina with a Research & Analysis Headquarters in Chennai, India. They also have a support research and analysis center in Rosario, Argentina and satellite offices in: Shenzhen—China, Hanoi—Vietnam, St Petersburg—Russia, Bucharest—Romania, Istanbul—Turkey, and Sao Paulo—Brazil.

Beroe offer a suite of services through their four business units namely: Intelligence, Source, Risk and Green. Figure 9 gives highlights of each of these units.

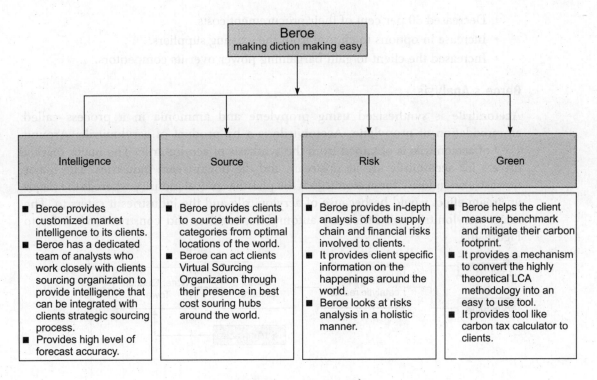

Figure 9 Units of Beroe

Case of Managing Acetonitrile

Shyam was looking at this company as one of the world's leading suppliers to the pharmaceutical, healthcare, and life sciences industries namely ABC Inc. It has a market share of around 7–8 per cent and is one of the leaders in Europe.

The Business Challenge

- In November 2008, there was a severe shortage of acetonitrile in the market and prices raised tenfold.
- The demand for acetonitrile from its downstream industries steadily increased which made the issue more complex.
- The management was facing a lot of trouble procuring acetonitrile at a cheaper price and from the right supplier. They were buying the material at an extremely high price.

The Solution

ABC Inc. decided to outsource it to a market intelligence company called Beroe Inc and results are follows:

- Decreased 30 per cent of their procurement costs.
- Increase in options to choose from the existing suppliers.
- Increased the client to gain bargaining power over its competitors.

Beroe's Analysis

Acetonitrile is synthesized using propylene and ammonia in a process called ammoxidation of propylene. Acetonitrile is a by product of acrylonitrile. Around 1.5% of acetonitrile is obtained from the synthesis of acrylonitrile. The major market drivers for acetonitrile are its upstream and the downstream industries. The major downstream industry for acetonitrile is the pharmaceutical industry whereas the major upstream effect would be because of acrylonitrile and the industries it caters to. The major acrylonitrile industries are automobile, textiles, and construction. (Refer to Figure 10.)

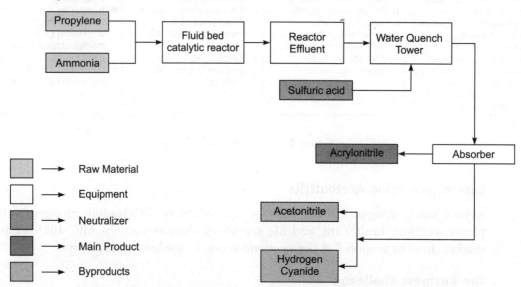

Figure 10 Value chain of acetonitrile

The major demand for acrylonitrile comes from the automobile industry. In 2008, the automobile and construction industries faced a sixteen year low and the demand for acrylonitrile decreased which directly influenced the acetonitrile market. Around 70 per cent of acetonitrile demand is from the pharma sector. The pharma companies were not majorly affected due to recession and there was a steady increase in demand in this sector, which increased the prices tenfold. Beroe played a major role in cutting down the client's cost. Beroe provided information not only about the existing market and suppliers, but also regarding the different regional suppliers providing at lower costs. The geographic options from where they could procure raw materials were also elaborated to the client. It provided sufficient information about the market which gave the client a better bargaining power.

The major challenge was to find the low cost sourcing opportunities. The region wise acetonitrile production (Figure 11) shows that Asia has been an ever-growing market for acetonitrile and the supply demand analysis (Figure 12) shows that India and China have more capacity than demand which shows that they export a lot of acetonitrile to other countries like USA which have excess demand and less capacity.

Beroe looked at the major low cost suppliers in this region and gives rating based on various factors to suppliers. The client would be guided towards the best supplier based on other supplier information.

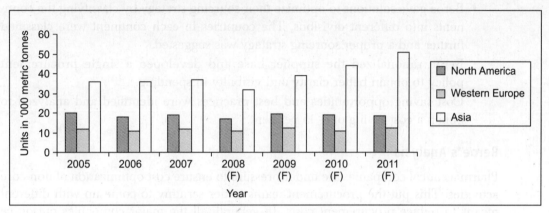

Figure 11   Region-wise acetonitrile production 2005–11

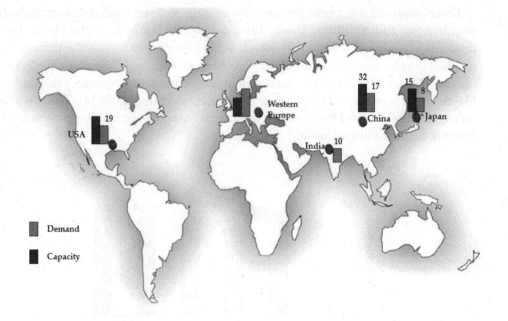

Figure 12   Acetonitrile region-wise capacity and demand

Case of XYZ Inc—A Biomedical and Pharmaceutical Company

XYZ Inc is one of the world's leading biomedical and pharmaceutical companies. XYZ Inc was procuring print management services from multiple suppliers and the procurement spend fell compared to the previous year. XYZ wanted to optimize their supplier base and sourcing strategy.

The company decided to outsource this job to a market intelligence company called Beroe Inc. The results are as follows:

- Beroe gave solutions to optimize their sourcing strategy by classifying the continents into different divisions. The countries in each continent were classified further and a proper sourcing strategy was suggested.
- Beroe rationalized the supplier base and developed a single procurement policy to obtain better clarity and visibility in spending.
- Cost saving opportunities and best practices were identified and analyzed to obtain a cost saving of 8–15 per cent.

Beroe's Analysis

Pharmaceutical companies are under pressure to ensure cost optimization of non-core activities. This put the procurement teams under scrutiny to come up with different means to reduce procurement costs. In general, all the major companies outsource their printing and other non-core activities. They outsource their printing facilities to a service provider who acts like a liaison.

Beroe analyzed the whole problem by looking at three main divisions: industries, competitors, and suppliers. Using this information Beroe gave the client the best practices available in the industry which helped them save reduce the printing costs.

The US print management industry has been growing at a rate of 3.1 per cent year on year (Figure 13). The print management industry caters to various other industries like financial services, retail, pharma, travel and telecom (Figure 14). There would be increase in the demand from retail and financial services sector. The growth from the Pharma sector would be around 3–4 per cent.

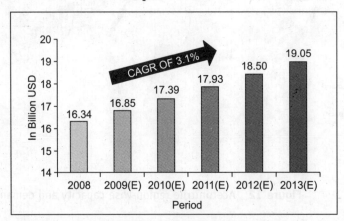

Figure 13 Market size of print management industry in US

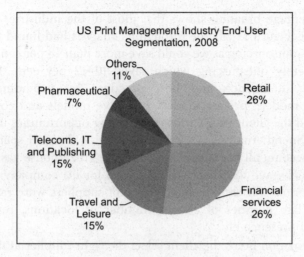

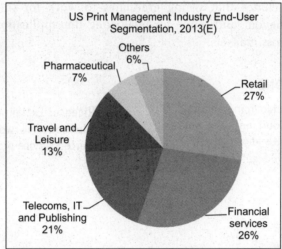

Figure 14 US print management industry segmentation

There are different sourcing options for print management (see Figure 15):

- In-House
- Semi-Outsource
- Outsource

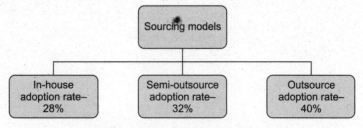

Figure 15 Sourcing models

The percentage breakup shows that most of the industries outsource it to print management (Figure 14). Beroe through its analysis had found that semi-outsourcing is better than outsourcing as we could save more than 18 per cent by semi-outsourcing than completely outsourcing which saves 10–12 per cent. Beroe also provided competitive intelligence and best practices by providing sourcing models, engagement models, pricing models, incentive models and contract models. Beroe also provided the client with various cost saving opportunities using the formula Best Practices + Spend Analysis = Cost Reduction. A detailed spend analysis was done taking into account all the factors including the green house gas emission and carbon footprint which gave the client a right model for his company. The detailed SWOT analysis was done for suppliers and different suppliers were rated based on various parameters like number of clients, number of locations, revenue, track record, geographical presence etc.

This information helps the client select the right supplier at the lowest price.

Shyam concludes that young graduates to work for the company as it gives international flavour and scope for evaluating the application of different analytics techniques across markets.

DISCUSSION QUESTIONS

1. What is procurement outsourcing and how is it different from outsourcing of sourcing intelligence? Explain with above cases.
2. What benefits one would get by outsourcing intelligence? Explain with above examples.
3. Explain how one would evaluate a sourcing outsourced service provider as in case of Beroe.

Scheduling of Transport Services for Employees in a Financial Services BPO in Pune

Mr Prem Raj, Planning Manager of Delta Travels, Pune received a call for discussion from Ms Sheela David—Head of Administration of Finright Services (P) Ltd (FSPL) which manages global back office of an MNC financial services company. FSPL which started in 2001 has grown in size and is currently a 4,000 employee's strong operation in Pune alone. They have two other centres in India, one at Noida, near Delhi and the other at Bangalore.

A financial services company generally works on multiple shifts as per time zones across countries based on location. A BPO would match staffing for serving a country within the time zone. For example, Singapore operates, say, between 8 a.m. and 5 p.m. from Monday to Friday and an Indian BPO serving the same will have to man employees between 5.30 a.m. to 2.30 p.m. IST for back office operations. As per the service level agreement (SLA) BPO must ensure required manpower is available in such slots as per time and number committed.

Like a typical BPO, FSPL Pune has its office in one of the growth centre of the city where IT & ITES companies are located. It is about 40 kms away from the hub of the city where employees live. Out of 4,000 employees of FSPL, 2,250 have opted for company pick up and drop where the company has taken responsibility of arranging buses and dropping them. The company would recover this cost from employees from the allowance payable to them per month. If an employee chooses to drive on his own his allowance would be to maximum of Rs 3,500 per month. This would involve risk and discomfort of driving especially if it is on a two wheeler. The other option which employees do is to pool among themselves and drive in their car where they share operating expenses and rotate car deployment from own resources.

David has to ensure that the employees who have opted for company bus are picked up on time from their designated place and dropped at an agreed time window. The condition should be that the employee must be there for beginning the shift fifteen minutes ahead of start time and must be able to leave work campus within fifteen minutes on completion of shift. Employees have a tolerance of fifteen minutes delay. There is no shift delay tolerance which can be permitted and route time may have addition time cushion of fifteen minutes for route planning.

FSPL has five shifts wherein employees work in all shifts with composition of company pick up and own arrangements equally split. The arrangement is that if for any reason an employee is delayed for the next shift, the then available employees would extend stay and handover as and when the other employee comes in next shift. These are exceptions and not to be considered for scheduling pick up and drop. Employees work for eight hours and one hour is provided for break and changeover of work stations wherever required between shifts. FSPL has following five shifts and employees distribution. (Refer Table 11.)

Table 11   Shift-wise deployment of staff

Shift no	Timing	Company	Self
I	6 a.m. to 3 p.m. (incl. break)	270	270
II	9 a.m. to 6 p.m. (incl. break)	540	540
III	2 p.m. to 11 p.m. (incl. break)	450	450
IV	6 p.m. to 3 a.m. (incl. break)	270	270
V	9 p.m. to 6 a.m. (incl. break)	720	720

David has the task of seat utilization and manpower availability per shift. There is a need to provide for peak capacity and 5 per cent extra. A seat has a cost of approximately Rs 30,000 per month inclusive of all overheads but excludes employee cost and other direct costs. Transportation costs for an operator are detailed as below in Table 12:

Table 12   Cost of transport operations for an operator

Cost of a bus (Rs.)	1400000
Life in years	7
Depreciation per annum	200000
Interest, insurance & other cost (Rs) per annum	140000
Driver & support staff salary per month	15000
Repairs & maintenance per annum Rs.	120000
Overheads	140000
Total costs excluding fuel	1011000
Fuel @ 5 km per litre On average, a bus covering	396000
165 kms for 25 days in a month	
Cost per employee per month	3127

It is also observed that all vehicles cannot leave/enter at the same time, since all the exit/entry to the campus has limited space for vehicle and say, four vehicles at a time may be leaving and spacing of entry and exit must be provided with a band of three minutes from one batch of buses to the other.

Gives shift-wise details of pick up and drop in terms on number of employees, distance for covering last point by empty buses and travel time of loaded bus.

1. You may help to prepare discussions points for Raj and David from different view points on number of buses to be deployed, start and end time and other dynamics.

2. Raj needs to find out the scheduling procedure and to come out whether the time first vehicles to start from campus for pick up, and the sequence?
3. How many buses are to be deployed?
4. Similarly, the sequence for post shift drop needs to be scheduled. He has preference of using the same vehicle and driver crew whereas David is looking for optimizing deployment.
5. David also requires your support on confirming his seat utilization factor and wants best seat deployment plan from you as additional input.

ANNEXURE 1

Route /Shift	Capacity	Last point distance in kms	No of pick ups	Time to last point distance in minutes	Pick & run time in minutes	Route	Capacity	Last point distance in kms	No of pick ups	Time to last point distance in minutes	Pick & run time in minutes
1/I	45	68	7	90	111	26/III	45	39	5	50	65
2/I	45	65	6	85	103	27/III	45	38	7	50	71
3/I	45	62	8	80	104	28/III	45	38	9	50	77
4/I	45	61	8	80	104	29/III	45	38	5	50	65
5/I	45	59	6	75	93	30/III	45	36	8	50	74
6/I	45	56	5	70	85	31/IV	45	36	9	50	77
7/I	45	55	9	70	97	32/IV	45	35	8	45	69
8/I	45	52	9	70	97	33/IV	45	35	6	45	63
9/I	45	50	8	70	94	34/IV	45	35	9	45	72
10/I	45	50	5	60	75	35/IV	45	34	7	45	66
11/II	45	49	6	60	78	36/IV	45	33	7	45	66
12/II	45	48	5	60	75	37/IV	45	32	6	45	63
13/II	45	48	8	60	84	38/IV	45	32	7	45	66
14/II	45	47	9	60	87	39/IV	45	32	8	45	69
15/II	45	46	8	60	84	40/IV	45	31	8	45	69
16/II	45	46	7	60	81	41/V	45	30	9	45	72
17/II	45	45	6	60	78	42/V	45	29	10	40	70
18/II	45	44	6	60	78	43/V	45	29	5	40	55
19/II	45	43	8	60	84	44/V	45	29	6	40	58
20/II	45	42	8	60	84	45/V	45	28	9	40	67
21/III	45	41	6	60	78	46/V	45	27	10	40	70
22/III	45	41	8	60	84	47/V	45	26	9	40	67
23/III	45	40	6	50	68	48/V	45	26	5	40	55
24/III	45	40	8	50	74	49/V	45	26	10	40	70
25/III	45	40	6	50	68	50/V	45	25	9	40	67

Index